CREATIVE
WRITING
for ‹‹‹‹‹‹‹‹‹‹‹‹
COLLEGE
STUDENTS

CREATIVE WRITING
for College Students

§~ A Summary of the Theory of Exposition,
Argument, Narration, and Description; *with
a Selective and Illustrative Anthology of College
Student Themes and of Selections from Literature.*

———————————————————————————

ROBERT WITBECK BABCOCK, Ph.D.
WAYNE UNIVERSITY

ROBERT DEWEY HORN, Ph.D.
UNIVERSITY OF OREGON

THOMAS HOPKINS ENGLISH, Ph.D.
EMORY UNIVERSITY

———

AMERICAN BOOK COMPANY · *New York* · *Cincinnati*
Chicago · *Boston* · *Atlanta* · *Dallas* · *San Francisco*

Made in U.S.A.

To
M.W.B.
C.H.H.
and
R.W.E.

MANY YEARS of facing students in several universities have indelibly impressed on us that the main thing a college writing course should do is to teach students how to write. By teaching them how to write, we mean simply to place the main emphasis on the more important forms, chiefly the expository and narrative, and thus stimulate young undergraduates to think in terms of whole creations, not of unrelated fragments, such as relative pronouns, attributive adjectives, finite verbs, correlative constructions, and topic sentences. In general, then, the point of view of this book is that most writing is essentially creative in intent, as is evidenced by the effort of mind it demands. This is true of bad writing as well as good since the former is only creative failure.

The purpose of this book is to discuss the types of discourse as directly and suggestively as possible and to set forth as attractively as possible what may be done with them. In order to accomplish these aims, we present, along with the discussion, first, student themes as illustrations of what other students have actually done with the types. Then, for comparison, we add examples from recognized writers, including both classical and modern masters. The primary purpose in printing the themes is to stimulate creative rivalry, for it has been our experience that most students do far better work if you put before them papers written by other students—papers which represent positive achievement in certain forms—and ask them if they can do anything like that. Then you are inviting them to attempt something clearly within the range of their own possibilities, and you will find them rising immediately to meet the challenge.

We do not mean to imply, though, that classical illustrations and handbooks should be thrown overboard. We have, as we have said, paralleled the student papers with professional illustrations and we assume, throughout, the use of a handbook of grammar and rhetoric. What we do want, however, is to see both classics and handbook subordinated to the main purpose of releasing the impulses and powers of these young students to *write!* "Writing out" is of supreme importance; to encourage it is our main objective in this book.

A word should be spoken about the narrative chapters. They are not intended to teach students to turn out marketable short stories, nor are they particularly concerned with the rhetorical features of narration. We have always thought that there is a middle ground between these extremes, and in these chapters we try to point it out. The student is told frankly that the ability to put people down on paper plastically cannot be taught by any instructor; it is a specific talent, which the most gifted novelist cannot quite explain. But it is possible to teach undergraduates the structural aspects of story writing and so lay a foundation for the play of imagination. Thus the chapters on narration develop the mechanical basis of plot by means of exercises on chronological plotting, climactic plotting, plotting a single characteristic, and plotting the effect of a given setting. By the time the embryonic writer reaches the end of this section, his attention has been focused separately on the three main elements of any story. The last chapter then suggests how plot, character, and setting may be put together; the student is not told to write an actual short story, combining all three elements, till the very end of his study of narration. We believe that this gradual progress toward a definite, artistic form provides a practicable writing program even for the student who has no special talent for narrative.

We have tried to keep constantly in mind the fact that this book is written for young college students. We have tried to remember the limitations of their experience. Our precepts and exercises are intended to be suggestive, to open avenues of possibility. This book aims mainly, therefore, to encourage college students to teach themselves to write by writing.

R. W. B.
R. D. H.
T. H. E.

⇛ Acknowledgments ⇚

For much generous aid from those who helped to make this book possible the authors wish to express thanks as indicated below.

To the authors and publishers who gave their very kind permission to reprint whole essays and stories:

Professor R. B. Anderson for his translation of Björnson's "The Father"; Richard Connell for "The Most Dangerous Game"; Clarence Day (prior to his death) and Alfred A. Knopf, Inc. for "Father Lets in the Telephone," from *Life with Father*, by Clarence Day; Doubleday, Doran & Company, Inc., for "The Cop and the Anthem," from *The Four Million*, by O. Henry, and for "The Poplar" and "The Kaleidoscope," from *Trivia*, by L. P. Smith; J. H. Driberg and E. P. Dutton & Co., Inc. for "Engato, the Hunter" from *Engato, the Lion Cub;* W. A. Dwiggins for "La Dernière Mobilisation"; Elizabeth I. Folsom for "Towers of Fame"; the proprietors of *The Graphic* for "The Pensioner," by William Caine; Christopher Gerould for "The End of the Party"; Harcourt, Brace and Company, Inc. for "Michel de Montaigne," from *Thirteen Worthies*, by Llewelyn Powys; Harvard University Press for "Cracks in the Clouds," from *Imitation and Other Essays*, by Professor Charles H. Grandgent; *Life* for "The Mighty," by Harry Evans; Robert Lynd and *The New Statesman and Nation* for "On Making Mistakes" and "Love at Its Last Gasp"; the *Nation* for "The Road to Peace" by Louis Fischer; the *New York Times* for "A World of Gold beneath a Vacant Lot," by H. L. Matthews; Mary B. O'Reilly for "In Berlin"; *PMLA* for "A Freshman Poem by Emerson," by Tremaine McDowell; *Reader's Digest* for "Pro and Con—Abolish Intercollegiate Football?"; Benjamin Rosenblatt for "In the Metropolis," from *Brief Stories;* and the Syracuse *Post-Standard* for "Death of Captain Eddie," by F. E. Dutcher.

To the many other authors and publishers who generously allowed the use of extracts from their works, most of them by direct and personal permission of the author:

Conrad Aiken, Sherwood Anderson, Willimina Armstrong (for W. L. Comfort), Morley Callaghan, Malcolm Cowley, George E. De Mille, Charles Caldwell Dobie, Alban Dobson (for Austin Dobson), Lady Conan Doyle (for Sir Arthur Conan Doyle), Walter Prichard Eaton, Walter D. Edmonds, Charles J. Finger, Waldo Frank, Hamlin

Garland, Philip Guedalla, Don Marquis, Vincent O'Sullivan, Professor T. E. Rankin, Laurence Stallings, Wilbur Daniel Steele, Professor E. E. Stoll, and L. C. Wimberly.

The American Review, D. Appleton-Century Company, Inc., Albert & Charles Boni, Inc., the *Chicago Tribune*, the *Detroit Free Press*, the *Detroit News*, The Dial Press, Dodd, Mead and Company, Inc., Doubleday, Doran & Company, Inc., E. P. Dutton & Co., Inc., Harper & Brothers, Harvard University Press, Henry Holt and Company, Houghton Mifflin Company, the *Junior League Magazine*, Alfred A. Knopf, Inc., Liveright Publishing Corporation, The Macmillan Company, Modern Library, Inc., the *New Republic*, Oxford University Press, Pitman Publishing Corporation, Random House, *Reader's Digest*, William Reeves, Bookseller, Ltd., *The Saturday Review of Literature*, Charles Scribner's Sons, and the University of Minnesota Press.

To Professor J. M. Steadman, Jr., of Emory University, for valuable comments on several chapters of Part I; to Mrs. Josephine N. Keal, of Wayne University, for technical advice in the chapter on Argumentation; to Mr. Otto Soglow, illustrator for *The New Yorker*, for the drawing depicting the structure of the "plot story"; to Miss Maritje E. Babcock for willingly giving sturdy and accurate aid in typing and retyping the manuscript; and to J. E. Tilford, Jr., Mrs. W. H. Jones, and Miss Vivian Byers for further aid in preparing the manuscript.

Not least, to the many student writers whose work is reproduced herein. The compilers wish to express regret that it has been feasible, at least so far as this book is concerned, to interpose only their initials between acknowledgment and anonymity. It is to be hoped that, in due time, their full names will appear elsewhere along with their further work. Some of the student pieces have been, by assignment, written in conscious emulation of professional writers. Every effort has been made, however, to avoid including work marked by indebtedness beyond such imitation. It is sincerely hoped that no infringements upon the ethics of authorship have crept in to cast reflection on the honor of student writers as a group. This book, written so largely by them, has been prepared for their use.

R. W. B.
R. D. H.
T. H. E.

≫ *Table of Contents* ≪

Preface vii
Acknowledgments ix

PART I

FORMAL EXPOSITION AND INFORMAL ARGUMENT 1

I   TYPES OF FORMAL EXPOSITION 3
II   EXPOSITION OF A PROCESS 10
III   THE CLASSIFIED SUMMARY 28
IV   THE SUMMARIZING RÉSUMÉ 47
V   DEFINITION OF THE ABSTRACT TERM OR IDEA 67
VI   GENERALIZED DESCRIPTION 98
VII   THE CHARACTER SKETCH 117
VIII   EXPOSITORY BIOGRAPHY 139
IX   CRITICISM 163
X   SHORT, INFORMAL WRITTEN ARGUMENT 196
XI   THE TERM PAPER 227

PART II

THE INFORMAL ESSAY, NARRATION, AND DESCRIPTION 275

XII   THE INFORMAL ESSAY 277
XIII   LINEAR NARRATION 320
XIV   THE PLOT STORY 347
XV   EXPANSION OF THE PLOT STORY 421
XVI   DESCRIPTION 459
XVII   THE THREE ELEMENTS TOGETHER—THE SHORT STORY 477
XVIII   THE FULLY DEVELOPED FORM 540

Index 587

xi

⇛ PART ONE ⇚

Formal Exposition and Informal Argument

CHAPTER I

Types of Formal Exposition

THIS BOOK will in large part be devoted to distinguishing good sentences from bad, and indicating how to write good ones. Opinions differ as to what constitutes a good sentence, but most people will agree that it cannot be mechanically produced by a formula or set pattern; its effectiveness will be determined by the purpose which it is to serve and its adequacy to that purpose, as well as by considerations of grammatical form. Here are four sentences.

BALL–CASED BEEBE EYES WEIRD DEEP
NEWSPAPER HEADLINE.

I first noticed the hurry and business-like scramble of the people on the streets and I thought of the hurry I would soon amongst going to and from classes not running if late but I would be because that is the custom of twenty century campus conduct.

STUDENT'S THEME, "On Returning to College."

It is a hard and nice subject for a man to write of himself; it grates his own heart to say anything of disparagement, and the reader's ears to hear anything of praise from him.

ABRAHAM COWLEY, "Of Myself."

The several towns and villages in which, in my time, I have pitched a tent did not please, for one obscure reason or another: this one was too large, t'other too small; but when, on a summer evening about the hour of eight, I first beheld Dreamthorp, with its westward-looking windows painted by sunset, its children playing in the single straggling street, the mothers knitting at the open doors, the fathers standing about in long white blouses, chatting or smoking; the great tower of the ruined castle rising high into the rosy air, with a whole troop of swallows—by distance made as small as gnats—skimming about

3

its rents and fissures;—when I first beheld all this, I felt instinctively that my knapsack might be taken off my shoulders, that my tired feet might wander no more, that at last, on the planet, I had found a home.

ALEXANDER SMITH, Dreamthorp and Other Essays.

Now ask yourself which of these four sentences best serves the purpose for which sentences are written. Does not the first arrest your attention, whether or not you identify the deep-sea naturalist, Dr. William Beebe, and his famous diving apparatus, the bathysphere? The second sentence is unmistakably bad. The hurried student who wrote it was suddenly confronted with an assignment involving an impromptu piece of writing. He had a vivid imagination, but the rush of ideas flooded his mental engine, his sense of grammatical and logical form. Still, how much could the statement be improved upon as an expression of the confused rush to and from classes? The third sentence is tightly drawn, from the grammatical point of view—a compound sentence offering no difficulties of analysis; but is it not more resistant to the mind than the fourth example, which is only a casual stringing out of phrases and clauses?

These sentences raise questions concerning form. Which one could be definitely called the *best?* Could any one serve as a model for the others, or for sentences in general? What is the more important factor, grammatical purity, or force of idea and image? If you gain in one, must you lose in the other? No one can give final answers to such questions. Your work with this book, and your whole course in composition, will be an effort to find your own answers; and the answers you prefer will show their effect in your way of writing, in your *style.* A writer's style is the particular personal quality or stamp which distinguishes his writing. It results from his own special manner of conveying his ideas and feelings in sentences.

Exposition, or "setting forth," is a blanket term which covers this effort at conveying ideas and feelings. It is the form of writing which is most used in college: the explaining of a laboratory process, the interpretation of a literary or historical character, the discussion of a philosophical idea, a social situation, a group of phenomena—or, rather often, the answering of examination questions requiring information and critical conclusions. But especially you will use the methods of exposition a great deal, because college instructors have a habit of requiring frequent papers and reports. The most popular of these is the term paper—a bit of research devoted to the investigation of a more or less comprehensive or complex subject. Upperclassmen may be confronted with as many as five or six of these in a single term. Hence, the first or second term of the first year may well be devoted chiefly to training in the art of producing a fairly long piece of expository writing, by way of anticipating the student's future needs.

Twenty-five thousand words! One hundred thousand! How would it affect the state of mind of the average student when he first steps into the atmosphere of ivy-hung walls that is to be his campus, if he knew that he would eventually be required to put such wholesale quantities of words into action on paper before he could add a college degree to his name? The bland statements in the catalogues hold out no threat of such obligations. If there are any wrinkles in his forehead, they are brought there by misgivings over the bank balance, the social correctness of details of personal appearance, or other more tangible considerations. Like the gay grasshopper, he may even escape serious work-worries for several weeks, but inevitably they will come. Usually they develop at just about the season of the first snowflakes, of frozen ground, fur coats and chrysanthemums, and the thud of the booted foot on pigskin. Ah yes, just when the grasshopper, with stiffening fingers, his fiddle clutched under a shivering arm, begins to knock at the door of the ant.

Still, with a bit of the ant's foresight, there is really no need to worry greatly about the long paper, for it can be mastered by slow and easy stages. It consists of a series of definite and simple steps, easy to follow once a few points about bibliography and note taking have been absorbed. The shorter themes at the beginning of the term become minor exercises in preparing sections of the long paper due at the end. The discussion of exposition in this book, therefore, involves two main aims: first, a gradual preparation in the steps toward the production of a long exposition, or term paper; second, an introduction to the fundamental types of exposition arranged in something like a climactic order, leading from the more formal and stereotyped to the more individual and literary. In general, as will be shown, these two aims are closely related, for the types of exposition here separately treated often are equivalent to minor sections of the term paper itself. Thus you are actually following the procedure of the long paper while writing the short ones, and it is perfectly possible— if the instructor permits—to split the long-paper subject into parts to be developed and submitted as short papers. This method is not wholly desirable, however, for some of the shorter papers represent types which will not be involved in the working out of specific subjects for long papers. Also, as the course proceeds, you may be acquiring new points of view which might modify your original ideas as expressed in the earlier, short papers.

Let us illustrate more in detail. In the first of the two columns below are listed eight formal types of expository writing. In the second column are listed six basic steps in the long paper. List A includes the short papers which you will probably be asked to write in the beginning of the first semester or during the first term. List B includes steps in the long paper to be submitted at the end of the semester, or at the middle of the second term.

A. *Formal Expository Types*

1. Exposition of a process or generalized narration
2. Classified summary
3. Summarizing résumé
4. Definition of an abstract term or idea
5. Generalized description of a type
6. Character sketch of an individual
7. Expository biography
8. Criticism [1]

B. *Steps in the Long Expository Paper*

a. Definition and limiting the subject
b. Citing history or sources
c. Division or listing of types, aspects, varieties
d. Comparison or contrast in relationship
e. Value—a critical estimate
f. Future—a prediction of changes and results

---

[1] Other types, definitely minor in importance, have been subordinated to the development of the above main types.

As has been suggested, there is a fairly close relationship between the types of exposition and the steps in the development of the whole article or long paper. For example, training for definition (a), the usual first step in the long paper, will result from the earlier analysis of an abstraction or type (4), (or in 3 and 5); training for history, the sources and development of the subject (b), is anticipated in expository biography (7); training for division (c) comes early, in the summarizing themes (2 and 3); for comparison (d), all the short themes help (especially 1, 2, 3, 4, and 5); and for value (e), criticism (8) leads the way. Future (f) is usually only a graceful and convincing conclusion, growing out of what has preceded.

Once the essential purpose of each expository type or step has been grasped, it is very easy to apply it in the investigation and development of a definite subject. They are actual aspects of our process of communication and thinking. All of the steps in the long paper can be included in miniature in a single sentence, as follows:

The pioneers, restless invaders of the ever-receding West (a), crossed the wild plains and mountains from the cultivated regions of the Mississippi Valley and eastward (b), prospectors and trappers often on foot, Indian fighters, soldiers, explorers, surveyors on horseback, families of farmers, settlers, town-builders in wagon trains (c), all turning their backs on the planted and urbanized regions of dwindling opportunities, tax collectors, and mortgages, of security and body comforts as well (d), to set up lasting and vigorous outposts of civilization to the very shores of the Pacific (e), where ultimately America may come to find her true national soul and reason for being as the bulwark of Western culture (f).

Of course, in theme writing you would usually split such long sentences into shorter ones, indicating the transitions carefully and working for a climax.

If you are among those who have followed the trail of the covered wagon in car and trailer, you may find it interesting to work out a series of papers on the pioneer. Or suppose you are interested in radio. Then a series of short themes can be written on (1) the operation of a radio, some new type of tube, short wave, or television, or else on the organization of a broadcasting station and programs; (2) types of radios, of radio performers, of programs, or of radio "fans"; (3) the résumé of an article on the radio or of an ideal broadcast; (4) the analysis of good voice quality or pleasing personality for the microphone; (5) the general types of radio announcer, master of ceremonies, or performer; (6) a character sketch of some admired or detested performer; (7) an expository biography of inventors, organizers, performers in radio, of Amos 'n Andy; (8) a criticism of radio news, of the relative value of radio concerts and actual concerts, of radio plays, of specific performers again, or of the qualities of a particular type or make of radio.

By the time you have conducted this much investigation of various aspects of the radio you can sit down and produce a comprehensive essay rather rapidly. Taking account of our six steps, you might have the following outline:

Improvement in the Social Value of the Radio

(a) Definition of social value in its practical and aesthetic aspects
(b) History of radio programs from the first rudimentary stages
(c) Types of programs compared: informative, comic, sentimental, political, etc.
(d) A comparison of radio programs with the newspaper, the moving picture, the lecture, the sermon, bridge, sports, dancing
(e) The value of the radio: education, amusement, news, social contact, etc.
(f) The future of the radio in any of the above aspects or all of them, or in its strictly mechanical developments

Possibly you have preferred some other general subject—handloom weaving, automobiles, superstitions, precious stones, types of government—but by this time you have learned a good deal about your chosen interest. You have produced a special study of it based on short themes and a body of notes taken in the course of the semester. In this modern world of specialization, you have dug a deep niche for yourself.

We do not say that this intense specialization is always advisable; more often it is not. You will be a better man—or woman—at the end if you dissociate the long theme, the term paper, from the shorter productions. You will have a more varied, a more liberal education, and you will have a better chance of not wearing out your reader's interest. Furthermore, you will need to be taking notes throughout the whole semester on the subject of the long theme, and since the material in these notes may not be exactly suited to the shorter papers, these preparatory themes may prove to be of little value when you come to work out the long paper at the end. The best general advice would be to choose at the beginning of the term a subject in which you are greatly interested, so that its investigation for a final term paper will in itself be a pleasure. Listen to the instructor's ideas on note taking and bibliography. Then go out and write the shorter themes on subjects that perhaps have less appeal than the term-paper subject, but which still have some distinctly individual interest for you. If this program is followed, you will perhaps be able to astonish yourself with the versatility of your mind and interests as you handle the different types of exposition.

We are now ready to examine in sequence the eight main types of formal exposition. After that we can turn to an informal type of argument—the controversial essay. A chapter will be devoted to each expository type, with professional extracts and student themes appended to illustrate the varying degrees of success of beginning writers with these types. Following all these chapters will appear a chapter on the term paper, with illustrative material on bibliography, note taking, and outlining. This chapter should perhaps be read at once, as an early introduction to the idea of the term paper, and it may well be re-read each week, especially in connection with conferences.

At the conclusion of each chapter we have supplied a list of suggestive theme subjects, chosen by our own students for the particular type of writing involved in each chapter; but you should never feel compelled to limit yourself to one of these topics. The main purpose of this book is to encourage you to write naturally by allowing you absolute freedom to exploit your own individual interests. If you write about what you want to write about, you may learn to write well.

CHAPTER II

Exposition of a Process

THE SIMPLEST TYPE of exposition is technically called generalized narration. In its usual form it involves merely the explanation of a process: how to make something, how to play a game or musical instrument, how a mechanical device works. Sit down and think of some game, machine, device, food, that interests you particularly and that you can explain easily because of your first-hand knowledge of it.

Here the chief difficulty of this type appears. You will know so much about it that you will assume the reader knows just as much, and in most such guesses you will be wrong. Hence be careful to explain specific, technical terms involved: for example, do not assume definite knowledge of "trick" in bridge, "strike" in baseball, "punt" in football.

In this type of exposition a diagram or picture will help considerably. Tennis, baseball, field hockey, work out very readily on this basis. Letter the diagram and follow it through. But once you have adopted such a device, do not deliberately drop it in the middle of the theme and forget to refer to it again. If it is a really valuable diagram, it will probably be usable throughout the paper.

Another very important feature of this type of exposition is the style. The structure is simple enough, for the chronological sequence generally determines it. In the case of a machine the fundamental principle can be given and the parts related to that. But the style of the paper often becomes extremely mechanical— a mere series of short, choppy, stenographic sentences, repetitious phrases and words (especially "then"), and perhaps a persistent use of the imperative mood. This last effect is common in recipes.

The main thing is gracefully to combine the short sentences, varying the beginnings; or else, where combination is awkward, stock yourself with co-ordinate connectives to replace the omni-present "then": for example, "next," "after this," "secondly," "following this," "to continue."

Guard against a too informal style, which may by its very flippancy detract from the clearness of the exposition. On the other hand, the dangerously mechanical aspect of this theme may be considerably redeemed by some freedom of style. The mere statement of a process is, after all, a peculiarly dry affair which usually begins, though it should not, with "I will try to explain," after a long introduction indicating why you happen to like base-ball more than hockey, or waffles more than sponge cake. Get the theme started quickly, write it straight through as vitally as you can, and then go back and eliminate the stylistic crudities. Revision will help more in this type of exposition than in any other.

One final bit of advice: do not write specific narration—that is, avoid telling specifically how you prepared for a picnic at Holmes's Woods on Saturday, June 15. After all, this theme is supposed to be *generalized* narration: an exposition of how such and such a thing is generally done or such and such a game is generally played. Contrast the extracts from *Lorna Doone* and *Moby Dick* in section B below in regard to the tendency to write a concrete narrative of a specific series of events. Although they occur, exceptions to the rules, or specific cases, are beside the point. They will come in readily enough in linear narration which is to be discussed later.

The themes appended to this chapter show how the students avoided or fell into the above-mentioned pitfalls. They are, in general, papers of superior quality and should be studied in com-parison with the professional illustrations before an attempt is made to write this type. Most students have very little trouble with process themes, so that not much time need be spent on them. For possible inspiration we submit a selected list of the subjects our students have generally preferred:

Tennis, Volley Ball, Bridge, Field Hockey, How to Grow To-bacco, Playing a Trumpet, Making a Charcoal Sketch, How an

Editor Edits, How to Save a Drowning Person, How to Preserve Eggs, Baseball, Copying a Picture with Oils, How to Pass a Course, Horseback Riding, Amateur Dressmaking, Making a Garden, Fashion Designing, How to Play the Harmonica, Ice Hockey, Basketball, The Gasoline Engine, The Radio, The Telephone, The Shotgun, the Linotype Machine, Grinding Valves, The Candid Camera, Hand-loom Weaving, Batik Making, Shooting Ducks, Building Stage Scenery, Making a Date, Wood-block Printing, Selecting Christmas Gifts.

⫸ A ¹ ⫷

Observe the clearness of this first paper.

MAKING CHOCOLATE FUDGE

Anticipation of the enjoyment of this delicious form of candy, tempered by the slight degree of uncertainty involved in its preparation, renders the making of chocolate fudge an interesting and pleasureable pastime. It is the favorite indoor sport of many a sweet-toothed person.

Because, at certain points in the process, even a slight delay may prove disastrous, it is well to have all the ingredients and the utensils in readiness before starting. Chocolate, sugar, milk, butter, salt, and vanilla are the ingredients usually used. The utensils ordinarily employed are: a saucepan, spoon, cup, grater, and shallow pans (pie tins are best). The saucepan must be large enough to prevent the contents from boiling over, and the shallow pans must be well greased inside with butter so the candy can be easily removed after it has cooled. Careful attention to these details at the beginning is important because the remainder of the work should be done without unnecessary delay.

The chocolate must be finely grated so that it will blend well with the other ingredients. It is then put in the saucepan and thoroughly mixed with the milk, sugar, and butter, which, like the chocolate, have been carefully proportioned according to the recipe that is being used. Next, this mixture is put on the fire and boiled until the final test shows that it has reached the proper stage for beating. This testing is the most important feature of the process, for upon it depends the success of the venture. It is done by frequently trying a

---

¹ In general, student papers will appear under this heading, and more formal illustrations under "B."

few drops of the mixture in a cup of cold water. If these drops can be formed into a soft ball in the water, the pan must be removed from the fire at once.

Salt and vanilla are then added, and the whole mass is stirred and beaten vigorously to make it smooth and creamy. As soon as it begins to thicken, it must be poured into the buttered pans to cool.

Cutting the candy into squares is the last step. This is done after it has hardened but before it becomes too brittle. A thin, sharp knife which has been greased with butter is best for this purpose. The butter prevents the candy from sticking to the knife.

Often, especially in rural communities, the making of candy and popcorn constitutes the chief entertainment of an evening social gathering, after which everyone gathers in the parlor and enjoys the results of his efforts that were made in the kitchen.

H. M. H.

It is possible to add stylistic smoothness to clearness.

HOW TO PLAY GOLF

A definition given in a book, but obviously not written by a golfer, reads: "Golf is an open-air game consisting of driving a small resilient ball successively into each of 9 or 18 holes arranged at varying intervals over a course, or links."

Sounds simple, but try it. Naturally the first requisite should be the implements of the game, and these should be chosen with a view to the effect you want to create. If it is your desire to impress others with your prowess or nonchalance, a matched set of steel-shafted clubs should be selected. These include two wooden clubs, six irons, and a putter. In addition, a leather bag for carrying the clubs is necessary; leather being chosen so that the entire weight, that is, bag and clubs, necessitates hiring a caddy, thus increasing the above impression of being a champion. It is also advisable to tip the caddy liberally, which will in time materially lower your score.

Next you should join as exclusive a club as money and your personality can command, and sign up for lessons with the club professional. He will explain, in a condescending manner, the form and swing required for the various shots. He will, however, fail to explain that a good many shots may cause your ball to fall into hazards, such as bunkers, sand traps, clumps of trees, or the local brook. After a few lessons and some practice, he may let you go around the course at an early morning hour when no other golfers are in your way (thus saving you a lawsuit).

You should then proceed to the first tee, a terrace-like mound of grass, from which your first drive is made. The ball is placed on a small wooden tee, pin-shaped with a tiny cuplike head, and is driven off with the driver. If your score card lists the first hole as 540 yards, par 5, the first shot has presumably, though not probably, travelled more than 200 yards down the fairway, which is the narrow strip of land between tee and green. If your ball really has travelled that far, you walk to where it lies and using your brassie, the slightly lofted wooden club, you again knock the ball toward the green. This time the ball may land in a sand trap near the green, and it can be played out in several ways. The most effective one is the explosion shot which you play with your putter or midiron, and strike for the sand back of the ball, thus exploding the ball out and on the green. The advantage of this shot is that the sand usually obscures the number of shots you take in the trap from your partner's view.

Now that your ball is on the green, the putter is used with a pushing stroke until the ball falls in the hole. The green is a large, fairly flat surface covered with closely clipped grass, on which is located the hole. Unless the course has been visited by thieves, you will find a medium-length bamboo pole with a flag attached to the top, bearing the number of the hole you are playing. This can usually be seen from the tee.

There are either nine or eighteen of these holes, of varying lengths and slightly different topography, on the course and they are played consecutively, the game being to reach each of the holes with the lowest possible number of strokes.

For the first few years, regardless of the number of lessons you take and the hours you practice, you will be tempted to quit the game and throw your clubs in the nearest lake whenever you make a poor shot. Your next shot is usually so much better, however, that you'll consider it worth while to go on and try again. It helps your feelings, somewhat, if you have at your command some strong expletives to be used after each poor shot, but a few years of golf will undoubtedly add much to your vocabulary in this line.

C. S. L.

"How to Solve a Cryptogram" is perfectly constructed, and shows how concrete illustration helps this type of theme.

HOW TO SOLVE A CRYPTOGRAM

Solving puzzles is one of the most interesting hobbies a person can have. I am not referring to jig-saw puzzles, mechanical puzzles, or any of the sort. I merely mean word puzzles. There are several types of these, among which are anagrams, rebuses, homonyms, and endless others; but the ones with which I am chiefly concerned are cryptograms.

Before explaining the solution, I suppose the logical thing is to tell exactly what type of puzzle it is. My definition is this: a cryptogram is a sentence or paragraph in which each letter of a word is substituted by another, the same symbol representing a letter each time it appears.

Here is a puzzle which I will use as an example:

GHMNPA KJ DCZJBEACHGF NF H GKDL OHFNOC BHFM BLHP FEQRNPA DCZJBEACHGF. POROCBLOQOFF BLO FEQKBNEP EI EPO NF GKDL GECO NPBOCOFBNPA.

The first step towards the solution is the taking of the frequency. This points out the rare letters and enables one to determine in a better way which letters are vowels, and which are consonants.

The frequency of this cryptogram is as follows:

A B C D E F G H I J K L M N O P Q R S̸ T̸ U̸ V̸ W̸ X̸ Y̸ Z

5 9 8 4 8 11 6 7 1 3 4 5 2 8 11 8 3 2   2

After the symbols have been counted for the frequency, the tentative vowels and consonants are marked by certain signs. A circle surrounds a letter appearing only once. Those letters that occur twice are shown by a square. Letters thought to be vowels are underscored with a small line, and consonants are designated by a small cross.

Here are a few suggestions that will help in deciding whether letters are to be vowels or consonants: the first letter in most words is a consonant; the second letter is generally a vowel; and a consonant preceded by a consonant at the beginning of a word is usually an "r," an "h," or an "l."

When the cryptogram has been completely marked, it will look something like this:

GH[M]NPA KJ DC[Z]JBEACHGF NF H GKDL OHFNOC BHF[M] BLHP FEQ[R]NPA

X— —XX —X XX XX—XX—XX —X — X—XX — —X——X X—X   XX—X X—X —XX

DC[Z]JBEACHGF. PO[R]OCBLOQOFF BLO FEQKBNEP E(I) EPO NF GKDL GECO

XX XX—XX—XX X— —XXX—X—XX XX— X—X—X——X —   —X— —X X—XX X—X—

NPBOCOFBNPA.

—XX—X—XX—XX

Guessing words, which is the most enjoyable process, follows this. Short words are good beginnings. For example, the symbol "h," uncapitalized, would probably be "a." The ending "NPA" is noticeable several times, and would likely be considered "ing" by the way it is marked (vowel, consonant, consonant). Of course this sort of ending and short words are found mostly in the easier cryptograms.

After the completion of three words, the cryptogram is practically solved. It is only necessary then to fill in the remainder of the symbols with the same letters.

The answer to the example, which is easily achieved after following the last few steps, is as follows:

MAKING UP CRYPTOGRAMS IS A MUCH EASIER TASK THAN SOLVING CRYPTOGRAMS. NEVERTHELESS THE SOLUTION OF ONE IS MUCH MORE INTERESTING.

The greatest reward for the solution of a cryptogram is the satisfied feeling one has at the completion of his work.

J. L.

The author of the following theme has engaged in some good research and written up the facts cleverly.

THE EGYPTIAN MUMMY

The ancient Egyptians are the only people known who have succeeded in perfecting the art of embalming. They believed that the soul would revisit the body after a number of years. Therefore, it was absolutely necessary for the body to be preserved if its owner wished to live forever with the gods. The soul was supposed to have its own body and be able to eat and to drink. After it left the body it was doomed to undergo a series of existences until it reached a fit state of purity to be absorbed into its original double.

The art of embalming is said to be of divine origin. It was unknown in the ages that followed the creation. Osiris was the first mummy, and from it the others were all copied.

There were three different ways in which mummies were made. In the first, the body was treated with perfumes, drugs, stuffs, amulets, and prayers. The result of this method was excellent. However, it was so long and so costly that only the princes and the great men were wealthy enough to pay for it. The second method, which did not involve such complicated operations, required less time and money, and was used for people of average means. The third method, costing only a very small sum, was for the poor. That meant about four-fifths of the Egyptian population.

The three methods were based upon the same principle. This was to extract from the body those parts which easily decayed. The remainder was saturated in salts and aromatics to prevent any change taking place in it. The drugs used were quite valuable, and the work very carefully done. The appearance of the mummy was more or less luxurious, according to the price given, but the result was the same in all cases. The body lasted instead of perishing, and its permanence guaranteed that of its double.

An examination of the mummies shows that many different processes were used at different periods in Egypt; also, that the Egyptians possessed a good knowledge of the use of medicines and of anatomy.

The corpse was first undressed, washed, and stretched upon the ground under the direction of a master of the ceremonies. After a prayer was said, a surgeon then passed a curved instrument up the left nostril with which he broke the divisions of the skull and withdrew the brain, piece by piece. A second prayer was said. This was followed by the scribe's tracing a line in ink upon the left side of the stomach, and another prayer. Then someone made an incision with an Ethiopian stone knife. Since it was considered a sacrilege to open a human body, the assistants attacked and abused the operator as soon as he accomplished his task. One of the embalmers rapidly removed the intestines, heart, and lungs. Another prayer was said, and the workmen carried the remains and plunged them into the bath of liquid natron in which they had to soak for seventy days.

When the body was taken from the brine, it was nothing but a skeleton covered with yellowish parchment-like skin. The cheeks were slightly hollowed, the lips thinner, and the nostrils slightly drawn, but the face was not changed. The natron had preserved in the limbs a suppleness. The embalmers took advantage of this and placed the feet closely together and crossed the arms. They stuffed the stomach and chest with linen and sawdust mixed with aromatic powders and then started the wrapping of the body.

During the bandaging of the corpse, amulets, dry flowers, blades of grass, and plates covered with hieroglyphics were placed on it. The master of ceremonies fastened at the dead man's throat a green scarabaeus. Rings of gold and of blue or green enamel were placed upon his fingers as amulets which gave him a correct tone of voice and enabled him to recite prayers.

After the body had been wrapped, it was usually enclosed in what

was called a cartonnage, if the person was of rank or a priest. The
cartonnage was a thin casing made of plaster and linen. It covered
the whole body, fitting closely.

The face was painted only, in the earlier days, but later, the face
and ears were often gilded, and the eyes, eyebrows, and lids made of
glass or porcelain. On the top of the head a scarabaeus or beetle was
painted. A number of scenes were painted on the cartonnages, depicting the deceased with Osiris and other deities. However, they
varied greatly, few being exactly alike. In the last days of the Egyptian
empire a portrait of the deceased was painted and laid upon the face
of the mummy. The hair was usually mummified, and wrapped in
bandages and laid at the foot of the corpse.

The mummy, arranged in its brightly painted cartonnage, was
then placed in a coffin or case of sycamore wood, which was made to
represent the form of a man. As the mummy, so the coffin was made
according to the amount the friends of the dead person could afford
to pay. The outer case of all was made of stone, and was sometimes
covered entirely with hieroglyphs, and at other times, different scenes
illustrated the "Book of the Dead."

When the body of the man was safely sealed in the coffin, his friends
and relatives breathed easier, for they knew he would then be quite
safe in the other world. The mummy was ready for his funeral and
tomb.

J. R.

»»» B ¹ «««

At its simplest, generalized narration will be objective; it will
not admit the personal element of imagination. Such types are
available in any cookbook, in laboratory manuals for experiments
in chemistry and physics, and technical works on the processes
of such arts and crafts as pottery making, weaving, and wood
carving. Some portions of an account of the method for making
linoleum cuts will illustrate the emphasis on facts and the plain
statement of procedure. There is little regard for paragraph
form here and none for stylistic effect. The selection is taken
from *Block-Cutting and Print-Making by Hand* (London, 1930)[2] by
Margaret Dobson. A very elementary treatment has been chosen

---

[1] This heading will be used to indicate sections containing more formal illustrations.

[2] Reprinted by permission of the publishers, The Pitman Publishing Corporation.

so that you may, if you like, follow directions and make a linoleum cut yourself.

For a First Experiment

For a first cut and print, the required tools and materials are surprisingly few.

A medium-sized water-colour brush;
Common or Indian ink;
Piece of linoleum;
Sharp pocket knife or vee-shaped gouge;
Printing ink made from Indian ink and flour paste;
Any variety of smooth paper upon which to print;
Plenty of newspaper;
Small piece of tracing paper;
A little white chalk;
Drawing paper. . . .

How to Transfer a Design to a Block

In thinking out a design with which to start a first cut, the simplest treatments are, if the knife is to be used as the tool, that of practically black silhouette, and, if the vee gouge is to be used as the tool, that of rich line. The whole of the desired effect of the print should be rendered on white paper so that it is known exactly what to expect from the print. The drawing should be of the same size as that which is to be cut out on the block, correct in every detail, all the parts, which are to print black, being filled in with Indian ink and a brush. . . . When the design according to the tool adopted is decided upon, a tracing is made on tracing paper, in outline, in pencil, from the inked drawing. When this is done, a little powdered chalk is rubbed with the finger over the back of the tracing. (Should the design not bear reversing, for it is always reversed in the print, as in the case of lettering, the tracing should be gone over on its other side with pencil and then the chalk rubbed on the right side, that is, on the top of the first tracing made.) The tracing rubbed, it is placed, chalk side downwards, on the face of the linoleum block. The left hand will hold the tracing paper steady while the right hand runs over the outlines again with a pencil. The tracing paper is then removed, when the outlines should show clearly on the linoleum as white chalk lines.

These chalk lines are not permanent, so the design should now be redrawn in full, masses and lines, exactly as in the drawing, with a brush and Indian ink. The chalk lines are for guidance.

Linoleum should never be drawn upon with any sharp point. The brush is the suitable implement for it.

With the design rendered in full on the block, greater certainty is assured in cutting. Otherwise, if in outline only, mistakes may easily occur with the cutting tool.

The ink is now allowed to dry thoroughly, when it should appear quite black. . . .

The ideal, of course, is to dispense with tracing altogether and either to draw straight away with the brush and ink on the block or to draw with the cutting tool itself. To work of this description there always comes a certain spontaneous fresh appearance which is usually lost if the design is taken through many stages. But, in a first cut, technique is of first importance, and the student is wise who does not attempt too much.

The inked block when thoroughly dry is ready for cutting.

The Cutting of a Linoleum Block

The cutting of linoleum is quite an easy matter. . . .

The tool should be used freely and an effort made to understand its possibilities. There is little use straining after impossibilities in cutting. Much intricate detail, even in an initially simple design, will only clog up and be submerged in printing. It very often happens that many parts must be simplified on the block. And, in cutting, it is advisable not to cut away too much. Lines should be left thick and masses broad. It is easy to recut into a part, but, once removed, it is difficult to replace.

Either method of cutting leaves in relief that part which is to receive the ink.

Care must be taken not to injure the edges and to steer the tool clear of them when removing backgrounds. A certain roughness is bound to result in gouging away large spaces, but this is of little consequence if it does not interfere with the paper too much when printing. It should be taken into consideration that large background areas require cutting to a greater depth than small areas. For very small areas, the usual depth of the trench cut is sufficient.

When the block is cut satisfactorily, it requires to be freed from the ink which was used in drawing the design on the block. A rush of cold water from the tap and a gentle rubbing with a sponge or soft cloth should suffice. The surface is then mopped dry with a towel. Printing may commence before the block is "bone" dry. In fact, a new block is often greasy and requires washing in tepid water with a little soda or soap before printing is commenced. But, in drying a block, beware of exposing it to any undue heat, even the sun, for the block warps easily.

Printing from the Linoleum Block

. . . In ideal circumstances the paper should be dampened, but printing can be done on dry paper, provided it is not too thick. The paper should be placed near the block in readiness.

Then the printing ink, placed also in readiness near the block, is prepared by having a tablespoonful or more of smooth flour paste, not too thin, in one saucer and some Indian ink poured out in another saucer.

Two or three folds of newspaper, of a size a little larger than the block, will serve as a baren or pad.

The ink is applied to the block by dipping the brush first into the saucer of ink, lifting a brushload and brushing it over the block, allowing the ink to settle on every part which is in relief. Then a little of the paste is lifted from its saucer by the same brush and it is brushed over the block so that the paste mixes well with the ink. Very little paste is required.

When the block is all covered with the ink and its paste, when the mixture appears lying on every part of the surface like cream, a piece of printing paper is placed, with a quick sharp movement, down on the top of the richly inked block. At once the wad of newspaper is applied to the block and its paper, it also being laid down with a quick movement on the top of the paper. Then the newspaper is rubbed with the fingers or the palm of the hand in a zigzag direction, from left to right, and up and down. Holding all the papers on the block steady with the left hand, it does not take a minute for the right hand to feel the design in relief telling through the wad of newspaper. Layers of the newspaper may be removed from the wad, until the pressure is applied with only one layer of newspaper on the top of the paper. A peep can be taken at the print by raising one corner. If it shows richly black, and the rubbing has been, as far as can be told, even all over, the newspaper is first removed from the block, then the paper, on which the print is, is slowly raised with the fingers of both hands by the bottom two corners. Prints should always be pulled away from the block rather warily.

In contrast to this matter-of-fact method, a few of the careful paragraphs of Richard D. Blackmore's romantic novel *Lorna Doone* will show that imaginative treatment is quite possible. When an enthusiast for fishing, such as Isaak Walton, for wood life, such as John Muir or Stewart Edward White, for book collecting, such as A. Edward Newton, or any devotee of a hobby or sport discusses his technique, we are certain to find his excitement affecting his language. Here, through his hero, John Ridd, Blackmore betrays his zest for the pursuit of the insignificant loach. Such exposition verges closely on the informal essay which we shall discuss later.

There are many people, even now, who have not come to the right knowledge what a loach is, and where he lives, and how to catch and pickle him. And I will not tell them all about it, because if I did, very likely there would be no loaches left, ten or twenty years after the appearance of this book. A pickled minnow is very good, if you catch him in a stickle, with the scarlet fingers upon him; but I count him no more than the ropes in beer, compared with a loach done properly.

Being resolved to catch some loaches, whatever trouble it cost me, I set forth without a word to any one, in the forenoon of St. Valentine's day, 1675–6, I think it must have been. Annie should not come with me, because the water was too cold; for the winter had been long, and snow lay here and there, in patches in the hollow of the banks, like a lady's gloves forgotten. And yet the spring was breaking forth, as it always does in Devonshire, when the turn of the days is over; and though there was little to see of it, the air was full of feeling. . . .

I never could forget that day, and how bitter cold the water was. For I doffed my shoes and hose, and put them in a bag about my neck; and left my little coat at home, and tied my shirt-sleeves back to my shoulders. Then I took a three-pronged fork firmly bound to a rod with cord, and a piece of canvas kerchief, with a lump of bread inside it; and so went into the pebbly water, trying to think how warm it was. For more than a mile all down the Lynn stream, scarcely a stone I left unturned, being thoroughly skilled in the tricks of the loach, and knowing how he hides himself. For being gray-spotted, and clear to see through, and something like a cuttle-fish, only more substantial, he will stay quite still, where a streak of weed is in the rapid water, hoping to be overlooked, nor caring even to wag his tail. Then being disturbed he flips away, like whalebone from the finger, and hies to a shelf of stone, and lies with his sharp head poked in under it; or sometimes he bellies him into the mud, and only shows his back-ridge. And that is the time to spear him nicely, holding the fork very gingerly, and allowing for the bent of it, which comes to pass, I know not how, at the tickle of air and water.

Or if your loach should not be abroad, when first you come to look for him, but keeping snug in his little home, then you may see him come forth amazed at the quivering of the shingles, and oar himself and look at you, and then dart upstream, like a little gray streak; and then you must try to mark him in, and follow very daintily. So after that, in a sandy place, you steal up behind his tail to him, so that he cannot set eyes on you, for his head is upstream always, and there you see him abiding still, clear, and mild, and affable. Then, as he looks so innocent, you make full sure to prog him well, in spite of the wry of the water, and the sun making elbows to everything, and the trembling of your fingers. But when you gird at him lovingly, and have as good as gotten him, lo! in the go-by of the river he is gone as a shadow goes, and only a little cloud of mud curls away from the prong he should have been on.

R. D. BLACKMORE, *Lorna Doone.*

Moby Dick (1851), the masterpiece of the American novelist Herman Melville, is no less a work of exposition than a massive piece of fiction. The story of the relentless pursuit of a white whale by the mad Captain Ahab is told with an earnestness equal to that of "The Ancient Mariner." Coleridge's tale is a mystical account of wrongdoing and penance. Melville's is a no less mystical epic of vengeance, for the whale had once sheared off Captain Ahab's leg, leaving him to support himself on an ivory peg, and an insatiable thirst for vengeance. In reading the work, however, you will become acquainted with all there is to be known about whales: their types (see the selection in the next chapter), their habits, the methods of their pursuit and capture, the processes in converting them into commercial products, and much more.

The following extract gives an account of the difficult method of capturing whales by hurling a spear from a small boat.

Of all the wondrous devices and dexterities, the sleights of hand and countless subtleties, to which the veteran whaleman is so often forced, none exceed that fine manoeuvre with the lance called pitchpoling. Small sword, or broad sword, in all its exercises boasts nothing like it. It is only indispensable with an inveterate running whale; its grand fact and feature is the wonderful distance to which the long lance is accurately darted from a violently rocking, jerking boat, under extreme headway. Steel and wood included, the entire spear is some ten or twelve feet in length; the staff is much slighter than that of the harpoon, and also of a lighter material—pine. It is furnished with a small rope called a warp, of considerable length, by which it can be hauled back to the hand after darting.

But before going further, it is important to mention here, that though the harpoon may be pitchpoled in the same way with the lance, yet it is seldom done; and when done, is still less frequently successful, on account of the greater weight and inferior length of the harpoon as compared with the lance, which in effect become serious drawbacks. As a general thing, therefore, you must first get fast to a whale, before any pitchpoling comes into play.

Look now at Stubb; a man who from his humorous, deliberate coolness and equanimity in the direst emergencies, was specially qualified to excel in pitchpoling. Look at him; he stands upright in the tossed bow of the flying boat; wrapped in fleecy foam, the towing whale is forty feet ahead. Handling the long lance lightly, glancing twice or thrice along its length to see if it be exactly straight, Stubb whistlingly gathers up the coil of the warp in one hand, so as to secure its free end in his grasp, leaving the rest unobstructed. Then holding the lance full before his waistband's middle, he levels it at the whale; when, covering him with it, he steadily depresses the butt-end in his hand, thereby elevating the point till the weapon stands fairly balanced upon his palm, fifteen feet in the air. He minds you somewhat of a juggler, balancing a long staff on his chin. Next moment with a rapid, nameless impulse, in a superb lofty arch the bright steel spans the foaming distance, and quivers in the life spot of the whale. Instead of sparkling water, he now spouts red blood.

HERMAN MELVILLE, *Moby Dick.*

Finally, the strict type of formal explanation may be seen in these extracts from a lucid and straightforward account of the procedure to be followed in making a rock garden.[1]

MAKING A ROCK GARDEN

Richard Sudell

You can make a rock garden anywhere if you are prepared to spend money. But there are some sites that are only suitable for a

[1] Reprinted from Richard Sudell, *The New Garden*, London, The English Universities Press Ltd., 1935, by permission of Charles Scribner's Sons.

definite type of rock garden, and the first thing to do is to consider the suitability of the available site, what it is capable of, and how much cost and labour it would entail to make the best of it. The best position for a good rock garden is on an open sunny site, quite away from the drip or shade of trees. If there are available slopes, it will be found that the easiest to keep bright and well-cultivated will be a slope that faces southeast.

Any rock garden will be built with varying slopes, some of which will be almost completely shady, while others will get the maximum amount of sunshine, but a site where sun is plentiful is the best to work on, and easiest to maintain. . . .

Weathered limestone is regarded as one of the best rock-garden stones, if not the best. . . . Red sandstone is delightful when well built and planted. . . . I am not one of those highbrow rock gardeners who despise substitutes for natural rock. I have seen gardens built with lumps of cement dug from old foundations, and with homemade rocks formed by running cement over beaten tins and broken bricks. . . .

It is not really possible to state how much stone is needed for any particular size of rock garden, but, for the smallest amateur's rockery, about a ton of stone will make up a surface of about nine square yards—i.e. three yards each way. In a larger rock garden a single stone might weigh a ton!

Now for the spade work. The type of rock garden must be determined beforehand. On a sloping site, the general lie of the garden will be suggested already. On a flat site, there are roughly two possibilities. You can pile up the soil and rocks into a mound, or mounds, large or small according to the amount of rocks at your disposal, or you can excavate a sunk path or paths, and pile the excavated soil at the sides so that the rockery slopes face each other.

The simple mound is generally chosen where the rock garden is very small, and only a part of the general garden—for instance, where a rockery is built on one corner of the lawn in order to focus attention there. The excavated winding path makes a larger rock garden, of greater interest, and, because of its form, it has in it the element of surprise which is most desirable in every garden design. . . . A further feature of a rock garden is the inclusion of water, either in the form of a stream, natural or artificial, running close to the sunk path, or in the form of pools at different levels, with tiny cascades from one to the other. . . .

When the general form of the rock garden has been decided, excavations can begin. Remember that the fertile soil of the garden is the top dark soil only. Do not bury any of this under rocks or piles of subsoil, but begin by stripping it off and stacking it in a heap elsewhere. Then roughly pile up the subsoil to the desired shape. On soil that is naturally light and well drained no special attention need be given to the foundations, but, should a rock garden be made on a heavy clay subsoil, build it over a six-inch layer of rough clinker or other drainage material.

Also, if the soil is clay, mix with it as much coarse grit as you can, to make it more porous. Faulty drainage will kill more rock plants than any other trouble.

When you begin on the actual work of rock building, have by you the rocks, more or less sorted out, and a quantity of prepared soil that is of an open porous nature, with some leaf mould, or other decayed organic matter, well distributed in it. . . .

Select a few of the larger rocks for key positions, and decide which way up they are to be set. This will to a large extent determine the positions of the other smaller rocks, for, as far as possible, the rocks should lie in the natural strata, as they would if they were a natural outcrop. That means that any lines or cracks on the rocks should generally lie in the same direction.

Begin to build from the base, tilting each rock inwards so that the rain falling on it would enter the soil and not be diverted down the outer side of the rock. Make each one quite firm before you leave it. To test each by standing on it is a good practice, for, when you come to planting and weeding, you may have to stand on the rocks to reach some of the plants, and not very pleasant for yourself!

Ram the prepared soil well behind and round the rocks, so that there are no air pockets left, for these are very dangerous for plant roots, and have been known to kill plants by causing the roots to dry out. Arrange rocks and soil so that there are pockets of varying sizes to take the plants—wide, flat pockets for gentians, vertical crevices for Ramondias, etc. Remember that for every rock plant that likes the shady side of the rock garden, there are half a dozen that prefer the sunny slopes, so, if you can, make the shady slopes more precipitous than the sunny ones. This will give you a greater area for the sun lovers. . . .

Colour is of importance in the rock garden, though in some types of rock garden colour is subdued to form. Colour is so easily obtainable in the spring that few rock gardens are dull at this season, when drifts of golden alyssum, purple aubretia, pink saponaria, white arabis, blue gentians and campanulas, and purple violas flower freely with no special care. But colour in the later months of the year—August and September—is more difficult to obtain, and many rock gardeners allow their gardens to become comparatively dull after the spring show. . . . It should be a point of honour with the keen rock gardener to keep up the colour and floral interest of his miniature landscape all through the seasons.

CHAPTER III

The Classified Summary

THE CLASSIFIED SUMMARY is another easy type of exposition to write, for its substance and organization are simplified from the start. In fact, the chief danger of the exercise arises from its very simplicity, and its main asset as a promoter of style evolves from the precise problem of covering up this extreme simplicity by a distinct individualization of the material. All one does is to sit down and think up types of guns, inventions, automobiles, cats, dances, etc., etc. The task then is to write them up so that the theme does not read like the catalogue of a mail-order house.

Obviously the first step is to choose a subject which interests you and which you know thoroughly. That will start you on the way to some individuality. Then write out a list of possible divisions of this subject—e.g., for dances: minuet, polka, waltz, two-step, one-step, tango, lame duck, turkey trot, fox trot, toddle, Chicago, Charleston, black bottom, varsity drag, Gary hop, camel's glide, Indiana slide, big apple. (A student once developed these in detail for a term paper.) It will be seen at once that it would be impossible to cover this whole list in a short paper (four or five hundred words), so that naturally you will choose the most distinctive dances—and this process of selecting the best illustrations will be another step toward individuality. In the above case the dances might be discussed in the order in which they became popular, but this chronological element will not always be present to help outline the paper.

After you have chosen an interesting subject and some concrete illustrations, the next thing is to put them together in a non-catalogue form. This requires art. Be wary of the dry one-two-three-four procedure, and watch carefully transitions from one

28

illustration to the next. The paragraphing will be simple enough because each illustration will generally receive one paragraph— the first paragraph being mainly devoted to introducing them all; but the style of the sentences with the paragraphs will have to be watched, as in the case of the process theme, to avoid monotony. Suggestions on varying sentence structure may be found in any handbook of composition. Co-ordinate connectives, as in the preceding type (Chapter II), are again important.

The main problem in this theme, then, is to avoid producing a flat, mechanical catalogue. Choice of subject and illustrations, organization and development, style—all will help to solve the problem. Diagrams and pictures may also be used in this type, but like headings for the various parts, they are something of a confession of inability to handle the material smoothly. A diagram may be necessary to make an intricate process clearer, but there will generally be no particular intricacy about the subjects of this second type of exposition. If a technical subject is chosen—such as types of wind instruments—probably some diagrams will help; in general, however, these shorter themes should be written on easily developed topics which will not require research; that particular aspect of the work is better reserved for the term paper.

Here are some subjects students have preferred for this type: Moving Pictures, Sea Weeds, Cheirognomy, Freshman Prejudices, Freshman Ambitions, Blind Dates, Liars, Varieties of Oaks, Winter Wraps, Types of Husbands, Friends, Taboos, Actors, Barbers, Sophomores, Cereals, Schoolteachers, "Lines," Brothers, Mustaches, Hats. The possibilities are innumerable, but it is important to distinguish between the casual subject, allowing for play of fancy and humor, as against the scientific, where close observation, research in the writings of authorities, and strict conformity to fact are imperative. Draw on your courses and instructors for such subjects. Examples might include: Earth Features (geology); the Planets (astronomy); the Greek, Roman, or Norse Pantheon of Gods and Goddesses (mythology); Races of Men (anthropology); the Three Orders in Greek Architecture or Features of Gothic (architecture). Scientific classification, the basis of manufacture and industry and invention itself, includes the whole universe of "shoes—and ships—and sealing-wax."

⋙ A ⋘

In "Types of Women" the style is natural, in the main. Notice that humor, blended with raillery, must above all seem casual. This example, unfortunately, displays certain faults in idiom.

TYPES OF WOMEN

It is practically impossible to give a complete analysis of all types of the female sex, but it is possible to give enough information to warrant one to be observant and careful—particularly careful. The character of a woman is like a leaf tossed by the wind from place to place—ever restless—never stopping until utterly extinguished. Man has made poor headway as the extinguisher.

Eve created the first and most common type when she gave Adam the apple. Now, instead of apples, women give bills. A slave to the god Vanity, her husband is given as sacrifice. To analyze this kind of woman we must go back into the past, and, piece by piece, build up her character to its present status.

First we will question the environment in her own home. What were her parents' attitudes toward each other? Their life in general? We can picture a big "butter-and-egg" man chased into marriage by an ambitious waitress; or probably a wealthy, over-solicitous widow, who in a frenzy to darn socks, snared into marrying her, a book-keeper who had always stayed home and done his homework.

The next type is not to be outdone in popularity. Everyone knows those stout women who go about groaning every minute of the day about certain pains in their body. Their complaints are always exaggerated to excite sympathy. She, who has labored all her life, painstakingly obeyed all phases of her religion, does not understand why she should be subjected by God to be in such pain. She is never happy if she has nothing to complain of. Her greatest ambition is to discover some strange malady in herself which her friends have never heard of before.

You may now relax; I am gradually coming into a more familiar field. You know the women that always say everything is darling, and everything is simply gorgeous. The kind who quote "Shakespeare" at a pinochle game, and the ones men love to choke.

The next is the "hard" type; the kind who should be in a ring instead of a home. The mother-in-law is a perfect example. I won't dwell on this kind very much; most of you have, painfully, received more information than I can ever give you.

The last and rarest type is the perfect woman; the kind you might find at a lonely wayside inn, or out in the desert. When you're lying in bed after a heavy supper, she'll probably come to you in a dream. Just like you pictured your wife before you married her.

I had better stop writing now, because if my wife sees this when she comes home, even all that I know about women won't do me any good.

H. R.

The next paper has novelty of material and imaginative handling. Compare it with Addison's *Spectator* paper in section B for qualities leading toward the familiar essay.

THE DOORBELL SPEAKS

Much has been said in the past about Nature's way of providing compensation for her handicapped. The blind develop a keener sense of hearing, and the deaf develop a keener sense of sight. So, too, do the senses of an invalid become sharpened and alert to small details. The range of sight of the invalid is usually limited to a single room so that his eyesight does not have very much opportunity to become keener. The sense, though, that does have this opportunity to become more alert is his sense of hearing, because he must rely so much upon this sense to know what is going on outside of his room. He hears all sounds and noises; none escape him. He listens for the airplane that passes over his house exactly at the same time every evening, and he sets his clock by it. He listens to voices outside his room and guesses to whom they belong. He tries to count the number of turns when someone dials on the telephone and attempts to determine the number being dialed. He tries to guess who it is every time the telephone or doorbell rings. It is a difficult task to guess who is calling on the telephone, because all calls come through the impersonal ring of the telephone operator or mechanism that treats all calls alike and has the same unvarying ring for all.

The doorbell, however, lends itself a little more easily to guesswork. There is more of the personal "touch" present when the person rings the doorbell in his own style. Most doorbell ringers have their own particular pattern. They all have one thing in common, however, and that is that they are all in a hurry. No matter whether the ringer has come to collect for the newspaper or whether he is going to spend four or five hours there, it is expected that someone will automatically appear at the door the second the bell is touched. Aside from all doorbells saying, "Hurry, hurry," they say other things. The invalid listens to the ring and, after some practice, he can guess with more than a fair degree of accuracy who is ringing.

Take, for example, the ringer who "sits" on the bell. He rings a long, loud ring which causes everyone in the house to jump. If he does not get immediate action, he repeats this ring, longer and more pompous than before. The ring says, "For *Heaven's* sake, please hurry. I do hope you realize whom you are keeping waiting. There are at least a dozen other places I could be right now, and here I am standing and waiting for some slow-poke to decide to open the door. Of course I won't stay but a few minutes, so every minute you keep me out here will be deducted from the time allotted to you. *I'm* a busy person."

An equally impatient ringer is the "pattern" ringer. His ring goes like this: two long rings, pause, two long rings, pause, and the little ritual is completed by two more long rings. By this time the eardrums of the listener are at least partially shattered, but he can still hear the bell saying, "I've been here before. You should know that from this very unique and clever way I have of ringing. I should think you'd be in as much of a hurry to receive this special-delivery letter as I am to get on my way. Such nerve—keeping the United States mails waiting."

There is also a female of this loud-ringing species. She rings three long, impatient rings in rapid succession. Her ring says, "Oh I can hardly wait to tell you something. Please open the door quickly. You'll just die when you hear what I have to tell you. It's really too good to keep. Please hurry."

In direct contrast to these ringers is the bashful ringer who "pecks" at the bell. His "peck" seems to say, "There's no reason for making a lot of noise when I ring the bell. I just have to let them know I'm here. I hope I haven't disturbed anyone. Maybe they're all taking a nap. I wonder if there is anything wrong."

The most challenging ringer is the one whose ring is never recognized because he never rings the same way twice. He may "sit" on the bell one time and ring more quietly the next. He may even have a series of short rings as though he were spelling out a short message in code. The poor invalid guesses him as anything from a collector of old magazines and newspapers to the Fuller brush man.

Is the ring really an expression of the personality of the ringer? If the personality of the ringer and his particular bell-ringing "style" were not known, would the rings be interpreted in the same way?

Might not the pompous ring, for instance, be thought of as a very business-like ring? Our guesser begins to think that maybe he is not such a good guesser after all. One thing is certain, and that is that there are a great many types of bell ringers.

E. L.

Research in objective material calls for clear judgment and staying power. Here is a graceful treatment of matter-of-fact content.

WEDDINGS OF OTHER AGES

The examples I have chosen of the early marriages will show you how elaborate these affairs were. I give you but three types of the many that were. Each country had its own ceremonies, customs, and superstitions. The subject is of such wide range, and the types of ceremonies are so many that it has been necessary to narrow it to this degree. Compare these with the marriages of the twentieth century.

Among the early Hebrews and the oriental nations, the choice of a bride depended upon the relations or friend deputed by the bridegroom for the purpose. His wishes were consulted and parents made proposals at the instigation of their sons. The consent of the bride was sometimes asked, but this was subordinate to previous consent of father or relation.

Selection of the bride was followed by the betrothal, which was a formal proceeding taken by a friend of the bridegroom and the parents of the bride. It was confirmed by oaths and accompanied by presents from the man to the woman. The act of betrothal was celebrated by a feast, and among the more modern Hebrews it was the custom to place a ring upon the intended bride's finger.

Between the betrothal and marriage an interval elapsed varying from a few days to a year. During this period the bride-elect lived with her friends and all communication between herself and her future husband was carried by the medium of a friend, who was termed "the friend of the bridegroom." She was virtually regarded as a wife, her betrothal having equal force with marriage.

On the wedding day the bridegroom dressed in festive attire, wore a beautiful turban and a crown or garland of gold, silver, roses, or myrtle, according to his circumstances and was highly perfumed with sweet powders. A distinctive feature of the bride's dress was a veil or robe of ample dimensions to cover her face and whole body. This was intended as a symbol of her submission to her husband. If she had not been married before, she wore her hair flowing and her robes were white. She was much perfumed and decked with jewels.

The hour was generally late in the night when the bridegroom set forth from his house, preceded by musicians and accompanied by men bearing torches. When he reached her house, he conducted her and her party back to his house with audible demonstrations of his gladness.

They feasted and danced at the bridegroom's house for several, and sometimes as long as fourteen days. All the friends and neighbors were invited to this celebration, which was the most essential part of the ceremony.

The last act of the ceremonial was conducting the bride, still completely veiled, to her bedchamber, where a canopy, which was of roses and myrtle, was prepared. This act was preceded by formal prayers.

Among the Moors in Africa, the tabola or large drum, is beaten to announce a wedding. A great number of people assemble. A woman beats the drum and the other women join in, in chorus, by setting up a wild scream. The wedding drum continues to beat, and the women to sing all night. About nine o'clock in the morning the bride is brought in state from her mother's tent, attended by a number of women who carry her tent, which is a present from the groom. They march, singing, until they arrive at the place designated for her residence, and pitch her tent. The husband follows with a number of men, leading four bulls, which they tie to the tent strings, and kill another which is distributed among the people. This action completes the ceremony.

Christian marriage was developed out of the marital customs of pagan Greece and Italy and also from the Jews. At first it was not a religious ceremony, the only necessary form of it being that the groom should go to the bride's house, and lead her to his home in the presence of witnesses. It was considered a civil contract by the church, and it was not until later that, in order to correct abuses, the priesthood introduced the custom of celebrating marriages before themselves and of giving the nuptial benediction.

The Anglo-Saxons contended that no marriage was lawful without the consent of the woman's father or guardian, who was called her Mundbora. For this consent the lover always paid a price, in the nature of a present, according to the rank of the lady.

The parties were solemnly contracted; her dowry was fixed and all the relations were invited to the marriage feast. Each one gave a present to the couple and the Mundbora gave them arms, furniture, cattle, and money. This was all the fortune that the groom received.

The day before the wedding, which was within six to eight weeks from the time of the contract, the feast was held. The next morning they went armed and on horseback to the bride's house to receive her and to conduct her to her husband. On her arrival she was received by the bridegroom and solemnly betrothed by her guardian.

The united companies proceeded to the church, attended by musicians. No marriage was lawful without the presence of the Mundbora and he gave the bride to the bridegroom saying, "I give her to be thy honor and thy wife." After the benediction both parties were crowned with flowers which were kept in the church for the purpose. A ring was used at the marriage as well as at the betrothal. It is said that the Mundbora presented the groom with one of the bride's shoes, as a token of the transfer of authority; and she was made to feel the change by a blow on the head with the shoe.

After the ceremony, all returned to the groom's house for the wedding feast. At night, the bride was conducted to her chamber and put to bed by the women, and the bridegroom was in like manner attended by the men. The couple both being in bed, their healths were drunk by all the company. The feasting continued until all the provisions were consumed and then having made presents to the husband, they departed.

This has but little in common with the procedure in connection with some of the ceremonies today. When the couple leave their offices at noon, on Saturday, they drive down to Toledo, madly search the favorite haunts of the license clerk. Then after locating him, they secure a license and begin the hunt for a justice of peace. When he has been located and their pledges made, the homeward journey is begun. Provided the act is not too much of a surprise to their families, one moves his clothes to the other's home. Thus, they proceed to live happily ever after, each returning to his job on Monday morning.

H. A.

There is always the student who writes almost absolutely correctly, in both mechanics and structure. But "Types of Dancers" also exhibits an excellent style of its own.

TYPES OF DANCERS

Many times one can enjoy a dance much more by watching the dancers than by participating in the so-called "gay event." There are many varieties of people who indulge in the terpsichorean art, and chief among them are the "rabbit" dancer, the slow dancer, the one who *adores* waltzing, and the perfect dancer, who is discovered at very, very rare intervals.

Dancing is a game to the "rabbit" dancer. He believes that to win the prize, one must cover as much territory in as short a time as possible. This area includes not only the horizontal, but also the vertical plane. He is the terror of other dancers, as he leaps joyfully up and down, to the side, and to the back, regardless of the poor beings who chance to be in his way. The unfortunate girl who is his partner is exhausted at the end of her first dance with him, as his efforts are a cross between a bounding jack rabbit and a Mexican jumping bean. He must set snares to trap his victims—or perhaps some people really think it's fun to gyrate in this manner.

Exactly opposite to the above-mentioned blithe spirit of the dance is the slow dancer. This gentle soul fairly walks around the floor. He is a very voluble talker and never quite gets the right rhythm. As he moves with a lazy gait, he pushes his long-suffering partner in a dull, monotonous version of the "light fantastic." Poor soul! perhaps he had a hard day, or he didn't get to bed early enough the night before. His bored air certainly corroborates these suppositions. However, he may be only a despairing husband whose wife delights in balls, and drags him thither much against his will.

Very often one meets the dancer who fervently loves to waltz. He assures you that waltzing is one of the things that he does best. But, alas, after a dance with him, you wonder just how he does those things in which he is not proficient. As soon as the first strains of a waltz reach his ear, he gathers his luckless companion into his arms, and commences to swoop, in what he believes to be a rhythmic fashion, about the dance floor. He dotes on the "hesitation" step, and at the moment that you both least expect it, he suddenly halts, stands perfectly still for at least two minutes, and then renews his swooping motion. Every little while he seems to forget that he is waltzing, and intersperses sundry fox-trot steps. When you finally escape from his clutches, you violently promise yourself that you will never waltz again—that is, if what you have just been doing is really waltzing.

Last, but certainly not least, there is the dancer who knows the different steps perfectly, and does them with just the right amount of enthusiasm. He dances without effort, and although he is not at all effeminate, he moves with a truly rhythmic grace. As a rule he is an intelligent conversationalist, but he does not feel it is necessary to relate his life history while dancing. This delightful person avoids most of the collisions in which other dancers seem to joy, and, if you ever have the good luck to encounter him, don't forget he is extremely rare in type.

M. M.

Finally, consider this splendid manipulation of comparison and contrast by use of concrete illustrations, and also the emotional rise at the end of a theme-type which is generally all too dry.

TYPES OF WINDOW DISPLAYS

Of course, *all* window displays (and many other things) fall into two large classes—the good and the bad. The determining factor in this case is the way in which a window display catches and then holds the eye of the public. In other words, to excite the attention of, and interest the casual observer, is one of the best ways to advertise whatever one has to sell.

Let us consider some good examples of this eye-catching quality. One of the best ways to attract attention to an object is to isolate that object and to bring it into strong relief to its background. In the window of Cartier, jewellers on Fifth Avenue, New York, is one string of perfectly graduated pearls. The entire window is draped in black velvet. The pearls are absolutely the only things in that window, and their color and texture are shown to the greatest possible advantage by the velvet. Contrast this window arrangement with that of any cheap jewelry shop on Seventh Avenue, for instance. Who wouldn't become dizzy after taking in a wild conglomeration of rhinestone bracelets, earrings, necklaces, pink-jade elephants, and alabaster ash trays! After passing a window like this, one is left with a hazy impression of rhinestone ash trays, earrings of pink jade elephants, and many spots before the eyes. A junky window never has much advertising value.

However, the objects displayed certainly need not be valuable to attract attention. When I was passing by Woolworth's the other day, my attention was attracted most decidedly by an artistic window display. Upon black steps, in a simple geometric pattern, were arranged rows of china skulls, all wagging their jaws in unison (by means of some ingenious spring contrivance which I cannot attempt to explain). My attention was attracted by the movement, by the unusual objects, and by the very strong contrast of dead-white china upon a black background. There was an almost sensational quality about this display, and sensation is used to very good effect in many other cases. For instance, at Tiffany's, New York, there was the largest diamond in the United States on window display for a short time. This was sensational in itself, but was augmented by the presence of two of New York's burliest policemen guarding it, one on each side. In the Dorothy Gray Beauty Salon, not far from there, was a "Temple of Beauty." The "Temple" consisted of four slender pillars, a roof, and an altar-like arrangement enclosed. Upon the altar burned a beautiful blue-green flame—a *real* one! Here the fascinating power of fire was used to draw attention. As another example, take Browning's Toy Shop. Waiving the fact that "Daddy" Browning is a bit of a sensation himself, his toy shop excites the interest of children and grown-ups alike. Tony Sarg, the well-known maker of marionettes, has made a number of figures from the *Arabian Nights* for the window. These revolve, one after the other, on a tread which causes them to appear before a screen, pass in front of it, and disappear behind it again. Here, movement, bright color, and unusualness combine to attract the attention.

There are "bad" types of sensational window displays, too. Everyone is familiar with the girl (a live one!) seated in a store window, waving her hair with "Marcella's Marvelous Mixture for Hair Waving"; or the man standing outside his shop door, inviting passersby to "step right in, folks, marvelous values—bargains—bla, bla, bla." Of course these seem to attract great crowds of interested onlookers, but as the crowd usually consists of those who have no better job than to stand and gape at such things, it isn't very good advertising.

One of the best window displays I ever saw wasn't in a window at all. It was down in that section of the New York ghetto known as "Brasstown." Out in front of the tiny shop were rows and rows of brilliantly polished copper and brass. It was a gorgeous bit of sunlight brought down to that murky street under the "L." The old Jew sat in the doorway with his little skull cap, long beard, and newspaper. Just to look at it all made me glad. I went into the tiny shop and bought so many things I could scarcely carry them home.

R. E.

⇛ B ⇚

There are two chief dangers in making a classified summary: one is that of having too many subdivisions, the other, that of not including all of the subject in these subdivisions. In making subdivisions avoid awkward enumeration, like that of the speaker who began with "firstly" and worked his way up to "eleventhly." If there are as many as eleven items, it is probable that careful grouping into three or four main divisions will be logical, and certainly it will help the reader to follow your analysis.

In his discussions of pleasures, the philosopher Bishop Berkeley restricts himself to two main classes.

It is of great use to consider the pleasures which constitute human happiness, as they are distinguished into natural and fantastical. Natural pleasures I call those, which, not depending on the fashion and caprice of any particular age or nation, are suited to human nature in general, and were intended by Providence as rewards for the using our faculties agreeably to the ends for which they were given us. Fantastical pleasures are those which, having no natural fitness to delight our minds, presuppose some particular whim or taste accidentally prevailing in a set of people, to which it is owing that they please.

The Guardian, No. 49.

Having made these definitions, Berkeley then illustrates each type of pleasures by illustrations and contrasts.

In his cynical review of human life the "melancholy Jaques" of Shakespeare's *As You Like It* lists seven ages; but the reader has examples of the familiar cycle, from infancy to senility, all about him to aid him in understanding the résumé. Observe the unobtrusive enumeration. Then try, in prose, to produce an equivalent picture of life as you see it.

> All the world's a stage,
> And all the men and women merely players:
> They have their exits and their entrances;
> And one man in his time plays many parts,
> His acts being seven ages. At first the infant,
> Mewling and puking in the nurse's arms.
> And then the whining school-boy, with his satchel
> And shining morning face, creeping like snail
> Unwillingly to school. And then the lover,
> Sighing like furnace, with a woeful ballad
> Made to his mistress' eyebrow. Then a soldier,
> Full of strange oaths and bearded like the pard,
> Jealous in honour, sudden and quick in quarrel,
> Seeking the bubble reputation

Even in the cannon's mouth. And then the justice,
In fair round belly with good capon lin'd,
With eyes severe and beard of formal cut,
Full of wise saws and modern instances;
And so he plays his part. The sixth age shifts
Into the lean and slipper'd pantaloon,
With spectacles on nose, and pouch on side;
His youthful hose, well sav'd, a world too wide
For his shrunk shank; and his big manly voice,
Turning again toward childish treble, pipes
And whistles in his sound. Last scene of all,
That ends this strange eventful history,
Is second childishness, and mere oblivion,
Sans teeth, sans eyes, sans taste, sans everything.

—*As You Like It*, II, vii.

Some classifications are more imaginative than logical; they require more of description than analysis and definition. In Addison's account of the noises of London are apparent the mingled affection for sound and bustle of the city dweller and the discomfort of the man of letters who prefers quiet.

The cries of London may be divided into vocal and instrumental. As for the latter, they are at present under a very great disorder. A freeman of London has the privilege of disturbing a whole street for an hour together, with the twanking of a brass kettle or a frying-pan. The watchman's thump at midnight startles us in our beds, as much as the breaking in of a thief. The sow-gelder's horn has indeed something musical in it, but this is seldom heard within the liberties. I would therefore propose, that no instrument of this nature should be made use of, which I have not tuned and licensed, after having carefully examined in what manner it may affect the ears of her Majesty's liege subjects.

Vocal cries are of a much larger extent, and indeed so full of incongruities and barbarisms, that we appear a distracted city to foreigners, who do not comprehend the meaning of such enormous outcries. Milk is generally sold in a note above *ela*, and in sounds so exceedingly shrill, that it often sets our teeth on edge. The chimney-sweeper is confined to no certain pitch; he sometimes utters himself in the deepest bass, and sometimes in the sharpest treble; sometimes in the highest, and sometimes in the lowest note of the gamut. The same observation might be made on the retailers of small-coal, not to mention broken glasses or brick-dust. In these, therefore, and the like cases, it should be my care to sweeten and mellow the voices of these itinerant tradesmen, before they make their appearance in our streets; as also to accommodate their cries to their respective wares; and to take care in particular that those may not make the most noise, who have the least to sell, which is very observable in the vendors of card-matches, to whom I cannot but apply the old proverb of "Much cry but little wool."

Spectator, No. 251.

In some cases the writer finds it impossible to reduce all his material to simple, specific subclasses. For example, the poet Robert Herrick (1591–1674) in "The Argument of His Book" chants:

> I sing of brooks, of blossoms, birds, and bowers,
> Of April, May, of June, and July-flowers;
> I sing of May-poles, hock-carts, wassails, wakes . . .

Nearly every one of the fourteen lines of this sonnet provides an example of a classified summary. For a modern expression of the poet's interest in the many varieties of experience read Rupert Brooke's deeply emotional poem "The Great Lover." It will prepare you for the essay by the critic Max Eastman called "Practical and Poetic People." Eastman shows the former individuals as looking forward primarily to an objective in the future, usually having to do with money in the bank; the latter enjoy the experience of living, watching the flight of gulls over the water, while the practical people sit below over the morning cigar and newspaper till the ferryboat docks.

Such distinctions as Eastman's are easy to make; often, too, they are false, or at least misleading. Our second danger signal warned against inaccurate division. Strictly, all classification should include the totality of the class being divided, and also no subdivisions should overlap. Avoid hasty generalizations. Be certain that your classes form neat compartments, distinct from each other. If you classify the means of travel, be sure that you include bicycles as well as steamboats, but do not put them in the same category.

As an illustration of more objective analysis examine the passage below classifying whales. To Herman Melville, author of *Moby Dick*, the whale was not only the object of tireless scientific study, but an object of profound, soul-stirring meaning as well. Observe the ingenious use of analogy. By basing the classification on the bookdealer's terms for book sizes (folio, octavo, duodecimo), Melville sustains interest and achieves clarity. Only portions of the chapter of Cetology (whale-ology) are quoted.

Now, then, come the grand divisions of the entire whale host.

First: According to magnitude I divide the whales into three primary BOOKS (subdivisible into CHAPTERS), and these shall comprehend them all, both small and large.

I. The FOLIO WHALE; II. the OCTAVO WHALE; III. the DUODECIMO WHALE.

As the type of the FOLIO I present the *Sperm Whale;* of the OCTAVO, the *Grampus;* of the DUODECIMO, the *Porpoise.*

FOLIOS. Among these I here include the following chapters: —I. The *Sperm Whale;* II. the *Right Whale;* III. the *Fin-back Whale;* IV. the *Hump-backed Whale;* V. the *Razor-back Whale;* VI. the *Sulphur-bottom Whale.*

BOOK I. (*Folio*), CHAPTER I. (*Sperm Whale*).—This whale, among the English of old vaguely known as the Trumpa whale, and the Physeter whale, and the Anvil-headed whale, is the present Cachalot of the French, and the Pottsfisch of the Germans, and the Macrocephalus of the Long Words. He is, without doubt, the largest inhabitant of the globe; the most formidable of all whales to encounter; the most majestic in aspect; and lastly, by far the most valuable in commerce; he being the only creature from which that valuable substance, spermaceti, is obtained.

. . . .

Thus ends BOOK I. (*Folio*), and now begins BOOK II. (*Octavo*).

OCTAVOS. These embrace the whales of middling magnitude, among which at present may be numbered:—I. the *Grampus;* II. the *Black Fish;* III. the *Narwhale;* IV. the *Thrasher;* V. the *Killer.*

. . . .

DUODECIMOS. These include the smaller whales:—I. the *Huzza Porpoise;* II. the *Algerine Porpoise;* III. the *Mealy-mouthed Porpoise.*

To those who have not chanced specially to study the subject, it may possibly seem strange, that fishes not commonly exceeding four or five feet should be marshalled among WHALES—a word which, in the popular sense, always conveys an idea of hugeness. But the creatures set down as Duodecimos are infallibly whales, by the terms of my definition of what a whale is—*i.e.* a spouting fish, with a horizontal tail.

BOOK III. (*Duodecimo*), CHAPTER I. (*Huzza Porpoise*).—This is the common porpoise found almost all over the globe. The name is of my own bestowal; for there are more than one sort of porpoises, and something must be done to distinguish them. I call him thus, because he always swims in hilarious shoals, which upon the broad sea keep tossing themselves to heaven like caps in a Fourth-of-July crowd. Their appearance is generally hailed with delight by the mariner. Full of fine spirits, they invariably come from the breezy billows to windward. They are the lads that always live before the wind. They are accounted a lucky omen. If you yourself can withstand three cheers at beholding these vivacious fish, then heaven help ye; the spirit of godly gamesomeness is not in ye. A well-fed, plump Huzza porpoise will yield you one good gallon of good oil. But the fine and delicate fluid extracted from his jaws is exceedingly valuable. It is in request among jewellers and watchmakers. Sailors put it on their hones. Porpoise meat is good eating, you know. It may never have occurred to you that a porpoise spouts. Indeed, his spout is so small that it is not very readily discernible. But the next time you have a chance, watch him; and you will then see the great Sperm whale himself in miniature.

BOOK III. (*Duodecimo*), CHAPTER II. (*Algerine Porpoise*).—A pirate. Very savage. He is only found, I think, in the Pacific. He is somewhat larger than the Huzza porpoise, but much of the same general make. Provoke him, and he will buckle to a shark. I have lowered for him many times, but never yet saw him captured.

BOOK III. (*Duodecimo*), CHAPTER III. (*Mealy-mouthed Porpoise*). —The largest kind of porpoise; and only found in the Pacific, so far as it is known. The only English name, by which he has hitherto been designated, is that of the fishers—Right-whale porpoise, from the circumstance that he is chiefly found in the vicinity of that Folio. In shape, he differs in some degree from the Huzza porpoise, being of a less rotund and jolly girth; indeed, he is of quite a neat and gentleman-like figure. He has no fins on his back (most other porpoises have), he has a lovely tail, and sentimental Indian eyes of a hazel hue. But his mealy-mouth spoils all. Though his entire back down to his side fins is a deep sable, yet a boundary line, distinct as the mark in a ship's hull, called the 'bright waist,' that line streaks him from stem to stern, with two separate colors, black above and white below. The white comprises part of his head, and the whole of his mouth, which makes him look as if he had just escaped from a felonious visit to a mealbag. A most mean and mealy aspect! His oil is much like that of the common porpoise.

HERMAN MELVILLE, *Moby Dick*.

In some instances the number of items will be indefinite, but in others a specific limitation will be set upon them. It is so in the following critical résumé of the nine symphonies of Beethoven. The style reflects an intense enthusiasm for the emotional and poetic factors in music. A section of the Introduction giving the ideas developed in the succeeding chapters of the book is quoted. Try a similar survey for a novelist, dramatist, poet, or artist.

If anyone were to make the attempt to convey, in one general review, an adequate idea of the wealth and variety of moods depicted in Beethoven's Symphonies, he would soon discover the hopelessness of such an undertaking. Great as is the number of symphonies which the world owes to Haydn and Mozart, it is possible to regard them all collectively, from one identical standpoint; their ideal centre being the same throughout. This, in the case of Haydn, may be characterized as a pure, child-like ideality; in that of Mozart, as a noble, harmonious humanity; all their symphonic works being but modifications of the one central idea. It is far otherwise with the symphonies of Beethoven. Their number is but small yet each represents a world in itself, with an ideal centre of its own. Thus in his first symphony we are introduced to a little idyl of the heart; the second presents to us a picture of the joyous vigour, and amorous strivings of youth; the third suggests a world of daring heroism; in the fourth the wonders of a romantic world are revealed to us; tragical conflict with fate, and eventual victory, is the theme of the fifth; while in the sixth we commune with ever kindly Nature; the seventh is a manifestation of joy in human existence; in the eighth the humorous element predominates; and finally in the ninth, both the *inferno* and *paradiso* of the inmost soul are unrolled before our eyes. . . .[1]

In the final selection the number of items is suggested by the names of leading European centers of architectural inspiration in

[1] From *Beethoven's Symphonies in Their Ideal Significance, Explained by Ernst von Elterlein*, London, William Reeves, 1896. Translated by Emily Hill.

the past. It might have been extended, of course, to include Spain, Sweden, and other countries. Notice that the classified summary has now merged into the development of the thought in the paragraph; we feel no longer the disposition to itemize and number, yet the process of classification provides the structure of the paragraph. You will find it interesting to compare the same writer's penetrating analysis of the spirit of Paris reprinted in Chapter V below.[1]

The extent and duration of the supremacy of the Gothic ideal among the different nations depended entirely on how deeply the ancient civilization had taken root. In Italy Gothic remained entirely on the surface, while in Spain it combined not so much with Graeco-Roman as with Moorish elements; its influence was strongest and most permanent in the Teutonic countries. In England the Gothic style has never quite died out, and the Gothic ideals of love, chivalry and vassaldom, and religion are even now a living force. A Gothic palace is as much the natural meeting-place for Parliament there as a classic temple is in France. In spite of the short-lived Roman occupation, ancient civilization has had little influence on the mental development of the English, the reason being that later foreign invaders, especially the Normans, did not, as in France, coalesce with the native inhabitants but kept them down. It is, however, on the Germans that Gothic had its most lasting effect. It was, and has remained, Germany's great experience. Germany having remained practically untouched by ancient civilization, the Gothic spirit had no resistance to overcome there. Hence it was able to develop to its fullest extent, but hence also the synthesis which France achieved was denied to Germany. That is the explanation of the German's perpetual yearning for the South and its classical spirit, which runs right through his history and literature without (apart from short-lived, isolated exceptions) attaining its end. But when a German wants to go back to a genuine German tradition, he turns to the Christian Middle Ages, the era of Gothic. The much-canvassed antithesis between the German and French characters is nothing more or less than the difference between the predominately Gothic ideal of one and the (in spite of an intermixture of Gothic) predominately classical ideal of the other. It looks as if the psychoanalytical doctrine, that first impressions by their overwhelming strength permanently deter-

---

[1] Reprinted from *The Spirit of France*, E. P. Dutton and Company, 1933, by Paul Cohen-Portheim and translated by Alan Harris, with the kind permission of the publishers.

mine the whole character, whereas subsequent experiences only touch the surface, were true of nations no less than of individuals. France's first waking impression was the ancient, Germany's the Gothic world, and Gothic could no more completely remould the French genius than the Renaissance and Classicism could the German.

CHAPTER IV

The Summarizing Résumé

ONE OF THE very best sellers on the newsstands is the periodical which condenses articles from current magazines. Sometimes books, usually non-fictional works, are also read and pre-digested for the time-pressed reader. The condensation, or, as it is technically called, the précis of an article makes particular demands on the writer's skill. The usual problems of order, arrangement, proportion, are already solved for him by the pattern of the article which he is condensing. On the other hand, the précis calls for the utmost in conciseness and clarity, the very essence of the expository manner. More than in the forms previously studied, it will be necessary in attempting this form to give attention to style.

The art of the précis might be too readily looked upon with condescension as a kind of making of molehills out of mountains. In reality it is a very exacting art, as is apparent in the various efforts to define it. As has been said, "The précis must contain the essence of the selection dealt with, but it must be *precise, accurate*, and *well-expressed*." [1] It demands sensitive, penetrating perceptiveness and business-like efficiency. Of course the good old-fashioned terms used above really describe qualities desirable in all writing. They tell us nothing of the methods for making the molehills which are to be precise, accurate, and well-expressed. This chapter is intended to point out the main aspects in the technique of producing the summarizing résumé, or précis, of a magazine article, particularly the expository, non-argumentative article.

[1] From Foerster and Steadman, *Writing and Thinking*, Houghton Mifflin Company, 1931. Reprinted by permission of the publishers. Compare Chapter I of Richard Nelson, *Précis, Notes, and Summaries*, Thomas Nelson and Sons, 1925; and A. W. Leonard and C. M. Fuess, *Practical Précis Writing*, Harcourt, Brace and Company, 1929.

The purpose of this type is fairly obvious, particularly as it relates to accurate, faithful restatement of given material. But, beyond mere fidelity to the given facts, it can aid in the mastery of one of the most valuable tools of criticism. It is important to observe that the précis excludes critical remarks; however, criticism always involves a close reading of the work being criticized and quite often a brief summary or exposition of its content. Practice in summarizing articles will be one of the most valuable aids for dealing with the problems of formal criticism later.

Précis writing requires careful thought and preparation. Before attacking the problem of writing the actual résumé, one should select the article with care, giving attention to stylistic qualities as well as to the scope and nature of the subject matter. Best results are obtained if each student actually procures a copy of the magazine and submits the article to the instructor for approval. It is helpful to underline passages, to annotate, or even to clip sections from the text, but these are unsocial, even criminal, practices when the magazine is not the property of the student. Also, in the matter of making a final choice, it is advisable for the instructor to restrict the whole class to two or three articles. Then, by aid of some brief discussion and reading of extracts, it will be possible for all to be familiar with the pieces which are being summarized and to criticize the quality of the summaries.

The style of the précis must satisfy the modern demand for clean-cut directness, brevity, speed, and yet completeness of statement. In short, this type calls for streamlining. The summary must not only be "precise, accurate, and well-expressed." It must be more than that. It must be a concise condensation of what the author wrote—most of it in *your own words*. The gist of what he said in a whole paragraph must be reduced to one brief sentence of your own, a very good type of mental exercise. Furthermore, the reduced summary must be kept in focus; that means that its proportions and emphasis must be kept true to the original. This requires, not only fidelity to the spirit and meaning of the author, but also the constant assurance in the reader's mind that the ideas of the summary belong to the author and not to the summarizer. This last effect can be attained by mentioning the author by name occasionally, and also by inserting bits of direct quotation. Never more than a few striking sentences should be inserted at a time, except at the very end, where the concluding paragraph, if it is a good one, may provide an effective conclusion.

In the case of very matter-of-fact material, some students use the device of quoting the author's topic sentence for each paragraph, then following with a summary of the paragraph. Used with discretion, this method can be extremely effective, but it easily becomes mechanical. However, the device of topic sentences is not employed by all or even the majority of writers. Wherever direct quoting is used, it is important to remember two primary laws of quotation. First, all quotations must be scrupulously indicated as such by the use of quotation marks. Second, the source must be quoted correctly both as to words and ideas. Every public speaker knows how inaccurate or partial quotation can viciously falsify his actual meaning.

The title of the précis will be the author's title. There should be a footnote at the bottom of the first page indicating the name of the magazine in which the article is to be found and also the date and page reference.[1] The summary may well open with a quotation to give the quality of the author's language. Then the point of view of the summarizer must be established, not by the use of critical remarks (these, above all, must be excluded), but by careful indication of the intention to condense. If at any point the summarizer wishes to insert a remark of his own within a quotation, square brackets must be used—*always*. Parentheses would imply that the remark came from the author, not the summarizer. If portions of a direct quotation are omitted, this fact may be indicated by the insertion of three dots. Thus, if the beginning of a sentence is dropped, the dots follow the quotation marks without the initial capital letter: e.g., ". . . all National Parks are affected," the Secretary maintains. Dots are used also where two quotations which do not follow in direct sequence in the original are presented. Particular care must be given to consistency in tenses in any shifting from the author's point of view to that of the summarizer, just as in the process of quoting.

Inasmuch as the summary is the one form of writing in which material is always drawn directly and entirely from published

[1] See p. 259.

works, special difficulties may easily arise. A rather stereotyped procedure must be followed, and yet the result must appear fresh and unstereotyped. The finest clues to the purpose and spirit of the précis may be found in poetry, for poetry is itself a précis of experience. A brief poem may often be seen as the condensation of a complete *potential* biography or novel. This power of condensing experience is notable in Shakespeare, the master writer. Observe the scope of meaning which has been packed into these phrases: "The April's in her eyes; it is love's spring," "After life's fitful fever he sleeps well," "Uneasy lies the head that wears a crown." Often Shakespeare condenses further one of his own already brilliantly "compacted" passages. Four words serve to sum up in *Antony and Cleopatra* a famous tribute in *Macbeth*. Malcolm graces the death of the traitorous Thane of Cawdor with the tribute that:

> Nothing in his life
> Became him like the leaving it; he died
> As one that had been studied in his death,
> To throw away the dearest thing he ow'd,
> As 'twere a careless trifle.

In the later play we find the simple phrase, spoken by Antony of his dead wife, Fulvia—"At the last, best." Again and again Shakespeare reduces whole episodes in legend or history to a brief passage or phrase.

A somewhat gruesome parallel to the précis may also be found in the art of the head-hunting tribes. Trophies of victory take the form of the preserved head of the victim, ingeniously reduced to the size of a small grapefruit, yet with all the features—forehead, nose, chin—kept in perfect proportion. The Japanese achieve similar effects in their art of dwarfing living trees, so that an aged forest "giant" may sustain a Lilliputian existence in a flowerpot. The technique in both cases involves the subtraction of elements not essential to the form or life of the original. While the art of the précis writer is less grisly than the head-hunter's, he must be equally meticulous in preserving the shape and proportions of the original; if he, like the Japanese worker with trees, can also preserve the life, then success is complete.

From a more practical point of view it may be useful to test out the completed summary on the basis of the following list of cautions. Trial and the avoidance of error will produce the best results.

1. Does the proportioning of the material fairly represent the balance and emphasis of ideas in the original? A common tendency is to produce a succession of short paragraphs which merely follow the outline of the original. In general, try to construct a compact, new form of your own which still preserves the skeleton of argument or exposition of the original.

2. Has the identity of the author been kept in mind? Is it clear to the reader that he is being presented with the ideas of that author and not your own? If the author is mentioned occasionally, are there possibly too many expressions such as "Jones says"?

3. Is the expository style original, or at least free from slavishness to the work summarized? Is it appropriate and consistent throughout in its method of making allusions, quotations, and points of emphasis?

4. Is there an effective proportion of quotations? Are they taken from the essential and best passages in the source? Are they carefully indicated by quotation marks, footnote references, and other acknowledgments?

5. Have irrelevant materials, incidental titles of works, statistical data, and the like been properly subordinated, in footnotes or otherwise? Often such items may be desirably reproduced, but if kept in the body of the summary they may throw it out of proportion.

6. Has the reader's attention been successfully guided to the content and point of view of the original? Is it free from the intrusion of the personality of the summarizer, from expository guideposts, or other factors in the mere technique of restatement? Is the introductory comment smooth and clear, and is the conclusion quick and unforced?

Convenient models for the résumé may be found in numerous periodicals. Some, such as those in *Time*, are primarily surveys of current works and events. The *Reader's Digest* has established a vogue for condensed articles and books. The method followed is, however, that of telescoped extracts rather than a combination of brief quotation and restatement. Good examples of précis writing abound in the periodicals which specialize in the reviewing of books and articles. One of the most interesting types of reading may be developed by following, in the reviews, the plays that flicker or flame across the New York stage. Many of these plays are given early publication; it is possible to read the play and compare one's own reactions with those of the reviewers. Often a filmed version of the play is also available for further comparison.

There is no need for a list of theme topics for the précis, but a few student examples of the type are presented. Their success may be judged by looking up the original article for checking according to the points listed above. After these there is reprinted a selection from Thucydides, famous Greek historian, followed by two student summaries based on it. Since this selection represents high art in prose, it involves the most difficult kind of task in restatement.

⟶⟫ A ⟪⟵

The following paper is a model of simple organization.

WHAT TO DO AT YOUR AGE TO PROTECT YOUR HEALTH

William S. Sadler, M.D.

This article, appearing in the *American Magazine* for August, 1929, contains health hints for people of any age. For the sake of simplicity and convenience, the author divides age into seven arbitrary divisions. These I shall list as given:

"1. Infancy and childhood—extending, let us say, to 13 or thereabouts.

2. Youth—13 or thereabouts up to 21. (A very trying period of adjustment for both boys and girls.)

3. The prime of life—from 21 to 35; when you feel ready to take on the whole world—the most robust and virile decade and a half (or it should be).

4. Middle age—from 35 to 50. (How some people in the late thirties will resent being called middle-aged!)

5. Advancing age—from 50 to 65.

6. Old age—from 65 to 80.

7. Advanced age—80 and upward."

Because of lack of space, very little is said about the first two divisions, childhood and youth. The only suggestion is that if, having been carefully brought up by sensible parents, one does not arrive at the prime of life "fit and fightin'," he should have a complete and thorough medical examination at once. Then, when the trouble has been discovered, he can set out immediately to correct it.

In speaking of the third division, Dr. Sadler begins by saying, "My first advice to you 'prime-of-lifers' is that you should get married around 25. [He goes on to point out the advantages.] . . . Responsibilities don't hurt you people in your prime—they steady you and develop you mentally and morally." He then cautions against "flying off the handle," pointing out that it is harmful to the nervous system as well as to success in business. Many people at this stage of life "curtail their physical activities too rapidly." They seem to think it is time to quit playing and to devote all of their time to making their fortunes. The author declares that this is a big mistake, and advises more or less strenuous physical exercise until one is "around forty years of age." Periodical visits to the doctor and the dentist should not be neglected, even though one feels perfectly well. The people in this division are also urged to guard against constipation, to take a *daily* sweat, to drink plenty of water, and to avoid overeating.

The first thing pointed out to those of middle age is the fact that overweight is a decided liability from that time on. We also learn that it is well for them to have an analysis made of their health. This should include, among other extraordinary tests, "an X-ray of every part of the body including the teeth." This research should be repeated when one is around fifty-five years of age. It may be advisable also to find out if the use of coffee, tea, tobacco, or alcohol is doing any harm, and to regulate their consumption, if any, accordingly. The Doctor warns against the possibilities of cancer at this age. He mentions some of the early indications: "such as neglected moles, sore tongues, unusual lumps in the breast, severe and unusual attacks of stomach disorder with sudden loss of weight." We are told that persons in the "mid-channel" of life must slow down on their physical exercise, with moderation, of course. An annual vacation is necessary at this age.

Among the most important hints to those between the ages of fifty and sixty-five is that of a daily rest period, to be taken around noon. One does not need to sleep, but should simply forget all about business during this hour. Reduction of weight now becomes imperative for those who have neglected it so far. Dr. Sadler also cautions the person of advancing age to watch his diet more closely, to have eyeglasses re-fitted at least once every two years, and to take two vacations a year, instead of one, if possible.

We are informed that the term "second childhood" doesn't refer to mentality but to diet. Hence, people who have arrived at old age must avoid eating the coarser foods. The daily rest period of the "middle-ages" now becomes more important than ever. If the blood pressure is high, it should be taken care of, but not worried about.

All that the last division is advised to do is to follow more closely the directions given the next younger group. The author states: "I firmly believe that seventy-five years should be the *average* length of life of the human species, and that a more intelligent and conscientious observance of the rules of living, as developed by modern science, would speedily enable the race to attain one hundred years as a common experience."

In closing, Dr. Sadler makes the interesting remark that it has never been his experience to witness a person, young or old, "passing out of this life resisting death and fearing the future."

H. M. H.

Note that it is possible to use the author's topic sentences to establish one's own organization.

BULBOUS IRISES [1]

"Of the several flowers which have been called 'poor man's Orchids,' 'out-door orchids,' and 'hardy orchids,' none comes so near really deserving this enviable title as the bulbous Irises." The gorgeously rich coloring, hardly surpassed by the Cattleya orchid, makes them desirable for every garden. Two reasons have prevented bulbous irises from gaining popularity in this country: namely, the reputation which they possess of being hard to grow; and the fact that the supply of bulbs was shut off by the federal quarantine.

"From my experience I should say that the most important types of the bulbous Irises are little more difficult to grow than the tulips." Irises, like tulips, except under the most favorable weather conditions, do not establish themselves as do the hardy daffodils, but they are extremely well worth what they cost, because one can be practically sure of one hundred percent results the first year. The northern-grown bulbs average somewhat smaller in size, but are of a firmer quality, which makes them more preferred by the florists for commercial usage.

"The differences between the bulbous Irises and perennial sorts" are easily marked. The shape of the flower, with its six petals ar-

[1] F. F. Rockwell, "The Beautiful Bulbous Irises Have Come Back," *House and Garden*, LV (November, 1929), 106, 140, 142.

ranged in two sets of threes, immediately marks them as being bulbous irises. They are much more graceful in growth, and the slim stems rise from a grasslike foliage to a height of eighteen or twenty inches. "The Spanish Irises have a dainty and fairy-like grace," and for this reason it is to be regretted that they are too fragile for wholesale growers. The more vigorous Dutch type of iris is more practical.

"In the culture of the bulbous Irises, the one most essential thing is not to have the soil freezing and thawing about the plants in late winter or early spring." Often this has been the real cause of failure where low winter temperatures have been to blame. A slightly elevated bed, with plenty of sand in the soil around and under the bulbs, will help to supply the conditions needed. Plenty of moisture must be supplied during the growth of the flower. Where one has only low soil with which to contend, he can put several layers of cinders or gravel beneath the surface, and this will greatly improve the drainage.

"Following the Dutch Irises in season of bloom come the Spanish." Of these the following varieties give a good range of color: "King of Blues, a very deep blue; Louise, porcelain blue; Queen Wilhelmina, pure white; Blanche Fleur, white shaded lilac"; and "Golden Lion, a lemon yellow with golden yellow falls." There are a great many ways of arranging the beautiful bulbous irises. One might suggest them in a mixed border effect; a border to a flag-stone walk; a border around a pond of water, and many other borders—for which they have become so well-known in landscape gardening, not only for their decorativeness, but because they are so immensely welcome in the early spring.

M. F.

The following paper reveals mature style and clever interpolation of quotations.

OUR "BEAUTIFUL YOUNG IDIOTS" [1]

The custom of the *Literary Digest*, as you probably know, is to present different points of view on all subjects by collecting and publishing excerpts from leading newspapers. This policy is beautifully illustrated in the criticisms of which this article is made up. They refer to Miss Edna Ferber's impression of modern youth as a whole.

Our editor tells us about this lady and just how she happened to form such an opinion of the younger generation. It appears that she has recently traveled in Europe and observed the conversation and

[1] From the *Literary Digest*, October 3, 1931.

action of the youth in the different countries. She has now returned home to find American boys and girls terribly lacking in brain power; in fact, the editor quotes her as saying, "If they'd only use their 'beans.'" He also gives us the contents of the interview secured by the reporters of the *New York Times*. She seems to think that the modern youth can make or break the future of our nation; she thinks that they can "do away with Prohibition and abolish war," if they use their heads. However, that is where the argument comes in. Miss Ferber contends that from her observations on shipboard, the American youth does nothing but drink gin and talk about football. (She admits that she adores gin herself.) The *Times* quotes her as saying, "In this country, to be serious is to be ridiculous," and that all the boys and girls say is "'Oh, yeah?' and that sort of thing." She calls them "beautiful young idiots."

Daniel de Guzman in the *New York Herald Tribune* takes up the defense of the young people by saying that he has had a great many conversations with the young generation of Americans that were nothing if not serious, and he believes these better represent the modern youths. The editor quotes him as saying, "We can't all go to Europe, and we can't all afford the unlimited gin drinking which is always ascribed to 'modern youth'." Also another quotation from him bears repeating, "We deplore prohibition, we deplore the hypocrisy that surrounds disarmament, we are greatly interested in the welfare of Germany, we do not understand France's viewpoint, the name 'Mussolini' is not always the cause for laughter, we are greatly interested in the great experiment . . . being carried on in Russia." Mr. de Guzman also insists that "the future is a product of the past," and that no one young person or group of them can control it. He maintains that middle-aged brains originate, govern, and applaud youth movements.

The editor also quotes Heywood Broun, in the *New York World-Telegram*, as saying that in the colleges of today there is much more interest in politics than there was in 1910, and that youth cannot be entirely oblivious of politics when they are discussed everywhere. The *Hartford Times* concedes that there are plenty of wild girls and boys, but they are not in the majority, and they existed in Miss Ferber's day as well as now. The *St. Louis Post-Dispatch* criticises the authoress for "adoring gin" and calls it "the lowest form of alcoholic recreation."

The article is concluded with an excerpt from the *Milwaukee Journal* stating that all of the blame is justly placed on the heads of the parents of the so-called "wildly modern" youth, and that thorough observation reveals that the serious-minded types of young people are from homes that are exceptional.

R. M.

A selection which we have employed as an assignment in précis writing is the noble tribute of Pericles to his native Athens, as reported by Thucydides, delivered in the course of a funeral oration on those who had fallen in the Peloponnesian War.[1]

1. Most of my predecessors in this place have commended him who made this speech part of the law, telling us that it is well that it should be delivered at the burial of those who fall in battle. For myself, I should have thought that the worth which had displayed itself in deeds, would be sufficiently rewarded by honors also shown by deeds; such as you now see in this funeral prepared at the people's cost. And I could have wished that the reputations of many brave men were not to be imperiled in the mouth of a single individual, to stand or fall according as he spoke well or ill. For it is hard to speak properly upon a subject where it is even difficult to convince your hearers that you are speaking the truth. On the one hand, the friend who is familiar with every fact of the story, may think that some point has not been set forth with that fulness which he wishes and knows it to deserve; on the other, he who is a stranger to the matter may be led by envy to suspect exaggeration if he hears anything above his own nature. For men can endure to hear others praised only so long as they can severally persuade themselves of their own ability to equal the actions recounted; when this point is passed, envy comes in and with it incredulity. However, since our ancestors have stamped this custom with their approval, it becomes my duty to obey the law and to try to satisfy your several wishes and opinions as best I may.

2. I shall begin with our ancestors: it is both just and proper that they should have the honor of the first mention on an occasion like the present. They dwelt in the country without break in the succession from generation to generation, and handed it down free to the present time by their valor. And if our more remote ancestors deserve praise, much more do our own fathers, who added to their inheritance the empire which we now possess, and spared no pains to be able to leave their acquisitions to us of the present generation. Lastly, there are few parts of our dominions that have not been augmented by those of us here, who are still more or less in the vigor of life; while the mother

---

[1] Translated by Richard Crawley. From *Thought in English Prose*, by J. C. Dent, Doubleday, Doran and Co., Inc., 1930. Reprinted by permission of the publishers.

country has been furnished by us with everything that can enable her to depend on her own resources whether for war or for peace. That part of our history which tells of the military achievements which gave us our several possessions, or of the ready valor with which either we or our fathers stemmed the tide of Hellenic or foreign aggression, is a theme too familiar to my hearers for me to dilate on, and I shall therefore pass it by. But what was the road by which we reached our position, what the form of government under which our greatness grew, what the national habits out of which it sprang; these are questions which I may try to solve before I proceed to my panegyric upon these men; since I think this to be a subject upon which on the present occasion a speaker may properly dwell, and to which the whole assemblage, whether citizens or foreigners, may listen with advantage.

3. Our Constitution does not copy the laws of neighboring states; we are rather a pattern to others than imitators ourselves. Its administration favors the many instead of the few; this is why it is called a democracy. If we look to the laws, they afford equal justice to all in their private differences; if to social standing, advancement in public life falls to reputation for capacity, class considerations not being allowed to interfere with merit; nor again does poverty bar the way; if a man is able to serve the state, he is not hindered by the obscurity of his condition. The freedom which we enjoy in our government extends also to our ordinary life. There, far from exercising a jealous surveillance over each other, we do not feel called upon to be angry with our neighbor for doing what he likes, or even to indulge in those injurious looks which cannot fail to be offensive, although they inflict no positive penalty. But all this ease in our private relations does not make us lawless as citizens. Against this, fear is our chief safeguard, teaching us to obey the magistrates and the laws, particularly such as regard the protection of the injured, whether they are actually on the statute book, or belong to that code which, although unwritten, yet cannot be broken without acknowledged disgrace.

4. Further, we provide plenty of means for the mind to refresh itself from business. We celebrate games and sacrifices all the year round, and the elegance of our private establishments forms a daily source of pleasure and helps to banish the spleen; while the magnitude of our city draws the produce of the world into our harbor, so that to the Athenian the fruits of other countries are as familiar a luxury as those of his own.

5. If we turn to our military policy, there also we differ from our antagonists. We throw open our city to the world, and never by alien

acts exclude foreigners from any opportunity of learning or observing, although the eyes of an enemy may occasionally profit by our liberality; trusting less in system and policy than to the native spirit of our citizens; while in education, where our rivals from their very cradles by a painful discipline seek after manliness, at Athens we live exactly as we please, and yet are just as ready to encounter every legitimate danger. In proof of this it may be noticed that the Lacedaemonians do not invade our country alone, but bring with them all their confederates; while we Athenians advance unsupported into the territory of a neighbor, and fighting upon a foreign soil usually vanquish with ease men who are defending their homes. Our united force was never yet encountered by any enemy, because we have at once to attend to our marine and to dispatch our citizens by land upon a hundred different services; so that, wherever they engage with some such fraction of our strength, a success against a detachment is magnified into a victory over the nation, and a defeat into a reverse suffered at the hands of our entire people. And yet if with habits not of labor but of ease, and courage not of art but of nature, we are still willing to encounter danger, we have the double advantage of escaping the experience of hardships in anticipation and of facing them in the hour of need as fearlessly as those who are never free from them.

6. Nor are these the only points in which our city is worthy of admiration. We cultivate refinement without extravagance and knowledge without effeminacy; wealth we employ more for use than for show, and place the real disgrace of poverty not in owning to the fact but in declining the struggle against it. Our public men have, besides politics, their private affairs to attend to, and our ordinary citizens, though occupied with the pursuits of industry, are still fair judges of public matters; for, unlike any other nation, regarding him who takes no part in these duties not as unambitious but as useless, we Athenians are able to judge at all events if we cannot originate, and instead of looking on discussion as a stumbling-block in the way of action, we think it an indispensable preliminary to any wise action at all. Again, in our enterprises we present the singular spectacle of daring and deliberation, each carried to its highest point, and both united in the same persons; although usually decision is the fruit of ignorance, hesitation of reflection. But the palm of courage will surely be adjudged most justly to those who best know the difference between hardship and pleasure and yet are never tempted to shrink from danger. In generosity we are equally singular, acquiring our friends by conferring not by receiving favors. Yet, of course, the doer

of the favor is the firmer friend of the two, in order by continued kindness to keep the recipient in his debt; while the debtor feels less keenly from the very consciousness that the return he makes will be a payment, not a free gift. And it is only the Athenians who, fearless of consequences, confer their benefits not from calculations of expediency, but in the confidence of liberality.

7. In short, I say that as a city we are the school of Hellas; while I doubt if the world can produce a man, who where he has only himself to depend upon, is equal to so many emergencies, and graced by so happy a versatility as the Athenian. And that this is no mere boast thrown out for the occasion, but plain matter of fact, the power of the state acquired by these habits proves. For Athens alone of her contemporaries is found when tested to be greater than her reputation, and alone gives no occasion to her assailants to blush at the antagonist by whom they have been worsted, or to her subjects to question her title by merit to rule. Rather, the admiration of the present and succeeding ages will be ours, since we have not left our power without witness, but have shown it by mighty proofs; and far from needing a Homer for our panegyrist, or other of his craft whose verses might charm for the moment, only for the impression which they gave to melt at the touch of fact, we have forced every sea and land to be the highway of our daring, and everywhere, whether of evil or for good, have left imperishable monuments behind us. Such is the Athens for which these men, in the assertion of their resolve not to lose her, nobly fought and died; and well may every one of their survivors be ready to suffer in her cause.

One obvious solution of the problem is a well-written analysis, in which the speaker is never forgotten.

SUMMARY OF PERICLES'S PANEGYRIC

The preceding speakers at the funeral services expressed their approval of speeches eulogizing the dead, whereas Pericles believed that worthy deeds should be honored also by deeds, such as a public, splendid funeral, "that the reputation of many brave men were not to be imperiled in the mouth of a single individual, to stand or fall according as he spoke well or ill"; that a panegyric usually aroused dissatisfaction or envy in the listeners: dissatisfaction in friends because, perhaps, some point had been slighted; envy in strangers because the praise of the dead ranked above that to which they themselves were entitled.

Since the custom had been made a law by his ancestors, however, Pericles tried to satisfy all his listeners with his panegyric.

He began his speech with the mention of his ancestors, honoring them for their contribution to the glory and power of Athens. For their addition to the empire, he sang the praises of the fathers of his generation, and, finally, he related the valorous deeds of the people of the nation, represented by his listeners, commended them for their deeds, and, as a fitting subject for discourse on the occasion, he announced the subject of the introduction to his panegyric to be the way in which the Athenians reached their position, the form of government under which their greatness grew, the national habits of their ancestors.

Instead of following the trend of the times, the Athenians adopted a Constitution which granted equal privileges to all people, regardless of social position or amount of wealth. In their private lives, the citizens enjoyed life in their own manner, neither molesting or being molested by their neighbors. They were a law-abiding race, paying strictest attention to all the laws, whether written in the statute book or simply a part of the unwritten code of behavior which cannot honorably be broken.

Among the diversions of his fellow citizens, Pericles listed athletic games, sacrifices, and the care and beautification of the home. That the Athenians, because of the great harbor they had made, were able to enjoy the fruits and luxuries of other countries as familiarly as they could their own, he also brought forth.

The people of Athens, in contrast to the policy of their enemies, invited visits from people of all nations to observe their modes of living and government and, in spite of this, were still able in most cases, though living easily and without constant anticipation of trouble, to defeat any of their adversaries, whether they came singly or combined.

Setting forth the admirable qualities of his city, Pericles proclaimed: "We cultivate refinement without extravagance and knowledge without effeminacy; wealth we employ more for use than for show, and place the real disgrace of poverty not in owning to the fact but in declining the struggle against it." He commented on the ability of the people, aside from public matters, to judge fairly and wisely before acting, on their ability to deliberate and to dare, on their ability to face hardships and dangers while knowing what it was to live easily. That the Athenians were truly generous and liberal, and that the reasons for many close friendships were the ties of generosity between the friends, he also proclaimed.

In closing, he said that as a city, Athens was the model of Hellas, that the Athenian was the most versatile of all men, that as a ruler or as a foe, Athens' name was one to be spoken of with pride, and that her actions were sufficient, in themselves, to be sung over the world without the flowery embellishments of great poetry. Of all the Hellenic governments, that of Athens was the most admired and this admiration would extend through the ages. For this wise, daring, admirable nation, those men had sacrificed themselves; that she might not be lost after the heroism of the dead, Pericles exhorted the survivors, his audience, to be ever ready to defend her.

J. J.

An attempt to summarize the excerpt in journalistic vein is, unfortunately, not altogether successful.

THE GLORY THAT IS ATHENS

A newspaper headline might give as a title to the first paragraph of this extract from Thucydides' *History of the Peloponnesian War* the caption "Pericles Breaks Custom As Regards Accepted Eulogy." It is the practice and law of the time to deliver a panegyric "at the burial of those who fall in battle," in which the dead are extolled. Pericles is averse to this policy for the reason that he believes "that the worth which had displayed itself in deeds would be sufficiently rewarded by honors also shown by deeds"; and because it is beyond man's privilege and scope to make a favorable or unfavorable reputation for an individual simply by speaking one way or another about him. Also he considers it very difficult to satisfy both friend and stranger alike on all points regarding the facts of this person's story.

Thus, being dissatisfied with the fashionable scheme for this speech, Pericles changes the order of the oration. He extends his praise to groups: that is, the ancestors are mentioned first, then the fathers of the existent generation, and finally, the existing generation itself. The fact is brought out that the mother country has been enriched by added possessions, and by "everything that can enable her to depend on her own resources whether for war or peace." Here Pericles declares his intention to relate of the "road" by which the Athenians, past and present, have reached their position, the system of government under which their glory developed, and of the "national habits" from which it emerged.

The title of the third paragraph of the selection is found in the phrase of the preceding one, "the form of government under which our greatness grew." It is my view that Pericles places more credit for the magnificence of Athens upon this item than he does upon the Athenians as individuals, since it is due to the existing form of government that the Athenians are what they are. This government is a democracy and "favors the many." Class and social standing are no bar to advancement from poverty and obscurity upward by reason of capacity and merit. In the main, the citizens conduct themselves in their individual manners, regardless of their neighbors, yet all obey the magistrates and the codes, written or unwritten.

Continuing, all is not business in Athens. There are plenty of recreations and luxuries (due to the world-wide trade which Athens carries on) present in this ideal city. Games and sacrifices are indulged in throughout the year. The grandeur of the residences is a constant source of pride and soothing enjoyment, all of which serves to keep the mind cheerful.

As regards the "military policy" of Athens, much of credit may be spoken. Nothing is kept secret from foreigners, which fact reveals the fearlessness and security of the Athenians, the secret of whose success (military) is this; because of their "native spirit" and inherent courage, they have the "double advantage" of not experiencing the worries of anticipation and of always being ready to face hardships undaunted.

Returning to the journalistic vein, the sixth paragraph of the piece might well be named "Pericles Contradicts Self." In speaking of the generosity of Athens in presenting gifts to other countries "not from calculations of expediency, but in the confidence of liberality" he speaks in antithesis to a previous statement which proves the *expediency* of donating gifts for the reason that the receivers of the favors are the debtors of the givers. Further, in this paragraph it is learned that all the Athenians are public-spirited and are ready and free to join in all discussions of public matters.

Pericles concludes the excerpt by a statement of the greatness of Athens: the fact that Athens is the "school of Hellas," and that no men are as versatile as the Athenians. It is for such a glorious city that men have nobly fought and died, their death in this manner, alone, conferring the highest of laudatory praise possible upon them.

W. M.

>>> B <<<

An example of the condensed summary from the *Reader's Digest* will show how a skilled writer can preserve stylistic smoothness and still reduce a fairly long article to small compass. Look up the original article.[1]

THE CULT OF CULTURE [2]
Winthrop Parkhurst

Man may be a noble animal, but he is also often a ludicrous one. Nowhere is he more ludicrously pompous than in those circles where his culture takes an airing; where, fearful of being thought an ass, he becomes a donkey.

But let me be concrete. As a cultivated person you have heard of Púshkin. Is not Púshkin the foremost Russian poet? Of course. Therefore, let us say, you mention Púshkin, taking care to give a juicy, rich *oosh* sound to the first syllable. Immediately the eye of your hearer brightens. "Ah," he exclaims, "Púshkin!" Your eyes meet in mutual understanding. You say no more. You have no need to say more than those magic syllables. And this is peculiarly fortunate for both of you, since exactly what might happen next, supposing you were compelled to stop pushkinning each other, is something that belongs to the world of nightmares.

Not long ago I had an experience of this order. For some reason or other, I mentioned Púshkin. I mentioned Púshkin easily, casually, with that air of mingled familiarity and reverence which marks the discourse of cultured persons on such occasions. The *oosh* fairly oozed cultivation; nothing could have beaten it for pure ooshiness. Indeed, for one perilous moment, it threatened to swallow me up like a bed of quicksand; it was nip and tuck between honesty and humbug. And then, I am proud to relate, I leaped out of the bog. Púshkin! Well, who really and actually *was* Púshkin? Did I know his first name? No. Could I quote a single line from his poems? No. What, then, did I know about Púshkin? Simply this: that his name was Púshkin. And why, knowing absolutely nothing about the man or his works, did I mention him? Simply because his name was one of those words which, plucked from the grab-bag, seemed to show a cultured background. This famous if utterly unknown Russian poet is a symbol. His name stands for refined humbug the world over, the sort of humbug we all practise daily.

Consider, for example, the way we secretly shudder over various

[1] Compare, also, our own condensation of the *Reader's Digest's* précis of a *Scribner's* article at the end of Chapter VI below: a précis of a précis!

[2] Condensed from the *Bookman* (October, 1932). Reprinted by kind permission of the *American Review* (formerly the *Bookman*) and the *Reader's Digest*, holders of the copyright.

trifling *gaucheries* of our fellow citizens. In most cases these *gaucheries* are very small ones. The crudity which makes our souls wince may be nothing more than a single misspelled word, a single mispronounced word, a single lapse in syntax; no matter: the offender goes silently on our blacklist. Let him spell thousands of other words with dazzling accuracy; let him pronounce thousands of other words with blinding elegance (even a few, perhaps, about which we ourselves feel uncertain); no matter: out comes our *Index Expurgatorius* and down goes the sinner on its pages.

Take, if you must be concrete, the word *irreparable*. Here we have a single word taken from the fifteen or twenty thousand words of an average vocabulary. One would not say that especially grave importance could be attached to it. As long as its meaning is conveyed, any pronunciation of the word would seem adequate.

To argue this, however, is to project yourself instantly beyond the pale of culture. For *irreparable* is no mere word: it is a symbol of profound social significance. Let a man place the accent on the second syllable, and you would ask him to dinner or let him hold your wallet without anxiety. Let him but shift the accent to the third syllable, however, and at once you take a secret oath that he shall aspire in vain for the hand of your daughter. True, he may possess sterling virtues; he may be as industrious as Sisyphus and as good as the day is long with daylight-saving time; you might even go so far as to vote for him in a political crisis, especially if his rival candidate gives the word no accent at all, being ignorant of it. No matter. In the single fell act of shifting the accent to the third syllable, he has wiped his mouth on his sleeve, by verbal proxy.

I do not profess to understand these strange matters; they puzzle me. Why should mispronouncing the adjective *irreparable* be a scandal in our eyes, seeing that mispronouncing the word *combat* is almost universal? Why do we laugh at the illiterate spelling *recieve* but fail to crack a smile at the illiterate spelling *dessicate?*

No, we can hardly wiggle out of the fact that we have made a cult of the vague commodity we call our culture. A background of haphazard data, hand-me-down dates, and pick-me-up allusions to art and science, an English king here, a Greek philosopher there, a correct emphasis of a certain syllable elsewhere: of such is the kingdom of our well-bred heaven.

Incidentally, one of the best ways of cultivating the capacity for close, critical reading is the composition of such condensations as this. You will find yourself penetrating to what the author *really* said.

The more general analysis of books is discussed in Chapter IX on Criticism. It is in the review that the condensed form of the summary is most used. Excellent examples of reviews of novels, poetry, drama, concerts and recitals in music and dance, painting, sculpture, and of new developments in science, discovery, politics, and international affairs, appear each week in the various classified sections of the Sunday *New York Times*. The *Christian Science Monitor*, the *New York Herald Tribune* and other great newspapers provide similar specialized sections.

CHAPTER V

Definition of the Abstract Term
or Idea [1]

THE VIEW is often expressed by professional writers that the core
of good writing is nothing more than a collection of facts plus
ideas. To produce a piece of writing of your own, you must
search for an idea and for the facts to substantiate it, to give it
body. Usually these two processes go so closely together as to
seem simultaneous; but in most cases the actual initial stimulus
will lie in the arresting force of an idea, or in the vivid, concrete
vigor of a fact. Ideas are the framework of the literary building,
facts the sticks and stones which compose the walls. Ideas must
have a tough, tensile strength; facts must have bulk.

It is common to refer to ideas as abstract. The Latin derivation reveals the essential meaning of this term: *ab*, *abs*, "from,"
and *trahere*, "to draw or take." Ideas, then, are *taken from* things,
from events, experiences, which supply the facts on which ideas
depend. Of course there are so-called ideas not derived from facts
either material or spiritual; these are really superstitions, prejudices, delusions, or at best pure playful fancies. Although in life
these are the false counterparts of ideas, they abound in writing,
especially fanciful and descriptive writing; but to be effective
there they must be given an imaginative reality. Even the immortal nonsense of Lewis Carroll's upside-down world keeps a
close parallel to what the real world leads us to expect. The
idea in the book wherein Alice walks through a looking glass de-

---

[1] Some ideas in this chapter are derived from Professor T. E. Rankin's excellent
book, *The Method and Practice of Exposition*, The Macmillan Company, 1917, with the
permission of both the author and the publishers.

lights us because of the astonishing number of familiar facts which are thrown into comical reverse. We enjoy meeting the White Knight because we recognize at once that he is the possessor of an eminently practical and logical mind.

We seldom have to present ideas pure and simple. Much writing labors to draw or wrench the ideas out of the mass of facts in which they are embedded. Such writing is usually expository. At other times the endeavor is to return the idea to the facts, to re-clothe it in them. Such writing is usually descriptive. But in either approach, expository or descriptive, the ultimate purpose is defini-tion. You will be presenting a fund or tissue of facts from which you wish to derive and define your idea; or you will be defining an idea in the first place, gradually adding factual details till you have an expository or descriptive expansion or application of it.

We must now observe how the processes of definition may be either the commonly recognized type in which the idea is stripped to its simplest, most naked statement, that is, the dictionary defi-nition; or the much more common, but less recognized type, in which the simple idea is elaborated and enriched into its fullest expression, at any length, from a paragraph to the six volumes of Gibbon's *Decline and Fall of the Roman Empire.*

When you hear the man in the street saying, "Now I have an idea . . .," what do you expect from him? Will it not be the recital of some series of experiences or a group of apparently re-lated facts? He will attempt to make these converge on some con-clusion or hunch: his suspicions concerning city-hall graft, the ideal cigarette lighter, a perfect system for handling traffic, or, if his mind is so inclined, some idea of a philosophical, economic, or critical nature. The important point to observe is that the power and clarity of his idea will really lie in its derivation from a coherent body of experience or research. Legends to the con-trary, ideas of real value have almost always come from pro-fessionals or devoted amateurs. They result from persistent efforts at isolating and shaping statements of derived truth—from defi-nition. Our need now is to consider the types and methods of definition.

In the first place consider the term *definition* closely. The easiest way to define any word, that is, to explain any idea or thing for which the English language has a word, is to go to Webster's Dictionary. You will find there also the derivation or etymology of the word, and this is often very suggestive. We noticed the derivation of the word *abstract* from the Latin. Search out the pedigree of ten words. (*Pedigree*—from the medieval French meaning "crane's foot," the shape of the heraldic genealogical trees.) From the Greek, for example, you will find many classes of words stemming from common roots. *Graph* from the word meaning "to write" combines with *bio* (life), *geo* (earth), *chiro* (hand), *phono* (sound, tone), *photo* (light), *tele* (far, far off), to produce familiar words. Knowledge of their sources gives them fresh meaning; often it makes obscure words intelligible.

But there are other methods of definition. A very simple one is to give *concrete illustrations* of the term. Macbeth, Julius Caesar, Napoleon represent one aspect of ambition; Lincoln, or the scientist who searches for a cure for cancer, may represent quite another. Characters in literature provide many types—Romeo and Juliet illustrate romantic love; the Nurse and Mercutio, in the same play, quite another conception of love; the Wife of Bath, Ivanhoe, Fagin, Sentimental Tommy—each suggests abstract human qualities expanded into a single character. The modern cartoonist makes much use of this device. Little Orphan Annie is artful innocence and Browning's Pippa in one; Popeye the Sailor combines Don Quixote and an enormous forearm; Major Hoople is the incarnation of bluff. In both fiction and the cartoon you are very likely to find directly opposed types: guileless innocence and crafty villainy; heroism and cowardice; or, as in Jane Austen's novel, pride and prejudice. Such an employment of abstract ideas almost invariably brings with it contrast and comparison.

But to go a step further, there is another type of definition generally called the *analytical definition*. In this case you sum up all possible varying aspects of the term at once, viewing it from different angles, telling what it is, what it is not. You explain the term from as many different points of view as possible, hoping that by one or two of your explanatory comments—not the same one or two—you will catch the attention and understanding of each particular reader. There are some very good illustrations of this type in the selections appended below.

There is also what is called the *synthetic definition*. This endeavors to show how over a period of years a term has changed in meaning, and so finally to indicate its meaning today in relation to its meaning years ago. For example, *chivalry*, which was an elaborate organization of society in the Middle Ages, today is nothing more than a social attitude, largely restricted in meaning to a man's behavior to a woman. Note the gradual, subtle change in the implications of the term over the centuries.

Some terms can be explained less by direct definition than by supplying words that are closely equivalent or opposite in meaning, *synonyms* and *antonyms*. This method will often bring out subtle shades of meaning which, except in the case of absolutely new words, are more useful than specific definitions. In the case of words of technical nature and foreign derivation, equivalents are often needed. To find these, do not go only to the dictionary; consult also Roget's *Thesaurus of English Words and Phrases*. The work covers the entire field of knowledge and classifies the words pertaining to each field. Under each heading—as for example, "No. 446. Visibility"—terms are classified under nouns, verbs, adjectives, and adverbs. In the adjacent column appears "No. 447. Invisibility," with the same classification of useful terms. There is no better aid in the practical building up of a working vocabulary than this book. Thus, it would be unnecessary to define such a word as *promise*, but the list of associated nouns alone is suggestive of useful variants.

"768. Promise.—N. promise, undertaking, word, troth, plight, pledge, *parole*, word of honor, vow; oath, etc. (*affirmation*) 535; profession, assurance . . . obligation; contract, etc. 769. engagement, pre-engagement; affiance; betroth, -al, -ment."

The numbers indicate equivalents leading into related fields of idea which may be located under sections so denoted.

The strictest procedure in definition requires a completely objective, impersonal type of statement. Dr. Samuel Johnson, virtual founder of the defining dictionary, occasionally relieved himself of the tedium of driving his six Scotch assistants by composing humorous definitions: "Oats, a grain which in England is generally given to horses, but in Scotland supports the people." The difficulty and futility of defining familiar terms are reflected in his famous definition of *network* as "Anything reticulated or decussated, at equal distances, with interstices between the intersections." Try yourself to compose definitions of *book, flower, chair,* or *shoe*.

It should be noted that the correct form for such definitions is that of the so-called *logical definition*. Such definitions have rigid rules controlling their form: they should be stated in one sentence only; they are composed of three elements, the *term*, the *genus*, and the *differentiae*. The *term* designates that which is to be defined, for example, *carburetor*. The *genus* restricts the term to a conveniently limited class, such as "a mechanical device." The *differentiae* include the details which differentiate or distinguish the term from the other members of the genus or class, that is, "for mixing air and the vapor of gasoline in proportions suitable for explosion in internal combustion engines." Combined in sequence the three elements given compose a complete definition. Certain suggestions are important. Avoid using the term or a derivative of it in the definition: "Hunger is a state of being hungry." Do not employ words that are unfamiliar, or so technical as themselves to require defining: "Apocryphal—that which is not canonical." Bear in mind that the definition must ordinarily be expressed in a single, complete sentence. It will be useful, also, to determine in advance whether the term should be defined with regard to purpose, as in mechanical devices; or appearance, as in types of clouds, pets, trees; or some other dominant feature, such as composition, value, quantity, derivation, etc.

The chief value in constructing the formulated type of definition is similar to the value in doing setting-up exercises. You gain muscularity, control, and precision in the use of words. The actual defining, however, which will be called for in term papers, examinations, and critical writing will not be of the spare, logical variety. While you may begin your discussion with such definitions if, for example, you are treating feudalism, or the comedy of George Bernard Shaw, your real work will lie in an elaboration which will present concrete examples, the atmosphere of names, description, color, the substance of the thing you wish to define. How can a logical, dictionary definition possibly convey all one wants to know or say about the Russian ballet, television, communism, Greek architecture, evolution, the grading system, Fascism, cosmetics, professional football, campus journalism, Paris, and the worlds of other things from which flow what we call ideas?

You now have a complete account of this subtle type of exposition; there remain some warnings to be given. Do not write a criticism of the term: that is, do not let emotions or mere opinions confuse the analysis. Do not preach about the beauty or ugliness, the preciousness or futility of what you are defining; explain it so clearly that it will reveal itself; that is enough. Do not neglect concreteness—an anecdote here and there, some proper names of persons, cities, streets, hotels, or a few technical words—all these arouse interest and provide atmosphere. Observe how Mr. Waldo Frank heightens the sense of the peculiar character of Spanish life and landscape by these devices in the illustration at the end of this chapter, yet without letting the method intrude itself. Generally several illustrations are better than one. Beware of quoting too much, particularly from a series of dictionaries. Vary the above methods; it may be possible to use two or three on the same term. Beware of balancing terms too much. An essay is included below which overdid this method: read the paper on "Conviction and Prejudice" and note that while for a page or two the balancing is effective, it later becomes monotonous. Finally do not hesitate to read up a little on the subject; you may not be able to handle it entirely out of your own mind.

We should prefer to divide this type into two exercises: the first on a personal abstraction, and the second on a philosophical (or scientific) idea, which is much harder. Certainly the type is worth two themes.

The subjects students have chosen for the personal type are: Refinement, Culture, Pride, Vanity, Insincerity, Greediness, A Sense of Humor, Chivalry, Fear, Poise, Jealousy, Common Sense, Avarice, Cleverness, Honesty, Hypocrisy, Puppy Love, Ambition, Frankness, Prejudice, Self-Reliance. For the philosophical type:

Humanism, Transcendentalism, Pessimism, Materialism, Buddhism, Socialism, Communism, Fascism, Beauty, Realism, Superstition, Unitarianism, Anarchism, Stoicism, Democracy, Atheism, Genius, Fatalism, Romanticism, Naturalism, Classicism.

->>> A <<<-

The Personal Abstraction

This first paper exemplifies the analytical method at its best. Note also the excellent construction—definition, sources, and value [1]—and the fine stylistic qualities.

PERSONALITY

"And she never knew!"

"Even your best friends won't tell you."—So say the advertisements of the day, thus ever trying to explain the secret of popularity. Among the many solutions to the problem, personality as the key to social success holds an important place.

Personality is that combination of characteristics in an individual which serves to distinguish him from all other persons. By negative definition it is that quality without which one is but a dull, uninteresting sort of mortal, making no impression whatsoever upon his surroundings. Again, it is the peculiar vitality or distinctive personal atmosphere which differentiates one human being from another. Personality marks the difference between a type and an individual. And so we could go on, enumerating formidable definitions, which, after all, are perhaps not very enlightening. An analysis of the quality under discussion would possibly be more helpful at this point.

In considering the sources of this intangible thing called personality it will probably be found that this most coveted quality can be attributed to nothing definite. Some people are born with it; others achieve it; still others have it thrust upon them. The first class certainly has the least to worry about. They simply cannot help making their presence felt. It is not especially to their credit if they are naturally friendly, cheerful, capable, interesting, or any of the other fine things which we would all like to be. On the other hand, indeed, they apparently should not be blamed for arrogance, boastfulness, boldness, vanity, or any of the other undesirable qualities with which a too decided personality has encumbered them. Achieving personality,

---

[1] See Chapters I and XI.

however, is really quite an accomplishment. The timid, sensitive, weak-minded person who through his own efforts attains poise, compatability, leadership, and a sympathetic nature, in so doing accomplishes something undeniably worth while. Finally, there are those upon whom conditions practically thrust personality. In this class it occurs to me to place school teachers, for I have noticed that they of all people have the most individualistic natures, brought out, probably, by their contact with hundreds of students, all different, probably nearly all annoying, and all requiring a different type of treatment. It is doubtful whether one thus endowed with personality is more to be congratulated or pitied.

From whatever source it comes, however, personality still remains the same interesting quality. It is not so essential to man as moral strength, and yet it is almost as popular a subject for discussion. It may not be so helpful as great intelligence, but it is much more comforting. It is not as unusual as a very poetic mind, but it is undeniably more sought after. In short, personality may be termed a non-essential but extremely desirable quality in human nature.

Of course, even great blessings may be abused, and so, too strong a personality may degenerate into a forward, hot-tempered, fussy, or stubborn nature, that is anything but desirable. This disagreeable sense of the word is not so common as the more pleasant sense, but it is none the less manifest. Needless to say, he who unfortunately possesses such an objectionable character should strive even harder than the "jelly-fish" sort of person to obtain the right kind of personality. Just how this may be accomplished those wiser in psychology than I must say.

Those possessing personality in its better form, however, are undeniably blessed. One of their outstanding assets is the ability to accomplish whatever purpose they may have in life. They can easily do whatever they set out to do—from being elected class president in their youth to selling the latest marvel from the patent office in their maturity. In old age, by sheer personality, they may marry their children to whomever they please. (Though, of course, they may not do so if their own personality does not equal that of their offspring.) Furthermore, people possessing this distinct vitality are much more satisfying to themselves. That is, a dynamic nature is more interesting even to its owner in his solitary hours than a listless nature is to its possessor. Finally, personality has its greatest value in its ability to attract and hold friendships, in its quality of forming true and lasting comradeships, for the person whom everybody admires, trusts, and loves is the person who possesses this strange, invaluable thing called person-ality.

A. G.

Here is an example of definition by direct exemplification.

THE SUPERIORITY COMPLEX

If someone discusses some question in which you are not very well versed, or if he gives you his opinion of your work, or even if he fails to compliment you in any way, he has a very bad case of superiority complex. But, on the other hand, if you tell someone a joke, or give him some hints, or show him just how you did "it," and then the reply consists of merely a mild "Yeh?," you may be sure that he also has been stricken with this disease. Therefore, "superiority complex" may be defined as a condition of the mind that affects everyone except one certain individual, and that individual is one's self.

Unlike many other personal characteristics, the superiority complex is permanent, and is not altered on the spur of the moment; but, it is similar to the others because it has quite a variety of different stages. Nearly everyone who is mildly affected is a beginner. However, many pretend to have this attitude in order to enable them to successfully perform their mission, as the following humble examples: a salesman giving a canvass, a social-climber playing bridge, a student talking to his instructor, a criminal begging a pardon from the governor, a waiter hawking for a tip, and a man giving another man a loaded cigar. A more advanced stage is pictured in street-cleaners, teachers, deaf-mutes, and plumbers, who are not more advanced because they are handicapped greatly by the lack of vocal power. The absolute degree of superiority complex, the ultimate aim of the amateurs, is characterized by the many conceited egoists with overworked jaw-bones and undernourished brains. These beings consist of: cops (or officers of the law), automobile drivers, football coaches, umpires, banana peddlers, and ninety-nine and forty-four hundredths per cent of all the women.

This disease is not useless, but it is, indeed, a great benefit to those who have it. It would be no easy task for an automobile driver to convince a police officer that he is absolutely guiltless, and that he would give the officer a five-dollar bill as positive proof, had he not this condition of the mind; and if the officer had not a superiority complex, it would be difficult for him to act as if he were convinced in the proper manner. Similarly, if a politician and a bootlegger wish to make an agreement, both are obliged to take the superior attitude in order to prevent havoc resulting when one of them is gypped. Then in one-sided affairs, such as a conversation between a man and a woman, an assignment given by an instructor, or a speech rendered by a congressman, the donor should have an air of predominancy about him. The usefulness of the superiority complex is made even more pronounced by its usage in speech, as it is a harmless substitute for many terms which may be the cause of disastrous or inauspicious results.

Superiority complex is one of the many contributions to human knowledge made by the science of psychology. One used to address a fellow being as "Sophisticated Sap," or "Conceited Ass," but now "You big superiority complex" has taken their places. In the bygone days, an author would have to write a decent book, but now, the moment he mentions psychology, the book is a best seller. It is hoped that science will invent a new word that will make everything formidable, and so make this little world a bigger and better place to live in.

J. H.

The synthetic method demands an effort of the imagination.

HORSE SENSE

How often have you heard this expression, "That fellow hasn't much of an education, but he has plenty of horse sense"?

I heard practically the same remark only yesterday and it started me thinking about the origin of the last term. There probably is a definition for *horse sense* somewhere, but I don't think it can be found in Webster. Of course, you could look up *horse* and *sense*, but, even if you put the two meanings together, I don't think you would have anything like a definition for *horse sense*, a combination of the two.

The expression is relatively new, probably having been first used by the western pioneers as the advantages of having good beasts of burden dawned upon them. Psychologists will tell you that one will naturally apply, for comparison, the objects with which he is most in contact, and form the most part of his routine of life, with new ideas or objects. A horse was decidedly the most constant companion of a westerner, and so he applied the traits of his horse to the things that commanded his attention. I can imagine the expression as starting in this manner:

"Thet fellow's ez smart ez my old hoss Bet, Hank."

"Yep, Bill, he's a right pert chap. Got a good hoss's sense."

Then, as the term spread, and the facilities of a good education became more common, there arose a need to distinguish the term, that had been used to denote brilliance when an education was a rare thing, from school-taught sense. A conversation between two farmers a little while later would probably have been like this:

"My son Jack's doing right well at his booklarning, but he don't know ez much 'bout plowin' ez my old mare Dobbin."

"Wal, Silas, thet's the way 'tis. Booklarning comes, hoss sense goes."

Now, a recognizable distinction has been made between the two terms, education and horse sense. While an education can be procured from books, horse sense must be gotten from practical experiences in everyday life. The criterion of a well-educated man is to be able to use horse sense. In conclusion, a definition of the term might be given somewhat in this form:

The knowledge and application, respectively, of the problems and experiences of everyday life.

C. B.

The writer here made excellent use of etymology but prolonged his balancing technique too far.

CONVICTION AND PREJUDICE

The word *conviction* is of Latin origin. The *con-* prefix denotes completeness or union. It is intensive in feeling. The root *vincō* means to conquer. Literally then to convince is to conquer completely or to overpower. Hence, it has come to mean to overcome or persuade with argument, to force to yield assent to truth, to satisfy with proofs, to demonstrate. A conviction, therefore, is a firm belief founded on evidence. *Prejudice* is also from the Latin. The prefix *pre-* means before; the root *iūdicō* means to judge or decide. Hence, a prejudice is a prejudgment, a decision reached before study or examination of the evidence, a preconceived opinion. Frequently prejudice implies a negative decision, since many unfounded opinions are adverse.

Conviction exists by knowledge; prejudice by ignorance. Conviction is the result of thought and study; prejudice is the product of associations and environment. Conviction is the evidence of mental activity; prejudice is the admission of mental stagnation. Conviction delves into truths, weighs evidence; prejudice shuts out facts and lives by opinions, beliefs, and habits. Conviction goes to the heart of truth; prejudice wants only externals, never goes below the surface, and rejects what it does not comprehend. Conviction is positive, constructive; prejudice is negative and destructive. Conviction is firm, reasonable, persuasive, analytical; it accepts only what it can prove. Prejudice is unfair, unjust, ignorant, bigoted; it rejects what it cannot understand. Conviction brings peace and contentment to the soul; prejudice brings fear, distrust, and hate into life. Conviction commands respect and attracts disciples; prejudice engenders opposition, strife, and conflict. Conviction builds its house upon a rock; prejudice builds upon the sand. Conviction has the earnestness and devotion of a scientist delving into the mysteries of existence; prejudice is the bigot, consumed with fierce and malignant passions. Conviction ennobles, purifies, deepens, enriches, gives color and meaning to life; prejudice corrodes, stupefies, dwarfs, destroys, stultifies. Conviction is the inspiration of noble service and sacrificial lives; prejudice breeds tyranny and persecution.

Conviction has been the solace of martyrs, the companion of saints, the vindication of the despised and outcast; prejudice has been the instrument of tyranny, the sword of persecution, the flame of martyrdom. Galileo stating boldly the revolutionary theory that the earth was not the center of the universe was actuated by conviction. Pope Urban VIII forcing the astronomer to recant his heretical doctrines was acting on prejudice. Conviction makes the idealist, the dreamer, the apostle, the leader; prejudice has the arrogant mien of a despot, the sneering supercilious aspect of a tyrant. Luther, facing the Diet of Worms courageously in the crisis of his career, was sustained by conviction. Philip II of Spain, who wasted his treasury, impoverished his nation, diminished his hopes of imperial power to extirpate heresy through the Inquisition, was prejudiced to the extent of fanaticism.

H. B. L.

THE PHILOSOPHICAL ABSTRACTION

The following theme shows the value of concrete illustrations.

SPIRITUALISM

The scene is a dim or completely darkened room. A group of people are seated around a table with their hands on the table, palms down, their fingers barely touching their neighbors'. Incessant rapping on the table, cobwebby feelings around the face, and cold breezes are the only signs of life in the room. This is not a Halloween party, but merely a spiritual séance.

Spiritualism is the belief that man survives death, and that communication between the living and the dead is possible through mediums. The word *spiritualism* is derived from the Latin word *spiritualis*, meaning "relating to spirit or breath." This conception, in so far as doctrine is concerned, is only about a half-century old. The Fox sisters in 1848 were the first to bring about a general interest in it. After fooling the public for years, they were finally discovered to be frauds. Much publicity was given them, and through this, spiritualism gained many followers.

According to W. J. Crawford, lecturer in the Municipal Technical Institute, Belfast, the entities from the departed world can work better in the dark because the ether light vibrations prevent the efflux of psychic energy from the bodies of the sitters at a séance, or prohibit the invisible emanations from the body of the medium. That is to say, the levitation of any object in the room is due to a thread-like loose structure, ejected from the medium's body, which structure attaches itself to the object that is to be moved. These thread-like structures are hollow tubes which are filled with gassy substance that is different from any gas we have on earth here. The gas is matter supplied by the spirits from the departed world and is injected into the tubes. The tubes are thus stiffened and are able to move light pieces of furniture about the room. The moving of objects about the room is one of the ways the spirits have of communicating with our world. First the medium establishes a code with the spirit, say two raps for "yes," and three raps for "no." The medium then asks questions and the spirits rock or tap the furniture accordingly.

Another common form of communication is by the planchette, which is a heart-shaped board resting on casters and fitted with a pencil, which traces words, supposedly from the other world. The following is an example of planchette writing that is given by Sir Wm. F. Barrett in his book on the phenomena of spiritualism:

"The planchette began to write as follows:

" 'David—David—David—dead 143 years.' Mr. Wedgewood, who was one of the sitters at the séance, suggested the name David Hume, who he thought had died about then, but after many trials, the planchette was finally able to spell out the name David Brainerd. It also went on to say that he had been a missionary to the North American Indians and that he knew where the secret gold of the Indians was located, but that some day it would be uncovered. Upon looking up the history of Mr. Brainerd, Mr. Wedgewood goes on to say, it was discovered that the above facts were correct, but as yet, there is no record of the gold having been brought to light. Why Mr. Brainerd thought it necessary for him to convey this valuable information to our world is another question."

There are other ways of communicating with the spiritual world, but I have just given two of the most common forms.

As yet, the believers in spiritualism have not been able to discover much about the appearance of the spiritual world. However, the operators (spirits from the departed world) declare that no one need be idle in their world, and that congenial duties are available for every-body. Music and art have higher expressions there than here. There is no orthodox hell, but there are dark spheres into which the worst of humanity pass at physical death. The operators also assert that, at death, entry into their world seems excessively wonderful, but not altogether unfamiliar, which keeps them from becoming bewildered.

The afterlife of the spiritualist is ideal, but I cannot picture myself as returning in spirit form to this world and attempting to move a twenty-pound table in the hope of comforting my loved ones on this earth.

I. A.

Research can produce such an excellent paper as "Voodooism."

VOODOOISM

In real Voodoo a priest, a priestess, and a snake are absolutely necessary. White Voodoo is satisfied with a cock or a goat for sacrificial blood, but Red Voodoo must have a human victim. In the secret rites of Haitian Voodooism the male priest is known as the *papaloi* and the priestess as the *mamaloi*. In the depths of West Indian and Haitian forests, where the dark and terrible Voodoo rites are still supposed to be practiced in secret, stands Honfou, the Voodoo temple, a straw hut of some size.

At the nocturnal service in the forest depths, a great fire burns beside a snake basket containing the reptile god. The *papaloi* assisted by his sub-priests, the *dijions*, cuts the throats of three goats, two black and one white, whose flesh is devoured and whose blood, mixed with rum, is consumed by the worshippers. To the mad beat of magic drums, the *mamaloi* then steps forward and stands on the snake basket. She wears a red kerchief about her loins, and one hangs over her shoulder. She begins the song of the divine snake whose chorus is repeated by hundreds of drunken lips. Then the Negroes crowd around to question the oracle: "Will I get a new donkey?" "Will my lover come back?" "Will my child get well?" Each one asks his question. The priestess, swaying, calls from time to time, "Houedo, the great snake hears you! Houedo, the great snake answers!" Then with downcast eyes she gives the answers inspired by the snake spirit. Suddenly the drums beat again. The priestess steps down from the basket and draws out the god, a long yellow-black viper, which winds itself about her arm. Chickens are sacrificed to it and then—the climax of the rite—come the priests of the demon-god, Cimbi-Kita. They wear devil masks, their bodies are stained with blood, and goat skins hang from their backs. They drag along, by a rope tied to her neck, a ten-year-old child. It feels no pain, for it has been intoxicated with rum, and the sacrifice takes place in a moment. No sooner has the *papaloi* strewn certain magic herbs on its woolly head, and set fire to it with a burning brand, than the *mamaloi*, with a terrible cry, seizes the child, and holding it high above her head, strangles it. Meanwhile the devil-priests sing a chant of triumph: "Ask the graveyard, it will tell you whether we or death sends it the most guests!" The cannibal meal is then devoured with draughts of raw rum and fresh blood.

It hardly seems possible that this horrible superstition still flourishes in the twentieth century. Yet it is said that, in the secret recesses of the Haitian jungle, victims are still devoured.

H. A.

->» B «<-

The Personal Abstraction

This type deals with what are commonly known as subjective or psychological aspects of personality. The so-called character writings illustrated in Chapter VI below are developments of it in the form of generalized character types. In the first selection the genial Oliver Goldsmith, without developing a single character, defines by analysis and illustration narrow nationalistic prejudice, showing its difference from genuine patriotism, while at the same time he gives significant meaning to the opposite attitude, that of the "citizen of the world."

ON NATIONAL PREJUDICES (1760)
Oliver Goldsmith

As I am one of that sauntering tribe of mortals who spend the greatest part of their time in taverns, coffee-houses, and other places of public resort, I have thereby an opportunity of observing an infinite variety of characters, which to a person of a contemplative turn is a much higher entertainment than a view of all the curiosities of art or nature. In one of these my late rambles I accidentally fell into a company of half a dozen gentlemen, who were engaged in a warm dispute about some political affair, the decision of which, as they were equally divided in their sentiments, they thought proper to refer to me, which naturally drew me in for a share of the conversation.

Amongst a multiplicity of other topics, we took occasion to talk of the different characters of the several nations of Europe; when one of the gentlemen, cocking his hat, and assuming such an air of importance as if he had possessed all the merit of the English nation in his own person, declared, that the Dutch were a parcel of avaricious wretches; the French a set of flattering sycophants; that the Germans were drunken sots, and beastly gluttons; and the Spaniards proud, haughty, and surly tyrants; but that in bravery, generosity, clemency, and in every other virtue, the English excelled all the world.

This very learned and judicious remark was received with a general smile of approbation by all the company—all, I mean, but your humble servant, who, endeavouring to keep my gravity as well as I could, and reclining my head upon my arm, continued for some time in a posture of affected thoughtfulness, as if I had been musing on something else, and did not seem to attend to the subject of conversation; hoping by this means to avoid the disagreeable necessity of explaining myself, and thereby depriving the gentleman of his imaginary happiness.

But my pseudo-patriot had no mind to let me escape so easily. Not satisfied that his opinion should pass without contradiction, he was determined to have it ratified by the suffrage of every one in the company; for which purpose, addressing himself to me with an air of inexpressible confidence, he asked me if I was not of the same way of thinking. As I am never forward in giving my opinion, especially when I have reason to believe that it will not be agreeable; so, when I am obliged to give it, I always hold it for a maxim to speak my real sentiments. I therefore told him that, for my own part, I should not have ventured to talk in such a peremptory strain unless I had made the tour of Europe, and examined the manners of these several nations with great care and accuracy: that perhaps a more impartial judge would not scruple to affirm, that the Dutch were more frugal and industrious, the French more temperate and polite, the Germans more hardy and patient of labour and fatigue, and the Spaniards more staid and sedate, than the English; who, though undoubtedly brave and generous, were at the same time rash, headstrong, and impetuous; too apt to be elated with prosperity, and to despond in adversity.

I could easily perceive, that all the company began to regard me with a jealous eye before I had finished my answer, which I had no sooner done, than the patriotic gentleman observed, with a contemptuous sneer, that he was greatly surprised how some people could have the conscience to live in a country which they did not love, and to enjoy the protection of a government to which in their hearts they were inveterate enemies. Finding that by this modest declaration of my sentiments I had forfeited the good opinion of my companions, and given them occasion to call my political principles in question, and well knowing that it was in vain to argue with men who were so very full of themselves, I threw down my reckoning and retired to my own lodgings, reflecting on the absurd and ridiculous nature of national prejudice and prepossession.

Among all the famous sayings of antiquity, there is none that does greater honour to the author, or affords greater pleasure to the reader (at least if he be a person of generous and benevolent heart), than that of the philosopher who, being asked what countryman he was, replied, that he was "a citizen of the world." How few are there to be found in modern times who can say the same, or whose conduct is consistent with such a profession! We are now become so much Englishmen, Frenchmen, Dutchmen, Spaniards, or Germans, that we are no longer citizens of the world; so much the natives of one particular spot, or members of one petty society, that we no longer consider ourselves as the general inhabitants of the globe, or members of that grand society which comprehends the whole human kind.

Did these prejudices prevail only among the meanest and lowest of the people, perhaps they might be excused, as they have few, if any, opportunities of correcting them by reading, travelling, or conversing with foreigners: but the misfortune is, that they infect the minds, and influence the conduct, even of our gentlemen; of those, I mean, who have every title to this appellation but an exemption from prejudice, which, however, in my opinion, ought to be regarded as the characteristical mark of a gentleman; for let a man's birth be ever so high, his station ever so exalted, or his fortune ever so large, yet if he is not free from national and other prejudices, I should make bold to tell him, that he had a low and vulgar mind, and had no just claim to the character of a gentleman. And, in fact, you will always find that those are most apt to boast of national merit, who have little or no merit of their own to depend on; than which, to be sure, nothing is more natural: the slender vine twists around the sturdy oak for no other reason in the world but because it has not strength sufficient to support itself.

Should it be alleged in defence of national prejudice, that it is the natural and necessary growth of love to our country, and that there-fore the former cannot be destroyed without hurting the latter, I answer that this is a gross fallacy and delusion. That it is the growth of love to our country, I will allow; but that it is the natural and necessary growth of it, I absolutely deny. Superstition and enthusiasm, too, are the growth of religion; but who ever took it in his head to affirm, that they are the necessary growth of this noble principle? They are, if you will, the bastard sprouts of this heavenly plant, but not its natural and genuine branches, and may safely enough be lopped off, without doing any harm to the parent stock: nay, perhaps, till once they are lopped off, this goodly tree can never flourish in perfect health and vigour.

Is it not very possible that I may love my own country, without hating the natives of other countries? that I may exert the most heroic bravery, the most undaunted resolution, in defending its laws and liberty, without despising all the rest of the world as cowards and poltroons? Most certainly it is; and if it were not—But why need I suppose what is absolutely impossible?—But if it were not, I must own I should prefer the title of the ancient philosopher, viz., a citizen of the world, to that of an Englishman, a Frenchman, an European, or to any other appellation whatever.

In the selection from Thackeray, definition may be seen at work in the service of satirical burlesque. *The Book of Snobs* (1848) appeared originally as a series of humorous papers in *Punch*. Gathered together, these papers form a sizeable volume, entirely devoted to the author's enthusiastic effort to hunt down the snob and poise him for inspection like a wasp on a pin, in other words, to classify and define an odious type. You will search the book in vain for a concise definition of the *genus snobbus*, but from the array of types and the bustle of Thackeray's style (he seems to write with a fly-swatter) you will get positive impressions of the genus which no brief definition could convey.

THE SNOBS OF ENGLAND [1]

William Makepeace Thackeray

. . . I have long gone about with a conviction in my mind that I had a work to do—a Work, if you like, with a great W; a Purpose to fulfil; a chasm to leap into, like CURTIUS, horse and foot; a Great Social Evil to Discover and Remedy. That Conviction Has Pursued me for Years. It has Dogged me in the Busy Street; Seated Itself By Me in the Lonely Study; Jogged my Elbow as it Lifted The Wine-cup at the Festive Board; Pursued me through the Maze of Rotten Row; Followed me in Far Lands. On Brighton's Shingly Beach, or Margate's Sand, the Voice Outpiped the Roaring of the Sea: it Nestles in my Nightcap, And it Whispers "Wake, Slumberer, thy Work is Not Yet Done." Last Year, by Moonlight, in the Colosseum, the Little Sedulous Voice Came to Me and Said, "SMITH, or JONES" (the Writer's Name is Neither Here Nor There)—"SMITH, or JONES, my fine fellow, this is all very well; but you ought to be at home, writing your great work ON SNOBS."

. . . .

I have (and for this gift I congratulate myself with a Deep and Abiding Thankfulness) an eye for a Snob. If the Truthful is the Beautiful: it is Beautiful to study even the Snobbish: to track Snobs through history, as certain little dogs in Hampshire hunt out truffles; to sink shafts in society and come upon rich veins of Snob-ore. Snobbishness is like Death in a quotation from Horace, which I hope you have never heard "beating with equal foot at poor men's doors, and kicking at the gates of Emperors." It is a great mistake to judge of Snobs lightly, and think they exist among the lower classes merely. An immense percentage of Snobs I believe is to be found in every rank of this mortal life. You must not judge hastily or vulgarly of Snobs; to do so shows that you are yourself a Snob. I myself have been taken for one.

When I was taking the water at Bagnigge Wells, and living at the Imperial Hotel there, there used to sit opposite me at breakfast, for a short time, a Snob so insufferable that I felt I should never get any benefit of the waters so long as he remained. His name was LIEUTENANT-COLONEL SNOBLEY, of a certain dragoon regiment. He wore japanned boots and moustachios: he lisped, drawled, and left the "r's" out of his words; he was always flourishing about and smoothing his lac-

[1] From "Prefatory Remarks" to *The Book of Snobs*.

quered whiskers with a huge flaming bandanna, that filled the room
with an odour of musk so stifling that I determined to do battle with
that Snob, and that either he or I should quit the Inn. I first began
harmless conversations with him; frightening him exceedingly, for he
did not know what to do when so attacked, and had never the slightest
notion that anybody would take such a liberty with him as to speak
first; then I handed him the paper: then, as he would take no notice
of these advances, I used to look him in the face steadily and—and
use my fork in the light of a toothpick. After two mornings of this
practice, he could bear it no longer, and fairly quitted the place.

Skeptics are usually good definers. Not only are they necessarily always on the defensive, thus needing well-phrased am-
munition to defend their positions, but they also often have a
clear, questioning point of view, unclouded by sentimental wish-
ful thinking. There has been no more incisive and laconic style
than Voltaire's, and no more devastating definer of human stupidity and pettiness than Voltaire. In him we learn that swift
statement, arrow-like in accuracy, constitutes the essence of definition, and of satire. In his famous narrative, *Candide*, he ridicules
pedantry and unthinking optimism. Here he defines one of the
hardest of hard words, incidentally making it up for his own
purposes, though we recognize that he is caricaturing empty
optimism.

Pangloss was professor of metaphysicotheologicocosmonigology. . . .
"It is demonstrable," said he, "that all is necessarily for the best
end. Observe that the nose has been formed to bear spectacles . . .
legs were visibly designed for stockings . . . stones were designed to
construct castles . . . pigs were made so that we might have pork all
the year round. Consequently, they who assert that all is well have
said a foolish thing; they should have said all is for the best."

                                                    VOLTAIRE, *Candide*.

It is said that the good die young; Voltaire (1694–1778) lived
to be eighty-four, a tireless gadfly to many narrow-minded people,
and it must be admitted, to some very well-meaning individuals
as well. The German philosopher Arthur Schopenhauer (1788–
1860) survived for seventy-two years, long enough to give vigorous
support to Voltaire's attack on those who fail to look at life and

conduct and thought without defining their elements in clear-cut, realistic terms.

Though Schopenhauer made his fame as a pessimistic thinker, you will find him here insisting on the primary value of thinking as against pessimism or any other *ism*. In this selection, definition, expanding into analysis, clearly merges into the philosophical type of essay. We are reminded that most articles in serious magazines and in the *Encyclopaedia Britannica*, most works on social, scientific, historical, economic, and such subjects, even biography with its analysis of the controlling factors in individual lives, in fact, most non-fictional writing—all these are essentially expansions of the method of definition.

THINKING FOR ONESELF [1]

Arthur Schopenhauer

A library may be very large; but if it is in disorder, it is not so useful as one that is small but well arranged. In the same way, a man may have a great mass of knowledge, but if he has not worked it up by thinking it over for himself, it has much less value than a far smaller amount which he has thoroughly pondered. For it is only when a man looks at his knowledge from all sides, and combines the things he knows by comparing truth with truth, that he obtains a complete hold over it and gets it into his power. A man cannot turn over anything in his mind unless he knows it; he should, therefore, learn something; but it is only when he has turned it over that he can be said to know it.

Reading and learning are things that anyone can do of his own free will; but not so thinking. Thinking must be kindled, like a fire by a draught; it must be sustained by some interest in the matter in hand. This interest may be of purely objective kind, or merely subjective. The latter comes into play only in things that concern us personally. Objective interest is confined to heads that think by nature; to whom thinking is as natural as breathing; and they are very rare. This is why most men of learning show so little of it.

It is incredible what a different effect is produced upon the mind by thinking for oneself as compared with reading. It carries on and intensifies that original difference in the nature of two minds which leads the one to think and the other to read. What I mean is that

[1] From *Parerga and Paralipomena*. Translated by T. Bailey Saunders.

reading forces alien thoughts upon the mind—thoughts which are as foreign to the drift and temper in which it may be for the moment, as the seal is to the wax on which it stamps its imprint. The mind is thus entirely under compulsion from without; it is driven to think this or that, though for the moment it may not have the slightest impulse or inclination to do so.

But when a man thinks for himself, he follows the impulse of his own mind, which is determined for him at the time, either by his environment or some particular recollection. The visible world of a man's surroundings does not, as reading does, impress a single definite thought upon his mind, but merely gives the matter and occasion which lead him to think what is appropriate to his nature and present temper. So it is, that much reading deprives the mind of all elasticity; it is like keeping a spring continually under pressure. The safest way of having no thoughts of one's own is to take up a book every moment one has nothing else to do. It is this practice which explains why erudition makes most men more stupid and silly than they are by nature, and prevents their writings obtaining any measure of success. They remain, in Pope's words:

"Forever reading, never to be read!"

Men of learning are those who have done their reading in the pages of a book. Thinkers and men of genius are those who have gone straight to the book of nature; it is they who have enlightened the world and carried humanity further on its way.

If a man's thoughts are to have truth and life in them, they must, after all, be his own fundamental thoughts; for these are the only ones that he can fully and wholly understand. To read another's thoughts is like taking the leavings of a meal to which we have not been invited, or putting on the clothes which some unknown visitor has laid aside.

The thought we read is related to the thought which springs up in ourselves, as the fossil-impress of some prehistoric plant to a plant as it buds forth in springtime.

Reading is nothing more than a substitute for thought of one's own. It means putting the mind into leading-strings. The multitude of books serves only to show how many false paths there are, and how widely astray a man may wander if he follows any of them. But he who is guided by his genius, he who thinks for himself, who thinks spontaneously and exactly, possesses the only compass by which he can steer aright. A man should read only when his own thoughts stagnate at their source, which will happen often enough even with the best of minds. On the other hand, to take up a book for the purpose of scaring away one's own original thoughts is sin against the Holy Spirit. It is like running away from nature to look at a museum of dried plants or gaze at a landscape in copper-plate.

A man may have discovered some portion of truth or wisdom, after spending a great deal of time and trouble in thinking it over for himself and adding thought to thought; and it may sometimes happen that he could have found it all ready to hand in a book and spared himself the trouble. But even so, it is a hundred times more valuable if he has acquired it by thinking it out for himself. For it is only when we gain our knowledge in this way that it enters as an integral part, a living member into the whole system of our thought; that it stands in complete and firm relation with what we know; that it is understood with all that underlies it and follows from it; that it wears the color, the precise shade, the distinguishing mark of our own way of thinking; that it comes exactly at the right time, just as we felt the necessity for it; that it stands fast and cannot be forgotten. This is the perfect application, nay, the interpretation, of Goethe's advice to earn our inheritance for ourselves so that we may really possess it:

"Was du ererbt von deinen Vätern hast,
Erwirb es, um es zu besitzen." [1]

The man who thinks for himself forms his own opinions and learns the authorities for them only later on, when they serve but to strengthen his belief in them and in himself. But the book-philosopher starts from the authorities. He reads other people's books, collects their opinions, and so forms a whole for himself, which resembles an automaton made up of anything but flesh and blood. Contrarily, he who thinks for himself creates a work like a living man as made by Nature. For the work comes into being as a man does; the thinking mind is impregnated from without and it then forms and bears its child!

Truth that has been merely learned is like an artificial limb, a false tooth, a waxen nose; at best, like a nose made out of another's flesh; it adheres to us only because it is put on. But truth acquired by thinking of our own is like a natural limb; it alone really belongs to us. This is the fundamental difference between the thinker and the mere man of learning. The intellectual attainments of a man who thinks for himself resemble a fine painting, where the light and shade are correct, the tone sustained, the color perfectly harmonized;

---

[1] What you have inherited from your fathers,
You must still earn in order to possess it.—*Faust*, 1, 329-30.

it is true to life. On the other hand, the intellectual attainments of the mere man of learning are like a large palette, full of all sorts of colors, which at most are systematically arranged, but devoid of harmony, connection, and meaning.

Reading is thinking with someone else's head instead of one's own. To think with one's own head is always to aim at developing a coherent whole—a system, even though it be not a strictly complete one; and nothing hinders this so much as too strong a current of others' thoughts, such as comes of continual reading. These thoughts, springing every one of them from different minds, belonging to different systems, and tinged with different colors, never of themselves flow together into an intellectual whole; they never form a unity of knowledge, or insight, or conviction; but, rather, fill the head with a Babylonian confusion of tongues. The mind that is over-loaded with alien thought is thus deprived of all clear insight, and so well-nigh disorganized. This is a state of things observable in many men of learning; and it makes them inferior in sound sense, correct judgment, and practical tact, to many illiterate persons, who, after obtaining a little knowledge from without by means of experience, intercourse with others, and a small amount of reading, have always subordinated it to, and embodied it with, their own thought.

The really scientific thinker does the same thing as these illiterate persons, but on a larger scale. Although he has need of much knowledge, and so must read a great deal, his mind is nevertheless strong enough to master it all, to assimilate and incorporate it with the system of his thoughts, and so to make it fit in with the organic unity of his insight, which, though vast, is always growing. And in the process, his own thought, like the bass in an organ, always dominates everything, and is never drowned by other tones, as happens with minds which are full of mere antiquarian lore; where shreds of music, as it were, in every key, mingle confusedly, and no fundamental note is heard at all.

Those who have spent their lives in reading, and taken their wisdom from books, are like people who have obtained precise information about a country from the descriptions of many travelers. Such people can tell a great deal about it; but, after all, they have no connected, clear, and profound knowledge of its real condition. But those who have spent their lives in thinking resemble the travelers themselves; they alone really know what they are talking about; they are acquainted with the actual state of affairs, and are quite at home in the subject.

This thinker stands in the same relation to the ordinary book-philosopher as an eyewitness does to the historian; he speaks from direct knowledge of his own. That is why all those who think for themselves come, at bottom, to much the same conclusion. The differences they present are due to their different points of view; and when these do not affect the matter, they all speak alike. They merely express the result of their own objective perception of things. There are many passages in my works which I have given to the public only after some hesitation, because of their paradoxical nature; and afterward I have experienced a pleasant surprise in finding the same opinion recorded in the works of great men who lived long ago.

The book-philosopher merely reports what one person has said and another meant, or the objections raised by a third, and so on. He compares different opinions, ponders, criticizes, and tries to get at the truth of the matter; herein on a par with the critical historian. For instance, he will set out to inquire whether Leibnitz was not for some time a follower of Spinoza, and questions of a like nature. The curious student of such matters may find conspicuous examples of what I mean in Herbart's *Analytical Elucidation of Morality and Natural Right*, and in the same author's *Letters on Freedom*. Surprise may be felt that a man of the kind should put himself to so much trouble; for, on the face of it, if he would only examine the matter for himself, he would speedily attain his object by the exercise of a little thought. But there is a small difficulty in the way. It does not depend upon his own will. A man can always sit down and read, but not—think. It is with thoughts as with men: they cannot always be summoned at pleasure; we must wait for them to come. Thought about a subject must appear of itself, by a happy and harmonious combination of external stimulus with mental temper and attention; and it is just that which never seems to come to these people.

This truth may be illustrated by what happens in the case of matters affecting our own personal interest. When it is necessary to come to some resolution in a matter of that kind, we cannot well sit down at any given moment and think over the merits of the case and make up our mind; for, if we try to do so, we often find ourselves unable, at that particular moment, to keep our mind fixed upon the subject; it wanders off to other things. Aversion to the matter in question is sometimes to blame for this. In such a case we should not use force, but wait for the proper frame of mind to come of itself. It often comes unexpectedly and returns again and again; and the variety of temper in which we approach it at different moments puts the matter always in a fresh light. It is this long process which is understood by the term *a ripe resolution*. For the work of coming to a resolution must be distributed; and in the process much that is overlooked at one moment occurs to us at another; and the repugnance vanishes when we find, as we usually do, on a closer inspection, that things are not so bad as they seemed.

This rule applies to the life of the intellect as well as to matters of practice. A man must wait for the right moment. Not even the greatest mind is capable of thinking for itself at all times. Hence a great mind does well to spend its leisure in reading, which, as I have said, is a substitute for thought; it brings stuff to the mind by letting another person do the thinking; although that is always done in a manner not our own. Therefore, a man should not read too much, in order that his mind may not become accustomed to the substitute and thereby forget the reality; that it may not form the habit of walking in well-worn paths; nor by following an alien course of thought grow a stranger to its own. Least of all should a man quite withdraw his gaze from the real world for the mere sake of reading; as the impulse and the temper which prompt to thought of one's own come far oftener from the world of reality than from the world of books. The real life that a man sees before him is the natural subject of thought; and in its strength as the primary element of existence, it can more easily than anything else rouse and influence the thinking mind.

After these considerations, it will not be matter for surprise that a man who thinks for himself can easily be distinguished from the book-philosopher by the very way in which he talks, by his marked earnestness, and the originality, directness, and personal conviction that stamp all his thought and expressions. The book-philosopher, on the other hand, lets it be seen that everything he has is second-hand; that his ideas are like the lumber and trash of an old furniture-shop, collected together from all quarters. Mentally, he is dull and pointless—a copy of a copy. His literary style is made up of conventional, nay, vulgar phrases, and terms that happen to be current; in this respect much like a small state where all the money that circulates is foreign, because it has no coinage of its own.

Mere experience can as little as reading supply the place of thought. It stands to thinking in the same relation in which eating stands to digestion and assimilation. When experience boasts that to its discoveries alone is due the advancement of the human race, it is as though the mouth were to claim the whole credit of maintaining the body in health.

The works of all truly capable minds are distinguished by a character of decision and definiteness, which means that they are clear and free from obscurity. A truly capable mind always knows definitely and clearly what it is that it wants to express, whether its medium is prose, verse, or music. Other minds are not decisive and not definite; and by this they may be known for what they are.

The characteristic sign of a mind of the highest order is that it always judges at first hand. Everything it advances is the result of thinking for itself; and this is everywhere evident by the way in which it gives its thoughts utterance. Such a mind is like a prince. In the realm of intellect its authority is imperial, whereas the authority of minds of a lower order is delegated only; as may be seen in their style, which has no independent stamp of its own.

THE PHILOSOPHICAL ESSAY

The effort to explain the full meaning of abstract ideas has been suggested already in the Schopenhauer piece above. It will be the serious, rather than the familiar, essay. Two brief selections are now given to show that there is ample play for the imagination in this type of writing. Associated with them are the illustrations for the chapters dealing with criticism, expository biography, and the informal essay.

John Ruskin (1819–1900), both art critic and imaginative writer, is here observing with a painter's passion for visual detail what might seem to be a subject for a meteorologist.

It is actually some two years since I last saw a noble cumulus cloud under full light. I chanced to be standing under the Victoria Tower at Westminster, when the largest mass of them floated past, that day, from the north-west; and I was more impressed than ever yet by the awfulness of the cloud-form, and its unaccountableness, in the present state of our knowledge. The Victoria Tower, seen against it, had no magnitude: it was like looking at Mont Blanc over a lamp-post. The domes of cloud-snow were heaped as definitely; their broken flanks were as gray and firm as rocks, and the whole mountain, of a compass and height in heaven which only became more and more inconceivable as the eye strove to ascend it, was passing behind the tower with a steady march, whose swiftness must in reality have been that of a tempest: yet, along all the ravines of vapour, precipice kept pace with precipice, and not one thrust another.

JOHN RUSKIN, *The Eagle's Nest.*

The next selection, defining a very elusive term, marks the transitional middle ground between objective, scientific definition and imaginative definition. It is more interpretive and tends definitely toward description. Archaic art, as you discover, is not determined by time; it is a quality attaching to the art of various peoples at various times. To define its quality, then, is not a simple matter. Not a logical definition, but a brief essay, is required. Ernst Buschor is led to this effort in a work on Greek vase painting,[1] an extract from which is here given in translation from the German.

Archaic art, the wonderful offspring of the contact of Greek civilization with the East, exercises its charm today more than ever. We have ceased to ascribe a unique saving grace to the classic period, the period of full bloom, and to allow no independent value to the preceding century except as an inevitable transitional phase. We love these archaic works of sculpture and painting for their own sake, not in spite of their crudities but just because of their unpolished hidden vigour, because of the precious combination of their essential features. The fetters of space, and the strong tradition of an ornamental early period give them a monumental effect, which has nothing of mummified stiffness but is kept ever fresh and youthful by an eminently progressive spirit and an energetic endeavour to attain freedom. The archaic style "with fresh boldness goes beyond its Oriental patterns, is ever making fresh experiments, and thus exhibits constant change and progress. It is always full of serious painstaking zeal, it is always careful, takes honest trouble, is exactly methodical: the language which it speaks always tells of inward cheerfulness and joy at the result of effort, the effect produced by independent exertion. There is something touching in the sight of archaic art with its childlike freshness, its painstaking zeal, its reverence for tradition, and yet its bold progressiveness. What a contrast to Oriental and Egyptian art, which are fast bound in tradition: in the one the sweltering air of dull coercion, in the other the fresh atmosphere of Freedom" (Furtwängler).

The subject of archaic art still brings up definitely concrete objects, statues, columns, vases. In the final two selections the subjects are less tangible. Notice the remarkable number of sug-

---

[1] *Greek Vase-Painting*, by Ernst Buschor, E. P. Dutton & Co., Inc., 1922. Translated by G. C. Richards, and reprinted by permission of the publishers.

gestive observations which the first writer makes about Paris. Yet he does not describe the city, even though any one of these observations might be elaborated into a detailed picture of French life. An expository central idea is the core of the whole analysis. The name Paris connotes an idea, a concept of an immensely subtle and complex atmosphere. Paris is much more than a large city which happens to be the capital of France. We see in the district around Paris, the Ile de France, a synthesis of north, south, east, and west—a balance of many factors which stand as a visible expression of the golden mean of truly civilized existence.[1]

It is not the North, if one thinks of England or Germany, nor the South, if one thinks of Spain or of Italy. It is neither flat plain nor mountain country, but a broad river valley bounded by hills. The soil is neither poor nor rich, but it produces the most delicate and perfect fruits; the sky is neither of an Italian blue nor of a northern dullness; it is a delicate blue-gray, full of fine shades and subtle variations. Nowhere is the natural colour scheme so little garish and yet so far removed from drabness. Sensuous but not animal, neither dry nor luxuriant, but charming, gracious and discreetly attractive, a blend of light-hearted gaiety and gentle wistfulness—that is the Ile de France, which has formed and moulded the European men and women who grew up in it till their genius has come to resemble that of the country in which they live—healthy without being robust, sensual but in a charming way, free from all extremes, capable of appreciating the finest shades, neither flat nor towering, neither strident nor dull, not too northern to understand the South nor too southern to understand the North, full of intelligence but without the capacity for feeling being impaired thereby, at once critical and creative; a genius in which all comers, from north, south, east or west, have found something akin to themselves, but also what was lacking in themselves; a harmony which transforms the inharmonious, an atmosphere which possesses the secret of enhancing everyone's particular individuality.

PAUL COHEN-PORTHEIM, *The Spirit of France*.

In much of your writing, as we have seen, your mind will need to be active in a double process. If you are wide awake, you will be both analyzing and imagining, observing and reflect-

---

[1] Reprinted from *The Spirit of France*, with the permission of E. P. Dutton & Co., Inc., publishers.

ing, discriminating and constructing. Out of this double process must come a unified impression if you are to achieve a good style. Such a style you will find in the final selection. Mr. Waldo Frank writes a prose that is as richly descriptive as can well be, yet it is devoted to the purpose of defining, of explaining the peculiar atmosphere of a particular region. If you are interested in Spain, look up the volume *Virgin Spain*, and you will find some new points of view. Also you will find brilliant expository-descriptive accounts of the Spanish bull fight, the Andalusian dance with castanets, the spirit of Madrid, the significance of Don Quixote, and many other subjects.

HINTERLAND IN SPAIN [1]
Waldo Frank

The sun is hidden from this dawn. The snow range is a crest to the south and east. Air, pouring over, cold and hard like pearls, is the dawn upon Spain. Tidy huertas [2] are green crystals in the dawn. Villages, orange-marged, make a pied flash in it. Fig and olive march in armies up the slopes of the Sierra, toward snow, toward dawn. When the sun stands at last in the ridge, the day is hot.

This is the south. After Guadix, toward the eastern sea, the human world grows dim. The carretera, [3] at the entrance of a town, slides in a slough of mud. Rain is rare and violent; it becomes a torrent from the impervious mountain. Dark men in black grimed capes walk beside laden donkeys. Women herd goats; the tuberous udders sticking on the mud. Children are rhythms in a maze of rags. The eyes of humans are like the eyes of burros.

The Sierras have disappeared behind the depopulous hills. The verdant valleys of Granada are folded back. Villages here are hard like the parched clay. The carretera is a swathe of dust, glittering in the sun. The land is sere as if a flame dwelt on it. The eyes of humans are velvet dark, like the eyes of a dream.

Murcia, now. Even the sparse irrigated huertas disappear. The barbarous abruptness of the soil turns to desert. Villages are a single eyeless street of houses, abject under the eye of the sun. The world is a turmoil of yellow waste. The villages are splinters of the waste. Only, to break the yellow, walls of cactus—a Maya-like green sculpture matching its lush planes with the harsh planes of the clay. Goats, dusty

[1] Reprinted from *Virgin Spain*, copyright 1926, by permission of the author and the Liveright Publishing Corporation.   [2] Orchards.   [3] Highway.

and crabbed, crop an invisible herb. The Barbary fig is the olive and the grape of this land. Villages grow lower, sparser—merge with the desert. Villages disappear.

Under the sky huge mounds of sterile hill rise now; and on their slopes, red and advancing with the mirrored sun, are serried shadows. Caves. Villages of caves. This is below Phœnicia in time. This is Iberia. A Spanish folk still dwells here.

The hills are steep. There is a row of caves, horizontally curved. Above each cave is a tiny aperture for smoke. Then comes another row. In the foreground, the cactus is cultivated for its fruit. There is a hooded well.

It is not yet noon. But the summer sun has turned the heaven into irradiant steel. Light and heat strike like solids on the solid soil, on the intricate levels of the hills. In their rebound, light and heat become polyphonous, weaving the world into their image.

The sun, rising, faints into its own immensity of heat. And the cave villages grow larger. Between them, the sterile hills leap in a monotone against the day's pressure. A cave town flings sheer to the ridge of a pyramidal mountain. A hundred threads of smoke thresh the air like filaments of wire. Caves are dark eyes that hide from the steel heaven. The eyes of the dwellers are caves.

Shadow is cold. Here is a town with houses. Where the sun strikes the street, horses, donkeys, moving forms of people gyre and funnel and become a fume in the sun. Signs on shops, blue shutters, yellow parasols of women tremble and swerve as if they were in flame. But shadow is cold.

Outside, there is desert and the sky has melted. All the steel strokes of the sun, beating down, beating up, are melted: heaven has fallen into waves. Villages live in this fierce element. Men and women, donkeys and goats live in this radiant sea.

Over the brow of a *despoblado*,[1] the sun goes. The desert flattens, like a sea after storm. The sterile hills are farther away, and on the even plain there is grass. The desert becomes a moor. Salt wort suggests the ocean. The road circles, catching the sun again. The sun splinters and breaks on the moor. Huge masses of dried dung, the fuel of these people, catch a last ray. There is a hill, dark-mottled. The hill is a city. At the height, there are caves and dwellings cut in clay. At the base, there is dust: and in the dust are streets.

Sordid wineshops, stores, squat in the dust. All is dust save the people who are clay; clay black-baked in the sun.

[1] Depopulated area.

CHAPTER VI

Generalized Description

THE EXPOSITORY PROBLEM in the previous chapter involved the defining of an *abstract* term or idea. As we approach nearer the *concrete* interests of our minds, we find a world of objects and of persons. Before you attempt the difficult task of accounting for these as individuals, it will be valuable to look at the broadest aspects, the typical qualities, which are the distinguishing marks of the group. For the first time we meet a form of exposition which deals with people, with human nature. True, the same technique may be applied to sports, hats, shoes, cars, foods, books, cities; but even when this is done, a large element of human interest is bound to intrude. To write of sports will be to emphasize sportsmen and their qualities. Hats and shoes will bring in wearers, sellers, buyers, and borrowers of these articles. And so for cars, foods, books, cities: types of car salesmen, of drivers and backseat drivers; types of waiters, gourmands, cooks, and soup-eaters; types of readers, reviewers, and booksellers; types of city builders, city dwellers, "city slickers." Each concrete element of life and experience will take the mind on to the human beings associated with it. Generalized description really proceeds toward actual literary composition, the imaginative treatment of the data of experience. It involves an emotional, creative impulse beyond the merely intellectual interests of scientific exposition.

In selecting a subject for generalized description, then, we must remember that certain aspects of the form are important. No one particular individual is to be described anywhere in the paper; but a composite impression is to be built up of a generalized type. Traditional with this form of writing is a definitely satirical, or sardonic, tone. Its invention is credited to the Greek disciple

98

of Aristotle, Theophrastus, who, in his *Ethical Characters*, dealt with human vices and virtues in a series of character sketches, of which the vices alone survive. Since his day the *character*, as this thumbnail sketch came to be called, has always been popular in periods of comedy and satire. Implicit in it is the spirit of penetrating, often disillusioning, insight that finds in human absurdity and pretentiousness occasion for open scorn or suppressed laughter. Pure expressions of this form survive from certain writers of the seventeenth century, Joseph Hall, Sir Thomas Overbury, John Earle, and Samuel Butler. Some writers, Hall among them, attempted to present virtues as well as vices; but the result was tepid. The skeptical and satirical, rather than the tender and approving, attitude seems to carry the secret of success for the character. The student with the most impersonal, perhaps coldest, nature and the most analytical mind will usually do the best work in this type of writing.

The title for this paper, in addition to pointing out the specific subject, should indicate the satirical emphasis. Thus, Earle in his *Microcosmography* writes not merely of "The Student," but of "The Plodding Student." The type can be summed up in one word, now somewhat old-fashioned, the Grind. The Campus Widow is also obsolete; but there are the Apple Polisher, the B.M.O.C. (Big Man on the Campus), and numerous species of the genus Coed. Generally the writer selects some type of person that irritates him and proceeds to itemize from top to toe the specific features that distinguish this type from all other disagreeable branches of the human race. His language may even become scurrilous; but he must not lose control of his emotions nor sacrifice his cool, detached manner. He scans his victim exhaustively, presenting first, and most important, what the type looks like; second, what it thinks about; third, its typical actions; and fourth, what its conversation generally consists of. Under no circumstances can the purely descriptive element be omitted, yet this descriptive feature must never become individualized.

It is possible, of course, to be too coldly analytical; then no picture evolves at all. There must be an emotional tone in this production. One student concocted a vicious exposé of "The Overstuffed Female Parasite," but when it was read to the class as an excellent example of the type, another student objected: "That doesn't produce any emotion in me; it just makes me sick with disgust." This remark called forth general laughter, because that was just the emotion the paper intended. The critic himself, when he essayed the type, wrote a cold analysis of "The Introvert," which had no emotional value at all. Both themes are included below for purposes of comparison. Read them together.

Some other warnings may be suggestive. Begin quickly—do not waste time on a long, formal introduction. Start off directly with the dominant tone of the type (see the chapter on description in Part II below), and use definite details to promote that tone: a satiric tone, we should repeat. Try not to shift this tone once you have it under way; that is, do not relent and point out that this character has a few angelic aspects, whereas up to this moment in the theme he has been something of a devil. Dialogue is dangerous: it breaks through the type and spoils the picture.[1] Keep your eye on the victim throughout. You must not let him get away. Above all, take a subject that both you and the reader can actually visualize, have actually seen, and can recognize as a type.

Two final suggestions as to style and structure. Both of these may become mechanical unless you are careful. Students tend to write too many parallel sentences in a row: his hair is this, his coat is that, his clothes are this, his thoughts are that. A little care will provide variation here, and also in the structure: the four aspects of the character given above (actions, appearance, thoughts, conversation) can be interwoven in such a way as to produce a varied structure but a single tone.

In conclusion, it may be helpful to use an individual as the basis for the generalized description, if necessary, but do not betray this device in the theme itself. And by all means avoid dilating on the future existence of the subject.

Some types preferred by students have been: The Coed, The Genius, The Henpecked Husband, The Haberdasher, The Apartment-House Janitor, The Road Hog, The Landlady, The School Teacher, The Boss, The Social Climber, The Old Maid, The Musician, The Soda-Fountain Girl, The Young Doctor, The Traveling Salesman, The Movie Hero, The Hard-Boiled Lover.

---

[1] Monologue can be used with three dots between speeches.

⇥ A ⇤

This first theme is totally useless, so far as this type is concerned. It has no emotional tone and is not developed properly.

THE INTROVERT

The introvert is one of those unfortunate individuals who is never understood, who never tries to make himself understood, and never fully realizes why he is so misunderstood.

A distinction must be made between an introvert and a person afflicted with, or who has acquired an inferiority complex. The introvert has qualities that will make his work outstanding, while the person with the complex seldom makes a success of life. Some persons, not knowingly, confuse the two subjects.

The qualities of the two can be most easily confused if the observer is not quick to notice differences in character traits and tendencies. The following are most typical of the introvert, and can hardly be applied to the person with the inferiority complex: the introvert inclines toward activities requiring care and detail; he is slow and deliberate about his movements and what he does; and he will not readily abandon an activity regardless of its success.

The introvert is usually a person of great intellect, and for this reason inclines toward care and detail. The writer, chemist, and physicist are all types of persons among whom the introvert is to be found. They take great pains with their work, always being sure of their results before making them known. His slowness and deliberateness in movement indicate his desire for perfection. He realizes that to go rapidly, headlong into an experiment or a thesis would be foolhardy. Instead he takes care and is slow about each step. Finally, if he does not readily achieve success, he will do over again what he has just failed in. In some instances failure at first will cause illness and desperation of the introvert, but sooner or later he will again take up the reins and tackle what has once proved to be a failure.

The misunderstanding between introverts and society is a most peculiar thing to observers. They do not realize the temperament they are dealing with; hence they cannot understand it.

This next theme was intended to provoke a decided emotional response in the reader.

THE OVERSTUFFED FEMALE PARASITE

Here she comes creaking down the stairs, her old bedroom slippers exposing one fat toe and one very dirty heel, her gray-looking night-dress hanging six inches below a dirty lounging robe, which is almost as red as her face. Her hair, carroty color, is tied back with a pick-a-ninny ribbon. Fat and floppy, dirty and sloppy, she sinks into an over-stuffed chair, panting and puffing, as she rings for coffee and lunch for two but service for one. She didn't eat any breakfast; she missed that by staying in bed. Consequently she eats double portions for lunch.

Having finished her luncheon, she reaches for a box of chocolates and picks up the latest *True Romance* magazine. Time flies and so do the chocolates. At two o'clock she orders tea and cakes, eats heartily, flounders upstairs and into the bathroom. She bathes, weighs, and dresses. Just as she is deciding which dress is the least soiled, the door-bell rings, and so she puts on the sloppy old lounging robe again and flops down to answer the bell. It is her calory-counting bridge friends. No apologies necessary for her floppy appearance now. They all know, only too well, how ill the poor good soul is, and how, except for such a wonderful doctor, she would be dead, even now, with heart trouble. And so they discuss their poor health, marvelous operations, superior doctors, and play *at* bridge.

The conversation turns to calories and refreshments are served. All declare they haven't eaten one bite all day, in order to justify an extra large serving or seconds on that famous dessert, "Angels' Delight." They continue with their famous indoor sport, counting calories, ad infinitum, but eating nevertheless, much, much more than they should. Time flies; the calory-counting friends disassemble at the front door as friend husband walks in at the rear. She explains to him that she has been sick in bed all day and has just now dragged her poor aching body down the stairs to greet him. They dress, dine again, and wander out to a few night clubs to distract her mind. Arriving home about twelve, they eat a midnight lunch and he retires.

There she goes, fat and floppy, dirty and sloppy, the overstuffed female waddling upstairs on the way to bed. She drags out the bath scales, weighs and mutters, "Two hundred and ten pounds. Oh, why can't I lose weight? I don't eat much. Well, tomorrow I will just starve."

J. N.

In the sketch which follows, humorous observation has produced a brilliant piece of work with plenty of varied touches. The details are vivid and suggestive.

THE DORM GIRL

Clad in a neglige of dazzling hue, with a very limp and dejected cigarette hanging at half mast from one corner of her mouth, the dorm girl vigorously polishes the nails of her right hand on the palm of her left, while her roommate bends over her solicitously, shaving her neck with painstaking care and, incidentally, a dull razor. All this—while time seeps by and with it the slightest hope of completing that reading report, revising that long overdue paper, or translating that troublesome French assignment.

At about ten-thirty or shortly thereafter, she becomes possessed of an urge for food; so, having donned her coat, and fastened it closely, for her costume beneath is almost always somewhat sketchy, she departs with a party of her fellow "dormitorians" for the nearest drugstore. Once there, she unfailingly selects the most indigestible item on the menu and tops it off, usually, with an assortment of salted almonds, maple taffy, chewing gum, and chocolate caramels. This later collection of delectables is, as a rule, eaten en route to the "dorm" and accompanied by much raucous hilarity. Then, feeling none the worse for her orgy of gourmandizing, she settles down to prepare those lessons for the following morning which are absolutely unavoidable. If it is, by this time, considerably after one, she may be able to pursue her erudite endeavors uninterrupted. Before that hour, however, concentration is practically impossible, for there is much slamming of doors and shrieking of informalities along the corridor. To put it roughly, it is between the hours of two and four-thirty that she finds most favorable for real study, but, since it is such an inconvenient time, she gradually develops the amazing feat of memorizing irregular verbs or penning her required thousand words while someone at her elbow is rendering "Where Are You?" with ukelele accompaniment, someone else is demonstrating the latest gyrations of the big apple, and still another is relating the sad tale of what she told Harold when he suggested the Tivoli.

During her residence at the dorm she inevitably develops an insatiable desire for letters and 'phone calls. She peers into the mailbox at irregular intervals all through the day, and, when there is nothing for her, as is usually the case, she makes no bones about examining other people's as to postmarks, stationery, and return addresses. If, when the telephone rings, the desired person is not in, she is oh, so eager to take the message. She might just as well carry on the entire conversation, for she usually knows exactly what it is all about anyway.

Indeed, she becomes so well-versed in the concerns of others that she regards everything from love affairs to laundry bills as common knowledge. This super-co-operative spirit applies, so far as she is concerned, not only to an acquaintance with others' interests, but to private possessions as well. Dresses, shoes, coats, hose, jewelry, gloves, hats, scarfs, purses, powder puffs—all become community property, used by the entire hall without the slightest misgiving as to their personal nature. Indeed, the only thing which retains its individual character is her toothbrush, and even that, under the stress of circumstances, might be resorted to by others than its rightful owner.

All in all, the dorm girl is an unusual creature, the product of an unusual environment—not that there is anything fundamentally wrong with her or it, but—well, shall we say, with the necessary apologies to Shaw, of course, that the dormitory, like marriage, is a faulty institution, tolerated only because it has no satisfactory substitute.

M. F.

"The Golf Bug" is practically a perfect paper, for this type of theme. Note its humorously satirical tone.

THE GOLF BUG

He is everywhere. You have met him on the streetcar or collided with him on the pavement and wondered at that blank, open stare that penetrates beyond. You have probably been startled at the mutterings of a fellow bus passenger. Don't be alarmed in the future. These are only golf-bug symptoms.

This particular fellow is entirely void of the appreciation of art—unless it's a landscape particularly suitable for golf. He doesn't like theaters—unless the Bobby Jones golf lessons are showing. He hates mathematics, particularly addition, and his favorite number is four. He has a peculiar habit of associating his golf with ordinary life. He doesn't like pie because it is sliced. He won't eat fish because they are hooked. When he was ill, his doctor caught him putting his pills into the inkwell. His reason is obsessed with golf; he reads golf, eats golf, and sleeps golf. He doesn't go in swimming because the beach reminds him of the sand trap that took ten strokes to get out of. His favorite literature is the pro and con on the balloon golf ball.

His clothes are neat, but his shoestrings are tied behind his ankles because they were tied that way when he broke one hundred. His eyes are squinty, and he always looks as if he were calculating the distance to the next corner, building, or whatever transfixes his nervous attention. His fingers are continually working, and seem to be trying to practice a grip on everything grippable. He walks with a quick, jerky tread, and he invariably carries his cane with the handle down.

When he eats, he cuts his food into large pieces so as to take the least number of strokes with his knife. It has been reported that this fellow played nine holes of golf on a swiss-cheese sandwich, using an aspirin tablet for a golf ball and a toothpick for a club. He counts the strokes of his brush, when washing his teeth, with as much ardor as if he were on the golf course. In short, golf to him is the main objective in life. To do eighteen holes in seventy-six would be the supreme goal of his life's efforts. Eating, working, sleeping, and all other worldly activities are, to him, mere secondary pursuits helping toward the worship of his one dominant god, golf.

C. B.

"The Country Doctor" is a rare specimen in that it actually applauds the type it describes.

THE COUNTRY DOCTOR

The country doctor's profession is as old as the daybreak of civilization. In every country he has almost been part of the natural surroundings; especially in America he has become an outstanding figure in the welfare and growth of the rural communities.

This ever-faithful and steadfast healer of mankind, whose thin, sure hands have guided a knife within a hair's breadth of instant death, is still found practising in out-of-way places. He is not a great politician; yet he knows his politics. His dislike for donning his Sunday best has kept him from attending the weekly hour of worship. Busy as he is— and there are few busier men around—he always has time and patience to listen to an old woman harping about her troubles. Even if it means going without something for himself, he will stop and "cure" the doll of some broken-hearted girl. He also has time to fix an unfortunate animal with his fine, delicately wrought, sympathetic hands that have soothed so many aching heads.

His office is plain, as is his method of doctoring. Upon his shelves are rows of test tubes, cases of instruments, and a line of bottles labelled with names of various mixtures (these doctors are chemists also). The doctor's books are few, and the only medical journals found in his office are sample copies. When his learning fails him, he is wise in silence.

In raiment he is not overadorned; yet his clothes are in excellent taste. Strong as they are of sickroom odors, they are the perfection of tidiness. He is usually several years behind in the city fashions, but to be in the present styles would brand him as affected in clothing.

The farther he travels, the less likely he is to collect his bills; but never a complaint is heard. Others may demand that the widow sell her cow, but if the doctor sues, he loses his respect and is met with a sour look from everyone. But whether in rain or snow, he travels the almost unpassable roads to help a less fortunate fellowman. Far into the night, and until dawn streaks the sky, his vigil continues; yet he receives no great honors bestowed upon him.

E. S.

It is our purpose in this chapter to emphasize the development of generalized description in relation to the portrayal of character. Description as applied to places and objects will be treated in Part II. However, two examples of city atmosphere are given, one a student paper, the other from Oliver Goldsmith. Observe that in each case no specific city is mentioned; the details, closely observed as they are, might apply to any city.

One danger in such studies is that of exaggeration for effect, forcing in details because they seem to help out the picture. Observe the unassuming opening and the conclusion by which the student gives a close unity to her paper. Tone is very important in such writing.

A MIDDLE–CLASS NEIGHBORHOOD

There are few more oppressive or more monotonous things than a street in a poor, middle-class neighborhood in a big city. House presses upon house in a prim, unvarying file. Block stretches after block, packed with dwellings of the same general type and made after the same plans. They are built so close together that people in adjacent houses can reach out of opposite windows and shake hands or punch each other's noses if they are so minded. People have been known to enter the wrong houses by mistake because of the appalling lack of originality of design. Practically the only things which distinguish one from the other are details such as the colors they are painted, the sizes, and slight variations in the dormer, the porch, or the window groupings. Indeed, in some factory districts and even elsewhere, one sometimes comes across whole blocks of houses which are as like as peas in a pod. Not a board is differently placed. Not a window varies by so much as a few inches.

Family flats and bungalows predominate, with a scattering of apartments and so-called "garage houses." In the apartment houses humanity is piled atop humanity in a needless and regrettable conservation of space. Their occupants have been aptly called "our modern cliff dwellers." The "garage houses" are, in a way, something of a relief, for they are so diminutive that the brief bit of land on which they are built appears to be something of a vast expanse. Truly a rare and precious phenomenon in this type of neighborhood!

Trees, grass, and shrubs are coaxed and petted to grow in the front and back yards of the houses. These patches of green and fresh pretty colors somehow help take the curse off the cramped quarters and uninspiring surroundings.

The summer is the most interesting period in a neighborhood of this kind. At this time, people, and especially the innumerable children, are outdoors most of the time. The center of interest becomes the street. Children laugh and shout, cry and fight here. All teaching in school and at home to the contrary, this is their main playground. It becomes tennis court, roller-skating rink, baseball diamond, scooter, bicycle, tricycle, and wagon track, race track, and almost everything else imaginable. It is a street merely as a sideline.

Lucky is the street which has an empty lot! For this helps relieve the pressure on the street. Here, even the older men may congregate of an evening for a game of horseshoes. Youngsters find it a fascinating place to make mud pies and sand castles, and young boys make it the site of the inevitable "bunk" or the mysterious local junior male fraternity.

There are various figures which are very familiar in a neighborhood of this type. Icemen idle along in their trucks, calling "Ice! Ice!" with a characteristic nasal, sing-songy intonation. With monotonous insistence and often in broken English, hucksters shout their wares. Agents wend their weary way from door to door, pathetically trying to maintain a semblance of enthusiasm and convincing sincerity. Hopeless beggars, some hypocritical, some apologetic, mumble their pleas and oft-repeated hard-luck tales to all who will listen. Bill collectors make their persistent demands for the money which often is not forthcoming.

Such is a general view of life in the average middle-class neighborhood.

E. MacG.

⋙ B ⋘

In "A City Night Piece" from *The Bee* (1759) Goldsmith presents general details such as might characterize any city at two in the morning, provided they were observed by a sensitive and humane person. The atmosphere of gloom is heightened by the sense of the sufferings of unfortunates. We have, then, not a description of specific city streets, but rather the personality of the city.

A CITY NIGHT PIECE
Oliver Goldsmith

The clock has just struck two, the expiring taper rises and sinks in the socket, the watchman forgets the hour in slumber, the laborious and the happy are at rest, and nothing wakes but meditation, guilt, revelry, and despair. The drunkard once more fills the destroying bowl, the robber walks his midnight round, and the suicide lifts his guilty arm against his own sacred person.

Let me no longer waste the night over the page of antiquity or the sallies of contemporary genius, but pursue the solitary walk, where vanity, ever changing, but a few hours past walked before me, where she kept up the pageant, and now, like a froward child, seems hushed with her own importunities.

What a gloom hangs all around! The dying lamp feebly emits a yellow gleam; no sound is heard but of the chiming clock, or the distant watch-dog. All the bustle of human pride is forgotten, an hour like this may well display the emptiness of human vanity. . . .

How few appear in those streets which but some few hours ago were crowded! and those who appear now no longer wear their daily mask, nor attempt to hide their lewdness or their misery.

But who are those who make the streets their couch, and find a short repose from the wretchedness at the doors of the opulent? These are strangers, wanderers, and orphans, whose circumstances are too humble to expect redress, and their distresses are too great even for pity. . . . Some are without the covering even of rags, and others emaciated with disease; the world has disclaimed them; society turns its back upon their distress, and has given them up to nakedness and hunger. These poor shivering females have once seen happier days, and been flattered into beauty. They have been prostituted to the gay luxurious villain, and are now turned out to meet the severity of winter. Perhaps, now lying at the doors of their betrayers, they sue to wretches whose hearts are insensible, or debauchees who may curse, but will not relieve them.

Why, why, was I born a man, and yet see the sufferings of wretches I cannot relieve! Poor houseless creatures! the world will give you reproaches, but will not give you relief. The slightest misfortunes of the great, the most imaginary uneasiness of the rich, are aggravated with all the power of eloquence, and held up to engage our attention and sympathetic sorrow. The poor weep unheeded, persecuted by every subordinate species of tyranny; and every law which gives others security, becomes an enemy to them.

Why was this heart of mine formed with so much sensibility? or why was not my fortune adapted to its impulse? Tenderness, without a capacity of relieving, only makes the heart that feels it more wretched than the object which sues for assistance.

But let me turn from a scene of such distress to the sanctified hypocrite, who has been talking of virtue till the time of bed, and now steals out, to give a loose rein to his vices under the protection of midnight—vices more atrocious because he attempts to conceal them. See how he pants down the dark alley, and, with hastening steps, fears an acquaintance in every face! He has passed the whole day in company he hates, and now goes to prolong the night among company that as heartily hate him. May his vices be detected: may the morning rise upon his shame! Yet I wish to no purpose: villainy, when detected, never gives up, but boldly adds impudence to imposture.

What qualities mark Goldsmith's characterization as being nearly two hundred years old? Taking its basic idea, try to catch the typical mood of your own college or university town as you have felt it after late studying or return from a one-o'clock dance.

We now return to the primary type of generalized description, to the dissection of character. As has been mentioned, this type of exercise, the so-called *character*, was especially popular in the seventeenth century, before the appearance of the novel in the next era with its strong emphasis on character delineation. While it was used chiefly for satirical purposes, sometimes it produced effects closely allied to fiction. It is not surprising, then, that Addison's famous glimpses of Sir Roger de Coverley should exhibit an important step toward the complete portrayal of character in action and setting. When these final steps had been taken, the novel in its true form had become possible.

In the following selections we offer three examples of the character from the seventeenth century. Do not be disturbed by the seeming quaintness of style in Overbury's description. Observe the details and their implications. Where would you find an equivalent of the gallant today? What comic writers, columnists, and cartoonists make capital of the type? Write an up-to-date version.

AN IMPROVIDENT YOUNG GALLANT

There is a confederacy betweene him and his clothes, to bee made a puppy: view him well, and you'll say his Gentry fits as ill upon him, as if he had bought it with his penny. He hath more places to send money to, then the Devill hath to send his Spirits: and to furnish each Mistrisse, would make him runne besides his wits, if hee had any to lose. Hee accounts bashfulnesse the wickedst thing in the world; and therefore studies Impudence. If all men were of his minde, all honesty would be out of fashion: hee withers his Cloathes on the Stage, as a Sale-man is for'ct to doe his sutes in Birchin-lane; and when the Play is done, if you marke his rising, 'tis with a kinde of walking Epilogue betweene the two candles, to know if his Suite may passe for currant: hee studies by the direction of his Barber, to frizle like a Baboone: three such would keepe three the nimblest Barbers in the towne, from ever having leisure to weave net-Garters: for when they have to doe with him, they have many Irons in th' fire. He is travelled, but to little purpose; onely went over for a squirt, and came backe againe, yet never the more mended in his conditions, 'cause hee carried himselfe along with him: a Scholler hee pretends himselfe, and sayes he hath sweat for it: but the truth is, he knowes *Cornelius*, farre better than *Tacitus:* his ordinary sports are Cock-fights; but the most frequent, horse-rases, from whence hee comes home drie-foundered. Thus when his purse hath cast her calfe, hee goes downe into the Country, where he is brought to milke and white cheese like the *Switzers*.

SIR THOMAS OVERBURY.

A common practice in character writing was to make studies of contrasting types. You are familiar with an example in poetry, Milton's "L'Allegro" and "Il Penseroso," the joyous-active and the melancholy-pensive types. Just such distinctions are being made by practical psychologists in our day. Try working out similar contrasts yourself, choosing types from students, land-ladies, librarians, professors, umpires, preachers, etc. Then pro-ceed to combine them with other types of writing, such as the fable. The Ant and the Grasshopper, and Chaucer's Dan Russel the Fox and Chauntecleer the Cock in the "Nun's Priest's Tale" are examples.

In the following selection from John Earle's *Microcosmography* (1628) you will find details contrasting with Overbury's Improvi-dent Gallant. Would these details fit the twentieth-century scholar? Try a character of him as you know him in office, laboratory, or classroom. How does he walk, carry his books, sit at his desk, handle his pen and glasses?

A CONTEMPLATIVE MAN

Is a Scholer in this great University the World; and the same, his Booke and Study. Hee cloysters not his Meditations in the narrow darknesse of a Roome, but sends them abroad with his Eyes, and his Braine travels with his Feet. He lookes upon Man from a high Tower, and sees him trulyer at this distance in his Infirmities and poorenesse. He scornes to mixe himselfe in men's actions, as he would to act upon a Stage; but sits aloft on the Scaffold a censuring Spec-tator. He will not loose his time by being busie, nor make so poore a use of the world as to hug and embrace it. Nature admits him as a partaker of her Sports, and askes his approbation as it were of her owne Workes, and variety. Hee comes not in Company, because hee would not be solitary, but findes Discourse enough with himselfe, and his owne thoughts are his excellent play-fellowes. He lookes not upon a thing as a yawning Stranger at novelties; but his search is more mysterious and inward, and hee spels Heaven out of earth. He knits his observations together, and makes a Ladder of them all to climbe to God. He is free from vice, because he has no occasion to imploy it, and is above those ends that make men wicked. He has learnt all can heere be taught him, and comes now to Heaven to see more.

JOHN EARLE.

After reading the next extract, Samuel Butler's analysis of what we should call a patent-medicine addict, examine Butler's greatest satirical portrait. You will find this in the rough-shod verses of his galloping poem, *Hudibras*, where he does full justice to the hypocritical type of Puritan. The work gave him fame and the sobriquet "Hudibras" Butler, but not fortune. Is there a "Last Puritan" left today?

A MEDICINE–TAKER

Has a sickly Mind, and believes the Infirmity is in his Body; like one, that draws the wrong tooth, and fancies his Pain in the wrong Place. The less he understands the Reason of Physic, the stronger Faith he has in it, as it commonly fares in all other Affairs of the World. His Disease is only in his Judgment, which makes him believe a Doctor can fetch it out of his Stomach, or his Belly; and fright those Worms out of his Guts, that are bred in his Brain. He believes a Doctor is a Kind of Conjurer, that can do strange Things, and he is as willing to have him think so; for by that means he does not only get his Money, but finds himself in some Possibility, by complying with that Fancy, to do him good for it, which he could never expect to do any other Way; for . . . his own Imagination is a better Medicine than any the Doctor knows how to prescribe, even as the Weapon-Salve cures a Wound by being applied to that which made it. He is no sooner well, but any Story or Lye of a new famous Doctor, or strange Cure puts him into a Relapse, and he falls sick of a Medicine instead of a Disease, and catches Physic, like him that fell into a Looseness at the Sight of a Purge. He never knows when he is well, nor sick, but is always tampering with his Health till he has spoiled it, like a foolish Musician, that breaks his Strings with striving to put them in Tune; for *Nature*, which is *Physic*, understands better how to do her own Work than those that take it from her at second hand. *Hippocrates* says—*Ars longa, Vita brevis*, and it is the truest of all his Aphorisms,

> For he that's giv'n much to the long Art,
> Does not prolong his Life, but cut it short.

SAMUEL BUTLER.

In the familiar essay type Charles Lamb finds a stimulus to his analytical powers, his resources of literary allusion, and his general working vocabulary that often leaves the reader gasping for breath. In "Poor Relations" [1] Lamb seems to have grown tired of the cloying sentimentalism of his day. We are printing only a portion of the essay lest it appear that the prince of familiar essayists had broken all the laws of the type, especially those calling for a casual, good-humored acceptance of things.

POOR RELATIONS
Charles Lamb

A Poor Relation—is the most irrelevant thing in nature,—a piece of impertinent correspondency,—an odious approximation,—a haunting conscience,—a preposterous shadow, lengthening in the noontide of your prosperity,—an unwelcome remembrancer,—a perpetually recurring mortification,—a drain on your purse,—a more intolerable dun upon your pride,—a drawback upon success,—a rebuke to your rising,—a stain in your blood,—a blot on your scutcheon,—a rent in your garment,—a death's head at your banquet,—Agathocles' pot,—a Mordecai in your gate,—a Lazarus at your door,—a lion in your path, —a frog in your chamber,—a fly in your ointment,—a mote in your eye,—a triumph to your enemy, an apology to your friends,—the one thing not needful,—the hail in harvest,—the ounce of sour in a pound of sweet.

He is known by his knock. Your heart telleth you "That is Mr. ——." A rap, between familiarity and respect, that demands, and, at the same time, seems to despair of, entertainment. He entereth smiling and—embarrassed. He holdeth out his hand to you to shake and—draweth it back again. He casually looketh in about dinner time—when the table is full. He offereth to go away, seeing you have company—but is induced to stay. He filleth a chair, and your visitor's two children are accommodated at a side table. He never cometh upon open days, when your wife says with some complacency, "My dear, perhaps Mr. —— will drop in today." He remembereth birthdays—and professeth he is fortunate to have stumbled upon one. He declareth against fish, the turbot being small—yet suffereth himself to be importuned into a slice against his first resolution. He sticketh by the port—yet will be prevailed upon to empty the remainder glass of claret, if a stranger press it upon him. He is a puzzle to the servants, who are fearful of being too obsequious, or not civil enough, to him. The guests think "they have seen him before." Every one speculateth upon his condition; and the most part take him to be—a tide-waiter.

[1] From the *Last Essays of Elia* (1833).

He calleth you by your Christian name to imply that his other is the same with your own. He is too familiar by half, yet you wish he had less diffidence. With half the familiarity he might pass for a casual dependent; with more boldness he would be in no danger of being taken for what he is. He is too humble for a friend, yet taketh on him more state than befits a client, He is a worse guest than a country tenant, inasmuch as he bringeth up no rent—yet 'tis odds, from his garb and demeanour, that your guests take him for one. He is asked to make one at the whist table, refuseth on the score of poverty, and—resents being left out. When the company break up, he proffereth to go for a coach—and lets the servants go. He recollects your grandfather, and will thrust in some mean and quite unimportant anecdote of—the family. He knew it when it was not quite so flourishing as he is "blest in seeing it now." He reviveth past situations to institute what he calleth—favourable comparisons. With a reflecting sort of congratulation, he will inquire the price of your furniture; and insults you with a special commendation of your window-curtains. He is of opinion that the urn is the more elegant shape, but, after all, there was something more comfortable about the old tea-kettle—which you must remember. He dares say you must find a great convenience in having a carriage of your own, and appealeth to your lady if it is not so. Inquireth if you have had your arms done on vellum yet; and did not know, till lately, that such-and-such had been the crest of the family. His memory is unseasonable, his compliments perverse, his talk a trouble, his stay pertinaceous; and when he goeth away, you dismiss his chair into a corner, as precipitately as possible, and feel fairly rid of two nuisances.

There is a worse evil under the sun, and that is—a female Poor Relation. You may do something with the other; you may pass him off tolerably well; but your indigent she-relative is hopeless. "He is an old humourist," you may say, "and affects to go threadbare. His circumstances are better than folks would take them to be. You are fond of having a Character at your table, and truly he is one." But in the indications of female poverty there can be no disguise. No woman dresses below herself from caprice. The truth must out without shuffling. "She is plainly related to the L——'s; or what does she at their house?" She is, in all probability, your wife's cousin. Nine times out of ten, at least, this is the case. Her garb is something between a gentlewoman and a beggar, yet the former evidently predominates. She is most provokingly humble, and ostentatiously sensible to her inferiority. He may require to be repressed sometimes—*aliquando suf-*

flaminandus erat—but there is no raising her. You send her soup at dinner, and she begs to be helped—after the gentleman. Mr. —— requests the honour of taking wine with her; she hesitates between port and madeira, and chooses the former—because he does. She calls the servant "Sir," and insists on not troubling him to hold her plate. The housekeeper patronizes her. The children's governess takes upon her to correct her, when she has mistaken the piano for a harpsichord. . . .

A particularly good modern illustration is the following extract.

OUR FIFTEEN–YEAR–OLD SOPHISTICATES [1]
Marian Purcell

They imitate one another to an extent that is appalling. Ruth, whose diction has always been excellent, is this year talking through her nose because Pansy talks through hers. They dress as nearly like twins as they can, and every time they go out together the jaunt is preceded by a long discussion over the telephone that runs something like this:

"What are you going to wear? Yep, I've got a brown one. Yep, I'll wear it. Yeah, I'll wear my brown hat, too. The orange chain. O.K., I've got one. And brown stockings and pumps? Watch me. What? Oh, he did, did he? Well, I've got my eye on that baby, too. Lay off. Let me have him a week, and I'll roll him over to you. Goo'bye. Don't forget to add to the population."

I once asked Ruth what she meant by the last verbal gem. She could only tell me that Betty had originated it and that it was the favorite slogan of her circle. She was deeply pained when I asked her to drop it.

During vacations Ruth spends most of her time at the telephone. The talk with the boy usually runs something like this:

"Yeah? Is that so? Says you. Uh-huh. You'd be surprised. Yep. Nope. Oh, he did, did he? Well, if I ever hear him say that it will be just too bad. Sure, I'll tie a can to him. Yep. Nope. Toodle-oo!"

Every 15-year-old girl I know now has a "boy friend," and her first duty toward him is to "treat him rough." Ruth's rudeness to some of her boy friends was unbelievable till I discovered and stopped it. Rebuked, she said:

[1] Condensed from *Scribner's Magazine*, August, 1933, by permission of Charles Scribner's Sons and the editors of the *Reader's Digest*, wherein it appeared in October, 1933.

"But, Mumsey, he expects it. All the girls treat the boys like that! Naturally we don't want the boys to think we *like* them," she ended simply.

Betty's line with her boy friends is a drooping languor. "You simply slay me," she murmurs at intervals, or a little later one hears her say, "How simply devastating," or "How disillusioning!" [1]

[1] Compare the vicious jabs at "Faculty Wives" and "Faculty Husbands" in *Harper's* for March and April, respectively, 1934.

CHAPTER VII

The Character Sketch

EXPOSITION now begins to call definitely on the aid of description. The character sketch is the direct opposite of the rather abstract generalized description. Instead of the mere type or class, one now has an actual, individual character in mind, preferably a close friend or relative. The purpose is to select his most prominent characteristics, good or bad, and to construct from them a single, unified portrait, to the end that some definite judgment may be established as to his value as an individual personality.

In contrast to the satirical tendency of the generalized description, the most effective item in the production of a successful character sketch is sympathy—sincere, innate sympathy. Here a subtle line must be drawn between mawkish sentimentality and sane understanding of human nature. Straightforward understanding comes most easily, perhaps, between friends; hence pick out a good friend and go ahead.

Mr. Clayton Hamilton once outlined eight methods of character portrayal, four of which he called direct, and the other four indirect. Exposition (by the writer), description, psychological analysis, and reports of other characters—these Mr. Hamilton called "direct"; the character's actions, speeches, environment, and effect on other characters—these he called "indirect." Here are the useful methods and materials, but they will require skillful employment to produce a good character sketch. They will enable you to arrive at your character's dominant traits or characteristics. In your composition focus on these characteristics, not on the methods by which you determined them; in other words, though you will use some or all of the above eight methods of approach, subordinate them consistently to the picture being drawn of one distinct individual.

You will do well to conceal the expository methods chosen, and not let any one predominate. A more complete sketch by Professor Grandgent is given at the end of the chapter, but observe in this thumbnail portrait that he uses nearly all the eight methods except the actual speeches of characters. From boyhood memories he is contrasting Mrs. Bigelow with other village folk who insisted upon his coming to visit them, without regard to his own desires.

Old Mrs. Bigelow was somewhat different. She lived all alone in a wee house that was a regular curiosity shop—Malay clubs, Chinese teapots, Indian lacquer, a baby crocodile (stuffed). I fancy Mr. Bigelow —for there must have been one, in the inconceivable past—was a sea captain. She was very kind, and ready to tell stories about her treasures. But one had to remember to ask her about her rheumatism. Each of these old people had some special infirmity that must be made a subject of inquiry, and that was something of a nuisance, especially as the answers were never very encouraging.[1]

As a rule, sum up your general impression of the character in the first sentence: "Jim is an incurable dreamer, except in emergencies." Perhaps it will not be possible to make it as short as that, but cut it down as much as possible; the reader wants a sharp, compact impression from the start. The problem then is to demonstrate both these contradictory aspects of Jim's nature. There will not be time to present more than four or five aspects of any character in the four or five hundred words which are generally allotted. Anecdotes will help the most, but beware of a straight, biographical development—that will come in a later theme. Beware also of blurring the character with too much description; use it chiefly when the main thesis about the character absolutely demands description as the distinctive feature of development. Above all, do not merely list the characteristics of the subject pro and con, and then add them up with mathematical precision at the end. The character sketch demands sympathy— intimate touches—and "philosophy will clip an angel's wings."

[1] From "Cracks in the Clouds" in *Imitation and Other Essays*, by Charles Grandgent, Harvard University Press, 1933, with the permission of the publishers.

Name the subject at the beginning,[1] and perhaps his very name will give the clue to the leading impression by which you can distinguish him: Frank, Willy, "Beetles" Brown, Maggie, Uncle Ed, etc. In developing feeling for nice points of character you are actually preparing for story writing later on.

Obviously it is impossible to list precise theme subjects for this type, but some students' papers may offer suggestions: A Preacher's Son, A Friend, My Aunt Helen, A Selfish Girl, My Grandfather D——, My Youngest Sister. It is best to name the character in the title. If you are not afraid of some research, historical figures offer excellent opportunities, besides characters already existing in novels and plays.

→≫ A ≪←

The following paper has hit the type precisely. Note the concrete anecdotes and sympathetic approach.

THAT DOBBS GIRL

She was not quite forty years old, but so aged was she in appearance that another twenty-five years would not find her perceptibly older. And to the people of St. Elmo she was still Nelle Dobbs, or "that Dobbs girl." Age in St. Elmo is not reckoned in years, but by marriage, and by children, and grandchildren.

It had never occurred to Nelle to leave St. Elmo because all the young men had gone away. So Nelle never married. She had been born in the big house at the foot of Elm Street; she had never lived anywhere else; she had never slept anywhere but in the black bed in the south bedroom. And at the age of twenty-five, Nelle inherited the big house, and with it the Darkey Tom. He was part of her inheritance. Her memory of him, like her memory of the big house, went back as far as her memory of herself.

Every winter evening, between seven and eight o'clock, Nelle lighted the glass-handled lamp, placed it on the marble-topped table in the parlor window, and sat down beside it. The faint light of this lamp gleaming through the snow-hung evergreen was the only sign that the big house was there and occupied.

The things that made the people of St. Elmo interesting to each

[1] A brief narrative beginning may serve as an introduction: e.g., a man walks up to you in a safety zone.

other and drew them together meant nothing to Nelle Dobbs. When she had become too old to be asked in marriage by anyone, she had stopped going to dances or sleigh rides, and no one asked her why. Then she had left the choir.

For fifteen years after Alfred Dobbs died, Nelle and Old Tom lived alone in the big house. Every Saturday morning, as her mother had done before her, Nelle went to the grocery store, and to the butcher shop. She always walked along the south side of St. Elmo Ave. Once every week Nelle made a batch of cookies, cutting the thin-rolled dough into the shape of leaves with an old tin cutter that had been her mother's. She put the cookies in the shiny tin can that stood on the shelf in the clothespress of the downstairs bedroom, because that was where her mother had always kept them. This was handy and it was also out of reach of the hired help. When Mae Pope's children came to her door on their way home from school, she gave them two cookies each, because her mother had always given two.

Nelle had an apple tree growing in the yard. The rosy apples were wonderful to the eyes of the children as they were to Nelle. One day instead of taking the cookies and hurrying home, their eyes round and big, they stood looking at the fruit. While Nelle went to the clothespress to get the cooky pail, Bill Pope "snipped" an apple from the tree. The youngsters were unnaturally still when Nelle came out. They did not rush forward to get the cookies. Nelle looked quickly at the partly hidden apple and then the pail of cookies dropped from her hands. She grabbed the two children nearest and shook them until their heads bumped together. Then she drove them out the front gate, which she slammed shut behind them.

Nelle, her hands trembling, her eyes hot, went back into the house. Well, there would be no more cookies, and Old Tom would not let the youngsters come in the yard again. Being one of the youngsters driven away, it will be impossible for me to relate any more of the happenings at the big house.

B. T.

In the following paper the anecdotes are effective.

MY GRANDFATHER

exposition

The perpetual cigar in his mouth, he sits there, day after day, in his own corner of the sunroom, patiently enduring his afflictions and just as patiently hoping they will clear up. My grandfather is eighty-four years old, has been partially deaf for fifteen years, and has gradually been going blind for the past three years. Now he is almost totally blind, and this plus his other affliction would give him cause enough to grumble, but he never does. This patience of his is very marked, and many have noticed it and commented on it; but if they say anything to him, asking him how he endures the inaction, he just says, "Oh, well, they'll probably clear up soon. They usually do in a few years."

Another of the sides of his character is his extreme sense of good humor. He always has a remark no matter what the occasion. In his earlier years he was an engineer on the Pere Marquette Railroad, and on his retirement he became a member of the Locomotive Engineers' Society. Every summer he attends their reunion, enjoying himself to the utmost, as it is the one event of the year to which he looks forward. Last summer he went to Island Lake, where the picnic was given. In the course of the day's events, there was held a contest to determine the oldest living member of the society, a liberal money prize being offered. Naturally he entered, and climbed upon the platform with some other old men. As the judges inquired of the men their ages, Grandfather was surprised to find a man who was eighty-five years old; but, when another man declared his age to be ninety-one, Grandfather stood up and said to those around him, "Well, I guess us kids had better get out of here."

To reveal another characteristic, this anecdote, which has been repeated for many years by engineers of the line, is told. On the night run from Saginaw to Detroit, Grandfather and his fireman were talking of commonplace activities when suddenly out of the dusk ahead loomed the back end of a freight train. Without a thought of jumping, but with the safety of all those lives in back of him in his mind, he set the brakes and prepared himself for the shock. Within a few feet, they were suddenly switched off onto another track and safety. Then Grandfather leaned over, tapped the fireman on the shoulder and said, "And how are all your folks?"

As I look into the sunroom and see him sitting there, I wonder of what he is thinking, the long and eventful past, or the future, where perhaps light is awaiting.

C. C.

The next sketch is also marked by sympathy. In contrast to the satirical approach of the generalized description, feeling for and with the character contributes much to the success of individualized characterization.

HANS BÄUMGART

exposition

The mystery that surrounded the man's life, the circumstances that led a man of his ability to accept a position in a small-town high school, and the peculiarities of the man's character will always remain sources of wonder to me. Perhaps it was his large, dreamy-blue eyes, or perhaps it was the way he wore that black string tie, the ends trailing with animate stubbornness from beneath his shirt bosom, resisting the valiant efforts of his thin, white hands to replace them. Whatever it was, I was strangely attracted to the small, frailly built German from the very first moment I saw him.

He came to the small town as a professor of physics. No one had heard of him. Even the Board of Directors knew nothing about him except that he was a graduate of a famous German university and had had several degrees attached to his name. He, of course, became the principal topic for the town gossips, and all sorts of fantastic stories about his life, disappointments in love, and so forth and so on, were batted about the town from coffee shop to barbershop, and vice versa. The real truth was that the barbed tongues could find nothing tangible about his past life to talk about. It remained closed as fast as the Book of the Seven Seals. As a result, he was soon ignored by the town, but he remained an object of fascination to me.

I could not even venture a guess at his age. His hair was snow-white, but his form was slender and straight, and his face was practically without wrinkles. His eyes reflected the wisdom of the ages, and always retained a deep, somber, pensive look. His voice was soft and carried, through some mysterious quality, to every corner of the schoolroom. His explanations of the intricacies of physics were astonishingly clear and concise. When the textbook was vague, a new law, a single statement, would often clear the whole matter immediately. He moved like a ghost, treading lightly and softly. He liked to walk, and often took long moonlight strolls on warm spring nights.

I had developed a rather pleasant acquaintance with him, and it was on one of these nights that I met him strolling on the precipice of Bishop's Hill. There was a full moon. We walked together in silence. I asked some trivial questions and he answered. Then began the strangest conversation that I have ever entered into. Nothing, no subject was too complicated for him to explain simply, easily, and in an understandable way. He philosophized on Nature, on the stars, on life—and in the midst of his conversation, he stopped to remove a snail from the path of passing pedestrians. He talked of sorrows, of happiness, and his definition of happiness has rung through my brain since that night. "Happiness," he mused, "is the foam on a wave. Whoever rises with it knows there is a valley behind." Then he smiled a slow, sad smile.

The term of school was nearly over when he received a letter from Germany. The next day after receiving the missive, he handed his resignation to the Board of Directors. That same day, he said good-bye to his classes, and I saw a new light, a light with something of a rapturous expression, in his eyes. It was as if he had received some new incentive. A few parting words, an adjusting of his tie, and he was gone.

C. B.

In the next paper the writer has attempted an historical subject, with considerable success.

"L'ÉTAT—C'EST MOI" [1]

"I love me." What an appropriate epitaph for the tombstone of King Louis XIV this would be! Everything connected with his majesty, from his ways to his women, was a result of his insatiable desire for flattery. All his other characteristics were almost negligible in comparison with his vanity, which became a byword to his court and people. Under the early influence of his Spanish mother, herself a vain and selfish creature, and of Mazarin, his guardian, he formed many bigoted opinions which led him to believe that he was the imperial agent of God. Though usually veiled in wit, good humor, and captivating affability, pure vanity was the basis of his policies in domestic and foreign affairs. Even when he decided to introduce uniformity of religion in France, it was only because he thought it would be a feather in his cap to be able to accomplish that which his ancestors could not.

In appearance, Louis XIV was not handsome. He had, however, grace, charm, and manners, and could assume a suave and dignified attitude which was very impressive. At social functions, he was more genial than imposing. He liked to be ostentatious and make speeches before women, often accompanied by a pat on the hand or a pinch on the cheek. Louis loved to admire himself. The walls of his palace at Versailles were hung with portraits. Each painting flattered him to such an extent that I am inclined to believe we would find slight resemblance between him and his supposed likenesses. But it was as

---

[1] "The state—It is I."

necessary to flatter Louis if one wished to remain in his favor, as it is necessary to eat in order to live. More than one painter had his head separated from his body because he had interpreted on canvas the real Louis, a vain and selfish man.

Not without good cause was the king nicknamed the "Great Lover." Many a loquacious courtier had ample food for gossip concerning the morals and chastity of their ruler. After the death of his first wife, he had many mistresses and favorites among the beautiful women of the court. He succumbed to their charms, one after another, and even his second marriage did not interfere with his "amourettes." Only affairs of state could interrupt his social life. For a king, Louis worked hard. He was conscientious and painstaking. Day after day he reviewed the details of administration, and sat in council with his ministers, watching over foreign affairs. "One reigns by work and for work," he once wrote to his grandson.

I feel certain that had Louis been raised under different influences he would have proved to be a good monarch as well as a "glorious" one. Although Louis meant well, there seems to be a stain on all his good deeds, simply because they were motivated by vanity.

L. W.

A good style is a tremendous asset.

A SKETCH OF AN ARTIST

She is a petite person with a small, neat figure and dainty feet, and her name is Penelope. She would resemble a little gray mouse if it were not for the three features which betray her underlying character to the world. First there are her hands, fine, beautifully modelled, with long, elliptical nails—artistic hands. There are her eyes, large and wide apart, which reveal the dreamer and the mystic. Finally, in direct contrast to these eyes, is the stubborn jaw. Somehow I never can reconcile these last two features to each other, but they combine to produce a very interesting set of features.

Let us first consider the qualities which make Penelope an artist (whatever that word may signify). Primarily, she loves beauty as she perceives it through her senses. She appreciates fine art, and knows it when she sees it. She knows and appreciates natural beauty a great deal more. I remember, once, we were both on the summit of a hill in northern New York State, overlooking a great panorama, so typical of that part of the country. We wandered along the crest of the hill, and suddenly Penelope stopped and said, "Look through that tree!"

It was a dead apple tree, and the limbs were gnarled so as to form a frame for the view. The picture was enhanced incomparably; I shall never forget it. Yet I would never have noticed it if Penelope hadn't. The world seems to be full of such things for her, for she has eyes to see them. What a wonderful life she must lead!

Sensations mean a great deal to her. She loves the feeling of wind and rain on her face. She likes to run her fingers over satin and fur, and to touch things with her hands.

As Penelope loves beauty, so she loves to create it. Usually she paints and dreams. Sometimes she writes poetry, sometimes she plays music. Wherever she goes, she creates a beautiful environment for herself. At home, her parents have been able to afford lovely things for her. She is away from home a great deal, but she always manages to buy charming things for her room, inexpensively, though how she does it is a mystery to me. Penelope loves to wander around queer little shops by the hour, and she comes home with the strangest assortment of purchases. Once it was a small Venetian lantern of brass, with colored panes of glass. Again it was a carved whale-bone fan, and a strange glass dragon of pale blue, with gold wings and a ruby tongue. But I could go on forever about Penelope's collection of lovely (and quite useless) things.

Along with artistic talent goes the regrettable artistic temperament. Penelope has plenty of this. She is subject to moods of depression, when she hates people, bores herself, and is utterly devoid of any creative ability. She can never explain these moods; they fall upon her from a clear sky, and lift as suddenly. Then she becomes gay, entertaining, and overflows with all sorts of ideas. Penelope is also very changeable in her pursuits and likings. Sometimes she draws, then she prefers to write, and again she devotes herself to the piano. The same holds true in regard to her liking of people; she likes to be with different ones at different times.

One of the sad points about Penelope's character is her failure to understand people, and her instinctive dislike of them at first sight. If anyone is willing to take the trouble to seek out the real Penelope, she responds quickly, and is quite ready to be friends, but she will never seek people out herself. However, Penelope is devoted to her friends and would do anything for them. She invariably is more loyal to them than they to her, and so she is invariably getting hurt. Perhaps it is this which makes her inclined to distrust people.

Now we come to the stubborn chin—and Penelope *is* very stubborn. She forms her own ideas, and no one on earth can change them. She has a profound contempt for almost everyone's opinion but her own. She accepts nothing without proving it for herself, and she firmly believes in doing her own thinking.

Penelope is lazy. She hates to have any responsibility thrust upon her, although she will take it upon herself occasionally, by her own volition. She prefers to sit back and let someone else handle a situation, if that someone else is handy. Along with this laziness goes a remarkable capacity for telling lies. She usually tells them for effect without meaning any particular harm, although I have known her to lie herself out of many situations. This again is pure laziness.

Adventure is in Penelope's soul. She loves to travel and to wander about strange places. She detests anything ordinary: "Let it be ugly or beautiful, but never commonplace!" Indeed, she really enjoys ugliness as a form of beauty. She loves the iron foundries of Pittsburgh, train yards on a cold, rainy night, the water front at Hoboken. She is fortunate.

This is the artist, Penelope. She loves and understands places better than people. She has a logical, yet aesthetic mind. She has the eyes of a mystic—and a stubborn chin.

R. E.

How could the following portrait be improved by rearrangement of details?

MY AUNT

In an unused room in our house there hangs a worn little miniature of a young girl. She is wearing a wine-colored dress with a dainty little ruffle at the neck. Her face is heart-shaped and there are little hollows in her cheeks. She has a tip-tilted little nose and longish grey eyes that stare out seriously at the world. They are lovely, thoughtful eyes and somehow seem very wise. Her hair is fine and very curly—almost kinky—and it lights up the whole picture. This is a picture of my great-aunt at the age of eighteen.

When I look at it, I think how different her childhood must have been from mine. My mind wanders back over a period of sixty years to a wide street in the fine old town of Cambridge, Massachusetts. It is a hot July day, and the large old elm trees that line the road are drooping with the heat. Back of them are big, neat colonial houses surrounded by white picket fences. In the dim shadows of the trees open windows may be seen with ruffled muslin curtains swaying coolly in, driven by a tired little summer breeze. Nothing is heard except the drone of the bees humming busily from flower to flower in the shady old gardens. A piano tinkles out a merry old waltz from one of the pleasant houses, and low laughter and voices float down from an open upstairs window. Occasionally a carriage passes, the horses' feet making a soft regular thudding sound in the loam of the road. Young girls in hoop skirts with lacy pantalettes peeping from beneath are strolling down the shady boardwalks arm and arm with their swains. It is a pretty scene, calm and tranquil—quite different from the Cambridge of today with its roar and bustle caught from the city across the river.

This is the atmosphere in which my aunt was brought up—a calm, sensible, restrained atmosphere. At the age of fifteen she had probably mastered every household art and was ready for marriage. She must have lived a life very much like that of the Marches in *Little Women*. Her mother died when she was quite young, and from the time of her death my aunt's life was one long sacrifice. Her younger sister was chronically ill; so she gave up her own life to devote herself to the sick girl and her father, who was ailing from a wound received in the Civil War. Years passed, taking the lives of her sister and father, and with her hopes of marriage and a family of her own utterly shattered, she went to live with my grandfather, where she became an essential part of the household. She cared for all the illnesses and had a helping hand in straightening out all the difficulties of three generations of our family. All this she did with fervor and actual enjoyment and with no thought for herself.

When I look at the old miniature, I think of the differences age made on her. When I last saw her, she was over seventy and was still attractive. Wrinkles, white hair, and a little shrinking of the skin about her mouth were the only changes time had brought. Her eyes were amazingly young and she carried herself with almost soldierly erectness.

Perhaps the most outstanding thing about her was her capacity for enjoyment. At seventy, movies, card games and games with children were her greatest pleasures. She loved to gamble, and in her later years played a good many hands of poker, betting rather moderately. I think she got more fun out of playing games with us when we were children than even we did. Parchesi used to be the most popular sport when she was at our house, and the combats were long and fiercely contested. I remember so plainly how she used to sit at the table in her plain black dress, drumming on the mahogany surface with her shiny fingernails while she waited for her turn to play.

She had a wonderful sense of humor and was a genius for mimicking odd characters. Her head was packed with droll sayings and fancies, and when she had a silly fit she would convulse everyone around her.

Violet water was a great weakness with her, and when she came to visit us she always brought a bottle for me. I still have a small bottle of it in my bureau drawer at home.

I never knew her to get really angry unless she thought that someone she was fond of was being abused. Sometimes, on rare occasions when the thread she was sewing with broke, she would say, "Damn!" in a loud sharp voice.

She was loyal and steadfast and combined with these qualities a keen judgment of people. Her verdict on character was always correct, and I don't see how she could tear a person apart so accurately because everyone was always at his best when she was about.

D. McC.

⇢⇢ B ⇠⇠

A few rarely gifted writers have had the power of making characters seem to leap into existence almost immediately. They sketch rapidly, catching the distinctive features in a few words. Some of them, Chaucer, Shakespeare, and Balzac, for example, preserve the normal proportions of the individual. Others, such as Dickens and numerous comic dramatists, Shaw, Barrie, and others, give the sense of vital force, but produce caricatures, marionettes that seem to respond in clever fashion only as their creators pull the strings. It is impossible to avoid the feeling that, once we have stopped reading, the characters are tossed back into the box, where they lie lifelessly till they are resuscitated by further reading.

Observe how Chaucer achieves his portraits with a few deft strokes: his Wife of Bath, with her gaudy red stockings; the Miller, big-boned, his mouth like a furnace; the Merchant with correct forked beard, "and no one knew he was in debt"; the manly Monk, out of his cloister, the bridle of his well-fed mount "jingling in a whistling wind as clear and just as loud as does the chapel bell." Notice too the contrasts in types: the Nun, a Prioress, "full simple and coy" (modest and quiet) in her smiling, dainty in her eating, in her speech, in her affection for her little dogs, cherishing her beads "gauded all with green" and her gold brooch; and then the Summoner, an insinuating, intrusive sneak, with one of the most loathsome faces in literature, a face so horrible it frightened the children.

Still, Chaucer's characterizations, fresh and clean cut as they are, give the impression of portraits rather than of free-moving persons. One passage from Shakespeare (*Henry IV, Part I*) will show how the dramatist creates the free character. We seem to learn all that is essential concerning the life and adventures of Robin Ostler:

> *Second Carrier:* Peas and beans are as dank here as a dog, and that is the next way to give poor jades the bots: this house is turned upside down since Robin Ostler died.
>
> *First Carrier:* Poor fellow, never joyed since the price of oats rose; it was the death of him.

It was such understanding of men that made possible the creation of Falstaff, and Cleopatra, and Hamlet.

In the seventeenth century the generalized character (illustrated in the preceding chapter) was popular. Evidences of the effort to portray the fully rounded character in prose begin to appear in the familiar figures of Sir Roger de Coverley in Addison's *Spectator* papers, Defoe's adventurous and diligent Crusoe, and the creations of a succession of great novelists. The character sketch outside of fiction flourished also, ultimately finding a magnificent development in modern biography. Boswell's *Life of Samuel Johnson* is a sustained character sketch. Less familiar than this portrayal of Johnson is the account in Fanny Burney's (Madame d'Arblay's) diary. A short excerpt will show how exact reproduction of speech vivifies a character.

> When we were summoned to dinner, Mrs. Thrale made my father and me sit on each side of her. I said that I hoped I did not take Dr. Johnson's place; for he had not yet appeared.
>
> "No," answered Mrs. Thrale, "he will sit by you, which I am sure will give him great pleasure."
>
> Soon after we were seated, this great man entered. I have so true a veneration for him, that the very sight of him inspires me with delight and reverence, notwithstanding the cruel infirmities to which he is subject; for he has almost perpetual convulsive movements, either of his hands, lips, feet, or knees, and sometimes of all together.

Mrs. Thrale introduced me to him, and he took his place. We had a noble dinner, and a most elegant dessert. Dr. Johnson, in the middle of dinner, asked Mrs. Thrale what was in some little pies that were near him.

"Mutton," answered she, "so I don't ask you to eat any, because I know you despise it."

"No, madam, no," cried he; "I despise nothing that is good of its sort; but I am too proud now to eat of it. Sitting by Miss Burney makes me very proud today!"

"Miss Burney," said Mrs. Thrale, laughing, "you must take great care of your heart if Dr. Johnson attacks it; for I assure you he is not often successless."

"What's that you say, Madam?" cried he; "are you making mischief between the young lady and me already?"

A little while after he drank Miss Thrale's health and mine, and then added:

"'Tis a terrible thing that we cannot wish young ladies well, without wishing them to become old women!"

Such characterization belongs to the so-called indirect method, although as in most examples of such writing there is a mingling of both types. In this method the author withdraws, leaving the character to reveal itself. In the drama we have it in its pure state. Some novelists have sought the impersonality of the dramatist. Among the most famous of these is the French writer Gustave Flaubert (1821–1880). Notice in the following excerpt from *Madame Bovary* how Charles Bovary is revealed in a state of gradual disintegration. A young medical student, he had been exceptionally industrious, but now the subtle influences of environment conspire to break down his will. Although character here is recessive, almost negative, our attention is focused on it so intently that we share the sense of the vagrant lure which causes Charles to fail in his examinations.

On the fine summer evenings, at the time when the close streets are empty, when the servants are playing shuttlecock at the doors, he opened his window and leaned out. The river, that makes of this quarter of Rouen a wretched little Venice, flowed beneath him, between the bridges and the railings, yellow, violet, or blue. Working men, kneeling on the banks, washed their bare arms in the water. On poles projecting from the attics, skeins of cotton were drying in the air.

Opposite, beyond the roofs, spread the pure heaven with the red sun setting. How pleasant it must be at home! How fresh under the beech tree! And he expanded his nostrils to breathe in the sweet odors of the country which did not reach him.

He grew thin, his figure became taller, his face took a saddened look that made it nearly interesting. Naturally, through indifference, he abandoned all the resolutions he had made. Once he missed a lecture; the next day all the lectures; and, enjoying his idleness, little by little he gave up work altogether. He got into the habit of going to the public-house, and had a passion for dominoes. To shut himself up every evening in the dirty public room, to push about on marble tables the small sheep-bones with black dots, seemed to him a fine proof of his freedom, which raised him in his own esteem. It was beginning to see life, the sweetness of stolen pleasures; and when he entered, he put his hand on the door-handle with a joy almost sensual. Then many things hidden within him came out; he learnt couplets by heart and sang them to his boon companions, became enthusiastic about Béranger, learnt how to make punch, and, finally, how to make love.

In the next selection from a story by Stephen Crane, "A Desertion,"[1] environment expands to include other characters in indirect characterization. Their speeches serve less to describe the girl than to combine with the yellow gaslight in forming a single, sinister atmosphere. In the same author's *Maggie* the method is elaborated into a powerful study of a tragic type.

The yellow gaslight that came with an effect of difficulty through the dust-stained windows on either side of the door gave strange hues to the faces and forms of the three women who stood gabbling in the hallway of the tenement. They made rapid gestures, and in the background their enormous shadows mingled in terrific conflict.

"Aye, she ain't so good as he thinks she is, I'll bet. He can watch over 'er an' take care of 'er all he pleases, but when she wants t' fool 'im, she'll fool 'im. An' how does he know she ain't foolin' 'im now?"

"Oh, he thinks he's keepin' 'er from goin' t' th' bad, he does. Oh, yes. He ses she's too purty t' let run round alone. Too purty! Huh! My Sadie—"

"Well, he keeps a clost watch on 'er, you bet. On'y las' week, she met my boy Tim on th' stairs, an' Tim hadn't said two words to 'er

---

[1] Reprinted from Stephen Crane's *Men, Women, and Boats*, The Modern Library, 1921, by permission of the publishers.

b'fore th' ol' man begin to holler. 'Dorter, dorter, come here, come here!' "

At this moment a young girl entered from the street. . . .

Direct characterization usually takes the form of exposition with descriptive elements; it may be presented by the writer himself or through the mouth of another character. The Russian, Anton Chekhov (1860–1904), was a master of delineation through rapid analysis which penetrated the minds of his characters. Olenka, in his story "The Darling," is presented as a girl who loves a weak man through pity.[1]

Olenka, the daughter of the retired collegiate assessor Plemyanikov, was sitting on the back-door steps of her house doing nothing. It was hot, the flies were nagging and teasing, and it was pleasant to think that it would soon be evening. Dark rain clouds were gathering from the east, wafting a breath of moisture every now and then. . . .

She was always loving somebody. She couldn't get on without loving somebody. She had loved her sick father, who sat the whole time in his armchair in a darkened room, breathing heavily. She had loved her aunt, who came from Brianska once or twice a year to visit them. And before that, when a pupil at the progymnasium, she had loved her French teacher. She was a quiet, kind-hearted, compassionate girl, with a soft gentle way about her. And she made a very healthy, wholesome impression. Looking at her full, rosy cheeks, at her soft white neck with the black mole, and at the good naïve smile that always played on her face when something pleasant was said, the men would think, "Not so bad," and would smile too; and the lady visitors, in the middle of the conversation, would suddenly grasp her hand and exclaim, "You darling!" in a burst of delight.

In the same story Chekhov illustrates the use of purely descriptive details in giving the essentials of character.

Three months afterwards Olenka was returning home from mass, downhearted and in deep mourning. Beside her walked a man also returning from church, Vasily Pustovalov, the manager of the merchant Babakayev's lumber-yard. He was wearing a straw hat, a white vest with a gold chain, and looked more like a landowner than a business man.

[1] Reprinted from *Best Russian Short Stories*, compiled by Thomas Seltzer, by permission of The Modern Library, holders of the American copyright, 1917.

Mrs. Gaskell's famous description of Charlotte Brontë, author of *Jane Eyre*, is a composite portrait. In attempting such characterization, avoid a lifeless, mechanical listing of details. Notice particularly that what seems to be direct description and exposition, is really in effect psychological analysis, Mr. Hamilton's third type of direct characterization.

This is perhaps a fitting time to give some personal description of Miss Brontë. In 1831, she was a quiet, thoughtful girl, of nearly fifteen years of age, very small in figure—"stunted" was the word she applied to herself—but as her limbs and head were in just proportion to the slight, fragile body, no word in ever so slight a degree suggestive of deformity could properly be applied to her; with soft, thick, brown hair, and peculiar eyes, of which I find it difficult to give a description, as they appeared to me in her later life. They were large, and well shaped; their color a reddish brown; but if the iris was closely examined, it appeared to be composed of a great variety of tints. The usual expression was of quiet, listening intelligence; but now and then, on some just occasion for vivid interest or wholesome indignation, a light would shine out, as if some spiritual lamp had been kindled, which glowed behind those expressive orbs. I never saw the like in any other human creature. As for the rest of her features, they were plain, large, and ill set; but, unless you began to catalogue them, you were hardly aware of the fact, for the eyes and power of the countenance overbalanced every physical defect; the crooked mouth and the large nose were forgotten, and the whole face arrested the attention, and presently attracted all those whom she herself would have cared to attract. Her hands and feet were the smallest I ever saw; when one of the former was placed in mine, it was like the soft touch of a bird in the middle of my palm. The delicate long fingers had a peculiar fineness of sensation, which was one reason why all her handiwork, of whatever kind—writing, sewing, knitting—was so clear in its minuteness. She was remarkably neat in her whole personal attire; but she was dainty as to the fit of her shoes and gloves.

Life of Charlotte Brontë (1857).

The ideal character sketch will probably combine some of the qualities of all types. The portrayal [1] of Jonathan Swift is part of one of Austin Dobson's sketches of famous eighteenth-century fig-

[1] From *Eighteenth Century Vignettes, Second Series*, Oxford University Press, 1894. Reprinted by courtesy of Mr. Alban Dobson and the publishers.

ures. The method is both direct and indirect by turns; Swift is described by the author, and then he reveals himself by his own actions and speech, while the atmosphere in which he is presented intensifies the details of the portrait. We see Swift at work on one of his quaint and memorable letters in the *Journal to Stella*.

A dim light was burning in the back room of a first-floor in Bury Street, St. James's. The apartment it irradiated was not an extensive one; and the furniture, sufficient rather than sumptuous, had that indefinable lack of physiognomy which only lodging-house furniture seems to possess. There was no fireplace; but in the adjoining parlour, partly visible through the open door, the last embers were dying in a grate from which the larger pieces of coal had been carefully lifted out and ranged in order on the hobs. Across the heavy high-backed chairs in the bedroom lay various neatly-folded garments, one of which was the black gown with pudding sleeves commonly worn in public by the eighteenth-century divine, while at the bottom of the bed hung a clerical-looking periwig. In the bed itself, and leaning toward a tall wax candle at his side (which, from a faint smell of singed woollen still lingering about the chamber, must recently have come into contact with the now tucked-back bed-curtain), was a gentleman of forty or thereabouts, writing in a very small hand upon a very large sheet of paper, folded, for greater convenience, into one long horizontal slip. He had dark, fierce-looking eyebrows, an aquiline nose, full-lidded and rather prominent clear blue eyes, a firmly-cut, handsome mouth, and a wide, massive forehead, the extent of which was, for the moment, abnormally exaggerated by the fact that, in the energy of composition, the fur-lined cap he had substituted for his wig had been slightly tilted backward. As his task proceeded, his expression altered from time to time; now growing grave and stern, now inexpressibly soft and tender. Occasionally the look almost passed into a kind of grimace, resembling nothing so much as the imitative motion of the lips which one makes in speaking to a pet bird. He continued writing until, in the distance, the step of the watchman—first pausing deliberately, then moving slowly forward for a few paces—was heard in the street below. "Past twelve o'clock!" came a wheezy cry at the window. *"Paaaaast twelvvve o'clock!"* followed the writer, dragging out his letters so as to reproduce the speaker's drawl. After this, he rapidly set down a string of words in what looked like some unknown tongue, ending off with a trail of seeming hieroglyphics: *"Nite, nown deelest sollahs. Nite dee litt MD, Pdfr's MD. Rove Pdfr, poo Pdfr, MD MD MD FW FW FW*

Lele Lele Lele Lele michar MD." Then, tucking his paper under his pillow, he popped out the guttering candle, and turning round upon his side with a smile of exceeding sweetness, settled himself to sleep.

AUSTIN DOBSON, *Eighteenth Century Vignettes.*

Were it possible to enter the mind of another person and walk about in it, like Alice in the garden, looking at the ideas, handling and comparing the appetites and emotions like solid objects, there would be little need of an author to tell us about a character. He would, so to speak, reveal himself. Such a technique of characterization has been developed by a modern school of writers. It is commonly known as the stream-of-consciousness technique. The internal, mental and emotional, life of the character is revealed to us as a ceaseless flow, a river of ideas, impulses, memories, desires. Hints of this technique appear in the soliloquies in Shakespeare's plays, in Melville's *Moby Dick*, and elsewhere. But it was the Irish writer, James Joyce, who exploited it to the full. Since his characters were taken from the shady side of Dublin life, many of their currents of thought were distinctly unsavory. As a consequence the chief work in which they appear, the novel *Ulysses*, has been, until very recently, banned in the United States. However, many passages provide brilliant examples of the technique we are considering.

In the following excerpt [1] you will find a characterization in which giblets and a cat play as important roles as any of the actual features of the man Bloom. Since *Ulysses* was published in 1922, the style is no longer novel. It is easy to imitate—badly; do not be too much fascinated by its apparent freedom.

Mr. Leopold Bloom ate with relish the inner organs of beasts and fowls. He liked thick giblet soup, nutty gizzards, a stuffed roast heart, liver slices fried with crustcrumbs, fried hencods' roes. Most of all he liked grilled mutton kidneys.

Kidneys were in his mind as he moved about the kitchen softly, righting her breakfast things on the humpy tray. Gelid light and air were in the kitchen but out of doors gentle summer morning everywhere. Made him feel a bit peckish.

The coals were reddening.

[1] Reprinted by kind permission of Random House.

Another slice of bread and butter: three, four: right. She didn't like her plate full. Right. He turned from the tray, lifted the kettle off the hob and set it sideways on the fire. It sat there, dull and squat, its spout stuck out. Cup of tea soon. Good. Mouth dry. The cat walked stiffly round a leg of the table with tail on high.

—Mkgnao!

—O, there you are, Mr. Bloom said, turning from the fire.

The cat mewed in answer and stalked again stiffly round a leg of the table, mewing. Just how she stalks over my writing-table. Prr. Scratch my head. Prr.

Mr. Bloom watched curiously, kindly, the lithe black form. Clean to see: the gloss of her sleek hide . . . the green flashing eyes. He bent down to her, his hands on his knees.

—Milk for the pussens, he said.

—Mrkgnao! the cat cried.

They call them stupid. She understands all she wants to. Vindictive, too. Wonder what I look like to her. Height of a tower? No, she can jump me.

—Afraid of the chickens she is, he said mockingly. Afraid of the chook-chooks. I never saw such a stupid pussens as the pussens.

Cruel. Her nature. Curious mice never squeal. Seem to like it.

—Mrkrgnao! the cat said loudly.

She blinked up out of her avid shameclosing eyes, mewing plaintively and long, showing him her milkwhite teeth. He watched the dark eyeslits narrowing with greed till her eyes were green stones. Then he went to the dresser took the jug Hanlon's milkman had just filled for him, poured warmbubbled milk on a saucer and set it slowly on the floor.

—Gurrhr! she cried, running to lap.

He watched the bristles shining wirily in the weak light as she tipped three times and licked lightly. Wonder is it true if you clip them they can't mouse after. Why? They shine in the dark, perhaps, the tips. Or kind of feelers in the dark, perhaps.

He listened to her licking lap. Ham and eggs, no. No good eggs with this drouth. Want pure fresh water. Thursday: not a good day either for a mutton kidney at Buckley's. Fried with butter, a shake of pepper. Better a pork kidney at Dlugacz's. While the kettle is boiling. She lapped slower, then licking the saucer clean. Why are their tongues so rough? To lap better, all porous holes. Nothing she can eat? He glanced round him. No.

On quietly creaky boots he went up the staircase to the hall, paused by the bedroom door. She might like something tasty. Thin bread and butter she likes in the morning. Still perhaps: once in a way.

He said softly in the bare hall:

—I am going round the corner. Be back in a minute.

JAMES JOYCE, Ulysses.

While Joyce's method of characterization may seem very novel and modern, the average writer will always return to the well-tried method of direct exposition. Notice in the final illustration how a New England type is presented. We see the man against the background of his period and locality. Would you suspect the author of this portrait [1] to be a distinguished authority on philology? Could you show that Professor Grandgent's profound knowledge of Dante and the severely disciplined art of the *Divine Comedy* had influenced his style?

It struck me as very strange that my uncle and aunt had no children. They were just the sort who ought to have some, they were so good to me. But my mother warned me that I must never, never mention the subject to them. Then the wonderment was all the greater, until one day I discovered a little grave in the cemetery behind the Baptist Church; and I understood.

My uncle had Billy, though, a spirited old horse who was kept like a spoiled boy. It was great fun to see him roll in the grass and kick his legs in the air, when uncle took him out to play in the evening. He had a stall four times as big as the ordinary, and lots of choice food; and a good time when hitched to the buggy, too, for he was a sport and my uncle was a fast and fearless driver. One had to be careful, because Billy, despite his excellences, was inclined to bite and kick. Like so many biters and kickers, he lived to a very ripe age; before he died, he had turned snow-white.

Uncle Franklin was a portly, courteous, dignified man, sometimes stern but habitually jolly—at least with my parents and me. He kept the village store, and sang bass in the church choir. When politics were propitious, he had the post office. Once a year, to lay in stock, he would make a pilgrimage to the city; and on those occasions we had the satisfaction of entertaining him in Boston. Really, he did not then appear particularly countrified, except his hair-cut.

I still love the composite smell of a country store, and I still love

---

[1] Reprinted from *Imitation and Other Essays* (1933), with the kind permission of the Harvard University Press.

the sight of rolls of cloth in proximity to suspended scythes. It made life so simple. Customers were not expected to come at mealtimes. If they (strangers, I suppose) were so indiscreet, they were authoritatively but politely told to wait until dinner should be over; and wait they did, although uncle never hurried. The most anxious person, on such occasions, seemed to be myself, who, not daring to leave my seat, would eagerly attempt, every time the dining-room door was opened, to peep into the adjacent store, to see whether the customers were manifesting impatience. Had they departed, we should have heard their boots, for the new refectory, where we sat, was but thinly separated from the older building.

CHARLES GRANDGENT, "Cracks in the Clouds."

CHAPTER VIII

Expository Biography

WITH GENERALIZED DESCRIPTION and the character sketch behind us, we are now ready to face a somewhat harder type, the expository biography. This is a type of literary production that is especially popular today. In the treatment of Lytton Strachey it has developed a satiric tone, somewhat like the generalized description above; as employed by André Maurois it has a distinctly romantic tendency. Neither school succeeds in presenting human characters with objective reality, for both exaggerate in different ways. It may be interesting to experiment with one method or the other; but in either case you should strive for a truthful presentation of the subject chosen, rather than an exhibition of cleverness.

Generally if a man's career is surveyed in the light of the characterizing elements mentioned in the preceding chapter, you will discover that one predominating influence—ambition, selfishness, interest, faith, belief—swayed the whole span of his life. Of course, it may not have governed every successive period, but in the long run, when you sum up his life, you will find this ruling passion in most of his actions. Every man, great or small, has generally some one dominating motif, and the problem is to exhibit it sympathetically. Perhaps it was not a good trait, but it is not your duty to moralize on the matter or sneer at the man, as Strachey maliciously flung jibes at Pope. If possible, try to find the reason behind this unfortunate motif and explain it sympathetically throughout the man's career. At any rate, this is the first step in writing the expository biography: find the centralizing motif and write it directly into the first paragraph. This is the best way to start.

You are then ready to survey the scope of the man's whole life, taking it period by period—all seven ages, as Jaques put it. In each of these ages you will probably find evidence of the dominating motif, in some ages more than in others. And as you go along, you will do well to narrate anecdotes in each period which serve to substantiate the main thesis of the career. These intimate anecdotes are important, and help tremendously to make the man live before us—for he must appear as an individual, not a type. Boswell, for example, gave them in the case of Johnson: little actions, sayings, scraps of letters or memoranda, comments to or by friends. The more you present the better—all of them introduced to give a sympathetic, intimate survey of the man's whole career.

It will probably be best to begin with the influence of heredity and environment on the development of the man's chief interest. Never start with "John Jones was born on October 7, 1910, at 5 o'clock in the morning." Expository biography is not a mere sequence of chronological events, but a definite thesis stating the central feature of a life. Sometimes such a thesis may contain two elements, even three: one student began a fairly successful theme with, "My friend M—— is noted for his keenness of mind, self-reliance, and aggressiveness." But he would have done far better with one of these, since they overlap somewhat.

The seventeenth century wrote biography in terms of panegyric or moral teaching. You will do neither. Try to be sympathetic toward your character in attempting to understand his controlling purpose; but do not use his career as a grand example of what to do or not to do. Above all, try not to forget that you are writing his life, a series of chronological events selected to support a thesis, and not a mere static character sketch or a criticism of the man's works. Cover all the periods—the seven ages—if possible, but the most important ones anyway. And do not lose the thesis in a mass of details.

It is best not to make up fictional biographies. Write first on people you know well, and second on public characters about whom you can do some reading. This means that this type is important enough to deserve two exercises, or more.

For the first theme, students have preferred: A Friend, A

Relative (named), The Self-Made Man, A Black Sheep, The Young Musician, A Tradesman, A Doctor, A Lawyer, A Merchant, A Politician. (Compare types in Chapter VI, now individualized.)

Among the public characters the following have been successfully treated: Benvenuto Cellini, Queen Elizabeth, Joyce Kilmer, Abraham Lincoln, John Hay, Ben Franklin, T. A. Edison, Edward Bok, Dr. W. C. Gorgas, Ben Jonson, Jane Austen, Disraeli, Robert Burns, Lord Clive, "O. Henry," Lindbergh.

⟫ A ⟪

Sympathy is the keynote of this biography which is based upon direct observation.

MY DAD

Born of common people, farmers, early in the year of '69, my father began his life of hard labor. The very term *hard work* brings to me a picture of his life. Every nut and bolt in his car has meant skin from his knuckles.

When about seven, he and his eight brothers and sisters were left orphans, and so shifting for himself began. He worked on one farm and then another, doing the chores, sometimes with the promise of pay which he never received, and most of the while with barely enough to eat. When working on one farm for a crabbed old pair, he was allowed only two pancakes for breakfast, and left the table, hungry, to watch the woman throw the rest of the steaming dish to the pigs, thinking all the while, "If I were only a pig." Later he worked for an old bachelor who was very fond of his beer and insisted that he wait up each night he went on a "toot" to unsaddle his horse. At the time my father was so small that he could not reach the nail to hang the saddle on, yet he must wait up for the man till he came in at twelve or one o'clock. Then, if the old devil felt in the mood, he would bite his ears till the blood ran. Poor Dad, standing erect and as tall as he could, bravely said, "There will come a day when you won't be able to do that to me," at which the man laughed. This prediction was fulfilled more than twenty years later when Dad was standing at a bar drinking a schooner of beer. The old fellow came up to him saying, "I guess you don't remember me." To which he replied: "Oh yes, I do. Do you remember the time I told you there would come a time when you wouldn't be able to bite my ears?

That time has come." Clank! went the schooner; out in the snow he went and four weeks elapsed before the old devil was able to get out of his bed.

After working all summer, when the fall came, he was asked—very graciously, I imagine—to leave, for the cold weather was coming and the farmer could do his own chores. So, starting out he knew not for where, he had the good fortune to run into a man who was starting out for the lumber woods. Upon learning the boy's predicament he asked him to join him. The kindest treatment of the boy's early years was given him by the uncouth men of the woods of northern Michigan. Those were the days when a hundred men were bunked in one large camp and another camp served as the dining room, where later in the evening they all gathered 'round the huge fire to sing and talk. My dad received fifteen dollars a month for this work, which was taken away from him by hook or by crook, by the farmer he worked for the following summer. So this was the way his early years were spent, drifting from one place to another, in the struggle for existence. I wonder what he thought of it all. I wonder how our city-bred youth of today would have stood it. Schooling was practically unheard of, and when he did go, it was only when there was no work to be done. I doubt if he has had one year of school in his whole life.

When he was eighteen years old, he came to Detroit and began to work for the Wabash Railroad. Beginning as a common wiper of engines he eventually became a fireman. One night after both he and the engineer had worked for thirty-six hours without rest, the engineer went to sleep. Directions to the engineer were always written, and this night the man very hurriedly glanced over them not noticing an ambiguous statement. Later, when the engineer was peacefully snoring, my dad reread the directions, why he never knew, and barely escaped a wreck by switching the train on a siding while the special whizzed through.

I really believe he must have an engineering mind, for from experience alone he has acquired a knowledge of machinery that is quite remarkable. What heights he might have reached had he had the education! Shortly after his marriage, he left railroading and began working in a large factory in the capacity of engineer. Then, for over twenty years, he was with the Michigan Steam Laundry, working twelve hours every week day and many Sundays as well. It is a mighty good thing that he likes to work or he would have been dead long ago. Now he is employed by the Board of Education as engineer in a public school, and, I can assure you, he is considered above many who have had several years of training in the field of mechanics. Even now, while he is ageing slightly, when he leaves his job on Saturday, he is wishing for Monday morning. Dear old Dad, he will die with his shoulder to the wheel!

H. A.

In "My Aunt" the thesis is stated quickly and developed with considerable concreteness.

MY AUNT

From the time she was four years old, my aunt has been following her ambition, which was to make money. Ambition is the one word which can explain all the experiences she has had. She started to earn money when she was four years old. Her mother was never strict with her, and Carrie was allowed to do just about as she pleased. It pleased her to go to the corner saloon and sing and dance and recite for the rough lumbermen. The minute she appeared, she became the center of interest, and one of the table-tops became her stage. The men gave her pennies, and they all loved her in their rude way. There wasn't one of them who wouldn't have died rather than let any harm come to Carrie.

When only ten years old, she again proved that she could make money. She read all sorts of books, and in one of them was a complete description of the gentle art of hanging. Being Carrie, she wanted to test the truth of what she had read. It happened that one of the neighbors had a stray hound which was fast becoming a neighborhood nuisance. There were no humane societies nor any other organization to take care of such dogs; someone would have to shoot it. The woman said several times in Carrie's presence that she would be glad to give anyone who would get rid of the dog ten dollars. Carrie got a rope from somewhere and she coaxed the dog off into the woods. She fixed the noose around its neck and then she proceeded to climb a young sapling, and when it bent to the ground because of her weight, Carrie quickly tied the other end of the rope to the tree-top. Of course the tree sprang upright immediately, and the dog was hanged. So she received the ten dollars. She wasn't cruel, but she felt that the dog would be better off dead, and it was an opportunity to earn some money and to test her ability.

When she was fourteen, she came home from school and announced that she was through with school and that she was going to teach. She pretended to be sixteen, which was the youngest anyone was supposed to begin teaching, and she took the examinations given by the school board. She taught school in northern Michigan until she was eighteen. Here she met the young Irishman whom she married. He had never attended school but three months, but had studied at home. She persuaded him to go with her to Albion, where they passed the entrance examinations, and in two years, graduated with honors. For the next two years they both taught school in Humboldt, Michigan. Soon after this they decided to go to Florida; here Carrie met the great Dr. Osler of England. She decided then and there that some day she would study medicine, and that it should be her career. Ambition for a larger earning capacity combined with a real love of the work made her choose this for a life work.

Carrie's health failed her soon after this, and she and her husband returned to Michigan. He soon went to Seattle to work for the post office, while she remained in the East. When her health had slightly improved, she left to join her husband. She stopped on her journey to Seattle at Kalispell, Montana. She meant to stay only a short time, but a vacancy occurred in one of the schools and she decided to teach a little longer. She taught for fifteen years there.

In the meantime, her husband had become a mail clerk on the "S. S. Dora" with headquarters in Valdez, Alaska. Carrie went to Alaska to join him, but she did not like it there, so she went to New York City. She replenished her wardrobe with some Paris importations and decided to try Alaska again. It didn't work; then she made up her mind that it was time to begin her career if she intended to before it was too late. Carrie was about thirty-five at this time. She went to St. Paul and studied medicine. After years of effort, and a large expenditure of money, she finished her course and began her practice. This was twenty years ago. Carrie now runs two offices, one in Santa Maria and one in Los Angeles. She is also the owner of a large fruit ranch in California, which she manages very successfully. Although sixty-four years of age, she is as active as most women of forty. With Aunt Carrie, money was the means to an end, never an end in itself.

M. D. R.

The following biography evolves a negative thesis.

"X"

He should never have been born; his death was a blessing to the community. "X"—this name will serve as well as any—was born of well-matched parents—his mother, a woman of the streets, his father a minor underworld czar, who derived his revenue from terrorism and petty racketeering. At the age of seven—he never had any schooling— he embarked on a life of crime whose beginning was the pilfering of fruit from unsuspecting hucksters and the swift flight to safety into one of the doors of the tenements, of which there were many in the neighborhood. He ran away from home when he was ten, neither parent caring to find him. "X's" stopping point, unknown at the start, turned out to be a district, just as bad, on the opposite side of the town. There he was quickly swallowed up as a minor member of a small gang of slightly older hoodlums who existed by the same type of petty thieving, carried on, however, in a more organized manner. Food was obtained in this way and any empty house served as shelter.

The reform school made his acquaintance at the age of fourteen, soon after he had been made gang leader, at a time when he had already begun to mature, his stunted figure broadening out slightly and his voice changing into one of deeper tone. In this place of criminal education he quickly learned the few remaining things that he had somehow missed in his early life. When sixteen, he with several other calloused youths formed a gang, purchased weapons from a mail-order house, and went after bigger money by holding up small stores and gasoline stations. They profited greatly through these operations and were well on the way to a local reputation when the police stopped them for two years.

Emerging from prison at the expiration of his sentence, "X" became a sworn enemy of organized society and joined the ranks of the local gang, whose leader controlled the liquor trade. Quickly he rose to a position of importance, and at the age of twenty-two he daringly struck out for himself. His reputation as a gangster with iron nerves had spread; consequently he had little difficulty enlisting followers. At twenty-five he dominated the local underworld, with three murders to his credit. When his career was at its height, he foolishly went out alone one night and was fatally shot by a woman whom he had deserted. He should never have been born; his death was a blessing to the community.

D. L.

The next two biographies illustrate the second type—that of the public character—as outlined above. In the first theme the thesis appears in the title (quoted from Matthew Arnold) and is well developed, but is it wholly sound?

SHELLEY: "THE BEAUTIFUL BUT INEFFECTUAL ANGEL"

One usually thinks of Shelley as a writer of beautiful verse, little knowing that his supreme ambition in life was to reform the world. He knew almost nothing of real life, for his thoughts dwelt in a world remote from ours—a world of ideals and beauty; therefore, he found it difficult to understand why there had to be misery, evil, and corruption among people. He desperately hated the existence of these things and retained the very extravagant idea that he could banish all evil from the world and leave beauty in its place. This wild ambition was a typical product of Shelley's impractical nature.

His appearance was in keeping with his character; he was a youth who was possessor of a beauty seldom found in men. He was always fascinated by the charm of women and the freedom and youthful simplicity of children. Yet this dreamy, romantic figure imbibed the spirit of the French Revolution and rebelled against the tyranny that met his eyes everywhere he turned them. Because of his belief in the freedom of expressing thoughts, he was expelled from Oxford after attacking religion in a little paper which he published under the title "The Necessity of Atheism." This disgrace caused his father to denounce him, the result being that he married a mere child of sixteen whom he felt to be as misunderstood as he. Both of the youngsters were reckless and irresponsible but very devoted to each other for the most part. However, the young wife, though a pretty and clever child, did not serve as sufficient inspiration to Shelley, so he sought it elsewhere: namely, in the charming atmosphere of the home of his friends, the Newcombes, where he chatted with the lovely creatures who also seemed attracted by the home of his friends. They flattered him by their spellbound attention to his conversation and his personal appearance. The marriage didn't last very long before a separation occurred.

All of his life, Shelley's main source of inspiration and the foundation of all his philosophy was found in a book written by a man named Godwin. Finally he determined to meet the man who had played such a large part in his life; so he went to the author's home, and it was only a very short time before the two were staunch friends, for the young poet had a surprisingly magnetic personality. But more important was the friendship, and later love, which was formed between Shelley and Godwin's daughter, a woman of astounding brilliance and character—the kind of person in whom the young man

could confide all his dreams of reform and who fully measured up
to his conception of the ideal woman. She too was a writer, her best-
known work being the classic *Frankenstein*. The part of his career
following his marriage to Mary Godwin marked the period in which
his best-known works were written. The happiness of these two fine
individuals was short-lived; for, while they were cruising with friends
on the Mediterranean, a small boat in which Shelley was riding cap-
sized and the poet, just thirty, was drowned. After about a week, his
body was recovered on the shore bordering that great sea; the body
was found, but his marvelous soul had fled to the land of immortality
to join that of his fellow-poet, Keats. Shelley is forgotten as a re-
former, but he will always be remembered as a poet of great merit.

R. M.

The chief asset of "Ludwig van Beethoven" is its concentrated
sympathy, as expressed in the first paragraph.

LUDWIG VAN BEETHOVEN

Beethoven's life began and ended with absolutely no personal satisfactions. It was a very sad and anxious one, filled with petty failings.
Even his music was a sad resource, for when his heart was heavy he
found refuge in composing.

Beethoven's father was a poor musician, who, discovering talent
in Ludwig, forced lessons on him at an early age. The boy hated to
practice and his father would beat him unmercifully. However, he
had such great genius that it soon started to influence him into loving
the music he played. When Ludwig was but seventeen, his mother,
the only loving and loved member of the family, died. Soon after this
his sister died, and then his father, leaving the poor boy to care for
his brothers.

Later in years Beethoven had a great many friends. He seems to
have been a guest in every home where art and music were loved.
He was a clumsy, awkward figure in a drawing room. But his queer
temper, peculiar clothes, and rudeness were easily outweighed by his
undoubted genius, his honesty, and his gentle and true heart. He had
a big head, a great shock of dark hair, soulful eyes, and brilliantly
white teeth. He cared nothing for his appearance, although he was
very fond of washing. When he was in the depths of writing a symphony, he would keep a basin filled with water and every few minutes
would wash his hands and arms violently, returning to his work with
renewed ardor.

His friends loved and humored him. For many years he lived at the palace of one of his admirers, Prince Lichnowsky. Although he knew these people intimately, he never wished to intrude upon them. Poor as he was, he bought a horse so as not to make any disturbance in using any of those from the royal stables. He even hired his own servant so as not to run the risk of ringing for one in the house at the same moment someone else did.

Beethoven never married, despite his passionate love for a countess who spurned him. Needing someone to make happy, he adopted his nephew, Carl. This boy was a wretch who broke Beethoven's heart with his cruelty and deceit. He toiled and labored so that the boy might have comfort and ease. He begged Carl to come and see him in his lonely hours, but the scoundrel was too vain and selfish, and unless it were for money he wouldn't spend any time with his uncle, whose ill health and disappointments were fast making him a fretful, melancholy invalid. Beethoven discovered the extent of Carl's badness, yet before he died the old love for the boy stirred him to name Carl as his sole heir.

Success and maybe even happiness were about to come to Beethoven when suddenly deafness struck him. He could still lead his own works in orchestras, but when the performance was ended he would have to be turned around to see the applause he could not hear. He had loved to play and compose, and by holding his violin very near his face, for some time, he was able to feel the sounds. But gradually these faded out, and not long after his deafness he became blind.

Not one loving word from the nephew Carl came to cheer his last hours, and he passed away, glad to arrive at the end of the life which had meant so much pain to him. He died without realizing that he was the greatest master of his art the world has ever known.

L. C.

≫ B ≪

Sir Sidney Lee, biographer of Shakespeare, has said that the chief feature of biography is its "power to transmit personality." As we have emphasized, good biography is not a mere chronology of events; it is the portrait and interpretation of a life. While certain recent biographers, such as Lytton Strachey, Emil Ludwig, André Maurois, and Gamaliel Bradford, have shown remarkable deftness in selecting and focusing the significant events of a life, no writers have surpassed the two greatest names in biography.

Plutarch (46?–120?) and James Boswell (1740–1795) both have contributed immensely to the fame of the illustrious persons of whom they wrote by bringing them to life, not as greater than they were, but just as they were, their absurdities and faults being given as well as happier details. A few men have been equally truthful in autobiography: St. Augustine, medieval saint, Benvenuto Cellini, artist of the Italian Renaissance, and Jean Jacques Rousseau, poet and social philosopher of the period culminating in the French Revolution, all antedate a period of almost desperate self-exposure in the age of psychoanalysis. You will find it interesting to look into all these writers.

Rapid miniature biography had as one of its most brilliant exponents Lord Macaulay (1800–1859) who, for all his Victorian way of handing out moral judgments, succeeded in packing a great deal into small space. In the following brief extract we seem to learn all that is essential concerning a man who, to Macaulay, was a dazzling failure.

No public man of that age had greater courage, greater ambition, greater activity, greater talents for debate or for declamation. No public man had such profound and extensive learning. He [Lord Carteret] was familiar with the ancient writers, and loved to sit up till midnight discussing philological and metrical questions with Bentley. His knowledge of modern languages was prodigious. The privy council, when he was present, needed no interpreter. He spoke and wrote French, Italian, Spanish, Portuguese, German, even Swedish. He had pushed his researches into the most obscure nooks of literature. . . .

With all this learning, Carteret was far from being a pedant. His was not one of those cold spirits of which the fire is put out by the fuel. In council, in debate, in society, he was all life and energy. His measures were strong, prompt, and daring, his oratory animated and glowing. His spirits were constantly high. No misfortune, public or private, could depress him. He was at once the most unlucky and the happiest public man of his time.

He had been Secretary of State in Walpole's administration, and had acquired considerable influence over the mind of George the First. The other ministers could speak no German. The king could speak no English. All the communication that Walpole held with his master was in very bad Latin. Carteret dismayed his colleagues by the volubility with which he addressed his Majesty in German. They listened with envy and terror to the mysterious gutturals which might possibly convey suggestions very little in unison with their wishes.

Walpole was not a man to endure such a colleague as Carteret. The king was induced to give up his favourite. Carteret joined the Opposition, and signalized himself at the head of that party till, after the retirement of his old rival, he again became Secretary of State. . . .

He was driven from his office. He shortly after made a bold, indeed a desperate, attempt to recover power. The attempt failed. From that time he relinquished all ambitious hopes, and retired laughing to his books and his bottle. No statesman ever enjoyed success with so exquisite a relish, or submitted to defeat with so genuine and unforced a cheerfulness. Ill as he had been used, he did not seem, says Horace Walpole, to have any resentment, or indeed any feeling except thirst.

T. B. MACAULAY, "An Admirable Crichton."

The rich biographical material in the next selection, from Dr. Axel Munthe's *The Story of San Michele*, flows with the informality and easy transitions of casual memories. Yet see what a lively picture we have of Miss Hall—a complete life is suggested without crowding the detail. Notice how the unconventional punctuation permits the canalizing of reminiscence. The commas really indicate pauses, as in speaking, rather than grammatical units. Dr. Munthe gives a valuable hint concerning autobiography when he remarks that "the simplest way to write a book about oneself consists in trying as hard as one can to think of somebody else."

MISS HALL [1]

Axel Munthe

Many of my patients of those days will surely remember Miss Hall, indeed once seen she was not easily forgotten. Great Britain alone, Great Britain at its very best, could have produced this unique type of the early Victorian spinster, six feet three inches, dry and stiff like a stick, *arida nutrix* of at least two unborn generations of Scotchmen. During the fifteen years I knew Miss Hall I never saw any change in her appearance, always the same glorious face enshrined by the same curls of faded gold, always the same gaily coloured dress, always the same bower of roses in her hat. How many years of uneventful life

---

[1] Reprinted from *The Story of San Michele*, copyright 1929, by kind permission of the publishers, E. P. Dutton & Co., Inc.

Miss Hall had spent in various second-class Roman pensions in search of adventure, I do not know. But I know that the day she met Tappio and me in the Villa Borghese her real mission in life began, she had found herself at last. She spent her mornings brushing and combing the dogs in my ice-cold back sitting-room under the Trinità dei Monti steps, only to return to her pension for luncheon. At three o'clock she sailed forth from Keats' house across the Piazza with Giovannina and Rosina, half her size, on each side of her in their wooden shoes with their red handkerchiefs round their heads and surrounded by all my dogs barking joyously in anticipation of their walk in Villa Borghese —a familiar sight to the whole Piazza di Spagna in those days. Giovannina and Rosina belonged to the San Michele household, better servants I have never had, light of hand and foot, singing the whole day at their work. Of course nobody but I could ever have dreamt of taking these two half-tamed Anacapri girls to Rome. It would besides never have worked had not Miss Hall turned up in time to become a sort of foster-mother to them, to watch over them with the solicitude of an old hen over her chickens. Miss Hall said she could never understand why I did not allow the girls to walk about alone in the Villa Borghese, she had been walking all over Rome by herself for many years without anybody ever having taken any notice of her or said a word to her. True to her type Miss Hall had never succeeded in saying a single word of comprehensible Italian, but the girls understood her quite well and were very fond of her, although I fear they did not take her more seriously than I did. Of me Miss Hall saw very little, and I saw even less of her, I never looked at her when I could help it. On the rare occasions when Miss Hall was invited to be present at my luncheon, a huge flower vase was always placed on the table between us. Although Miss Hall was strictly forbidden to look at me, she nevertheless managed now and then to pop her head over the flower vase and have a shot at me from the corner of her old eye. Miss Hall never seemed to understand how beastly selfish and ungrateful I was in return for all she did for me. Considering her limited means of communication—Miss Hall was not allowed to ask me any questions— she succeeded somehow in finding out a good deal of what was going on in the house and what people I saw. She kept a vigilant eye on all my lady patients, she used to patrol the Piazza for hours to see them coming in and out during my consultations. With the opening of the Grand Hôtel, Ritz had dealt a final blow to the vanishing simplicity of Roman life. The last invasions of the barbarians had begun, the Eternal City had become fashionable. The huge hotel was crammed with the smart set from London and Paris, American millionaires and leading rastaqouères from the Riviera. Miss Hall knew all these people by name, she had watched them for years through the society columns of the "Morning Post." As to the English nobility Miss Hall was a perfect encyclopedia. She knew by heart the birth and the coming of age of their sons and heirs, the betrothal and the marriage of their daughters, the dresses they had worn when presented at Court, their dances, their dinner-parties, their journeys abroad. Many of these smart people ended by becoming my patients whether they wanted it or not, to the huge delight of Miss Hall. Others, unable to be alone a single moment, invited me to lunch or dinner. Others called at Piazza di Spagna to see the room Keats had died in. Others stopped their carriages in the Villa Borghese to pat my dogs with some complimentary words to Miss Hall how well they were groomed. Gradually Miss Hall and I emerged hand in hand from our natural obscurity into the higher spheres of society. I went out a good deal that winter. I had still a lot to learn from these easy-going idlers, their capacity for doing nothing, their good spirits, their good sleep puzzled me. Miss Hall now kept a special diary of the social events of my daily life. Beaming with pride she trotted about in her best frock leaving my cards right and left. The lustre of our ascending star grew brighter and brighter, higher and higher went our way, nothing could stop us any more. One day as Miss Hall was walking with the dogs in the Villa Borghese a lady with a black poodle on her lap signalled to her to come up to her carriage. The lady patted the Lapland dog and said it was she who had given Tappio as a tiny puppy to the doctor. Miss Hall felt her old knees shaking under her, it was H. R. H. the Crown Princess of Sweden! A beautiful gentleman, seated by her illustrious side, stretched out his hand with a charming smile and actually said:

"Hullo, Miss Hall, I have heard a lot about you from the doctor."

It was H. R. H. Prince Max of Baden, the husband of nobody less than the niece of her beloved Queen Alexandra! From that memorable day Miss Hall abandoned the smart set of the Grand Hôtel to devote all her spare time to royalties, there were at least half-a-dozen of them that winter in Rome. She stood for hours outside their hotels waiting for a chance to see them coming in or out, she watched them with bent head driving on the Pincio or in the Villa Borghese, she followed them like a detective in the churches and the museums. On Sundays she sat in the English church in Via Babuino as near to the Ambassador's pew as she dared, with one eye on her prayer-book and the other on a Royal Highness, straining her old ear to catch the particular sound of the royal voice in the singing of the congregation, praying for the Royal Family and their relations in every land with the fervour of an early Christian.

Soon Miss Hall started another diary, entirely devoted to our associations with Royalty. The previous Monday she had had the honour to carry a letter from the doctor to H. R. H. the Grand Duchess of Weimar at the Hôtel Quirinale. The porter had given her an answer adorned with the Grandducal crown of Saxe and Weimar. The envelope had been graciously presented to her by the doctor as a precious souvenir. On Wednesday she had been entrusted with a letter for H. R. H. the Infanta Eulalia of Spain in the Grand Hôtel. Unfortunately there was no answer. One afternoon, as she was with the dogs in the Villa Borghese, Miss Hall had noticed a tall lady in black walking rapidly up and down a side alley. She recognized her at once as the same lady she had seen in the garden of San Michele, standing motionless by the Sphinx and ooking out over the sea with her beautiful, sad eyes. As the lady passed before her now, she said something to her companion and stretched out her hand to pat Gialla, the borzoi. Judge of Miss Hall's consternation when a detective came up to her and told her to move on at once with the dogs—it was H. I. H. the Empress of Austria and her sister Countess Trani! How could the doctor have been so cruel not to have told her in the summer? Only by a mere accident did she know much later that a week after the lady's visit to San Michele the doctor had received a letter from the Austrian Embassy in Rome with an offer to buy San Michele and that the would-be purchaser was no less a person than the Empress of Austria. Luckily the doctor had declined the offer, it would indeed be a pity if he should sell a place like San Michele with such unique opportunities for seeing Royalties! Had she not last summer for weeks been watching at a respectful distance a granddaughter of her own beloved Queen Victoria, painting in the pergola! Had not a cousin of the Tsar himself been living there for a whole month! Had she not had the honour to stand behind the kitchen door to see the Empress Eugénie pass before her at arm's length the first time she came to San Michele! Had she not heard with her own ears H. I. H. say to the doctor that she had never seen a more striking likeness to the great Napoleon than the head of Augustus the doctor had dug up in his garden! Had she not several years later heard the commanding voice of the Kaiser himself lecturing to his suite on the various antiquities and works of art as they passed along accompanied by the doctor who hardly opened his mouth! Close to where she stood hidden behind the cypresses, H. I. H. had pointed to a female torso half covered by the ivy and told his suite that what they saw was worthy of a place of honour in his Museum in Berlin, for all he knew it might be an unknown masterpiece by Phidias himself. Horror-struck Miss Hall had heard the doctor say it was the only fragment in San Michele that was not good. It had been dumped upon him by a well-meaning patient who had bought it in Naples, it was Canova at his worst. To Miss Hall's great regret the party had left almost immediately for the Marina to embark on their dispatch boat Sleipner for Naples.

A propos of the Empress of Austria I must tell you, that Miss Hall was a K. C. of the Imperial Order of St. Stefan. This high distinction had been bestowed upon Miss Hall one day by me when my conscience must have been particularly bad, as a reward for her faithful services to me and my dogs. Why it had been bestowed upon myself I had never succeeded in understanding. Miss Hall received this decoration from my hands with bent head and tear-filled eyes. She said she would take it with her to her grave. I said I saw no objection, she was sure to go to Heaven anyhow. But that she would take it with her to the British Embassy I had not anticipated. I had succeeded in obtaining from Lord Dufferin an invitation for Miss Hall to the reception at the Embassy in honour of the Queen's birthday, all the English colony in Rome having been invited except poor Miss Hall. Overwhelmed with joyful anticipation Miss Hall had been invisible for several days, hard at work with her toilette. Judge of my consternation when on presenting Miss Hall to her ambassador, I saw Lord Dufferin screw in his monocle and stare speechless at Miss Hall's sternum. Luckily Lord Dufferin was not an Irishman for nothing. All he did was to take me aside with a roar of laughter and make me promise to keep Miss Hall out of sight of his Austrian colleague. Miss Hall told me as we drove home that it had been the proudest day of her life. Lord Dufferin had been most gracious to her, everybody had smiled at her, she felt sure her toilette had been a great success.

Yes, it is all very well to make fun of Miss Hall! But I should like to know what will become of Royalty when Miss Hall is no more there to keep a diary of their doings, to watch them with shaking knees and bent head driving on the Pincio and in the Villa Borghese, to pray for them in the English church of Via Babuino? What will become of their stars and ribbons when mankind will have outgrown playing with toys? Why not give them all to Miss Hall and be done with them!

We have had occasion to refer at various points in this book to the personality and writings of Montaigne. He was one of the earliest and greatest of modern writers. He stands among writers as does Rembrandt among painters or Mozart among composers, a complete man, finding complete satisfaction in his chosen art. Notice how adequately he is portrayed in the following selection. It is not a mere character sketch, but a biography in miniature.

MICHEL DE MONTAIGNE [1]
Llewelyn Powys

On a lichen-covered wall of an ancient château which for long ages had stood "amid the fat noonday Gascon scenery," these words, carved deeply in the crumbling masonry, were to be read by the curious for many generations: "In the year of our Lord 1571, at the age of thirty-eight, on the last day of February, being the anniversary of his birth, Monsieur de Montaigne, long weary of the service of the Court and of public employments, while still in his full vigour, betook himself to the bosom of the nine learned virgins." Could anything have been more significant of the character, tastes, and sturdy Epicurean aplomb of the man to whom they owed their origin?

In every sense that the gracious phrase implies, Montaigne was first and last "a good European" and not one inclined to set aside the true values of life. A generous lover of leisure, of spiritual and physical well-being, of curious meditations, of quaint erudition, he was by no means a man to suffer his days to slide by unnoticed because of an overzealous preoccupation with the illusive activities that belong to everyday life. It is said that Montaigne was an eleven months' child, and indeed in his shrewd, slow-moving constitution—so full of a mature sanity—there is something that goes to suggest a longer time in the making than is granted to most mortal men.

He was born in a turbulent and unsettled age, an age as bewildered with difficulties and confusions as is our own, and yet was able to reach to an adjustment with life which for civilized poise has scarcely been surpassed before or since. He was fortunate in his upbringing. He owed his lifelong enthusiasm "for the greatness of old Greek and Roman life" to the eccentric theories of his father, who, while Michel was a child, would have no word spoken in the château, not even by

[1] *Thirteen Worthies*, Harcourt, Brace and Company, 1923, reprinted by permission of the publishers.

the servants, except it was Latin. Indeed, so thoroughly was the rule kept that a hundred years later certain Latin nouns were found to have lingered on in the mouths of the ploughmen and vine tenders employed about the eighteen farms that constituted the broad estates of the castle.

It has been remarked that another refining influence invaded the spirit of the sun-tanned, broad-mouthed *seigneur*—his meeting with Estienne de la Böetie. It happened, so it always seemed to Montaigne, "by some secret appointment of Heaven," and without doubt it did more than anything else in his life to impart to his jocund, earthbound nature a suspicion that there might be, possibly, after all, abroad in the world an unutterable something above and beyond what his eager and insatiable senses saw and felt. The memory of his dead friend was never out of his mind. Twenty years later, he tells us, when he was bathing in the waters of Lucca, the thought of the irremediable loss he had sustained by this death swept suddenly over his soul with unrebated bitterness. It was the one experience of his life that perplexed and astounded the old skeptic, the one experience capable of endowing his style with a new tone of passionate inspiration. There is a certain pathos in observing how rattled and put about the old egoist was by this tragic and unexpected revelation—the old red fox caught at last in the gin of the absolute! Craftily he scans the familiar landscape of his mind. How could this be? The explanation of this! what was it? "Because it was he, because it was I" is all that he, the master "idealclast," finds it in him to say.

For the most part, however, he was able to survey the grotesque panorama of human life with a massive and indelible satisfaction. It pleased him mightily to hold discourse with two aboriginals from the New World whom he lit upon in Rouen. They had come, he tells us, "to learn the wisdom of Europe" and were "men of dignity, although they wore no breeches." He liked to note the fact that "tortoises and ostriches hatch their eggs with only looking on them, which infers that their eyes have in them ejaculative virtue," that "Xerxes was a coxcombical blockhead," that "Carneades was so besotted with knowledge that he would not find time so much as to comb his head or to pare his nails," and that there existed a certain nation that fed on spiders—"Yea, made provision of them and fed them for their tables, as also they did grasshoppers, mice, lizards, and bats; and in a time of a scarcity of such delicacies a toad was sold for six crowns, all which they cook and dish up with several sauces." It amused him to observe that when the vines of his village were nipped with frost "his parish priest presently concluded that the indignation of God is gone out against *all the human race.*"

But his interests were by no means confined to such objective observations. There was nothing that diverted him so much as to mark down his own peculiar tastes and idiosyncrasies, whether at home in his cheerful, sunlit tower, or abroad on horseback, wrapped about in the dark, threadbare mantle that had belonged to his father, "because it seemed to envelop me in him."

Nobody prognosticated that I should be wicked, but only useless; they foresaw idleness, but no malice; and I find it falls out accordingly.

I never inquire, when I am to take a footman, if he be chaste, but if he be diligent; and am not solicitous if my muleteer be given to gaming, as if he be strong and able, or if my cook be a swearer, if he be a good cook. . . .

The generality of more solid sort of men look upon abundance of children as a great blessing; I and some others think it a great benefit to be without them.

I love stout expressions amongst gentlemen and to have them speak as they think.

I love rain and to dabble in the dirt as well as ducks do.

I give great authority to my propensions and desires. To be subject to the stone and subject to abstention from eating oysters are two evils instead of one.

I have ever loved to repose myself whether sitting or lying, with my heels as high or higher than my seat.

I do not remember that I ever had the itch, and yet scratching is one of nature's sweetest gratifications . . . I use it most on my ears, which are often apt to itch.

We have in us notions that are inconsistent and for which no reason can be given; for example, I found radishes first grateful to my stomach, since that nauseous, and now again grateful.

At the little jerks of oars, stealing the vessel from under me, I find, I know not how, both my head and my stomach disordered.

'Tis indecent, beside the hurt it does to one's health and even to the pleasure of eating, to eat so greedily as I do. I often bite my tongue and sometimes my fingers, in my haste.

To the end that even sleep itself should not so stupidly escape from me, I have formerly caused myself to be disturbed in my sleep, so that I might the better and more sensibly relish and taste it.

I have never put myself to great pains to curb the desires by which I have found myself beset. My virtue is a virtue, or rather an innocence, which is purely random and accidental.

From these and similar utterances what a vivid picture is evoked of the genial, philosophic old aristocrat. His short, thickset figure, tough and individual as one of his own gnarled vine stumps, is never out of our sight as we review the various events of his life. There he stands superintending the construction of the lighthouse at Bordeaux for the better direction of the mariners returning from that New World which had so intrigued his imagination; there he sits, goose quill in hand, composing the letter in which he proffered his resignation from the mayoralty of the city, for no better reason, forsooth, than the personal apprehension that he felt with regard to the plague. "For my part, I am of the mind that if a man can by any means avoid danger, though by creeping under a calf's skin, I am one that would not be ashamed of the shift." We see him on his travels observing how ill-favored were the faces of German women, buying a new fur hat at Augsburg, or rating a Swiss tavern keeper because his table was ill provided with crayfish! We see him at Rome attending Christmas Mass, or walking the streets, which through his reading were as familiar to him as those of Paris, impatient sometimes of the Renaissance buildings which cluttered up the monumental foundations that were so dear to his heart. They resemble, he thinks, the martins' and jackdaws' nests that adhere to the shattered fragments of the churches in France which had been brought to ruin by the ravages of the Huguenots.

Two volumes of his *Essays* were found in his trunks and fell into the hands of the ecclesiastical censor. He was brought to task by Pope Gregory. He himself willingly enough condemns them beforehand, out of hand, "if so be anything should be found in his rhapsodies contrary to the Catholic Apostolic and Roman Church into which I was born and in which I shall die," and then returns to France to publish from the safe retreat of his castle the very passages to which exception has been taken. He visits the unfortunate Tasso in his convent at Ferrara, and in the papal library peers curiously at the writing of St. Thomas Aquinas, which he observes to be even more illegible than his own. "I cannot even write properly myself, so that when I have finished a scrawl I had rather rewrite it than give myself the trouble of deciphering it." He makes friends with Anthony Bacon, a brother of the great Francis, and embarks upon a correspondence with him. His zest for life is insatiable. He indulges the fancy of being given the full citizenship of Rome. To be a Roman citizen! One can understand how of all others he would covet that distinction. He pursues his purpose "with all his five natural senses" and is accorded the honour. He goes about glancing now at this damsel, now at that, never failing to allow due credit for beauty and charm.

But, of course, it is at home, in his serene and hospitable château of St. Michel de Montaigne, that we are able to envisage him best. Here, within those cool, stone-flagged courtyards, the gates of which stood ever open to welcome king or beggar, "having no other guard than my porter, no other sentinel than the stars," his extraordinary personality, "virgin from all law suits," and "harbouring but a perplexed and uncertain knowledge about his money," found full scope for placid, unhampered development. Alternately, to and fro across the neighboring countryside, the warring factions passed, devastating all that came in their way. But it would seem that both Catholic and Huguenot felt a strange reluctance to trouble the residence of the old, indulgent, philosophic opportunist, who, as he himself declares, would be as ready, at a pinch, to carry a taper "before the Dragon as before St. George." Decade followed decade, and still the château of Montaigne remained intact on its green eminence, a symbol of civilized humanism and happy tolerance amid a crazed and distracted world.

In the famous room of his tower, surrounded by a library of over a thousand folios, Montaigne passed his days in peace, disturbed only by the reverberating echoes of the great bell above him as it was rung morning and evening for the Ave Marias to be held in the castle chapel below. Here it was that the stout, good-natured, weather-beaten philosopher, crossing himself, as he tells us, whenever he yawned, composed his essays, played with his cat, or interviewed that honest lad that he had to his tailor, "whom I never knew guilty of one truth," or ate his bread without salt, or drank the wine "that they mix in the buttery two or three hours before 'tis brought in," and even then, old hedonist that he was, "not willingly out of common glass, but in those that are clear and transparent."

We are made to see the passing of his easy, indolent days almost as clearly as if we ourselves had shared with Henry of Navarre the privilege of being his guest. Sometimes, when the mood was upon him, he would go down into the great hall and play cards with wife and daughter, or take a stroll in his secluded orchard. Then, again, with whimsical, incredulous eye, he would stand watching his long-suffering lady busying herself with her aromatic simples and medicinal herbs, or the inexpedient ways of the governess with his daughter, Léonore. Tired of this, he would go riding abroad over his lands, and although, as he confesses, he had "no manner of complacency for husbandry," he would while away his time talking to this or that familiar rustic, for he always, as he tells us, "had an inclination towards the meaner sort of people." Wherever he went there beat under his doublet a spleenless and generous heart, a heart unexpectedly tender, as, for instance, when he assures us he could with difficulty watch a chicken being killed or hear the cries of a hare in her agony when the dogs had got her. Always simply enough dressed in black and white "in imitation of my father," he would return from such homely excursions to the perusal of his Plutarch or even to the reading of Cicero, though he remarks that an hour with this latter formal stylist "was a great deal for him."

Little enough is known of his wife, the Lady Françoise de la Chassaigne. It is apparent that Montaigne's attitude toward her was one of indulgent tolerance not unmingled with contempt.

> Feminine policy has a mysterious course and we must e'en let them go on their own way.
>
> There is a natural feud, a fray, between us and women; the closest agreement that we have with them is more or less turbulent and stormy.
>
> I see and I am vexed to see, in several families I know, Monsieur about dinner time comes home all jaded and ruffled about his affairs when Madame is still pouncing and tricking up herself, forsooth, in her closet. This is for queens to do, and that's a question too; 'tis ridiculous and unjust that the laziness of our wives should be maintained with our sweat and labour.
>
> The pains of childbearing, said by the physicians and by God himself to be very great, *and which our women keep such a clutter about* —there are whole nations that make nothing of them.
>
> I for my part went ever the plain way to work.
>
> I love to lie hard and alone, yea, even without my wife, as kings do.
>
> And as great a libertine as I am taken to be, I have in truth more strictly observed the laws of marriage than I either promised or expected.
>
> Who for seeing me one while cold and presently very fond towards my wife, believes the one or the other to be counterfeited is an ass.

There have been many who have had it in them to dispute Montaigne's claim to be considered as a serious philosopher. They are mistaken. If wisdom is philosophy, what a rich store of it is contained in these quaint, closely written pages. It is Shakespearean wisdom, a wisdom that is simple and that springs as naturally from the pasturelands and parks of Warwickshire as from the vineyards of Guyenne.

When we loiter near some place full of suggestions of age-long human usages—a graveyard perhaps, or a sheep-shearing barton, or a black-smith's forge when horseshoeing is in progress—and overhear some pithy comment that seems to have the very sap of life in it, we are listening to the voice of Montaigne. John Cowper Powys, in his *Suspended Judgments*, has after his poetic manner expressed this most excellently:

> The wisdom of Montaigne is the wisdom of lazy noons in spacious corn-fields, of dewy mornings in misty lanes and moss-grown paths; of dreamy shadows in deep grass when the apple boughs hang heavily earthward, and long nights of autumn rain have left amber-coloured pools in the hollow places of the trees and in the mud trodden by the cattle. . . . It is the wisdom of the earth itself; shrewd, friendly, full of unaccountable instincts; obstinate and capricious, given up to irrational and inexplicable superstitions, sluggish, suspicious, cautious, hostile to theory, enamoured of inconsistencies, humorously critical of all ideals, realistic, empirical, wayward.

Montaigne himself affirmed that there should be "nothing more airy, more gay, more frolic, and I had like to have said more wanton, than philosophy"; and certainly if one takes some of his utterances at random one is astounded at the deep, laetificant sagacity which they reveal. In the mean, famished period in which we live, wherein ill-bred industrial commercialism masquerades as civilized life, how consoling, how infinitely restorative they are, as it were like great dripping combs of golden honey gathered from I know not what distant blossoms!

> Man (in good earnest) is a marvelous, vain, fickle, and unstable subject, and one on whom it is very hard to form a certain and uniform judgment.

> I would always have a man to be doing . . . and then let death take me planting my cabbages, indifferent to him and still less to my garden's not being finished.

> They begin to teach us to live when we have almost done living. . . .

> There is indeed a certain low and moderate sort of poetry, that a man may well enough judge of certain rules of art; but the true supreme and divine poetry is above all rules and reason . . . it does not exercise but ravishes and overwhelms our judgments.

> All whimsies as are in use amongst us deserve at least a hearing. . . .

Women are not in the wrong when they refuse the rules of life obtaining in the world; it is the man who made these laws without them.

The for and the against are both possible.

I am a man and nothing human is alien to me.

So taken was Montaigne himself with the last two sentences that he caused them to be engraved upon the ceiling of his tower. It seems he was often in doubt concerning the intrinsic value of his writings, though he never allowed such misgivings to ruffle his accustomed equanimity. "I do not, nevertheless, always believe myself; I often hazard sallies of my own wit, wherein I very much suspect myself and shake my ears; but I let them go at a venture." After all, what did it matter? "If I should have a long life my memory is so bad that I believe I shall forget my own name. So greatly do I excel in forgetfulness that even my writings are forgotten. The public dealeth me blows about them, and I do not feel them." Should his papers eventually be used as wrappers he makes little of it: "I shall at least keep some pats of butter from melting in the market."

Montaigne died at his château in his sixtieth year. The grapes that covered so closely those sun-drenched, hand-cultivated slopes had already been harvested, and already the trees that held with so firm a root to the opulent soil of his broad acres were changing colour. "In the last piece between death and you there is no pretending; you must speak French."

On 13 September, 1592, Michel de Montaigne, having distributed certain legacies to his servants, summoned his parish priest to his bedside, and there in his curious room with the swallows already gathering on the leaden gutters outside, he heard Mass said for the last time in the company of certain of his neighbours. With due solemnity the blessed sacrament was elevated, and at the very moment that this good heretical Catholic and Catholic heretic (unmindful for once of his nine learned virgins) was raising his arms in seemly devotion toward the sacred morsel which in its essence—*que sçais-je*—might, or might not, contain a subtle and crafty secret, he fell back dead.

CHAPTER IX

Criticism

CRITICISM IS ONE of the forms most popular with modern readers—and one of the most difficult to write successfully. It requires wealth of cultural background and maturity of judgment as well as skill in expression. George Jean Nathan, one of our cleverest dramatic critics, remarks: "For every hundred men who have succeeded in writing good drama, you will be at pains to discover one who has succeeded in writing good dramatic criticism." The mathematics of this statement may be slightly inaccurate, but something of the sort is true of other types of criticism. As Pope more conservatively put the matter, "Ten censure wrong for one who writes amiss." Both authorities point to the particular dangers in the critic's adventure—the threat of easy error. In other kinds of prose there are "nine and sixty ways," to quote Kipling, "and every single one of them is right." In critical writing there seem to be a million ways to be wrong.

Nevertheless, there is no reason why the rudiments of the critical method should not be learned as early as possible. There is nothing better than critical study of good, bad, and indifferent writing to sharpen one's sense of word and phrase. We are not concerned here with the philosophy of beauty or with the history of criticism. Interesting and valuable as they are, they are not essential in learning to write simple criticism. On the other hand, it is useful to know something of the rather distinctive types of criticism. There are at least six of these, each representing a special purpose and manner. These will be discussed briefly; but only the latter three are of importance for the daily work of serious critical appraisal, and for the first ventures in critical writing.

First, there is what may be called purely *impressionistic criticism*.

163

This type is highly subjective, and usually it takes the tone of rather extravagant rhapsody. When the critic lavishes on his object a flood of tender and luscious language, he is indulging in an extreme manifestation of the impressionistic method. The true spirit of criticism has been lost. The critic has substituted his own emotional nature, his ego, for the elements that are actually in the work. It should be remembered, though, that the tone of bitter disillusionment of modern criticism is often just as false as the gushing that was once the fashion. Impressionistic criticism can have value only in proportion to the mental stability and integrity and the vital experience of the critic. Where it is successful, as with Coleridge and Walter Pater, it reveals the powers emphasized in less personal types of criticism.

A second type to be avoided by the novice is *bibliographical* or *textual criticism*. This type, immensely important, is also highly technical. It involves the study of manuscripts and various editions of a work with the aim of producing as correct an edition as possible. While there are sometimes questionable and varying versions of recent works, the main field for this type of criticism is in connection with older authors, notably Shakespeare. Most of the plays were not even printed in Shakespeare's lifetime; and those that were printed often appeared in widely differing texts. The textual critic tries to get a text as close as possible to what Shakespeare wrote, or intended, for *Hamlet, Romeo and Juliet, Richard III*, or other plays which offer endless puzzles by conflicting readings in various versions. Obviously this type of criticism belongs only to advanced study.

The third type, *genetic criticism*, is also the province of the specialist. Called by the French "explication du texte," it seeks to trace the minutest details of idea and expression in a literary work, scrutinizing even the separate word to determine the ultimate origin of the impulse that led to its selection. This microscopic method reveals many secrets of the style and habits of thought that are the core of an author's art. While formal writing of this type of criticism should perhaps not be attempted by the beginning writer, it is useful to examine even such papers as have been written in this course for genetic details. What is the source of the ideas? What sources have been used with best effect, and how can they be amplified by wider reading or closer observation? We are all inclined to ask ourselves, now and then: "Now where did I get that idea?" That is the starting point of the genetic approach.

There remain, now, three types of criticism, any one of which can be learned and used, not only in literary study, but for history and the multifarious social studies as well. The first may be called *interpretive criticism*, or, for a more limited term, *thesis criticism*. It is essentially a sane appreciative criticism, free of the objectionable intrusions of personal feeling that marred impressionistic criticism. The critic sets down in the first paragraph a point of view, pro or con, with regard to the object of his criticism. Then he attempts to substantiate this view, or thesis, in the remainder of his treatment. Thus, in one of the student themes in this chapter you will find the writer criticizing the critics for their varying and conflicting theses concerning the romantic novel *Anthony Adverse*. Yet it would be impossible for any critic to deal with every detail of such a notoriously long work; he can only drive home one or two points that seem to him most significant. Criticism exists in an atmosphere of conflicting tastes and convictions. It is the function of the critic to attack or defend. Thus he may develop the thesis that "Thackeray's *Vanity Fair* is a fine novel because its characters are alive and real," or he may press the negative view that "*Vanity Fair* is a faulty novel because its structure is loose." He is not attempting to state the *whole* truth, but to establish *a* truth, one that seems to him vital to a clear understanding of the work. This type of criticism should be supported, not alone by firm conviction, but by ample evidence as well.

The next useful type of criticism is *judicial criticism*. The judicial critic views the problem in terms of established law and recognized precedent. Here a large element of sound judgment is necessary, as the law does not interpret itself. The critic must often select the standards which he is to apply himself, and always he must apply them in as impartial and disinterested a manner as possible. Matthew Arnold's "A Study of Poetry" will illustrate this type of criticism. Another excellent example is the article "Poe as a Critic," parts of which have been reprinted below.

The first step in writing judicial criticism is to set down a list of reputable standards pertinent to the general class within which the object of criticism lies. For example, if the criticism is to deal with a mystery story, establish a set of standards which cover the ideal requirements for such stories; and then decide, step by step, whether the story in question meets these standards. The same technique can, of course, be applied to a critical examination of the newest automobile, a candidate for public office, the conduct of youth, or any other subject of current interest. The chief danger involved in the writing of judicial criticism lies in the possibility of getting an inadequate or faulty set of critical standards. Aside from this difficulty, the actual working out of the criticism is usually simple. In order to arrive at a final statement of truth, however, it is necessary to take pains to avoid being biased or arbitrary.

The final type, *historical criticism*, is the most difficult and yet perhaps the most interesting to attempt. It lies closest to the heart of the modern attitude toward experience, for it is primarily concerned with the "why" of things. Modern Shakespearean criticism, a good gauge of the shifts in critical attitudes, is saturated with it. It pervades much current writing on all manner of subjects. Hence college students should know about its methods and use it as early as possible.

Historical criticism is the attempt to judge an event, a character, or a work of art, in terms of the standards and influences of its own age. The writer must project himself in imagination back to the period in which the object of his interest belongs, and interpret its value in the proper perspective. While analogous methods will have to be worked out for non-literary subjects, it will be useful to point out six prominent modes of approach in dealing with poetry and prose. These are listed in diagram form to facilitate comparison.

1. The author's language. Shakespeare must be interpreted in terms of Elizabethan usage, not ours.

2. The author's life. Biography may reveal aspects of the work not ascertainable by other means. The "love life" of the author is a preoccupation of much recent criticism; but professional interests, such as Hardy's training in architecture, may be highly important.

3. Literary sources. Extensive reading in works of seafaring lie back of *Robinson Crusoe* and "The Ancient Mariner." Light on the tragedies of Shakespeare may be derived from knowledge of earlier plays.

4. Historical background. Events, political, social, and religious ideas, the general outlook of a period, must often be understood before the work can be validly interpreted. Without this knowledge, Swift's *Gulliver's Travels* is a child's wonder book; with it, a brilliant satire full of social meaning.

5. Other works of the same period. Comparison may show that devices that appear to be strange or implausible (for example, the thin disguises, the asides, and soliloquies of Shakespeare) were used by his contemporaries and were quite within the expectations of the audience. Extremely sentimental language and ideas in a novel may be merely the normal expression of a sentimental period, such as the age of social reform and emotional letdown following the Napoleonic Wars.

6. History of the text. Often successive productions of a drama or publications of a novel bring about changes, excisions, additions, revisions. Thomas Gray was polishing the churchyard "Elegy" over a period of at least seven years. There are four stanzas which were not even included in the final version. Manuscripts of novels often have strange adventures before they reach a "definitive" edition.

All in all, historical criticism embraces a variety of possibilities; and often a profound problem, such as the conduct of Prince Hamlet, may call for the best utilization of all of them. While the type has been sketched here for literary works, as has been pointed out, it need not be restricted to these. Public achievements, economic and social theories, inventions and fads, in fact anything that is subject to evaluation (including judicial criticism itself) may be judged by the methods of historical criticism, provided, of course, that the subject lies far enough back in the past to have historical status, that is, usually before 1900.

It should be remembered that the prime objective of criticism is to explain, to establish clear meanings, not to produce pure types of the six or more modes indicated above. It is quite possible, of course, to apply all three of the preferred types, interpretive, judicial, and historical, to the same subject. Thus *Vanity Fair* can be criticized with the thesis approach, as mentioned above; or, in turn, it can be studied in terms of judicial standards for the social or psychological novel; or, finally, it can be analyzed in terms of the historical conditions in England of the day it describes, the period of Waterloo, the events of Thackeray's life, his reading, or other external forces that may have affected the actual working out of the novel. Choice of the method to be used may be determined by the nature of the work, or it may merely be a matter of the writer's personal preference.

It is always helpful to have a definite schedule of procedure in writing criticism. The following pattern may be used until the critical method has been fully grasped.

   I. Statement of Thesis or Set of Judicial Standards
   II. Descriptive Summary
   III. Proof or Application of Thesis
   IV. The Other Side
   V. Conclusion: Back to the Thesis

This requires some explanation. Part I is explained in the paragraph just above on the three possible ways of approaching *Vanity Fair.* Part II is pure exposition[1]—the kind of exercise discussed above in Chapter IV. You will have to tell the reader just what the mechanical object is that you are criticizing (an autogyro, for example), or, if you are judging a literary work, you will have to summarize its content briefly. Note that we said *briefly;* this section must be short and concise. Part III is the central— and longest—feature of the theme; in it you give the evidence which will substantiate your point of view as set forth in Part I. If you have decided that *Vanity Fair* is a good novel because of its real characters, here is the place to adduce illustrations of the realistic characterization. If you have set up precise standards in Part I for a good automobile, here is the place to apply them to the Ford car. If you have pointed out in Part I that Hardy's descriptions are too technical because of his architectural training, here is the spot to bring in the descriptions which prove your point. Part III, then, is the most important section of the whole criticism: by it the thesis stands or falls.

Part IV gives "the other side." It will be hard, sometimes, to

---

[1] No critical adjectives or adverbs should be injected into this section.

see another side. You have decided that the object is either very good or very bad, and you will perhaps be so intensely sure of this point of view that you will not succeed in seeing anything of the opposite tendency in it. But criticism must be fair and "disinterested," as Arnold put it. Nothing is so bad generally that some good cannot be found in it; similarly nothing is so exquisitely perfect that it contains no flaws. In IV, then, point out that though the characterization of *Vanity Fair* is as a whole admirable, there are one or two characters who have become mere caricatures (Sir Pitt Crawley, Sr., for example). The Ford car may be a fine car and meet most of the standards required, but it will probably fall short in one or two respects. Hardy's architectural training may have injured his descriptions, but, on the other hand, it may have given him a sense of structure which is generally apparent in all of his novels. Be fair in IV; try to see the other side; but do not see too much of the other side, or your original contention will appear to have been wrong. Part IV saves your criticism from argument—especially from contentiousness.

Part V, the conclusion, merely returns to the main thesis as the parting corroboration of your decision. It may consist of no more than one sentence, often attached to the final paragraph of IV. With regard to the division of the other parts, I and II generally have one paragraph each, while III has several. But your own judgment will often vary this part of the construction; your main task is to write an effective criticism, not a dull categorical list of remarks.

Obviously this is a mechanical presentation, but it will be found useful at least in the early stages of critical writing. A few hints and warnings are also in order.

First take a worth-while subject and begin at once with a distinct statement of Part I. In writing thesis criticism, try to pick out the main aspect of the subject, that is, the most significant thesis—whether good or bad—and in Part I state why it is good or bad. After you are thus started, do not prolong II and do not merge II and III; furthermore, make II perfectly clear to the ordinary reader, especially in the case of a technical subject. In III give plenty of evidence—the more the better—several quotations if necessary. Try not to become contentious, however, or too rhapsodic. After all, it is well to follow the advice of Matthew Arnold and be "disinterested."[1] When through with III, do not forget IV, and under no circumstances make it equal in length to III, unless you have adopted such a thesis of equality in I, a procedure which will be rare. Obviously you should not reverse the positions of III and IV, though students often try to do it. Do not omit V; an apt conclusion will increase the effect of unity in the presentation.

In the case of judicial criticism, be sure to test the validity and comprehensiveness of the standards adopted before going ahead to apply them. It is doubtful whether you can write judicial and thesis criticism in the same theme; in general keep the methods separate. At the end of a judicial criticism do not forget to state your decision based on the application of the standards—in other words, do not forget Part V.

In the case of historical criticism, write out the historical thesis directly in Part I. For example: Thackeray's life did not train him in the knowledge of high society, so that *Vanity Fair* fails on this score. In II summarize briefly both Thackeray's life and *Vanity Fair*. Then go ahead with III. But you have to *relate* the man's life to his work, not simply give an account of his career and then an outline of his work. Often historical criticism is largely an *explanation* of some aspect of the work: thus in Part I you may note that the politics behind *Gulliver's Travels* make it an excellent satire. Part II summarizes the politics and the plot of *Gulliver's Travels* briefly, and in III you will put the two together: showing Walpole, Carteret, Nottingham, Middleton behind the apparently innocuous names of Flimnap, Reldresal, Bolgolam, and Munodi. However, do not stop with mere historical exposition; your historical thesis should generally point out a positive or negative value to be derived from this historical study of the work.

As to subjects: literary problems should perhaps be reserved for a second- or third-term theme; but the methods of criticism apply to any subject involving values and differences of taste and opinion. Subjects may be taken from lists in previous chapters. Students have effectively used such subjects as: An Athletic Coach,

[1] See Matthew Arnold's "The Function of Criticism," in *Essays in Criticism* (1865).

College Fraternities, Jazz Music, The Ford, The League of Nations, Fraternity Rushing, Player Pianos, Prohibition, Apartments, Professor D——'s Methods of Teaching, Bridge Fiends, Stenography, Co-education, Installment Buying, Superstition, Behaviorism, Women's Hats, Socialism, Campus Politics.

->>> A <<<-

Here is an example of successful thesis criticism, perfectly constructed.

THE CONCRETE BEEHIVE

Recently, a prominent beekeeper in this district invented a new type of concrete beehive which seems to have many advantages over the old wooden hive. The new hive greatly reduces the care the beekeeper has to give to his bees, especially during the wintertime.

The ordinary beehive is a square box with no top or bottom. This box has a ledge at each end on which the racks that hold the combs rest. The hive sits on a wooden or concrete base with an opening at one side to allow the bees to enter and leave. A top of wood completes the house. The new concrete hive is exactly like the older form except that the square box, the main part of the hive, is made of concrete with a layer of Celotex imbedded in the walls.

The main advantage of this new hive is due to the insulating effect of the concrete and the Celotex within the walls. In the summertime a thermometer was placed in both a new hive and an old hive sitting side by side. The temperature of the concrete box was about seven degrees cooler than that of the wooden box. In the wintertime, when the bees have to eat a lot of honey to keep the hive warm, the new hive reduces the danger of the food giving out and the bees freezing to death, because the walls keep the heat within the hive. The concrete hive also reduces the expense of packing the bees during the winter, since they can be left right where they stand.

The great disadvantage of the new form is that it is hard to handle, since it is much heavier and easier to break. Once a colony is placed on a stand it cannot be moved without a great deal of weight lifting.

The reduction of the loss of bees during the winter and the subsequent earlier strength of the bees in the spring seem greatly to outweigh the disadvantages due to the weight. In a few years the new hives will probably come into greater use, because of this saving.

L. L. M.

The next criticism seems to have gained fluency from a negative attitude induced through irritation. A response from some veteran stamp collector might bring forth a sample of spirited "positive" criticism,—that is, in favor of the type.

THE STAMP COLLECTOR

The rabid stamp collector is a nuisance to his friends (with the exception of other philatelists) and the despair of his family.

The stamp collector to whom I refer is not that individual who is occasionally stricken with the collecting fever, but who soon recovers and becomes normal again. I refer to the overly enthusiastic collector who is so intensely interested in stamps that he thinks stamps, talks stamps, dreams stamps, and almost eats stamps.

His conversation is punctuated with references to "perfs," watermarks, shadings, issues, first-day covers, and commemoratives—all of which is only an unintelligible gibberish to the uninitiated (and uninterested) outsider. Whatever or wherever the group of which the philatelist is a part, or whatever the subject under discussion, he eventually turns the conversation into stampy channels. Then he is happy.

He rushes home from his work of the day, hastily and almost unconsciously swallows a well-cooked and delicious meal, and then disappears into his stamp room. "Oh well," you say, "if he spends his time in a stamp room and keeps all his stamps there with him, he surely does not bother his family." But he does not stay in his stamp room, and he does not keep his stamps there. No indeed! He scatters his precious little pieces of paper hither and yon through the rest of the house, and is most astonished when he cannot find each and every one of them.

It is almost impossible to keep the rest of the house in order. No papers can be thrown out, for, in all probability, they are the corners of old envelopes containing stamps of unusual coloring or markings— and such stamps are valuable. No strong breezes must be created or allowed in a room containing stamps (and every room *does* contain them), for a strong breeze will blow the flimsy, fluttery little papers away.

Visitors to the stamp collector's home, as well as members of his own family, must be careful about sitting down suddenly. Oh no, this is not because of the stamps lurking here and there. It is because of the stamp tongs, magnifying glasses, perforation gauges, catalogues, and what not, which he continually leaves in unexpected places and positions. Of course he tries to keep his stamps and utensils in his stamp room but they do get scattered, and if people will only be a little careful and considerate, he will get them all put in order soon. His intentions are of the best, but his actions are a trifle disconcerting, to say the least.

The books which such a stamp collector reads are stamp books, the papers he buys are stamp papers, the plays or entertainments he enjoys are those in which some reference is made to stamps. When subjects foreign to philately are mentioned, he nods vaguely, and resumes his eternal searching for the unusual stamp. A clever writer has described the fanatical stamp collector thus:

> "Stamps are here, stamps are there,
> Lovely stamps—they're everywhere.
> Stamps are buzzing in my brain,
> Almost driving me insane.
> All the girls I've quite forgot,
> Other loves are simply not.
> Stamps—the luring little stamps,
> In my heart like gleaming lamps,
> Burn all day, glow all night.
> Stamps, you are my heart's delight."

Of course, stamp collecting has its commendable qualities. It is an interesting hobby, and often a profitable one. The occasional collector is quite bearable, and makes enjoyable company when he forgets stamps for a time.

It is the constant stamp collector, the collector who lives solely in the interest of stamps, who is a nuisance to his friends and the despair of his family.

C. S.

The next paper makes a rather precise use of judicial procedure. Was it the ideal method for this particular subject?

COLONEL J——, LIBRARIAN

Miss J—— is not an ideal librarian.

The ideal librarian should be courteous and agreeable; pleasant, both in manner and appearance; and above all, she must have some understanding of human nature. She should be willing to bestir herself, if necessary, to find reference books for readers.

Miss J——, then, is obviously not an ideal librarian because she is the possessor of none of the above qualities. She is neither courteous nor agreeable. She is unpleasant, and whatever psychology she may have learned during her years of training, she has evidently forgotten, or else she does not deign to practice the precepts of this science on the vulgar rabble about her in the library.

Miss J——'s belligerent traits have led frequenters of the library to speak of her as "Colonel J——." This librarian has shown surprising lack of tact in dealing with the younger generation. It is no uncommon thing in a small community library for those coming in to stop and talk a moment with friends already seated around the various tables. In a few seconds, greetings have been exchanged and comparative quiet again reigns, but for Miss J——, who is always willing to quibble over mere technicalities. She steps to the fore, telling the offenders that if they must talk, they can step into the other room (she means the little vestibule by the door). She not only gains a lot of ill will in this way, but what is more to the point, she seems bent on acquiring more and more of it.

For all her knowledge of books, Miss J—— has never found out that the Bible says, "A soft answer turneth away wrath." I remember one night when two little boys were unknowingly causing a little disturbance by their somewhat noisy remarks. Miss J—— went over to the boys and threatened forcibly to eject them if they didn't keep still! Now no self-respecting little boy could let a mere woman get away with anything like that, and so the fray was on! The boys made their remarks louder and funnier (at least it seemed that way to the high-school students in the back of the room who had long suffered her tyranny). In fact, the remarks were getting personal; all of which didn't detract any from the general hilarity. Miss J—— made good her threats and the boys got up to leave, but the last word was theirs. As they went out of the door, they shouted, "You're nothin' but an old crab." A loud snicker on the part of the audience followed this sally, and poor Miss J——, her face livid with mortification, went back to her desk, simply writhing in agony.

Miss J—— is not to be condemned too heartily for her bad breaks. She was not born in America. In her native country, discipline is more strict than in America, and she cannot acclimate herself to this laxity with regard to American young people. Then, too, her home life is far from cheerful; her mother is an invalid.

M. E.

We now present a good example of historical criticism.

SERGEI RACHMANINOFF

The gloomy passion that pervades the music of Sergei Rachmaninoff is understood when one considers the intense melancholy of his nature, and the weird environment that influenced him. He grew up in an odd provincial atmosphere which developed the moderation of his spirit. The life in Moscow, which was decidedly Bohemian with a very prominent bourgeois touch permeating, determined his aesthetics. The famous Moscow restaurants and gipsy choruses were characterized by an "atmosphere of continuous dissipation in which perhaps there was no merriment at all, but on the contrary, the most genuine, bitter, and impenetrable pessimism." What this life demanded of music was not harmony, but passion, feeling, languor, and heartache. It is not surprising then, that Rachmaninoff's music took this form. As conservatism was his standard, it was only natural that he should hate the Russian school of innovation in St. Petersburg. But as time went on and modernism took a firm hold of Russian music, it was inevitable that Rachmaninoff's compositions would, to a certain degree, have a modern tone of innovation. Examples of this are his student opera, *Aleko*, and his symphonic poem, *The Cliff*.

The Bohemian life with its ensuing temptations and dissipation had much to do with the spasmodic nature of his work. Also, the Conservatory of Moscow concentrated on music but did not give a general education which would enrich the culture of its students. Lack of culture limited the artistic horizon of the student, and great genius that Rachmaninoff is, his artistic efforts are limited because of that.

Rachmaninoff's *C-Sharp Minor Prelude* is an expression of his whole attitude toward life, the facing of a terrifying and unconquerable power, fate, or destiny. It shows his helpless horror before it, and his lapses into a dreaming state in order to escape from it. A great change took place in Rachmaninoff's music when he had himself cured of his Bohemian dissipation by a famous hypnotist physician named Dal'. Then the composer could view his passionate morbid moods in an impersonal manner, from an objective point of view, which is so necessary to every artist in his creative work. Soon after this, he composed his *Second Concerto*, which is much more gloomy and pessimistic, but, nevertheless, has an impenetrableness and majesty. Rachmaninoff suffers intensely when he is composing. Each one of his compositions is achieved at the cost of a part of himself. The intense sincerity of the man is evident in all his compositions.

S. S.

The comparative study is another type of historical criticism.

BARABAS AND SHYLOCK

The Jew of Malta, written by Christopher Marlowe a few years prior to Shakespeare's *Merchant of Venice*, is in some respects its prototype. Like Shylock, Barabas, the Jew of Malta, is stripped of his wealth by the Christians and has a daughter in love with a Gentile; yet here the resemblance ends. Barabas is so inhuman in his revenge that he inspires nothing but horror and aversion, while Shylock creates in us a feeling of sympathy and compassion.

The direct source of Barabas's character is not known, although there is a parallel between his life and that of Juan Marquis who lived in Portugal in the sixteenth century. After persecution in Portugal, Marquis fled to Constantinople, taking refuge with the Turks, allied himself with them, and used his wealth to gain revenge on the Christians. Shakespeare is indebted to Marlowe's *Jew of Malta*, *Il Pecorone*, and *The Orator* for his material. The plot of *The Merchant of Venice* when taken apart is found to belong to several widespread and very old traditions. The right to take payment in flesh of an insolvent debtor is admitted in the Twelve Tables of Rome drawn up in 451 B.C. The story of the bond is also found in Buddhist legend. The only actual record of a pound of flesh being claimed was in Rome. The claimant was a Christian and the victim a Jew. In this instance, the Christian demanded the pound of flesh, and Pope Sixtus hearing this, sentenced Gentile and Jew to death, later pardoning them. This incident took place in 1585, nine years before *The Merchant of Venice* was written.

The plot of *The Jew of Malta* consists of a number of crimes and improbable events loosely strung together, and not interwoven with any great dramatic skill. This play has been called "a masterpiece of inhuman horror." No humor relieves its gloom as in *The Merchant of Venice*. A cross section of Barabas's character may be gained from what he says after he has poisoned all the nuns in the convent, one of whom is his daughter. He says: "How sweet the bells ring now the nuns are dead." And again: "I grieve because she lived so long a Hebrew born and she would become a Christian"—thus referring to his daughter.

Now let us turn to Shylock. During the time of Shakespeare, Shylock was presented as a comic character. In 1741, Charles Macklin, an Irish actor, defied tradition and played Shylock in a tragic mood. Since then Shylock has been portrayed variously. Shylock is really pitiful, even though Shakespeare did not intend that construction or interpretation of him. Throughout the whole play he is made the butt and target of the witticisms of the Christians from highest to lowest; he is treated with contempt on all sides, even by those who are his debtors; his daughter is ashamed of him and deserts him when he needs her the most. Barabas, on the other hand, cannot be pitied. There is no element of pity in him, and he is depicted as an inhuman and bloodthirsty monster. He does not demand sympathy even when thrown into a boiling caldron, as he remains unrepentant, heaping maledictions on the Christians. Shylock when sentenced to lose his property or turn Christian, accepts Christianity. After all, humanity is inclined to cringe and repent when placed in the shadow of death by torture, or accept compromises when about to be deprived of all possessions. On the whole, Shylock is the more human of the two characters. We cannot sympathize with Barabas as he is beyond our power of understanding, but we can pity Shylock because he is so downtrodden and so human. He possesses many of our own failings.

H. T.

This strictly literary criticism is in the light judicial manner. Its humor and informality lead easily into the material of the chapter on the informal essay in Part II.

"CAME THE DAWN"

"And the hero came pounding up in a cloud of dust just in time to rescue our lovely Nell from a fate worse than death at the hands of the sleek villain, Lord Dangerfield."

It's an old phrase, and hackneyed, I grant you; for it has been employed in like situations since literature began. Sir Thomas Malory probably threw it in at the climax, when his mailed knight took the enemy castle and rescued the fair maiden from the dungeon. It reigned in the "mauve decade," when the top-hatted gallant arrived at the scene of the outrage in a dashing coach-and-four, and challenged his adversary to a duel at sunrise for the insults which the hobble-skirted heroine had undergone. When the fearless private raided and captured the German machine-gun nest single-handed, and saved the beautiful American spy from torture for her refusal to reveal military secrets, "came the dawn" introduced the final dramatic moment. And after the war, when Louie the Lug and his thugs stormed the hangout of Butch and King Pin and grabbed off Louie's moll, what phrase could more appropriately indicate that the loving pair lived happily ever after?

Only modern cynics, masquerading under the guise of realists, have begun to suspect that perhaps the good old literary stand-by has become labelled, dated, and generally undesirable. "Why," they reason, "should the climax always arrive with the dawn?" They determine that if they are to be realists, they will be realists—gol dern it—and represent life as it is. Nineteen thirty-four drawing-room "draymas" even intimate that the crucial moment which used to be thus indicated has been known to occur before midnight. The more daring playwrights admit that it *might* even take place in the afternoon. To date no one has come out flat-footed and allowed the hero to do his rescuing until he has at least consumed a good lunch. This final piece of debunking is left to the fearless dramatists of the future.

But today's stories seem to lack something, and I believe that this literary rabbit's foot is what is missing. For twenty centuries audiences and readers have thrilled to the situations heralded by subtitle, "came the dawn." Knight or cavalier, private or racketeer, the hero satisfied some vital need of human society when he swept the heroine into his arms at the critical moment and carried her off, leaving the villain foiled and snarling. Nowadays such a scene would be laughed off the stage, say the writers. Sophisticated drawing-room comedy is what the public wants, they say. Plays with box-office appeal are those with plots which resemble froth. To be really successful, the aspiring young author is told, a play must mix its drama thoroughly with comedy. A divorced couple and their respective second mates meeting on their honeymoons in an ideal musical-comedy setting, is the general idea of the modern play. Wine, women, and song are liberally mixed in a dozen different titles, such as *Double Honeymoon*, *Meet the Missus*, *So Nice Seeing You*, *Matrimonial Exchange*, and so on.

But no matter how you slice it, it's still boloney, and no matter how you mix these ingredients, they are still the same, and after a while even the playgoing public begins to wake up and realize that it is being fooled. The writers and producers should have realized long ago that variety is more than the name of the magazine of the profession. Any form of life, if fed on one kind of diet too long, grows dyspeptic and loses its appetite. The rule of nature is the same whether the diet is bread and milk or pineapple tarts and champagne, although one might expect the former to be more healthful than the latter. Perhaps that explains why the plain old category of "came-the-dawn" plays lasted longer and were better than the ultra-modern drawing-room farces. Perhaps it was because the "foiled-again" villain and the "you-cad" hero did satisfy a fundamental need of the man-in-the-street's soul, as bread and milk satisfy fundamental needs of the human body, that they lasted so long and could be hashed up in so many different ways. The people may have realized that they were being fooled, but they loved it. Though a child may cry for the rich and frothy diet, he will soon tire of it, and if it is continued too long it will make him ill, and this is exactly what has happened to the playgoing public.

Gaze upon the theater page of the paper and what do you see? Every new play is introduced as "the smartest of the smart, sophisticated, laughable, clever, the most modern of plays," and is plastered on the billboards and advertised in blazing lights; so that it may take its place among all the other "smart, sophisticated, laughable, clever, modern" plays of the season. The playgoer may well feel that there is sophistication to the right of him and sophistication to the left of him, and over and under him. Never does he see a good old-fashioned "came-the-dawn" play, although that is exactly what he needs, if he but knew it.

"But can we go back?" the reviewers ask. The modern public would laugh little Nell off the stage and like as not applaud the villain, no matter how indecently he curled his mustaches. And they would probably boo the upright hero.

Certainly we cannot go back. One can never go back to anything. The things we have left are no longer there for us to find. We must go on and ahead, hoping only that life will swing us in time back around the circle of the years to what has been. In this progression we can take what was the best of the "up-and-at-'em's" and what we find the least undesirable in the "oh-really?" atrocities, and mixing them to the proper consistency, turn out something rather good. To be fair to either form of art we must do justice to both.

This can hardly be prophesied to be a Utopia of the stage, but at least it may bring the theater out of its dark doldrums to a state where we can say of it—"came the dawn."

V. S.

One of the best ways to stimulate the critical sense is to read criticism. A good deal of friction in book reviewing is produced by the differences between the judicial and the appreciative approaches. The object of criticism in this next review, which is of a contemporary best-seller about which much was written at the time when it first came off the press, is this conflict in criticism itself.

WE LIKE THEM SHORT AND SWEET
Being a Criticism of the Critics of "Anthony Adverse"

Anthony Adverse came into the American limelight quickly, gracefully, and daringly. What the destiny of the novel will be rests with America, and the future. Peter Monro Jack, in the *New York Times*, ventures that it ". . . may become the best-loved book of our times."

Mr. Allen, in releasing three separate volumes under one cover and title, seems to have placed a chip on his shoulder. The challenge was quickly accepted by the critics. Typical of the attitude taken is this conservative statement in the *London Times Literary Supplement*, ". . . it would be dishonest criticism not to insist that a pruning would have done this free-growing plant no harm."

There was but one to come forth and say that the work was not superbly written. This was Dorothy Van Doren, writing for the *Nation*. She writes: "The book has all the meaninglessness of life, which is unendurable in art." Everyone else followed the general pattern of Ben Ray Redman's review in the *Saturday Review of Literature*, which in content says, ". . . if he [the reader] is capable of enjoying a picaresque for the yarn's sake, and of appreciating a vigorous, vivid, and convincing reconstruction of times past, based apparently on a wealth of knowledge and sympathy, he will enjoy himself long and thoroughly."

On the face of it, it appears that the average time a reviewer deems it necessary to spend at a novel of one thousand two hundred and twenty-four pages is the few minutes required to study the content of the flyleaf, and the pattern of a rival's review. The pattern of the reviews could almost be traced on paper, so clearly are they defined.

The critics seem to be too stunned to do more than give a brief résumé of the sequence of events within the story and add a paragraph of praise at the conclusion. Surely Mr. Allen had something more in mind than a sequence of events, when he set out to produce this work. Certainly he had a higher motive than the amusing descriptions abounding in all the chapters, the tragedy that courses through the work like some invisible gas, the pathos that is introduced by Toussaint, the little French clerk.

Although it may be that Mr. Allen's philosophies struck home surprisingly well, in fact so well that the critics are too surprised to admit it, I think that the average reviewer is simply at a loss to find time, or space, to review the book adequately.

Here I would like to state my stand against the critics, public and private. The book is criticized on its objective content alone. The

material factor of length is constantly imposing itself into any suggestions that arise. What seems to me to be the real thought of the book
is left absolutely alone. That there is a thought is obvious.

The closest that anyone has touched, so far, upon really criticizing
this work is the statement that was made in the review in the *New
Republic:* "If Anthony were less of a hero and more of a man, his adventures would matter less and his story would matter more."

This is hardly the time to defend the other side of the argument.
Let it suffice that I merely say that in a work where all the emotions
that a human being can possibly experience are meant to be portrayed, what better way is there than to have a central figure to experience them? Five or six persons, with the emotions divided up
among them would create havoc, and tear down the sense of unity
and rhythm that Mr. Allen has caught throughout his book.

An interesting study in the expectations of the American public is
presented here. The majority of the critics seemed to think that it
was a mistake ever to print *Anthony Adverse* because it is so full of
detail, and the movies could work such wonders with it. No doubt,
America wants a story like that of *Anthony Adverse;* but they want it
held over the fire until the juice has steamed off. Five hundred thousand
words is more reading than the average American does in a year, exclusive of the newspapers and cheap magazines. America wants something light, something that will make it laugh out loud, something
that it can read at night, and forget the next day.

Anthony Adverse is one of those books that is a best-seller because
people like to have "that book that everyone is talking about" on
their living-room tables. Perhaps they dabble a little in the passages
that are most amusing, and skip over the heavier pages. After all,
the story is the thing. Philosophy is out of place in the modern novel.
Excitement, romance, adventure, sex—these are the things that the
American public expects from reading.

The critics in the press, and the critics in the home, are crying out
—"we like them short and sweet."

J. S.

Interesting confirmation of the vast amount of planning and
reflection that went into the making of this huge work ("there
were to be three novels, three books in each novel, and three
themes running through the entire work") is available in an
article by Mr. Allen in the *Saturday Review of Literature*, January
13, 1934. He shows how his materials are drawn from thousands

of books, many of them specified, and assembled by years of effort. After years of preliminary work, the total scheme was placed in the hands of the publishers; but four years more of steady work preceded the final completion of the novel.

-»> B «<-

Impressionistic criticism appears in its most extravagant form in the opening paean of Mrs. Jameson's chapter on Juliet in her *Characteristics of [Shakespeare's] Women*. The writer seems to be seeking emotional exhaustion rather than clear ideas. Actually she provides some acute analysis of Shakespeare's heroines in her book, criticism that is sanely appreciative, but this is usually smothered in luxuriant and ecstatic phrasing. This style belongs to the Romantic decadence of 1832.

O Love! thou teacher, O Grief! thou tamer, and Time, thou healer of human hearts!—bring hither all your deep and serious revelations! And ye too, rich fancies of unbruised, unbowed youth—ye visions of long-perished hopes—shadows of unborn joys—gay colourings of the dawn of existence! whatever memory hath treasured up of bright and beautiful in nature or in art; all soft and delicate images—all lovely forms—divinest voices and entrancing melodies—gleams of sunnier skies and fairer climes—Italian moonlights, and airs that "breathe of the sweet south,"—now, if it be possible, revive to my imagination—live once more to my heart! Come thronging around me, all inspirations that wait on passion, on power, on beauty; give me to tread, not bold, and yet unblamed, within the inmost sanctuary of Shakspeare's genius, in Juliet's moonlight bower and Miranda's enchanted isle!

Brief illustrations of the three major types of criticism will serve to show the contrast between balanced judgments and such effusions. Genuine appreciative criticism is apparent in Dryden's tribute to Shakespeare. The statements have scarcely less emotion than those of Mrs. Jameson, but here feeling is justified and clarified by positive ideas concerning Shakespeare's style.

To begin, then, with Shakespeare. He was the man who of all modern, and perhaps ancient poets, had the largest and most comprehensive soul. All the images of nature were still present to him, and he drew them, not laboriously, but luckily; when he describes anything, you more than see it, you feel it too. Those who accuse him to have wanted learning, give him the greater commendation: he was naturally learned; he needed not the spectacles of books to read nature; he looked inwards, and found her there. I cannot say he is eve ywhere alike; were he so, I should do him injury to compare him with the greatest of mankind. He is many times flat, insipid; his comic wit degenerating into clenches, his serious swelling into bombast. But he is always great when some great occasion is presented to him; no man can say he ever had a fit subject for his wit and did not then raise himself as high above the rest of poets,

Quantum lenta solent inter viburna cupressi.[1]

The consideration of this made Mr. Hales of Eaton say, that there was no subject of which any poet ever writ, but he would produce it much better done in Shakespeare; and however others are now generally preferred before him, yet the age wherein he lived, which had contemporaries with him, Fletcher and Jonson, never equalled them to him in their esteem: and in the last king's court, when Ben's reputation was at highest, Sir John Suckling, and with him the greater part of the courtiers, set our Shakespeare far above him.

JOHN DRYDEN, *Essay of Dramatic Poesy* (1668).

The true spirit of criticism is detached, impersonal, objective. It lets the subject reveal itself as fully as possible and then stand or fall on its own merits. Sometimes this involves examination of opposing views, as in the essay on O. Henry by O. W. Firkins. "There are two opinions concerning O. Henry," he begins. "The middle class views him as the impersonation of vigor and brilliancy; part of the higher criticism sees in him little but sensation and persiflage."

The famous concluding passage of Dr. Johnson's essay on Addison from *The Lives of the English Poets* shows the solid judgment of a master critic feeling out the path between conflicting ideas. Here is judicial criticism at its best.

His prose is the model of the middle style; on grave subjects not formal, on light occasions not grovelling; pure without scrupulosity, and exact without apparent elaboration; always equable, and always easy, without glowing words or pointed sentences. Addison never deviates from his track to snatch a grace; he seeks no ambitious orna-

---

[1] As the cypresses tower among the humbler trees of the wayside.

ments, and tries no hazardous innovations. His page is always luminous, but never blazes in unexpected splendour.

It was apparently his principal endeavour to avoid all harshness and severity of diction; he is therefore sometimes verbose in his transitions and connexions, and sometimes descends too much to the language of conversation; yet if his language had been less idiomatical it might have lost somewhat of its genuine Anglicism. What he attempted, he performed; he is never feeble, and he did not wish to be energetic; he is never rapid, and he never stagnates. His sentences have neither studied amplitude nor affected brevity; his periods, though not diligently rounded, are voluble and easy. Whoever wishes to attain an English style, familiar but not coarse, and elegant but not ostentatious, must give his days and nights to the volumes of Addison.

Here is a brief example of judicial criticism, taken from Matthew Arnold's provocative essay, "The Study of Poetry."

The specimens I have quoted differ widely from one another, but they have in common this: the possession of the very highest poetical quality. . . . The characters of a high quality of poetry are what is expressed *there*. They are far better recognized by being felt in the verse of the master, than by being perused in the prose of the critic. Nevertheless if we are urgently pressed to give some critical account of them, we may safely, perhaps, venture on laying down, not indeed how and why the characters arise, but where and in what they arise. They are in the matter and substance of the poetry, and they are in its manner and style. Both of these, the substance and matter on the one hand, the style and manner on the other, have a mark, an accent, of high beauty, worth, and power.

Having thus prepared his ground, Arnold proceeds to criticize, in sequence, Chaucer, Dryden, Pope, Burns—all with relation to the above standards.

Or let us look at an excerpt from an *American Mercury* article [1] on Poe, a brilliant critic as well as poet and short-story writer. You will note that the author is giving you three views of judicial criticism: (1) he is describing judicial criticism in general; (2) he is pointing out Poe's methods as a judicial critic; (3) and he is using judicial criticism himself.

[1] Reprinted from its later version in *Literary Criticism in America* (1931) by special arrangement with the author, Mr. George E. De Mille, and the publishers, the Dial Press. Originally published in *The American Mercury* for April, 1925.

POE

George E. De Mille

II

. . . Turning first to Poe's reviews, let us look at his critical method. In spite of his pronounced Romantic leanings, his criticism is in at least two important respects in the full Eighteenth Century tradition. It is invariably judicial. Poe had very definite opinions as to the merits of the authors he read, and no hesitancy whatever about expressing those opinions flatly. And these opinions always appear, not as the result of pure inspiration or of innate taste, but as reasoned conclusions from general principles.[1] Does he wish to deny high poetic rank to Drake? He first sets up a distinction between the fancy and the imagination. (All respectable critics of the early Nineteenth Century did this. Poe's distinguishing mark is that he makes sense of it.) On the basis of this distinction he proceeds to show that Drake has only the lesser quality. Does he wish to form a judgment of Hawthorne's tales? He preludes his essay by a definition of the prose tale. Does he wish to condemn the didacticism of Longfellow? He must first limit the respective provinces of truth and beauty in poetry.

No one could say of Poe, as has been so often said of modern reviewers, that he was not in the habit of reading the books he reviewed. Once he had made his definition, stated his general law, established his major premise, he proceeded in logical fashion to prove his case, not by vague generalizations, but by a most minute examination of the books under review. Nothing was too small to escape his critical eye, no detail too trivial, no analysis too technical. Consider, for instance, his article on Longfellow's *Spanish Student*. He begins by discussing the general theme of the play, endeavoring to find out how far Longfellow's conception is original.[2] From the theme, he proceeds logically to the plot. Here his first move is to give a synopsis of the whole story. Then follows a discussion of the relevancy of certain scenes, Poe taking pains in each case to show just why the incident in question adds nothing to the advance of the plot. After this, he points out half a dozen inconsistencies in the conduct of the story. Finally, he shoots the whole plot full of holes by naming incident after incident

---

[1] All destructive critics make a parade of doing this. But one does not feel that with Poe, as with Lowell, the reason comes after the conclusion. [*De Mille's footnote.*]

[2] This obsession with originality was one of Poe's worst critical defects, due, I think, to his lack of knowledge of literary history, which would have taught him the rarity of originality, even among the greatest. [*De Mille's footnote.*]

that is as old as the hills and as stage-worn as the familiar missing will. The plot thus disposed of, Poe attacks Longfellow's attempts at humor—mainly by the simple yet effective device of quotation without comment. Finally, the facts being all presented, he arrives at the conclusion that the whole piece, while containing here and there a line of passable poetry, is as a play quite unworthy of any critical respect. . . .

. . . .

Now all this makes Poe a good critic, but it also makes him extraordinarily hard reading. He is technical, and rightly so; but that is not all of criticism. . . . It is, however, a necessary part, especially for the kind of criticism Poe was attempting. The foundation of judicial criticism, if the judgment is to be worth anything, must be an examination of technicalities. Unfortunately the ordinary intelligent reader, to whom literature is an amusement, is not interested in technicalities. A few pages of the sort of thing I have quoted put him to sleep. And here we have a second reason why Poe stays on the shelf. [The first reason, given earlier, was Poe's tendency to choose minor authors as subjects for criticism.]

III

Max Beerbohm once divided critics into two classes, those who feel and those who think. To the former group Lowell belongs. . . . Poe is here again his exact opposite. At first glance, one would unhesitatingly class the author of *The Fall of the House of Usher* and *Annabel Lee* as an emotionalist—and correctly. But when the emotionalist, or even the sensualist, can reason in any sort, he is apt to reason with unequalled power and clearness. Poe himself noted and commented on this frequent and yet surprising combination of faculties. "The reasoning powers," he asserted, "never exist in perfection unless when allied with a high degree of the imaginative faculty." In his tales, his poems, his life, Poe appears to the superficial student as the incarnation of the popular notion of the literary man—a creature of pure feeling, of sensitive, tingling nerves, unordered by reason. In his criticism we are more often reminded of the man who offered to solve any cipher the readers of his magazine might send him—and who did it. . . .

IV

But, since Poe was always systematically judicial, his likes, whether right or wrong, were of less importance than his dislikes. Systematic judicial criticism is primarily a means, not of discovering truth, but of exposing error. The particular function of the judicial critic, the thing that he can do and that no one else can do, is the flagellation of bad authors. . . .

V

But important and valuable though this process of demolishing shaky reputations was, it is not the best nor the most important side of Poe's criticism. His particular excellence as a critic lies in his almost unique ability to apply a keen and marvellously logical thinking machine to the problems of literary theory. When there is a question of pronouncing on the merits of a particular author, intelligence is not enough. There Poe often fails. But criticism does not consist merely of bringing authors before a court of review and there passing judgment on their evil deeds. It also has its philosophical and scientific side. And here Poe excels. Looking over as much of the field of literature as he knew, he constantly exercised his powers of analysis to induce from literary phenomena the general laws that govern them. . . .

The task of the literary generalizer is analogous to that of the natural scientist. Gathering as many facts as he can amass, he must endeavor to discover in them some common denominator, some guiding principle. Obviously, the value of his generalization will depend largely on the completeness of his collection of facts. Poe's collection was woefully incomplete. . . . Nowhere does Poe give much evidence of possessing the historic sense—that invaluable corrective of hasty opinions. That with such an imperfect equipment as this, Poe managed to develop theories so essentially sound, is one of the greatest evidences of the innate power of his mind.

His theory of criticism can best be set forth by standing aside and allowing Poe to speak for himself.

Of one who instructs we demand, in the first instance, a certain knowledge of the principles which regulate the instruction.

When we attend less to authority and more to principles, when we look less at merit and more at demerit, we shall be better critics than we are.

Criticism is not an essay, nor a sermon, nor an oration, nor a chapter in history, nor a philosophical speculation, nor a prose-poem, nor an art-novel, nor a dialogue. We would wish to limit literary criticism to comment on Art. A book is written, and it is only as the book that we subject it to review. With the opinions of the author the critic really has nothing to do. It is his part simply to decide upon the mode in which these opinions are brought to bear. And this art now no more than in the days of the *Dunciad* can, without neglect of its duty, dismiss errors of grammar, or hand over an imperfect rhyme or a false quantity to the proof-reader.

In general, we should not be overscrupulous about niceties of phrase, when the matter in hand is a dunce to be gibbeted. Speak out—or the person may not understand you. He is to be hung? Then hang him by all means; but make no bow where you mean no obeisance, and eschew the droll delicacy of the Clown in the play—"Be so good, sir, as to rise and be put to death."

There is something like a whole system of criticism contained in these brief passages. . . . Furthermore, Poe, unlike the vast majority of critics, actually made his system work.

Even more impersonal is historical criticism. It is definitely scientific in spirit, seeking facts of any sort which may bear on the man or work which is being studied. Often it serves to correct or refute prejudiced or false judgments. Above all, to quote Dr. Johnson again, it seeks to form its impression of the man in terms of "the state of the age" in which he lived and wrote. In the next selection Hazlitt is making a plea for a fair view of the neo-classic style of Pope in an age of such romantic revolutionaries as Shelley and Victor Hugo.

Pope's correctness, smoothness, etc., are very good things and much to be commended in him. But it is not to be expected, or even desired, that others should have these qualities in the same paramount degree, to the exclusion of everything else. If you like correctness and smoothness of all things in the world, there they are for you in Pope. If you like other things better, such as strength and sublimity, you know where to go for them. Why trouble Pope or any other author for what they have not, and do not profess to give? Those who seem to imply that Pope possessed, besides his own peculiar exquisite merits, all that is to be found in Shakespeare or Milton, are, I should hardly think, in good earnest. But I do not therefore see that, because this was not the case, Pope was no poet. We cannot by a little verbal sophistry confound the qualities of different minds, nor force opposite excellences into a union by all the intolerance in the world. We may pull Pope in pieces as long as we please for not being Shakespeare or Milton, as we may carp at them for not being Pope; but this will not make a poet equal to all three. If we have a taste for some one precise style or manner, we may keep it to ourselves and let others have theirs.

HAZLITT, *Lectures on the English Poets* (1818).

The great French critic Sainte-Beuve achieved a balance of sympathetic insight and clear-eyed judgment which is attained only by the best minds. His understanding is as impartial as is possible when an insatiable zest for the objects of criticism is involved. The swift glimpse into the complex nature of Voltaire is only one of the facets of a brilliantly carved gem of criticism.

One sees how in practical matters, as well as literary, or in society, indeed everywhere, Voltaire entered with head high, sure of his way, putting people in their places and asserting himself boldly, like a prince in the realm of the mind. Say what you will of this faculty of Voltaire's,—at twenty-four to write tragedies, compose an epic, and to carry on in *business!* He foresaw that it was necessary to become rich first in order to be independent later. However, to this he added the polished manner of the man of the world.

Voltaire's fiery spirit was always impetuous. Even when he had complete leisure, he never attained really sober vision; his spirit was always constantly at war with itself. . . . Yet, even though the worlds of intellect and fashion made rival claims upon him, they also served in some respects to make of him a poet of lively and easy turn of phrase, a writer of fine taste and a very natural quality of elegance. When we consider only the ideal of charm, the flower of fine raillery and urbanity, it is pleasant to picture Voltaire enjoying the pleasures of that society of which he often dreamed, in which he sometimes appeared, but from which he was always fleeing. "Mon Dieu, my dear Cideville," he wrote to a friend of those happy days, "what a delightful existence it would be to lodge with three or four men of letters, gifted but free of petty jealousies, to enjoy one another, culti- vate one's art, to talk it over together, to work out our ideas com- pletely! I picture myself living in such a paradise someday; but I insist that you shall be the god over it."

Causeries du Lundi (Monday Chats) October 20, 1856.

Contrast Sainte-Beuve's style with the modern academic de- tachment in the next selection. It is taken from a work by one of the most stimulating and influential of historical critics, Pro- fessor E. E. Stoll, a monograph on *Hamlet* (1919).[1]

Now the Kydian revenge play had recently come back into favor. . . . He [Shakespeare] always followed the tradition of the stage, he never

[1] Reprinted by permission of the University of Minnesota Press and of Mr. Stoll, who edited the following excerpts for us himself. Mr. Stoll's *Art and Artifice* (1933) contains a more recent discussion of *Hamlet*.

ignored or defied it. . . . It thus appears that two great improbabilities in the play as we have it lay imbedded in the story when Shakespeare took it over. . . .

The present Hamlet theory arose and was developed far away from every tradition and echo of the stage. . . .

And the charges of remissness and neglect of duty brought against Hamlet (our present concern) are quite similar to those brought against Hieronimo [in a play by Thomas Kyd which has many of the features like *Hamlet*]. However all these devices [of the soliloquies] may have been further developed by Shakespeare, they are, then, nothing new; and as used by others before him, they were not meant, as we shall see, to indicate a weakness in the hero's character. . . .

Likewise Hamlet's doubt of the Ghost has been taken for no honest doubt. It is remarkable that scholarly critics continue to do this, although it has long been known that the doctrine that ghosts masquerading as devils was then the enlightened Protestant opinion. . . .

In contrast to the formal styles in criticism we now offer one example of up-to-the-minute reviewing. Notice, however, that even in this racy criticism, so briskly written as to be not entirely free from inconsistency, there is still the basic structure which we outlined in this chapter. The five steps are indicated: thesis, summary, proof, the other side, conclusion.

THE MIGHTY [1]

Harry Evans

[Sect. I] This being He-Man Week at *Life*, we will celebrate by reporting films featuring the nation's two most popular roughnecks— George Bancroft and Victor McLaglen.

There are many nice things to be said about Mr. Bancroft in "The Mighty." He is, unquestionably, the screen's most personable and efficient gangster, and in this one he offers a performance that has more general appeal than anything he has done since "Underworld." [Sect. II] The plot is a sure-fire tale of a gangster who refuses to answer the draft call, and is dragged into the World War very much against his will. Once in the scrapping he finds the killing business right down his alley, and his exploits soon make him a national hero. When the armistice is declared, he returns home where the city fathers welcome him with open arms and offer him the job as chief of police. George

[1] Reprinted from *Life*, January 24, 1930, by permission of Life Publishing Company.

sees in this an opportunity to make a clean-up with his old "mob," but after taking over the work he develops a conscience with interesting results.

[Sect. III] Outstanding in a cast of unusual excellence is Raymond Hatton, a film player whom we have yet to see give a poor performance. Mr. Hatton's film value is enhanced with the chance to use his speaking voice. Warner Oland is impressively sinister as the gang leader, and. Dorothy Revier, as the gangster's "moll," displays one of the few very pleasant feminine voices we have heard on the screen. Esther Ralston is adequate if not exciting as George's heart interest. And speaking of the sex feature of the picture, it might be well to let the romance lovers know that the affection between Esther and George, if any, takes place after the picture is over. Fortunately, Mr. Bancroft is one of those big strong men who are able to convince their audiences of their possibilities for passion without giving demonstrations, and the latent heat of his wooing is a relief after watching countless screen lovers struggle to work themselves into a higher temperature than their glands will honestly support.

[Sect. IV] In commending "The Mighty" as worthy entertainment, we must add that the director has not made the most of the opportunities presented by the story. We are naturally a peace-loving person, but we must admit that the steadily increasing cadence of the plot led into a hopeful anticipation of a violent climax that was not fully realized. There is also one of those annoying scenes during which the hero and heroine, after barely escaping from death by a machine gun, stand up and make a fuss over each other, thereby presenting a perfect target in case the shooting party should happen to decide to try again.

[Sect. V] "The Mighty" is the kind of entertainment this department likes to endorse. We guarantee that it will furnish you with a mighty pleasant evening.

You will doubtless feel, after examining the various kinds of criticism, that the best will combine certain qualities of all of them. In Professor Kittredge's unassuming work on Chaucer you will find the sympathy and responsiveness of interpretive criticism, the deliberation and balance of judicial criticism, and the essential objectivity and fidelity to known facts that distinguishes historical criticism. Study this synthetic approach in the two selections following.[1] How do they reveal varying aspects

[1] Reprinted from *Chaucer and His Poetry*, by George Lyman Kittredge, Harvard University Press, 1915, with the permission of the publishers.

of Chaucer as poet? (He is generally regarded as being second only to Shakespeare in his understanding of feminine nature.) What traces of the various types of criticism do you find?

The *Book of the Duchess*, with all its defects, is a very beautiful poem. There is a haunting charm about it that eludes analysis, but subdues our mood to a gentle and vaguely troubled pensiveness. The mind is purged, not by the tragedy of life, with its pity and terror, but by a sense of the sadness which pervades its beauty and joy. Ours is a pleasant world of birds and flowers and green trees and running streams, and life in such a world is gracious and desirable, and nothing is so good as tender and faithful love, which is its own reward. But the glory of it all is for a moment. Alcyone prayed to Juno to send her a dream, that she might know whether her long-absent husband was alive or dead. And the drowned Ceyx came while she slept, and stood at her bed's foot, and bade her bury his body, which was cast up on the shore:—

> "And far-well, swete, my worldes blisse!
> I praye God your sorwe lisse.
> To litel whyl our blisse lasteth!"

Now this thought—that life and love and happiness are transitory—is not, with Chaucer, a commonplace reflection, with which he has only a concern that is conventional and impersonal and external. Nor is it, again, a dogma of experience, to which he has dispassionately adjusted his philosophic scheme. It is an element in his nature: it beats in his heart, and flows in his veins, and catches in his throat, and hammers in his head. All men are mortal, no doubt, but seldom do we find one in whom mortality is a part of his consciousness. And such a man was Chaucer—yet so sound of heart, so sane and normal, so wholesome in his mirth, so delighting in the world and his fellow-creatures, that no less a critic than Matthew Arnold, speaking with limited sympathy and imperfect comprehension, would exclude him from the fellowship of his peers on the strength of a formula, because he lacked "high seriousness." Whether Chaucer saw life whole, I do not know. One thing I know—he saw it steadily.

G. L. Kittredge, *Chaucer and His Poetry.*

Notice how easily the critic turns his mounting fervor and culminating indignation to a luminous interpretation and defense, without for a moment losing his own balance. The second selection, taken from the same source, is perhaps more objective, but no less warmed by understanding. It represents true critical insight, which does not strain for subtlety yet which constantly interests and illuminates.[1]

Chaucer's own birth and station, as I reminded you in my opening lecture, had brought him into easy contact with both high and low; and his experiences as burgher, soldier, courtier, officeholder, and diplomatic agent had given him unparalleled opportunities for observation, which his humorously sympathetic temperament had impelled him to use to the best advantage. Mankind was his specialty. He was now a trained and practised writer, with a profound sense of the joy and beauty, the sadness and irony, of human life. He has already studied the whole world from the point of view of two of the ruling passions:—the desire for reputation (in the *House of Fame*) and passionate love (in the *Troilus*). In both of these great works, however, his approach had been, so to speak, oblique or indirect: by symbolism or allegory in the one; in the other, by way of a return to the days of old. Now, at length, in this Canterbury Pilgrimage, with its nine-and-twenty contemporary human creatures, he has recognized his crowning opportunity. He will show life as it is; he will paint "what he sees"! But I am wrong. It is not showing (or exhibition); it is not painting (or delineation): it is dramatic action. And so he makes himself one of the Pilgrims, in order that we may understand that they are as real as he is. Chaucer existed, thus we instinctively syllogize, and therefore the Prioress existed, and the Reeve, and the Manciple, and the Monk, and the Knight, and Harry Bailly, the incomparable innkeeper, to whom, and not to Geoffrey Chaucer, the conduct of the drama is entrusted. Chaucer reports, but Harry Bailly is the dynamic agent. The action of the piece is largely due to his initiative, and to him are referable the details again and again. Sometimes, to be sure, the play gets out of hand, but not for long; and usually, on such occasions, he is content to let go the reins, since the team is guiding itself.

The Host, as we know, is the appointed leader. He nominates himself for the office, as many a good politician has done before and since, but not until after supper, when his social qualities have been fully tested. He is well fitted for the office—a fine large man, handsome after his florid fashion, merry, afraid of nobody—"of manhood him lakkede right nought"—loud-voiced and free-spoken. It is not by accident that Chaucer calls him as fair a burgess as there is in Cheap; for London was an *imperium in imperio*, and the citizens were persons of

---

[1] *Chaucer and His Poetry*. By courtesy of the Harvard University Press.

importance, not merely in their own eyes, but in the estimation of all orders and even of the king. Chaucer himself, who was always in politics,—would that we had his political autobiography!—is a first-rate example of a "king's man," a sort of courtier who was also a burgher by descent and in actuality. Once a Londoner, always a Londoner, no matter what else you might become.

But Harry Bailly was not only a fair and seemly burgess, bold of his speech. He was "wise and well ytaught": that is, in modern parlance, a discreet man, with plenty of tact, one who "knew his way about"; he had some education and was thoroughly versed in the usages of society. His hearty and sometimes boisterous manner must not deceive us. It is partly temperament, partly professional technique, and he forces it a little now and then, for a very special purpose—to see if he cannot irritate some pilgrim or other into revolt; for whoever gainsays his judgment must pay an enormous forfeit, no less than the total travelling expenses of the company.

> "Whoso wol my juggement withseye
> Shal paye al that we spenden by the weye."

Harry is the legitimate ancestor of many a jovial and autocratic inn-keeper in our literature; but we must not confuse him with such roaring eccentrics as Blague the landlord of the George at Waltham in the *Merry Devil of Edmonton*, or even mine Host of the Garter in the *Merry Wives*. "Ha!" cries Blague, "I'll caper in my own fee simple. Away with punc-tilios and orthography! I serve the good Duke of Norfolk. Bilbo! *Tityre tu patulae recubans sub tegmine fagi*." Blague, it appears, is "well ytaught," for he can quote Virgil, with a prophecy, one is tempted to conjecture, of the *Tityre-tu's* of the next generation; but after all he is only a kind of substantial and well-esteemed buffoon. He is not Harry Bailly—scarcely more so than Sir John Falstaff (rest his soul!) is Chaucer's Knight. For Harry has his own dignity: he knows the times and the manners. Here, as ever, Chaucer is quite specific. The landlord of the Tabard, so he tells us, was

> a seemly man with-alle
> For to han ben a marshal in a halle.

Such as he had been master of ceremonies many a time when our Knight had "begun the board," or sat at the head of the table, at high chivalric festivals.

Yet, despite the Host's autocracy, the ruler of the company is actually the Knight. It is he that asserts himself whenever the case requires an appeal to the controlling forces of the social world. One of these crises arrives when the Monk gets halfway—a quarter, who can tell?—through his list of tragedies, or tales of men and women fallen from their high estate. The Monk belonged to the "gentles," and the Host was not so ready to interrupt him as in the case of Chaucer, who was a somewhat ambiguous personality, even to the omniscient Bailly. Not altogether because Harry was considerate. He stood in no awe of Dan Piers; the preliminaries demonstrate that. He was simply at his wit's end. This roll of dismal biographies must close sometime; but it is like many a sermon: at every pause, one thinks the peroration has passed, only to discover that the preacher has got his second wind, or his thirteenth; and one feels a certain reluctance to imitate the historic Scotswoman and throw a footstool at the parson's head! Besides, Harry Bailly was well taught, and he was rather a Saxon than a Celt. He did agnize a natural and prompt alacrity he felt in boredom. It is all very well to be entertained; but now and then there is a time for edification, and anything that's stupid must be edifying. In my part of the country we call this the New England conscience. Hence Harry was hesitant. "Lucifer, Adam, Zenobia, Croesus, Pedro of Spain, Bernabò Visconti,"—these be good words! *Rusticus exspectat!* Patience! the river will flow by if we wait a bit. In short, Harry was "out of his epoch"; the situation was just a trifle beyond his control; and so the natural leader asserted himself, as many a time on the perilous edge of battle when it raged.

Chaucer, they tell us, is very modern. So he is; this crisis proves it. You can translate his situations into our own at any given moment. Darken the theatre for a second—then turn up the lights. Vanishes the road to Canterbury; vanish the Pilgrims on their way to St. Thomas's shrine. Appear at table a party of gentlemen; a helpless toastmaster, twirling his eyeglasses and stealing glances at his watch. Time flies, death urges—and there are several speakers left on the list which he has scribbled off upon his cuff. And here,—intrenched, unassailable, standing like Teneriffe,—is the lord of the ascendant, the after-dinner platitudinarian, droning on and on, his ten minutes elongated by imperceptible gradations to five-and-twenty, and still no sign that he is nearing the seamark of his utmost sail! And this is precisely the address that will be reported at greatest length in the morrow's newspaper, and that a grateful constituency will hold it a precious privilege to read.

KITTREDGE, Chaucer and His Poetry.

CHAPTER X

Short, Informal Written Argument[1]

For formal argument, or the technique of debating, you will go in these modern days to the speech department of any college or university. We are here going to propose merely a brief exercise in written, informal argument, involving of course some of the principles of formal argument, but confining itself to the limits of such a piece as you may wish to contribute some day to magazines like the *Nation*, the *New Republic*, the *American Mercury*, and their other less vigorously militant contemporaries, such as the *Forum*.

The general development of this exercise will be somewhat like that of the preceding chapter, on Criticism. That is, it will be Criticism with section IV (the other side) left out, for section IV will now become "Refutation," an attempt to eliminate completely the value of whatever ideas or arguments appear to be on your opponent's side. Similarly, too, neither type will permit an influx of contentiousness or violent prejudice to mar the clear-cut decisiveness of the exposition. So far, then, superficially, the two exercises, Criticism and Informal Written Argument, are very much alike. But Argument really has a few terms and implications of its own that should be considered.

Argument goes a little beyond mere criticism in purpose: it aims to induce the reader (or listener) to *act* as a result of his acceptance of the ideas of the writer (or speaker). This feature may also be partially true of the editorial in the field of pure criticism, but the evidence involved in developing an argument and the persuasive trickery sometimes employed are a little

[1] Or The Controversial Essay. We are indebted to Mrs. Josephine N. Keal of Wayne University for some technical advice in this chapter.

beyond the normal mild editorial and certainly beyond the more disinterested literary criticism. Types of evidence may become problems of study in themselves, and the formal principles of logic may involve the writer of pure argument in intricacies of thought far beyond the scope of the present chapter. However, even in casual writing and thinking, where positive truth is claimed, an important principle may be observed, a principle of truth and error. Simply stated, it recognizes that truth is single, error multiple. For every truth a legion of potential errors exists. Hence, the writer in asserting a truth must guard against numerous possible errors, or fallacies, in his own reasoning. It will be useful to examine the structure of logical assertion and some of the parasitic fallacies which beset it before looking into the actual procedure of argumentative writing.

Since Aristotle (384–322 B.C.) the essential pattern of logical reasoning has been described in the form of the Syllogism. The syllogism restricts the development of reasoning to a series of steps which proceed from the known, or at least accepted, truth to a derived truth. We stand on one assertion, throw out another ahead of us, step to it, then reach behind us for a portion of the first assertion, and throw it out still farther ahead for a new position— quite like a man crossing a shallow stream by means of stepping-stones. The security of our new, third position always depends on the soundness of those preceding. Thus, we begin with the first step, called the major premise ("All men are mortal"), advance to the minor premise ("Socrates is a man"), an intermediary truth which is a portion or derivative of the major assertion, and last, step to the conclusion ("Socrates is mortal"). This final assertion, usually prefixed with the label "therefore," has advanced us in our thought process. To continue on our way we can formulate our conclusion into the major premise of a new syllogism.

Much of our conscious life rests on hidden syllogism. We go our way, living, voting, arguing, making decisions; yet few of us realize how much of this activity is based on the structure of syllogistic reasoning. By early training, codes of honor and duty, religious, moral, legal, and general social standards, we are equipped with a set of accepted truths. These stand as axioms or principles which provide the major premises in shaping our attitudes and our very lives. Perhaps the relative maturity of our minds can be measured in no way better than by the degree of our critical awareness of such truths as the basis of our social order.

Of course, as we know from the Middle Ages, syllogistic reasoning can be exceedingly rigid, blind, dogmatic. Where authority dictates the premises, or general truths, which must be accepted, we lose the essential element in free inquiry. Inquisitive, restless, and skeptical minds are always stirred to pry into and challenge such abuses of the right to freedom of thought. Still, for most of us, the menace to sound thinking lies more in our own susceptibility to false arguments than in the restrictions of authority. Superficiality, shallow catchwords and slogans, confusion of issues, the craft of the advertising expert and the political orator, all conspire with our own credulity and mental laziness to impose on our logical faculties. We accept unconsidered judgments, false values, and half-truths under the stimulus of appeals to our desires and vanity just as we buy inferior drugs and foods without knowing their real content.

The best protection against unsoundness in our own thinking as well as against the barrage of propaganda with which we are assailed is a knowledge of some of the most common diseases or distortions of reasoning, that is, the logical fallacies. The most persistent ones are listed and described briefly below. Look for examples of each in advertisements, editorials, speeches, or, better still, in the arguments and interchanges of opinion in the classroom, on the street, or wherever spontaneous argument may flourish. Logical fallacies fall into two broad types: fallacies of equivocation in which there is confusion or deception in the terms used, particularly in the statement of the premises, and fallacies of unwarranted assumption in which a conclusion is asserted on the basis of inadequate, irrelevant, or unsound evidence or assumptions.[1]

I. *Fallacies of Equivocation.* Avoidance of the fallacies in this group requires a clear defining of terms and careful distinction between various fields of thought and types of objects and ideas.

---

[1] A more complete discussion of logical procedure and fallacies will include Mill's *Canons of Logic*, numerous aspects of syllogistic mechanics, and the familiar distinctions between types of reasoning. This material is available in any standard work on logic, Sellars, Whately, and others.

1. Ambiguity and Amphiboly. These fallacies arise where more than one interpretation of important words and statements is possible. In discussing labor, poverty, crime, and similar abstractions it is important to define a specific meaning and then hold to that meaning. Amphiboly often produces humorous double meanings. Here the confusion lies in the sentence structure, for example the familiar type ("Wanted: experienced housekeeper with puppies").

2. Composition and Division. In these the error results from making an assertion concerning the whole which is true of only the part ("America is not a safe country because of the menace of gangsters.")— the fallacy of composition; or the attribution to the part of what is true only of the whole ("George Gershwin cannot be called a great composer because he wrote in jazz rhythm.")—the fallacy of division.

3. Accident and Accent. These fallacies give a false impression by emphasizing a general principle without allowing for qualifying circumstances ("Share the wealth." "Card playing is wicked." "The moving picture is a tool of the devil."), or by placing the emphasis on the wrong word or idea—most frequently by quoting only a portion of a speaker's words so that an essential part is omitted. (Professor Stuart P. Sherman used to tell of a headline to a news account of one of his public addresses: "College Professor Shows Need of Higher Education." A speaker may be quoted as saying "Democracy will fail," when his full statement was that "Democracy will fail only if we demand of it more than any existing type of government can achieve.")

Fallacies of equivocation are largely confined to phrasing and to choice of terms. The most severe effects of unsound reasoning are more often found in the second group where fallacious reasoning may undermine the whole argument.

II. *Fallacies of Unwarranted Assumption.*

1. *Assumption of the point to be proved.* The most common form is called *Begging the Question.* Usually a term of condemnation or praise is introduced so as to take for granted what is to be proved. ("The *lazy* college students of today should be compelled to study under supervision." "We —ists stand for progressive ideas." "This *contemptible*, *moth-eaten* old scoundrel has the *audacity* to claim that he is innocent!") To call names or sing praises proves nothing, even though political campaigns are often greatly affected by mud-slinging tactics or "sloganeering" methods that "beg the question" at issue, that is, the essential capacity of the candidate.

In long arguments the inconsistency of assuming the point which is to be proved may be carried to the extreme of *arguing in a circle*. Not only is the truth of the major premise assumed—it is also used as the basis of a conclusion which is later brought in again to prove the original premise from which it has been derived. Such procedure suggests the inconclusive musical "round," such as the "Three Blind Mice." For example, the arguments of some European countries seem to proceed as follows:

a. We need to increase our population and territory; hence
b. Many more workers and soldiers are needed to make our nation rich and powerful; therefore
c. We need wealth and military might to secure the well-being and happiness of our over-crowded millions of people.

Such arguing frequently develops in the effort to justify already existing desires. The boy urging his father to buy him a new bicycle, the woman trying to persuade herself of the need of an expensive fur coat, earnest student bodies campaigning for an expanded athletic program, in fact, anyone who is seeking to strain the budget, is in danger of circular reasoning. The effort is to prove that what we want is needed because we want it. Elaborate verbiage conceals the real motives or the lack of sound ones.

2. *Irrational evidence.* A rather large family of fallacies results from the appeal to the emotions, prejudices, or other irrelevant factors of the mind instead of advancing cogent reasons.

a. *Argumentum ad hominem.* Attack is made against the character of a man even though his possible moral blemishes have no bearing on the point at issue. Gossip and slander play a large part in legal battles even though effort is made to rule them out as "irrelevant and immaterial." The writer of biography or criticism sometimes prejudices the analysis by emphasizing moral defection. A Victorian critic questions the poetic power of a writer because he is wayward in love; a modern critic attacks a Victorian writer for being inhibited by concern for virtue.

b. *Argumentum ad populum.* Here is the open appeal to feelings, prejudices, or passions which are beside the point. Popular feeling and mob psychology are particularly pertinent here as this fallacious appeal is usually used as a deliberate means of swaying groups by whipping up sudden hysteria or at least unreasoning response. The writer can be guilty of misusing statistics or lurid details just as the crafty attorney plays on emotions by use of the widow's tears or the blood-stained garments of the murdered man.

c. *Argumentum ad vericundiam.* Finally in this group there is the appeal to the reader's or listener's sense of modesty. This approach is often effective since the sane, reasoning person is often inclined to be reserved in judgment, modest about his own opinions, and considerate of the judgments of others. Thus he gives undue weight to evidence or authority, particularly when that authority comes from highly esteemed sources. The writer of argument, on his side, should avoid this fallacy by a strictly logical use of authority. Achievement in one field does not in itself entitle an individual to act as judge in another. It is inconsistent to elect a man to a public office and then permit the prestige which the office gives him to serve to justify his laying down judgments on music, art, history, and other complex matters outside his own field. One of the most prevalent uses of this fallacy is the testimonial advertisement in which prominent persons in society, sports, or the movies tell us how to determine our purchases.

3. *Argument beside the point.* A final group of fallacies is particularly important for the writer of argument. Often the undergraduate learns to his chagrin that the instructor is convinced that he has not proved anything at all, or at least not what he set out to prove. His intentions were good, he has advanced much wholesome truth; but, the instructor insists, he has not proved his case. He may be like the dazed halfback who made a brilliant eighty-yard run to his own goal line—brilliant but irrelevant to the scorekeeper's tally.

a. *Irrelevant conclusion.* "True, but beside the point. . . . Very good, but what of it? . . . Interesting, but not what we are looking for." Such comments, often heard, challenge the most well-meant and earnest efforts to win assent. They are the logical equivalent of Kipling's terse criticism: "It's pretty, but is it art?" To prove that unemployment is prodigious, or even that the distresses of the unemployed are acute, does not necessarily prove the validity of a legislative program of economic reform. To prove that a certain country has a huge army and navy is not to prove that it has intentions of attacking us. To establish that there is commercialism in athletics is not to prove that football is undesirable.

b. *Non sequitur:* "It does not follow." This fallacy is different chiefly in emphasis. As with others of this group, it is more likely to result from a mental blind spot, particularly in long-winded arguments, rather than from any deliberate intent to mislead. Usually it is the champion of the argument who is deceiving himself; but, as with all fallacies, it is important for the reader or listener to be on his guard and to be able to diagnose unsound reasoning. *Non sequitur* occurs frequently in connection with a series of perfectly logical and well-documented arguments; the train arrives, but it is simply the wrong train, or else it is on the wrong track. Thus, it does not follow that, because the candidate is a good churchman and the head of a family, he may be an efficient officeholder.

c. *False analogy.* Legitimate use of analogy, that is, comparison on the basis of common qualities, provides one of the most vivid and forceful tools of argument. It acts in the same way that simile and metaphor do in poetic description. Thus when Carlyle attacks the legislative and economic experiments of his day as reckless, he uses the phrase "shooting Niagara." Such concentrated appeal to the imagination is found in the slogan, often with fallacious effect. Hence, Carlyle's phrase may or may not be accurate; but it will be no less forceful in either case. The justness of analogy will depend upon the existence of significant common qualities between the two objects of comparison, and, equally important, upon the absence of vital points of difference between them. Before we call Uncle Sam a Shylock for expecting payment of war debts, we need to be certain not only that his claims are just, but also that the desire for a pound of flesh nearest the heart of the debtor countries is also present.

d. *Unsound generalization.* As with analogy, generalization is a valid type of argument, fallacious only when abused. Here, too, we have a form which provides pitfalls for the earnest writer. He is eager to establish certain general views concerning athletes, fraternity men, the grading system, campus clothes, the rights of students, and in consequence makes hasty and sweeping statements about them. If he is hypersensitive, he may be obsessed with the notion that the members of this or that group are snobbish. However, one or two instances in which he has been snubbed do not prove the point at all. Realizing this in part, he may seek to bolster his contentions by use of analogy supported by other fallacies, particularly those which are addressed to the emotions.

False generalization is a relatively juvenile error, perhaps a carryover from the childish disposition to gain force by exaggeration, by saying millions where at most a dozen were meant. The writer may guard against this fallacy by being sure that he has collected a sufficient number of cases to make his claim sound. Beyond this he must be certain that there are no exceptions which will invalidate his contention. He must test the validity of the general truth and then scrutinize closely its application. Often the fallacy lies chiefly in the use of terms that are too extreme. "Did I say all?" Browning asks at the end of the "Pied Piper." The one surviving child, only a little cripple, is the exception that proves the rule—all the children are gone. Words such as *all*, *every*, *absolutely*, *completely*, should be watched closely. The strength of the argument may be just as well established by the use of *most*, *the majority of*, *usually*, *typically*, and the like.

In turning from the reasoning process to the actual written argument it is important to remember that this type of writing introduces a competitive element. Whether there is an actual debate or the mere desire to convince the reader, there is the impulse to win. Fair play and sound thinking demand that winning be achieved without sacrifice of consistency and healthy logic. The writer may forget the names of specific fallacies, but he should bear in mind the fundamental principles of good reasoning. Finally, argument as a form of writing in itself has some specific terms and, to some extent, a structure of its own which should be applied, partially at least, in the development of this informal written exercise.

The outline of an argument is generally called a Brief. It consists normally of three divisions, the Introduction (stating the occasion and history of the question and defining terms), the Body (giving the proposition now limited and carefully defined, the direct proof, and the refutation), and the Conclusion ("Therefore you ought to believe in democracy," or whatever the proposition has been). Formal discussion of Argument often obscures the real process beneath an elaborate set of rules. However, for the essentials a few simple instructions should suffice. These are based on the three parts of the brief, or outline, as indicated above. The relation of the ideas, usually set down in complete statements, is expressed by the normal outline symbols: I A 1 a, etc. The typical connectives of argument, "for" and "because," are used in the Body, or Proof, but not in the Introduction. Each subhead proves the preceding heading and contains generally only *one* proposition. The functions of the Introduction and Body have already been expressed. We should perhaps add as an obvious fact that the Conclusion should propose no new evidence nor qualify what has gone before. It often contains, however, a summarizing of all the main arguments.

Sometimes it may be well to state the issues of a proposition before attempting to formulate the outline to be followed. For example, consider the following questions about fraternities and sororities:

Are they more expensive than dormitories?
Are they undemocratic?
Are they demoralizing?
Are they productive of lasting friendships?
Are they of value in later life?
Are they socially valuable in college?
Will they be superseded by clubs anyway if dropped?
Are local clubs more dangerous than national fraternities and sororities?

Such a list of issues, then, might help you to determine an outline, or brief, of the proposition: "Fraternities and sororities should be abolished."

The arguments themselves may appear in various forms, the most typical of which are these:

1. Deductive, or syllogistical
   All clubs are expensive; fraternities are clubs; hence they are expensive.
2. Inductive
   Brother Jones "flunked" chemistry.
   Brother Phillips "flunked" history.
   Brother Price "flunked" English.[1]
   Hence (or therefore) fraternities must be intellectually demoralizing.
3. Argument from example
   The Z B house is up for taxes; two of its members were recently expelled; etc.
4. Argument from analogy
   Harvard College dropped national fraternities, and very exclusive clubs sprang up immediately. This same process will occur whenever fraternities are dropped; is it an agreeable development?
5. Argument from statistics or printed authorities
   The grades of non-fraternity and fraternity men should be compared over a period of ten years, or reliable authorities cited.

---

[1] But merely a *few* instances will not establish the inductive argument.

And there are of course others; try, for example, to develop arguments on the above proposition from cause to effect, effect to cause, effect to effect, etc.

In all these cases the evidence must be carefully tested for validity before it is introduced. A witness, or source giving the facts, may be prejudiced, may be incompetent morally or intellectually. The above fallacies will thus arise in the arguments and must be eliminated. You cannot say that *all* fraternities are bad because *one* fraternity "goes bad." You cannot bluntly *assert* that the Z B house is bad because you personally simply *know* it is. You cannot state a proposition as unfairly as this: "Our generally immoral fraternities must be eliminated." You cannot announce that because Jim Jones went to town last night and got violently intoxicated, his fraternity *caused* Jim Jones to go astray like that. You cannot casually *assume* from the start that all fraternities consist of wealthy men or all sororities of social butterflies. You cannot argue by analogy that the same rules applied to fraternities as are applied to men's athletic clubs in big cities would "clean up the fraternities," for the two situations are quite different; here, incidentally, you are committing *two* fallacies: false analogy and begging the question (that is, assuming, unjustly here, that fraternities *need* "cleaning up"). These are some of the dangerous fallacies that may creep into any otherwise well-developed argument. You will have to watch for them, and for the others listed above, which any handbook of formal argument will tell you more about.

Your refutation, whenever it appears, must be fair and to the point, with a line of attack hitting the fallacies just indicated above. Further, throughout the argument you may be able to introduce from time to time various devices, or sources, of more or less subtle persuasion. For instance, if you can anticipate your reader's attitude toward the proposition, his general habits of mind, his level of intelligence, his susceptibility to emotion, you can play upon these facets of reader-interest to develop an attitude in your favor. And of course there is nothing better than a smooth, vital, individual style to help arouse such an interested attitude in the reader; hence it is up to you, so to speak, to revise your work several times before releasing the final version.

We present now, in conclusion, a purely suggestive, and perhaps biased (it is written by a graduate of an eastern men's college) model brief of an argument on co-education (one of the most popular topics in modern college life). Analyze the sequence of the arguments for types of evidence, for possible fallacies, for development of the refutation—in short, for all of the ideas given above for the writing of short, informal argument. We suggest that you yourself develop a brief proving the proposition from precisely the opposite direction, even as below we have printed an interesting argument developed from two directions at once: "Pro and Con: Abolish Intercollegiate Football?" Then we suggest that you apply these principles of briefing to the list of modern subjects soon to be given, to the student themes in section A, and to the professional illustrations in section B. If you wish more details now on the development of Argument—in its more formal aspects—we refer you to any specialized handbook of argumentation and to the speech department of your particular college or university.

THE BRIEF

Co-education Generally Demoralizes Young Men

(*Introduction*) I The occasion: Another sophomore boy has been "flunked" out of college; basic reason: a fraternity pin (or diamond ring) was thrown back at him by a coed.

(*Body*) Proposition: Co-education generally demoralizes young men, for

II The average male student in a co-educational institution is emotionally dominated by the female, for

    A. Girls are far more emotionally mature at eighteen than are boys at that age; and

    B. The boy's inborn deference to womanhood leads him naturally into emotional submission to coeds in general; and

    C. Most coeds come to college to get a husband and so put undue emotional pressure on the boys.

III The boy's college work suffers as a result of such close contact with women, for

    A. The average amorous young coed (and there are many such) can absorb three love affairs at once and maintain her scholastic standing, while the average young freshman or sophomore male student cannot manage more than one ring of the college circus at once; and

B. The coed spends considerable time "working on" the boy, or various boys, to sponge what she can of ideas for courses, and the boy chivalrously cannot refuse, but loses considerable time in the process; and

C. The lively sorority life at a co-educational college cuts the boy out of many valuable week-end study hours.

IV The coeds can "handle" the instructors and professors more easily than can the boys, who immediately develop a feeling of resentment toward this whole situation and "lie down on the job."

V The idea that co-education is more normal than the more sequestered type of education is untenable, for

A. A normal existence depends on normal development of the faculties unhindered by special pressure, not on mere close contact of opposite sexes; and

B. An abnormal sex pressure is brought to bear on a boy not yet fully developed emotionally just when he should be let alone to develop his mental faculties in training for a future career to support these very women who are seeking not a career but a husband; and

C. The normal "hunting ground" of the female is home life in the ordinary city or village, not an educational institution.

(*Conclusion*) Therefore, young men should go to men's colleges, if possible, and not to co-educational institutions.

In this short brief, specific subordinate arguments and illustrations should be inserted by the student himself under the "A," "B," "C" subdivisions. Obviously the whole proposition could be developed from the opposite point of view, and we suggest now that you try just such a procedure.

A List of Modern Subjects for Short, Informal Written Argument

1. Private Ownership of Modern Newspapers Is Subversive of Democracy.
2. Prohibition Should Be Brought Back.
3. Jazz Music Is as Valuable as Classical Music.

4. Our Forests Must Be Saved.
5. Is Divorce Too Easy Today?
6. College Hazing Should Be Eliminated.
7. Modern Automobiles Go Too Fast for Safety.
8. Education Should Control the Radio.
9. Should Sit-Down Strikes Be Eliminated?
10. Is the Supreme Court the Constitution?
11. *Tobacco Road* Should Be Taken off the Stage.
12. The New Deal Is a Failure.
13. The Anti-Lynching Law Should Not Pass.
14. Is the Welfare Haven Destroying the American Spirit?
15. The Airplane Will Beat the Battleship.
16. Should Democracy Survive?
17. Is Fascism More Effective Politically than Nazism?
18. Should the S.E.C. Be Given Greater Powers?
19. Is International Law Worth Anything Now?
20. Can a New World War Be Avoided?
21. Why Not Suppress Modern Art?
22. Psychoanalysis Is Dangerous Quackery.
23. Has the Farmer Been Pampered Too Much?
24. The University of Chicago Plan of Undergraduate Education Should Be Imitated.
25. Is Modern Socialism a Failure?
26. Should the United States Join the League of Nations?
27. The Commercialization of College Football Should Be Stopped.
28. The Government Is Crushing the Utilities.
29. The Political Lobby Should Be Outlawed.
30. What Should Be Done with the Railroads?
31. Should Fraternities and Sororities Be Abolished?
32. Freshmen Should Not Be Initiated into Fraternities or Sororities.
33. Visual Education Substitutes Machinery for Ideas.
34. Advertising Adds to the Cost, but Not the Value, of Goods.
35. The Movie in Technicolor Is a Failure.
36. The Government Should Greatly Expand the Force of G-Men.
37. Fascism and Communism Bring the Same Threats to Individual Liberty.
38. Beauty Contests Are Pernicious.
39. The Center Jump in Basketball Should Be Restored.
40. Slang Enriches the Language.

⋙ A ⋘

This first theme exhibits a direct and matter-of-fact presentation of a subject that was much discussed not long ago. There are more simple assertions than points of evidence, but the writer was able to assume a general unanimity of opinion on the problem.

TRANS–OCEANIC FLIGHTS

For the last fifteen years, more flights across the ocean or around the world have been attempted each year. Many of these flights have been completely successful, but entirely too many were unsuccessful.

A successful flight is, of course, a progressive advancement of aviation. A successful flight tends to increase the confidence of the public in the safety of aviation. It is a true test of the equipment and the skill of the pilot. The knowledge attained from such flights can be used to increase the safety and speed the development of aviation.

An unsuccessful flight, on the other hand, seems to do more damage to the progress of aviation than one hundred successful flights over the same route would do to aid aviation. One hundred to one may seem large odds to some people, but the average person does not want to gamble his life upon one-hundred-to-one odds.

The United States Department of Commerce governs all flights from the United States to foreign countries. Before one can fly from the United States to Paris, for example, he must receive the approval of the Department of Commerce.

The Department of Commerce has no definite policy toward these flights. Until recently its approval of a flight was simply an exercise that one went through before a flight to a foreign country. But recently several flights have failed to receive its approval.

The Department of Commerce should state a definite policy toward dangerous flights to foreign countries. It should decide whether the United States should spend its money to send its ships and aeroplanes in search of missing flyers, whether a flight that is just for fun, that would be of no scientific importance although successfully completed, should be approved, or whether only flights of importance to science, in which all possible precautions are taken to insure the safety of the flyers, should be approved.

A person should do what he pleases only as long as his pleasure does not harm the interests of others. But a flight across an ocean affects more than the pilot who is in the plane. The result of the flight has a profound consequence upon the progress of aviation.

The government should encourage flights that are made for scientific purposes and in which the proper precautions have been made. Such flights are necessary to the progress of aviation. Without these pioneer flights aviation would not have reached its present state of development.

A flight such as the one just completed by the *China Clipper* to Ireland differs in many respects from a flight over the same route by a land plane which one or two people would pilot. The modern aeroplane has been developed to such a state of near perfection that the majority of accidents which occur on commercial airways are traceable to mistakes on the part of the pilot. A plane such as the *China Clipper* has a crew of six men. The pilot is relieved of the problems of navigation, which cause the majority of accidents.

The government of the United States should enact laws that would protect a man who is attempting to make a flight that has a worthwhile scientific value to aviation. The government should approve such flights and support any flights that it approves. But flights that are not of scientific value should be discouraged and made illegal.

C. M.

What types of argument are used in the following well-poised paper? Note the careful introduction and the restrained refutation.

AMERICA SHOULD JOIN THE LEAGUE OF NATIONS

In the past there has been great controversy as to the advisability of the United States joining the League of Nations. Since the establishment of the League, the Republicans and the Democrats in alternating order included the controversy over the League as a major issue at the times of presidential elections. And till today the United States has steadfastly refused to join. Yet, despite all the political opposition, the United States should become a member of the League of Nations.

The League of Nations is pictured by the average American as an awful "bogeyman" who will surely get the United States into trouble. "The League is only machinery for the co-operation of Nations when the Nations see fit."[1] And they should see fit to co-operate at all times. The purposes of the League, as expressed in the preamble of the League's covenant, are "to promote international co-operation" and "to achieve international peace and security." It is obvious that the

[1] Dr. B. W. Rust, Lecture, "The League of Nations."

League needs the United States to promote international co-operation.

Let us look now to see why our country ought to become a member of the League of Nations. In the first place, the League was conceived by an American—President Woodrow Wilson—and was established by the Treaty of Versailles with the co-operation of American statesmen. But despite its American origin, the United States continuously turns "thumbs down" on the proposal of joining the League.

Secondly, our country participates in many of the peacetime activities of the League in full co-operation with the League. For example, the problem of health is one of the activities in which the United States takes an active role. We send medical authorities and financial support to the League Health Division to cope with international health problems. One of the duties of the international health authorities is to prevent pestilence from being carried from infected areas to countries abroad. For example, whenever a ship is about to leave the port of Shanghai, it is thoroughly investigated by health authorities to see that no pestilence will be carried to American or other ports. For there is always the danger that a ship, leaving the port of Shanghai, may be carrying some person or goods infected with the horrible plague pestilence which is so abundant in Asiatic countries. Another problem that we have a leading role in solving is the control of the opium traffic. The United States is more interested in this problem than any other country and is therefore seeking not only to control the traffic of opium, but also to regulate the cultivation of the poppy plant and the production of the drug. Therefore, the United States realizes the importance of international co-operation in these problems, and she should realize the necessity of international co-operation in other problems.

A third argument in favor of joining the League is that there would be no discrimination against the United States for her stubborn refusal to join. The United States would receive and wield the same power in the League as England, the leading member at the present time. We would receive a permanent seat (as only the great powers do) in the Council, which generally directs the affairs of the League.

Finally, in rebuttal to those who believe that membership in the League will only cause us to become entangled in some war, there is this argument: All resolutions made by the League must be adopted by unanimous vote or else the resolution does not pass. Therefore, if the United States were a member and the League proposed some measure, such as to send troops of League members to the present war-torn area of China, our country, even if it were the only country opposed to such a measure, could hold up the passage of the proposal and subsequently cause its defeat. This statement shows the absurdity of the belief that our country would go to war just because she was a member of the League and some other member country demanded that she go. So why not join?

Of course, the opposition claims that joining the League of Nations would be useless because the League is ineffective. It is admitted that the League has failed to settle the three major disputes of recent years— Japan's conquest of Manchuria, Italy's conquest of Ethiopia, and Japan's present invasion of China—but since the League's existence it has settled approximately seventy disputes between nations. The League may be ineffective, but in order to be effective it must have wholehearted international co-operation, and that is what it lacks.

Therefore the United States should join the League of Nations. America would lose nothing, gain a little, and would help international relations a great deal.

C. J. W.

Is the following "Refutation" wholly logical? Is it ever contentious?

A REFUTATION OF THE POPULAR OPINION THAT CITY LIFE INCREASES THE NUMBER OF NEUROTICS [1]

Life in the great American city has been described both tenderly and viciously, but always colorfully. "The pace that kills" has become synonymous with the tempo of the city. It is only logical to expect that being continually subjected to the terrific chorus of city noises— the riveting machines, the radio loud-speakers, the motor horns, the shouts of newsboys, the roar of traffic—and to the restrictions imposed upon us all by artificial civilization, to the whip of business and social competition—that all this would result in neurotic men and women, who could find release only in insanity or suicide; it is only logical to believe that human nerves can be stretched just so far and no farther, or they will break. This fact is so logical that it is easily understood why the conclusion has won such widespread belief. It may be logical and popular, but it is utterly and ridiculously untrue.

This noise of the city, about which there has been so much talk of late, does not make people neurotic. The truth of the matter is that

[1] A neurotic is a person who is at least of average mentality, but who is incapable of exerting emotional self-control.

only neurotic people are uncomfortably aware of city noise. Such people usually forget their noisy environments when they become absorbed in something which deals with the primary instincts, such as hunger and love. If the noise and movement of cities made people neurotic, all our traffic policemen would be raving mad, and our taxi-drivers would go insane, for they are subject to greater periods of noise than anyone else. Yet one never hears of an epidemic of neurosis among them. They are so busy performing their duties that they are not aware of the noise. Noise which really goes with life in the city —traffic, jazz, and the like—as often soothes as it irritates.

You have no doubt heard it said that there are more neurotics in the city than in the country. That is most certainly true, but the city has also more healthy persons. It has, in fact, more inhabitants of every nature than the country. I do not believe, however, that, speaking relatively, there are more neurotics in the city than in the country.

The rest cure of the country will not rid a man of his neuroses, since neurotic conditions are due to emotional reasons; they are a form of mental and not physical sickness; moreover, the city is a better place for the neurotic than the country, since it offers him more opportunity toward the release of these supercharged emotions. Not only is city life harmless to neurotics as well as to the average healthy person, but it is genuinely beneficial to both, since it provides men with two essentials for happiness—interesting work and comparative freedom from monotony; therefore I believe that the popular opinion that city life makes people neurotic as well as injures people already neurotic, is utterly and ridiculously untrue.

B. B.

The following theme develops an historical proposition. Is any new evidence introduced in the conclusion?

THE BRITISH MONARCHY DURING THE EIGHTEENTH CENTURY

The British Monarchy, which included England, Wales, Scotland, and Ireland, during the Eighteenth Century was in fact both corrupt and oppressive.

The kings were still the rulers of their kingdom, at least in theory. But they had continued to lose their power, and retain only their dignity, thus becoming mere figureheads. Parliament, therefore, had gained those powers which the king had lost: namely, the right of free speech for its members, with the power to levy taxes, to make laws, to remove or retain judges, and to determine the policy of their country in war or peace.

And yet, this Parliament, this so-called representation of the people, was most undemocratic. It consisted of two houses, the House of Lords and the House of Commons, but it is very probable that the statement that each Lord had his dummy in the lower house is true to the highest degree. It was, therefore, representative of the people only in name. For during the Eighteenth Century the majority of the people had no voice in choosing their representatives. True, two knights were elected for each shire, but it was done largely by the buying of votes by a rich noble.

Again there was no means of representation for all towns. And yet towns which had diminished to a population of two or had entirely disappeared were entitled to two representatives, while new towns which had sprung into existence were entirely without representation. And since no method for election was prescribed by law, the nobles practically ran the voting. This in time gave rise to corruption. Thus it was that seats in Parliament were bought and sold like boxes at the opera and seats at the stock exchange.

Surely there was need for reform. When a country is overrun by paupers supported by the government, when poor people might be shut up in the poor house and see their children carted off to factories, when sailors were kidnaped for the royal navy, when the farm hand was practically bound to the soil as a serf, when religious intolerance was prevalent, and when such minor offenses as stealing a shilling or cutting down an apple tree were punishable by death—then, I say, that there is something wrong. No matter how much praise the French gave the English monarchy; no matter that it was used as a model in politics; there can easily be seen by close observation the corruption and oppressiveness of the whole institution.

H. E.

➤➤➤ B ❮❮❮

The following professional illustrations have been chosen particularly for their vital, up-to-date flavor. We suggest special study of the debate on intercollegiate football, which should certainly stimulate emulation. Apply to both sides the list of fallacies given above in this chapter, in order to determine for yourself which arguments are the most logical. Note that the affirmative side has made a liberal and effective use of statistics.

PRO AND CON—ABOLISH INTER-
COLLEGIATE FOOTBALL? [1]

*In the following debate Mr. Pro and Mr. Con thresh out this issue with no
holds barred. All attitudes treated are derived from acknowledged experts and
all facts have been gathered by a skilled investigator.*

So, when the smoke has cleared away, what do you think?

YES, SAYS MR. PRO:

"American football is a splendid game. That is why some of us
would like to see the game given back to the boys before the over-
enthusiastic public squeezes it to death. Here is evidence of the impending suffocation:

"Thanksgiving Day used to end the season. Now, the big inter-
sectional post-season games are played on New Year's Day. Spring
practice begins in another four months. Many college players spend
their summers at manual labor conditioning for the September opening of the season. That adds up to seven or eight months a year. College football isn't a game any longer—it's a job.

"The University of Texas recently hired a first-flight football coach
on a 10-year contract at $15,000 a year. How many college presidents
receive as much?

"Radio advertisers paid college athletic associations some $400,000
this season for exclusive rights to broadcast their football games.

"The ultimate comment on football's present absurdities was made
when Elbert Hubbard wrote that 'Football bears the same relation to
education that bull-fighting does to agriculture.'

"Francis Wallace, realistic and intelligent friend of the game, summarizes the situation:

"'The colleges enter the open market and bid against one another
for the year's crop of athletes. They pay these boys and masquerade
the payments. They present these athletes in great outdoor stadia and
charge all that the traffic will bear. Football, as now conducted by
most of our great universities, is, at best, semi-professional—as much
show-business as Broadway.'

"*Colleges do not need football profits to pay for the rest of their athletic
programs.* Stevens Institute of Technology abolished intercollegiate
football in 1924. Since then it has maintained intercollegiate competition in full schedules of all other standard sports and provided an

[1] Reprinted from *Reader's Digest* for January, 1938, by permission of the editors.

intramural program which takes in all undergraduates. Exclusive of maintenance on buildings and grounds, the annual cost to the college is around $10 per undergraduate.

"On that basis, the salaries of a high-powered football coaching staff (say $30,000) plus graduate manager and press agent (say $10,000) would pay for such a program for a male student body of 4000.

"Massachusetts Institute of Technology, rid of intercollegiate football these 30 years, finances an extensive athletic program at much the same figure as Stevens from a student tax ($5.80 a year) and general college funds. This includes crew, the most expensive of college sports. Neither alumni nor students ever agitate for the return of intercollegiate football.

"*Football victories are not necessary for keeping alumni and public in a financially generous frame of mind.* An expert survey of representative colleges between 1921 and 1930 showed that those conspicuous for football success had increased their asset values by 117 percent, their endowments by 125 percent. Those going light on football did just a trifle better: assets were up 125 percent, endowments 126 percent.

"*The publicity values of football have little to do with stimulating enrollment.* The curve of increasing enrollment of male undergraduates at Columbia forged steadily upward in both the period when football was abolished (1905–15) and since it has been restored. The curve dropped after the depression, in spite of the college's developing football success.

"The enrollment of Reed College, without intercollegiate football, has grown steadily since the war. Its proportion of male students has increased and the student body compares favorably in height and weight with Pacific Coast students in general.

"*Subsidizing of football players handicaps intelligent boys lacking conspicuous athletic ability, and loads colleges with a dead weight of the less intelligent.* When athletes of Pennsylvania colleges, large and small, were given tests measuring intelligence and information, football players rated lowest. Football-playing Phi Beta Kappas are always rare enough to get publicity. The rank and file of paid football letter men are crammed and bullied into passing grades, or passed by professors who know better than to hold them to usual standards.

"Most of the scholarships that disguise subsidizing were really intended to help intelligent boys without money to get an education useful to society. A fast-running but slow-thinking halfback may be keeping out of college a bright lad who isn't so good at snagging passes.

"Many college jobs, usually the easiest ones, are reserved for athletes. The non-athletic poor boy gets what is left. Athletes are often paid far more than non-athletes for certain jobs.

"Francis Wallace wrote that he stopped scouting talent for big-time football colleges because too many of the football boys he had wangled into college graduated only to be too good for hard work and not quite good enough for the easy jobs they had expected.

"The days when a star end could count on a soft berth in a broker's office died with 1929. Professional football will pay a player only some $1200 a season for the few years he lasts—provided he measures up to professional standards, which are terrific. Radio stations were mobbed this season by bewildered gridiron heroes hoping for soft work as football announcers. Most of them would have been better off if they'd never had the financial chance to die for alma mater.

"Guesses on how much went into football pools in 1937 range between $50,000,000 and $75,000,000. Nobody knows exactly. But everybody knows that the whole huge total, along with other large sums bet on individual games, is handled by the lowest type of racketeers.

"A boy who is living a lie learns a lot about cutting corners. Now put these facts together: big money staked every week—chiseling gangsters—players made cynical by a dishonest system. Those are the makings of what might be the nastiest athletic scandal since the Black Sox.

"Many admirers of football deny heatedly that the college game could be fixed. According to highly responsible authority, it is already being fixed right along in at least one football-crazy section of the country. When some such scandal does break wide open, the public will have finished its job of wrecking.

"The colleges will do much better to beat fate to the draw by performing the indicated surgery while there is yet time. All the college color in the country could hardly make up for the disillusioning spectacle of alma mater's young heroes pulling the kind of fast ones that class them with crooked jockeys.

"Football would still survive as a lusty game played, as at Emory University, for fun among intramural teams.

"Or, for the athletic connoisseur, it would survive in the professional leagues which are drawing more money and attention every season.

"But it would no longer pervert the atmosphere of higher education, warp the athletic programs of colleges and set a flagrant example of chicanery for American youth."

No, Says Mr. Con:

"This agitation is old stuff. Way back in the day of bone-crushing mass plays, several important colleges bowed to public opinion and dropped football. Most of them have since restored it, as the game, opened and speeded up, became far less brutal.

"The public has responded to the change by filling huge stadia at high prices. The same public is discovering—and not minding much— the fact that one way or another colleges subsidize many of their players. It is learning to take them cordially for what they are—husky kids, using athletic skill to pay for education—and to honor them for their grit, skill, and perseverance.

"It also knows that, since dumb beef long since went out of football, the modern college player must be as quick on the uptake as he is on the charge.

"There is no way to repeal this popular enthusiasm for the spectacle of game youngsters fighting a wholesome, thrilling, mimic warfare because they enjoy it and because it helps some of them to an education.

"If intercollegiate football were abolished, the public would seek spontaneous color and drama in some other intercollegiate sport— and find it. The net effect would be merely the elimination of the most colorful and characteristic American spectacle.

"Professional croakers charge that 'College football has turned into big business.' So it has. And a darn good thing too for the American college and the American student.

"For receipts from football buy equipment, pay transportation, hire coaches and build facilities for basketball, baseball, track, hockey, swimming, lacrosse, tennis, squash, boxing, wrestling, fencing, rowing, and everything else.

"Every football player who is subsidized is only getting back a fraction of what he contributes in cash and inspiration to the physical good of the whole college community.

"Without football, college athletic associations owing large debts on new stadia would have to default on their bonds, which would outrage the sports-minded alumni who bought those bonds out of devotion to alma mater.

"Conversely, each football victory ties the alumnus closer to alma mater, and makes things far simpler for the college president when he needs funds for new dormitories. Where colleges are dependent on state funds, it works the same way on state legislators.

"College presidents know that live youngsters, recognizing successful football teams as signs of energy and enterprise and of that electric comradeship known as college spirit, are attracted to big-time football colleges.

"Football is the keystone of college sport. Its glories foster a vigorous athletic psychology inspiring every youth, dub or not, to play some game as best he can, building up a healthy habit of strenuous play that will pay him dividends the rest of his life.

"Since football demands a maximum of courage, discipline and perseverance, it is a superlative training for later life. Many a famous college tackle, now a success in his chosen career, testifies that the moral training he got from Coach So-and-So was more valuable to him than all the rest of his college education put together.

"Now that the cuss-and-bully type of coach is passing out of the picture, that factor's still more important. The modern coach is usually intelligent, smart with boys, soft-spoken, shrewd—perfect for leading and training youth.

"The healthiest thing that ever happened to intercollegiate football is the present tendency to admit subsidization and ask, with all the logic on one side: 'Why shouldn't needy boys be paid for their grueling battles in the interests of the whole college?'

"In a few years most colleges will have candidly brought things into the open. Already the members of one large conference have an agreement defining and limiting the amounts and number of athletic scholarships. All over the country various mutual agreements on talent-scouting and maximum rates of pay are gradually building up a code of ethics that will eventually either correct the worst abuses of intercollegiate football or put colleges that refuse to observe the code off the schedules of institutions that play fair in scouting and paying players.

"Stringent financial pressure on college athletic associations that are still paying off on boomtime stadia and other buildings is already lessening as the bonds are retired.

"By applying honest and realistic regulation to the present situation, the game can still be saved for the old grad, the student and the public, with all its pageantry and excitement and its nation-wide fostering of a healthy attitude toward physical courage and hard knocks. To abolish the game on account of its present minor extravagances would be to burn the house down to roast the pig."

Peace strikes have been popular in colleges recently. What do you think of the arguments in Mr. Fischer's paper? Does he successfully sustain his thesis? We print it merely to stimulate debate.

THE ROAD TO PEACE [1]
Louis Fischer

The outstanding fact in the world today is that wars are raging in three countries—in China, Spain, and Ethiopia. The greatest fallacy of our political thinking suggests that this situation offers only two alternatives: to stay out and allow the aggressor to have his way, or to go to war and stop him. If I thought so I should be an isolationist. I should say: let the aggressor run amuck; it will be years before he gets ready to strike at us, and any respite is a blessing. I have seen so much of the horrors of war in Spain during the last eighteen months that I would even be ready to advocate peace at any price. But I am convinced that isolationism is a greater menace to peace and to democratic institutions in this country than a wise American foreign policy based on free international collaboration with a view to preventing war.

The aggressors have been made bold by their successes. Manchoukuo, the Rhineland, Abyssinia, Spain, China—and now Austria. Nor does Austria bring the story to an end. In August the *Angriff*, official Nazi organ, said: "Money is being collected in Czechoslovakia for Soviet Spain. And who will later collect for Czechoslovakia?" The implication is obvious: Czechoslovakia is next. Why not?

France, England, the Soviet Union, and the smaller states are therefore alarmed, and announce unprecedented accelerations of already unprecedented rearmament programs. We do the same. The more progress Japan makes in China and the farther Italy and Germany penetrate into South America, where their support of Spanish fascism has earned them many friends (what happens in Spain is quickly reflected in the Spanish-American republics), the more feverishly the United States will arm. We shall have a large military establishment, mobilization of industry for war purposes, greater surveillance of individual citizens, more repression, more reaction. Successful aggression stimulates the world arms race. So does the prospect of successful aggression. There is no use asking for smaller army and navy subsidies while wars are in progress or while aggression pays.

[1] Reprinted from the *Nation* for February 26, 1938, by permission of the editors.

As the aggressors advance they must reach a line which the opposing armed giants, if they are to protect their national interests, cannot allow them to cross. And then a major conflict will ensue. This is the gravest implication of fascist conquests. Isolationists may believe that America can remain aloof. This immature notion is not shared by those who understand the complicated pattern of international relations. Once war has started, Ludlow amendments will not help. War must be prevented long before it becomes imminent. Measures like the Ludlow amendment would tend to draw us away from a policy of war prevention and toward one of stopping a war in the eleventh hour.

The road away from armaments and back to appeasement and peace must start in a conscious attempt to stop the assaults of totalitarian states upon unoffending peoples. The first duty of the true pacifist is to take the profit out of aggression. If one aggressive war ended in failure thanks to collective action, a second would be less likely. The choice lies between mad rearmament, plus frail dams like the Ludlow amendment to hold back the inevitable flood, and the re-establishment of peace by a policy of war prevention.

Peace can be re-established by nonviolent measures. The assumption that Germany or Italy or Japan would, if subjected to economic pressure, strike back in desperation is based on an error not difficult to disprove. Ever since October, 1936, the Soviet Union has helped Loyalist Spain with munitions. If it had not, fascism would now be triumphant in Spain. Have Germany or Italy attacked Russia in retaliation? No. France today pursues a pro-Loyalist policy which is immediately translated into greater Spanish war costs for Italy and Germany. Have the invaders of Spain moved against France? No. Hongkong is the gateway through which a broad stream of British and other war materials is entering China. The Japanese have not yet attacked Hongkong, or French Indo-China, or Soviet Siberia, whence the Chinese are now receiving airplanes and other weapons to defend themselves against invasion. The fascist nations have not struck back because they cannot. They are too weak. We often mistake their audacity for strength. They are merely made brave by other nations' passivity.

Poor Loyalist Spain, which began the war with no army and with political disunity, has been able to resist Franco, Hitler, and Mussolini. Germany and Italy have helped the rebels as much as their resources, their preoccupations, and the international situation permitted. Italy has had 200,000 soldiers in Spain. The two dictators have sent 1,800 airplanes to the disloyal generals and equipment for an army of half a million. Franco, according to the London *Financial News* of January 10, owes Rome two and a half billion lire and Berlin eight hundred million marks. Germany and Italy will try to do more but it will not be enough. Their arm is too short. Meanwhile, the fascist investment in Spain has so weakened the investors as to prevent them from launching a European war. This is the Loyalists' contribution to world peace.

The Nazi *Frankfurter Zeitung* said on December 28 that when the rebels rose in Spain no one thought that the war would last longer than a few months. The Japanese were similarly mistaken about the war in China. The German theory of the short war has been exploded. Continued Chinese resistance will increasingly undermine Japan's economy. Will aggressor nations which cannot conquer their weak victims assume the additional task of attacking great powers which are helping those victims? The fact is that the powers which are aiding Spain and China have not been attacked although they are within easier reach of the aggressors than the United States.

Not only do the fascist states hesitate to fight the large countries. They even retreat when hard pressed by diplomacy. The Nyon conference against submarine piracy was one case. Again, a year ago, the French were disturbed by the German penetration into Spanish Morocco. On January 11, 1937, François-Poncet, the French ambassador in Berlin, told Hitler that these activities would have to stop. They stopped. No force was used. No force would ever have to be used. The moral and economic influence of the pacific nations would suffice.

America's contribution to this peace policy would be safe and inexpensive. It would consist, chiefly, in withholding from aggressors the materials which they need to pursue their murderous adventures. On January 11, 1938, the German steamer *Crefeld* sailed down the Delaware River with 200 aerial bombs. Its destination was a German port, where part of the cargo was to be unloaded, probably for reshipment to Spain. The remaining bombs were to be sent on to Japanese army depots in China. This was the first shipment of a 2,500-ton order of bombs for Germany and Japan. About the same time President Roosevelt appealed to the Red Cross to give a million dollars in relief to Chinese civilians.

It is not neutral to assist the stronger side. In accordance with the Neutrality Act we deny arms to Franco and to the Loyalists. Franco, however, needs no American munitions. He receives all he needs from Germany and Italy, and we sell arms to Germany and Italy.

But the legal Spanish government suffers, and Spaniards die in thousands in air raids because the government is short of arms. Apparently impartial, we are in fact anti-Loyalist. We take sides by doing nothing. Though the sympathies of the American people are undoubtedly with China, we facilitate Japan's war on China.

The Neutrality Act should be repealed or at least amended so that it does not aid the bully and penalize the underdog. Does any danger of war lurk in such changes? Suppose we sold arms to the Loyalists. Would Franco or Hitler or Mussolini attack the United States? At worst they could seize the foreign ships in which those arms would be carried. The same applies to shipments of weapons for China. And always it must be kept in mind that nations are actually supplying China and the Loyalists without getting themselves into the slightest trouble.

United States government policy and the private attitude of Americans as expressed through a boycott can foster peace by making it clear that aggression will receive no encouragement or aid from America. We could, if necessary, proceed independently of others. But American efforts might be correlated with similar measures by the bourgeois democracies and the Soviet Union. The French and British have been guilty of imperialist robberies. They have bombed peaceful inhabitants in the Northwest Frontier of India, in Palestine, and elsewhere. I am under no illusions regarding the reactionary potentialities of these countries. But they want peace, for they know they can gain nothing from war. This is not a very idealistic reason, but it is all the more reliable since it is a selfish one.

We dislike hearing about struggles for democracy because Woodrow Wilson in 1917 camouflaged an ugly combat between rival imperialisms as a lofty crusade to make the world safe for democracy and to end all wars. Ever since we have been zealously on guard against such hokum. Now in Spain a feudal military clique, inspired and supported by reactionary foreign dictatorships, is trying to snuff out a democracy where civil liberties have manifested remarkable virility even in war conditions. China, painfully seeking to become a nation, is threatened by a neighbor who would make it a slave. England and France, in the past, did similar things. Yet France sympathizes with the Loyalists for national-defense reasons. England looks with disfavor on the Japanese thrust for imperialist reasons. We do not approve the reasons but we welcome the result.

In international politics, which is a hard-boiled game, motive and consequence do not always match. For instance, Soviet assistance in

Spain stimulates revolution in Spain and contributes to the downfall of totalitarian fascisms, but it also aids the bourgeois imperialisms of France and England. The naïve and malicious have contended that each of these effects is deliberately sought. The discerning realize that one effect is not obtainable without the others. So, too, the capitalist democracies may set out to defend their sordid interests and end by buttressing true democracies with advanced social programs.

It has been argued that if the fascist nations cannot obtain the raw materials they need and solve the problem of their excess inhabitants they will explode. I do not accept the facile division of the world into haves and have-nots. Was it to *have* that Mussolini took Abyssinia? Then why, before he had even finished fighting there and before he began economic exploitation of the country, did he plot to invade Spain? If Italy needs new lands because it is overpopulated, why does the Duce distribute prizes to encourage large families? In *Mein Kampf* Hitler objected to colonies for Germany, and wisely. For in 1913 Germany's total trade with its colonies—and it had held some of them for more than thirty years—amounted to $25,000,000, or .005 of its total exports and imports. It got practically no important raw materials from its colonies. Yet it was rich and powerful. First Hitler wanted no colonies. Now he insists on them. First he proposed autarchy, or national self-sufficiency. He still has his four-year plan for substitutes and armaments, but he has also struck out for foreign-trade expansion. Mussolini too talks of self-sufficiency and in the next breath of empire. The two aims are at odds. The point is that fascism seems to be the last chance for these countries to solve their problems within the present social system. Frantically they take up with first one panacea, then the other, then they merge the two; finally they appear to achieve partial success in both and nevertheless continue to pursue the same goals with a madness that suggests the eternally ungratified.

Japan, in 1931, asserted that it coveted Manchuria for its surplus population and as a source of natural wealth. Yet Manchuria's economic surface was scarcely scratched when Tokyo occupied northern China, and that enterprise was far from consolidated when it launched its present assault on all of China. The motive is not economic. It is insanity born of futility. Even in Poland, with its tremendous stretches of sparsely settled land, a large Polish organization, officially inspired, directs a movement to acquire for Poland distant domains in Africa, South America, and Asia.

Czarist Russia was a colossal empire. Yet it neglected opportunities for internal development to absorb vast new provinces in Central Asia and the Far East. Russia was a big "have," but it wanted to have more. The revolution in Russia changed the have which wanted expansion to a have which needs none. But fascist states are have-nots by their very political nature, and no Van Zeeland plan or raw-material redistribution will help them.

The millions in Germany and Italy who thought and voted liberal or democratic or Socialist or Communist are neither all dead nor all converted. Outside opposition to fascism heartens internal opposition, whereas foreign political victories for the dictators depress it. Domestic discontent cannot yet cause the collapse of Hitler or Mussolini, but it must be put down on the debit side of the ledger when the totalitarian governments count up the pros and cons of initiating a major war. In this calculation, too, the neutrals appear as assets. If European fascism were certain that the United States would refrain from helping the democracies, it would feel less reluctant to challenge them. If Hitler and Mussolini were certain that America and England would remain neutral, France would be in danger. The goal of Nazi foreign policy has been to foster American isolationism and to separate England from France, and France from the Soviet Union. Similarly, Japan, Germany, and Italy have sought to cripple the League of Nations lest it become an instrument of common action against aggression. The bitterest opponents of collective security are not American isolationists but Hitler and Mussolini. In May, 1935, Hitler urged that when hostilities break out between two nations "the other nations withdraw at once from both sides." This is his idea of neutrality. Germany attacks Czechoslovakia, for instance. All other nations withdraw from the conflict. Germany wins. Hitler marches into France. Everybody remains neutral. Germany wins.

The aggressors seek to drive isolationist and neutral wedges between their potential enemies. At the same time, however, the aggressors themselves unite for collective insecurity under the guise of the "anti-Communist pact." This device fools some people, for communism is a very popular red herring. Yet the three fascist militarisms are concerned first of all with Great Britain, and it is British interests that have suffered most in Abyssinia, Spain, and China. Those who believe that collective security is a Soviet machination are taking the anti-Communist pact at its face value and Hitler and Mussolini at their word.

Even in their union, however, the fascist aggressors lack complete cohesion. Germany and Italy cannot come to an agreement on strategy in Spain. Germany and Japan have not the same interests in China. Moreover, the fact that each of the aggressors is at war—Italy on two fronts—lessens the practical aid they can give to one another. The task of checking fascist aggression, while not easy, must therefore not be exaggerated. France and England must before long awaken to the necessity of resistance, and America's role would consequently be a minor one. If China and the Loyalists fight on for another year, the aggressors will be incapable of disturbing the peace much longer. Today collective security means help for China and Spain in stemming invasion. America could give this help without expanding its navy. But if past and present aggressions make us build a bigger fleet, people who don't like it ought to do something to oppose aggression.

For oratorical effects in persuasive argument consult the selection printed in this book in Chapter IV: Pericles's *Oration*, as reported by the historian Thucydides, and translated by Mr. Richard Crawley. Excellent modern material for short arguments on vital political subjects of the hour appears from month to month in the *Congressional Digest: the Pro and Con Monthly*, edited by A. G. and N. T. N. Robinson at 2131 Leroy Place, Washington, D. C. Other interesting "pro-and-con" arguments on contemporary subjects can be found from time to time in the *Reader's Digest*.

CHAPTER XI

The Term Paper [1]

THE TIME has now come for a more sustained piece of writing. While the term paper need not be a Herculean labor, it does call for the use of varied abilities. There will be an opportunity to combine many of the shorter types of writing that have been introduced in the preceding chapters; for the term paper is simply a more complex problem in exposition, in "setting forth." Two primary aspects of the type should be borne in mind. One is that it calls for an element of sheer length; it is a kind of test flight to display efficiency, staying power, demonstrable ability at the end of the training period. The other point is that the term paper is essentially an investigation in its content, and a piece of strict exposition in its style. That is to say, it is only indirectly imaginative, if at all, its nearest professional parallel being the informative magazine article. If its objective tone is lost, the term paper tends to merge into the informal essay, the type that is to follow as the first of the definitely imaginative forms of writing.

Seasoned commanders never try to take cities by single assaults. They divide the work into stages of careful preparation and successive attacks. Similarly, the long paper involves several months of siege before the final stroke. The process may be divided into four steps, and, inasmuch as these are distributed throughout the term, several of them will be discussed here "after the fact." In sum, these steps are as follows: selection of subject, location of material, reading, actual composition.

[1] The basic idea of this chapter is to some extent derived from Professor T. E. Rankin's *The Method and Practice of Exposition* with the permission of both the author and the publishers. All footnotes in this chapter will follow *A Manual of Style*, University of Chicago Press, in form, not the permission-line form used necessarily elsewhere in this book.

First, two or three weeks after the beginning of the course, the general subject should be chosen. Perhaps the instructor will want to submit his own ideas; if so, these will be best to follow. He may even wish to have all the members of the class write on various aspects of a large centralizing interest: Nationalism, the Fine Arts, or the Orient. Seventy-five broad possibilities are listed in this chapter. Probably he will let you make the final choice closely in line with your own interests and particular fund of knowledge. Sometimes students choose a subject of which they know nothing, just to educate themselves a little; but this procedure is not advisable, particularly where the subject involves subtle defining of elusive abstractions or the handling of advanced technical matters. Some shifting is possible, even healthful, but it should not be protracted. The final choice should be made by the middle of the term, at the latest, and life will be much smoother if it is established at the beginning. The energetic student who works at the abstract problems of Socialism and then finally switches to the concrete type of subject, such as Training Hunting Dogs or Types of Dancing, can make no use of the materials which he has rejected. The selection cannot be made too carefully—or too early.

After the subject has been determined upon, there will then be time allowed for the second step. The materials must be located. This will require further close thinking about the subject; but this will be stimulated by the task in hand, the collecting of facts and locating of the best authorities, in books, encyclopedias, magazines, newspapers, etc. At the end of this period of study the student should be able to submit to the instructor an outline of the main divisions—the Roman-numeral divisions—of the paper, and as complete a bibliography as he has been able to build up for the subject. This bibliography should be recorded on cards, one item per card, in a form that will be explained in detail in this chapter.

The third step will require more time, since there will be a number of short papers for the student to write in this period as well. The problem here is to read and collect notes preparatory to a long personal conference with the instructor at the end of this stage of the preliminary work. It is not necessary to have all the reading and notes completed at this time; part of these will fall in the last weeks, but the sooner they are all in hand, the better.

The final, fourth step—the actual writing of the finished version—comes near the end of the term. It should be presented to the instructor by the middle of the month; then he can go over it, preferably in a second conference. Thus the task is completed in four easy stages and, provided all work is done on schedule, without noticeable strain. By developing an easy, conversational grasp of the subject, the writer should be able to work out the complete paper swiftly and directly. If possible, it may be most effective to do this at one sitting; there will be a gain in cogency and stylistic smoothness. A few hours of persistent effort, with perhaps a few cups of coffee for the hours when most good citizens are in bed, will often produce a clean-cut result and save days of worried frittering.

Now, to recapitulate the four steps in producing the term paper more in detail: The subject for the term paper should involve investigative treatment, that is, research. The length of the paper may be about two thousand words; but the instructor may ask for a paper of such scope as to involve a potential five thousand words, only two thousand of which—or perhaps two major sections—will actually be written out. As the hunter of big game knows, there is nothing in mere length or size which need by itself inspire fear; and, as a matter of fact, many a casual telephone conversation extends well beyond two thousand words. But, once more, there is real value in sustained effort with the brain as well as the muscles. Hence, the subject should be chosen, at least to some extent, in accordance with the demands and limitations of the prescribed space. The following have been chosen by students and may give some idea of the type: The Elizabethan Theaters, The Beginning of Printing, The Short Story, The Evolution of the Piano, Henry Ford in Industry, Oriental Rugs, A History of Detroit, The Panama Canal, The Development of Opera in Europe, Thirty Years of Dancing (1900–1930), Christmas, The Five-Year Plan (in Russia), Music in the Shakespearean Era, Nursing, Advertising, The Stock Market, The Development of Early English Drama, Pioneer Broadcasting, Airships, Some Dickens Originals, Psychology, The History of Aviation. Since this is an English course, some of the subjects above are related to the field of English literature. Most instructors will probably make similar suggestions, but the student should consider primarily his own capabilities and interests.

Once the subject has been chosen, the next step is to look up material on it and arrange this material in some coherent outline form to present to the instructor. You will now require various bibliographical aids, which the librarians will be glad to explain if you ask intelligent questions. The most obvious source of material is the library card catalogue; go to it first. Then there are the various encyclopedias—some are for special topics such as religion, science, agriculture—and also dictionaries, which contain a surprising amount of information. For articles in magazines look up your subject in *Poole's Index*, *The Reader's Guide*, and the *International Index*. For some specialized material in English and American literature and history you may consult the *Dictionary of National* [British] *Biography*, the *Dictionary of American Biography*, the *Cambridge History of English Literature*, the *Cambridge History of American Literature*, and C. S. Northup's *Register of Bibliographies of the English Language and Literature*. If you really want to choose a subject in English literature, you will find further sources of material in T. P. Cross's *Bibliography and Methods of English Literary History*, in *The Year's Work in English Studies*, and the annual bibliography of the Modern Humanities Research Association. But for more general subjects the librarians will perhaps let you look at John Minto's *Reference Guide* or I. G. Mudge's *Guide to Reference Books*. To proceed further, there are the English and American catalogues of books published, Whitaker's *Cumulative Book Index*, the H. W. Wilson *Cumulative Book Index*, and the *American Library Association Index*. The reference librarian will show you how to use these and other available helps and guides.

The outline of the most important divisions of the paper will come next, but keep in mind that it is to be merely a *general* outline. In Chapter I this outline was anticipated in the discussion of the relationship of the short papers to the term paper. There we noted that an outline of any general subject involving some study would normally include six divisions: (a) Definition, (b)

History or Sources, (c) Division, (d) Comparison and Contrast,[1] (e) Value, and (f) Future. You will recall that these six points were applied to a study of radio: thus the outline will in most cases be merely a restatement of the above six items *in terms of your own subject*. But this may not be always absolutely inevitable. In the case of the short themes you have already discovered that the chapters on "The Abstract Term," "The Classified Summary," and "Criticism," for example, have developed a detailed study of three sections of this tentative outline for the term paper (sections a, c, and e). We even suggested, in Chapter I, that the term paper might be written in sections like these for short papers and assembled at the end, *à la* the Ford car, to be presented as a whole. It is possible, too, that the whole term paper may be an expansion of merely *one* of these six sections, with other sections subordinated entirely to this one. Consider, for example, three subjects actually chosen by students: Oriental Rugs, Jazz, and The History of Aviation. Here you have sections c, a, and b, respectively, developed in detail for the term paper, and there is no reason why the whole paper could not be written on a criticism, a comparison, or the future of the subject chosen. Nevertheless we return to the six sections noted above as the foundation for the outline to be submitted to the instructor before the middle of the term. Whatever modification may be needed in this form will be determined by the subject chosen and by the instructor's individual suggestions.

There remains only to indicate the form to be used on the various bibliographical and index cards. Each of the cards—the three-by-five-inch size is best for general use—should have a separate entry. All the cards when put together finally should run in alphabetical sequence. The entry for a book should read:

> McMurtrie, D. C.
> The Book; the Story of Printing and Bookmaking.
> New York: Covici-Friede, Inc., 1937.

The punctuation should follow this model precisely, and the title of the book should be underlined.

---

[1] That is, comparison with something similar in another classification: e.g., radio and phonograph, airplane and motorboat—not types of radios or types of airplanes. The latter would be "Division."

For a magazine reference:

> Brounlow, E. B.
> "The Structure of the Sonnet."
> <u>Poet Lore</u>, VIII (1896), 593–601.

Again note the punctuation. Here the title of the article is in quotation marks, and the title of the magazine is underlined. The volume of the magazine is in Roman numerals, the date in parentheses, and the pages inserted after the parentheses. In case of both these forms an anonymous entry should be indicated with [Anon.] in place of the author's name, and the entry belongs at the beginning of the alphabet.[1]

You are now ready for the hardest task of all, the submission of notes in a particular form. There is an excellent book written on this by E. W. Dow, entitled *Principles of a Note-System for Historical Studies*,[2] but it is a hard book to read. Let us try to simplify Mr. Dow's ideas.

To return to the outline, with its six tentative divisions, you will now think of each one of these six as a major heading to be indexed on a large card (preferably the four-by-six-inch size). Now sit at your desk with a supply of blank cards before you, prepared to take notes on a book or magazine article first in your list. Spread out the cards on the farther side of the desk, and start to read.

Supposing your subject to be the "Ford Car," you may, as you read, suddenly come across an item on the early history of the Ford. Selecting one of the blank cards, you will now write, in the upper left corner, the major heading, "History"; in the upper right corner you will write the word "Early." This is now the subtopic for this card, and from this moment, this particular card is dedicated to notes on the early history of the Ford, and *no other topic*. It looks like this left-hand diagram.

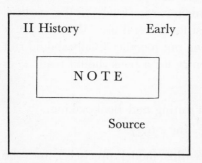

---

[1] For other variations, such as those covering encyclopedias, newspapers, etc., see the University of Chicago *Manual of Style*.

[2] D. Appleton-Century, and Company, Inc., 1924.

A few hours or days later, in a totally different book or magazine article, you will probably run across another note on the early history of the Ford car; pull out the card dedicated to this subtopic and write the new note below the other: the back of the card can be used if necessary. Clip all such cards on this one subtopic together, if you run beyond a single card. Your card now looks like this:

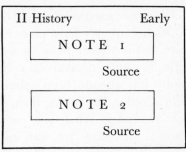

But let us go back to the original situation, with you at the desk reading the first book or magazine article. In it you presently run across a remark on the Ford as compared with the Chevrolet. Take up another blank card and enter a new note. See note at left. This card is now henceforth dedicated to all remarks comparing the Ford and Chevrolet. If you find another car compared with the Ford, make a new index card for this new subtopic.

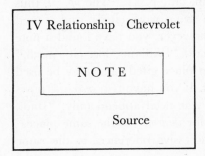

You continue reading. Sooner or later you will perhaps find something about the cheapness of the Ford car. See note below.

And so you proceed, the subtopics appearing one by one, like new pictures, as you read, so that you never need worry about the detailed division of your major outline: the whole thing unrolls as you read, and at the end you have a pack of cards which can be shuffled into any order you please. All there

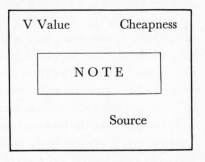

is to do then is to write straight through the cards, turning them face down as you write. This new system of note-taking organizes your material as you find it in your reading, and at the same time stimulates you to more intelligent reading and thinking.

One more suggestion should be given—about the word "source" on each card. We have placed it at the bottom of each separate note, but obviously these "sources" are not all the same. Their form, however, depends on certain fixed principles. The bibliography has already been submitted to the instructor in alphabetical order. He knows, then, what books and magazine articles you are using. When you come to write out notes from these sources, therefore, you can cut down the identification of the source to a minimum. Thus, to use the two illustrations given above—"Jones" for the book and "Williams" for the magazine article—if you have derived a note from Jones, your source will be written simply: "Jones, op. cit., p. 41." The *op. cit.* thus underlined, stands for *opere citato* (from work cited), and is used only for references to books. If, however, you have found a note in Williams, your source will read: "Williams, loc. cit., p. 58." The *loc. cit.* is for *loco citato* (from place cited) and may be used for reference to magazine articles. If you have two *successive* notes from either Jones or Williams, you need append only, "Ibid., p. 42," or "Ibid., p. 59." *Ibid* is for *ibidem*, "in the same place." But this can be used only for successive references to the same book or article.

This form for sources on index cards is used also for footnotes, if you need these in the theme itself. You are not likely to be asked to give footnotes for much more than direct quotations and direct ideas in the theme proper. Your notes will generally be summaries, *in your own words*, of the ideas of the source; only once in a while are you supposed to quote directly from this source. Of course deliberate insertion into the theme of material actually quoted *without quotation marks* constitutes definite plagiarism, which in writing is the unforgivable sin.

This theme, like the process, can make use of diagrams or pictures. Footnotes will often help to explain technical terms used in the text. Do not depend on merely one source; the instructor will expect you to submit at least two or three books and four or five magazine articles on the subject you have chosen. Beware of too broad a subject.[1] One student submitted the subject "Spain," another "English Drama"; but only one aspect of Spain or of English drama can be discussed to advantage in a two-thousand-word theme. In general avoid attempting such vague subjects as the "Existence of God," though one student did rather well with it. A biography, if this type is chosen, must be an *expository* biography. The introduction to any long theme should strive to appeal directly to the reader's interest, for your subject may be a hard one to get across. Concrete anecdotes and illustrations will always help to enliven a subject that may look very dead. If you are going to type this theme, double-space it by all means—the instructor will thank you from the bottom of his heart. Watch transitions from one large section to the next; indicate them carefully, but smoothly; perhaps a brief paragraph will be the best transition. Above all, choose a subject that really interests you, so that you can keep up your enthusiasm throughout the whole long procedure.

In later years even freshmen will be thankful for early training in writing the term paper, because with this preparation five or six papers a semester will never bother them as sophomores, juniors, and seniors.

→≫ A ≪←

"The Art of Block Printing" (compare Chapter II) is a perfect illustration of the development of all six divisions suggested for the term paper. It also exhibits an excellent style and perfect footnote form.

THE ART OF BLOCK PRINTING

Wood-block printing is one of the oldest arts known to mankind. This process consists of cutting away, or hollowing out from a block of wood, that part of the design which in the finished product will appear white. George T. Plowman defines wood engraving as a relief process in which "the design is drawn on or transferred to a block of wood and a knife is employed to cut away the surface of the block between the lines." [2] Another type of block printing, which is used a

[1] An unwieldy subject is often cut down in the process of the reading: e.g., Dogs → Small Dogs → Spaniels.

[2] G. T. Plowman, *Etching and Other Graphic Arts* (New York: John Lane Co., 1914), p. 38. [The *first* reference to a source should be complete in this form.]

great deal by modern artists, is the linoleum block. The technique of carving this is essentially the same as that of the wood block. However, it is much easier and faster, since the linoleum is so much softer than the wood. Schools very often give instruction in this branch of the art, and many young people have in this way, and through their researches, discovered the remarkable cuts executed by the ancient masters in both Europe and Asia.

The origin of wood engraving is lost in the dim shades of the past. However, it is known that the ancient Egyptians and Babylonians used wood blocks to indent bricks, the Romans printed letters with them, and, of course, the Chinese used them for many, many centuries, both to print books, and to form designs on fine materials.[1] It is evident that the Chinese pursued this art, and developed it to a much greater extent than any of the aforementioned peoples. To China goes the credit for the most ancient printed book of which any knowledge at present is recorded. This book, the *Diamond Sutra*, taken from the Buddhist scriptures, was printed and decorated with woodcuts by the Chinese in 828 A.D. Other sources state that as early as 300 B.C. in Cathay books were printed from wooden engravings.

Japan probably originated the color print—a form of block printing in which many blocks, often several hundred, are used, each block printing only one shade. This form was developed so highly by the Japanese that some of their color prints have never been excelled.[2] In contrast with their originality in the creation of the color print, the Japanese craftsmen commenced a practice which was later used by European artists. A block print was the product of two or more men— the artist who drew the design, the skilled cutter who hollowed out the blocks, and perhaps another skilled craftsman who printed the various shades, for the printing of the color blocks was an art in itself.

Wood engraving was first introduced into Europe about 1420, and for a time only religious subjects were used for prints. Still in existence are many old woodcuts depicting various Biblical scenes. Indeed, many of the old copies of the Bible, painstakingly transcribed by the monks, were illustrated in this way, and, as men became more proficient in the art, the letters themselves were printed from wood blocks. It is probably through the gradual development of this primitive printing that the printing press was invented.

---

[1] F. H. Vizetelly, ed., *New Standard Encyclopaedia of Universal Knowledge* (New York: Funk & Wagnalls, 1931), XXV, 290.

[2] R. W. Polk, *Essentials of Linoleum Block-Printing* (Peoria, Illinois: The Manual Arts Press, 1927), p. 11.

One of the greatest of the early masters of the woodcut was Albrecht Dürer, a German. As did most of the great wood engravers, he introduced new features which simplified and strengthened the cuts. Formerly, the prints had been mostly outline figures which were colored by hand. Dürer replaced these with dark and light lines which gave the effect of color and did away with the necessity of tinting.[1] Moreover, his technique was so excellently shown in his prints that others could better their own techniques by simply studying one of Dürer's woodcuts. After Dürer's death, no one appeared to take his place. In consequence, German wood engraving declined, and never again reached the high level Dürer had attained.

Ernest Knaufft calls Thomas Bewick, of England, who lived from 1753 to 1828, the "father of the modern woodcut."[2] Until his time, wood engravers had used pear or apple wood, and had cut with the grain. Bewick originated the use of boxwood, which he cut across the grain with a burin or graver. Also, he developed the white-line method of printing. This means that the print showed as white lines on a black ground, instead of the reverse, as it had formerly. Although modern woodcutters have a much wider range of subject, and use a bolder, cruder, more expressive technique, the fundamental wood-engraving methods of Thomas Bewick have not changed enough to be conspicuous, except in the instances when photography is used in the transference of the design to the block.[3]

American artists adopted the use of wood engraving, and, during the period from 1870 to 1900, became so excellent that they greatly influenced that art in many European states. Moreover, extraordinary progress has been made in the linoleum-block form of printing which was first practiced in the United States in 1910. Woodcuts and linoleum prints are used for every purpose imaginable today, and their field is ever widening. Every artist develops his own technique, with the result that the finished print is often extremely modern and grotesque—the cynosure of all eyes. The trend today, moreover, is toward a striking solidity of form, and great force in the execution of the subject.

As I have mentioned before, there are two types of block printing—the wood-block print, and the linoleum-block print. Color prints, which might be called a third type, can be made with either a wooden or a linoleum block. The wood block is, of course, the much older form,

---

[1] Vizetelly, *op. cit.*, XXV, 291.
[2] E. Knaufft, "Woodcuts," *Golden Book*, IX (March, 1929), 76.
[3] Plowman, *op. cit.*, p. 39.

but the linoleum block has rapidly developed many advantages over the former. The material is much easier to work upon, and costs much less than the wood. Also, the tools and other equipment needed are few, and inexpensive. For these reasons, the linoleum block is used much more for advertising and commercial purposes than the wood block. However, the latter still holds its place in the realm of decorative art.

Color prints, as developed by the Japanese, are also used, mainly for ornament. The color print actually is the most difficult of the block prints to make. Each block, printing only one shade, must exactly match the other blocks.[1] For instance, if one were to print a picture of the sun setting over a mountain peak, one block would print only the sun, another one, part of the mountain, another, its snowy peak, and probably two or three blocks would be needed to portray effectively the gloriously tinted sky. Such a print would be only a very simple one. The immense care and skill needed to make a more complex print can readily be seen. Some of the Japanese prints are so delicately shaded and matched that one could never guess they were made from hundreds of different blocks all meeting perfectly.

The uses of block prints are many and varied. In the Middle Ages, they were, of course, used to illustrate religious texts, and later on to print the texts themselves. They are employed extensively today for commercial purposes, such as second-color plates for maps and charts, graphs, monograms, letterheads, designs for cloth and wrapping paper, bookplates, posters, and programs.[2] F. Morley Fletcher says that "learning how to make a color print trains students to design with economy and simplicity for modern printing processes." [3] In addition to the practical uses of block prints, they are of value in supplying an atmosphere of serenity and charm to a room. For Mr. Fletcher further states that "a single print well placed in a room of quiet color will enrich and dominate a whole wall." [4] Also, art teachers have found that the making of block prints gives their students an opportunity to originate an individual technique.

Etching and block printing arose together in Europe, and have been developed by men who usually were masters in both arts, although etching is regarded as the opposite of woodcutting. For in the former, the lines are bitten into the metal surface by acid, while in the latter,

---

[1] Plowman, *op. cit.*, p. 41.

[2] Sallie Belle Tannahill, *P's and Q's* (New York: Doubleday, Page & Co., 1923), p. 41.

[3] F. M. Fletcher, *Wood-Block Printing* (London: J. Hogg, 1916), p. 8.

[4] *Ibid.*, p. 6.

the spaces of wood between the lines are cut away by tools fashioned for that purpose. However, the very fine wood engravings sometimes resemble etchings, even though the methods differ so greatly. Albrecht Dürer was the first to develop the etching, and since his time, the two arts have been rivals, with etching sometimes regarded as the better. They both require highly skilled masters to obtain worth-while results, and, although at present, etchings are of more value than wood-block prints, it is doubtful if they will remain so for many years.

Block printing will probably never cease to be an active and original medium of expression.[1] Moreover, if the public can be educated to appreciate this form of art, it is certain that artists in their efforts to please the world will improve and reach new heights in it. In the field of commercial art, block prints have only made a small beginning. More and more uses for them will be found, with the result that good design and unity will play an even greater part in advertising than they do today. I believe that I may safely say, even though the present tendency is to return to the method of reproductive art,[2] that the value of block printing has only begun to be appreciated by the modern age.

M. M.

Reading and research are not absolutely necessary for the preparation of the term paper; equally useful materials may be drawn from practical experience and observation. The following theme is basically a generalized narrative. (See Chapter II.)

AMATEUR DEEP–SEA DIVING

On any warm summer day there are apt to be several young men walking around on the bottoms of various rivers and lakes with from twenty to fifty feet of water over their heads.[3] This difficult feat is accomplished by having a strange-looking device, called a diving helmet, over their heads, an airtight cylinder that is supplied with a constant fresh supply of air from a pump overhead by means of a rubber hose. The helmet probably saw long usage as a hot-water tank, or gasoline tank, before it was ever made into a helmet. It is merely cut so that there is a slot for the shoulders, and a chest plate and back plate, fitting snugly at all points except the back, where the excess air

[1] M. C. Salaman, *The New Woodcut* (New York: Albert & Charles Boni, 1930), p. 4.
[2] Plowman, *op. cit.*, p. 40.
[3] Most articles advocate fifty feet as the maximum depth of amateur diving operations, but we frequently make dives from sixty to seventy feet deep without serious difficulty.

bubbles out. It must bubble out the back, or the air bubbles will interfere with the vision through the front glass window. A rubber hose connects the helmet with the air pump, and there has to be a valve somewhere in the hose to prevent air from coming out as fast as it is pumped in. If the valve is at the connection of the helmet with the air hose, the air remains in the helmet in case of a broken air hose. The glass plate in the front of the helmet[1] becomes steamed up by the person's breath if it is not coated with some oil or grease. The reason the air cannot escape is that any tube, if thrust upside down in the water, will not fill up with water. Pumping air in from the top causes the excess air to bubble out the bottom at the highest point of opening. The diver is not encumbered by any kind of weights attached to his body, all the weight needed being in the helmet. In case of emergency, the diver can always leave the helmet and swim up to the top, if the water isn't too deep. For extra protection, and for guiding and signaling from the top, a rope is fastened around the diver's body.

The best depth of water is from twenty to thirty feet, for any deeper water is too cold, dark, and "heavy"[2] for comfort. The shallower the water is, the better the visibility and temperature are. The warmer water allows longer dives, because one does not notice the effects of cold and artificial air so soon. I do not know how deep it is possible to go, but on one occasion, while testing for the bottom of one of these "bottomless"[3] gravel quarries, we descended so far that the darkness and coldness of the water became too extreme to continue on down to the bottom. It was on this escapade that we discovered, quite painfully, that it was impossible to go down without some kind of ladder, or weighted rope to guide us. I happened to be the first one to try floating down to the bottom, and found that the weighted helmet sank more rapidly than my body, and I was soon floating down up-ended, with the water pouring into the helmet.

The best type of bottom is a sand-beach bottom. Seaweed not only

[1] Some of our earlier helmets had a celluloid window which would be crushed in by the pressure of the water. This never happened after we began to use plate-glass windows.

[2] I am sure that there is quite a pressure at great depths, because talking is difficult and it is impossible to whistle, showing that the air is "thicker," or as it is sometimes called, "heavier." Deep water throws such a pressure on the body that your eardrums hurt and "sing." We have found that swallowing in our throats, while in deep water, causes our eardrums to go back to normal behavior. I am not sure just why this is so, but I suspect that it is the result of swallowing sufficient quantities of air to even up the pressure inside and outside our bodies.

[3] "Bottomless" is used to describe a lake that does have a bottom, but is so deep that no one has ever reached that bottom. We never did reach its bottom.

cuts and scratches, but masks the real nature of the bottom, allowing one to fall into holes and step on unpleasant things that heave up and scurry away. I think they are turtles, but even a turtle can give one a scare under water. It is often hard to see objects clearly under water, because on some bottoms there is a fine black silt that is stirred up in clouds by the feet of the diver, and even in clear water, there are peculiar wavy outlines to everything, due to the refraction, or bending, of light by the water. Because it becomes so dark in deep water, we have tried water-tight lights, but they did not seem to help much.[1]

It is difficult to dive in swift currents, because walking against the current requires a good footing; and the current also causes one to lose his sense of direction and become lost. When this happens, the diver has to depend almost entirely on signals from the handlers, who are handicapped by the limited number of signals possible to impart through the life line.

We have already tried a telephone hook-up between the diver and his handlers, and found it impracticable. It requires bulky batteries and entangling wires, and the telephone voice cannot be heard by the diver in the helmet unless the air is momentarily shut off, eliminating the hissing noise of the incoming air.

As far as danger goes, there is not much chance of serious accidents. A person may swallow a little water now and then, but every swimmer is used to that. A break in the air-pumping equipment is really not very serious, for there is enough air in the helmet to last the diver while he is being pulled up. The diver can hear when the hissing air stops coming in, and easily tell when his supply of air has been used up.[2] And most people can hold their breath at least a minute, which is ample time for hauling them up to the surface.

There is a much more tense situation that sometimes arises, that of getting tangled in spiles under a dock. Good handling of the signal line makes such a situation unusual, but sometimes, when we are diving from a ladder leading down into the water from a dock, the diver who has lost his sense of direction and is being led back by the signal line, misses the ladder and walks right under the dock. Between the cables and jumbled spiles under most docks is a veritable maze of passages.[3] But, here again, the chief danger lies in losing the helmet.

[1] The darkness is that kind which seems like fog, and through which lights don't seem to penetrate.

[2] Shortness of breath and quick breathing show that the air is no longer pure.

[3] Docks and piers catch under them all the drifting logs and debris that float down the river.

The diver can almost always come up if he leaves the helmet down. Some work can be done in leading the diver out, if the water isn't too deep, by ordinary swimmers, who, through a succession of quick dives and pulls on the diver's lines usually lead him out.

The bottoms of most rivers close to town are strewn with glass, wrecked cars, and especially barbed wire and sharp rocks. The bottom of the Detroit River, near shore, looks like "no man's land," with its wires, old water-logged trees, and wrecked cars.[1] In this respect, the only thing the diver can do is wear boots, or some kind of footwear, and proceed very cautiously.

There should be a lot of practical work for helmet divers to do, for they are well fitted for any type of salvage jobs. Our only salvage job, to date, was the successful rescue of an outboard motor, lost in thirty-five feet of water, and in difficult currents. The only drawback to salvage jobs is the fact that, although many valuable articles are lost under water each year, most of them are not worth recovering after a short time under water.[2]

All under-water structures, such as bases of bridges, large ships, piers, and docks, shipping channels, and cables, about whose soundness any doubt is felt, can be easily inspected by a helmet diver.

The only chance I ever had to gain fame—and perhaps save a life—with my helmet was at a lake beach last year when a man drowned, and although everyone knew the approximate location of his body, none of the swimmers could reach it. By the time police and grappling hooks arrived, it was too late. The body was found exactly where everyone believed it had gone down, and I am absolutely sure that I could have found him a few minutes after he went down, if I had had my diving helmet with me.

R. Z.

Compare the unique footnotes in the preceding theme with those in the first paper. The next two themes will be given without footnotes. "Chippendale Furniture" illustrates the value of research and diagrams in a summary theme (see Chapter III).

[1] It was in these old wrecked cars that I saw the only fish that we have ever observed under water. Schools of bass often hide in these old wrecks, and when the car is touched they go like a streak of light. I have often wanted to go down in some of these fish-hatching lakes where there are so many, and they are so tame that they eat out of your hand. It would make an interesting under-sea picture.

[2] Watches and keys seem to be the things lost most often. Both are such small objects that they are hard to recover. Unless we dive for them immediately after they are lost, there is not much chance of finding them.

CHIPPENDALE FURNITURE

In eighteenth-century London, an extremely fashionable rendezvous for the belles and beaux of the court of the early Georges was the furniture salon of Thomas Chippendale in St. Martin's Lane. Chippendale was the son of a country wood carver and cabinetmaker. Born in 1705, he came to London in 1727, and by a forceful personality and shrewd business sense, he soon made himself liked by the right people, and managed in a short time to build up a distinguished clientele. At his shop, the lords and ladies met in search of furniture, probably, but never missed the chance to discuss matters of the moment, the fall of Walpole, the resignation of Pitt, the chances at Culloden, or more likely, the latest escapade of the Lady X, Y, or Z.

It is not difficult to imagine the court dandies, wigged and powdered, competing with each other for a smile or the tap of a fan, from the reigning belles in their silks and satins, by telling them the latest scandal from the coffee houses. The bright, rich colors of their clothes must have perfectly set off the fine mahogany of the "Louis Quinze" or "Chinese Chippendale." No doubt many of the prototypes of the characters in *The School for Scandal* were personally known to this clever old tradesman.

Thomas Chippendale may be regarded as the pioneer of the movement which eventually resulted in the evolution of our late eighteenth-century furniture. In his designs, he used ideas often and without hesitation from many sources. At one time, he emphasized the "Gothick" as it was then called, at another the Chinese, and again the Dutch, and very nearly always kept up on the French designs. For instance, several sources have been discovered from which Chippendale borrowed. He used a book of designs by Jacques Androuet, called "du Cerveau," from which he copied the common claw foot with the carved top. The famous "ribbons" for chair backs are traced to a book of designs by Berain. All Chippendale's clockcases were borrowed from designs by Maret. However, it has been said that it matters little where you take the idea; it matters much what use you make of it, and Chippendale at his best made better things from what he borrowed. Unquestionably, his merits shine forth most in chairs; so let us see just what these chairs are.

Chairs are the most tricky and versatile members of the furniture family, and by far the most important. With chairs it is not necessary to study the whole piece, for only the backs are distinctive. Even the masters borrowed a leg here, a foot there; but no matter how many designs are there, it is the back which determines its type. Then, too, Chippendale worked entirely in mahogany, and his only decoration was his exceptionally beautiful carving.

Chippendale's chairs may be listed as follows: the "Ribbonback," the "Ladderback," the "Fret-back," and the "Roundabout" chair. The "Ribbonback" was evolved from a Dutch design, but Chippendale broadened the back out, and bent the top rail into a Cupid's bow. Sometimes he turned down the ends of the bow into the uprights like the original Dutch chair, but more often he finished them upward in a curve. In the Dutch chair the center splat had been plain or with a very simple design cut into it, but Chippendale lost no time in making it over into something distinctly "Chippendale."

RIBBONBACK   LADDERBACK

He kept the old vase shape, but inside that outline, he put in design upon design. Some were simple; some of them became involved intertwining of "ribbons" and "C" curves and Gothic figures. These backs are a never-ending variety of designs, and have always been a treasure chest for designers ever since Chippendale first used them. Chippendale has no superior when it comes to carving, and when one adds to the fine carving on the back much carving on the feet and knees of the cabriole legs, one has a very beautiful chair. Sometimes, too, he used perfectly plain, square, straight legs, and these seemed to enhance the beauty of the backs even more.

Another favorite design was the "Ladderback." This was worked out upon the slat idea, and consisted of three or four wavy, ribbon-like horizontal slats carved to match the top rail. These "Ladderback" chairs are most popular today.

Chippendale turned to good use a craze at that time for furniture in the Oriental style. Most people feel this style was overornate.

Some of this furniture is obviously in bad taste, but from this period come the lovely chair backs filled from corner to corner with delicate fretwork, and these well make up for the rest of this furniture. Of course this type is called the "Fret-back."

The "Roundabout" is an odd member of the chair family, and had been around for some time when Chippendale found it and, of course, made a design of his own for it. These chairs are just square chairs turned cornerwise, with a leg in front, one on each side, and one in back. The corners are usually rounded, and the low back rail is supported on three uprights from the three corners.

There, in a general way, are the Chippendale backs. So when you see a chair generously made, in mahogany, with a back like any of

FRET-BACK   ROUNDABOUT

these, and either straight, square legs, or bandy ones, carved about the knees and with the ball and claw foot, you may safely judge that it is Chippendale.

It is perhaps to be regretted that there are no great cabinetmakers today. The reason is easily found in the fact that the present-day furniture makers are so occupied with the technical side of the craft that they have no time to study styles and principles of design. The factories in which art is considered as much as commercialism are rare exceptions. The subdivision of labor, new tools, time and labor-saving machinery tend to make the craftsman into a mere machine. In times past, one man completely carried through the construction of a job, but now in ninety-nine out of one hundred cases, every part that can be is shaped and cut by machinery. The result is, of course, a complete loss of individualism in the work; but even this has its compensations, for now, as never before, the common people can have tastefully designed and solid furniture.

However, even though modern furniture is well-built and well-designed, the demand for the originals of the great cabinetmakers, or exact reproductions, is increasing. The name of Chippendale is always on the lips of all who pose as authorities on old furniture, and from the respect paid it by the section of the community who acquire their knowledge from the household art guides in the women's magazines, one would conclude that Chippendale was the most highly endowed cabinetmaker of his day.

Be that as it may, we can sum up Chippendale's work by saying that he took the main shapes as he found them, somewhat plain and severe; he left them decidedly better proportioned, lighter, more decorative, yet not less useful than they were. The ideas reduce themselves to a matter of artistic feeling, a sense of proportion which recognizes, for instance, that the breadth of a chair splat is too great or too little for the empty spaces on each side of it. It seems a small affair, but such affairs make all the difference between the ugly and the beautiful.

F. D.

Here is an excellent expository biography,[1] without documentation, however.

EUGÉNIE, QUEEN OF SORROWS

One day in the middle of August, 1920, a little old woman of ninety-four died very quietly in England, and this very practical and unromantic old world paused for a moment to gaze dreamily back into the vistas of a half-century ago, and to muse on the idiosyncrasies of that stern thing called Fate. It seemed strange that this familiar old lady in black was gone, that she would never again watch the Royal Guards parade on Napoleon's Day, or slyly and wistfully pluck the forbidden blooms in the gardens of the Tuileries; strange, too, was the almost-forgotten history of this tear-stained rose of long ago.

Doña Eugénia Maria de Montijo arrived on this earth in the midst of an earthquake in 1826 in Spain, a circumstance to which many people attribute the strain of melancholia in her character and in her life. Be this as it may, the peculiar curse of sorrow which was to follow this unhappy individual all through life seems to have been with her from the start. When Eugénie was but eight years old, her father and mother, who had never gotten along wonderfully well, were estranged, and the mother, the Countess de Montijo, took her

[1] Compare Chapter VIII above.

two girls to France. There Eugénie saw Louis Napoleon being taken into exile in England, and the sight, which she never forgot, touched her childish heart deeply. Shortly after this her father died suddenly, his whole fortune passing to his wife and children. And that's where the story really begins.

Eugénie and her sister were both very beautiful, and had many admirers. Chief among these was the Duke of Alva, who was diplomatic enough to be equally attentive to both of the young ladies. Finally the Countess demanded that he choose one or the other of her fair daughters. Eugénie, who believed herself very much in love with the Duke, was hiding behind a curtain and overheard her lover's proposal to her sister, who accepted him. Poor Eugénie, really quite heartbroken, immediately went to her room and took poison. When her folly was discovered, she could not be induced to take the antidote, until the Duke, bending over her bed on the pretense of consoling her, whispered, "Give me back my letters!" This so infuriated her that she decided to live for the sole purpose of revenge. This incident, seemingly childish and unimportant later on, nevertheless left a deep impression on the chief actress, and was the first severe shock to that implicit trust in everyone which was so characteristic of her.

For a brief period following this she and her mother were attached to the Spanish court, but after three months, because of real or imaginary misdemeanors, they were asked to relinquish their cherished positions as ladies-in-waiting. Now Eugénie, bored with life and shocked at the coldness and ugliness of a supposedly friendly and beautiful world, decided to renounce society and become a nun; but when she reached the convent, a crazy old woman stopped her at the gate and exclaimed, "My daughter, do not seek for rest within our walls; you are called to adorn a throne!" And so Eugénie turned from a life of peace and probable happiness to step again into the world that was to treat her so harshly in years to come.

The Countess and her daughter traveled from one fashionable resort to another, where Eugénie's incomparable beauty, wit, and charm caused men to love and women to hate her. The jealousy of these women gave rise to many criticisms and insults, which, though unavenged, were not unnoticed and unfelt by the fair victim. Among the men who proposed to her on these travels was Louis Napoleon, who was even then pulling strings and setting stages preparatory to overthrowing the Republic and becoming Emperor of France. In 1848 he was made Prince-President of the Republic, and Eugénie awaited developments. In 1852 Napoleon effected a coup d'état and became

Emperor. Then the ambitious young heroine accepted his proposal, and although this was not made public immediately, it was suspected, and various of Napoleon's lady friends in their jealousy insulted her so much as to leave her weeping bitterly. To settle matters and, in a measure, to quiet these sharp-tongued ladies, Napoleon formally asked the Countess de Montijo for the hand of Eugénie. The Countess gladly accepted, but wrote to a friend: "Eugénie is to be queen over your France, and, in spite of myself, I remember that with you queens have but little happiness. In spite of myself, the thought of Marie Antoinette takes possession of me, and I wonder if my child will not have the same fate?"

Eugénie de Montijo became Empress of France on January 29, 1853, at the age of twenty-seven. The ceremony took place in the Hall of Marshals in the Tuileries. The bride was dressed in a beautiful gown of white satin and lace with many costly pearls. A Spanish lady implored her to remove these, for there is an old Spanish superstition that the more pearls a bride wears on her wedding day, the more tears she will shed throughout the rest of her life; but Eugénie, usually so superstitious, insisted upon retaining the jewels, and the ceremony went on. The following morning Napoleon took his bride to the beautiful old cathedral of Notre Dame for the religious ceremony. The couple was taken there in a glass coach which had first been used for the coronation of Napoleon I and Josephine. There was a curious repetition of an incident which had occurred at this first coronation; as the coach started, the gilt crown surmounting the roof suddenly toppled over and fell to the ground. Many spectators viewed this as an evil omen, and it was rather disturbing to Eugénie. But without further mishap they reached the cathedral, which was gorgeously decorated. During the service the Empress was almost overcome with emotion. And when the long ceremony was finished, and the couple drove back to Paris between the cheering crowds which lined the road, the strain began to tell on Eugénie. She began to have an awful premonition. She was wearing the crown jewels that the ill-fated Marie Antoinette had at first worn so happily, and the pale, tragic face of the poor lady seemed to stare from the crowds at the couple. But the Empress had to keep on bowing and smiling to the eager people. The next day she begged to see Marie Antoinette's testamentary letter, written just before the Queen rode to the gallows; the letter moved her deeply, and from that time on, Marie assumed a strange fascination for her, a fascination which was not unlinked with dread of disaster.

Throughout the seventeen years of her Empress-ship Eugénie was subjected to a species of boycott by her sister queens and empresses. When foreign rulers visited Paris during Napoleon's reign, they invariably left their consorts at home. The only lady of high sovereign rank who ever was their guest at Paris was Queen Victoria of England, who was induced very reluctantly to visit them by her ministers. While in Paris the Queen developed a kindly interest in Eugénie, largely as a result of the deference the Empress showed to her. This interest soon grew into a real friendship, which continued till the death of the Queen of England. At one time a particularly violent quarrel between the imperial couple caused Eugénie to flee to England vowing never to return. Through the Queen, a complete reconciliation was effected, and possible scandal averted by transforming the flight into a perfectly innocent social visit. Except for the Queen of England, however, all sovereign ladies held themselves aloof. Eugénie's submission to snubs was pathetic. She could not defend herself against royalty, but she suffered impertinences from women of much lower than royal rank. For instance, the wife of the Austrian ambassador remarked before her, "Oh, but my sovereign is a real Empress!" And again, when Eugénie complained to the Princess Clothilde of Savoy of the fatigue and tedium of a court function, the Italian answered amiably, "We do not mind; you see, we are born to it." The old French nobility was likewise unfriendly; the Empress tried in vain to attract them to her court, but, with few exceptions, they remained aloof to the end.

Two other incidents helped to add to the fear and sorrow of these years as Empress of France. The first was an attempt on the life of Napoleon as the imperial couple was en route to the opera. Orsini, a hired assassin, threw a bomb which killed ten spectators and wounded some one hundred and fifty others, but did not accomplish its purpose so far as Napoleon was concerned. Eugénie's dread of an unknown and tragic fate was heightened by this incident, and she was always secretly fearful for the safety of her husband and her small son, whom she loved above all else.

The other incident was the death of her sister. It happened that Napoleon and Eugénie were in Algiers when the Emperor received news of the death of his sister-in-law, the Duchess of Alva. Knowing that they could not possibly return immediately, he did not tell his wife of the dispatch. Just before sailing for home, he told her that her sister was seriously ill. The poor Empress was so perturbed that they made an unadvisable passage, in which their ship was almost lost with all on board. Finally, when they had trouble in making train connections also, the Emperor told his wife the truth as gently as possible. They were too late even for the funeral, and Eugénie never entirely recovered from the shock.

Meanwhile clouds were gathering. In his Italian War Napoleon had followed Eugénie's advice with success, but in 1866 the revolt of Prussia served to prove that the prestige and influence of the Empire was a hollow sham; the internal situation went from bad to worse. There was an increasing hostility to the Empress. In 1869 the throne was obviously in danger and a desperate remedy in demand. The impending war with Prussia assumed the guise of this remedy for the salvation of the throne. It is believed that Eugénie was highly in favor of the war. She is even quoted as saying proudly, "This is my war!" At any rate, she helped to bring it on. Napoleon marched off to the front, and she became Empress Regent of France. There were a few victories and then came Metz, and failure. It was Eugénie who stopped MacMahon's highly strategic retreat to Paris and ordered him to make a flanking movement toward the Belgian frontier. Napoleon went with him to Sedan, where he became a prisoner in German hands on September 2, 1870. The end had come. Two days later the French Republic was proclaimed, and the Empire came tumbling down about the ears of poor Eugénie.

When the news of Sedan arrived, Paris went mad. Riotous mobs stormed the Tuileries and howled imprecations on the head of their former Empress; firmly convinced that her life was in peril, she finally fled in disguise from the palace by way of the Louvre and, accompanied only by a lady-in-waiting, made her way to the home of Dr. Evans, an American dentist. "They have all forsaken me; you can save me; you must save me!" she wailed. And he did. He drove her to Deauville in his carriage, and she managed to get a small boat to take her to England. There, though it hurt her pride, she lived quietly as the guest of Queen Victoria. She was joined later by Napoleon, but he died two years afterwards. Her only hope was now in the son she loved so well. She formed an Imperialistic party in Paris, based on this hope, and directed it from England. But in 1879, just when it seemed that that son had finally gained the opportunity of restoring the power of the Bonapartes, he joined an expedition to Zululand and was killed in a skirmish. Needless to say, this was the last straw. When she regained consciousness after receiving the dreadful news, poor Eugénie exclaimed, "Fate is very cruel; I feel now that I shall live a hundred years!"

The ex-Empress, now bereft of all that life had given her, began her restless wanderings over the face of the earth. She was at liberty to come and go in Paris, where she always stayed at the Continental, overlooking the Tuileries, where once she had reigned supreme. She visited all the scenes of her former grandeur—Biarritz, the French Riviera, St. Cloud—seeming drawn there by a strange fascination. But always she returned to England. She built at Farnborough Hill the memorial church in which both her dead are buried. Every morning for the rest of her life, when in England, she visited the church to pray and to scatter on the tombs fresh violets, the symbol of the Bonaparte family.

Near the end of her life, the ex-Empress lost the sight of one eye, and she was fearful of becoming totally blind. She begged to be able to visit Spain once more before it was too late. Her wish was gratified, and while there she submitted to an operation on her eyes by a certain Dr. Barraquin, who performed a miraculous cure. Then Eugénie really smiled for the first time since the death of the Prince-Imperial, as she said gratefully, "Thanks to you, I shall have been born twice in Spain!"

And still a relentless fate seemed to guard her life. All the signs of her former glory had disappeared, and her old friends and confidents with them. The World War came on, and Eugénie found momentary consolation in it. She said, "This is my revenge. Were the Emperor only here now! May God protect France!" The war dragged on and finally ended. Then one day in 1920, a half century after the fall of the French empire, Fate tired of her cruel game, and put Eugénie to sleep, never to wake again. With the passing of this woman ended a romantic career almost unparalleled for the heights of its glory and the depths of its tragedy.

The world woke from its day dream and hastened about its business, for this age is a restless and practical one, and time is valuable. There is small space for dreaming, and so we close the doors of the Past on that pitiful and tragic beauty whom we know as Empress Eugénie, Queen of Sorrows.

V. B.

»» B ««

Suggested Topics

The essence of the term report is the organized statement of the results of investigation and discovery, that is, of research. It has been suggested that good examples of the type would include articles in technical journals and in serious magazines dealing with social, aesthetic, and similar problems which involve controversy or critical interpretation. It would be an excellent idea to locate two or more periodicals and a group of writers to follow systematically for articles on a chosen topic—Russia, contemporary poetry, social service, or intercollegiate sports, but particularly on the subject which you are investigating for your term report.

When you have found a subject of interest and a group of writers on that subject, follow them as a bloodhound traces the scent. Make of yourself an inquiring specialist in the subject; talk about it with whoever is willing and able to discuss it with you. You will want to know who are the leading authorities and where their writings appear. You will want to know the earliest treatise, the best, the latest; whether there are museum specimens; illustrated books and monographs, catalogues, specialized bibliographies—in short, any sources of material which might increase your knowledge.

Instead of quoting here from writers, we are offering a list of seventy-five possible topics. These are intended to be only suggestive. If you choose one, consider possible variations or analogous subjects. The topics have been intentionally mixed; you must determine the proper classification of any choice. Probably the best advice to offer on making a selection would be this: choose only the topic which stirs at least some feeling of curiosity. Does it suggest positive questions for which you would like to find answers? The search for material, the first attack in the campaign, will involve the search for the best source of answers.

Occasionally writers and works are mentioned. In most cases the writer cited has so completely identified himself with the particular subject as to make any reference to it call up his name.

SUBJECTS:

1. Relationships between the Life of Ludwig van Beethoven and his Symphonies. See Grove's *Dictionary of Music* and Emil Ludwig's *Beethoven*.

2. The Crusades: their religious and social significance. Religious, economic, political, social factors. Actual results.

3. The Development of Bridge Building. Relate this to some specific project such as the Golden Gate bridge.

4. The Norsemen: wars and conquests, discoveries and explorations, colonies.

5. Honoré de Balzac: artist and lover. Good biography by René Benjamin. Are his works autobiographical?

6. The Gothic Cathedral: how built, relation to medieval Catholicism, location of the finest. Read Henry Adams, *Mont-Saint-Michel and Chartres*. The cathedral in America; collegiate Gothic.

7. The Forty-Niners: the discovery of gold in California. Spanish California, the American immigration, building of San Francisco.

8. The Stratosphere: new worlds being conquered.

9. Frédéric Chopin: music as the expression of romantic personality. Read James Huneker. Study the preludes or nocturnes as a sequence.

10. Modern Painting: impressionism, Picasso, recent American painters, Matisse, Cubism.

11. St. Francis of Assisi: medieval holiness. Read *The Little Flowers of St. Francis*. Look up Giotto's paintings.

12. Russian Ballet: Anna Pavlova, Diaghilev, Karsavina, Nijinsky. Read André Olivéroff's *The Flight of the Swan*, Arnold Haskell, Lincoln Kirstein.

13. Confucianism: origin and ethical values. Does its character as a religion help to explain the Oriental mind? Compare Taoism.

14. The Aztecs: prehistoric culture in America. Recent archaeological discoveries in Mexico.

15. Bret Harte: tale-teller of the West. Read a group of stories.

16. The Conquest of Disease. See Paul de Kruif. What are the most dangerous diseases? What is the history of great plagues?

17. The Invention of Printing: Gutenberg, features of early presses, modern representatives of fine printing.

18. Porcelain: Wedgwood, Rosenthal, spode, bone china, willowware; methods of manufacture.

19. Free Verse: experiments and forms. See Louis Untermeyer, Max Eastman. What are the newest movements in poetry?

20. The Eighteen-Nineties: art and epigram, the Pre-Raphaelites, Oscar Wilde, George Bernard Shaw, the *Yellow Book*. Read Holbrook Jackson's *The Eighteen Nineties*.

21. The Story of Tristram and Iseult: poetry, romance, opera. Look at Edwin Arlington Robinson's poem, *Tristram*.

22. Comets and Meteors: scientific theories, famous examples.

23. Life of the Esquimaux: or the Polynesians, the cliff dwellers, head-hunters.

24. Nürnberg: cultural center, Albrecht Dürer, Hans Sachs. Other single cities, such as Bruges, Stockholm, Prague, Peiping, Buenos Aires.

25. Penguins: their habits and types, especially the emperor penguin. Read *Cold*, by Laurence M. Gould.

26. Cardinal Richelieu: reasons for his extraordinary power. See Sainte-Beuve. Talleyrand, Metternich, Mazarin—why do such names trouble the pages of history?

27. An Afternoon in Court: judge and jury, questioning the witnesses, pleading the case, the verdict.

28. Mark Twain: pessimism and humor in the raw eighties.

29. The Making of Violins: Stradivarius, Amati, modern methods.

30. Television: try to make it intelligible to the average reader.

31. The Traffic in Drugs: how grave are the dangers? Methods of restraint. The role of the League of Nations in policing.

32. The Detective Story: varieties in technique of three prominent practitioners.

33. The Associated Press: its organization, methods of securing news.

34. The Ugly in Art: Gothic gargoyles, grotesques, satirical cartooning; why do we enjoy it?

35. The Last Ten Years in Egyptian Archaeology: also archaeology in Greece, the Holy Land, Assyria, Mexico for the same period. The same for developments in aviation, big league baseball, German political life, women's styles, League of Nations.

36. Leonardo da Vinci: type of universal genius. Rachel Taylor and Merezhkovski have spirited biographical treatments.

37. The Novel as a Means of Escape from Life: Scott, Cooper, Stevenson, Sabatini.

38. Buccaneers and Pirates of the Past.

39. Japanese Wood-Block Printing: exquisite art of Utamaro, Yeishi, Toyokuni, Hokusai, Hiroshige; methods and artistic value.

40. Charlemagne: the man and the Emperor of the West. Was he great in himself or for what he accomplished, or for both?

41. Philately: commonly called stamp collecting; also collecting coins, rare books, snuffboxes. What are the best standards of beauty or value? Who are noted collectors?

42. The Operas of Richard Wagner: themes, musical genius of the composer.

43. Primitive Man: how do we know about the Neanderthal man and his skull?

44. Lord Byron: "Outlaw of his own dark mind." See biography by Maurois.

45. The Taj Mahal: the religious ideas lying behind a costly tomb.

46. Theories of Biography: see the chapter above on this subject (Chapter VIII).

47. The St. Lawrence Waterway: an international project, political and commercial significance; future. Muscle Shoals, the Bonneville Dam, other great public works.

48. Henry Wadsworth Longfellow: story-teller and moralist. What did his own time think of him? What of his later fame?

49. The Battle of Marathon; of Blenheim, Trafalgar, Waterloo, Gettysburg, the Marne; significance, strategy, consequences.

50. The Philosophy of the Stoics: what values for a modern mind, sources, great representatives?

51. Waste: statistics on fires, accidents, crime, inefficiency.

52. The Feudal Ideal: its principles and values; organization of feudal society; the castle, the baron, and the serf. Read Davis, *Life on a Medieval Barony.*

53. Fraternities: history of their development; statistics as to property, membership, distribution. The same for lodge organizations, labor unions, nationalist movements.

54. Henry VIII: personality; a great ruler or a Bluebeard?

55. Antarctic Exploration: discovery and conquest of a new continent; Amundsen, Scott, Byrd, Ellsworth.

56. The Spectroscope: one of the subtlest instruments of science.

57. Rembrandt: the painter as master of life. See H. Van Loon's *R. v. R.*

58. Witchcraft: persecutions, quackery, survivals.

59. Religion: a serious study of the history and doctrines of any particular faith or denomination.

60. Heinrich Heine: his lyric poetry, his wit, his tragedy.

61. Mexico of Today: customs, geography, art; study as a prospective country to visit. Stuart Chase and others.

62. The Cure of Cancer: recent progress; centers of study.

63. Cotton: where and how it is grown, cotton manufactures, economic problem of the cotton states. Wheat. Sugar beets. Cattle.

64. The Home of the Future: new architectural styles, lighting, air conditioning, low-cost homes, apartments. Century of Progress Exposition, Chicago, 1933–34. New York World's Fair, 1939.

65. Hypnotism: anecdotes, history, the verdict of science.

66. Organization in Animal Life: apply to fish, such as the salmon; insects, such as the bee; or mammals, such as the beaver; habits, instinctive ingenuity, adaptiveness.

67. The United States Marine Corps: origin, organization, function.

68. Production of Rare Commercial Substances: ambergris, jet, mercury, radium, helium.

69. Production of a Moving Picture: casting, direction, filming, cutting. Animated cartoons.

70. The Wit of a Present-Day Writer: George Ade, Dorothy Parker, Noel Coward, Corey Ford, Stephen Leacock, Gertrude Stein, Robert Benchley, Alexander Woollcott.

71. The Auto Trailer: touring, camping. Trailer towns.

72. Modern Stage Design: study the work of one man, Max Reinhardt, Gordon Craig, Adolph Appia, etc. Read Lee Simonson, *The Stage Is Set* (1933).

73. The Autogiro: construction and technical advantages.

74. The Art of a Contemporary American Poet: Amy Lowell, Robert Frost, Edgar Lee Masters, Edna St. Vincent Millay, Edwin Arlington Robinson, Carl Sandburg, Robinson Jeffers, T. S. Eliot, Stephen Vincent Benét. Read a large proportion of his work; select a limited group of poems for critical analysis. Find the best biography.

75. New Orleans: charm, atmosphere, historical background, future. Similarly for San Francisco, Quebec, etc.

After you have selected your topic and defined its limits, you will then gather your material in the manner described in the main portion of this chapter. The final job will be the ordering of this material to make the actual article, or term paper, and this final result will take on a rather well-defined shape and appearance. Before examining further specimens of research articles, you will find it useful to review the mechanical and technical factors in shaping the completed paper. Here, perhaps, more than anywhere else in this book, it will be necessary to specify a precise way of doing things.

This concluding discussion of the preparation of the long term paper will be presented under the four headings: Purpose, Appearance, Form, Research.

THE PREPARATION OF TERM PAPERS

I. *Purpose.* As the final, climactic piece of work in the course, the term paper serves to show ability to produce an extended composition. Make every effort to demonstrate that you can gather reliable information on a specific subject, organize it, and present it so that it will be clear and cogent to the reader.

In itself the paper should, by its content and organization, stand as the result of a definite period of research. You will not present mere opinions. Nor will you attempt to convince the reader that you have a very sensitive and remarkable imagination. Here is an opportunity to prove that you can turn out a hard-headed, dependable piece of writing. If you can do this, your chances of excelling in the short story or informal essay will be much greater; for you will prove to yourself that you can command your own mind and the English language as a means of conveying what is in your mind.

II. *Appearance.* You expect a first-class department store or business office to be well-organized, with a place for everything and everything in its place. You expect the same of your daily newspaper, of your best friend's personal appearance, of a piece of machinery; then why not insist upon it for the paper which is to be the certificate of your abilities as a writer? Cultivate the habit early of an almost military exactitude in handling materials and in the final dressing-up of your papers. It is no secret to say that it will have a remarkable effect on your critic instructor. The following precise directions are designed to aid you in producing papers that will have the finish that is insisted upon by all publishing houses.

1. The paper should consist of from about 15 to 45 typed (or carefully written) pages. Incidentally, do not be miserly in the use of paper. If a page is ugly with corrections and poor spacing, do it over.

2. Use the standard $8\frac{1}{2}''$ x $11''$ typewriter paper. Use black typewriter ribbon, and black or blue ink if you write with pen.

3. Number the pages in Arabic numerals (1, 2, 3, 4, etc.); if any prefatory matter precedes the body of your paper, you may follow custom and use small Roman numerals (i, ii, iii, iv, etc.).

4. Preserve even margins on all sides of the page: at least an inch on the right and at the bottom, and, as a rule, nearly two inches on the left and at the top. In single-space typing, leave a double space between paragraphs. Indent for paragraphs. For long quoted sections indent farther and use single-space typing without quotation marks. For short quoted bits use quotation marks and no special indentation.

5. Use a separate title page, outline, or table of contents. In each case space carefully and check for accuracy.

III. *Form.* The formal elements of the paper may be numerous, but only six, perhaps, should be found in every paper. These are italicized in the list which follows. (a) Preliminary: *Title*, Preface, Table of Contents, Outline, *Introduction;* (b) Body of the Paper: *Development* of theme or subject stated in Title, *Documentation* in the form of quotation and footnotes, *Conclusion;* (c) Supplementary: Appendices, *Bibliography*, Index, Corrections. The indispensable, italicized elements will be given detailed notice.

1. *Title.* The length of the title will vary, but it should be long enough to limit the range of your subject. The wording should reveal something of the nature and intent of the paper, and at the same time interest the reader in it. For a long paper or formal thesis use a separate title page. Otherwise place the title at the top of page 1, underline it, and *do not repeat it* on succeeding pages.

2. *Introduction.* You may wish to prefix an introduction of one or more pages as a separate section of the paper. If there is no special reason for doing so, this element will occupy the opening paragraph. There is no better introduction than a clear, precise statement of what you intend to do in your paper. Do not try to ape a toastmaster here. Be direct, simple, matter of fact. Getting started is often difficult because of the impulse to open with a fanfare. Remember the importance of first impressions. The fate of the entire paper may often be determined in that first paragraph.

3. *Development.* Here of course is the substance of the paper. But that substance itself is composed of what has been found in the sources —in articles, technical works, encyclopedias, files of newspapers—and of what is added from your own knowledge, reflection, and speculation. Here you will profit by an outline. Many a good paper has been written by gradual amplification of a growing outline.

Development means at least two things: first, the clarification and bringing out of what is implicit in an idea or theme, just as the photographer develops his films so as to bring out the markings on the negative; and, second, the enlargement, strengthening, growth of an idea, theme, or thing, just as muscles develop with stiff exercise. Bring out the best there is in your subject; amplify it so as to give it substance and strength.

4. *Documentation.* If you are discussing Chinese immigration, bridges, the music of Debussy, you cannot depend solely on your own knowledge and experience. You will call in witnesses; you will seek out evidence.

Your documents, then, are sources of evidence and authentic information: diaries, autobiographies, studies by authorities, letters, legal instruments, photographs, maps, and whatever materials bear on the subject.

Use quotations, in the main, for the information they contain, not
for decoration. If possible give quotations entire; otherwise indicate
omitted portions by use of three dots. There are two notorious types of
literary imposture. One, less common, is the mutilation or clipping
of quotations so as to make them state the opposite of their real intent.
The other, plagiarism, sadly frequent, is perhaps not often really in-
tentional. To plagiarize intentionally is, of course, a particularly unpleasant kind of dishonesty. If you use the precise wording of the
source always set the passage off in "quotes" or by indentation and
introductory acknowledgment. Often a paraphrase is more practicable; here again acknowledgment is necessary. Quotations longer than
four lines should be single-spaced and blocked on the page.

The final important aspect of documentation is the footnote. Footnotes should be useful, not mere tags to indicate that you are being
scholarly. They are used chiefly to give exact references to works you
have quoted, and as subordinate repositories for bits of incidental information or supplementary material which do not properly claim a
place in the body of your paper. Again, you need to cultivate the
habit of being consistent and accurate in using footnotes, since they
are one of the mechanical, stereotyped factors in writing.

Place footnotes at the bottom of the pages on which the citations
appear. It is best to mark them off from the body of the page with a
solid line, typed or inked from margin to margin. Single-space the
notes, and preserve the same margin as is used in the body of the text.

Number the citation in the body of the text with Arabic numerals
(1, 2, 3, 4) and number the corresponding footnote with the same
number. Some publications number footnotes consecutively throughout
an article, or chapter, but for the term paper we recommend that you
start your numbering anew on each new page. This makes it possible
to shift pages. If it is ever desirable to place all footnotes at the end
of a paper or chapter, then a continuous numbering may be carried
through the whole piece.

The first footnote reference to a source or work should include the
full name of the writer, initials first, or the full name if possible; the
complete title of the work, underlined; and the place, publisher, and
date of publication in that order.[1] Thus you have:

[1] For a magazine reference: Leicester Bradner, "The First English Novel: A Study
of George Gascoigne's *Adventures of Master F. J.*," *PMLA*, XLV (1930), 543–52.

1. Ned Wayburn, *The Art of Stage Dancing* (New York: The Ned Wayburn Studios of Stage Dancing, Inc., 1925), p. 10.

2. André Olivéroff, *The Flight of the Swan* (New York, 1932), p. 50.

Subsequent footnote references may be shortened or abbreviated, but take care not to sacrifice clearness in doing so. Limit abbreviations and symbols to those in common use. These include *op. cit.*, *loc. cit.*, *ibid.*, *supra*, *sic*. All of these except the last indicate a work or place cited. *Supra* indicates a general location in what has gone before. [*Sic*] indicates that the writer calls attention to some error in the passage he is quoting as not being his own. *Ibid.* is by far the most useful symbol. It saves you from having to repeat the full title when, but only when, you are making successive references to the same work. Thus, if a footnote has referred the reader to: G. L. Kittredge, *The Poetry of Chaucer* (Cambridge: Harvard University Press, 1925), your next footnote, when references to other works do not intervene, may read *Ibid.*, pp. 136–42. If reference to another work and author has intervened, you may still use *Op. cit.* 136–42; but be very sure that your reader will understand what *opus* or work you are citing.

Finally, be careful to note and indicate volume numbers (in large Roman numerals), chapter numbers, if needed (in small Roman), and always page numbers. Thus—Edward Gibbon, *The Decline and Fall of the Roman Empire*, II, xlvii, 462–64. For very careful documentation there may also be section numbers or other indications which are desirable. For such a famous work as Gibbon's the title can safely be shortened to *Decline and Fall*, but in such works it is often very important to note the precise edition with the date.

5. *Conclusion.* So to speak, the introduction is the entrance and the conclusion is the exit. You may wish to put the latter element in a separate section. But its most important use is as a careful summing up of what you have demonstrated. It should be brief and pointed. It is your good-bye to the reader; do not keep him standing impatiently on the platform.

6. *Bibliography.* This section may often contain evidence of the largest part of your work. Externally it is only a list of the works which bear on your subject, or only those you have actually read in part or entire. But actually a good bibliography maps out the field of your inquiry; it is a plan showing where the reader himself can learn what you have learned before him.

Beyond listing your source works on slips, your problem is to classify them. Your system of classification will depend on the number of items and the nature of your subject; generally it will consist of primary and secondary references, with some subdivision of the latter. Within any group in your classification, list the works alphabetically by authors. In this arrangement the last name is placed first—

Gibbon, Edward. *The Decline and Fall of the Roman Empire*. New York: Modern Library, 1932.

Sometimes it is necessary to indicate the editor of a work, such as a new critical edition of Goldsmith's Works; and, once more, remember the need of recording the precise edition with the date so that your reader can locate the reference if he wishes to do so. A handy aid for all such matters of mechanical form is *A Manual of Style*, published by the University of Chicago Press.

Of the optional elements the most important is the outline. This serves several purposes, and there is no surer sign of control of material than the ability to work out an objective outline. If you include an outline, you will give the reader a definite aid in understanding what you have to offer, a sort of preview which enables him to survey the ground; you will provide a more detailed table of contents than the mere list of section or chapter titles will supply; and you will make up for the lack of an index, as the reader, or you yourself, can locate particular points in the discussion by reference to the outline. But of course the greatest value in the outline is in compelling the writer to organize his material, to arrange it in the order in which it may best be presented to the reader, and to determine whether he has fully and adequately covered the ground indicated in his title and theme. The detailed subdivisions will appear as you take notes.

IV. *Research*. This word has become something of a fetish. It indicates to some people an army of stoop-shouldered drones working themselves gray over musty manuscripts which are invariably stored away in damp, half-lit cellars. Actually, it means something much more like the exciting activities of Sherlock Holmes. The researcher is a detective, a follower of clues which he hopes will lead him to a place the precise whereabouts of which he cannot more than guess at. His materials are bibliographies, encyclopedias, biographies, even unpublished manuscripts, if he is lucky enough to have access to them.

In order to impress this fact upon you and to encourage you to investigate the possibilities of the library, we are offering a kind of equivalent of the game of Murder. Follow out the exercise, trying to waste as little time and motion as possible. Be sure to remember your trails, as you may be following them again when you are on a real case.

You will be given three "cases" which involve running down clues that will lead to information concerning "suspects." That is, you know or assume that somewhere in the library are to be found specific facts or general sources of new insight into an event, a character, or a literary work. Each case will call for its own special technique. You will have to work out the approach to the problem and follow it out in your own way. Unlike the detectives of fiction, however, you can easily work on all three cases at once, inasmuch as their trails may frequently cross.

The completed form of your report will consist of the analysis of your procedure, while in at least two cases the clues will be presented in footnotes. The completed form will look like the critical article on Emerson which is quoted below. You will present the steps which you followed in reaching your "solution," showing how one bit of information led to another. The titles of reference and source works which you use will be recorded in the footnotes.

Now take *Case I*. Who's Who? Investigate an important, or at least notorious, individual. He may be a diplomat, general, inventor, musician, statesman, business executive, writer, adventurer, or gangster.

The Problem: You are to assume that a nationally known magazine has offered a prize for the best essay on the figure you have chosen. It is your problem to locate the best material concerning him which has appeared in a definite period up to the present. This period may be five, ten, even twenty-five years. You are to collect a bibliography of titles and give some idea of what recent opinion concerning your man has been.

Sources of Information:

The Card Catalogue of your library. Record the call numbers of important works. Notice the difference in numbers for various classifications.

The Reader's Guide to Periodical Literature and its Supplement. Locate at least five articles, and trace two of the periodicals in which they are found.

Poole's Index to Periodical Literature.

Who's Who; Who's Who in America; Who Was Who (1931) for persons who died 1897–1928; similar publications for other countries, such as the German *Wer Ist's.*

Dictionary of National Biography [British].

Dictionary of American Biography.

Lippincott's Universal Pronouncing Dictionary of Biography and Mythology; Century Cyclopedia of Names, etc.

SUGGESTED NAMES:

Honoré de Balzac, John Barrymore, Sandro Botticelli, Andrew Carnegie, Benvenuto Cellini, Charlemagne, Charles Dickens, Theodore Dreiser, Albert Einstein, Robert Frost, Mahatma Gandhi, Heinrich Heine, Jean d'Arc, Nikolay Lenin, Charles Lindbergh, Benito Mussolini, Nero, Eugene O'Neill, Ignace Paderewski, Anna Pavlova, Max Reinhardt, Cecil Rhodes, Saladin, Sun Yat Sen, George Bernard Shaw, Alfred Tennyson, J. M. Whistler, Count Zaharoff.

Case II. Magazine Resources.

Fill out the following outline for five magazines: one general monthly, one weekly with political opinions (*Nation* and *New Republic* are typical), one technical (engineering, art, sport, etc.), one foreign language, one popular (humor, fashions, theater, etc.).

The outlines are to be suitable for a file containing sources for running down material on subjects relating to current interests. As a research detective, it is part of your job to be able to locate articles on all imaginable human pursuits, products, technical methods, and, in fact, everything that is known or that people might wish to know. By avoiding duplication, the class could prepare a useful file including most of the periodicals available in the library.

Name of magazine.

How often published? Approximate size. Price per issue and year.

Name of editor. Publisher. Place of publication.

Name of five or ten typical contributors.

Date of one specific number examined for this outline.

Subjects covered in the magazine: travel, history, biography, humor, criticism, stories, poems, social questions, education, fine arts, household arts, book reviews, politics, etc.

List five leading articles by author and title.

Name special departments and sections: cooking, bridge, advice to investors, gardening, questions and answers, etc.

Illustrations: general type and quality.

For what type of reader is the magazine designed? (Such a fact can be useful to detectives.)

What particular features of the magazine seem most interesting and valuable?

General comments not covered by the above items.

For choice of magazines it is best to go directly to the magazine room of your library. Casual examination of a variety of periodicals will open up new interests.

Case III. Historical Events.

Your problem here is to take some well-known historical event or important event of recent interest and to discover some new point of view concerning it such as might interest the average reader. Thus, try to determine the sentiment of the "other side," such as the state of mind of the White Russians during the Soviet Revolution or of really high-minded loyalists during the American Revolution; try to discover the immediate reaction to the discovery of the X-ray, to the first automobiles, or to the flight of the Wright brothers at Kitty Hawk; investigate the state of public feeling following the sinking of the "Lusitania," the Armistice which marked the end of the World War; or explore material concerning the completion of some great engineering project, Brooklyn Bridge, the Panama Canal, Boulder Dam, the San Francisco bridges, Bonneville Dam.

For each case it will be important to look up some aspect that will be of definite interest to the reader, probably a feature that will prick his curiosity or awaken the strong interest in human nature. Final choice will be determined by your own preferences and the nature of available material. The following list of sources will serve for all three cases. Follow trails closely as they lead from one clue to another, from article to book to encyclopedia and back to book and article, wherever the best material is to be found.

General Sources:

1. The library card catalogue. The subject index is usually placed under separate headings. If you know the authors of useful books, find them under their respective names.

2. Periodical guides—as listed under Case I.

3. Bound files of magazines and copies of current magazines containing pertinent articles. Do not forget the review periodicals.

4. Technical and historical encyclopedias. Among these:

> *The Encyclopaedia Britannica.*
> Freeman and Chandler, *World's Commercial Products.*
> *Harper's Book of Facts.*
> Haydn, *Dictionary of Dates.*
> Larned, *History for Ready Reference.*
> Low and Pulling, *Dictionary of English History.*
> McLaughlin and Hart, *Cyclopedia of American Government.*

New International Year Book.
Ploetz, *Manual of Universal History.*
Statesman's Year Book.
United States Official Congressional Directory.
United States Statistical Abstract.
World Almanac.

The following piece is reprinted from a scholarly journal to show the function and form of footnotes. Note the various types of footnotes and the use of three dots for omissions. Find a use of [*sic*].

A FRESHMAN POEM BY EMERSON [1]
Tremaine McDowell

During 1817–1818, Ralph Waldo Emerson furnished himself with lodgings at Harvard College by serving as the president's Freshman. His activities as messenger to President John Thornton Kirkland and to the faculty reached their high point when Emerson, at the close of the college year, formally distributed to his classmates official notices of their class standing and of their honors.[2]

Not long after this event came Commencement. The class of 1821, having performed their final scholastic exercises in "the hall of Minerva, philosophy's shrine," duly celebrated their release from such duties by a supper. For this occasion, the president's Freshman composed a song, which was transcribed by Emerson's classmate, Josiah Quincy, in his college common-place book, followed by this note: "The foregoing song was written by Ralph Emerson to be sung at the class supper of my class at the conclusion of our Freshman year, 1818." A copy of the song was presented to the Massachusetts Historical Society by Josiah P. Quincy in 1885; it is printed herewith from that transcript, with the courteous permission of Mr. Julius Tuttle, librarian of the Society. Since the first surviving volume of Emerson's journals (that numbered seventeen) dates from the year 1820, few of his verse compositions written before this poem have appeared in print.[3]

The text of the poem, as copied by Josiah Quincy, follows:

[1] From *Publications of the Modern Language Association*, XLV (March, 1930), 326–329. By permission of the editor.
[2] James E. Cabot, *A Memoir of Ralph Waldo Emerson* (Boston, 1887), I, 50.
[3] For a verse rendering of lines 19–53 of Vergil's fifth Bucolic, translated while Emerson was a pupil in the Boston Latin School, see George W. Cooke, *Ralph Waldo Emerson: His Life, Writings, and Philosophy* (Boston, 1881), pp. 18–19.

SONG

written for the Supper of the Freshman Class,
at the close of the College year 1818
by Ralph Waldo Emerson.

To bless the glad year as it closes tonight
Let Friendship and Reason and Pleasure unite,
To its close let Philanthropy bear it along
With the god of the vine and the spirit of song.
                    Derry down, &c.

In the hall of Minerva, Philosophy's shrine,
Recitations we've offered the goddess divine;
In the temple of Bacchus we'll finish the day,
And libations to his plump divinity pay.

Fill high then the wine cup, and think upon those
Who have caused us so oft multifarious woes;
Some screws were of iron, and others of brass,
Sparks [1] came from the first, and from Brazer [2] the last.

Sore evils hath life; yet were none broken-hearted
When first from our early friend Grotius we parted;
Yet perchance they were few who collegii in jugo
Grew pale pouring [sic] o'er the delectable Hugo.[3]

Though the eloquent Grecian of Macedon's age
Seem'd pictured anew in our own Grecian sage,[4]
Yet alas there were many of soberest face
Who had rather been there where the word was Ho-ráce.

Then drink to the sprite of satirical Flaccus,
The first we heard hymning the praises of Bacchus;
He left us the precepts we practise tonight
And his "Nunc est bibendum" we never should slight! [5]

We repeated in Euclid A.B.C. at random,
And when tired exclaimed "Quod erat demonstrandum,"

[1] Jared Sparks was tutor at Harvard from 1817 to 1819.—*Catalogus Harvardianus* (Cambridge, 1821), p. 11.

[2] John Brazer was Professor of Latin Language from 1817 to 1820.—*Ibid*, p. 8.

[3] Hugo Grotius, *De Veritate Religionis Christianae* (Boston, 1809). This edition was dedicated to the president and faculty of Harvard.

[4] "The eloquent Grecian" was Aristotle, whom Emerson had met in Andrew Dalzel, *Graeca Majora* . . . (Cambridge, 1811). "Our own Grecian sage" was Edward Everett, Professor of Greek Literature from 1815 onward.—*Catalogus Harvardianus*, p. 8.

[5] An expurgated edition of Horace was used at Harvard; apparently the only such edition available in the United States was *Opera Expurgata, Notis Anglicis Illustrata* . . . (Philadelphia, 1815).

But we never have proved it impossible yet
By first book or second to take a dead set.[1]

But obey not Rhetorical Walker's direction,
Nor give to your glasses the falling inflection,[2]
While the Friend of the Class, and the Friend of the Nine,
Our tutor revered claims a bumper of wine.[3]

Not poets dread more the strict Scottish Reviews
Than we did the Greek with concomitant screws,[4]
Though Lowth kindly came to enliven the day
And alternately Tacitus bore us away.[5]

Unsung we must leave historic Millot [6]
With Thucydides, Xenophon, Hesiod, & Co:
Ciceronian fame bless today's declamation;
The Senate in embryo! Hope of the Nation!

Yet still we may fill a few scattering lines
With lots of reproofs, admonitions, and fines,
While some sadly count in the list of their wrongs
Four dollars, for shaking a shovel and tongs.[7]

And a trifle for making an easier path—
T'was [*sic*] sacrilege sure—to the Government [8] bath,
And a thousand small fines very like in their features
To those troublesome tribes surnamed mosquitoes.

Freshmen's evils are many; yet leave them at rest,
And remember the maxim "tis all for the best;"
Now to Bacchus commend them, both great ones and small,
And in one cordial bumper amnestify all!

Elementary geometry was included in Samuel Webber, *Mathematics, Compiled from the Best Authors* . . . (2nd ed.; Cambridge, 1808). Webber was president of Harvard from 1806 to 1810.

[2] John Walker, *A Rhetorical Grammar; in which the Common Improprieties of Reading and Speaking are Detected* . . . (Boston, 1814).

[3] Samuel Gilman was Freshman tutor from 1817 to 1819.—*Catalogus Harvardianus*, p. 11.

[4] Robert Lowth, *A Short Introduction to English Grammar* (Philadelphia, 1775).

[5] Since history and antiquities alternated with English grammar during the third term of the Freshman year, it is probable that in alluding to Tacitus, Emerson had in mind Alexander Adam, *Roman Antiquities; or, an Account of the Manners and Customs of the Romans* (2nd American ed.; New York, 1814).

[6] Claude François Xavier Millot, *Elements of General History* (Worcester, 1789).

[7] "If any make tumultuous, troublesome, or indecent noises, to the dishonour or disturbance of the College, or of the town, or any of its inhabitants; . . . they subject themselves to a fine, not exceeding two dollars."—*Laws of Harvard College*, p. 16.

[8] "Government" was a cant term applied by the students to the college administration; see a satirical account of life at Harvard in 1819 in the anonymous poem, *The Rebelliad; or the Terrible Transaction at the Seat of the Muses* . . . (Boston, 1842).

The poem is primarily of historical interest. Here Ralph Emerson, aged fifteen, paid his respects to those members of the faculty of Harvard under whom he studied as a Freshman: John Brazer and Samuel Gilman, Jared Sparks and Edward Everett. Here he commented on the difficulties which he had encountered in the course of study for the first year: Latin and Greek, theology, mathematics, rhetoric and grammar, history and antiquities. And here, finally, he alluded to the boyish pranks of his classmates, in which he apparently did not participate, but by which he was evidently amused.[1] Throughout the song, the youthful Emerson reveals that urbanity of spirit which, in later years, led him to deprecate the pugnacity of such contemporaries as John Brown and Henry Thoreau. As poetry, the composition is entirely without distinction; if these lines are representative of Emerson's college verses, it is not surprising that in 1821 he was chosen class poet only after seven of his fellows had declined the honor.[2]

The above essay contains no references to lines of a play or verses of a poem. Footnote form for such references is as follows:

As You Like It, III, ii, 405–15. In William A. Nielson, *The Complete Works of William Shakespeare* (Boston: Houghton Mifflin Company, 1906), p. 222.
An Essay on Criticism, vv, 21–2. ["l" for "line" is confusing numerically when typed.] [For the rest see form for play above.]

In contrast to the intensive research paper involving the paraphernalia of footnotes, we are offering an article of the opposite type. In this case the value of the content lies in its novelty, rather than in the character of precise, logical combining of carefully isolated facts. Instead of documentation, interesting presentation is the objective. Of course the facts must be authentic; but they are secondary to the appeal they make to our imagination, their human interest. This article is typical of thousands that are available to you in bound and current issues of the *New York Times*, and in other papers and periodicals, as well as in encyclopedias and reference works belonging to the various technical fields.

---

[1] Concerning Emerson at Harvard, his classmate, J. B. Hill, made the following statement (quoted in Cabot, *op. cit.*, I, 63): "He was mirthful, and, though never demonstrative or boisterous, keenly enjoyed scenes of merriment."

[2] Josiah Quincy, quoted in Oliver Wendell Holmes, *Ralph Waldo Emerson* (Boston, 1884), p. 44.

A WORLD OF GOLD BENEATH A VACANT LOT [1]

Herbert L. Matthews

Paris

It is hard to think of more than 80,000,000,000 francs of gold as anything but an arithmetical figure with as much validity as the 3,000-odd light years of distance between us and the Milky Way. That much money to the average wage earner is not only incomprehensible but unreal—a mere convention used by international bankers. Even to walk along a corridor and look at the gold in its compartments carries little conviction in itself.

And as for the place within which it is kept, one gets above all that vague sensation of something fantastic and even horrible which mechanical perfection always arouses. For the strong rooms of the Bank of France constitute a world in themselves, a self-sufficient microcosm that can go on functioning by itself for eighty days. To visit that most modern of catacombs is to leave, for a while at least, the prosaic world of a busy, noisy city for a place completely apart from the routine existence going on some thirty yards overhead.

Nothing could look less distinguished than the bare plot of ground adjacent to the Bank of France building, about two and a half acres in size, surrounded by a plain wooden fence, past which thousands of people walk every day without giving it a thought. Yet there has been more concentrated mechanical ingenuity lavished on that spot than on any similar area in Paris, if not in the world.

The reasons for that extraordinary expenditure of time, money, and effort are, of course, perfectly logical. Of all metals, gold is the most negotiable. A collection of more than $3,000,000,000 worth of it constitutes a treasure without doubt greater than any gathered together in one place in the history of the world. No precaution can be too great in safeguarding such a hoard.

* * *

It may seem rather far-fetched to worry about thieves making off with anything so colossal, both in value and in weight, as 80,000,000,000 francs in gold bars and coins. As a matter of fact, the directors of the Bank of France are not worried about burglars. They are thinking of the years from 1914 to 1918 when a hostile army fought its way almost to the gates of Paris. They are thinking of bombers and Big Berthas, of devastating fires, and, above all things, of revolutions.

[1] Reprinted from the *New York Times Magazine*, September 25, 1932, by the kind permission of the *New York Times*. The asterisks are used to mark the various divisions of the paper, and do not indicate any omission of material.

In a world where established order seems dangerously near to crumbling, when distress is making certain elements of society uncomfortably restive, even France—solid, bourgeois France—cannot shut her eyes to the possibility of some future date, no matter though it be far distant, again providing the spectacle of a French revolution.

It may be asked how any fortress, however powerful, can withstand the destructive forces available in modern attack. Nothing can, of course, for an indefinite length of time, but the builders of this gigantic safe have performed the extraordinary task of constructing a subterranean stronghold which can exist as a world apart for two and a half months. During that time much might happen: a rebellion might be put down or an invading army driven away. If this did not eventuate there would be an end of the Bank of France in any case, so that there would no longer be any justification for guarding its gold.

* * *

The lesson that the World War taught was taken to heart. In those days the strong rooms were very much smaller and only seven yards under the ground. When Big Bertha started her bombardment in 1918, and it was thought for a while that the city was facing a severe attack of some sort, work ceased in the bank proper and the personnel descended underground to carry on their tasks in safety.

Though the attack did not materialize, the war generally gave the directors of the bank so many things to worry about that it was decided a bigger and stronger place must be constructed as soon as possible. The chance did not come until 1925, when 1200 laborers were set to work night and day to build an underground fortress that not a hundred Big Berthas or an entire army could successfully storm—in less than two and a half months of uninterrupted attack.

The better to understand the workings of this most ingenious of refuges let us pretend that a sudden uprising of discontented miners and agricultural laborers has taken place in the provinces and an army of revolutionaries has started to sweep down on Paris. In the building of the Bank of France clerks and cashiers and directors are working at their desks and in their offices when suddenly an alarm is sounded. Every man and woman knows exactly what to do, just as the employees of any large factory in the United States would know how to act in case of a fire alarm.

Bankbooks, bonds, securities, valuable papers, and cash are all put into certain recesses in the walls, from which they slide swiftly through tubes to the strong rooms far below. Meanwhile the procession has already started by stair and elevator toward the subterranean haven. From museums all over the city—the Louvre, the Cluny, the Luxembourg and others—automobiles are rushing some of the greatest art treasures in the world—statues, paintings, jewelry, manuscripts. On arrival at the bank these objects are hastily sent down to a series of rooms especially set aside for them.

All the bank's employees must go the same way, for there is only one entrance. It is seven stories under the ground, and whether you walk or take the elevators it is a zigzag journey, for the engineers are taking no chances that a lucky bomb dropped from a plane should go straight down to the level of the strong rooms before exploding. If you are on the third floor of the bank, for instance, you first take an elevator to the ground floor, then another three flights underground, and finally a cagelike lift going down through a great steel shaft around which wind two sets of stairs.

* * *

The two officials who alone have the open sesame of this modern treasure cave have swung back the immense steel door of the entrance— a solid piece of metal weighing 17,500 pounds and as thick as a man— showing a narrow passage in the midst of which is a revolving steel turret. The refugees go through in single file; there is no room for two abreast. When all are in, the directors follow, and the great door is swung to and locked.

But that door, powerful though it is, is not the greatest of the obstacles which keep the invader from entering. Once the employees are inside, the passageway is cleared. Five yards back is an immense steel block seven feet high and nearly as wide, weighing more than a ton and a half. An official presses a button, starting an electric motor behind the block, driving it forward into the passage, where it stops at the turret. A lever is manipulated: the block swings in a half turn and the passage is bolted as if by a gigantic lock. Should the electric current fail, the block is so disposed that it can be moved easily by hand.

To get in, then, is not only a question of blasting open the first great door but of literally hewing through seven feet of immovable steel.

Should the invaders, instead, seek to dig and blast their way through the ground from the vacant lot above, their task would be even greater. Thirty yards, not only of plain rock but of rock through which water is continually seeping, separates the strong rooms from the surface. Military engineers have guaranteed that that rock is protection against any known explosive. There is so much water, in fact, that the subterranean fortress had to be encircled with a double wall of cement filled in with an impermeable material.

* * *

The personnel of the Bank of France are now in a haven of refuge where no one can disturb them for at least eighty days. Save for their own talking and shuffling about, the quiet is something men generally never experience. For these Parisians, whose ears are attuned to the roar of a great city, whose every breath of air contains gasoline fumes or smoke or dust, this is a peaceful spot—though death and destruction might be raging thirty yards overhead.

All is spotlessly clean. Steel cement forms the outer walls and partitions, and inside are 750 columns of reinforced cement. The air the tenants breathe is pure and fresh, pumped from the outside by one of three great Diesel engines, off to one side of the fortress. It comes through hundreds of conduits in the masonry, whose locations are one of the many carefully guarded secrets of this fantastic world within a world. These ventilators are not built as continuous tubes, but zigzagged, so that even if the enemy found a dozen or so and dropped hand grenades down, they could do no damage. Or if they tried to send down poison gas, there is a device to reverse the current and send it back. The air that comes through is filtered, moistened from the water in the rock and heated so that the temperature of the place is always comfortably kept between 65 and 68 degrees Fahrenheit.

From the Diesel engines, too, comes the power to give the light and serve whatever other purposes electricity is needed for. There is sufficient oil to keep them going for two and a half months.

* * *

Now that everyone is safely in, and reassured, work can be recommenced. There are desks ready for all, and plenty of office supplies. The work is redistributed, and soon the scratching of pens and pencils and the rustling of paper is heard. There are accounts to be kept, business to be planned ahead. Meanwhile, off to the side, in the "factory" where all the mechanical devices are, a number of chefs and scullery maids are busy preparing dinner in a kitchen as modern and complete as the finest Parisian restaurant's, run by electricity from the Diesels. Food supplies, too, will be plentiful for two and a half months, and water can never give out, for it is ingeniously pumped from the surrounding rock.

Because the "factory" generates and uses heat, and thus makes a fire, or explosion, possible, a wall of the original moist rock, covered with steel cement, has been left between it and the rest of the fortress.

And when night comes there are dormitories, and comfortable beds, and quiet that cannot even be imagined by the noise-harassed population on the earth above. Perhaps, though, there will be the faint but reassuring noise of soldiers pacing slowly up and down in a special gallery completely surrounding the strong rooms. They are listening intently—though rather helplessly—for the sound of drilling and blasting which would mean that the enemy was coming. But most of all they are alert against poison gas; if they smelled it an alarm would be sounded.

Perhaps there are those who could toss about fitfully in the presence of so much riches. Misers are not alone in knowing this mystic fever. "La mystique de l'or" is the French expression for the irresistible appeal of the golden metal. One of the wakeful might rise and creep to the door of the rooms of gold. A mere grating separates him from this greatest of all earthly treasures. The touch of a finger to an electric switch and the room springs to light; not only the crude glare of electric lights, but the rich, warm glow of gold—gold gleaming in rows of bars, behind compartments of wire-netting starting at the ground and rising far overhead—red gold from the Rand, yellow gold from Alaska.

*   *   *

When the rooms are open one can stroll through corridors with gold heaped upon either side, stacks and stacks of it, stretching to the ceiling, hundreds of millions of dollars within easy reach. It staggers the mind. One thinks, in ludicrous self-defense, of bolts of silk in a department store, or boxes of shoes—something homely, and reassuring, and comprehensible. But there is always the tantalizing gleam—rich and warm— that only gold possesses, and one can imagine our sleepless gazer turning swiftly away with appetite grown by what it fed on.

Back to bed he goes, and once again the amazing silence returns, save for the muffled sound of a soldier's tread. Perhaps that soldier has stood guard there every night for two months and a half. Perhaps he has heard the ominous noise of drilling and blasting come ever closer. Perhaps at last he sees the wall beginning to crack and water starting to seep through.

All is over—yet not quite all. He sounds the last alarm. Everyone is awakened and ordered to dress quickly. In ten minutes those who have lived and worked there all that time gather in the central room. They have done their part like good soldiers. It is the time that must come to one side or the other in every battle—the time to retreat.

But retreat to where? Two men know, and only two, for the most carefully guarded of all the secrets in this strange place is the hidden exit. Where it starts, and where it goes, only they know; but it may be presumed that it takes these people to a spot from whence they can disperse unsuspected—revisiting a world that had been as far from them as another planet.

And this is not a fantasy. It is a simple description of a real place, built by certain hard-headed men who are taking no chances.

≫ PART TWO ≪

THE INFORMAL ESSAY, NARRATION, AND DESCRIPTION

CHAPTER XII

The Informal Essay

THERE COMES a time in the life of every college student when he feels the impulse to "let go." After the grind of meticulous formal exposition, the urge to burst the bonds and reveal his own personality is likely to be the strongest. But how, he asks, is free expression of personality possible without violating stringent rules of construction and standards of formal presentation? The answer may be found in the casual, time-honored familiar essay—the comfortable battered old hat in the literary clothes closet. Informal, it is usually called, and yet it can be brushed up to serve for almost all occasions.

Not much is to be gained by trying to tell anyone how to write a familiar essay. The masters themselves, from Montaigne in Shakespeare's time to Christopher Morley in ours, have talked genially on the subject but have told little. Certain traits of the essayist and his product are fairly persistent. Among these is one that is well nigh a mathematical "constant": it has been isolated by Mr. Morley as the "bookish micro-organism." The essayist need not be, like Charles Lamb, an addict to well-rubbed, leather-bound old volumes, but he must have the bookish germ in his blood stream. A background of cultural reading, easy literary allusion, and the atmosphere of books and authors will go far toward assuring success in writing the informal essay.

In addition to the bookish infection, there is also prominent in the familiar essay the free play of personality, the two often being blended into one quality. In connection with the vexed matter of personality two axioms may be helpful. First, personality is universal; everyone has it, and even the most recessive type may be effective in the very human world of the essayist.

Second, personality is to be measured by quality, not quantity; it may be, but need not be, huge, loud, or neon-lighted. In writing, it is essentially to be recognized as a quality of self; really any old self that one happens to have on hand at the moment will do. But let it not be a matter of forced draft, synthetic coloring, or "copycatting."

By tradition most of us are taught that we have both good and bad selves. The essayist accepts this genially—that is his good side—and gives expression to both. Usually he mixes them in a kind of good-humored grumbling about things, or a slightly peevish satisfaction in them. He wants to enjoy things, but not to be submerged by them to the loss of his sense of self. The best route to the expression of personality is through the concentration of likes and dislikes. The essayist, who so often lives a kind of bachelor existence, is sensitive to what he doesn't like. To like anything, he knows, is to dislike a great many other things, particularly things that get in the way and keep him from enjoying his likes.

The typical essay, then, will be saturated with reflections of taste and distaste. Since we Americans are notoriously clamorous and eloquent in asserting our personal rights in the face of grievances, particularly fancied or petty grievances, a good way to begin is to single out a pet peeve. Then swing the axe on it and let the chips of formal expository structure fall where they will. To get your inside self outside, on the paper, is now the important thing. Generally the writer will expose his pet aversion to ridicule, inviting the world to laugh at it with him. At all events he will get it out of his system. Now and then, of course, there may creep in some object of admiration; the good self may even capture a whole essay for the beneficent or good-humored mood. But such moments must be guarded against unfashionable sentimentality. Even when the essayist does chant praises, he is usually crying down some aversion. He hovers over the beauty of country meadows, humming like a well-fed, happiness-drugged bee; but there is back of this some irritation at the town and its offensiveness. If he becomes tender about children, or kittens, or kippered herring for breakfast, it is because he has been shocked by the coldness of the world toward these appealing things.

To be sure, this dog-in-the-manger quality of the essayist must not be emphasized too much. Once ease of expression has been gained, it is always possible to turn from dislikes to likes; but a highly desirable loosening up of one's style can often be attained by calling in the aid of such emotions as indignation, or at least amusement at little absurdities. After this has been accomplished, it is safe to turn to the more theoretical aspects of the informal essay. To prevent informality from becoming too formless, a plan of procedure may be used for a time; but in this form, more than any other, such a plan is only temporary, to be thrown away when it is outgrown.

There are a multitude of books on the informal essay. One of the best is W. M. Tanner's well-tested *Essays and Essay Writing* (Atlantic Monthly Press, 1917). In the introduction Mr. Tanner gives a tentative definition and brief history of the essay. We are not interested in the latter, which, of course, goes back to Montaigne in 1580, but we are concerned with defining the type. In the third section of his introduction Mr. Tanner calls the informal essay "a composite fabric delicately woven upon a slight framework called the theme or unifying idea"; it is "a species of soliloquy." Most authorities have emphasized this importance of personality in the essay. Christopher Morley (in *Modern Essays*, First Series) says that "the essay is a mood rather than a form"; it has "a tendency to generalize—to walk around the subject and view it from several vantages . . . the perfection of the familiar essay is a conscious revelation of self done inadvertently." Samuel Johnson, suspicious of informality, called it "a loose sally of the mind, an irregular, indigested piece, not a regular and orderly performance." So much for the form.

Mr. Tanner, thinking of the content, goes on to list five types of essays: "I—Personal Experiences, Confessions, and Self-Analysis; II—Reflections and Comments on Life, Human Nature, Customs, and Experience; III—Observations and Discoveries in the Familiar and Commonplace; IV—Nature; V—General Observations, Comments, and Opinions of the Author." Mr. M. J. Curl in his admirable chapter on the essay (*Expository Writing*, Chapter VII) is content with three types of essays: People, Things, and Nature. We have compromised on four, combining

Mr. Tanner's II and V under one head, Philosophical Essays, and asking students to write this type last, as the hardest. Our list, then, is: (1) Personal Experience, Confession, or Self-Analysis; (2) Observation on Some Aspect of Everyday Life; (3) Nature; (4) Philosophical Reflections.

Here we can fall back on the device given in the chapter on criticism—a schedule for writing informal essays. Of course this is a somewhat dangerous thing to do because of the nature of the form; but an accumulation of suggestions—and they are little more than that—gathered from many sources and placed on one small card for reference will do more than anything else to start the student on his way—a way which in the case of the informal essay is a definitely uncharted sea. The schedule looks something like this:

1. Personality: Allusions. Style. Naturalness.
2. Central Mood: Humorous. Whimsical. Pathetic. Serious. Satirical.
3. Slight Framework.
    Something of a theme running through.
4. Beginning very important.
    Crisp sentences. Paradox. Quotation.
5. Development.
    View subject from several angles.
    Leisurely—discursive—use psychological association.
    Literary allusions and references. Anecdotes.
    Clearness—concreteness. Details.
6. Effective Close.

Beware of "being too ostentatiously quaint" (Christopher Morley). Beware of preaching.

This schedule is, of course, only suggestive and is made as flexible as possible. Themes and published essays included below will illustrate its various features. Most students, once they have it in their hands, can go ahead readily. Only a few warnings and hints are necessary.

For nature essays explore the neglected Leigh Hunt. His essays in this type have kept fresh. If you are worried about the matter of literary allusions, use Bartlett's *Familiar Quotations* or Burton

Stevenson's *Home Book of Quotations.*[1] It is probably not heresy to say that the average student of today does not have his head filled with apt quotations, and yet the sayings of the poets and the wise seem to be as vigorously popular as ever. Sometimes a quotation can be humorously adapted to fit the subject, even as one student, writing on "Shattered Romances," began, "My heart leaps up when I behold proposals in the sky"—with apologies to Wordsworth rather necessary. Literary allusions will provide an essential flavor, but they should be brought in as gracefully as possible. Punning has its perils.

Guard against scientific terminology, except for mock-serious flavor; technical language will blight the tone. Most frequent in the familiar essay is the whimsically humorous manner, quite removed from the spirit of cold science. Similarly, avoid formal analysis. Do not take a subject and split it up as you did in pure exposition: "Four Types of Friends," for example. In the nature essay do not classify descriptive features; in fact do not let these features dominate as such. They merely serve to awaken those personal associations which are the core of the essay. Concrete anecdotes and plenty of intimate details, dropped in here and there, will add tremendously to the interest; but beware of too much straight narration.[2] Stop and give comments and associations now and then. Finally, watch the style; it should be perfectly frank and straightforward—never affected or slangy—and should reveal your real personality. For, after all, personality is the main aspect of the informal essay, and you do not want to cover it up. Do not, then, lose the first-person pronouns.

Some subjects students have preferred are as follows:

Type I. The Trials of Being Small, Why I Am What I Am, On Being Efficient, My Cleverness, When I Grow Up, On Being Timid, On

---

[1] There are many editions of Bartlett. Try to get the Eleventh Edition, revised and enlarged, edited by Christopher Morley and Louella D. Everett, xlviii + 1578 pp., Little, Brown and Company, 1937. Burton Stevenson's volume is even larger. The Second Edition, Dodd, Mead & Co., 1935, contains more than 71,000 quotations, verse and prose, from nearly 5,000 authors both classical and modern. In the alphabetized table of contents appear such recent names as ex-Mayor Walker, famous for his quips, and Mayor La Guardia, both of New York City. The volume boasts xliv + 2605 pages.

[2] The same holds true for excessive description. Always break it by introducing personal associations and reminiscences.

Being Undignified, Big Feet, On Freckles, My Views on My Length, On Making Up My Mind, On Being the Youngest Child.

Type II.[1] The Church Choir, Pea Green, Letters, Operations, Sponges, Old Maids, Sewing, Ice, Whistling, Chewing Gum, Liars, Noses, Streetcars, Neighbors, Bachelors, Alibis, Clothes, Soup, Stockings, Bells, Voices, Walking, Clocks, Hats, Eyes.

Type III. Moonlight, The Exhilaration of Winds, The Sea, Rainy Days, The Country Road, Trees, Autumn, Stars, Twilight.

Type IV. Death, Beauty, Fame, Women, The Work We Do, The Glamour of the Past, Love, This World of Ours, Man, Life, Our Shallow Pleasures, The Uses of Imperfection, Fear of Poverty, Curiosity, Charity, Chance, Time Flies, Golden Wedding, Over and Over and Over Again.

>>> A <<<

TYPE I. *Personal Confession.* This should be the writer's own sincere confession, not that of a fictitious character. But it is possible to imagine oneself as too fat or too thin, etc., if necessary.

"A Spasm on Spectacles" illustrates the effectiveness of various angles of approach.

A SPASM ON SPECTACLES

"Opportunity knocks but once." I gladly seize it, for I must unburden myself of my feelings regarding eyeglasses.

At a very young age, a noble nickname was bestowed upon me— "Foureyes." Since a human being with four eyes must be considered a phenomenon, I accepted the name gladly. But my immature mind soon grasped the fact that having such eyes was a deplorable affair. My friends greatly aided me to this knowledge.

My tomboyish traits were soon to disappear. I had to become that most horrible of all things, a little lady. And why? Because I couldn't fight without my glasses, for my blows would fall upon the air instead of the mouth. If I wanted to fight with my glasses perched upon my nose, the standard of sportsmanship held the others back.

My heyday was over. There would be no more rough and tumble games for me. I decided to obtain some compensation for my affliction. I aroused the tender sympathies of my relatives with sorrowful, brave looks. My gain was considerable. I well remember how quickly the number of nickels and dimes increased. Alas! The relatives were soon wise to my trick.

[1] Notice that most of these subjects are plural in number or generalized. A subject like "Our Kitten" may become too descriptive and lead you astray.

Because of the infernal glasses, everyone judged me to be a very proper and sedate person. *That* was too much! I could endure no more—I smashed the spectacles! I "danced along with vague, regardless eyes." The results were plentiful: I mistook my enemies for friends, I received zeros in all my classes (a usual occurrence), and last but not least, I suffered my parents' revenge. I had to stand up for weeks.

I became intensely interested in books. I was determined to find a near-sighted heroine. I had given up in despair when I found Lily Christine, a very beautiful and charming woman who was killed in an automobile accident. She had forgotten to wear her eyeglasses. This knowledge deadened my desire to find a heroine.

Yet there were heroes. Perhaps there existed one whose eyes burned with the fever of love behind a pair of horn-rimmed spectacles. Ah! I could find no traces of such a being. Love was not for me.

Foolishly, I sought spiritual solace. Verily, "those eyes were spiritual and clear." For two days I gazed upon a wicked world—a world whose strong eyes continually looked for more pleasure. This sin became so enticing that I soon ended my hermit existence.

In high school, no boy would ever proclaim the fact that my eyes were as "stars of twilight fair." How my heart bled for such words! But no. My eyeglasses were there to mock and scold me for my dishonorable thoughts. They flung questions upon me. "Have we not served you in good stead? Didn't your teachers think you were scholarly because of your studious appearance due to us?" What could I answer? I had to admit that they did deserve some praise.

One great hope sustained me. Perhaps, I could, at some time, stop wearing the precious things. With this fervent belief came another firm determination. I would marry a young eye doctor. What a marvelous solution to all my woes! These beautiful thoughts died a horrible death. I could fool myself no longer. I had never met or known an oculist who had the spirit of youth. All were decrepit, weak creatures who continually pronounced these words: "You must wear your eyeglasses, forever."

College has brought no changes. I now realize the worth of that scholastic look; I use it in classes. At times I am successful, but why are professors so discerning?

Not only does sleep "knit up the ravelled sleeve of care" but it is also my saviour. I can thankfully close my unprotected orbs and dream of some dashing knight who may see me in that glorious state.

The noble poet who once said

"Drink to me only with thine eyes
And I will pledge with mine"

would be at a disadvantage, I'm afraid, for my four eyes might weaken
him until he would reach the blessed state of intoxication.

C. H.

"My Views on My Length" has the same variety of approach,
with more humorous results. Have there been no tall women in
literature?

MY VIEWS ON MY LENGTH

"My, Frances, you're getting to be a great big girl," so I hear
every time I meet a family friend. An instinctive respect for my neck
prevents me from doing anything rash. Nevertheless, in my imagination I subject all such tactless people to all sorts of fitting punishments.
I know I'm tall. Why tell me about it? However, there is one consolation. I shall always look down upon those poor unfortunates; they
will always look up to me.

Being tall had its features from the first. Those high kitchen shelves,
the Waterloo of so many jam-seeking children, never thwarted my
ravenous desires. In spite of my sex, my height made me, in turn, a
general of worthy repute, the chief of a band of lusty Indians, and
the leader of a gang of decidedly desperate desperadoes.

In those days, as now, I was the despair of my mother's heart. I
outgrew clothes as fast as she could make them. She never purchased
garments for me with the intention that I should wear them two
seasons. Indeed no; it was unusual if they still fitted me after a period
of two months.

During my high-school career my height played an important part.
It aided me in obtaining the much-coveted center position on our
basket-ball team. But, when I desired to be the charming heroine in
our class play, I towered three inches above the leading man; therefore, I had to take the part of a freakish, eccentric spinster.

I seem to form an invariable Mutt and Jeff combination with my
girl friends. Is it the attraction of opposites? I don't know. As to men
friends, there's where the rub comes in. My man must be tall; I refuse
to go a step with a man shorter than I. I have a unique measuring
system at the front door of our house. My mother opens the door;
I remain behind a partly closed door. As the victim enters, I carefully
gauge his stature. If he reaches the top mark, I come tripping merrily

out from my ambuscade. If he reaches the second mark, I quickly change into shoes with Cuban heels. My appearance in Oxfords signifies that the poor man barely hits the third mark. If the dear soul fails to make any of these marks, I remove all traces of rouge; and next I plead a headache, or what have you?

As I enter a rumble seat, or a bathtub, I must coil myself in much the same manner as does a snake. I must occupy an aisle seat in the theater in order to have plenty of space for my lengthy framework. In a classroom I must have a front seat (on account of my thirst for knowledge, of course)!

In a crowd a small person can easily avoid another person whom he does not wish to see. Not me! I stand out a half a head above the tallest of them. No slinking away for me; I must face the music. Come to think of it, I'd make an excellent target for a gunman's bullet. A shorter person has some chance; even the poorest of shots could hit me.

Long length has its advantages, too. On a crowded bus I can read the newspaper of the person in front of me without ungracefully and impolitely stretching my neck. A horse would find it difficult to throw me. I have merely to lock my feet under the horse's belly. He may kick and rave; I'm there to stay. If I were marooned on a desert island, I would not have to climb a tree and hang out a distress signal. I could tie it on my head, and yet be sure of detection, so long as I remained standing.

My hygiene teacher tells me that I shall continue to grow until I am twenty-five years old. Heaven forbid! If I grow any taller I'll cease to be useful, except as a tent pole. If I were a man, I could go to England and join the King's Guards. Or, at least, I could challenge Primo Carnera. At my present rate of expansion, at the end of my seventh remaining year of growth, I should be able literally to look into the domestic affairs on Mount Olympus.

F. S.

One can "let go" without calling in literary allusions, as the next essay demonstrates.

WHY I HATE BEING THE YOUNGEST CHILD

I'm the youngest child of a large family, but I wouldn't brag about it. My mamma used to think I was great and from the time I was hitting all four till I went to school and learned things, she always presented me as "my youngest little dear" and then I'd be exposed to an avalanche of slobbering kisses by mammoth women who loved the "little angel." Little angel, indeed! If they only saw the faces the "little angel" made at them from behind closed doors, they would sprain the central fissure of their brain changing their minds. But now, mamma knows her child and when she presents her to company, she leaves off the "little dear" and substitutes just plain "daughter."

At home, my family being large, the line-ups to the newspaper, kitchen, and sink are enormous. Where do I, the youngest child, find myself in these mob scenes? I find myself at the end of the line.

Take the matter of clothes. Do I ever get anything new? I should say not. I always look like I've been put through a knothole, because my big sisters get new clothes and pass their old discarded rags to me. Mamma thinks they are simply wonderful to keep my wardrobe replenished. Ye gods! It's no wonder girls leave home.

When I want some money, I get myself all prepared for an attempt to wheedle some out of papa. I walk up bravely, smile sweetly, and say, "Why, papa dear, is that a new hair I see growing on your head?" Instead of saying, "How much?," he says, "That's just what Jerry used to say." And phooey goes all my technique.

Now you may wonder where the youngest daughter entertains her boy friends. Let me enlighten you. In the first place, the oldest daughter, by heritage, obtains the right to use the davenport in the living room. Papa and mamma, by hypothesis, have the right to play checkers in the dining room. The second oldest daughter gets the sun parlor for no reason at all. The third oldest daughter gets the back porch for the same reason. And the youngest daughter may have not only the whole kitchen, but the dog, cat, and silverware thrown in for good measure.

The way my family treats me is terrible. Some day I'm going to give them a piece of my mind, but first, I'm going to get a head start and run like—well, I'm going to run fast. Maybe, for the sake of my old mother, I'll drop a line saying that I've decided to take a vacation at the Thousand Islands and that I'm going to stay a week at each one.

F. S.

TYPE II. *Everyday Life.* It is easy to choose topics that are too serious for this type of essay. Well-balanced people, however, take most of the concerns of life with a dash of humor or sentiment. This type of essay, then, makes its effect by appealing to that instinct in all of us by which we lighten the load of life by discovering as many interests as possible in the mere routine of living.

The effect of the opening sentence is very important. Pertness is achieved in the opening of an essay called "The Church Choir." "What is so rare as a choir in tune? Nothing, except a choir that assembles on time." Often it is effective to link the opening and the close as in the essay on "Voices."

There are many voices, but only one Voice.

. . . .

And then, there is the Voice of conscience—with us all the time. This inner Voice comes to us without sound, but it is so capable of influencing us that its sound may be louder than the trumpet of Gabriel. The human being says, "I will," and the Voice says, "You won't." Sometimes the Voice wins, and oftentimes the voice does. It is all a matter of which can hold out the longest, the voice, or the Voice.

The following illustrates the effective use of short sentences for a crisp opening.

SPRING COLDS

Trees shed old bark for new. Pale green, spindly grass pushes away old brush and twigs. And you, most innocent of bystanders, burst forth with a new spring cold. Why must you do this when other people are messengers of spring? Dogs shed their hair, girls pop out with new freckles, and men don checked coats. Baby snakes slither around stubby weeds. Gophers pop up in young green fields. What would you give for a rifle, but no, your arms are too shaky to do justice to a BB gun.

That glittering look comes into your eyes. You feverishly hack with a jumpy cough. Many boxes of Kleenex find their way to your nose, and thence to the fire.

You snivel and droop wearily, abjectly, fiercely cursing the fate of the gods. Of course, you didn't play your first spring game of golf in inconsistent, spattering rain. Mud slushed oozingly around your ankles. The ball you drove from your favorite green, perfect with a sizzling back spin, fell plunk into juicy black mud. You plowed out to give it a withering blow and splattered mud and water all over your feet and ankles. And now you have a cold.

Suddenly you stumble on some unfortunate comrade in the same condition. Misery loves company, and you blithely hail each other, brothers under the skin after all. Unhappily you stagger along your miserable way together.

But your uncontaminated fair-weather friends avoid you as a farmer does a summer frost. Very obviously your nose burns and your eyes itch. There is a lump in your chest and bugs whiz about your head. In your solitude you can almost believe in Heine's melancholy,

> "Death is but a long, cool night
> And life's a dull and sultry day."

L. M.

In "A Chewing-Gum Romance" there is evidence of unusual talent. Note its realistic clearness.

A CHEWING–GUM ROMANCE

> When first he met her, she was fair
> And chewing chewing gum.
> A rosebud nestled in her hair;
> He breathed his love unto her there,
> And she—she smiled a smile so rare
> While chewing chewing gum.

You have seen her, haven't you? Of course, you have. With her eyebrows elevated a matter of inches above their natural location, and her mouth moving in great sweeping circles with a definite halt and swallow at the end of each gyration, she sits comfortably on the elevated train chewing furiously and reading the *American's* evening installment of "The Petter." Directly over her head, beaming down on her benignly, is Wrigley's ad bearing the words, "One of the Evidences of Refinement," and showing a mammoth package of Juicy Fruit with a number of devilish little imps gamboling over it. "After every meal," the slogan of which our dear friend, Peter K., is so fond, means nothing to her. She chews it day, night, and in between times.

> She listened as he urged his suit
> Still chewing chewing gum.
> He vowed her charms had made him mute
> And tuned his passions to a lute
> While she declared that it was "cute"
> Still chewing chewing gum.

Have you ever gone in to a ribbon counter and found the girl behind chewing gum with a vengeance? I have, and almost invariably, as she shows you her display of ribbons, she takes the pins from the rolls, puts them in her mouth, and, when she is ready to return the rolls to their case, draws them rather gingerly from their place of safety—to find them artistically capped and blunted by a covering of nice gray gum.

> At last she blushed and murmured, "Yes"
> Still chewing chewing gum.
> He wrapped her in a fond caress,
> And then she said, "'Tis time I guess
> I saw about my wedding dress."
> Still chewing chewing gum.

Telephone operators, too—especially the species that are in charge of hotel switchboards—are staunch supporters of this new cult of masticating modern. They have that fascinating mannerism of gazing coyly at the salesmen sauntering by, and of displaying, with every chew, any and all dimples or pearly teeth with which they happen to be blessed.

> She strode in state a-down the aisle
> Still chewing chewing gum.
> He met her with a happy smile
> And they were wedded there, the while
> She wept in pretty bridey style
> Still chewing chewing gum.

I suppose it does have its uses though. In fact, I know it has. Not more than two weeks ago, one of the rhinestone buckles on my only pair of silver pumps very inconsiderately dropped off without the slightest provocation. It left me in a rather sad predicament, for my escort was (I trust) patiently waiting and had been for some thirty minutes. Luckily, I remembered that I had half a stick of gum in my possession, and, having chewed it to the proper degree of stickiness, I used it as glue, securing the buckle quite satisfactorily.

> Today I saw her down the way
> Still chewing chewing gum,
> Three children joyous, blithe, and gay
> Were shouting in their merry play
> And they were hers I know for they
> Were chewing chewing gum.

M. F.

The revelations in the next essay come from a Swiss girl who had recently come to America. Her allusions are unique, and her mistakes in idiom are very few. What aspects of the essay are European rather than American?

THE TRUTH ABOUT OLD MAIDS

The bachelor who says that he is perfectly happy is a fibber. First, perfect happiness does not exist in the world. And if this bachelor is relatively happy, it is not because he is not married, but because he has a happy disposition, and would be just as happy whether he were married or not. This is true for bachelors, old maids, and married people.

Most persons think that bachelors are very happy, and old maids very unhappy. This is a prejudice resulting from the vast amount of talk done by men. The French say: "Les gens heureux n'ont pas d'histoire." Then, if there is no story, there is nothing to say. But bachelors have very much to say; this proves that they are not so happy as they want us to believe.

Anybody who has good sense will confess that it is much easier for a woman to live alone than for a man. A girl is able to adapt herself to her surroundings, and feel at home almost everywhere. One knows how particular bachelors are about their habits.

There is no bachelor or old maid, who, some dreary winter evening, did not wish for a home, for love, and for a good home-cooked meal. But the dream was soon discarded by the unmarried man at the thought of the bills to pay, the furnace to take care of, and the same woman to love. In woman's mind, the dream was given up even quicker. A home, what a beautiful thing, but the next day there is housecleaning. And love, how divine in the beginning, but there are children and other women to share with. Good things to eat! What about dishes to wash? Mrs. Mille Gade Corson, the only mother to swim the English Channel, says that what kept up her courage and gave her strength to swim across was that she was thinking of how many dishes she would have to wash if she did not make it.

If people could appreciate the peace of mind and the relief of an old maid who has given up trying to play the game to win or keep a sweetheart, they would not feel sorry for her. There are many girls who are not married because they are afraid of marriage, and I do not blame them when one knows that men's creed concerning love can be expressed by the following lines by Tom Moore:

" 'Tis sweet to think that where'er we rove,
　　We are sure to find something blissful and dear;
　　And that when we're far from the lips we love,
　　We've but to make love to the lips we are near."

But beyond the dishes to wash, and the house to clean, there is the monotony of married life which has always seemed dreadful to me. My life has been so far a great adventure, and I cannot conceive the possibility to settle down to live at the same place, in the same house forever, and see the same man come home every night.

My feelings, and I think those of many other old maids, are very well described in the following little Spanish folk song:

"If marriage a day and night lasted,
Or even a week or so,
Why then I too could marry
But forever? No, no, no!"

N. T.

The student who began her essay by parodying Wordsworth had an effective device for securing attention. Frankly, she rather overdid the trick of humorous quotation.

SHATTERED ROMANCES

My heart leaps up when I behold
Proposals in the sky:
So was it in my girlhood daze
So is it now that I wear stays.

Yes, I still get a thrill out of proposals, even if they do seem to end disastrously.

My first one occurred in my early adolescent days. The male ensnared was "a lovely youth! I guess the panther in the wilderness was not so fair as he." Ah! those tender days, with their misty glances and shy blushes! Finally, he popped the question one lovely night. "At length," cried she, "I'll marry: what should I tarry for?" The romance was blooming in its fullness, when suddenly one day it withered without warning. We had just returned from skating, and as Albert complained of cold feet, mamma insisted on removing his shoes and stockings, much to the great discomfiture of both Albert and me. This modesty seemed ridiculous—hadn't we been swimming together many times? Yet feet, somehow, were different, and not the least bit romantic. And, furthermore, love, blind as it is, didn't prevent me from seeing a large hole in the toe of Albert's sock. Thus, ended my first affair of the heart.

"Five years have past; five summers; with the length of five long winters! And again I hear"—the plaintive lover's voice. But this time it was in the form of one whose chief occupation in life seemed to be that of boasting of his great wealth. "He was like a cock who thought the sun had risen to hear him crow." But the mortgage on the old homestead was long past due, and anyway, my family wanted me to marry the old bloke, as I was their only hope of gaining riches. So, here was I ready to sacrifice my young life for the good of the cause. Proclaiming myself a subdued and adoring creature, I soon held this victim in my clutches, and was even beginning to think myself "how well I had feathered my nest." Well, here's what happened this time. After having most effusively welcomed Mr. Jyppe one evening, my dear family (yes, the whole seven of them) retired, into the darkened dining room, to greedily await the crucial moment.

"My dear," cried Jasper, as soon as the last of the tribe had disappeared, "since I know you really love me and are so eager to become my wife, I will tell you the truth now. My phantom wealth was only a decoy, and I have always been penniless. I'm poor but oh my!"

He was interrupted by despairing screams which came from the next room. The parlor door burst open and mamma crashed to the floor in a dead faint. As for Jasper Jyppe, he certainly was "a phantom of delight when at last he gleamed out of my sight."

The next scene took place in Lugano, Switzerland, where we were visiting friends last year. We spent one evening at a neighboring villa, to which I was requested to bring my violin and play for the people. My performance must have had a terrible effect on one young handsome Italian, for he rushed up feverishly, and asked to escort me home. (That is, to where we were staying, not to America.) I was startled when he suddenly proposed marriage to me! Although I didn't even know his name, I managed to find out, in the course of the short walk, that he owned several large vineyards, besides a villa. He spoke English quite well, so I'm sure I didn't misunderstand him when he said, "Ah, my sweet carrot, be my wife, be the mother of my children."

I managed to escape with the promise that I would come the following morning with the family and the answer. Of course everyone grew hopeful when I told them of the exciting news, and the next morning we presented ourselves at the home of our suitor. Upon being admitted we heard a great din and clatter, and suddenly many, many children appeared. Cheerfully, yet fearfully I glanced at my parents, as we waited for the Italian. Then he entered the room, beamed on us, then said,

"Now children be quiet, here is your new mamma!"

Now, dear friends (just everywhere),

> "Have I not reason to lament
> What man has made of man?"

L. C.

Type III. *The Nature Essay.* In the following brief sketch there are perhaps too few allusions; but the mood and the details are emotionally affecting. Can you suggest a quotation or two from literature that would fit the text at some point?

FARMHOUSE AT NIGHT

Those unfortunates who have never lived in the country have missed one of the peaceful places on this earth. To me a farmhouse at night is balm to a troubled spirit. I love to lie under a low roof and listen to the steady, soothing beat of the rain, close above me. In the barnyard, fowls stir restlessly in the low branches. Far across the fields a frog croaks dismally. Mice scamper through the walls close by. The atmosphere is charged with a feeling of rest after labor, of preparation for the day to come. I can readily see how these sounds would be hateful to some, but to me they are dear.

The country at night is so untroubled that most cares become trivial. In contemplation the world and its anxieties seem far off. My little room constitutes, for the time, my all. Life is good, and I want only to rest that I may enjoy it fully tomorrow. I wish that I could explain the utter detachment and repose that I feel.

Nights in the city are utterly dreadful. City noises are harsh and insistent. Few would call the rattle of a trolley car peaceful or soothing. There sleep is broken—at least for me. As for meditation, I find it difficult with a street light glaring in my window and patrons of the night club across the street noisily enjoying themselves. Night in the city is not for rest. As little as is possible is used for physical and mental repose, and even that little is used grudgingly.

I wonder how many busy men and women would give much of their worldly goods just for a place in which to find peace. For so many, there is no stopping the rush and hurry of everyday affairs. It would be interesting to know what would appeal to different personalities. The man who, as a little boy, longed to "go down to the sea in ships" probably would seek his haven in a rowboat on a quiet lake. So change our youthful ambitions.

Those who lived in and loved the country in their youth always feel a strange urge to go back, if not to stay, at least to enjoy it for a while. For them nature is the answer to their need for a refuge. "Nature never did betray the heart that loved her" has been proved true again and again. I am glad that I have so early found the place that affords me perfect peace.

B. J. H.

The author of "The Country Road" has an excellent feeling for the value of tone.

THE COUNTRY ROAD

There is something very alluring to me in a winding strip of country road. I am thinking just now of a certain little country road located away up in the highlands of Scotland. It was late in the month of September that my eyes looked upon that never-to-be-forgotten sight.

The road was narrow, winding, and very uneven. It wound in and out among the heathered hills. On one side of it ran a mountain stream, on the other side towered the high hills covered with gorgeous, purple heather. A drove of snow-white sheep were following their leader down the accustomed path that led to a distant cottage on the hill. An aged shepherd brought up the rear. He carried an old leather sack over his back for the wool, and a staff in his hand to guide the wandering sheep. Strange wild flowers nestled here and there along the quiet roadside. In the west the sun, like a great ball of fire, was slowly sinking beyond sight.

There is something in a scene like this that acts like magic on my soul. I find myself suddenly transformed from a nervous, fidgety being into a calm, purposeful person. It makes one long to get out and do things. It is soothing to the senses, and, at the same time, exhilarating to every fiber of one's being. To tread such a road alone is to think, and to reason, and to muse over the great, good things of life. I never see a country road but that I think of a little red school, a toiling student, and—eventually, a great man. An open country road speaks to me of opportunities ahead. A busy city street seldom speaks of the future. It is essentially a creation of the present. I never have been able to do much thinking on a city street save those thoughts of self-preservation which are, in reality, of basic instinct. But give me a long stretch of country road with open fields on either side, with the sun of early June overhead, and with the joy of youth in one's heart— that is living!

The country road is to all appearances fast becoming a thing of the past. Swift cars fly along smooth pavement where formerly the horse and wagon jaunted along at a somewhat easier pace. Do I advocate horse and wagon in place of automobiles? No. Nor do I speak for more and more country roads. What I do warmly announce is the fact that with the coming of these things, and the accompanying gasoline streak in the middle of the road, the beauty and solemnity of the country road is, to my mind, forever gone. One can never sense the fragrance of the newborn blossoms, one can never drink in the beauties of the fields of yellow corn, one can never pause and drink from the sparkling, bubbling spring with half so much pleasure as when traveling on foot along the country road.

J. M. T.

TYPE IV. *The Philosophical Essay.*

ADVICE

"Nothing is given so profusely as advice"—and nothing is quite so completely disregarded. I have never yet met a person who was dissuaded from something he wanted to do by advice. "Many receive advice, but few profit by it," said a pre-Christian era Roman, showing how little ideas have changed on some subjects through the centuries. It seems the nature of us beasts not to profit by the experiences of others. But even though we won't take the advice of anyone else, we insist on passing our own out freely. Then when the poor mere man who disregarded our advice comes to grief, we sit back complacently, and with a very self-satisfied, holier-than-thou expression, calmly say, "I told you so!" Some people are terribly audacious in their advice-giving habits, invading fields of which they have no understanding or appreciation. Let us take, for example, the thirteenth-century scholar who remarked, "Had I been present at the Creation, I would have given some useful hints for the better ordering of the universe." Now I am not a religious fanatic or anything of the sort, but how anyone could invade the sanctity of God himself and say, "Brother, you did a bum job; now here's what I wouldda done," is beyond my comprehension. And the label of the old fellow who said this was Alphonso the Wise! Can you imagine the magnificent self-importance the man must have attached to his intellect? That, it seems to me, is one of the bad results of advice-giving on a grand scale. For when the person who does not accept our advice goes wrong, we are imbued with a feeling of our own great mental capacity and foresight.

Furthermore, most of us can't ourselves follow the advice we give others. "We may give advice, but we cannot inspire the conduct." For example, Polonius gave his son Laertes some very good advice: "Give thy thoughts no tongue"; and again: "Give every man thy ear, but few thy voice; Take each man's censure, but reserve thy judgment." Polonius himself was, however, one of the biggest gossips in the Danish court. Is there any wonder that tales floated back to Polonius about some of Laertes's exploits in France, including some of the things he was advised against?

Thus, it seems to me that advice is one of the most futile things we have. Even in this modern stoveless age, it seems that everyone must sometime touch a hot stove and learn from experience. And so my parting advice to each and every one of you is:

STOP GIVING ADVICE!

J. T.

Consider the effectiveness of the vocabulary and allusions in "The Glamour of the Past."

THE GLAMOUR OF THE PAST

When one ponders on the glories of the past, he is apt not to think of the flesh and blood humanness of the various eras, but he is carried away by vague pictures of universal beauty, chivalry, alluring romance, and plotting intrigue perpetrated by fascinating characters whose real lives have been distorted by fiction. It is more pleasant to think of "les précieuses ridicules," that whimsical French group of the seventeenth century who carried graces and gallantries to rather foolish extremes, than to suffer with the greatly abused French peasantry of the same period. Glamour appeals to us above harsh reality. We are, in truth, looking out of

"Charmed magic casements, opening on the foam
Of perilous seas, in faery lands forlorn,"

searching only for the beauty and simple exquisiteness of the past, while in our ignorance we disregard the beauty which existed in the humble, even as it does now.

Truly, "distance lends enchantment to the view." We drift so far from real life in our constant seeking after glamour that eventually everything pertaining to the past is mistily obscured by myopy. After all, it is only human to gloss over unpleasantness and dwell only on sweeping crinolines, demure smiles, thrilling Indian raids, moon-drenched Southern gardens, and stalwart young heroes marching off to spectacular wars. It is an interesting fact that ever since the Napoleonic wars the men of France have been almost a foot smaller in stature than before the great romantic hero's conquests. This is due to the commandeering of tall men for armies, leaving only short men at home to raise families. We would not be apt to think of this in our consideration of the glamorous past.

These various and sundry pictures of past life present to our vision an endless pageant of kaleidoscopic nuance and brilliance. Undoubtedly the motion pictures have led to this aspect, for they over-exaggerate romance and glamour. One seldom finds a truly natural humorous character in a costume drama, a fact which tends to prove that the picture is padded out on the romantic side. The motion-picture magnates have found out that the great American public likes the past shown with a heavy sugar-coating.

Probably almost everyone, at some time or other, has wished that he might have had his existence in former times. In this "groaning ever for the past," we seldom stop to realize that we would have vexations and troubles, although they would be in somewhat different guise.

A. McK.

The next paper shows how the essay may make use of a narrative element, just as the nature essay draws heavily on descriptive resources. It is an effort at imitation of an essay by Max Beerbohm, "William and Mary," in the volume *And Even Now* (1920). The basic episode is taken from the writer's own experience.

FULFILLMENT

"Theirs is a love grown perfect through understanding," I remember thinking as I had watched Dennis and Mary working side by side in the garden, he hoeing the ground and she walking beside him, her blue apron gathered up in her hands and filled with seeds that she sprinkled in the furrows he was making. It was mid-morning, and the sun had tangled itself in the glory of Mary's black Irish hair that hung, unbound, to her waist. All the neighbors said that Mary Catterly was a fool to do anything that Dennis wished, like letting her hair hang free down her back and spending all her time working in peasant dress and apron in the gardens of the old farm they had restored, instead of living in town part of the time and spending some of the money that Dennis made from his successful plays on lovely gowns and smart apartments.

Dennis had loved Mary's hair, and he had never wanted her to do it up with restraining pins and ribbons; so she, who would look at the tall man she loved so greatly and murmur Irish love songs—"Beloved, with the light of stars in your eyes"—went about her home with quiet pride, never hearing the laughter of neighbor folk who chanced to see her picking strawberries for Dennis's breakfast, her dark cloud of hair rippling smooth in the sunlight.

For three summers now we had rented the farm next to theirs, and I had known the generous happiness of youth in another's love. I used to sit long hours in the plum tree, watching Dennis and Mary working together beyond the hedge, and wonder if some day I too should know the all-fulfilling love that had drawn them together.

All these thoughts were with me now as Mother was telling me that Dennis had been killed by a speeding car on his way back from the village that morning, and that she and the other neighbors had just come from helping Mary. My heart was sad, and I could have cried aloud when Mother said, "Mary doesn't seem to mind very much, because she hasn't shed a tear. When they came to her with the news, she just turned and walked into the house, and when she came back to the yard she had screwed her hair tightly back into a knot that she had pinned high on the back of her head."

I could have cried aloud because of the unshed tears in the heart of this lovely woman whose sorrow knew, as her devotion had known, strange expression.

P. A.

As Izaak Walton showed, it is possible to blend nature, the feeling for everyday life, and philosophical reflection, at least where there is a man on one end of a fish pole and even the faintest possibility of a fish on the other. This is only a portion of a paper that extended to nine typed pages.

FISHIN'

There's a calendar hanging on the wall, and it has been turned to the month of April. A bright red pencil marks a particular day, the opening day of the fishing season. It is 'long about January when the wind howls down the chimney that the first symptoms appear. The fisherman will finger the pages of an old sport magazine, lay it aside and sigh, fidget in his chair, pick up an angler's guide and pore over it with an increasing show of restlessness. He lifts his eyes and stares into space. He takes down his fishing jacket, goes through the pockets, and brings out his last year's license and other relics—tangled leaders, water-soaked matches, something unpleasant like stale gravy in the bottom of the pocket. That's where the chocolate bar disappeared to. An old handkerchief, smelling of fish, also comes out.

The urge of springtime is a real force in our lives, whether we realize it or not. Early in March, even while the blizzards are raging about the house and the mercury hovers around zero, we get out our rods and prepare them for the coming season. Dreary March is a nightmare, a month of mere possibilities. Sitting before the fireplace, the fisherman catches more fish than he does all season.

So, busily and happily employed, dipping into angling books and the like, the days pass, and soon it is opening day. Because opening day arrives so early, insect life is conspicuous by its absence; but fish will take worms, so what's the difference? I am a fly fisherman; but I dare confess that I do use worms in the early spring and grasshoppers in the summer. No doubt one can take a few fish on a fly in April, and I have done so, but this is not real fly-fishing. Where is the difference between a deeply sunken fly and a spinner? It is easier to make a great display of flies and fly books, while we carry a baking-powder can of worms in our coattail pocket.

When the cares of life press, business irks, and everything seems wrong, go fishing, go trout fishing. Seek out some stream where the trout are jumping, crazy for the fly. Even if you succeed in taking no fish, would it be such a catastrophe? Some of my best days have been days of failure. The important thing is to get out where the cool breezes blow, where you can cure your restlessness and forget your cares.

The pungent fragrance of the balsams and pines at sunrise, the startled flight of birds, the resounding splash of a hungry trout on a still lake, the quality of the early morning hush—all these are a part of fishing. Fishing goes deep into a fellow's soul and does something. Only the fisherman knows. One can never tell what is going to happen. Lady Luck turns the wheel. There is always something new, some surprise in trying to outwit the finny tribe. If you doubt it, just go out and try.

In the evening, just at sundown, when the shadows are deepening in the woods and the crickets are tuning up their fiddles for their all-night serenade, the big trout quit their hidden lairs beneath the rocks in the deep pools and come forth in search of food, and the smaller ones dart across in play. When you see the water break into a ripple and broaden out in disappearing circles, you may know that one of the smaller fry has risen to the surface, only to dart away frightened. But where you see the quiet surface of the pool suddenly part with a swirl, and you catch a gleam of silver and red in the fast fading light, and hear the heavy splash that follows, you may know that a prince of the realm has seized upon the tribute he extorts from the inhabitants of the insect world. In that pool is the place to cast your fly.

There are many things that appeal to me at these hours, so many thoughts that come to me; it is the hour when a congenial soul is welcome and company is much desired. I have never been able to decide which part of the day appeals to me the most, the gray dawn or the dim, shadowy twilight. You arise in the very early morning while it is yet dark, half grumbling at the hour and with sleep hanging on your eyebrows. A douse of cold water brings you to your senses and clears the cobwebs from your brain; you pick up your rod and can of bait, sling your basket over your shoulder, and start out for the stream.

M. J.

⋙ B ⋘

In spite of its name, the informal essay does not always achieve the quality of informality. If we allow for the passage of over three hundred years, the style of the real inventor of the type shows a conversational ease that is much more genuine than the studied informality of Lamb or Hazlitt. Michel de Montaigne (1533–1592), as a skeptic leading the way out of medieval dogmatism, learned to accept life with a sane equanimity by being content with what his own mind could give him. He asked questions, but did not insist on having the answers. He sought independence of mind, an enjoyment of aesthetic satisfactions, a healthy cheerfulness; and he attained these by building his philosophy on the basis of an honest doubt. The selection below reveals something of the inquisitiveness, shrewdness of observation, and the alert tolerance of the master of those who are not taken in. Ignore Dr. Johnson's advice concerning the style of Addison, and spend a few days and nights with Montaigne. You will find a living personality, and discover that there lies the true source and determinant of style. He says[1]

I speak into paper as to the first man I meet. . . . I never travel without bookes, nor in peace nor in warre; yet doe I passe many dayes and moneths without using them. It shall be anon, say I or to morrow, or when I please; in the meane while the time runnes away, and passeth without hurting me. For it is wonderfull, what repose I take, and how I continue in this consideration, that they are at my elbow to delight me when time shall serve; and in acknowledging what assistance they give unto my life. . . . At home I betake

[1] From the *Essays* of Michel de Montaigne, the Third Book, Chapters I and III. Translated into English by John Florio (1603).

me somwhat the oftner to my library, whence all at once I command and survay all my houshold; It is seated in the chiefe entrie of my house, thence I behold under me my garden, my base court, my yard, and looke even into most roomes of my house. There without order, without method, and by peece-meales I turne over and ransacke, now one booke and now another. Sometimes I muse and rave; and walking up and downe I endight and enregister these my humours, these my conceits. It is placed on the third storie of a tower. The lowermost is my Chapell; the second a chamber with other lodgings, where I often lie, because I would be alone. Above it is a great ward-robe. It was in times past the most unprofitable place of all my house. There I [passe] the greatest part of my lives dayes, and weare out most houres of the day. . . . My thoughts are prone to sleepe, if I sit long. My minde goes not alone as if [legges] did moove it. Those that studie without bookes, are all in the same case. The forme of it is round, and hath no flat side, but what serveth for my table and chaire: In which bending or circling manner, at one looke it offreth me the full sight of all my books, set round about upon shelves or desks, five rancks one upon another. It hath three bay-windowes, of a farre-extending, rich and unresisted prospect, and is in diameter sixteene paces void. In winter I am lesse continually there: for my house (as the name of it importeth) is pearched upon an over-pearing hillocke; and hath no part more subject to all wethers then this: which pleaseth me the more, both because the accesse unto it is somewhat troublesome and remote, and for the benefit of the exercise which is to be respected; and that I may the better seclude my selfe from companie, and keepe incrochers from me: There is my seat, there is my throne. I endevour to make my rule therein absolute, and to sequester that only corner from the communitie of wife, of children and of acquaintance. Elsewhere I have but a verball authoritie, of confused essence. Miserable, in my minde is he, who in his owne home, hath no where to be himselfe; where hee may particularly court, and at his pleasure hide or with-draw himself.

MONTAIGNE, Essays.

Just as any study of lyric poetry should not ignore the music of Goethe and Heine, so any study of the shrewd, pliant prose of the essayist cannot ignore the writings of the French. The strain of skepticism and irony is almost continuous, from Montaigne through Voltaire (1694–1778) down to Anatole France (1844–1924). Perhaps you looked up the whole essay on Voltaire by the critic Sainte-Beuve, an excerpt of which is given in Chapter IX above. In contrast to the virtual aloofness of Montaigne, the eighteenth-century Frenchman attacks the degradations and miseries of human life with bitter, mocking laughter. Like Swift he sees the pettiness and misery of man and despises him for them. Voltaire's most famous pronouncement urges every individual to "cultivate his own garden," not to hope for much from life except by rejection of it.

In his turn Anatole France questions and mocks but with much more good humor. Yet of one of his characters it is said, "His great heart was big with all the virtues born of pride: frankness, courage, constancy in trial, indomitable hope." It is characteristic of the French mind to find a place for many of the qualities which the Anglo-Saxon at least affects to condemn. The pride that defies humdrum moral and social codes produces more positive and more human virtues.

Such mental keenness as is found in these French essayists is not a common feature of English writers in the field of the essay. In the latter we find less exercise of the intellect and more of a tendency toward enjoyment of moods, the whimsical, passing fancy, such ideas as come to a man who is relaxed in an easy chair or sauntering along country lanes. As in the case of Lamb, he may enjoy the bustle and color of the city, but his instincts even then are for the cozy. He collects impressions and stores them neatly away, or else tosses them into the drawers from which he casually pulls his essays. He likes the old, the quaint, the unnoticed. In him we have the true amateur, writing of things because of his sheer affection for them.

The indolent romanticist, Leigh Hunt (1784–1859), is typical. Life, especially Nature herself, seems to prick and stir him just sufficiently to set his pen going in an effort at self-justification. You will easily sympathize with his protests in the essay "A 'Now' —Descriptive of a Cold Day." [1] Less commonly known is his "A 'Now'—Descriptive of a Hot Day," in which he surveys in mock-heroic vein the features of a hot day:

Now the rosy- (and lazy-) fingered Aurora, issuing from her saffron house, calls up the moist vapours to surround her, and goes veiled

[1] See below in Chapter XVIII.

with them as long as she can; till Phoebus, coming forth in his power, looks everything out of the sky, and holds sharp, uninterrupted empire from his throne of beams. Now the mower begins to make his sweeping cuts more slowly, and resorts oftener to the beer. Now the carter sleeps a-top of his load of hay, or plods with double slouch of shoulder, looking out with eyes winking under his shading hat, and with a hitch upward of one side of his mouth. Now the little girl at her grandmother's cottage-door watches the coaches that go by, with her hand held up over her sunny forehead. Now labourers look well resting in their white shirts at the doors of rural alehouses. Now an elm is fine there, with a seat under it; and horses drink out of the trough, stretching their yearning necks with loosened collars; and the traveller calls for his glass of ale, having been without one for more than ten minutes; and his horse stands wincing at the flies, giving sharp shivers of his skin, and moving to and fro his ineffectual docked tail; and now Miss Betty Wilson, the host's daughter, comes streaming forth in a flowered gown and ear-rings, carrying with four of her beautiful fingers the foaming glass, for which, after the traveller has drank it, she receives with an indifferent eye, looking another way, the lawful twopence. . . . Now grasshoppers "fry," as Dryden says. Now cattle stand in water, and ducks are envied. Now boots, and shoes, and trees by the roadside, are thick with dust; and dogs, rolling in it, after issuing out of the water, into which they have been thrown to fetch sticks, come scattering horror among the legs of the spectators. Now a fellow who finds he has three miles further to go in a pair of tight shoes is in a pretty situation. Now rooms with the sun upon them become intolerable; and the apothecary's apprentice, with a bitterness beyond aloes, thinks of the pond he used to bathe in at school. Now men with powdered heads (especially if thick) envy those that are unpowdered, and stop to wipe them up hill, with countenances that seem to expostulate with destiny. Now boys assemble round the village pump with a ladle to it, and delight to make a forbidden splash and get wet through the shoes. Now also they make suckers of leather, and bathe all day long in rivers and ponds, and make mighty fishings for "tittle-bats." Now the bee, as he hums along, seems to be talking heavily of the heat. Now doors and brick-walls are burning to the hand; and a walled lane, with dust and broken bottles in it, near a brick-field, is a thing not to be thought of. Now a green lane, on the contrary, thick-set with hedgerow elms, and having the noise of a brook "rumbling in pebble-stones," is one of the pleasantest things in the world.

LEIGH HUNT, *The Indicator*, June 28, 1820.

No American writer has responded to the impulse to escape to nature more strikingly than Henry David Thoreau (1817–1862). In the selection given below he reflects the personality of a man whose instincts are, you may feel, strikingly American.[1]

When first I took up my abode in the woods, that is, began to spend my nights as well as days there, which, by accident, was on Independence Day, or the Fourth of July, 1845, my house was not finished for winter, but was merely a defence against the rain, without plastering or chimney, the walls being of rough, weather-stained boards, with wide chinks, which made it cool at night. The upright white hewn studs and freshly planed door and window casings gave it a clean and airy look, especially in the morning, when its timbers were saturated with dew, so that I fancied that by noon some sweet gum would exude from them. To my imagination it retained throughout the day more or less of this auroral character, reminding me of a certain house on a mountain which I had visited a year before. This was an airy and unplastered cabin, fit to entertain a travelling god, and where a goddess might trail her garments. The winds which passed over my dwelling were such as sweep over the ridges of mountains, bearing the broken strains, or celestial parts only, of terrestrial music. The morning wind forever blows, the poem of creation is uninterrupted; but few are the ears that hear it. Olympus is but the outside of the earth everywhere.

. . . .

I was seated by the shore of a small pond, about a mile and a half south of the village of Concord and somewhat higher than it, in the midst of an extensive wood between that town and Lincoln, and about two miles south of that our only field known to fame, Concord Battle Ground; but I was so low in the woods that the opposite shore, half a mile off, like the rest, covered with wood, was my most distant horizon. For the first week, whenever I looked out on the pond it impressed me like a tarn high up on the side of a mountain, its bottom far above the surface of other lakes, and, as the sun arose, I saw it throwing off its nightly clothing of mist, and here and there, by degrees, its soft ripples or its smooth reflecting surface was revealed, while the mists, like ghosts, were stealthily withdrawing in every direction into the woods, as at the breaking up of some nocturnal conventicle. The very dew seemed to hang upon the trees later into the day than usual, as on the sides of mountains.

This small lake was of most value as a neighbor in the intervals of

---

[1] From *Walden: or, Life in the Woods* (1854).

a gentle rain storm in August, when, both air and water being perfectly still, but the sky overcast, mid-afternoon had all the serenity of evening, and the wood-thrush sang around, and was heard from shore to shore. A lake like this is never smoother than at such a time; and the clear portion of the air above it being shallow and darkened by clouds, the water, full of light and reflections, becomes a lower heaven itself so much the more important. From a hill top near by, where the wood had been recently cut off, there was a pleasing vista southward across the pond, through a wide indentation in the hills which form the shore there, where their opposite sides sloping toward each other suggested a stream flowing out in that direction through a wooded valley, but stream there was none. That way I looked between and over the near green hills to some distant and higher ones in the horizon, tinged with blue.

H. D. THOREAU, *Walden.*

What the fable is to the story the tiny vignettes of Logan Pearsall Smith are to the usual essay. They are really slight incidents, usually with a not-too-withering moral, that seem to hang suspended in the mind of the writer, sensitive in response to existence, yet restrained to an unassuming brevity. The two selections appear in *Trivia*.[1]

THE POPLAR
Logan Pearsall Smith

There is a great tree in Sussex, whose cloud of thin foliage floats high in the summer air. The thrush sings in it, and blackbirds, who fill the late, decorative sunshine with a shimmer of golden sound. There the nightingale finds her green cloister; and on those branches sometimes, like a great fruit, hangs the lemon-colored Moon. In the glare of August, when all the world is faint with heat, there is always a breeze in those cool recesses, always a noise, like the noise of water, among its lightly hung leaves.

But the owner of this Tree lives in London, reading books.

THE KALEIDOSCOPE
Logan Pearsall Smith

I find in my mind, in its miscellany of ideas and musings, a curious collection of little landscapes and pictures, shining and fading for no

---

[1] Reprinted from *Trivia*, by Logan Pearsall Smith, copyright 1917, by permission of the publishers, Doubleday, Doran & Company, Inc.

reason. Sometimes they are views in no way remarkable—the corner of a road, a heap of stones, an old gate. But there are many charming pictures, too: as I read, between my eyes and book, the Moon sheds down on harvest fields her chill of silver; I see autumnal avenues, with the leaves falling, or swept in heaps; and storms blow among my thoughts, with the rain beating forever on the fields. Then Winter's upward glare of snow appears; or the pink and delicate green of Spring in the windy sunshine; or cornfields and green waters, and youths bathing in Summer's golden heats.

And as I walk about, certain places haunt me: a cathedral rises above a dark blue foreign town, the colour of ivory in the sunset light; now I find myself in a French garden, full of lilacs and bees, and shut-in sunshine, with the Mediterranean lounging and washing outside its walls; now in a little college library, with busts, and the green reflected light of Oxford lawns—and again I hear the bells, reminding me of the familiar Oxford hours.

If there are distinctive qualities of American humor, they undoubtedly include straight-faced and ironic exaggeration. Among the masters of this irresistible blend is Robert Benchley.

HOW I CREATE [1]
Robert Benchley

In an article on How Authors Create, in which the writing methods of various masters of English prose like Conrad, Shaw, and Barrie are explained (with photographs of them in knickerbockers plaguing dogs and pushing against sun-dials), I discover that I have been doing the whole thing wrong all these years. The interviewer in this case hasn't got around to asking me yet—doubtless because I have been up in my room with the door shut and not answering the bell—but I am going to take a chance anyway and tell him how I do my creative work and just how much comes from inspiration and how much from hashish and other perfumes. I may even loosen up and tell him what my favorite hot-weather dishes are.

When I am writing a novel I must actually live the lives of my characters. If, for instance, my hero is a gambler on the French Riviera, I make myself pack up and go to Cannes or Nice, willy-nilly, and there throw myself into the gay life of the gambling set until I really feel that I *am* Paul De Lacroix or Ed Whelan, or whatever my hero's

[1] Reprinted from *No Poems, or Around the World Backwards and Sideways,* copyright 1932, by permission of Harper & Brothers, publishers.

name is. Of course this runs into money, and I am quite likely to have to change my ideas about my hero entirely and make him a bum on a tramp steamer working his way back to America, or a young college boy out of funds who lives by his wits until his friends at home send him a hundred and ten dollars.

.   .   .   .

This actually living the lives of my characters takes up quite a lot of time and makes it a little difficult to write anything. It was not until I decided to tell stories about old men who just sit in their rooms and shell walnuts that I ever got around to doing any work. It doesn't make for very interesting novels, but at any rate the wordage is there and there is something to show the publishers for their advance royalties. (Publishers are crotchety that way. They want copy, copy, copy, all the time, just because they happen to have advanced a measly three hundred dollars a couple of years before. You would think that printing words on paper was their business.)

.   .   .   .

I find that, while working, a pipe is a great source of inspiration. A pipe can be placed diagonally across the keys of a typewriter so that they will not function, or it can be made to give out such a cloud of smoke, that I cannot see the paper. Then, there is the process of lighting it. I can make lighting a pipe a ritual which has not been equaled for elaborateness since the five-day festival to the God of the Harvest. (See my book on Rituals: the Man.)

In the first place, owing to twenty-six years of constant smoking without once calling in a plumber, the space left for tobacco in the bowl of my pipe is now the size of a medium body-pore. Once the match has been applied to the tobacco therein, the smoke is over. This necessitates refilling, relighting, and reknocking. The knocking out of a pipe can be made almost as important as the smoking of it, especially if there are nervous people in the room. A good, smart knock of a pipe against a tin wastebasket and you will have a neurasthenic out of his chair and into the window sash in no time.

.   .   .   .

And so you see now how we creative artists work. It really isn't like any other kind of work, for it must come from a great emotional upheaval in the soul of the writer himself; and if that emotional upheaval is not present, it must come from the works of any other writers which happen to be handy and easily imitated.

A sketch by Clarence Day which originally appeared in *The New Yorker* shows what results from a more subtly restrained exaggeration of real events. The humor, since it is less deliberate, seems to be more in the nature of things.

FATHER LETS IN THE TELEPHONE [1]
Clarence Day

Up to the late eighteen-nineties, when Father walked in the front door of his home and closed it behind him, he shut out the world. Telephones had been invented but, like most people, he hadn't installed one. There was no way for anybody to get at him except by climbing up the front stoop and ringing the bell; and if the bell rang late at night, Father looked out of the window to see who it was. He thought nothing of this—homes had always been shut off since men began building them, and it seemed only natural.

Once in a long while a messenger boy would bring him or Mother a telegram—maybe two or three times a year. As this generally meant bad news, they were nervous about getting telegrams.

No telegraph poles were allowed on Fifth Avenue, but long rows of them grew on other thoroughfares. Old Margaret, our cook, was mystified by all those wires, up in the air. We had wires in our house, to be sure; they had been strung inside the walls to ring bells with; but they were good, honest, old-fashioned wires and to make them work we had to pull them. There was none of this dangerous stuff called electricity anywhere in our house, and neither we boys nor Margaret could make out what it was.

After a while the telegraph company persuaded Father to let them install a new invention close to one of our bedroom windows, where it couldn't do any harm. This was a small metal box with a handle. A wire led from it which was connected with one of those on the poles, but the company said it was safe. The handle was made to look like those on the bells we were used to. By pulling it, we could make the box buzz, and somehow that sent a signal to the nearest telegraph office, where a row of little messenger boys was supposed to be waiting. The office then sent a boy to our house ready to run any errand.

This "Buzzer," as we called it, seemed almost as remarkable to us as that lamp of Aladdin's. By giving some extra pulls on it and making it buzz enough times, the directions said, a policeman could be summoned, or even a fire engine.

How long it would have taken for a policeman to come we never had occasion to learn. It took a messenger boy from twenty to thirty-five minutes—that is, if we were lucky. The branch office was nearly a mile away and it had only one little benchful of boys. If the boys were all out when we buzzed for one, the manager had no way to tell us. We might be impatient. He wasn't. He peacefully waited till some boy got through other errands.

On stormy days sometimes, when a friend wished to send us a message or break an engagement, a messenger would surprise us by coming without being buzzed for. He stood outside the front door, with a black rubber hood dripping with rain hanging down from his cap, blowing on his cold fingers and stamping, and ringing away at the bell. And when one of us opened the door, the boy would thrust in a wet letter and hoarsely ask us to sign the name and the hour on a small, smudgy slip.

All these delays were more or less put up with, however. There was no other service to turn to. And anyway we seldom used messengers—they were not only slow but expensive. We ran our own errands.

When the telephone was invented and was ready to use, hardly anybody cared to install one. We all stuck to our buzzers. Messenger boys were quite enough of a nuisance, coming every month or so with a letter and expecting an answer. People admitted that telephones were ingenious contraptions and wondered just how they worked, but they no more thought of getting one of their own than the average man now thinks of getting an airplane.

As a matter of fact, for a long time they were of little use in a home. Since almost nobody had them but brokers, there was no one to talk to. The telephone company mailed circulars in which they made large claims: they said that an important department store now had a telephone, and three banks had ordered one apiece, and that some enterprising doctors were getting them. But though people saw vaguely that a telephone might be a convenience if every household installed one, they decided to wait in a body until everyone did.

Father had to have one downtown, but he wouldn't use it himself; he had it put in the back office, where the bookkeeper dealt with it, bringing Father the message if necessary. There was another new machine, called a typewriter, in the back office, too. But the idea of putting these business conveniences in a home seemed absurd.

Mother agreed with Father—she didn't like telephones either. She distrusted machines of all kinds; they weren't human, they popped or exploded and made her nervous. She never knew what they might do to her. And the telephone seemed to her, and many other people, especially dangerous. They were afraid that if they stood near one in a thunderstorm they might get hit by lightning. Even if there wasn't any storm, the electric wiring might give them a shock. When they saw a telephone in some hotel or office, they stood away from it or picked it up gingerly. It was a freak way to use electricity, and Mother wouldn't even touch the queer toy. Besides, she said, she had to see the face of any person she talked to. She didn't want to be answered by an invisible and indistinct voice coming out of a box on the wall.

Little by little, however, and year by year, telephones came into use. Some of the large markets and groceries installed them. The livery stable. Some druggists. And once in a while, when Father had a bad cold and couldn't go to the office he saw it would be a business convenience to have one at home.

After ten or fifteen years, in spite of his still having misgivings, he got one. It was put on a wall on the second floor, where everybody could hear its loud bell. We didn't give it much of a welcome. It seemed to us rude and intrusive, and from the first it made trouble. It rang seldom but it always chose a bad moment, when there was nobody on that floor to answer. Mother would pick up her skirts and run upstairs to it, calling loudly "I'm coming! I'm coming!" but the fretful thing kept right on ringing. Father couldn't regard it as inanimate either. He refused to be hurried like Mother, but he scolded and cursed it.

The outer world now began intruding upon us at will. This was hard to get used to. Even Mother felt there was too much of it. As for Father, he met these invasions with ferocious resentment. When somebody telephoned him and he couldn't make out at once who it was, and when there was nothing he could shake his fist at but a little black receiver which was squeaking at him, he said it was horrible. "Speak up, speak up, damn it!" he would shout at the telephone, getting red in the face. "What is it, who are you? I can't hear a word you are saying. I can't hear a damned word I tell you."

"Clare, give me that telephone!" Mother would cry, rushing in.

"I will not give you this telephone!" Father would roar in reply, without taking his lips from the transmitter. "Will you let me alone, I am trying to find out who the devil this person is. Halloa! I say halloa there, do you hear me? Who are you? Halloa! . . . What's that? . . . Oh, it's you, Mrs. Nichols." Here his voice would grow a little less forbidding, and sometimes even friendly. "Yes, Mrs. Day's here. How are you? . . . Oh, do you wish to speak to Mrs. Day? . . . Eh? . . . Very well then. Wait a moment." And he would at last allow Mother to get at the box on the wall.

When Father called a number himself, he usually got angry at "Central." He said she was deaf, she was stupid, he told her she wasn't attending to her duties in a suitable manner. If she said a number was busy, he'd protest: "I can't sit here waiting all day. Busy? Busy be damned!"

He always assumed when the bell rang that it was a message for him. The idea that it might be a call for Mother or one of the rest of us seemed wholly improbable. If he let anyone but himself answer, he would keep calling out and asking who it was and what it was all about anyhow, while we tried, in the midst of his shouts, to hear some of the message. When it was something that didn't concern him, he was incredulous, and had to have it explained to him to make sure.

One day some new friends of mine, who lived in a settlement house in the slums, telephoned to invite me to lunch with some visiting Russians. Father answered the telephone. "Yes, this is Mr. Day. Speak up, damn it! Don't mumble at me. Who are you? . . . *What?* Come to lunch? I've had lunch. . . . Next Friday? Why, I don't want to lunch with you next Friday. . . . No. . . . Where? Where did you say? . . . In Rivington Street? The devil! . . . Yes, my name is Clarence Day and I told you that before. Don't repeat. . . . Lunch with you in Rivington Street? Good God! I never heard of such a thing in my life! . . . Russians? I don't know any Russians. . . . No, I don't want to, either. . . . No, I haven't changed. I never change. . . . What? . . . Goodby, Madam. Damn!"

"I think that was a friend of mine, Father," I said.

"A friend of yours!" he exclaimed. "Why, it sounded to me like some pushcart peddler's wife this time, arguing with me about lunching with her somewhere down in the slums. I can't stand it, that's all I have to say. I'll have the damned thing taken out."

You may have observed that Clarence Day's style is marked by an ease which preserves the indispensable quality of personal charm, and yet which does not reveal any of the studied quaintness so often apparent in essay styles. A surprising number of good essays are constantly appearing in our magazines, grave and gay. The writers combine a casual tone with a genuine concern for stylistic finish which they generously season with shrewdness and wit. Their acknowledged *maestro* is Christopher Morley. Look up some of his essays in the volumes *Shandygaff, Mince Pie,* or the *Christopher Morley Omnibus.*

Robert Lynd, like Mr. Benchley and Mr. Day, belongs to the happy band of gay essayists. An example of the more reflective type of essay appears in Chapter XVIII; but Mr. Lynd's two following essays represent types I and IV, in our classification above.

ON MAKING MISTAKES [1]
Robert Lynd

If you take down a dictionary of quotations—and I am lucky enough to possess a review-copy of one of these excellent books—no one but a snob would have mentioned the fact that it was a review-copy, by the way—and if you open it at "Mistakes," you will find that E. J. Phelps said in 1889: "The man who makes no mistakes does not usually make anything." You will also find that S. Smiles said in *Self-Help:* "Probably he who never made a mistake never made a discovery," and that Archbishop Trench said in *The Study of Words:* "To make mistakes as we are on the way to knowledge is far more honourable than to escape making them through never having set out to seek knowledge." Again, J. Pomfret wrote in *Love Triumphant Over Reason:*

> The best may slip, and the most cautious fall;
> He's more than mortal that ne'er erred at all.

And Young observed, a little more irrelevantly, in *Love of Fame, Sat 6:*

> With skill she vibrates her eternal tongue,
> For ever most divinely in the wrong.

There is not much consolation to be got from the last quotation, but the others are all of a kind to bring peace to the souls of those who have to write a great deal, who, therefore, are almost certain to make an occasional mistake, and who are lucky if that is the worst that can be said of them. I, myself, have from my youth up lived in a perpetual horror of making mistakes. I have a passion for accuracy, that, if I had the time, would keep me continually referring to encyclopaedias and dictionaries as I write. I hate to wake up in the morning and see in print that I have put the Battle of Hastings in the twelfth century or that I have made Nelson win the Battle of Waterloo. To be per-

---

[1] From *The New Statesman,* December 19, 1925. Reprinted by permission of the author, and the editor of *The New Statesman and Nation.*

fectly candid, I do not think that I could go so far as to make a mistake about the dates of either of these battles, but they are the only two battles in history, except the Battle of the Boyne, in regard to the dates of which I feel something approaching absolute confidence. If you met me in the street and suddenly demanded the dates of any of these battles, I should be willing to bet £100 to a penny that I could tell you all three without a blunder. But who won the Battle of Naseby, or when, or if there was such a battle, I am not nearly so certain. I could tell you—or, at least, I think I could—in whose reign the Battle of Agincourt was fought, but I could not undertake to be more precise than that. As for Crécy and Poictiers, I once knew all about them, and could even have told you who won them, but if I wished to write about them—and one never knows what one may find oneself writing about—I should have to look them up in a history, and I remember only enough about them to know that I should be more likely to find them mentioned in John Richard Green than in Gibbon's *Decline and Fall of the Roman Empire*. Yet time was when I could have repeated the dates of all the kings of England and given you the names of all the kings' wives and of all the queens' husbands, if any. Now, all this noble array of facts is vanished, and I have only the dimmest notion of who married whom throughout the ages. All the great figures are mixed up in my mind, like the animals in a Noah's Ark, and I shall never be able to sort them out and pair them correctly without assistance.

And, if this is so in regard to English history, which was drilled into me against all my instincts at school, you may be sure the case is worse when it comes to the history of the great nations of Europe. Aegispotami is only a name to me—a name that, for all I know, I may have made up myself. I have heard of Mantinea, but what happened there I could not tell you for a thousand pounds. I am capable of making mistakes about Marathon, and I know as little about the battles fought by Julius Caesar—if he ever fought any real battles—as I do about the Wars of the Roses. Persons I remember better than battles, and Epaminondas is a very real person to me, though I could not tell you what century he lived in. Even about Julius Caesar I know something—that he either crossed or did not cross the Rubicon, that he was bald and was annoyed about it, that he was murdered and had two very fine speeches about him, that something happened to him—I am almost sure of this—in 55 B.C., and that his wife had to be above suspicion. But for the most part these historical figures are to me as dateless as the characters in fiction. Who knows the year of Silas Wegg's birth? Or of the death of Little Nell? How many scholars could tell you in what year Mr. Collins was appointed to his first curacy, or in what year Mr. Jorrocks said: "When I dines I sleeps." And to me, in this respect, Alcibiades and Mr. Jorrocks are all one, and Mr. Collins sleeps in the same grave of datelessness with princes. Yet such is my passion for accuracy that I should lie awake all night if I thought I had made an erroneous statement about Alcibiades, and I had rather find that I had libelled the character of Darius than that I had confused him with Xerxes. The melancholy truth is that I always confuse Darius and Xerxes, and, if I could, would avoid mentioning either of them for the rest of my life.

It is all the more comforting to know from S. Smiles that these things do not greatly matter. What is good enough for S. Smiles ought to be good enough for you and me. And, after all, if blunders were enough to condemn a writer, every writer for whom we have any respect would stand condemned, and no one but a pedant would ever dare to take a pen in his hand. Dr. Johnson was content to make mistakes even in a dictionary, and gave the noble excuse: "Ignorance, madam, pure ignorance." From Shakespeare to Goldsmith, and from Lamb to Mr. Chesterton, you will find a long procession of errors, the discovery of which has greatly added to the happiness of scholars. You might compile a dictionary of misquotations from the works of great authors that would almost equal in size the ordinary dictionary of quotations. Even Macaulay, who knew everything, once made a mistake, when he spoke of *The Vicar of Wakefield* as one of the less-read books of Oliver Goldsmith, putting *The Vicar of Wakefield* in place of the *History of England* by a slip of the pen. And one can scarcely take up a paper or a book today in which, however ignorant one may be, one does not come upon some recognisable mistake or misstatement. A lady novelist made Aston Villa score a try in a football match. "Q," unless I am mistaken, once made the sun rise in the west. Who that has ever written has not perpetrated similar blunders? I confess I never write a description of a ceremony in a cathedral that I do not lie awake wondering what lunacies of error may have crept into my sentences. For I know nothing about chasubles; and albs and copes and mitres are all abracadabra to me. Yet it is impossible to write about great ceremonial occasions without dipping, however gingerly, into this perilous vocabulary. You cannot be content to write that a priest was wearing a sort of white thing, or that a bishop was wearing a kind of goldy coat and a queer-shaped hat. There is great satisfaction in using the other sort of words, which certainly add a touch of verisimilitude to a description of any lordly ritual. And, then, besides the names of the costumes, there are all sorts of other words, like reredos and chancel and even high altar, that dance in the brain, appealing not to be left out in the cold. It is impossible for anyone who was brought up a Presbyterian ever to be quite sure what a reredos is, but, when you are writing about churches, the temptation to mention the reredos is well-nigh irresistible. I think I usually make the choir sing in it, or the bishop step down from it to bless the congregation.

Yet, no sooner have I finished writing than I begin to verify—to consult reference-books or to telephone to someone who knows—and in the end I usually manage to drive the choir from the reredos and to put the bishop's mitre on his head instead of round his shoulders. How often, after telegraphing a description of a ceremony, I have hurried back to the post-office to send a further telegram: "For 'chasuble' read 'surplice' and for 'deacon' read 'dean.' " This love of correctness is a torture to me even in small things. If I have described black smoke pluming out of a factory-chimney, I must at the first opportunity go out and look at a factory-chimney, and if I find that the smoke is brown I must immediately send an amending telegram. There is a pedant buried somewhere in me who is continually rising from his grave to denounce my ignorance. If I had not to earn a living, I am sure I should spend all my life looking things up for fear of making mistakes about them. As it is, I never put pen to paper without the risk of making a "howler" such as schoolmasters would write joyfully to the papers about if it were made by a boy at an examination. Yet the odd thing is that none of us objects if someone else makes an occasional "howler." We hate a sloppy or lazy inaccuracy, but we concede to every writer his allowance of errors, knowing that the eye may be deceived and that the memory is frail; and we distinguish, like the church, between mortal and venial error. And in this, let us rejoice, we have S. Smiles on our side, and J. Pomfret, author of *Love Triumphant Over Reason*. There is, fortunately, no chance that I have misquoted either of these great authors. Dictionaries of quotations, unlike the rest of us, do not err.

Y. Y. [Robert Lynd]

Mr. Lynd's essays are still appearing from week to week in the *New Statesman and Nation*. For Type II read "Spelling Bees" in the issue for March 26, 1938; and for Type III see "Country Walk" May 14, 1938. The next essay represents Type IV.

LOVE AT ITS LAST GASP [1]
Robert Lynd

Count Keyserling has told us that love is dying in civilised countries. I forget the course of his argument, but I gather that he believes that the Amazons are upon us, and that woman in parting with her inferiority has parted with her superiority as well. I can never understand how publicists can come so easily to conclusions about the future of the human race or even about the present condition of the human race. It is by no means easy to be sure even whether the world is a better place today than it was a hundred years ago. If we concentrate on a certain number of things—the growth of external freedom, the greater distribution of material comfort, the spread of the rudiments of education—there is good ground for optimism. But has discontent decreased in proportion to the decrease of servitude and discomfort? Are human beings so very much better or happier? We have no means of being certain of this. Those who praise today most confidently are usually those who can see nothing but the black spots in yesterday's sun. Our judgments are all based on fragmentary and arbitrarily chosen evidence, and, though each of us is nine-tenths ignorant of the life that is going on in his own street, this does not prevent us from generalizing boldly on life as it is being lived throughout the civilised world. What on earth can any one man know about love as it is experienced by millions of people? How can he tell what was the normal temperature of love in the age of Elizabeth, or what proportion of men and women were capable of a grand passion in different ages? He may deny that the appearance of a Cleopatra or a Juliet is possible in the modern world, but there were never very many Cleopatras or Juliets, and the theory of a loveless age does not survive the spectacle of a pair of lovers.

That love has not yet lost its power over the imagination of at least one sex is suggested by the prospectus, which I saw in a friend's house the other day, of a work called *Fascinating Womanhood*. In these modest pages love is represented, in the old fashion, as "woman's whole existence," and, as it apparently pays to publish the work at twenty-five shillings, we may presume that the world is not yet entirely given over to apathetic Amazons. Here, for sale, are all the rules by obeying which a woman can capture a man, and it will come as good news to women, if not to men, that a woman who makes herself

[1] From *The New Statesman*, February 1, 1930. Reprinted by permission of Robert Lynd and the editor of *The New Statesman and Nation*.

"mistress of psychology" can capture almost any man she sets her cap at. The prospectus tells its female readers on an early page:

> Semiramis, Cleopatra, Madame de Staël, Madame du Barry, Empress Eugénie—some were beautiful, some were homely, some were witty, some were dull; but all knew the fine points of man's psychology, and profited by that knowledge.
>
> Some were born with an intuitive grasp of the subject; some won their knowledge from long years of hard experience; but you can get, in a few days or weeks, from *Fascinating Womanhood*, all the psychological information which made them invincible in the social world.

To be invincible in the social world, like Semiramis, is not everything, however; and the eight volumes that make up this great work appear to instruct the reader in the art of winning a husband rather than in social fascination. They "picture in detail," we are told, "the five psychological stages of winning a man. . . . You will learn hundreds of methods, modest but skilful, maidenly but sure, of winning a man's admiration." Beauty is, one gathers, of minor importance. Beautiful clothes are equally irrelevant. Psychological strategy is everything, and, "as one of the many thousands of girl readers of the course wrote, 'It's just like a pleasant game to be played.' " Clearly this is a work that ought to be read by men as well as women, so that they may beware of those who, not content with their natural wiles—which are considerable—are here instructed in other wiles still more dangerous. What man can read without apprehension an account of the eighth chapter in which "fourteen of the most effective stratagems" are discussed?

> Fourteen of the most effective stratagems by which they fascinate men are here described in detail, so that the reader can use them on the different men she meets. These fourteen stratagems alone are worth many times the cost of the course. Any girl who is mistress of them can just about do with men as she pleases.

What man, on reading this, will not, for the sake of his defenceless sex, grimly set himself to the task of inventing fourteen still more effective counter-stratagems in the same spirit in which men invented anti-aircraft methods of defeating attacks from the air which for a time had found them helpless? The very title of one of the chapters, "Stage Two (continued): Undermining the Man's Reserve," contains a threat to our entire sex, and it is no pleasant thought that almost any girl after reading a series of books—justly described as "the most remarkable set of books ever published"—can compel almost any man to "pour out his very soul before you, until the last vestige of his reserve has disappeared, until he will trust you absolutely and unequivocally with everything he holds sacred."

Having triumphantly passed through the first two stages of arousing the man's attention and arousing his interest (the second of which includes undermining his reserve), the practical female psychologist goes on to the third stage of "arousing worship, adoration and love." Here, it seems, is the Becher's Brook of the Grand Marital Steeplechase:

> This stage is the most delicate of all, a false step here will kill his interest forever. Many a girl can bring a man through the first two stages—attention and interest—but just as she is about to win his love she finds him growing indifferent. This chapter shows how you can manage this critical period, how you can prevent the falling off of the man's interest, how you can intensify his feeling toward you until "his arms ache to fold you in them forever."

How much more cheerful history, poetry, and fiction would have been, if women throughout the ages had known this! The course of true love never did run smooth, but only because women were not conversant with the contents of these precious volumes. On the other hand, if the volumes had been published just after the expulsion from Eden, and translated into all languages after the fall of the Tower of Babel, poetry and fiction might have become painfully monotonous. Every story would then have been the same story—a fascinating woman's progress from the stage of interest to the stage of adoration and so on to the conclusion of a happy marriage. Variety would have been possible only if more than one woman, having studied the secrets of fascination, had wished to marry the same man. Presuming—as we cannot help presuming—that they were all equally fascinating after reading this work, we must agree that there are the makings of an intricate plot in the situation. But how could the story ever end except with the flight and suicide of the man? No man, not even the vainest, could endure the strain of being fascinated equally, by a dozen women at the same time. Possibly, in an ideal world, there would be a law which would protect a man from multiple fascination of this sort. But, till such a law was passed, one would not envy a Romeo in a world that contained millions of fascinating female psychologists.

Even as it is, the young man of the present age may well feel nervous when he realises that love is no longer the divine accident he once thought it, and that the simple-looking girl who is sitting beside him at a dinner-party may all the time be practising the fourteen effective stratagems. Were I young and attractive, I should quail in my shoes on reading of "Stage Five: Inspiring the Proposal"—the section "devoted to different methods of getting a man to propose." It is clear that at this point the man has no chance against the well-instructed woman:

> How to prevent delay when in the proper mood, how to create romantic situations, how to make it practically impossible for the man not to speak out at the proper time, constitute the most amazing revelation of feminine fascination ever published. Page after page you read the absorbing details showing how clever women have handled different types of men at this delicate stage.

And employers as well as potential husbands should be on the lookout for danger, since the reader of this work will find it as easy to exercise her triumphant wiles in the world of business as in the pursuit of a husband. The extent of her powers may be measured by the sentence which informs us that "she will know how to win her employer as well as the office-boy, how to win the kind of a man to be proud of when she says, 'he's mine.' "

Men's only hope of safety, it seems to me, lies in an appeal to the finer spirits of the feminist movement. They cannot protect themselves, but I am sure there are enough disinterested feminists in the world to forbid the subjugation and subjection of a whole sex by their fellow-women. Nature abhors sex domination, or, if it does not, it ought to do so. It may be true that the "fourteen little exercises in fascination . . . will just simply thrill you," if you are a romantic young woman, but the thought of them will just simply terrify you if you are a romantic or even a hard-headed young man. They will make you hope that Count Keyserling is right and that love is dying. Perhaps it is. Perhaps the fact that so many people nowadays need books to tell them about the elements of it is a sign that it is already at its last gasp.

Y. Y. [Robert Lynd]

CHAPTER XIII

Linear Narration

THE FUNDAMENTAL FEATURE of narrative writing, which is simply the recounting of an event or series of events in actual sequence of occurrence, is the element of time. All narration is essentially chronological. But the time element is not so much concerned in the long run with the putting of events in their direct order as with the compression of these events within certain fixed limits. Hence the problem to be solved ultimately is not the mere ordering of events, which is a simple matter, but the determination of the sum total of time to be occupied by a certain plot in order to make it most effective.

The simplest form of narration, however, is obviously merely the ordering of events, and this should be given preliminary study, for two very cogent reasons. First, it will impress indelibly the importance of time in telling a story, and second, it will provide sources for plots. It will be quite necessary, we should say, to write out some form, or better, perhaps, several forms of this type of narration before you attempt to construct plot stories, the germs, in turn, of the prevalent literary form today, the short story.

We have arbitrarily called this simplest form of narration *linear*. Perhaps it might better have been called *horizontal-linear* narration, for the action of the story runs along a straight line which neither rises nor falls emotionally to any great extent. It might be graphed something like this: --∧-∧-→ with varying rises and falls in emotion, but generally moving steadily in one direction along the dotted line as indicated.

Such narration, by its very evenness, is practically devoid of the highest creative value, for it is generally rather matter-of-fact;

it rouses neither high nor sustained interest, and requires no great artistic skill in construction. It is the best type to attempt first, for it gives free scope to individual likes and dislikes, experiences and dreams, powers and capabilities. If you cannot handle this form with some ease, you may have to give up hope of notable success with the other two steps of narration, the plot story and the short story. But success in this form of narration should inspire you with confidence to proceed. You will learn that you can recount simple events easily, and you will also discover that you have a few things to write about.

The various types of linear narration will be found arranged in their ascending order of importance. Doubtless a few minor ones may be omitted, but the fundamental types are here. They are grouped quite arbitrarily, according to future usefulness in story work.

The first and least important group contains the laboratory notebook, the history or chronicle, and the report in general. A laboratory notebook recounts in direct chronological sequence the results of an experiment, and is perfect linear narration. It is generally useless, however, so far as models for artistic narrative are concerned. The history or chronicle offers more possibilities for a plot story, because the writing or reading of history will impress upon you the idea of time; otherwise it is a rather thankless procedure. Suppose you are to chronicle the conspicuous events that took place in some country during one particular year, in a theme of absolutely no more than four hundred words. If you choose Panama, you will face the problem of expansion; if you take Spain, you will face something quite opposite. In both cases you will learn that the length of your story will conform somewhat to the time duration of your action, exclusive of conspicuous breaks.

The same lesson will appear from the writing of a report, on the development of television, let us say, or on the operations of the C.I.O. in the year 1937. If you are given the same limit of words for both reports, you will probably rise in wrath before the affair is concluded. At any rate you will learn the great element of proportion; you will probably never write a four-hundred-word plot story later based on your total summer experiences.

The second group of types of linear narration is by far the more important, and should be put into practice as soon as possible. This group includes the newspaper story, the biography, the diary or letter, and the autobiography. There is no reason why you should not go to work at once writing up for a mythical newspaper a detached and straightforward account of some incident that has recently occurred in your particular neighborhood. You need not begin with a "lead," in newspaper parlance, but you can recount the event as graphically and effectively as possible without becoming at all personal about the affair. It will be good for you to efface yourself like this; the secret of art is the effacement of the artist. Be impersonal and state merely the facts, from a totally unbiased point of view. Finally, the newspaper story will also teach compression within a fixed limit of words, with special attention to emphasizing only the important features of the event. In fact, all these preliminary exercises should be short and to the point.

Biography—with the expository thesis excluded—is straightforward linear narration, of about the same value as newspaper writing. The essential difference is that here emphatically is the basis for future character study. An experienced writer often actually writes out an imaginary biography of his imaginary character before he begins to write a story involving that character. The result is, obviously, that the writer comes to know his character quite thoroughly. But such a close study of character at this stage is unnecessary and even detrimental, because it will distract attention from the fundamental task of plot building. Writing brief biographies will provide good preliminary work, mainly for exercise in the compression or expansion of details, in achieving a strictly impersonal point of view, and in collecting possible plot sources to be denoted later.

A diary is an interesting bit of self-revelation.[1] It is here set apart from the autobiography because essentially it is a more detailed piece of work, involving a smaller scope of time and a more intimate revelation of facts. Keep a diary for a few days, lay it aside, and after a few weeks prepare an edited version of it. In

---

[1] Similarly, the letter, addressed to a distinct individual, may also be suggested, although its scope is limited by the interests of the addressee.

the revised version you will naturally compress some incidents and expand others as they have come to seem less or more interesting than they did at the time of first noting them. From this exercise you will learn the faculty of instinctively choosing and placing the emphatic incidents of a story you may wish to write later. Furthermore, a diary does a rather startling thing, though quite accidentally. It wheedles you into jotting down realistic details which will go far toward enlivening and vivifying your subsequent stories. Too often beginning writers fail to visualize definitely. Sometimes this failure arises from a lack of visualizing power, but more often it is due to carelessness. Every event in life is complicated by a mass of detail, significant and insignificant. The art of narration consists in relating the event with a sure choice of the significant detail. Any exercise that will teach you to note detail may help you to master the art of narration.

There is another point in which a diary may be useful a little later, and that is in teaching you to transcribe dialogue accurately. Prolonged dialogue should not be attempted until the technique of the plot story is mastered. As a matter of fact, dialogue is an affair of character, and you are not quite ready to handle the intricacies of such a study until you are absolutely sure of the plot. Therefore, to return to the diary, the various remarks of other people jotted down from time to time may be a future steadying influence when you come to need dialogue. If you have been trained by a little diary writing to transcribe *exactly what was said to you*, you may be able to guide yourself by such remarks from such a character later on. But again, it should be distinctly noted that prolonged dialogue will demoralize the beginning story writer. It will be better if you use it as infrequently as possible.

Finally, one of the greatest functions of a diary is, of course, its service as a source for future story plots. That function will be taken up in a later chapter; but certainly you will handle best the material with which you yourself are intimately familiar. The most striking thing is that generally you do not believe such material is worth writing about.

An autobiography will suggest varied lines of attack for future story plots, and perhaps that is its chief function in a narrative course. One intrinsic feature of autobiography deserves some notice. It will teach you automatically the element of rising interest, the parabolic curve that describes most of the vital experiences in life. Your childhood is so far back that you will relegate it to an insignificant amount of space—quite properly. The present and particularly the future are of vital interest to you. Thus you will automatically throw a more vital style into your discussion of them. Normally you will also show a rising vitality of style as you approach these periods of your life. So you are doing automatically exactly what you will do later in plot building: intensifying yourself and thence your style as you approach the climax or highest pitch of your story. The point to remember in the writing of autobiography, then, is that, as an undergraduate, you are *not* ready to die. You may think that you have had all the thrills, that life holds no more for you. But you must write *up* to your present and future. Otherwise you will drop a story later in exactly the same way—before you have got yourself warmed up, and hence before you have the reader much interested.

Finally, the autobiography, much better than the diary or anything else that has preceded, is a splendid exercise in developing the memory. Those little events that happened in childhood are hazy and require a mental effort to recover. What was the name of that woman who always gave you cookies out on the farm? Who was that first sweetheart; what was the color of the family's first car; what was the name of the street where your pal used to live? The very exercise involved in this persistent recollecting will come in well later on, for the scenes of the stories, the characters, and above all the incidents to be used, can all be vivified by names or places remembered from childhood and jotted down now in this invaluable autobiography. In fact, to sum up, both you and the instructor will find an autobiography almost indispensable for future plot building.

Inasmuch as students frequently choose the diary in preference to all other linear forms, we suggest that you watch the following points. First, the identity of the person who is writing the diary must be clear from the beginning. Most diaries include more than two or even three entries, and they must have a distinct tone; a mere catalogue of happenings will not do. That is, they will be happy, morose, serious, philosophical, whimsical, etc.—they have a dominant mood. Nor are the entries equal, generally, day by day. This suggests, further, that not much time should elapse in the course of the diary—at least, the less the better. Write complete sentences, generally, for stenographic style is dangerous. The main thing seems to be to choose a plausible character [1] and then plunge in.

In conclusion, the chief value of all exercises in linear narration lies in the absence of consciousness of characters and setting. You will be writing either impersonally or about yourself (except in the case of biography, where the character is already predetermined for you); hence you will never worry about the creation of character. Similarly the setting, or scene, of your narrative will be automatically chosen for you, and thus you can concentrate all your attention on relating the incidents. Therefore this preliminary chapter leads directly into a more complicated discussion of plot building—or the manipulation of incidents—and only much later will focusing on character or setting be discussed, for that is mature creation. The obvious next step is to analyze the building of the plot story, a step which will be taken in the succeeding chapter.

➤➤➤ A ⦉⦉⦉

The following paper is a history blending narration and exposition. Has the author proportioned the space effectively?

THE HISTORY OF THE SHOE

Ages ago, when primitive man stalked the hairy mammoth in the semitropical forest of Europe, he walked in his bare feet. The climate was warm. His feet were tough. He had no need of foot coverings. But a day came when it grew colder. Man snatched his wives' fur mattresses to keep himself warm. The climate was changing from semitropical to temperate. Perhaps one morning a cave man woke up to find his toes frozen. They hurt. He wrapped a skin around his foot. Ah! That felt better. It kept him warm. Thus the savages of

---

[1] If you pose as a newsboy or racketeer, you will have to edit the language. But you could plausibly project yourself back a few years and write your diary as a boy or girl of fifteen or less. In this case give an explanatory introduction in brackets.

Europe grew to use a boot made of a single piece of hide and fastened with a thong. These they wore until that evil day when they first saw the Roman nose.

The early rock pictures of Egypt show the Egyptians wearing sandals. They made these sandals of palm leaves, straw, or papyrus. Imagine straw or paper shoes! The heroes of the Bible wore sandals, too. In fact, all the people who lived in warm climates wore sandals or soft slippers. Today they are still wearing them.

The Greeks wore beautifully ornamented dress sandals, but for war they invented iron or brass-soled boots. We can well imagine the wounded heroes of Thermopylae kicking off their iron shoes and gasping with their last breath, "Well, that's over."

The Romans recognized their officials by the color of their sandals. Consuls wore black shoes, senators, red, and so on. When the Romans met the baa-baas (as they called them) the history of the shoe really began, for a shoe is the combination of a sandal and a one-piece boot.

During the Dark Ages men were proud of their brawn, not of their dress. But the gradual intellectual awakening of the Middle Ages brought a sense of beauty and a desire for ornamentation. Shoes were elaborately trimmed with fur and straps. Men loved color so much that they wore a yellow shoe on one foot and a red shoe on the other, or, perhaps, a pink and blue combination. At this same time the French reached the height of idiocy. Big feet were esteemed! A prince could wear shoes two and a half feet long. Barons, being less noble, wore shoes two feet long. But the poor knights were allowed tiny shoes of only eighteen inches in length.

Just before the time of Columbus, points were introduced. These became longer and longer until it was really an effort to walk. Consequently, the flopping points were tied to the knee. Sometimes they were curled out, giving a super-Charlie-Chaplin effect.

Queen Elizabeth introduced the heel. The shoes of her furbelowed court were covered with jewels and had heels three inches high. Frenchmen of this period wore red heels from three to five inches in height.

We all are familiar with the Colonial shoe and its big buckle. Only common men, however, wore these. Gentlemen wore boots of a vile yellow color.

About 1800 people longed to look like Greek statues; so they wore flowing draperies. The shoes were quaint, flat affairs, tied around the ankles with ribbons.

During the latter part of the nineteenth century, people wore pointed shoes with buttoned cloth tops.

Today we see every kind of shoe. Girls teeter on high heels, looking as though a slight breeze would blow them over. Flat, mannish shoes stride by. The materials are numerous and often curious. This is indeed a Golden Age for shoe-lovers.

M. H.

"My Dramatic Career" shows how the scope of an autobiography can be limited to meet a required length.

MY DRAMATIC CAREER

Recollections of my first dramatic attempt are very vague. The only things I remember distinctly are the way Eleanora and I had to struggle to arrange a curtain which would open when we wanted it to do so, and that the play dealt with a farmer, a boarding-house landlady, and some eggs. It was presented before a very select audience consisting of our long-suffering parents and relatives.

My next successful attempt in the dramatic field was in a play called "The Courtship of Dr. James." Because of the lack of masculine members in that section of the country, I played the part of the doctor. A most charming one I made, if I do say so myself, with my Palm Beach suit, red silk handkerchief, cane, and drooping mustache. This part must have had some bearing on my future career, since I played only masculine characters for a number of years. One night, shortly after the Dr. James affair, we produced two more plays. In one, I was the irate old father; and in the other I was one of the two young men who possessed but one pair of shoes between them. As a result, only one could go out at a time, and much trouble arose between the otherwise friendly pair.

There was also the time when I took part in a Thanksgiving program. One of the important items on the program was a pageant of all the states in the union and of Columbia. We wore long, flowing, Grecian robes of filmy cheesecloth, crowns of gold paper, and broad bands of the same material with the name of the state we represented printed in black letters. Each one had to carry some product of the state she impersonated. As Nevada, I had to carry a basket of silver nuggets. No one could tell me where to secure these nuggets; I simply was told to get them. At last someone suggested that I cover chunks of coal with silver paper. It was quite effective, even if not as valuable as the real thing.

A number of years ago, Olive, my sister, and I organized a society. The name of this famous organization was the Society of PaP, signifying poets, authors, playwrights society. As the appellation suggests, we not only had to write poetry, essays, tales, and novels, but we had to produce plays. It took us a long time to choose a play. We had to reject many as being unfit for production by such an illustrious society as the PaPs, since in our preamble we definitely stated that we were forming a new society in order to "improve, benefit, and perfect the literature of the United States and also that of the World." Finally, after deep contemplation, we selected two: "Gimme Them Papers," "some syncopated sob-stuff"; and "Who's Crazy Now?", "a rapid-fire farce." I was chosen to play the part of Harry Hamme, the Handsome Hero, opposite Patricia Punque, the Perfect Peach. I refused. It was necessary for me to do so or I would have continued playing Mr. This or That indefinitely. In the end, I was given the part of Velma Vail, the Vicious Vamp, co-operating with Willie Wynne, the Wicked Willian. The scene was laid in the cruel, cruel world and the entire play was filled with action. In reality, it was a satire on the ancient melodrama. It required a great deal of ingenuity on our part to fix up the stage for the two plays. I had to devise a stairway and landing out of a number of packing boxes. To make them more realistic, I painted them green. Something was wrong with the paint as everything stuck to them for the next two weeks. We were in despair, at first, when we learned that a tree was necessary to complete our stage setting, but Irene went out into the forest and secured a branch of a tree.

"Who's Crazy Now?" was quite different, being decidedly modern. My part was that of Charlie Smooth, alias the Kidder, an escaped convict. Olive was an old maid, and Irene was Snowdrop Leblanc, a dancing pick. There was a Professor Twitters, an expressman, and an officer also. It took us a long time to rehearse, as a great deal of time was occupied in giving the high sign and in discussing our progress in the intellectual field. Then, too, it took us a long time to get the correct presentation of the scene between Abigail Sniffen and myself. She had placed an advertisement in a matrimonial magazine and thought that I had come in answer to it. We all enjoyed this scene so much that we could not stop laughing long enough to speak our parts.

The height of my career was reached in my senior year at Schurz. Our Spanish class presented a play, "Los Castillos de Torresnobles," in which I took the part of a marchioness. Everything was Spanish, the setting, the costumes, the music, and the speaking. Our audience probably did not understand us since the hero himself told me that he did not know what he was saying a good deal of the time. However, he was a wonderful actor and with everything else, such as bullfights, balcony scenes, street dances, and duels combined, the audience enjoyed itself thoroughly.

In looking over this array of plays, it seems as though I have acted in a goodly number and that I ought to be a fairly good actress. I fear, however, that it was more from necessity than from choice that I secured my parts in these plays. Because of this presentiment, I do not believe that I shall devote my entire life to a dramatic career.

C. G.

The following well-written paper, in newspaper form, contains a germ for a plot story, but could the conclusion be improved? How?

DR. WILHEIM'S CONDITION UNCHANGED

San Francisco, Calif., Feb. 14, 1934.

Physicians here at St. Lowood Sanitorium reported that the condition of Dr. Albert A. Wilheim, famous surgeon of cases involving the brain area, remains critical and unchanged since the removal of the doctor here from his home on February 12, 1934.

Dr. Wilheim who is rapidly approaching the age of sixty, has worked very strenuously during the past few months, and has undertaken more than his share of responsibility as staff member at the Russel Jennings Hospital. One of the nurses at this hospital said that, on February 10, Dr. Wilheim performed four operations requiring the utmost technique and ability. During the last of these, surrounding physicians and nurses detected signs of overstrained nerves on the part of Dr. Wilheim. It seems that the doctor questioned the completeness of preparation for the operation, and was hesitant to continue working for fear that he should err. After several minutes, the staff members hastily decided to substitute Dr. Phillip Marks for Dr. Wilheim to complete the operation begun, and thus prevent any disastrous outcome for the patient.

Strangely enough, the patient died only a few hours after the operation, although medical authorities intimated that the chances for the patient's recovery were slight, being only about one in ten. Nevertheless, the report greatly affected Dr. Wilheim mentally, who believed that his few minutes in the operating room were sufficient to incur the fatal result, and that he had momentarily erred in his procedure.

However, physicians emphatically assert that the removal of Dr. Wilheim was not due in any measure to faulty procedure on the latter's part. It was rather to prevent any serious mishap which might have resulted had Dr. Wilheim remained to continue the work under physical strain.

The butler at the spacious Wilheim home, located on North Wilshire Drive, told newspaper men that, on the night of February 12, he noticed signs of insanity in the doctor's actions—that he heard frequent mumblings, and exclamations to the effect that he was responsible for the death. Believing that the doctor was merely overtired, he took him into the drawing room and made it comfortable by lighting a cheery fire in the grate. A few minutes later, the butler reported, "Dr. Wilheim summoned me and said that the house was on fire, and that hell was burning up his soul for his crime." At this point, the butler realized the seriousness of the doctor's condition and called the hospital to which he was removed immediately.

Physicians with whom Dr. Wilheim has been associated during the past twenty years have nothing but words of commendation for him, and remark that such service as Dr. Wilheim has rendered at the Russel Jennings Hospital has been unprecedented.

C. E.

The author of the next paper has a very original subject.

IF EVE HAD KEPT A DIARY

1st day of the New Moon.

Since that serpent of an apple salesman caused our ejection from the beautiful estate of Eden, troubles unceasingly oppress us. Adam isn't the happy-go-lucky fellow he used to be, and today I found three grey hairs among my golden tresses.

2nd day after the New Moon.

I was up very early this morning, gathering figs and other fruit with which to bake cakes for the children. I could not get the fire to burn, and Adam never leaves enough wood; he does not like the idea of a woodpile—afraid of snakes. If he thinks I'm going to try to keep house in this ramshackle place, I'll tell him plainly what I think of him.

3rd day after the New Moon.

Adam and I have quarreled. He did not come home until the stars were waning this morning, but I was waiting for him. He resented

my attitude, and flung himself down on the skins with the children—
and he knows how I hate sleeping alone. The brute, he'll be sorry.

4th day after the New Moon.

My husband came home early this afternoon, and the dear man
had a stunning leopard skin thrown over his shoulder. Of course I
paid no attention to him; but he came right up to me, said he was
sorry, and gave me the skin. I was thrilled and surprised; it's the most
beautiful skin I've ever seen, honey-beige with flashing black and
white polka dots, and I know it will look wonderful on me. Then he
gave me a necklace of lion's teeth, white and sparkling. He is such a
good husband, I'll never complain again.

5th day after the New Moon.

Little Abel wandered off alone today, and we could not find him
anywhere. Finally Cain came upon him sitting in a shallow mountain
brook not far from our dwelling. He was playing with a frog and two
little water snakes. I cautioned Cain not to mention the snakes to his
father, for Adam cannot overcome his horror for these reptiles.

6th day after the New Moon.

Wonder of wonders! While I was gathering fruit today, I found a
small, round red berry that I had never seen before. As I bit into it
the juice spread over my lips and hands, and unconsciously I rubbed
my cheeks with my wet fingers. When Adam saw me, he exclaimed,
"Eve, what have you done to yourself? You are more beautiful than
I have ever seen you! Come here, my rib, and tell me where you got
such rosy cheeks, such ruby lips?" In astonishment I ran to the pond,
and on its quiet surface saw myself reflected. I couldn't believe my
eyes—I looked so much younger and even my hair seemed lighter
and fluffier. How I shall cherish those little, red berries; they will
keep me looking young and lovely always.

7th day after the New Moon.

I wore my new leopard skin today, and even the children admired
me when I put it on. We went for a long walk, and Adam showed us
a lovely nook where he intends to build our new home. We have just
finished supper and Adam is putting the children to bed. From the
back door I can see the great sun slowly sinking, and the sky is like
a rainbow of beautiful colors. I am so happy. We are going to talk
over the plans of our new house, and Adam says I can have a special
room for my pet monkeys. That will be so exclusive; I know I shall
never be unhappy again.

H. O.

In the following diary there is only one entry, but brevity aids in keeping the tone of a humorous sketch.

THE DIARY OF A LADY'S LAP DOG

February 14:

Dorothy said to me tonight, "Now, Fifi, oo must be a dood 'ittle doggie, 'cause Jerry is calling on me tonight. I'll tell you a secret, but don'tcha tell anyone. I fink he is going to bring me a valentine, so oo must be extra, extra sweet." Snuggling her curly hair in my face and giving me a hug, she put me on my best pillow of yellow chiffon velvet. She tied a huge pink bow around my neck to match my nose and set off the milky white of my hair.

Of all Dorothy's vanishing Americans who hold down the upholstery on the davenport, Jerry gripes me most. He's the kind of guy who pats my back in front of her face and slaps my face behind her back. Dorothy pays absolutely no attention to me when he's around. She makes the other fellows take me out for an airing and kiss me, but for some uncanny, inexplicable reason, she just laughs when Jerry refuses to entertain poor little me.

I had a sneaking feeling this valentine thing would be another excuse for total darkness in the living room. Consequently, when Jerry invited himself in, I smelled his running gear and had a good notion to sink my teeth in his pet corn, which, by the way, is my latest discovery of his weaknesses. I noticed a red box in his hand. It smelled pretty good. When he laid it down, I decided to investigate. The ribbon came off easily and what do you suppose I found when I tore the cover off? There, in the box, was my very favorite chocolate candy. Maple walnut creams, cherries in cordial cream, nuts, fruits, and stuffed dates made up symmetrical rows of pleasing eye-teasers. I do not like the chocolate covering on candy too dark or too light. I like it just medium. That is just the kind of covering these bonbons were coated with. As I was marveling at Jerry's good taste in choosing my favorite color, Dorothy, released from a huddle, pounced down upon me and boxed my ears. I was terribly hurt. Dorothy never treated me this way in front of the other fellows. Besides, how was I to know the candy was not meant for me? I tried to tell her this, but she just could not understand me. Deeply hurt and insulted, I slunk into a corner and gave both of them dirty looks that could be understood in any language. They sat on the davenport as usual and were more sick looking than ever. Believe me, when Dorothy has that dreamy appearance and Jerry gazes at her with the look of a dying calf, that's when a feller needs a friend.

F. S.

In "A Letter of 1671" appear the possibilities of letter-writing as linear narration.

A LETTER OF 1671

Chantilly, April 26, 1671

Dearest Marie:

This is Sunday, and at last I have found time to answer your letter. This is not really a letter, but an account of what has happened during the visit of our king at Chantilly.

The king and his party arrived Thursday in the early evening. They seemed very pleased to be here, but since the party was rather tired, all retired early except the servants, who were preparing for the forest fete on the morrow.

The next day was glorious, and the grounds were beautiful. The promenade, the collation in a spot carpeted with jonquils—all was going to perfection. Then came supper and the roast failed at one or two tables, probably due to the large number of unexpected guests. Vatel was very upset, and he said several times, "My honor is lost; this is a humiliation that I can not endure." Later, this prince of cooks met Gourville, who was in charge of all the preparations for the king's visit, and he said, "My head is swimming; I have not slept for twelve nights. Help me to give my order." Gourville did his best to console him, but the roast which had failed, not at the king's table, but at the twenty-fifth table seemed to haunt his mind.

He was so upset that Monsieur le Prince went to Vatel's rooms and said, "Vatel, all goes well; there never was anything so beautiful as the king's supper." Vatel answered, "Monseigneur, your goodness overwhelms me. I know that the roast failed at two tables."

"Nothing of the sort," said Monsieur le Prince. "Do not disturb yourself; all is well."

Midnight came, and the fireworks (which cost sixteen thousand francs) failed because of a cloud that overspread them.

Saturday morning at four o'clock, Vatel is wandering about the grounds, while everyone is asleep. He meets a small purveyor with two loads of fish and asks him, "Is this all?" "Yes, Sir," said the man who did not know that Vatel had sent to all the seaport towns in France. Vatel waits for some time, but the other purveyors do not come. He becomes excited, and thinks that there will be no more fish. He finds Gourville and says, "Sir, I shall not be able to survive this disgrace." Gourville only laughs and goes on his way.

Vatel returns to his rooms and runs a sword through his heart.

Meanwhile the fish are arriving from every side and people are seeking Vatel to distribute it. Finally they go to his rooms; they knock and when there is no answer, they break open the door. When his death is reported to the king and the prince, they decide that it all came from Vatel's having his own code of honor, and they praise his courage highly even while they blame him.

Thus ended the king's visit to Chantilly, but not as Vatel had believed. We had a splendid breakfast of fish, and everyone was happy, for the day was so splendid, and the jonquils so enchanting.

Your loving sister,

Hila

H. S.

The following tracing of moods shows the possibilities that lie in commonplace experience.

CLASSROOM SOLILOQUY

I came to my one o'clock class with the best of intentions. I had studied my lesson thoroughly and felt that I could make a suitable reply to any question that might be put to me.

I walked into the classroom and sat down in my seat near the window, feeling pleasantly sure of myself. Presently the professor came, shut the door, and settled himself in a chair. He took out a textbook and cleared his throat in preparation. I mentally braced myself for what might come. Nothing came. He commenced reading a selection from the text. It had to do with woman's economic independence, and I settled myself to listen attentively.

I listened carefully to the first two or three paragraphs; then gradually my thoughts wandered to other, more intriguing fields, and in a little while I felt the usual insidious classroom drowsiness creeping over me. I pulled myself up with a start and listened intently to the next paragraph. Then again I was enveloped by drowsiness. To divert myself I looked out the window. A boy and girl were standing on the corner. They were in earnest conversation and obviously were in love. The girl had on a sleek, rust-colored sport dress, and I wondered idly if I would look well in that color. Finally, after settling some apparently important question, they wandered off down the street, hand in hand.

I sighed, and focused my attention on a fly that was struggling up the window pane. He was having a dreadfully hard time climbing up the slippery surface. Several times he almost reached the top, only to lose his balance and tumble back to the little ledge at the bottom of the pane and lie sprawling there on his back with his furry little legs waving helplessly in the air. I carefully turned him over and began reflecting on the futility of his efforts. Then I thought how generally futile life was, and finally came to the conclusion that the future was, for me, just a long piece of grey woolen.

I was quite charmed by this metaphor and wrote it down in my notebook. However, after reading it over several times, I became less and less convinced of its merit.

At this point the heat of the room seemed to close in on me and I was overwhelmed by drowsiness. I decided that I could listen equally well with my eyes closed; so I arranged myself in a more comfortable position, with my feet upon the rungs of the chair in front of me and my head supported with one hand. I was deliciously comfortable and the faraway drone of the professor's voice lulled me farther and farther away into the realms of sleep.

Suddenly the drone ceased, and there was a silence which buzzed in my ears.

D. McC.

The sense of character and situation in this picture of country life is so vivid that an interfering factor, some element of plot complication, seems constantly about to appear. The blending of movement and descriptive detail is very successful.

AN AFTERNOON IN SPRING

Judy was awakened by the creaking of the horses' leather harness as they made the narrow turn between the row of gooseberries and the grape arbor.

Yes, it was a sure sign of spring when old Thomas borrowed a team and plowed the garden. In all of her six years, Judy remembered, the day of Thomas's spring plowing had always been an important event in her life. So, in accordance with her usual custom, she put on her shiny-black high rubber boots with the red tops and ran out the back door into the warm sunshine.

What fun it was to follow Thomas down the seamy rows from which clouds of vapor were rising. She ran along, following Thomas's big tracks, stumbling over the great rolls of soil when she ventured too far from the straight line of the seam.

They paused for a moment under the scarred old plum tree in the corner of the garden. In spite of its age it surpassed all the other trees on the place in the profusion of its blossoms. Thomas seemed to enjoy standing beneath it, inhaling its delicate fragrance, and listening to the lazy droning of the bees.

Judy was impatient, waiting for old Thomas to come out of his reverie. Days like this always reminded him of his old home in Italy, of the terraced vineyards he had cultivated as a boy.

Soon the horses were released from the plow and hitched to the little harrow, which seemed like a toy in comparison to their great bulk.

Thomas improvised a seat for Judy out of an old broken apple box and placed it in the center of the harrow. Judy felt grander than any queen, perched upon her rickety throne and clutching the reins in the middle, while Thomas walked behind her like a page, holding the ends.

Tiring of her ride, Judy ran across the yard to watch her mother clean out the flower beds. Only the violets were in bloom, but under the last year's dried stalks one could see thousands of little bright green plants. In the center of a circle of sticks placed upright in the ground, Judy found two long, slender, pointed dark-green leaves mottled with huge brown spots. She recognized the lamb's-tongue lily that she had herself transplanted from the woods into her own garden the spring before. Inspecting the daffodils, Judy saw on some of them green conical caps which reminded her of the dunce caps she had seen pictures of in her storybooks.

A loud shout from Thomas brought Judy to her feet and sent her bounding across the grass to the barnyard gate where the horses stood hitched to the wagon, ready to be driven home. Thomas lifted Judy up on the high wagon seat beside him, and the old wagon slowly creaked out of the yard and down the road in the direction of the house.

Just as the sun was disappearing behind the farthest mountain range, Judy and Thomas drove back into the yard in old Thomas's rattling Ford. As Judy ran up the walk to the kitchen door, she could smell the sweet scent of the violets at the doorstep, mingled with the aroma of the ham frying in the kitchen.

D. D.

⇶ B ⇜

CHRONICLE AND HISTORY

The following is taken from the *Anglo-Saxon Chronicle*. Could you build a story out of these entries?

A.D. 435. This year the Goths sacked the city of Rome; and never since have the Romans reigned in Britain. This was about eleven hundred and ten winters after it was built. They reigned altogether in Britain four hundred and seventy winters since Gaius Julius first sought that land.

A.D. 449. This year Marcian and Valentinian assumed the empire, and reigned seven winters. In their days Hengest and Horsa, invited by Wurtgern, king of the Britons, to his assistance, landed in Britain in a place that is called Ipwinesfleet; first of all to support the Britons, but they afterwards fought against them. . . .

It was with material like this excerpt from Holinshed (1577) that Shakespeare worked.

Shortly after, happened a strange and uncouth wonder, which afterward was the cause of much trouble in the realm of Scotland, as ye shall after hear. It fortuned as Macbeth and Banquo journeyed toward Fores, where the king then lay, they went sporting by the way together without other company, save only themselves, passing through the woods and fields, when suddenly in the midst of a land, there met them three women in strange and wild apparel, resembling creatures of elder world, whom when they attentively beheld, wondering much at the sight, the first of them spake and said: "All hail Macbeth, thane of Glamis." . . .

Note the picturesque style and details of this selection (1837) from Carlyle.

To describe this Siege of the Bastille (thought to be one of the most important in History) perhaps transcends the talent of mortals. Could one but, after infinite reading, get to understand so much as the plan of the building! But there is open Esplanade, at the end of the Rue Saint-Antoine; there are such Forecourts, *Cour Avancée, Cour de l'Orme*, arched Gateway (where Louis Tournay now fights); then new draw-bridges, dormant-bridges, rampart-bastions, and the grim Eight Towers; a labyrinthic Mass, high-frowning there, of all ages from twenty years to four hundred and twenty;—beleagued, in this its last hour, as we said, by mere Chaos come again! Ordnance of all calibres; throats of all capacities; men of all plans, every man his own engineer; seldom since the war of Pygmies and Cranes was there seen so anomalous a thing. Half-pay Elie is home for a suit of regimentals; no one would heed him in coloured clothes; half-pay Hulin is haranguing Gardes Françaises in the Place de Grève. Frantic Patriots pick up the grapeshots; bear them, still hot (or seemingly so), to the Hotel-de-Ville; —Paris, you perceive, is to be burnt! Flesselles is "pale to the very lips," for the roar of the multitude grows deep. Paris wholly has got to the acme of its frenzy; whirled, all ways, by panic madness. At every street-barricade, there whirls simmering a minor whirlpool—strengthening the barricade, since God knows what is coming; and all minor whirlpools play distractedly into the grand Fire-Maelstrom which is lashing round the Bastille.

And so it lashes and it roars. . . .

T. CARLYLE, *The French Revolution.*

In *The Duke*[1] (1931) Guedalla relives the life of his character and the situation in which his character finds himself.

The Duke, as usual, was everywhere, fighting his line along the ridge as a commander fights his ship in action. He rode "Copenhagen"; and all day long the chestnut carried him along the lanes of weary men. Each shift of the interminable battle elicited a gruff comment or an order scrawled on a scrap of parchment. He saw the Nassauers pressed out of Hougoumont and acidly observed to an Austrian General, "*Mais enfin, c'est avec ces Messieurs là qu'il faut que nous gagnions la bataille,*"[2] put in the Guards to retake the position with "There, my lads, in with you—let me see no more of you," and watched Mercer's guns dash into place between two squares with an appreciative "Ah! that's the way I like to see horse-artillery move." When the Life Guards charged, a deep voice was at hand to say, "Now, gentlemen, for the honour of the Household Troops,"; and when they rode back, a low cocked-hat was raised with "Life-Guards! I thank you." At one moment he formed a line of shaky infantry himself, like any company-commander, within twenty yards of the flash of an oncoming French column. And as the tide of cavalry was ebbing down the trampled slope, he asked the Rifles in his quiet manner to "drive those fellows away."

The light was failing now; and he rode down the line before the

[1] From *The Duke*, London, Hodder & Stoughton, 1931, reprinted by permission of the author.

[2] "But after all, it is with such gentlemen as that that we have to win the victory."

Guard was launched in the last charge of the Empire. The shadows lengthened from the west, as the tall bearskins came slowly on behind six Generals and a Marshal walking (for it was Ney) with a drawn sword. . . .

PHILIP GUEDALLA, The Duke.

For further reading try Carlyle's essay "On History." Macaulay, Froude, and Trevelyan are other extremely readable historians.

THE NEWS STORY

The editor himself called this first selection "a gem":

DEATH OF CAPTAIN EDDIE [1]

F. E. Dutcher

It is an unwritten law that a captain never deserts his ship, but gives his life, if need be, in an effort to save her. Captain Eddie Anderson, 5, died true to the traditions of the sea. He gave his life in trying to save his ship.

A sheet of water covered part of Valley Drive, brought down by the March thaw. Winds roughened it, and in this sea Captain Eddie launched his craft and set sail. He was a bold captain and it was a gallant bark. It raced before the wind, sails spread, and he who was captain and crew watched that it was not dashed upon the rocks.

Back across the sea it went again and into the very teeth of danger. Bearing down upon it, plowing through its little sea and sending flying spray was a streetcar of the Valley line. There was one thought in the mind of the little captain. He must save his ship. Directly in front of the car it sailed on its last voyage, and dashing after it, its captain.

Captain and ship went down together. The tiny craft will have its treasured place for the years to come in the home where its captain lived. It will be put away where "The little toy-dog is covered with dust, but sturdy and staunch he stands; and the little tin-soldier is red with rust and his musket molds in his hands."

The body of the lad, who died early yesterday morning in Crouse-Irving hospital from injuries suffered when he was run over Tuesday afternoon by a streetcar will be taken to the family home, No. 508 Valley Drive, today by A. C. Schumacher, undertaker.

The Syracuse Post-Standard, March 6, 1924.

[1] Reprinted by permission of the editor of the Syracuse *Post-Standard*.

BIOGRAPHY

Before beginning this section you will do well first to read Carlyle's essay on Biography. Boswell's *Life of Samuel Johnson* (1791) is one of the most famous of biographies.

At last, on Monday the 16th of May, when I was sitting in Mr. Davies's back parlour, after having drunk tea with him and Mrs. Davies, Johnson unexpectedly came into the shop; and Mr. Davies having perceived him through the glass-door in the room in which we were sitting, advancing towards us,—he announced his awful approach to me, somewhat in the manner of an actor in the part of Horatio, when he addresses Hamlet on the appearance of his father's ghost, "Look, my lord, it comes." I found that I had a very perfect idea of Johnson's figure, from the portrait of him painted by Sir Joshua Reynolds soon after he had published his *Dictionary*, in the attitude of sitting in his easy chair in deep meditation; which was the first picture his friend did for him, which Sir Joshua very kindly presented to me, and from which an engraving has been made for this work. Mr. Davies mentioned my name, and respectfully introduced me to him. I was much agitated; and recollecting his prejudice against the Scotch, of which I had heard much, I said to Davies, "Don't tell where I come from."—"From Scotland," cried Davies, roguishly. "Mr. Johnson, (said I) I do indeed come from Scotland, but I cannot help it." I am willing to flatter myself that I meant this as light pleasantry to soothe and conciliate him, and not as an humiliating abasement at the expense of my country. But however that might be, this speech was somewhat unlucky; for with the quickness of wit for which he was so remarkable, he seized the expression "come from Scotland," which I used in the sense of being of that country; and, as if I had said that I had come away from it, or left it, retorted, "That, Sir, I find, is what a very great many of your countrymen cannot help."

The following selection is of more modern origin. Compare it with Boswell's technique.

BARRETT WENDELL [1]

Walter Pritchard Eaton

The first time I ever saw Wendell, or at least ever heard him, he came into a freshman course designed to take us from Beowulf to

[1] Reprinted by permission of the author and *The American Mercury*.

Browning in a single winter. Somebody else had got us through Beowulf and Chaucer, and Wendell appeared on the platform one morning to initiate us into the splendors of the Elizabethan age. A rather short, immaculately dressed figure, a reddish beard, a voice that hesitated, broke into queer squeaks, had outlandish accents—that is what we saw and heard. And some of us tittered. A boy's first impression of Wendell was of a terrible ass. Nor did he ever do anything to lessen this impression. He used it, rather, as a weapon to attract attention. Presently he began to quote. As he quoted, he became excited. He pulled one end of his watch chain from his pocket (I think there was a gold penknife attached) and began to twirl it round and round. Then he began to walk rapidly back and forth across the platform.

Stamp-stamp-stamp; twirl-twirl-twirl; and—

> " 'Full fathom five thy father lies . . .
> Nothing of him that doth fade,
> But doth suffer a sea-change
> Into something rich and strange.'

Ah, gentlemen, that is beauty! That is art!"

An absurd performance? No—for suddenly, here and there astonished freshmen forgot to watch the twirling penknife, forgot the Oxford-atte-Back Bay accent, and realized that this *was* beauty, this *was* art, and that was what made this ridiculous professor so excited about it. It was so fine he was willing to make an exhibition of himself over it. Again the artist!

The American Mercury, August, 1925.

DIARY OR JOURNAL

The style of this first selection is chatty and gossipy.

Jan. 11th. [166 5/6]. At noon to dinner all of us by invitation to Sir W. Pen's, and much company. Among others, Lieutenant of the Tower, and Broome, his poet, and Dr. Whistler and his son-in-law Lowther, servant to Mrs. Margaret Pen, and Sir Edward Spragg, a merry man, that sang a pleasant song pleasantly.

Jan. 12th. I and my Lord Brouncker by coach a little way, for discourse sake, till our coach broke, and tumbled me over him quite down the side of the coach, falling on the ground about the stockes, but up again. To my poor wife, who works all day at home like a horse, at the making of her hangings for our chamber and the bed.

Jan. 13th. Home with his Lordship to Mrs. Williams's in Covent Garden, to dinner, the first time I ever was there, and there met Captain Cocke; and pretty merry, though not perfectly so, because of the fear that there is of a great encrease again of the plague this week. . . .

Jan. 16th. Mightily troubled at the news of the plague's being encreased, and was much the saddest news that the plague hath brought me from the beginning of it; because of the lateness of the year, and the fear we may with reason have of its continuing with us the next summer. The total being now 375, and the plague 158.

SAMUEL PEPYS, *Diary.*

The next selection [1] shows great emotional intensity, culminating in bitter tragedy at the close.

Monday, March 19 [1912].—Lunch. We camped with difficulty last night, and were dreadfully cold till after our supper of cold pemmican and biscuit and a half pannikin of cocoa cooked over the spirit. Then contrary to expectations, we got warm and all slept well. Today we started in the usual dragging manner. Sledge dreadfully heavy. We are $15\frac{1}{2}$ miles from the depot and ought to get there in three days. What progress! We have two days' food but barely a day's fuel. All our feet are getting bad—Wilson's best, my right foot worst, left all right. There is no chance to nurse one's feet till we can get hot food into us. Amputation is the least I can hope for now, but will the trouble spread? That is the serious question. The weather doesn't give us a chance—the wind from N. to N.W. and − 40° temp. today.

Wednesday, March 21.—Got within 11 miles of depot Monday night; had to lay up all yesterday in severe blizzard. Today forlorn hope, Wilson and Bowers going to depot for fuel.

Thursday, March 22 and 23.—Blizzard bad as ever—Wilson and Bowers unable to start—tomorrow last chance—no fuel and only one or two of food left—must be near the end. Have decided it shall be natural—we shall march for the depot with or without our effects and die in our tracks.

Thursday, March 29.—Since the 21st we have had a continuous gale from W.S.W. and S.W. We had fuel to make two cups of tea apiece and bare food for two days on the 20th. Every day we have been ready to start for our depot *11 miles* away, but outside the door of the tent it remains a scene of whirling drift. I do not think we can hope for any better things now. We shall stick it out to the end, but we are getting

[1] From *Scott's Last Expedition*, copyright 1913, by Dodd, Mead & Company.

weaker of course, and the end cannot be far. It seems a pity, but I do not think I can write more.

R. SCOTT.

For God's sake look after our people.

Scott's Last Expedition, arranged by Leonard Huxley.

For further reading see Evelyn's *Diary*, Swift's *Journal to Stella*, R. W. Emerson's *Journals*, Hawthorne's *American Notebooks*, *The Diary of A. C. Benson*, Thoreau's *Early Spring in Massachusetts*, etc.

AUTOBIOGRAPHY

Note the value of the anecdote in this selection from Trollope.

I do not know that I should interest my readers by saying much of my postoffice experiences in those days. I was always on the eve of being dismissed, and yet was always striving to show how good a public servant I could become, if only a chance were given me. But the chance went the wrong way.

On one occasion, in the performance of my duty, I had to put a private letter containing banknotes on the Secretary's table—which letter I had duly opened as it was not marked private. The letter was seen by the Colonel, but had not been moved by him when he left the room. On his return it was gone.

In the meantime I had returned to the room again in the performance of some duty. When the letter was missed, I was sent for, and there I found the Colonel much moved about his letter, and a certain chief clerk, who, with a long face, was making suggestions as to the probable fate of the money.

"The letter has been taken," said the Colonel, turning to me angrily, "and, by G—! there has been nobody in the room but you and I." As he spoke, he thundered his fist down upon the table.

"Then," said I, "by G—! *you* have taken it," and I also thundered my fist down; but, accidentally, not upon the table. There was a standing movable desk, at which, I presume, it was the Colonel's habit to write, and on this movable desk was a large bottle full of ink. My fist unfortunately came on the desk, and the ink at once flew up, covering the Colonel's face and shirt-front.

Then it was a sight to see the senior clerk, as he seized a quire of blotting paper, and rushed to the aid of his superior officer, striving to mop up the ink; and a sight also to see the Colonel, in his agony, hit right through the blotting-paper at the senior clerk's unoffending stomach.

At that moment there came in the Colonel's private secretary, with the letter and the money, and I was desired to go back to my own room. This was an incident not much in my favour, though I do not know that it did me special harm.

ANTHONY TROLLOPE, *Autobiography* (1883).

Compare similar material in T. H. Huxley's *Autobiography*, *The Memoirs of Edward Gibbon*, *The Autobiography of John Stuart Mill*, and the more modern autobiographies of Jane Addams, Michael Pupin, Theodore Roosevelt, W. H. Hudson, Mark Twain, etc.

The following selection [1] illustrates how dramatic a section of an autobiography can be.

My mother, who had left the stage for upward of twenty years, determined to return to it on the night of my first appearance, that I might have the comfort and support of her being with me in my trial. We drove to the theater very early, indeed while the late autumn sunlight yet lingered in the sky; it shone into the carriage upon me, and as I screened my eyes from it, my mother said, "Heaven smiles on you, my child." My poor mother went to her dressing-room to get herself ready, and did not return to me for fear of increasing my agitation by her own. My dear Aunt Dall and my maid and the theater dresser performed my toilet for me, and at length I was placed in a chair, with my satin train carefully laid over the back of it; and there I sat, ready for execution, with the palms of my hands pressed convulsively together, and the tears I in vain endeavored to repress welling up into my eyes and brimming slowly over, down my rouged cheeks—upon which my aunt, with a smile full of pity, renewed the color as often as these heavy drops made unsightly streaks in it. . . . At last, "Miss Kemble called for the stage, ma'am!" accompanied with a brisk tap at the door, started me upright on my feet, and I was led round to the side scene opposite to the one from which I saw my mother advance on the stage; and while the uproar of her reception filled me with terror, dear old Mrs. Davenport, my nurse, and dear Mr. Keely, her Peter, and half the *dramatis personae* of the play (but not my father, who had retreated, quite unable to endure the scene) stood round me as I lay, all but insensible, in my aunt's arms. "Courage, courage, dear child! poor thing, poor thing!" reiterated Mrs. Davenport. "Never mind 'em, Miss Kemble," urged Keely, in that irresistibly

[1] From *Records of a Girlhood*, by Fanny Kemble, Henry Holt and Company, 1884. Compare Margaret Armstrong's *Fanny Kemble*, The Macmillan Company, 1938.

comical, nervous, lachrymose voice of his, which I have never since heard without a thrill of anything but comical association; "never mind 'em! don't think of 'em, any more than if they were so many rows of cabbages!" "Nurse!" called my mother and on waddled Mrs. Davenport, and, turning back, called in her turn, "Juliet!" My aunt gave me an impulse forward, and I ran straight across the stage, stunned with the tremendous shout that greeted me, my eyes covered with mist, and the green baize flooring of the stage feeling as if it rose up against my feet; but I got hold of my mother, and stood like a terrified creature at bay, confronting the huge theater full of gazing human beings. I do not think a word I uttered during this scene could have been audible; in the next, the ballroom, I began to forget myself; in the following one, the balcony scene, I had done so, and for aught I knew I was Juliet; the passion I was uttering sending hot waves of blushes all over my neck and shoulders while the poetry sounded like music to me as I spoke it, with no consciousness of anything before me, utterly transported into the imaginary existence of the play. After this I did not return into myself till all was over, and amid a tumultuous storm of applause. . . .

Fanny Kemble, Records of a Girlhood.

The Letter

The correspondence of public persons, particularly men of letters, provides a rich source of narrative material.

Charles Lamb is often more animated in his letters than when, as an essayist, he wears the garb of the gentle Elia. The following is a portion of a letter to Mrs. Hazlitt, written in November, 1823.

Dear Mrs. H:

Sitting down to write a letter is such a painful operation to Mary, that you must accept me as her proxy. You have seen our house. What I now tell you is literally true. Yesterday George Dyer called upon us, at one o'clock (*bright noonday*), on his way to dine with Mrs. Barbauld at Newington. He sat with Mary about half an hour, and took leave. The maid saw him go out, from her kitchen window, but suddenly losing sight of him, ran up in a fright to Mary. G. D., instead of keeping the slip that leads to the gate, had deliberately, staff in hand, in broad open day, marched into the New River. He had not his spectacles on, and you know his absence. Who helped him out they can hardly tell, but between 'em they got him out, drenched thro' and thro'. A mob collected by that time, and accompanied him in. "Send for the doctor," they said: and a one-eyed fellow, dirty and drunk, was fetched from the public-house at the end, where it seems he lurks, for the sake of picking up water practice; having formerly had a medal from the Humane Society for some rescue. By his advice the patient was put between blankets; and when I came home at 4 to dinner, I found G. D. a-bed, and raving, light-headed, with the brandy and water which the doctor had administered. He sang, laughed, whimpered, screamed, babbled of guardian angels, would get up and go home; but we kept him there by force; and by next morning he departed sober, and seems to have received no injury. All my friends are open-mouth'd about having paling before the river; but I cannot see, that because a lunatic chooses to walk into a river with his eyes open at midday, I am any the more likely to be drowned in it, coming home at midnight.

NARRATIVE ANECDOTE

IN BERLIN [1]

(*1915*)

Mary Boyle O'Reilly

The train crawling out of Berlin was filled with women and children, hardly an able-bodied man. In one compartment a gray-haired Landsturm soldier sat beside an elderly woman who seemed weak and ill. Above the click-clack of the car wheels passengers could hear her counting: "One, two, three," evidently absorbed in her own thoughts. Sometimes she repeated the words at short intervals. Two girls tittered, thoughtlessly exchanging vapid remarks about such extraordinary behavior. An elderly man scowled reproval. Silence fell.

"One, two, three," repeated the obviously unconscious woman. Again the girls giggled stupidly. The gray Landsturm leaned forward.

"Fräulein," he said gravely, "you will perhaps cease laughing when I tell you that this poor lady is my wife. We have just lost our three sons in battle. Before leaving for the front myself I must take their mother to an insane asylum."

It became terribly quiet in the carriage.

The above is little more than a narrative sketch, but its emotional power is obvious. The author has written us that she composed it in the interest of peace *versus* war.

[1] Reprinted by the kind permission of the author.

CHAPTER XIV

The Plot Story

THE SOLE DIFFERENCE between the plot story and the finished short story is the factor of emphasis. We supply the *action* alone, a bare sequence of correlated events, similar to a synopsis or the framework of a building. For the moment, then, we ignore the development of the *characters* and *atmosphere*—the two elements which ultimately draw all the components of the story into a unity. Thus we do not show that what takes place arises from the traits and intentions of the persons in the story, or how it is affected by time of day or night, the weather, or the subtler atmosphere of gloom, hope, uncertainty, which accompany striking events. The bare framework or pattern of the action concerns us here, while common sense and an analytical habit of mind take the place of the imagination. The main questions are only: What is to happen, and when, and in what order? Later we shall ask: Who would do these things? Why are they done? In what atmosphere would they arise and develop? What mood would these events produce in characters and reader?

1. PLOT: DEFINITION AND ANALYSIS

The term *plot* is important. It suggests an intrigue, an action in which one person is pitting his wits against another, usually to do him mischief. A cup challenger in tennis plots the overthrow of his opponent; a district attorney plots a campaign of attack on organized crime; revolutionists plot the overthrow of a government. All employ strategy, foresight, and all hope the story will turn out as a defeat for the entrenched enemy. Unlike simpler linear narration, the incidents in the plotted action do not pursue a more or less even, horizontal sequence. Instead, conflict causes them to rise rapidly in interest to a distinctly high pitch where the reader is intensely worried as to whether the devil or the good angel (which have both been playing their conflicting parts in the ascending incidents) is going to win the day.

A plot, then, is a series of incidents of rising interest, involving positive and negative forces which conflict steadily with varying success, until at the critical moment, the most intense incident of all, one of the two forces (generally the positive) suddenly prevails. The German critic, Freytag, suggests all this when he asks us to think of a rubber band which is stretched tighter and tighter between our two hands. Each jerk increases tension and suspense, until, at the moment of greatest tension, the band snaps. Romantic fiction, from Dumas's *The Three Musketeers* to Margaret Mitchell's *Gone with the Wind*, proceeds by this method. Beneath the broad surface of the tale is a series of such plots centered in the career of a single individual.

Beyond the factor of conflicting forces, the chief thing to note in this theoretical exposition of plot is the absence of conspicuous character values and of a dominating setting. These highly important elements will be treated by themselves later. The point to remember now is that the plot story, a strictly elementary form of narration, has little to do with distinctly individualized characters or detailed settings. It is thus the logical form to undertake at this time, because it is easy and because it will provide an ideal framework, a skeleton, or automaton which you may later endow with specific characteristics and a definite locality if you wish to. After a study of the plot story, construction of plot will become so natural that you should pass smoothly on to the complete short story.

In order to visualize the emotional and narrative steps in the plot story, we shall first present a sequence wherein the actual setting provides a graph of its movement.

The University of Wisconsin is situated on a large lake. Along the shores of this lake there have been built swimming piers with floats and apparatus for high diving. The picture is intended to represent one of these floats. At *A* is the float, or raft. On it is erected a scaffold with steps *B*, *C*, *D*, and *E*. At *F* is attached a springboard, with the jumping-off place at *G*. Around *A*, of course, are the deep waters of the lake.

O. SOGLOW

On this float, one hot July afternoon, are gathered a number of students, both men and women. They have been diving and swimming, and now they are ready for diverting deviltry. One particularly young girl (remember that for the plot story we do not need to know whether or not she is blonde or her bathing suit orange, though that much might be revealed) has her foot on the first step *B*, and is wistfully looking up the ladder. Someone spies her and dares her to go up and dive. After some hesitation, and considerable "daring," she accepts the challenge and steps up on *B*.

The girl's succeeding steps up the ladder will become slower and slower as her fear becomes more and more intense. Opposing her fears are the taunts from below, acting as stimuli to her courage. Thus the devil and the good angel are at work, and the successive upward steps on the ladder provide increasing interest.

At *F* fear and pride are in a desperate struggle. It is here that our rubber band begins to show extreme tension. As the girl walks out on the springboard toward *G*, the band seems dangerously near snapping. Will she dive or will she "funk it"? Will the good angel or the devil triumph?

Now comes the moment when the elastic band must snap, when a decisive event cuts sharply into the action. The girl must be made to do something—quickly. Several things may happen. She may slip unexpectedly, but catch herself and straighten out into a perfect dive. (The writer's sympathy will perhaps make her do that.) She may turn around to come back, a sudden shout may confuse her, and she may fall off backwards. She may, again, be fooling them all (like the socially triumphant, self-taught piano or saxophone player of the advertisements), actually make a beautiful dive, and come up to laugh at their chagrin. Or the board may break down as she springs on it. At all events something happens quickly—and the girl's good angel or devil triumphs. She has come to the crisis, probably has taken the plunge from *G*. The story is ended.

Let us go back now to the diagram and, in a more technical fashion, describe the development of the typical plot story. *A*, the raft or float, is the "prelude" or "introduction" to the story. *B* is the "moment of interest," the point where the interest in the story is first actively engaged—the first moment of clash between opposing forces. *A* and *B* taken together may be called the "basic situation." *C*, *D*, and *E* are incidents of increasing "suspense,"[1] leading up to the "climax," *F*, which, in turn, is followed swiftly by the "solution," *G*, which is now really the girl's plunge from the board. (There may be a brief "conclusion," also, to be noted later.) Such, simply told, are the terms applicable to the form and development of the plot story. Actually they apply almost equally well to the fully developed short story.

Before further discussion of this narrative form, we should repeat that in the above story neither the character of the girl nor the details of the lake setting were of prime importance in the development. Interest was chiefly concerned with the bare incident. The following examples of exceedingly simple narrative will demonstrate this point even more conclusively.

It is our intention now to remove the story proper from the graphic setting of the raft, and to develop a plot which will more generally exemplify the same ladder-diving-board structure.

Succeeding chapters will treat in detail the steps in the ladder of suspense, but here it will be useful to examine a few plots in order to observe the function of the complete framework. This process will be much like lifting the spine and ribs of a nicely fried brook trout with your fork; the meat will be laid aside for later notice.

The first example will show how simple it is to create human interest and suspense, and how important ingenuity is in supplying the proper turn at the end so as both to release the tension and to justify our having been held by it. George Ade, famous for his *Fables in Slang*, perfected the art of lifting out the skeleton of the story, which he exhibited by itself, garnished only with his pungent slang. Other writers had long concentrated their efforts on the meat of realistic detail, characterization, setting. Ade very cleverly and ironically revealed the banality of things by isolating the stereotyped factor in age-old story types. Notice what he does with one of the most venerable of them, the tender romance. This is the boy-and-girl story, with the romantic element thrown into a new light. The steps are indicated.

---

[1] Each of these incidents will generally occupy one short paragraph. At least the story should be paragraphed by change in incident as the narration progresses.

(1) The Prelude: a youth and a maiden are sitting together on a davenport. The lights are dimmed. It is Monday evening. Both are somewhat nervous, the youth, of course, much more so than the maid. There are four cushions between them.

(2) Moment of Interest: the girl removes, almost by accident, one cushion.

(3) Incidents of Suspense: Tuesday night the girl removes a second cushion, Wednesday night a third, and on Thursday night, the fourth and last. Friday and Saturday nights follow with further progress toward—

(4) The Climax: for now a proposal is obviously inescapable. The boy's malicious devil, which would make him propose, and his good angel, which would save him, are at grips. Sunday is the proper day for the last terrific struggle. The boy is now on his knees—on one of the cushions which has dropped into a convenient position. He has his mouth open to— He must be saved somehow; and so we come to—

(5) The Solution: as George Ade did it, the girl's mother suddenly missed her cue and appeared. She weighed three hundred pounds! The boy took one look at her, and at the girl, and jumped out the window.

So the story is finished. It has followed the regular structure, step by step—but something else is needed, the sixth and most difficult item. And here George Ade's cleverness shows itself in—

(6) The Conclusion: soberly, he adds a concluding comment: "Moral—Never marry a girl until you have seen her mother."

Notice the quickness of this conclusion, like the snapping of a spring lid. It is a dangerous step for the undergraduate writer. He is easily led into writing several paragraphs of explanation of what has happened *after the story*. In general, drop the story as abruptly after the solution as possible. Try to get the clean-cut, flashing finish with which tap dancers turn off their acts.

George Ade's fable technique makes the bare bones of the story stand out by themselves. You could take the skeleton and build it up with any characters and settings you chose, just as a good dancer creates afresh the pleasure of rhythmical movements on the basis of the prescribed steps of the tango or waltz. Similar to the fable is the fairy tale. Both are story types built on well-understood formulas. Here again the characters are mere types; the plot is the thing. Many a writer of fiction and moving-picture scenarios has retold the story of Cinderella or of Beauty and the Beast in expensive new penthouse or Palm Beach settings.[1] Examine the tale of "The Nix of the Millpond," by the Brothers Grimm, for example. Conflict in this story is produced by the ancient interest of the spell (a nix is a water sprite endowed with witch powers) such as is central to the tale of Achilles and his fatal heel, or of Balder, who was immune from harm by all things— except one shrub from which his enemy made a fatal dart. Here is the skeleton of the story.

(1) Prelude: a miller, after living for years in contentment with his wife, is struck by ill luck. One morning at sunrise he is wailing by his millpond, despairing over his condition.

(2) Moment of Interest: a beautiful woman rises from the water. She calms the miller's fears, questions him as to his distress, and promises him great riches—on one condition. He must deliver to her the young thing which has just been born in his house. He believes it will be only a kitten or puppy which he must forfeit, and readily agrees.

(3) Incidents of Suspense: on returning to the house the miller finds that his wife has just given birth to a boy. He is in despair. Still he does not take his son to the Nix, but teaches him to stay far from the water. Even so, prosperity comes to him; and as the years pass the youth continues to grow, is apprenticed to a huntsman, and finally marries the beautiful, true-hearted maiden who is the huntsman's daughter.

(4) Climax: but one day the youth pursues a stag in the forest. Not noticing his whereabouts, he goes to the fatal millpond to wash the blood from his hands. As he touches the water, he is seized by the long arms of the Nix and drawn under. His wife finds his hunting pouch on the bank, and is left to mourn his loss.

(Were this a story of just vengeance, in which we might sympathize with the Nix, the ending might come here, and the story be complete. But in a fairy tale we expect a happy solution; so there follows a new sequence of events in which the wife is the central figure.)

[1] Compare the movie, "Snow White and the Seven Dwarfs."

(5) Solution: this takes the form of a dream which leads to a visit to an old woman on a mountain. Her knowledge of spells enables the wife to regain her husband.

(6) Conclusion: "They embraced and kissed each other, and no one need ask if they were happy."

One more illustration of the raft and diving-board structure, this time from a student's paper, should make the steps entirely clear. The following abstract, by the way, is of a story by an Iowa engineer, who insisted that nothing worth writing about had ever happened to him. Then he told the following actual experience, of the previous fall. The moral is obvious: look into your own past and use what you find there.

(1) Prelude: a boy is out hunting for deer. He carries a heavy rifle and is alone. The region is mountainous, but he is well acquainted with it; he is a good woodsman and ready for any emergency.

(2) Moment of Interest: he sees a bear cub on the other side of a huge log. He climbs the log to get it, and is confronted by the mother bear. She rises on her hind legs, pushes the boy over, and stands over him growling angrily.

(3) Incidents of Suspense: he tries to reach his rifle, but it has been knocked from his hand—he cannot reach it. The bear is snarling in his face. He yells, trying to frighten the bear—uselessly. The bear's anger is only growing. He tries to move slightly so as to grope for the rifle—the bear snaps at him and places her paw on his shoulder, where the claws dig in sharply. He decides to shove the bear with his foot and scramble away to run for it. The bear sits down on his legs, snuffs his body, and takes his head in her mouth. As the jaws begin to crush, he has the usual fleeting visions of childhood.

(4) Climax: he is in blinding pain and his head seems ready to burst.

(5) Solution: he drops his right hand in despair. It falls on the rifle, at the trigger, which he pulls quickly. The sudden report startles the bear, she drops him, leaps up and lumbers off, with the cub at her heels.

And *no more*—the story is done. Never mind how the boy got home. That is another story.

All these independent stories have followed the normal plot structure as indicated by the raft device and the applied story. In each may be noted three very important features, one of which will be treated in detail in the subsequent sections of this chapter. The first was the predominant length of the division headed Incidents of Suspense: this point will be discussed below. Second, there was no emphasis on character or setting, except possibly the millpond setting in the story of the Nix. The girl and boy, the miller, and the hunter were types. The davenport setting was not unique, nor was the forest unusual in the bear story (you will recall, for example, that the boy was not lost). Finally, a point to be noted particularly now, two of the above stories fairly preserved the three unities—old-fashioned, perhaps, but very applicable to the structure of the plot story—of time, place, and action, single and unchanging. Either a single scene of action or minimum of time (or both) was preserved throughout. There was a thread of action, with a beginning, a middle, and an end, and there were no complicating subplots. The bear story compressed time to its smallest bounds. If the others had concentrated on one single moment—George Ade to one evening, the Grimm Brothers to the moment of final restoration of the lost husband—the effect might have been much more powerful. However, each extension of time provided significant factors of interest. The humorist chose to follow the pattern of the days of the week to protract the amusement; and the tellers of wonderful tales increase our sense of mystery and suspense by stretching out the time.

With these examples before us the structure of the plot story should be fairly clear. Now the various elements will be taken separately and in the order in which they will normally present themselves. The three main divisions of the plot story are basic situation (prelude and moment of interest combined), suspense, and climax (with the solution). They will be taken up in that sequence with cross references from section to section whenever possible, in an attempt to follow the actual conception and putting together of a normal plot story. As noted long since, one of the chief troubles in beginning such a story is to find a source. Once the germ of a story has been discovered, the actual construction by the raft formation is fairly simple for a resourceful mind. (And even an unresourceful, unimaginative mind can devise tricks of suspense once it has been given a few hints, such as will be provided later.) Hence at the beginning of the next section, dealing with basic situation, we shall revert briefly to the material of the chapter on linear narration, to show how sources of stories may be discovered.

2. The Basic Situation: Prelude and Moment of Interest

One can never overestimate the importance of the *beginning* of any story, whether plot story or fully developed short story. In it lies the key to the whole narrative, and from its impact upon him the reader decides whether or not he will proceed further. The beginning establishes both the tone and the point of view. If it is not short, clear-cut, and decisive, the whole story may fail to make its effect. The climax itself will be feeble and pointless if the basic situation does not suggest to the reader a story worth reading, a situation worth unfolding, questions worth answering. And he is the final judge.

Consider, for example, what was termed, in Chapter XIII, an unpromising source for plot stories—the laboratory notebook. In itself it is useless, because the general tone, or atmosphere, involved in the matter-of-fact writing up of an experiment is flat, uninteresting. But it can be charged with interest, and heavily. If you are working on substances that may explode and maim a person for life, you immediately have possibilities for a plot story. Basic situations which are both exciting and novel: accidental discovery, revenge, fatality, and other avenues of development are open to you. The experiment with explosives or dangerous gases, unlike harmless laboratory routine, has tone, a keynote of danger; hence the reader will be caught at the beginning.

This matter of tone at the very start of the story deserves more notice. What first impressions mean in meeting new people, tone stands for in the opening of a story. It is the sign of vitality, color, fresh, original appeal. It demands that the story be raised by some compelling force, derived chiefly from the moment of interest, above the dull, flat, commonplace, and uninteresting. It means at the same time, of course, a pervading atmosphere (humor, pathos, irony, foreboding, gaiety, etc.); but primarily it should be labelled *force*. Whatever the mood, there must be a decisive, energetic opening to grip the reader's attention and *compel* him to read on to the end of the story.[1]

A plot story beginning with the account of a circus parade in G——, Ohio, as the basic situation, will not strike the proper tone. But if you choose as the basic situation a written threat against the life of one of the riders in the parade, perhaps from a jealous rival who has been displaced as favorite feature performer, you will have tone enough to attract the average reader. He will wonder how it all turned out. Such an item might come from a newspaper account. In using such a source be sure to distinguish for story tone. An item on President X——'s platform will lack tone. But, perhaps in the adjacent column, you will find a news story of a stenographer's foiling a check forger, of a dog's rescue of a child, of a girl's sacrifice for her lover, or a scientist's dying as a result of his efforts to discover a serum. Similarly, in drawing on biography, it is essential to discriminate between the normal routine of everyday life and the moments of tension. (You will catch those trout in the rough water, or at least in the riffles.) A famed opera singer at her country home, and the same woman at the point of going on the stage, represent two different people. A race driver, a senator, a mail pilot, a ballet dancer, Theodore Roosevelt, Lord Byron, Beethoven—all these individuals have moments when they provide story situations, but only moments, which must be detected and captured. Always there must be the

---

[1] Robert Louis Stevenson said: "For my part, I liked a story to begin with an old wayside inn where, 'towards the close of the year 17—,' several gentlemen in three cocked hats were playing bowls. A friend of mine preferred the Malabar coast in a storm, with a ship beating to windward, and a scowling fellow of Herculean proportions striding along the beach; he, to be sure, was a pirate. This was further afield than my home-keeping fancy loved to travel, and designed altogether for a larger canvas than the tales that I affected. Give me a highwayman and I was full to the brim; a Jacobite would do, but the highwayman was my favorite dish. I can still hear that merry clatter of hoofs along the moonlit lane . . ." (From "A Gossip on Romance," published by Charles Scribner's Sons. Reprinted by permission of the publishers.) However, Stevenson's formula easily leads to the melodramatic emphasis, more suitable to romance and balladry. See, for example, Alfred Noyes's popular narrative poem, "The Highwayman."

compelling force to provide the proper basis for beginning your story.

Probably your preference for story sources will be the diary and autobiography. Here will be incidents and characters within your own experience and understanding. Here again tone must rule the choice. From a day's account in your diary, the purchase of a pair of gloves would be cast aside for a pursuit for speeding. On the same day a girl may have a "permanent" and drive off a bridge into a lake—a girl who cannot swim well. You may find that you played tennis all one morning, and in the afternoon went for a ride in the country and were detained by a broken axle, while you were due back for an important appointment at five. On another day you may nonchalantly break a date in the morning and in the afternoon discover that it was with someone whom you were eager to meet. In every case you must select for tone, so that the story may begin with a drive. Remember that in the diary the incident that affected your life most will be the one which will provide the most tone, or force, at the beginning of your plot story. Use that incident, and concentrate your energy and interest upon it from the start. Then you will have your reader with you at once.

The same principles apply to the autobiography as a source of story material. Again, choose for tone so as to attract the reader at once. Substitute for the first day at school the fall into the creek; for the Christmas-tree service at the church the three-legged race at the Sunday-school picnic; for the success at grade school the first big fish that got away; for the changes in hair styles the first harmless affair of the heart; for the subjects you studied in high school the sophomore raid on the junior banquet; for the routine of vacation loafing the lost-in-the-mountains incident. And so on: there will be plenty of episodes stored away in your memory which involve tone. List some of them before worrying as to just how you are to make a story out of them. For example: the night raid on the melon patch, the burning of the garage, cramps while swimming, hunting and fishing episodes, surreptitious smoking or explorations of forbidden property, first encounters with real danger or broken bones, games and rivalries at school, comedies and tragedies at home—all of these should have an intrinsic force which will attract the reader and hold his attention from the very beginning. To that end, they must above all mean something to you.

In all cases, then, the problem of tone, or force, must be faced in the first paragraphs of the story. Thus, no matter what characters and general theme you decide upon for your story, you must carefully select some feature of the action which will provide a definite, compelling moment of interest to assure impetus at the opening. Do not depend merely on the moral value, the seriousness or greatness of the theme, to awaken interest. Notice the difference in the opening sentences of three of Hawthorne's tales. The first, written in 1835, begins:

There was once a time when New England groaned under the actual pressure of heavier wrongs than those threatened ones which brought on the Revolution. James II, the bigoted successor of Charles the Voluptuous, had annulled the charters of all the colonies, and sent a harsh and unprincipled soldier to take away our liberties and endanger our religion.   "The Grey Champion."

The second (1844) opens:

An elderly man, with his pretty daughter on his arm, was passing along the street, and emerged from the gloom of the cloudy evening into the light that fell across the pavement from the window of a small shop. It was a projecting window; and on the inside were suspended a variety of watches, pinchbeck, silver, . . .
                          "The Artist of the Beautiful."

And the third (1851, the year following *The Scarlet Letter*, and the same year as *The House of the Seven Gables*):

Bartram the lime-burner, a rough, heavy-looking man, begrimed with charcoal, sat watching his kiln at nightfall, while his little son played at building houses with the scattered fragments of marble, when, on the hillside below them, they heard a roar of laughter, not mirthful, but slow, and even solemn, like a wind shaking the boughs of the forest.

"Father, what is that?" asked the little boy, leaving his play . . .
                          "Ethan Brand."

Hawthorne is writing a distinctly literary type of story, usually with a symbolic and didactic intent. But, as the fine artist, he instinctively moves toward a more and more arresting presentation of his theme. Study him as the artist and avoid overloading your story with revelation of deep truth—unless you want to attempt a George Ade moral at the very end.

After the tone has been determined, our next important problem, as we have noted in the first paragraph of this section, is the adoption of a specific point of view. And here again, we might theorize at length. Professor C. L. Maxcy,[1] for example, notes three points of view: (1) the angle of some person in the narrative; (2) the focus of several angles; and (3) a wholly external angle. Mr. Clayton Hamilton suggests two: (1), the internal, which subdivides into (a) that of a leading character, (b) that of a subsidiary character, (c) that of different characters alternating, or (d) the epistolary; and, (2), the external, which indicates (a) the omniscient, (b) the limited, and (c) the rigidly restricted. But all this theory seems to involve too much excess baggage for the writing of a simple plot story. In actual practice the point of view will determine itself fairly well. Both you and your reader must be sure what it is, and you must maintain or change it consistently.

The simple plot story, as we are treating it, employs only two main points of view. Inasmuch as the majority of your plots may be taken from the diary or autobiography, the point of view will generally be strictly personal. The stories will generally be related from the angle of the first person—the pronoun *I*—that is, the internal angle with you as central character. However, for variation, it is easy to project yourself outside the picture and pose as an onlooker of your own actions—and of those of all the other characters, for that matter. This means adopting an external point of view, either the omniscient, or the restricted, as preferred: you may know all that happens in the minds and lives of the characters, even before it is revealed in the story; or, like Jim Hawkins, of *Treasure Island*, in the apple barrel, you become aware of events only as they occur. Finally, when you have gained sufficient control of narrative technique, vary the point of view even more by presenting the story from the point of view of several characters in alternation, in dialogue, letters, or by such means as ingenuity and the nature of the events may suggest. However,

[1] In his *Rhetorical Principles of Narration*, Houghton Mifflin Company, 1911.

always bear in mind one principle: there will be *very few*—preferably not more than two or three—characters in these plot stories. And even these few should require no elaborate delineation.

To illustrate these three points of view precisely: A touring car is parked at the top of a short, steep hill, slippery with rain or ice, and at the bottom there is a grade crossing. You and your dog are lolling in the rear seat, while your friend the driver, having just parked the car, dashes into a store on an errand. A speedy interurban train is approaching in the distance. The brakes of the car have been hastily set; perhaps because of the vibration caused by the train, the car suddenly starts down hill and the emergency brake jams.

Now choose a point of view. First you can go through the experience in the car as "I." Second, you can station yourself on the corner at the top of the hill as a witness, and watch yourself and dog go down to that crossing. Or, third, you can tell the story from the point of view of a man at the bottom of the hill, of the engineer on the approaching train, or even of the dog, with varied results. It will be apparent, though, that the point of view which is most vitally tense is that of the helpless person in the car who expects to be cut to bits. Even the omniscient method is limited: you will fail to identify yourself sympathetically with the action, and a tone of indifference may result. In this case you may fail to convey fully the terror of the occupant of the car. And further, if you select an external point of view, stranger, engineer, or dog, you will have to project yourself *into their characters* in order to comment on the incident vividly, and this requires considerable extra, perhaps futile, exertion. Hence the important fact at once appears—*the choice of point of view is linked up inextricably with the tone of the story*. Having chosen an incident with a distinct tone or force of a certain type—in this case, the horror involved in the descent of that runaway car toward the train—adopt a point of view so related to that tone as to support it as fully as possible. In this case the internal "I" is obviously the best. The omniscient external will rank second; and the others will have to be rejected. In practically every case involving a plot story, the "I" point of view will create the most tenseness. So consider that point of view first, with the omniscient as second choice.

With the tone and point of view decided, the story can now be started on paper. We have established our basic situation; now we come physically to the problem of the prelude and moment of interest. We say "physically," because both have been determined mentally by the choice of the tone. The problem now is simply to get them down in the quickest and most effective manner. But, even before pen is put to paper, the factor of suspense, and the climax and solution also, ought to be predetermined. In other words, the plot story should not be written out piecemeal, section by section, without being wholly conceived mentally beforehand. Careful preconception will produce a more unified and compact effect, with the emotional elements of suspense and surprise much more artfully calculated and placed. In general, never commit a prelude and moment of interest to paper and then wander like Lowell's "musing organist." Improvising is the legitimate amusement of the master technician. The fact remains, however, that for experimental and theoretical purposes, the prelude and moment of interest can be written down without the slightest thought of the succeeding stages from suspense to climax to solution. So we shall now discuss these two preliminary features further by themselves, showing three possible methods of presenting them in the narrative.

Of the three, the most conventional method is to state the salient facts of the situation just before the opening action occurs. This more leisurely approach is usual with Hawthorne. Give a sense of the scene; the characters (age, sex, condition must be perfectly clear), and presumably what they are doing at the moment; the time, perhaps even the hour and minute; and any significant details that may suggest and intensify the tone. For example—jotting them down at random before writing: dimly lighted, deserted street; midnight; man and woman at a door, the man fumbling with a key; light snow falling in the street; Christmas Eve; bells tolling; lights in windows. That is enough. In an outline, which should be submitted for every story in the early stages of the work, these details can be jotted down just like that. Written out, they would take an order dependent on what was going to happen the next moment, that is, at the moment of interest. If we were to follow the order listed above, obviously the tone would be determined already, for the "dimly lighted, deserted street" and "midnight" would give a sensation of uneasiness as to what might be about to happen. Incidentally, you may find in your preliminary list some details which are inconsistent with the tone, such as "lights in windows." This detail would have to be discarded, or reserved for later use. Finally, the prelude should be brief. It should not occupy more than one short paragraph in the average four-hundred-word story such as you will write.

The moment of interest should follow and be consistent with the tone which is struck in the opening. In reality, however, it is determined mentally even before the tone in your preconception of the story. One sentence should serve for this second element in the story structure—a short, powerful, driving, perhaps even brutal, sentence. In the above hypothetical story, for instance, we could follow the details, as ordered, with something lurid, like this: "Across the street a small, rat-like man sprang from a basement entrance, leveled a revolver at the woman, fired, and sped rapidly down the street." Though distinctly melodramatic, this action clinches the tone; and, while the puff of smoke is drifting upwards in the frozen air, you will have your reader jumping with you to follow the owner of the revolver down the street. Once you have the reader on the run, you have won your point. The work of the prelude and moment of interest has been done; the basic situation has been established. The game now is to work out the incidents of suspense which lead on to the climax and solution.

The other two types of opening for the plot story may be suggested briefly, for they are essentially variations of the above. Some writers prefer an explosive opening. This is really a reversal of the usual order: the moment of interest is put before the prelude. "Cra-a-ack! I had fallen through the ice!"; then the prelude proper is turned into exposition, explaining briefly how I had happened to be on the ice at that particular time (after dark) and in that particularly dangerous spot (the middle of the millpond, a short cut home from basket-ball practice). Immediately a return is made as quickly as possible to the actual story, that is, to the incidents of suspense. There is no objection to this shifting of order, provided it be well handled. The relative lengths of the two divisions remain the same. But the tendency of this type is to exhaust the reader's interest too abruptly, with a resulting monotony to follow; or else there is likely to be too decided and violent a tone and a melodramatic unreality. For plot-story construction it provides merely a useful variation from the first method.

The third type of beginning consists in prefixing to the first type—it could not be done smoothly with the second—a sort of Aesopian moral, to be exemplified by the subsequent story. Thus, George Ade's conclusion—"Never marry a girl until you see her mother"—might be the opening sentence of the story, followed by "I'll tell you why." Or consider the following: "You may say men will do anything for money—men, not women, of course. But I doubt it. For example I was . . ." Then go ahead with a story of an ultimate strain of honesty in a crook. The moral which adorns the tale at the beginning no doubt gives a degree of tone, for it acquaints the reader with the theme of the story to follow. But at the same time it may destroy curiosity; and, except in the hands of an expert (Kipling or O. Henry, for example), it may too much suggest the sermon and obliterate interest instead of arousing it. Hence, like the second method, it should be used sparingly for variety and special effects. Both of these types, too, must inevitably be opened, if not entirely written, in the retrospective past tense.

Tone and point of view, both applied to a short, effective writing out of the prelude and moment of interest, will start the plot story off with a driving momentum and attract the reader at once. Normally in a physical development, suspense is the next element in the sequence of plot elements. However, climax and a surprise solution are of greater importance, and usually should be *thought out* before the suspense is actually developed. They represent the end toward which the suspense aims, and to a large extent govern the direction in which the action moves. They are simpler, too, to determine, being single events, whereas suspense requires concentrated thinking to build up increasingly higher waves of emotional tension. For the moment, the importance of climax and solution may be grasped, with regard to their functions in the structure of the story, if the student asks which is the most important period in an initiation ordeal—or a "blind date"—the beginning, the middle, or the end?

→» A «←

Four of the student stories in this chapter have been split up, the various elements, prelude, suspense, etc., being distributed in the appropriate sections. These are as follows: "A Narrow Escape Boating," "The Fugitive," "Buck Fever," and "A Lynch Victim's Last Minutes." The complete story may be reconstructed simply by turning to each successive stage.

The following story presents a perfect example of clean-cut beginning (prelude followed by moment of interest); but students have objected that the ensuing rescue could not take place in the time allowed by the hundred yards of water before the dam would be reached.

A NARROW ESCAPE BOATING

The folks had gone to town, and our nearest neighbors were two miles away. Paul and I thought that this would be a good time to take the motor boat, which we had always been forbidden to touch.

I took the wheel, and we were soon sailing full speed down the stream. With the aid of the current and the power of the boat I believed that I could give Paul a real thrill. We were within one hundred yards of the dam, and I could see he was growing uneasy. I gave the wheel a sudden turn, expecting to scare Paul, but in doing so I broke the guide ropes to the rudder. We were now helplessly drifting toward the falls.

E. F.

"The Fugitive" starts quickly (moment of interest followed by exposition); the basic situation is sufficiently powerful. See whether the point of view is consistent with the treatment of suspense as presented in the next section.

THE FUGITIVE

Two shots, a groan, a diabolical laugh—then silence. Once again, Old Joe's gun had barked, after five years of silence while he had been serving time in the penitentiary; and now he was again a fugitive from the law.

G. V.

It is not absolutely necessary to maintain a fixed point of view throughout: the story may be broken into numbered sections for shifting points of view. The following story was originally written without sections indicated; the sectioning improved it.

BUCK FEVER

I

A shot broke the deep silence of the great forest. A shot which echoed and re-echoed, tossed from tree to tree—a plaything of the whims and fancies of nature. A moment of silence, and then four more shots followed in rapid succession. Out in a little clearing, the figure of a man shuddered and quivered with the impact of the swiftly moving death missiles, and then sank to the ground in a shapeless huddle—lifeless and inert.

II

A hunter tramped through the woods, with a song in his heart and a smile on his face; for this was his first hunting expedition, and the first chance he had ever had to get venison for himself. Suddenly, as he neared a small, cultivated clearing, which broke the monotonous expanse of treetops, his attention was focused by the sight of a magnificent buck which was slowly sauntering across the open—not a hundred yards from him. The hunter quickly raised his gun, but could not aim because a sudden trembling had seized him. He jerked the rifle to position and fired in the general direction of the unwary deer. With a bound, his now frightened quarry leaped into the safe refuge of the trees and was gone; but there in the clearing before the startled eyes of the hunter was a human being into whom the bullet had gone. Panic filled the hunter's breast—he had killed a man! . . .

M. S.

The potential terror in the situation presented in the next story is heightened by its presentation from the inside of the mind of the character. The technique is essentially what is known as "stream of consciousness," the source a newspaper episode.

A LYNCH VICTIM'S LAST MINUTES

"I know I'm to blame. I know I'm guilty. Thurmond wouldn't of had the guts to do it without my leadin' him. Listen to that crowd —and it's me they want.

"But they won't get me, they won't—they won't. I won't die yet;

they can't kill me. I still have my rights; I haven't been convicted. They can't hang me without giving me a trial—an' a jury too. . . ."

A. T.

⇥ B ⇤

The following professional illustrations use the normal order:

There is a hotel on Broadway that has escaped discovery by the summer-resort promoters. It is deep and wide and cool. Its rooms are finished in dark oak of a low temperature. Homemade breezes and deep-green shrubbery give it the delights without the inconveniences of the Adirondacks . . .

. . . .

In this July came to the hotel one whose card that she sent to the clerk for her name to be registered read "Mme. Héloise D'Arcy Beaumont."

O. Henry, "Transients in Arcadia." [1]

Denis de Beaulieu was not yet two and twenty, but he counted himself a grown man, and a very accomplished cavalier into the bargain. . . . He had put up his horse with due care, and supped with due deliberation; and then, in a very agreeable frame of mind, went out to pay a visit in the gray of the evening. It was not a very wise proceeding on the young man's part. . . . For the town was full of the troops of Burgundy and England under a mixed command. . . .

It was September, 1429; the weather had fallen sharp. . . .

R. L. Stevenson, "The Sire de Malétroit's Door." [2]

Notice how quickly the following story begins:

Before nine o'clock it was pretty well known all along the river that the two parties of the "Amity Claim" had quarrelled and separated at daybreak. At that time the attention of their nearest neighbor had been attracted by the sounds of altercations and two consecutive pistol-shots. . . .

Bret Harte, "The Iliad of Sandy Bar." [3]

The next two illustrations show a reversed prelude and moment of interest.

[1] From *Voice of the City*, by O. Henry, copyright, 1904, by Doubleday, Doran & Company, Inc. Reprinted by permission.

[2] Reprinted by permission of the publishers, Charles Scribner's Sons.

[3] Reprinted by permission of the publishers, Houghton Mifflin Company.

"It happened just as I have said," Fernet reiterated, tossing the wine-dregs from his glass.

The company at the table looked instinctively toward the kitchen. Berthe was bringing a fresh pot of coffee. They all followed Fernet's example, lifting their empty glasses for her to serve them in their turn.

The regular boarders of the Hôtel de France, after the fashion of folks who find their meal a duty to be promptly despatched, had departed, but the transients still lingered over their *café noir* and cognac in the hope that something exciting might materialize. . . .

C. C. Dobie, "The Open Window." [1]

Thirty days lost in jail because of a woman's vanity. Because Anna whined that she wanted a hat. He'd see to her. Didn't the Bible say that a man should be master of his own household? Just wait until he got home.

It had happened this way . . .

Elise M. Rushfeldt, "A Coffin for Anna." [1]

The first-person point of view is simple:

The thousand injuries of Fortunato I had borne as I best could, but when he ventured upon insult, I vowed revenge. . . .

Edgar Allan Poe, "The Cask of Amontillado."

It was twenty years ago, and on an evening in May. All day long there had been sunshine. . . .

Only at sunset did I leave the house . . .

George Gissing, "Christopherson." [2]

It was a hard jolt for me, one of the bitterest I ever had to face. And it all came about through my own foolishness too . . .

Sherwood Anderson, "I'm a Fool." [3]

But the third-person point of view is quite as popular.

Snow falling over London; a great blur of zigzagging flakes; the embankment was deserted; the streets half-filled; in the houses of Parliament long windows etched themselves in light; Westminster Abbey was almost obliterated by the downfall, its time-stained crevices had filled, like cups, with drifts of snow.

[1] Reprinted by permission of the author.
[2] Reprinted by permission of the publishers, E. P. Dutton & Co. Inc., from *The House of Cobwebs and Other Stories.*
[3] Reprinted by permission of the author.

Out of the obscurity and the snow a soldier approached Westminster.

He paused a moment on the opposite side of the street. . . .

SUSAN M. BOOGHER, "An Unknown Warrior." [1]

His greatest pleasure in life came always at dusk. Its prelude was the reading of the evening paper in the train that took him out of the city . . .

CONRAD AIKEN, "The Dark City." [2]

A moral in the opening sentence is sometimes effective. It appears in two, at least, of Kipling's stories, "The Man Who Would Be King" and "Thrown Away." O. Henry also could get the right effect with it, as in "A Municipal Report," or in the opening of "A Service of Love: [3]"

When one loves one's Art no service seems too hard.

That is our premise. This story shall draw a conclusion from it . . .

Similar in effect to the moralistic beginning is the following opening. [4]

"It's a queer thing," said Terence O'Meara, with a wink at his brother Jack and a glance at the bald spot on the top of his father's head; "it's a queer thing that the Irish let the English and the French, the Spanish and the Dutch, all get ahead of them in exploring and settling America."

DON MARQUIS, "O'Meara, 'The Mayflower' and Mrs. MacLirr."

The next example [5] uses a unique type of conversational atmosphere, though it is not conversation.

You don't like a small town? Well now that's odd. You can give me one every time. In a big place you can be born and grow up and marry a fortune and then die maybe and leave it all, and nobody is any the wiser or gives a damn. But in a little burg you've got everybody spotted and they've got you spotted. . . .

L. C. WIMBERLY, "White Man's Town."

---

[1] Reprinted by permission of the editor of the *Junior League Magazine*.

[2] Reprinted from *Bring, Bring*, by permission of the author and of The Liveright Publishing Corporation, publishers.

[3] Reprinted from *The Four Million*, by O. Henry, copyright, 1905, by permission of the publishers, Doubleday, Doran & Company, Inc.

[4] Reprinted by permission of the author and Doubleday, Doran & Company, Inc. holders of the copyright.

[5] Reprinted from *The Forum* (1931) by permission of the author.

Compare also S. V. Benét's "Uriah's Son," Sherwood Anderson's "Alice," and Peter Neagoe's "Shepherd of the Lord," for other recent illustrations.

3. SUSPENSE

The word suspense is derived from the Latin *suspensus*, meaning "hung up" or "dangling." Thus the power of suspense keeps the reader dangling in anticipation as he strains toward the final moment—the end of the race, the verdict of the jury, the moment of victory, or defeat. According to the nature of the story, a chain of crises, surprises, reversals, clashes of force, or other emotionally gripping episodes holds the reader's attention. This hold must be carefully calculated and sustained from the moment of interest to the climax, the final breaking point. To exaggerate a bit, suspense is a kind of craftily preconceived torture for both characters and reader. The writer simply sits back and, with the moment of interest, climax, and solution already in mind, somewhat fiendishly plans out as many things as he can think of to impose upon his character before he permits the final cry of despair (climax) and the immediate relaxation (solution). This cold, deliberate tantalizing, like cat and mouse, demands a will for devising situations. Anyone who has felt his heart speed up and his spine stiffen at a thrilling film can cultivate such a will by studying the effects which result from the teasing suspense calls for.

Popular with students are situations involving danger. These awaken the most deep-seated and powerful instincts, notably self-preservation. It is instructive to begin with such situations, where emotions are in the "crude" state—later equivalent urges to social self-preservation, involving reputation and self-esteem, fall naturally into line. However, these merge into the field of character, beyond the strict plot story.

To illustrate, we shall now outline the sequence of suspense for two plot stories. One, the "lost" story is slow in movement, basing suspense on prolonged agony; the other, a story of "sudden danger," represents a quick, abrupt tempo. At the end we shall recapitulate the devices used and their effects.

First, the "lost" story: *Prelude* and *Moment of Interest*—at five P.M. on a winter day; boy of sixteen hunting in deep woods with his dog; after shooting a rabbit and a partridge, he finds himself lost; *Climax*—the fourth day of helpless wandering; totally exhausted, famished, nearly frozen, he has given up in despair; *Solution*—(external type) the dog he drove towards home on the second day brings help, or (internal type) he contrives a message, sends the dog out with it, and is found unconscious. (Devise others yourself—see section 4 below.)

The following traces the stages in suspense. Notice that external forces, the obstacles and threats to the boy's safety, come first, while the corresponding psychological reactions follow. Thus incidents roughly alternate between positive and negative.

1. The boy scans horizon for familiar contours in the mountains.
   After several moments he gives up with a shake of the head.

2. He climbs a tree for clearer view.
   Useless—he recognizes no landmarks.

3. He tries to follow moss on trees.
   Darkness stops him.

4. He lights a fire and cooks the rabbit.
   Dog must be fed—this emergency worries him about food.

5. He prepares spot for the night.
   Has no extra clothes, and not enough loose wood for long fire.

6. He cuddles up with dog and tries to sleep.
   Too cold: almost sleepless night.

7. Morning comes and he shares remainder of rabbit with dog, and sets out to follow moss and sun.
   Sun goes behind clouds, and trees finally confuse him.

8. At noon he eats again—the partridge. (He may drive the dog away now if Solution I is to be used.)[1]
   His last bit of food.

9. In afternoon he tries to hunt up food and keeps eye on one specific mountain on horizon.
   Finds his shells all dampened during night. Is getting exhausted.

10. He sits down to dry the shells.
    Matches are wet (or lost, preferably).

11. He stops to find suitable cover for the night.
    He is hungry, tired, and faces freezing. (Some psychology.)

[1] For types of solution, see section 4 below.

12. He tries to settle down to sleep.
    The weather grows colder—he is afraid to sleep and walks about all night.

13. Near morning he catches a partridge on limb and eats part of it raw. (Do not forget dog if Solution II is to be used.)[1]

14. He picks out another mountain and sets resolutely forward.
    Snow comes, obscuring the landmark.

15. He stops to rest.
    Psychologically now he is preparing to give up—hungry, cold, tired, discouraged.

16. He hits a squirrel with a stick.
    Cannot find it in snow. (Remember the dog, though, may be there.)

17. He eats bark.
    It sickens him and weakens him.

18. He sees a rabbit.
    Goes after it so eagerly he falls and breaks his leg and his gun.

19. He prepares shelter for night.
    His resistance is now so low he knows he may die. (He may be aware, too, that sometimes men go mad after being alone in the woods a few days. Use this psychology.)

20. In the course of dragging himself along during night he stumbles on a logger's hut.
    It is empty of everything he hoped to find.

21. He is sheltered from snow during night.
    Morning finds him physically and psychologically at the——

Climax: Here he may send dog back, if internal solution is used, and relapse into unconsciousness.

Solution: When he awakes, the dog is licking his face, and a searching party is at hand.

Throughout this consciously formulated scheme of suspense the "torture" is constantly increased. Artful handling of the boy's state of mind keeps the reader dangling in hope of his survival. On the fourth day the fatal straw would break the camel's back— that is, now the solution must enter to account for death or rescue. A steadily rising emotional tension, with the devil of despair constantly getting the better of the good angel of hope,

---

[1] See section 4 below.

results from the tricks of suspense. External forces and psycho-logical tremors of mind produce an oscillating effect like that of the alternating current. All the essentials of suspense are there.

Now that story was long. The suspense was sustained purposely. For a shorter story the twenty-one situations might be reduced by half; as a matter of fact there was no need whatever for using *all* those incidents. Our intention was, as every writer's intention should be, to get down on paper (*before writing*) as many situations as possible, then to *choose discriminately those which will produce the ultimate effect (the tone) we wish to create:* horror, pathos, grim irony, and so forth. The above program of suspense would develop into a plot story of two thousand words or more. To cut it down to a thousand, it is necessary only to cut down the time—the number of days or hours—and concentrate a few of the incidents in one day instead of four. However, as we noted in the previous chapter, the diary will provide better incidents for a short plot story. The type of story outlined above would probably be derived from an autobiography.

Our second development of suspense, then, illustrates the briefer incident from a diary: threatened drowning. The problem now is to whip up suspense quickly, within five or ten minutes' reading time.

Moment of Interest: You fall out of a boat beyond your depth and cannot swim, or else are suddenly seized with cramps.

Climax: the third time down.

Solution: external—someone dives after you; or internal—you grab the anchor rope and pull yourself up or the cramps disappear. (Devise others yourself.)

Suspense: 1. You call for help.
Nobody is in sight, and you get a mouthful of water.

2. You tread water violently—instinctively.
Your arms give out.

3. You try to grasp boat.
You miss it.

4. You see somebody.
You start going under.

5. You hit bottom hard the first time and push up.
You just miss reaching the seat of the overturned boat.

6. You manage to get rid of some water but cannot shout.
   You go down a second time—negative psychology now in action.
7. Nearing top again you come up under the boat and manage to push it around a bit.
   Your finger slips off the seat and you start going down for the third time. Use all the negative psychology possible.

Then *Climax* and *Solution*.

People who have actually been threatened with drowning will be able to develop the suspense much better than this. We have only jotted down what survivors and imagination tell us might happen in a few minutes, and the items are sufficient for only a very short plot story. Again, emphasis is on external forces at the beginning and on psychology at the end. And once more, the principle of the alternating current is mechanically applied. Obviously, though, it is not necessary to balance positive and negative elements so regularly. They may go in waves of fortune and misfortune, in groups, that is. But always the negative factor should neutralize, or even outweigh, the preceding positive group of events. Always, too, the character should, by the neutralizing of the positive, be endangered more and more. Thus suspense is always rising and the outcome grows increasingly dubious. Ultimately (both character and reader feel) tension may reach the breaking point; persistent dread of this pulls the reader farther and farther into the story. If you once relax that dread too much, that is by slighting negative incidents and thus helping the character, the story is lost; for the reader must be held by suspense to the very end.

Finally, note two important features of suspense—the relative length and convincingness. In proportion to the other divisions of the story, suspense is by far the longest. In a sense the suspense *is* the story, particularly in the plot story. The longer the emotional span of suspense, the higher the pitch of interest at the climax, provided no lapse of interest has been allowed to creep in. The following graph shows the structure of a simple plot story, rising on a straight line from prelude to conclusion. Note that more than half of the line is devoted to suspense alone.

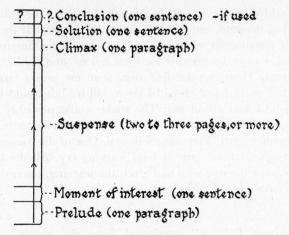

.-?-Conclusion (one sentence) –if used
--Solution (one sentence)
--Climax (one paragraph)

--Suspense (two to three pages, or more)

--Moment of interest (one sentence)
--Prelude (one paragraph)

The final element is convincingness. For example, in the "lost" story above we had written down as the negative feature of the sixth sequence: "Wolves." We left it there for a moment and proceeded. But something about it worried us. It was not quite logical—too much of a coincidence. It did not convince us at all. So we went back and substituted, "Too cold." Ask yourself whether you do not think we saved the story right there so far as convincingness at that spot was concerned. And what do you think of our 7th, 13th, and 17th sequences in the same story? Should they be changed? Should one or two be omitted? What happened to the "almost blind" denoted in our preconceived climax? And would that boy eat so fast at first? Such are the questions you must put to yourself on your own suspense sequence *before you begin to write out the story.*

>>> A <<<

After a good start the author of the following ruined the suspense by getting herself into a safe situation at the end of the first paragraph. Had she fallen down and broken her ankle at the beginning, there would have been a real story.

THE COMBAT BETWEEN THE SNAKE AND THE COCK

It was a fine summer morning, and, as it was my last vacation day at my uncle's farm, I thought I would wander about and take a last look around the place. Feeling full of pep and song, I strolled around saying good-bye to the household animals. I came to the poultry yard and stood at the gate, watching the hens and roosters eat their breakfast. While standing there and watching, I heard something rustling on the ground. I turned around to see what it was—and my heart leaped to my throat. There, several feet away from me, was a large rattlesnake. What could I do? Should I try to kill it—but would I succeed in killing it? I was afraid not. The snake would probably be upon me before I could get ready to strike it. I opened the gate and ran into the poultry yard. The snake followed. One of the roosters, seeing the snake approaching, gave a loud warning cry. All the hens and roosters, except the one who had given the warning, hurried into the large hen house, and I with them.

O. K.

"A Narrow Escape," continued from the previous section, creates excitement without sacrificing naturalness of language.

The first thing that came to my mind was to yell for help, but I remembered that no one could possibly be near. Then I thought of jumping and swimming for shore, and, motioning to Paul to leap, I stood on the side of the boat. He immediately rushed to my side, saying that he couldn't swim a stroke. We were drifting sideways toward the dam, which now was only fifty yards away. I climbed down and began using my hand as a rudder and paddling vigorously, but the determined current swept us on. The roar of the water falling became louder and the possibilities of escape less.

Realizing that every minute counted, I then jumped overboard and, grabbing the front of the boat, I tried to pull it for shore. I saw that I made no headway except that I was able to turn it. I called Paul to start the engine, and told him that I would remain in front and steer. He spun the flywheel several times, but shouted frantically that he couldn't start the motor. I saw the sticks and leaves dropping out of sight over the falls, only a short distance away. I knew that it was only a matter of a few minutes until we too would go over the falls and be crushed with the boat in the undercurrent below. I managed to climb back into the boat, and at the same instant Paul started the motor. We were headed straight for the dam, and only twenty-five short yards separated us from our doom.

"The Fugitive" concentrates the suspense within the mind and actions of the character. (See the beginning in previous section.)

He took to a small trail leading to an old mountain hideout, which he remembered before the rest were caught, with the thought that at last he had gained his revenge on the man who had caused his conviction. For the first time, however, Joe's gun had not been true, and by morning he knew he was being followed. Down in the valley he heard the baying of bloodhounds. He knew what that meant. Those critters would follow a man to his grave. However, he might be able to shake them at the little mountain stream he must cross, before reaching the hideout.

A short time before noon he reached the stream, and, though the icy waters made him catch his breath, he waded up the center of the stream for almost a mile. Coming out on the opposite bank, he struck out through the dense underbrush and shortly regained the trail. He had listened with great apprehension to the hounds, but soon after he hit the trail he noticed they stopped quite suddenly. An evil smile spread over his face as he chuckled to himself in outwitting the law. He went on with lighter heart, but his ease was short-lived.

The tracking party had broken up where he entered the stream. Some went up, the others down, and one of the hounds picked up the scent where he had climbed the bank, and immediately gave tongue. It seemed to spur him on, and, though the way became more rugged and the trail harder to climb, about three the following morning he reached the end of it and his destination. For the first time he realized that he had had nothing to eat, but Joe knew the hideout, and very soon he was feeling much better after a cold meal. His next move was for his defense against those who followed. He soon had his munitions placed, and then he sat down to watch and wait.

If they wanted him they would have to come and get him, and from the mouth of the cave, which had been remodeled into a miniature fortress, he commanded the whole trail. The trail was about six feet wide, in the shape of a crescent, and from an enormous boulder about one hundred yards down, which Joe called Guardian Rock, there were only a few scattered heaps of stone, which offered little protection. On one side a sheer wall of stone rose straight to the sky, while below on the other could be seen the treetops.

The dogs' baying came louder; they could not be far away now. A rifle lay across his knees and the finger on the trigger twitched spasmodically, as though eager for action. It was lightening, far across the valley in the east, when a man stepped past Guardian Rock and stopped at the situation before him. The end of the trail was in sight, but well he knew what probably lay behind those few rocks which lay at the mouth of the cave. He drew back. A conference was called, a decision reached; Joe must be taken, and anyone else with him.

Joe was all attention now. His gun rested between two rocks and he watched carefully and eagerly for some movement along that trail. He had not long to wait. In the early morning dusk, his keen eye soon picked out the sliding form of a man, working his way upward along the trail. Joe's gun spoke, the form lay still, then three bullets rattled on the rocks before him. He chuckled. They were coming for him, eh—well, he'd give them a few of his lead calling cards. Another movement; Joe's gun spoke again, and he heard the barrel of the other's gun drop against the stone. It was getting lighter. They would have to get him soon, or they would all be dead. There was a man lying like a stone near the ledge of the trail. A lead messenger found him too; he staggered to his feet, then pitched over into space.

From its beginning with a wholly unpremeditated crime, "Buck Fever" carries on to what the Germans would call a fate tragedy.

Self-preservation, however, was his first cowardly instinct, and so with a fear born of despair—fear that he would be convicted of murder —he desperately fired the four remaining shots into the still swaying body of the man, and watched the figure slowly sink to the ground. Through the mist in his brain he kept repeating the words, "Dead men tell no tales!"

Back in the city, the hunter became the hunted. His conscience dogged him unceasingly, and made his very existence miserable.

"I was justified in those last four shots," he would say aloud; "the first bullet killed him, and it was only accidental anyway."

"You lie," shrieked that small accusing voice, "the man was not dead. You could have saved him, but your own miserable fear made you think of your own safety first."

He could no longer work, because of his tormented mind, and, as a result, lost his position. His fear of discovery made him remain in hiding all day and gave him only the nights to seek his sustenance; for, like all criminals, he had left some evidence behind. His brown hunting cap, with his name inside, had fallen from his head when he had fired the first shot, and still lay at the edge of that little clearing— an open book to the identity of the murderer.

Seeking relief from this situation, he decided to revisit the scene of his crime, and get his hat: to destroy all evidence of his work by burying the body of that gruesome figure in the slouch hat which haunted his every hour; but he no longer had the means to undertake that long trip, and he was far too terrified to leave the safety of his garret hide-away if he did have the means.

A green mist floated perpetually before his mind's eye, in which a shrieking maniac seemed to appear and disappear; to lie slumped in a shapeless mass, and then to take shape and enlarge until it became enormous. The fog swirled and churned, and the figure in it was never the same, never still. It contracted, enlarged, and bulged, like an image formed by a row of distorting mirrors. Its eyes never changed. They were horribly distended and mocking, and in them glowed a strange red light—the only variation from the sickly green mist which enveloped everything.

Too great expansion of time is fatal to suspense. In contrast to the preceding narrative, notice the compact, sustained suspense in the continuation of "A Lynch Victim's Last Minutes."

A shower of stones struck the walls with a deafening roar. The crowd grew larger each minute; each newcomer added his voice to the clamor. The sheriff and his officers battled stoutly, but to no avail. There was no stopping that maddened throng of human wolves howling for bloody vengeance. In a last desperate effort the peace officers hurled tear bombs among the rioters. Choking, blinded, over-come by the powerful gases, the people drew back; but only tem-porarily. They were waiting for the fumes to lift a little. In the next cell Thurmond cowered in a corner, whimpering foolishly like a youngster surrounded by savage dogs.

"He wouldn't o' done it if it hadn't been for me. Just seventeen days ago he was working in his service station. Now Hart is dead. . . . The fool! Hiding in a corner! A lot of good that will do him if *they* ever get in!—But they won't get me; I'll fight. . . . Damn 'em anyway, I didn't do anything to them . . . only to young Hart. . . . What do they care about him?

"The air's getting clearer; they'll be back in a few minutes. Why don't they take us away? Why don't they shoot at that crowd? We've still got our rights. They're back! They're in! They're in! They've broken in the door. Here they come. Oh, God! it's up now; it's all over! They'll be here in a minute. . . .

"Look, they're asking for Serpa. Maybe they'll take him and Thurmond and be satisfied. Maybe they'll leave me alone. I didn't do anything to them; I didn't hurt them . . . only Hart! . . . No! They don't want Serpa. He only shot a ranchman; they don't want him. Here they come—they'll take Thurmond; he's next.

"Look at the fool. Look at him; he's not fighting. Look at him beg and whimper. A lot of good his whimpering will do now. They're beating him. He's senseless; he's knocked down. There they go, draggin' him after them. They won't get me that way. I'll fight. I won't let them drag *me* out like that an' hang me. They can't do that to me. . . .

"You can't take me out of here. I didn't do anything to you. You can't unlock that door. DON'T DO THAT. . . . There, maybe that'll teach you. . . . There's too many of them. If there was only one or two, I'd have a chance to get loose. If I escape from one, another grabs me. . . .

"If I could only get loose and run—run. Here in the park I might get away, in the darkness and the confusion.

"What's that? What's that white thing up there? that white thing dangling at the end of a rope. My God, it's Thurmond; it's Thurmond. They've hung him already.

"What are they doing now? What are they trying to do? They've got a rope over that limb. They're trying to put it around my neck! It is around my neck! I've got to get it off—got to—. There, that's better. I can breathe again, now. Now what are they up to?"

"Mischief Will Out" is a rather dramatic story, the suspense depending on the dramatic motif of foreknowledge given the reader. Dramatic suspense can also be secured by the use of such devices as overhearing and disguise.

MISCHIEF WILL OUT

Bud was a youth with a quaintly un-modern penchant for intrigue. Timidity, however, held in check this inclination to the extent that most of his escapades took place where most of them do—in his imagination. But these latent leanings cropped forth in a burst of initiative when he saw, on a table in his girl friend's house, the back of an envelope on which was the return address of a young lady in New York state. So he filched the address, and wrote a very engaging and slightly mysterious letter, cautiously giving his last name as Mack, which was only half the truth. Since no normally romantic girl can resist a winning letter from an unknown man, a correspondence began.

R. H.

There is plenty of suspense in the following two paragraphs; consider the fact that the swimmer is now in an underground cavern and has to swim *back*, presumably. How will he get out?

We stopped the boat near one of the larger openings, which was about three or four feet in diameter and ten feet under water. I stepped up on the bow of the craft and examined the cavern carefully. All of us thought that it would be best to dive for the entrance itself, since it was so far under water. Taking a deep breath, I plunged down, down into the cave. Before I realized my predicament, I was caught in a powerful current and swept through the passage. I clutched wildly to stop myself, but there was nothing to which I could hold, the walls having been worn smooth by the water, and now it was too late to turn back. My only hope was to swim forward in the expectation of coming to the surface of the water inside. Suddenly the tunnel made a turn upward. By this time I began to feel my need of air, and my lungs seemed almost bursting. The two minutes I had been under water had seemed like years to me. I became more terrified at the thought of drowning, and I pictured my corpse being taken from the lake. Then came the terrible feeling of despair and slowly I began to let out my breath.

Just as I was about to give up, my head came out into pure air. I gasped in the welcome oxygen and staggered, through the darkness, up a gradual incline until the water was only knee deep. I sat down exhausted and inhaled deeply until I had overcome the effects of my underground journey.

C. L.

The author of the following has the ability to put emotional suspense on paper. Does the title spoil the situation? Is the dialogue perfectly natural? This is a complete story.

IT'S ALL A MISTAKE

I bit the end of my tongue violently, as our roadster swerved sharply to the right just in time to avoid a head-on collision with an approaching car.

"Peter Hanley," I shrieked at the figure beside me, "will you stop acting like an idiot and drive on your side of the road!"

"Shut up," snapped Peter, and hunched down still farther over the wheel, never once slowing down.

"That's right," I shouted inelegantly over the roar of the motor; "kill us both." And I glared through the night's darkness at my companion's face.

"Well, why not?" came back the answer.

At this unreasonable reply my exasperation overcame me, and I said something for which I was immediately sorry.

"Well, I'll tell you 'why not.' Just because the doctor said you haven't long to live is no reason for killing me."

My mean-spirited words had the desired effect. The car slowed down and Peter looked contemplatively at the road ahead of us.

He turned to me.

"Do you want to go home?" he asked, much more considerate than he had been for the last few hours.

Immediately I was seized with contrition.

"Yes—but I'm sorry, Peter."

"Bah!" yelled Peter, and his foot came down on the accelerator. Our wild ride was resumed.

I settled resignedly down in my corner of the car and inwardly vowed that I'd wait until I was safely home before offering any more sympathy.

I'm not hard-hearted, but I had been riding most of the late afternoon and the early part of the night at just that speed, and the strain was beginning to affect my nervous system.

Little did either of us think when we started out at noon that the day would end so unpleasantly. Peter had suggested that we make a pleasure jaunt out of his trip to the Tager Hospital. He would see the doctor, get his report, and then we would take a ride through Barton Hills.

But the doctor hadn't been there, and the stupid interne had blurted out the nasty truth, handed Peter his report, directed him to the Lincoln Hospital, and turned to the next waiting patient. The interne couldn't be expected to sympathize, I suppose, since he had probably never even seen Peter before.

But I *did* sympathize. I had been looking through the open door of the office, had seen Peter grab the report, thrust it in his pocket, and dash blindly to the door. However, it's hard to get sympathy into one's voice over the roar of a motor, and after repeated attempts I had given up.

My thoughts were rudely brought back to the present as we skidded in a hair-raising way around the first of the dangerous curves of Barton Hills.

I shivered as I gazed at the sloping declivity to my right, with nothing to separate it from the narrow road we were on. Peter increased the speed of the car.

"Peter," I pleaded desperately.

Then in a split second we rounded the last curve and came face to face with two cars racing abreast. The brakes shrieked. I lurched heavily against the windshield, bounced back against the seat and felt myself sinking numbly to the floor. Half-consciously I felt our car hesitate on the edge of the hill for a moment and then hurtle down through space.

Fear rendered me powerless. I tried to scream—then I lost consciousness.

I came to, with a dull ringing in my ears and a dull ache to my whole body. I opened my eyes to see a group of people surrounding us. Evidently someone had come to pull us out.

There was Peter, not far from me. He was sitting up and arguing with a man who had been searching his clothes for a mark of identification. Finally, he grabbed a paper from the man's hand and waved it at me.

"Marge," he shouted, "this isn't my doctor's report at all. It's for someone by the name of Peter Hansen. It's all a mistake."

I felt of my aching body and wondered just how much of a mistake it (the report) had been after all. By the looks of things—and I gazed at the wrecked car and Peter's bleeding shoulder—by the looks of things the interne hadn't been so far wrong, after all!

M. G.

Note that from the evidence of this last story you will be most successful with dialogue when you choose for speakers characters of about your own age and experience.

→≫ B ≪←

Consider the one-two beat of "An Occurrence at Owl Creek Bridge," [1] which begins thus:

A man stood upon a railroad bridge in northern Alabama, looking down into the swift water twenty feet below. The man's hands were behind his back, the wrists bound with a cord. A rope loosely encircled his neck . . . his executioners—two private soldiers of the Federal army . . .

The preparations being complete, the two private soldiers stepped aside, and each drew away the plank upon which he had been standing . . .

He closed his eyes in order to fix his last thoughts upon his wife and children.

. . . .

---

[1] From *In the Midst of Life*, by Ambrose Bierce, Albert & Charles Boni, Inc., copyright, 1909. Reprinted by permission of the publishers.

As Peyton Farquhar fell straight downward through the bridge he lost consciousness and was as one already dead. From this state he was awakened—ages later, it seemed to him—by the pain of a sharp pressure upon his throat, followed by a sense of suffocation. . . . The power of thought was restored; he knew that the rope had broken and he had fallen into the stream. . . . he knew that he was rising toward the surface. . . . "No; I will not be shot; that is not fair." . . . he was trying to free his hands. . . . The cord fell away . . . [he] pounced upon the noose at his neck . . . tore it away . . . his lungs engulfed a great draught of air . . .

He had come to the surface facing down the stream . . . he saw . . . the soldiers upon the bridge . . .

Suddenly he heard a sharp report and something struck the water smartly within a few inches of his head, spattering his face with spray . . . this one had missed. . . . "Attention, company! . . . Shoulder arms! . . . Ready! . . . Aim! . . . Fire!"

Farquhar dived—dived as deeply as he could . . . yet he heard the dulled thunder of the volley and, rising again toward the surface, met shining bits of metal, singularly flattened, oscillating slowly downward . . .

As he rose to the surface, gasping for breath, he saw that . . . the soldiers had almost finished reloading . . . .

The hunted man saw all this over his shoulder. . . .

An appalling plash within two yards of him [was] followed by a loud, rushing sound. . . . The cannon had taken a hand in the game. . . .

Suddenly he felt himself whirled round and round—spinning like a top. . . . He had been caught in a vortex and was being whirled on with a velocity of advance and gyration which made him giddy and sick. In a few moments he was flung upon the gravel at the foot of the left bank of the stream. . . .

A whizz and rattle of grapeshot among the branches high above his head roused him from his dream. . . . He sprung to his feet, rushed up the sloping bank, and plunged into the forest.

All that day he traveled. . . .

AMBROSE BIERCE, "An Occurrence at Owl Creek Bridge."

Consider this sequence from the same author, the solution of which appears below in section 4:

The snake had not moved and appeared somewhat to have lost its power upon the imagination. . . . It was as if the creature, assured of its triumph, had determined to practise no more alluring wiles.

Now ensued a fearful scene. The man, prone upon the floor, within a yard of his enemy, raised the upper part of his body upon his elbows, his head thrown back, his legs extended to their full length. His face was white between its stains of blood; his eyes were strained open to their uttermost expansion. There was froth upon his lips; it dropped off in flakes. Strong convulsions ran through his body, making almost serpentine undulations. He bent himself at the waist, shifting his legs from side to side. And every movement left him a little nearer to the snake. He thrust his hands forward to brace himself back, yet constantly advanced upon his elbows . . .

AMBROSE BIERCE, "The Man and the Snake." [1]

The same intensity appears in W. L. Comfort's "Fear," [2] the solution of which is given in the succeeding section. It is another snake story, with the huge python pursuing Hilliard and the black boy:

Once he turned. The python had looped and lowered. . . . He laughed and seemed to see his own face as he laughed. It was as if he were already dead. All he knew was that he must push the boy forward step by step, yard by yard until . . .

It was as if they were running a treadmill, making no actual progress, or like children escaping from a giant . . .

As the wet spongy footing hardened at the edge of the clearing, a great shadow lifted above them from behind. Hilliard's face upturned. The python had already chosen. The head hovered above them; the endless undulation was soft and slow, compared to his own and the boy's frenzied effort. The mouth was not open; the thin, loose, lateral lips were wet but calm; the eyes quiet, the ease of it all transcended . . . The choice had been made.

Fitz-James O'Brien's "What Was It?" [3] provides plenty of suspense!

While I was lying still as a corpse, hoping that by a perfect physical inaction I should hasten mental repose, an awful incident occurred. A Something dropped, as it seemed, from the ceiling, plumb upon my chest, and the next instant I felt two bony hands encircling my throat, endeavoring to choke me.

---

[1] From *In the Midst of Life*, Albert & Charles Boni, Inc. Reprinted by permission of the publishers.

[2] Reprinted by permission of Willimina L. Armstrong.

[3] Reprinted by permission of the publishers, Albert & Charles Boni, Inc.

I am no coward, and am possessed of considerable physical strength. The suddenness of the attack, instead of stunning me, strung every nerve to its highest tension. My body acted from instinct, before my brain had time to realize the terrors of my position. In an instant I wound two muscular arms around the creature, and squeezed it, with all the strength of despair, against my chest. In a few seconds the bony hands that had fastened on my throat loosened their hold, and I was free to breathe once more. Then commenced a struggle of awful intensity. Immersed in the most profound darkness, totally ignorant of the nature of the Thing by which I was so suddenly attacked, finding my grasp slipping every moment, by reason, it seemed to me, of the entire nakedness of my assailant, bitten with sharp teeth in the shoulder, neck, and chest, having every moment to protect my throat against a pair of sinewy, agile hands, which my utmost efforts could not confine—these were a combination of circumstances to combat which required all the strength, skill and courage that I possessed.

At last, after a silent, deadly, exhausting struggle, I got my assailant under by a series of incredible efforts of strength. . . . [He finally manages to light the gas burner] . . . Yes; I had one arm firmly clasped round a breathing, panting, corporeal shape, my other hand gripped with all its strength a throat as warm, and apparently fleshly, as my own; and yet, with this living substance in my grasp, with its body pressed against my own, and all in the bright glare of a large jet of gas, I absolutely beheld nothing! Not even an outline—a vapor!

Jack London's "To Build a Fire" illustrates the hope-despair sequence perfectly. In seventy-five degrees below zero a man falls through some ice and wets his legs almost to his knees. He manages to light a small fire, but he has exposed and numbed his fingers. The fire, however, will thaw them out; but unfortunately he has built it under a tree laden with snow, which falls off and puts out the fire. He prepares material for another fire, but his numbed fingers drop all the matches in the snow. He tries to light one with his teeth, succeeds, but coughs from the fumes, and loses the lighted match in the snow. He manages to light seventy matches all at once and actually starts another little fire, but "A large piece of green moss fell squarely on the little fire." The fire is lost. He decides to kill his dog and warm his hands inside the carcass; but after a severe struggle in getting hold of the dog he discovers his hands are too numb to kill it. In despair he starts running, but his feet are frozen. He reflects (psychological element) on the coming of death, goes to sleep, and dies. It is all a perfect sequence of hope always blasted by quick disaster—the "one-two" idea in building up suspense.

4. Climax and Solution

Κλῖμαξ is the Greek for "ladder." From it we moderns derive the final, decisive rung in the ascending ladder of conflict—climax. Recall now the raft structure of a plot story, with the scaffold erected to denote suspense, climax, and solution—but with a difference. The original Greek denoted the *whole* of the ladder; but climax here is the *top rung* only.

Consider a man balancing himself at the top of a long, swaying, unsupported ladder. You have seen it done in circuses, vaudeville, and the movies. The chief element involved in the picture is perhaps humor, and the man is dressed to fit the scene. But suppose that on one side of that ladder is a precipice of sheer two hundred feet, and every time that ladder sways in one direction the man is swinging far over the edge, with a drop to rocks below him. Then you will have a fairly good idea of the modern concept of climax. An overbalance—the last dominant pull of positive or negative forces—one way or the other will precipitate the man into safety or destruction. So the Greek word for "ladder" can well be adopted for our transferred meaning of climax.

Another aspect of the swaying ladder will help to indicate a further important feature of the modern climax. From the bottom to the top, as the ladder sways, is an ever-widening series of arcs, until at the top of the ladder appears the widest arc of all. The longer the ladder, then, the wider will be this topmost arc, and correspondingly the more intense will be the reader's interest in the climax: the last terrific struggle of the good angel versus the devil, pulling against each other in a sweep like that of Poe's famous pendulum. Actually, then, the climax is the most intense incident of suspense, the culmination of suspense—the point where the ladder is just ready to overbalance one way or the other.

We have changed the figure from the raft structure merely to make use of the derivation of the word climax. The original figure still remains, for the girl at the top of the scaffold on the raft *is* swaying back and forth in the last wide sweep as surely as if she were on a swaying ladder. The only difference is that her swaying is mental, not physical. And so at the climax will appear most naturally, *written out on paper*, the girl's psychological struggle forced upon her by her situation. She may even cry aloud in her final agony of suspense, for here if anywhere sharp dialogue can be used. To this last tense moment, also, it will certainly be wise to give sufficient space, even more, probably, than to the prelude. So much for theory. Now let us choose some examples from the linear narration types denoted in the first chapter.

In the laboratory the addition of the last and most dangerous compound to an explosive mixture will indicate a climax. If too little or too much is added—if the ladder sways a bit too much either way—the mixture may behave most disagreeably. But it would require a sure knowledge of chemistry to describe such a climax as this.

History offers unlimited examples of climax. Two suggestions might be useful. First, people are remembered in history chiefly for action or for reflection and decision. For a sharply defined climax, take a man of action, John Paul Jones or Theodore Roosevelt, at a moment requiring reflection and decision, and take a man of reflection, Galileo or Woodrow Wilson, at a moment compelling action. Thus you will bring his real nature into relief. Second, avoid, as a rule, the towering heroes of history. They do well for biographical essays; but, since the reader is already familiar with the famous episodes in their careers, you will be handicapped in trying to make a portrayal of them convincing. Explore some such work as Thackeray's *The Four Georges*, carefully ignoring the Georges, and you will find plenty of clashes of human wit and will between individuals who will make excellent story material, and still be new to the reader. Similarly, instead of writing about Napoleon, hunt out some officer or court lady who lived under his shadow.

An investigation, such as a Congressional report, offers material for climax, less tense than the cavalry charge or naval battle of history, but often sufficiently thrilling. A wild, last-minute effort of certain senators to forestall or railroad through preferred legislation on the Supreme Court, for example, might serve as the climax of a session of the Senate. Exposure of oil scandals, banking frauds, lobbying—back of these activities are human conflicts of man against man, reputation against reputation, and ultimate smashing climax. Study a crime wave, such as kidnaping. The discovery of insulin or of the new serum for infantile paralysis in the medical field is a fitting climax to a series of life-saving investigations. The deadly triumph in the perfection of a fatal gas or projectile for military purposes; the Olympic games or a championship series in athletics; the announcement of the verdict in a noted jury trial: in every case the widest sweep of the ladder is represented.

Biography is even more prolific with examples; but here, again, remember the warning given in connection with history. Antony at Actium, Hannibal at Zama, Napoleon at Waterloo—all were at the peak, the tensest moment, the climax, of their careers. But do not expect the name alone to give the story force. With any individual facing life or death at a moment of decision—whether Joan of Arc before the English, Edith Cavell before the Germans, or a poverty-stricken girl before an irate or hard-hearted employer—you have the element of climax. But your chances of success in treating it are probably better with the less imposing figure.

In the newspaper field appear examples daily. The mine wherein seventy miners have been entombed for a week will be opened today. A round-the-world flier has been lost three days off the Howland Islands. A prison outbreak sweeps ten convicts into the open country. The foreman of the jury arises to announce . . . Today is the day set by a self-appointed prophet for the end of the world. Tomorrow is Election Day. In every case appears a climax, of more or less tensity. Remember the possibilities in bound volumes of leading newspapers. The element that makes news will serve to keep it potentially interesting long after the World's Series has been won or Public Enemy Number One has been captured and sentenced.

Finally, consider the two most popular fields—the diary and the autobiography. Here will be found a full cupboard. The difference between them, so far as climax is concerned, is slight.

Still there is some distinction—a matter mainly of gravity and time involved, of weight and extent. Do not overlook this latter item. If asked to write a story of four hundred words, choose the diary for an example of climax. For a longer story the auto-biography will serve better, since it will involve more preparation through time preceding the actual climax. Fit your incidents to the space to be used; *time* is your basis of measure.

From the diary: the third time down in deep water; point-set-match, and one minute to play; the last lap; end of the ninth inning, three on and two out, with the score a tie; the dormitory fire; a student falls into a deep gravel pit on a field trip. Or consider this series: caught by a motor-cycle policeman; caught at a dance by a girl you broke a date with; caught breaking holy campus traditions, and the like. You should, of course, have the solutions in mind before you begin to write.

From the autobiography recall the third day lost; a fever of 105°; the night of the big debate when the speech notes had been lost; "buck fever" as the deer approaches; the wounded hunter found in the mountains; final examinations. Or again there may be a series of "getting-caught" situations: in the melons, or in some building forbidden, perhaps containing some inventor's hopes or some dark secret such as a criminal hide-out; getting a forbidden "permanent," using the car on sister's night for the third time, and so forth. All can be the goal, the climax, of stories of more length than is usual with those taken from the diary.

And here, before going farther, we should insert a word about drawing climaxes, or plots as a whole, from reading or from moving pictures. You may vividly recall the climactic moment in some "Western"—such as the cowboy with the tarantula crawling over him as he lies by the fire, together with the line: "It's all over, boys; he's coming toward my throat." If you choose such a climax, involving a shudder of horror or terror, try to con-centrate it into a brief, tense moment. G. A. Henty's old thrillers are full of such moments which can be reset. But we should advise you to avoid depending too much on reading or movies for sources. In the first place, the procedure leads to the danger of plagiarism, besides the easy consequence of the loss of spontaneity; and this latter is really more serious so far as the progress of your writing

is concerned than is the matter of technical dishonesty. It is almost impossible to invent new situations, but keep your imagination free in developing those you choose. Then, in the second
place, lifting situations from books and films easily leads to the
development of a crop of sensational episodes such as never have
grown, or could grow, in the soil of reality. To hold the reader's
sympathies, your work must have an element of common sense
and downright plausibility.

The solution is more technically known as the catastrophe,
from the Greek καταστροφή, a "turning down." One hesitates to
use this word, for it tends to call up the vision of a railroad wreck,
a general holocaust swallowing up a hotel and several city blocks,
the slaughter of the Texans at the Alamo, or the shelling of
Madrid or Shanghai. But the Greek derivation really means a
quick "turning down," or plunge, in the motor sense of positive
action or change of position. Thus, we fall from the top of the
ladder of suspense, from the point of climax. The ladder has
swayed suddenly too far one way—the girl has plunged abruptly,
and the reader can relax and breathe freely again.

We cannot emphasize this element of quickness too strongly.
When you have decided on the method of extricating your victim
from the situation in which he is involved at the climax, do it
with a swiftness that will startle and amaze your reader. Shakespeare's *Cymbeline* and *Winter's Tale* are famous for the bewildering
rapidity with which sudden turns of fortune, restorations of lost
persons, and other surprises wind up the action, or rather un-
tangle the knots, in the last few scenes. Examine Thackeray's
final striking effect in that famous chapter of *Vanity Fair:* " . . . for
George was lying on his face dead, with a bullet through his
heart." Then follow the climax immediately with the bell that
summons your victim "to heaven or to hell." In that way only
will you succeed in leaving the reader with a distinctly effective
impression of the story. By comparison with other elements in the
plot story, the solution becomes the most vital and approaches
nearest in brevity to the moment of interest, a single sentence if
possible—"a short, powerful, driving, even brutal sentence," as
we said above.

There are three popular types of solution applicable to plot stories. The first is hackneyed and a frank admission on your part of incapability to think. The second is better, but still weak, involving no foresight in construction. The third, the best of all, is an original idea, planted in the story from the beginning, or an inspiration of the *character himself* at the most critical moment of his career (the climax). In every case the solution must be logical, or the reader will merely sit back and laugh.

The first type is sheer trickery and a lazy man's device. For example "It was all a dream"; "Then father fell asleep"; "The next page was torn out"; "Then static shut us off"; "Then teacher made us finish it"; "To be continued"; "Then the film broke"; etc., etc. Such an ending may occasionally be funny or otherwise effective, but it must always be used with caution.

The second type involves *external* aid to save the character at the climax: the tarantula in that horror story above was shot off the man's chest by another cowboy; the pitcher passes you in the ninth inning with three and two, two out, and three on; your sweetheart may cheer you on the last lap of a race and inspire you to heroic activities. Or external aid may be used whenever the character is in direct difficulty: surrounded by wolves, drowning, in a forest fire, lost, etc., etc. This is always a legitimate solution and may be encouraged, especially if the external aid can be introduced (planted) innocently somewhere back near the beginning of the story.

Finally the most interesting solution of all is the *internal* or *original* type. In this case either the writer or the character involved at the climax (preferably the latter) suddenly conceives an idea which projects him quickly out of his difficulty. (Often the preparation for this idea is planted previously in the story, and the character merely grasps at it at the last moment by recollecting it or suddenly having it thrust before him again.) For example: caught in switch with train at hand—remove your shoe; lost—use fire signals remembered from Boy Scout days; lost—cross same stream repeatedly until the idea suddenly comes to follow the stream down to a lake, where a hut is found; the fish slips under boat—dive over after it; in a forest fire—you recollect a large pan fallen over while running, go back, get it, and bury yourself under it in a pond. This is by far the best type. In the other form the *writer* has the saving idea: if you are caught in the switch, the train whirls by, switched off on the other track; you are swimming ashore and totally exhausted far from land—you drop your feet and find that the water is only three feet deep (a sand bar); there is a rattlesnake on your chest—it is artificial, wound up and placed there to torment you; chased by a bear— you find it was tame; a man catches you in a melon patch—he is your brother, trying to be funny.

The solution is by far the most interesting feature of any story. It should be logical, original, and, above all, come as a surprise. The reader must never be allowed to gain the faintest idea of what the solution will be, though after it has been sprung on him he must nod, smile, and admit its possibility. Further it must permit him to relax completely, if possible, from the strain of the climax, and hence quickness of solution is a vital element. Like a blow in the dark it must crumple up the reader into a laugh or a gasp. And so if you will write an effective plot story, prepare for an effective solution the moment you have decided on your tone, for on the solution will ultimately depend success.

➤➤➤ A ◄◄◄

This first piece has a purely external solution, for the victim plays no vital part in his own rescue. In the ancient theater, from the time of the Greeks even to Shakespeare's day, the rescue was often performed by a god let down in a kind of elevator, the *deus ex machina*. Here the effect is much the same.

TRAPPED IN A BURNING FOREST

I was burnt all over, my beautiful long curls were gone, and one foot was in a particularly bad condition. I had heard that death by fire was one of the most terrible ways to leave this life, and my agony confirmed this. I wondered about God's wisdom, and asked Him what I had ever done to deserve such a fate. I envied the unconscious girl we had left under the tree. She had not suffered, and was probably burned to a cinder by this time. What a pity; she had been wearing such a pretty silk dress. All my sensations melted into one, that of intense pain. I heard shouts and opened my eyes to see if I was dead yet. I saw a man leap through a wall of flame. He saw me and ran to my side. I did not recognize him, but he called me by name, and picking me up, wrapped me in his lumberjack's coat, and ran straight into the flames again. When we reached the other side, I asked him if he was sure this was Heaven.

"No," he replied, "you are going home to your mother."

L. G.

The writer deliberately brings about the solution of "The Fugitive," which has been presented in previous sections; yet there is a sense of Fate in the life and death of the man Joe.

Bullets rained about the mouth of the cave, and Joe decided he would shift his position. It was his undoing; Fate played an awful prank. One more shot from the cave, one more notch for Joe, and then the movement of the men went unheeded.

They found him by his second gun, his finger on the trigger, a bullet hole in the side of his neck. The bullet had caromed off one of his sheltering rocks.

The writer's solution in "A Narrow Escape," while it is true to life, lacks emotional tension.

Luckily I glanced toward the back of the boat, and there I saw about four inches of the guide ropes that were exposed just before going through to the rudder. I grabbed one of these and pulled furiously. The boat turned, and we missed the edge by a few yards and headed back up stream.

"Buck Fever" carries its story of a guilt-crazed consciousness through to the character's solution, but has still a conclusion to be presented in the next section.

Finally, in despair, he decided to give himself up to the police;— to find relief from his tortured condition. The vision of himself beaten and humiliated by the police and public was too much for him, and his nerve failed him at the last moment. Then in the agony of his condition, half starved, and thoroughly miserable, he decided on the only way out. He sat down at his rickety table and laboriously wrote out a full confession to the police. Then blowing out the flame from his gas light, he sat down to wait for eternity—calm at last, after days of agony.

III

A thoroughly frightened landlady called in the police. They found the body of a man slumped over a little table, with a serene smile of contentment on his horribly emaciated face. On the table they found a note which read, "I murdered a man in cold blood, near T—— in the great forest section. You will find his body in a little cultivated clearing about five miles north of town.

R——"

In "A Lynch Victim's Last Minutes" there is a sense of finality in the solution that makes any further conclusion unnecessary. The emotional tension is well sustained to the very last word.

"They're tying my arms; they're trying to tie my arms so I can't get the rope off. They've got it around my neck again. You can't do this. You —— can't hang —— me. . . . That's better,—it's off again.

"Won't you guys ever stop? I didn't hurt you any. What'd I ever do to you?—They're all quiet. A minute ago they were all yelling.— What's wrong with them? Maybe they'll quit. Maybe they'll let me go. Maybe the police reinforcements have come. No—they've got the rope again; they've got the rope.—I can't breathe—It's too tight —— tight —— the ground's gone, gone . . . gone . . ."

"Professional Courtesies," which is printed complete, shows how the solution may be effected by an idea in the mind of a character—the idea being based on a clever "plant" slipped into the second paragraph. Keep your eyes open to detect, if possible, the "plant" in advance of the solution.

PROFESSIONAL COURTESIES

In all my experience of newspaper writing, I was never sent on an errand that bored me as much as did this one. Would I never reach my destination? From its location on the map, Kremmling seemed only a short distance from Denver; so, shortly after our train left Denver, I proceeded to prepare myself to leave the train. My feet had swelled, as they always do when I keep my shoes off too long, and while I sat there waiting for my toes to adjust themselves to their usual cramped position I pondered about the many different types of humanity surrounding me.

I felt as though I knew my fellow passengers intimately, although I had not spoken to any of them. The man and woman across the aisle were on speaking terms again, much to my regret. He was evidently at fault for their two-hour estrangement, because when the train stopped for fifteen minutes at Denver he purchased a corsage of flowers and a large bag of peanuts. She was cracking the shells and eating peanuts while she talked even faster and louder than she had talked before. Again the story of the shameful way that they were treated by his people after the funeral fell upon my unwilling ears. The two men in the seat behind me were still talking. The one without the hiccoughs was telling that he heard about an organized gang of thieves that had grown so large that they were using a password, which he believed to be "bulldog," the name of their leader. Their friends and relatives were given this information and advised to use it if necessary.

How ridiculous all this conversation sounded. The woman across the aisle was arguing again. I couldn't help wishing that her husband had purchased some gum drops instead of peanuts. They would have been less noisy, and without the odor that I detest in peanuts. This ride was certainly getting on my nerves. The conductor was calling the name of the next town. I couldn't hear the name because the baby near the rear of the car was demonstrating its lung power to its fullest extent, but I was quite sure the place was Kremmling, and was willing to get out and walk the rest of the way, if it turned out to be some other town.

My first impression of Kremmling was that it was a quiet place, and that thought encouraged me. I walked towards the only automobile in sight. A card which read "for hire" dangled carelessly over the windshield. The driver knew where the Aster Hotel was located, of course, and after demanding my fare in advance and watching me while I removed several bills from their place around some bills of smaller denomination, he took his place behind the wheel and, with a violent jerk, we were off.

I didn't like the appearance of this fellow, but one can't be too choosey about drivers when they are so scarce. He was very young, perhaps less than twenty, with a very independent, carefree manner. I imagined that his most serious trouble in life was that of growing his mustache. With each turn of his head the thing seemed to take turnabout in appearing and disappearing. But yes, it was there: one could see it by looking hard.

The thought occurred to me that he was using an indirect way of driving to the hotel, but I knew nothing about the town and did not become alarmed until he increased the speed of the car and we were traveling so fast that I was compelled to hold on to the seat in order to remain in one position. I called out to him, but with no result. I could have opened the door and jumped, but that meant certain death, at the rate of speed we were traveling. If only someone would appear on the road or a car would pass us, so that I might attract their attention, but that was only a hope.

Aha! a car was following us. This looked like help and removed the terror that had surged within me. What was that? The driver of my car was signaling to the occupants of the car behind us. That meant that they were friends, accomplices. What could I do? In my terror-stricken condition, my mind failed to act. They were after my money, of course. And unfortunately I had considerable cash with me, and the loss of this money would greatly inconvenience me, besides affecting my financial status.

Things were happening very rapidly. We had evidently arrived at the designated spot for the holdup. The car I was riding in skidded about ten feet when the driver suddenly applied the brakes. The driver jumped from his place, produced a gun, and opened the door, in one short second. The second car pulled up beside us, but the occupants remained inside. When they noticed that I was a woman, and alone, they probably realized that their help would not be necessary. My abductor was trying to be as courteous and polite as was possible. He advised me that all they wanted was the large roll of bills I had displayed, and that I could avoid delay by handing it over at once.

I pleaded with him, saying that this was all the money I had, and being far away from home I needed it badly. His sympathy was not aroused, however, and his tone became more crude when he answered that I had better hurry, and not compel them to use force in getting the money. They were going to leave the car for me, he added, and I could use it to get back to town. "The owner is probably looking for it now," someone in the other car said, laughingly. My purse was then snatched from my arm. My pockets were being searched. Even my rings were jerked from my fingers. How terrible it was. A girl's voice called from the other car, requesting that my coat be taken. So I was compelled to remove my coat.

This thing was maddening. The man was walking away with everything of value I owned, and the door of the other car was opening to receive him. Like a flash, the conversation about the password, which I had heard on the train, came to me. Without the slightest hope or confidence in the result of my next act, I called, "bulldog." With puzzled expressions, but few words, my money, coat, and rings were returned to me, and I was very graciously and comfortably escorted back to town and to my destination.

A. F.

⇢⟫ B ⟪⇠

External aid saves the tortured man in Poe's "Pit and the Pendulum":

I felt that I tottered upon the brink—I averted my eyes—

There was a discordant hum of human voices! There was a loud blast as of many trumpets! There was a harsh grating as of a thousand thunders! The fiery walls rushed back! An outstretched arm caught my own as I fell, fainting, into the abyss. It was that of General Lasalle. The French army had entered Toledo. The Inquisition was in the hands of its enemies.

Compare also the end of W. L. Comfort's "Fear" [1]:

There was an almost invisible tug of the head, a hurling strike past Hilliard's shoulder and the boy bowled forward—a black rush of the python's length following, the vast mid-coils thrusting Hilliard aside. The rest for an instant was a huddle, a kind of nursing. Then Cantrell was there and a double shot. The dust rose vast and explosively. In the great threshing there was nothing to see. . . .

The python was looping and whipping itself back toward the jungle with a riddled head. . . .

(The directly preceding part of this story is in section 3 above.)

The writer's idea solved the climax in the following illustrations. The lonely bad-man, Sam Folwell, finds his mortal enemy in New York.

There was a sudden spring, a ripple in the stream of passers-by and the sound of Sam's voice crying:

"Howdy! Cal! I'm durned glad to see ye!"

And in the angles of Broadway, Fifth Avenue and Twenty-third Street the Cumberland feudists shook hands.

O. Henry, "Squaring the Circle." [2]

Ambrose Bierce himself solves the problem of "The Man and the Snake" [3] at the end (see section 3 above for the suspense in this story):

[1] Reprinted by permission of Willimina L. Armstrong.

[2] From *The Voice of the City*, copyright, 1904, by Doubleday, Doran & Company, Inc. Reprinted by permission.

[3] Reprinted from *In the Midst of Life*, by permission of the publishers, Albert & Charles Boni, Inc.

"Died in a fit," said the scientist, bending his knee and placing his hand upon the heart. While in that position he chanced to look under the bed. "Good God!" he added, "how did this thing get in here?"

He reached under the bed, pulled out the snake and flung it, still coiled, to the center of the room, whence with a harsh, shuffling sound it slid across the polished floor till stopped by the wall, where it lay without motion. It was a stuffed snake; its eyes were two shoe buttons.

This, however, is very close to a trick solution—a clever twist. In "How It Happened"[1] the man in the auto crash, having landed on some brushwood, reflects:

I was quite unable to move. . . . They were taking no notice of me . . . they did not seem to hear me. . . .

Stanley laid his hand upon my shoulder, and his touch was inexpressibly soothing. I felt light and happy, in spite of all.

"No pain, of course?" said he.

"None," said I.

"There never is," said he.

And then suddenly a wave of amazement passed over me. Stanley! Stanley! Why, Stanley had surely died of enteric at Bloemfontein in the Boer War!

"Stanley!" I cried, and the words seemed to choke my throat— "Stanley, you are dead."

He looked at me with the same old gentle, wistful smile.

"So are you," he answered.

ARTHUR CONAN DOYLE, "How It Happened."

A solution made by the character himself is probably the best type. Stevenson's Markheim makes his own decision:

He confronted the maid upon the threshold with something like a smile.

"You had better go for the police," said he: "I have killed your master." [2]

R. L. STEVENSON, "Markheim."

A solution of the same type is effected by the decision of Rainsford, the central figure in "The Most Dangerous Game." This story is reprinted complete in Chapter XVII below.

---

[1] Reprinted from *Danger and Other Stories*, 1918, by permission of Lady Conan Doyle and the publishers, Doubleday, Doran & Company, Inc.

[2] Reprinted by permission of the publishers, Charles Scribner's Sons.

"Nerve, nerve, nerve!" he panted, as he dashed along. A blue gap showed between the trees dead ahead. Ever nearer drew the hounds. Rainsford forced himself on toward that gap. He reached it. It was the shore of the sea. Across a cove he could see the gloomy gray stone of the chateau. Twenty feet below him the sea rumbled and hissed. Rainsford hesitated. He heard the hounds. Then he leaped far out into the sea. . . .

RICHARD CONNELL, "The Most Dangerous Game."

In Kipling's "The Mark of the Beast" the men take things into their own hands. Similarly, in Stevenson's "The Sire de Malétroit's Door" the man and woman themselves solve the story.

5. THE CONCLUSION

The purpose of a conclusion is to conclude. When you write a plot story, stop when through and do not give more than one final pat (if even that) to your brain child. If too much time is spent at the end fussing over and tucking in the child, you will find your reader beginning to dislike it or else developing an intense disgust for the sentimental parent who cannot stop petting his remarkable offspring. In fact, a slightly overlong conclusion will often spoil the whole preceding story, excellent though it may be.

A conclusion, if managed properly, does two things. First it completes the relaxation begun by the solution; it lets the reader down emotionally to pursue the even tenor of his way. Second, it puts the final artistic touch to the story. That is, it rhythmically closes a piece of work which, if dropped abruptly after the solution, would leave a harsh or shrill note in the reader's ears. The story can often be tapered off by the addition of a single sentence, and the reader will feel then that his aesthetic sense has been much better satisfied. Both these functions of a conclusion involve considerable skill on the part of the writer, and so we have generally advised you to beware of a conclusion. You can, nevertheless, by observing the simple types of conclusion given below, readily approximate, we believe, the effectiveness of an artistic and relaxing conclusion.

First, however, consider the omission of a conclusion. Two types of solutions, given in section 4, do not generally, we should say, require conclusions. The reader is actually let down and the

THE PLOT STORY 401

story is effectively closed by the very nature of the solution. If you conclude, "Then I woke up," or "The next page was torn out," obviously there is nothing more to be done. You have used a rather silly solution, as noted above, but you have avoided all worry about a conclusion. Similarly if the *writer's* inspiration idea is used in the third type of solution, a conclusion will seldom be necessary. "The water was only three feet deep"; "The train shot by on the *other* track"; "The bear was tame," etc. These two types of solution are about the same in finality, the second, of course, artistically is better than the first. In neither case is a conclusion absolutely necessary. The reader is definitely relaxed and the story effectively closed by the solution itself.

Nevertheless, with the second type of solution mentioned in section 4 (the external aid) and with the *character's* inspirational idea in the case of the third type, a short conclusion may be advisable, often necessary. And here we should be inclined to subdivide the types of conclusions into four: (1) simply an effective closing sentence; (2) the addition of a moral; (3) an echo of the beginning of the story; and (4) a surprise twist. Of these the fourth is the cleverest. All of them will fulfill the double function of a conclusion: "letting down" and "tapering off."

First consider the closing sentence. After the chase by the wolves, with the rescue: "A wolf in the bush, I decided from the moment, is worth at least ten in a cage." After the "lost" incident: "I reflected then that a compass might not be a bad thing to take along in the future," or with type three solution (saved by smoke signals): "So Father got his subject for his speech to the Boy Scouts." After the pitcher passed you in the ninth inning: "Verily, in the words of the sage, it is always darkest before the dawn." A touch of mild humor will complete the reader's relaxation and at the same time carry off the story with some degree of smoothness. You might try for that, at least.

The second type, the moral, *à la* George Ade, may produce the same results. "Moral: A compass will encompass many a difficulty!" "Moral: A base on balls is as good as a single when the sacks are full." Actually, though, this is not a type to be often used. Unless the moral comes off neatly, the story will be left flat at the end.

The third type of conclusion, echoing the note struck at the beginning of a story, rises, together with the fourth type, into the field of the professional writer. As such perhaps it had better not be attempted too blithely, but students have hit off both types with considerable aplomb, and as a result of these few successful experiments we venture to note the two types here.

A gem of a story appeared in *McClure's* a long time ago called "Out of the Night." It began something like this: "The clock above the Herald Building struck twelve in long muffled strokes. Out of the darkness across the snow-covered street rushed a girl and bent over the crumpled form of a fallen boy." The story continued with the girl's helping the sick boy to a restaurant, feeding him, hiding him (a thief) for a few days, and sending him *out of her life* to South America with *her* earnings. Then it closed with (again we paraphrase): "The clock above the Herald Building struck twelve in long muffled strokes. Out of the darkness across the snow-covered street shuffled a girl, who stopped and looked up at the stars and dreamed—and dreamed—." Of course these excerpts hardly suggest the brilliance of the effect which the author achieved, but there was certainly present a remarkable union of relaxation and smoothness. And it was not a happy ending either.

We might give other examples of this particular type. O. Henry's "Between Rounds" is gloriously funny, as its very title suggests. The story is about a lost child, whose disappearance abruptly stops an Irish domestic row. As soon as the child is recovered, however, the plates begin to fly again as at the beginning. And consider such nonprofessional work as this: "Through the darkness the snow sifted down lightly on the blind man's shoulders. He shifted his pencils to his left hand and rubbed his cold right leg. Pulling himself up with the aid of his broken cane, he shook the snow from his beard and tapped slowly down the dimly lighted street." In the course of the story he tries to shoot a man to prevent discovery of the fact that he is *not* blind at all. The revolver backfires and flares into his eyes; then you have him *actually* blind. Conclude now with the above lines and note the effect.

The final type of conclusion is the best, but it is a hard thing to do. Generally called, somewhat vaguely, the "O. Henry twist," it serves the purpose of an ordinary conclusion remarkably well: it both relaxes the reader completely and tapers off the story. In application it goes best with the finest type of solution, that is, the character's inspirational idea (see section 4). For example: you have dived under the boat and saved the fish—it is five inches long. You have suddenly overcome that "buck fever" and shot the deer—it is a sheep (you may think that is impossible, but it happens). You took your shoe off in the switch—the train was not on that track at all. You follow the stream down the lake when lost—you were only fifty yards from the outside of the woods anyway. You get away from the guardian of the melon patch after a terrific chase—the melons are all sour. And so forth. In every case the reader is left gasping, generally laughing.[1] And the story has got across by virtue of its most insignificant element— the conclusion.

One predominant feature is evident in all these types of conclusion: humor. There is nothing that will carry off a story better, and if you hesitate to attempt the humorous, you might better start in at once studying conclusions for every type of solution, to develop, if possible, some idea of the technique. Of course, there is always the tendency to carry such an effect to an extreme, to a discordant guffaw, but the experiment is worth trying, for without some humor you will find some conclusions difficult to achieve. So we again come back to our original injunction: in general, beware of conclusions. If you must use one, use the simplest types, as denoted above. And finally, if you must use one, make it short. Its function is to taper off the story and complete the relaxation of the reader begun by the solution. Both things can and must be done quickly. If you want, for example, to see what a deadly thing an unbalanced conclusion can be, read the final paragraph of the story, called "The Gift of the Magi," written by that expert in conclusions (plus denouements), O. Henry. There is no doubt whatever that such a conclusion as this would be better omitted.

[1] This conclusion can be bitterly ironical, however; see "Buck Fever" in this section. Another illustration appears below on pp. 405–6 (see E. W.'s "Five Months to Live"). But even an ironical conclusion often involves an element of satirical laughter.

→» A «←

"Buck Fever" comes to a swift and ironical conclusion. Such a conclusion will have value exactly in proportion to the degree of tension which precedes it in the stage of suspense.

The police captain, with two special investigators, boarded a train for the great woods, and when they arrived there, began an immediate search of the vicinity. After a four-hour search they finally found a cultivated opening, and on one edge they found a brown hunting cap with the name of the suicide written in the flap. On the far side of the clearing the captain saw something which made his hard old face show pity. There on the ground, in a shapeless heap, lay the bullet-riddled body of a scarecrow.

The endings of stories in preceding sections may be compared for surprise effect. See especially "Professional Courtesies" in section 4, and "It's All a Mistake" in section 3.

"Betty Gold" ends with a deliberate echo of the prelude. As the tone indicates, it is a story of frustration.

BETTY GOLD

The reek of onions and the stale stench of garlic pervaded the dinky hall of Marconi Mansions on East Tenth Street. An old black clock, standing on a worn telephone table near the rickety banister, bleaked out seven discordant chimes. At that same moment the screen door creaked, groaned, then banged as Miss Betty Gold walked slowly in.

(Betty tries to become a dancer on the stage, but ends up with a job in a clothes factory. She then falls in love with one Jack Wilson, a new boarder at the Marconi Mansions. Hope springs, only to be blighted at the end when she learns that Jack not only is a criminal, out on bond, but also has a wife! Then the conclusion.)

The reek of onions and the stale stench of garlic pervaded the dinky hall of Marconi Mansions on East Tenth Street. An old black clock, standing on a worn telephone table near the rickety banister, bleaked out seven discordant chimes. At the same moment the screen door creaked, groaned, then banged as Miss Betty Gold walked slowly in.

L. W.

Another distinctly ironical conclusion appears in "Five Months to Live." Students are fond of such unhappy endings, particularly the ironical.

FIVE MONTHS TO LIVE

"You have a lesion of the heart," said the specialist slowly in a cold, dispassionate voice. "You have five months to live. You will not suffer any pain; you will not be bedridden; you may even go about your business—but in five months your heart will cease to beat."

Without the slightest betrayal of emotion, Howland heard his doom, a doom as certain as if it had been pronounced by a judge.

"Sure you haven't made a mistake, Doctor?" he asked calmly enough for a man doomed to die.

"Not a chance," replied the doctor. "I gave you a very thorough examination."

The specialist rose to signify that the consultation was over, walked to the door, and held it open. Mechanically Howland passed through the door into the waiting room, put on his hat and coat, and went into the street.

"So this is the end of it all," he said to himself. "As the gates to prosperity are about to open, as I am about to live and enjoy the fruits of my efforts, I must die. For ten years I've worked night and day, worked and striven in the hope that I might some day partake of the good things in this world. For ten long years I've denied myself proper food and lodging in order that I might put my invention before the world. On the very threshold of fame everything has been taken away from me; but in these last five months I'll live," he cried fiercely. "I'll crowd into these five months the pleasures that have been denied me in the past ten years. Nothing shall stand in my way. The world shall pay for what it has denied me."

True to his word, Howland threw himself into the whirlpool of unbridled and licentious living. His conscience cried out against the life he was leading, but with the aid of John Barleycorn, it was soon silenced. When his money began to run out, he gambled. When he couldn't win honestly, he cheated.

"Why shouldn't I cheat?" he asked himself. "I've been cheated. The whole world is a cheat. The man who never was born never missed a thing, that's sure."

Howland slowly opened his eyes, and gazed fixedly at the ceiling. A feeling of horror and dread stole over him. He tried hard to collect his thoughts. Suddenly, everything came back to him. He had shot a man last night, killed a man in an argument over a game of cards. The police would probably find him any minute. It was just by mere chance that he had eluded his pursuers last evening. He reached for a bottle of liquor on the dresser. That feeling of horror was becoming more and more frequent lately. It had to be stifled. What difference did it make if he was hanged for murder. He would be cheating the gallows anyway. In two weeks the five months would be up. As for the fellow he had killed, well, he was no worse off than himself.

"I hardly know myself," he said aloud, as he gazed into the dresser mirror. "Five months of perpetual drunkenness certainly have put their stamp on my features. Well, the whole of me will soon be below the sod, so what's the odds?"

As he was about to turn away from the dresser, his eyes fell upon a letter addressed to himself. He tore off the end of the envelope, opened the letter, and read aloud: "Dear Mr. Howland: In going over the records of Doctor Johnston, I found you listed as one of his patients. Doctor Johnston is now in an insane asylum. For the past year he has been suffering with a peculiar mental malady which was discovered by the merest chance. For some time he has been diagnosing the ailment of all his patients as heart disease. Invariably he told them that they would not live over five months."

A loud knock sounded on the door. The letter fell from his nerveless hands. With a cry he fell over on the bed and buried his face in his hands.

E. W.

→≫ B ≪←

Indefinite, but clever, conclusions have been used:

The question of her decision is not one to be lightly considered, and it is not for me to presume to set myself up as the one person able to answer it. And so I leave it with all of you: Which came out of the opened door,—the lady, or the tiger?

F. R. Stockton, "The Lady, or the Tiger?" [1]

Compare also H. G. Wells's dream solution in "Under the Knife." Sometimes a closing sentence will do it well:

"Brrr! that fellow got on my nerves," he said; and we made no further allusion to the matter.

[1] Reprinted by permission of the publishers, Charles Scribner's Sons.

But as the train, moving slowly, passed a gap which brought us again in sight of the town, we saw a tongue of flame stream into the sky. .

VINCENT O'SULLIVAN, "Master of Fallen Years." [1]

And so I left him there in the shadow of the mountain, staring at the impassable sea.

WILBUR DANIEL STEELE, "The Shame Dance." [1]

The general made one of his deepest bows. "I see," he said. "Splendid! One of us is to furnish a repast for the hounds. The other will sleep in this very excellent bed. On guard, Rainsford." . . .
He had never slept in a better bed, Rainsford decided.

R. CONNELL, "The Most Dangerous Game." [2]

Compare the conclusions of E. Granberry's "A Trip to Czardis" and W. Duranty's "The Parrot." But contrast O. Henry's bad full paragraph conclusion to "The Gift of the Magi."
The use of a moral at the end is sometimes good:

"Naughty boy!" she said, fondly, "Did I say a peach? I think I would much rather have had an orange."
Blest be the bride.

O. HENRY, "Little Speck in Garnered Fruit." [3]

. . . I wanted them to quit their damned foolishness and tried to explain, but it was no use. You can't teach a mob to have sense. Well, adios. But remember this: Don't be too cocksure.

C. J. FINGER, "The Lizard God." [4]

An echo of the beginning is often very effective. O. Henry's "A Service of Love," [5] the beginning of which was given above in section 2, effectively utilizes the same line in the conclusion:

"When one loves one's Art no service seems—"
But Delia stopped him with her hand on his lips. "No," she said—"just 'When one loves.' "

---

[1] Reprinted by permission of the author.
[2] Reprinted in full in Chapter XVII below by permission of the author.
[3] From *The Voice of the City*, copyright, 1904, by Doubleday, Doran & Company, Inc. Reprinted by permission.
[4] Reprinted by permission of the author.
[5] From O. Henry's *The Four Million*, copyright, 1905. Reprinted by permission of Doubleday, Doran & Company, Inc.

Similarly Susan M. Boogher's "An Unknown Warrior" [1] echoes its beginning, given in section 2:

Snow was falling over London, a great blur of zigzagging flakes . . .

The same technique appears to some extent in W. D. Edmonds's "Water Never Hurt a Man" [2]:

He trudged with his hands tight fists in his pockets, his head bowed to the wind and rain. Ahead of him in the darkness, so that he could hear the squdge of their hoofs, the towing team bowed their necks against the collars . . .

. . . .

He reached down and took it from its peg, recoiled it, and tossed it ashore. The boat went ahead, slowly, with a sound of water, and of rain falling, and of wind.

The simple completion of a circuit is represented in the following beginning and ending of Laurence Stallings's "Gentlemen in Blue" [2]:

When they found those old embroidery scissors under that stump today, I went a long way back in memory. To memories of blue. I remember how blue their uniforms were. . . .

. . . .

When they found the embroidery scissors under that old stump today, it made me think of all this. I still remember how blue his jacket was when he lifted the gray over the picket fence and came down the gravel walk between those little button chrysanthemums.

What do you suppose takes place between the following extracts from Morley Callaghan's story, "The Red Hat," [2] from *The New Yorker?*

It was the kind of hat Frances had wanted for months, a plain little red felt hat with the narrow brim tacked back, which would look so smart and simple and expensive . . .

. . . .

And just thinking of it, sitting there, she felt an eagerness and a faint elation; it was a plain little red hat, the kind of hat she had wanted for months, elegant and expensive, a plain felt hat, but so very distinctive.

[1] Reprinted by permission of the editor of the *Junior League Magazine.*
[2] Reprinted by permission of the author.

Compare for a similar technique Konrad Bercovici's "The Death of Murdo," Katherine Mansfield's "The Wind Blows," and Sherwood Anderson's "Alice."

Always one of the most popular conclusions with students has been that with a surprise twist. This type is almost synonymous with the name of O. Henry. Notice, for example, the ending of his "The Skylight Room." [1] A half-starved girl has held nightly communion with a particular star which she has named "Billy Jackson." Finally she collapses and—well, let O. Henry do it:

. . . a little news item . . . recounted the reception into Bellevue Hospital of a young woman who had been removed from No. 49 East —— street, suffering from debility induced by starvation. It concluded with these words:

"Dr. William Jackson, the ambulance physician who attended the case, says the patient will recover."

The astringent note of suppressed tragedy and irony is common in Maupassant. Its power is hard to surpass. In his "Deux Amis" (Two Friends) we have such an ending. Two men, who are lovers of fishing, become bored by the long imprisonment brought about by the siege of Paris by the Prussians in 1870–71. Impelled by a crisp January day and a visit to a wineshop, they resolve on a reckless sortie to the banks of the Seine outside the city to indulge in a day of fishing. Passes are secured, and soon they are happily busy in filling their basket with fish. But when the time comes for their return, they find themselves cut off by gun fire, and suddenly they are captured. They are brought before an arrogant Prussian officer who offers them safe return if they will only betray the password. This they refuse to do, and both are mercilessly shot at the command of the officer and their bodies flung into the very waters where they have just been fishing. Remember that Maupassant held it as his artistic ideal to prevent his own personality from intruding upon the story in any way—to attain complete objectivity of statement.[2]

The water splashed, bubbled, quivered, then became still, while some little ripples came quite up to the bank.

[1] From *The Four Million*, by O. Henry, copyright, 1905, by Doubleday, Doran & Company, Inc.

[2] This excerpt from "Deux Amis" was translated by the editors.

A bit of flesh floated.

The officer, always serene, said quietly: "Now the fish will have their turn."

Then he turned back toward the house.

Suddenly he noticed the string of fish in the grass. He picked them up, examined them, smiled, cried out: "Wilhelm!"

A soldier came on the run, garbed in a white apron. And the Prussian, tossing him the catch of the two men who had just been shot, commanded: "Fry these little fellows for me at once, while they are still alive. They will be delicious."

Then he returned to lighting his pipe.

MAUPASSANT, "Two Friends."

6. Do's and Don't's in the Plot Story

The theory of the plot story is now complete. Its fundamental principles can be applied later in all the more intricate types, particularly the short story. But before taking the next step forward, we should rehearse some notes pro and con on the plot story — notes equally applicable to the more complex types to be discussed in subsequent chapters.

Obviously it is much easier to criticize than to construct. And yet constructive advice is much more helpful. Hence let us speak negatively first and positively afterward. And in the final summing up, the latter type of advice will generally predominate.

First, as to structure: There are five points to comment on, by way of warning. Begin quickly: don't write three or four paragraphs before arriving at the moment of interest, which actually carries the story into action. For example, you are going to have a boy lost in a snowstorm. There is absolutely no point in beginning with a description of the boy, then his careful preparation for a journey, then his starting out, and finally the first mile of the hike. By that time the reader will be half asleep or reading another story. The instructor will draw a long blue line through all of your methodical introductory material and write at the end of the blue line: "Begin here." In short, have the boy realize he is lost as near the actual beginning of the story as you can.

You now have the story under way; your moment of interest, coming early on the first page, has set the reader on the trail.

Now two dangerous temptations may face you at once. You may suddenly want to change the point of view (or perhaps you will be accidentally led into such a change), and you may very well slight the element of suspense in order to get quickly to that very clever solution you have thought out ahead of time. But if in one detail you disregard the fact that you are telling the story from the point of view of the main character, you may make this slip several times, and the reader will then become hopelessly confused. Furthermore, if you fail to stir him sufficiently—if you fail to torture him with the ever-increasing sense of suspense for the story hero—your clever solution will fall ridiculously flat. Hence you must realize that you cannot flit back and forth from the people in the house to the hero outside the house, continually shifting the point of view, without losing the essential directness of the story; and, further, that you cannot let your character go down only once instead of three times in a drowning incident without making the rescue a rather ludicrous, unexciting procedure. Look carefully to your moment of interest, to a fixed point of view,[1] and to a well-developed suspense.

Meanwhile, in the course of this most important middle of a story you cannot afford to mar or break your tone—that is, single effect—in the slightest possible degree. If the story begins on the keynote of horror, there must be no jokes emanating from a serious character's closely pressed lips—for, of course, such a story will have no humorous character. And it will tolerate no horseplay either. Singleness of tone must be maintained in plot, character, and setting. A murder should be committed by a leery-eyed maniac on a moor at midnight. There can of course be some slight modifications of this, for contrast, in more complex stories.

We are now again at the climax and solution, and at once the warning must be issued to keep the two physically close together: that is, the second must follow the first like the one-two punch in boxing. The idea of suspending a reader in mid-air at the climax until he becomes thoroughly exasperated, as well as emotionally exhausted, will be fatal to the solution, the effective-

[1] But see the modification given above for "Buck Fever," in sections 2 and 3. The suspense, therefore, can be presented in sections, from various points of view.

ness of which depends on a quick emotional rebound from the climax. Hence the psychology, or thought-sequence, of the character at the climax must not be too prolonged. The grip of the story depends on incident. Let the solution happen as quickly as is accordant with psychological effectiveness; that is, gauge the character's mind and reader's endurance most carefully.

The solution is over. Now *end* the story, if the solution has not already done so. Don't let the boy wander home after the drowning incident and drop in tears at mother's knees, to murmur, "I cannot tell a lie, mother dear; I did go down to the swimming hole with the big boys." Your story is over the moment the boy is saved. Never mind what he does afterward. Take up your pen and go elsewhere.

So much for structure. Now some points on what may be called the mechanics of the plot story. For example, personal comments of the writer—smart or otherwise—are absolutely barred. The character in the story may make a clever remark or evolve a brilliant train of thought—*but not the writer*. If you must let off steam, study the methods of G. B. Shaw and Oscar Wilde and express yourself through your characters. In general, though, it is best to stifle such a tendency to personal pyrotechnics.

This advice applies also to digressions of all sorts. One cares not who are the father and mother of the boy who is drowning. Omit all such irrelevant details. Stick to the story, and introduce nothing, personal or otherwise, out of keeping with the tone, the single effect to be produced.

There is always, too, the tendency to overload a story with too much description, psychology, or exposition. The first will either kill the vitality and action value of the character, or, if setting is involved, it will descend rapidly into mere sentimental or irrelevant detail. Too much psychology will also negate action, and is to be used sparingly (1) for character delineation and (2) for intensifying the climax. As for exposition, a brief paragraph of it, introduced *after* the moment of interest, will generally suffice. If not used in such a beginning, it must be subordinated by scattering it cleverly and unobtrusively throughout the early stages of the story, *never* after the suspense is well under way.

Long speeches must be avoided. Break up a speech—if dialogue *must* be used—by inserting a gesture or an expression of the speaker. If a long speech must be rehearsed, give it in indirect discourse, in your own words as the writer, as a kind of psychological synopsis. Dialogue, when used, should appear at *tense* moments and should be staccato, clever, and brief. The use of the introductory word "said" must be watched, though there are dangers in seeking ingenious ways of avoiding it. In general, avoid dialogue, but if you need to resort to it, go back to your diary and resurrect exact speeches of people *whom you know*, or who are about your own age, and then use both those people and their speeches (compressed if possible) in the emotional moments of your story.

We have nearly finished the negative advice. In concluding, we want to preach a brief sermon of good New England flavor. Avoid immorality, profanity, pessimism, and all other arts of the Devil. "Look not thou down but up," warns Rabbi Ben Ezra. Keep your gaze out of the gutter and your thoughts out of the sewer. Modern literature can stand a little uplifting. Begin your missionary work at home—you need not relate every detail of the kitchen and parlor indiscriminately. Imagination, not bad odors, counts in writing.

To turn now to the positive advice, first consider the three elements of a story. The plot must have an element of surprise, and a psychological tenseness at the climax. It is not enough to carry the character by incidents alone into a distinctly disagreeable situation. He must be allowed—in fact, *made*—to reflect on his predicament at the very moment when the clouds are thickest. He would do this normally: there is truth in the idea that a man's mental activity increases proportionally to his physical danger. He may move into a region of intense calm just before the final blow, but he cannot avoid the preceding mental turmoil. Hence let him philosophize for the sake of intensifying the climax. The only point is that, as noted above, the man's cerebral possibilities must be proportionate to his character as depicted up to that point; and at the same time the reader must not be pushed to emotional exhaustion, where supercharged nerves will be quite insulated to the electricity of the solution.

As for the element of surprise, we have already suggested the importance of that. It must not be forgotten that the reader expects, anticipates, and yearns for a surprise. You must give him one—you cannot disappoint him. If you let him down with a flat solution—hackneyed or impossible—he will sit back and laugh, or say something very unpleasant. All through that story he has been working his head off to beat you at your own game: that is, guess your solution before he gets to it. If you give yourself away too soon, he will drop the story, but if you have no adequate surprise in store for him at all, you have broken one of the cardinal rules of the game, and he will never play with you again. And, remember, your surprise must be a logical outcome of both the incidents and characters involved. Stuart P. Sherman's greatest tribute to O. Henry was this: that O. Henry's amazing twists evolved logically from the characters, not merely from plot legerdemain. Try to merit similar praise.

The characters should normally be of positive moral value, and your attitude toward them should be sympathetic. In short, there is no point in your going out of the way to drag yourself through the catacombs of the underworld, whose exotic or sordid denizens you neither know nor understand. Write from your own point of view first, and then if you must shift, look at the world from the eyes of the people you know (remember the diary)— and know well. The frantic desire to straddle social strata will get you nowhere and dissipate creative energy into idealistic mist and twaddle. Plant your feet solidly in your own front yard.

One element of character portrayal troubles students considerably—that is, description. No one can give a definite formula for that problem. But if you have intensely created and intensely realized a character before you put him down on paper, the description will flash in with instinctive strokes (compare Chapter XVI below). In the plot story normally you will need little description—in fact, if you are using your own point of view, none. But if it must be introduced, pick out the salient features, not all the painfully minute details; for you must look at this character from the point of view of the average man. And those salient features must harmonize with the tone of the story, that is, the emotional effect to be produced on the reader.

Setting is a matter of local color, so far as the plot story is concerned. Pick your own home town or any locale that you know thoroughly. Don't wander off into the sheik-ridden Soudan or the newest war zone. You will be surprised to see what you can do with incidents developed on the old county-fair grounds or the Toonerville golf course (see Chapter XV below).

Other *Do's* in the plot story should involve the title, the names, the unities, outlining, and revision. Obviously the title must be stimulating. Sometimes a quotation will suggest a title: "The Glimpses of the Moon," "The Heaven-Kissed Hill," "Ever Soft, Gentle, and Low"—to draw upon Shakespeare. But a quotation has its dangers. Not everyone will recognize it, and then your hopeful cleverness will be wasted. Reference to well-known stories, legends, or myths may go better: "A Descendant of the Magi," for example. But humorous, punning titles will go best of all: "Pieces of Hate," "The Widow's Might," "The Bridal Reign," etc. O. Henry provides endless examples. Doubtless others will do as well, but a writer should neglect no opportunity to attract attention with the first words of any story—that is, the title. Finally, the title should harmonize with the tone of the story.

Names should to some extent, either by rhythm or connotation, suggest the people they denote, for names are to the characters what the title is to the story. Edith Wharton, author of the compact masterpiece, *Ethan Frome*, said that in writing her stories she first searched for a name for her central character, and that from the sheer suggestive power of that name she derived her story, at least in large part. Personal qualities, frankness, guile, pliability, aggressiveness, good humor, the slightest shadings of character can be suggested in the name. The art lies in avoiding obvious and deliberate labeling. Not much originality can be shown by calling your ingenue Betty or your happy-go-lucky boy hero Jack. Only the shallowest movies still label their characters like canned goods; Dick Armstrong (hero), Reynard Trask (villain), and the like.

As the quality of the character is condensed within the name, so the action must be compressed within the brief plot. There are many devices for telescoping action; some have been suggested. Certain stories demand a slow tracing of events; but in most a rapid advance to a powerful climax is imperative. Letting the alphabet serve as a diagram of the events in a story, we may say it is best to begin the actual action at somewhere from F to M, accounting for previous events by exposition—with a letter, after-dinner conversation, or straight summarizing by the narrator—and then to build up to a strong climax at T to W. But even in stories where the opening events, A to E, are essential, one principle should control the presentation—concentration. In dramatic criticism the principles of the "three unities" of time, place, and action have been discussed since Aristotle and the Renaissance. A tale stretched over a long period of time is in danger of losing momentum and unity; persistent changing of place may confuse the reader and blur the climax; discontinuity in the action, if obtrusive, will shatter emotional tension. Work, then, for a well-integrated beginning, middle, and end, a unified narrative. Much of the success of the story will depend on the careful focusing of the alphabet of events, as if those events were letters spelling out one compact, clean-cut, meaningful sentence.

Outlining is by far the most important step in the actual preparation of the plot story, or any story. Before writing the first sentence, block out on paper the story in your mind, according to the divisions noted in sections 2, 3, 4, and 5. Section 3 already contains suggestions as to the outline form for the prelude and moment of interest. The remainder of the outline we have developed in the same section, in the treatment of the "lost" story with the sequences of suspense—except that the climax and solution should be noted in the outline *after* the suspense. The mental preconception of the story merely places them before. A conclusion, if necessary, can be derived from section 5.

Substantially, then, the outline of your complete story will take the form of a few jotted remarks for the prelude, a single sentence for the moment of interest, a long series of sequences for suspense (which according to the diagram in section 3 will be at least two-thirds of the outline), and a single sentence each for the climax, the solution, and the conclusion. This, of course, is but a rough, mechanical contrivance. It can be modified somewhat for more complex types of stories to be introduced presently. For the plot story, however, it will serve the purpose admirably. If such an outline is submitted to the instructor some days ahead of the story proper, it may be revised by his criticism.

When we take up the subject of revision, we immediately encroach upon the realm of style, that is, the word-clothing of the story idea. A few suggestions are then in order, which may be applied before the story is written or afterward. There must be free use of active verbs—*veni, vidi, vici*—and this triad arrangement will often be useful. "Jack raced down the hill, slipped on his skates, and sped out to the open hole in the ice where his brother was clinging desperately." "She leaped back, braced herself, and smashed the ball across the court like a rifle bullet." In both cases appear active verbs and a triad construction.

Similarly most narrative should be written in a loose style, with relatively short sentences. "If he comes, I'll fight him," is not loose but periodic. Turn it around so that the subordinate clause comes last: "I'll fight him if he comes." Most narrative sentences are like that, with the subordinate elements trailing loosely. And they are generally short, although the great problem is to vary their length enough within narrow bounds so that the reader never gets the impression of jerkiness. To secure smoothness you will need a wealth of connectives at your finger tips. You will do well to enlarge on your store by gathering synonyms from a thesaurus; then put as many into immediate use as you can. Connection may also be secured by repeating the idea in different words, and sometimes by repeating a word from the preceding sentence. Often the thought sequence is so swift and tense that the writer need not worry about connectives at all. This is especially true as the story approaches the climax, where action, psychology, and diction are all tremendously intensified.

Rhythm is the most elusive of all elements of style. Success in this feature is totally dependent on the writer's individual musical or metrical sense and the extent of his vocabulary. Consider the following, for example:

"The parlor was like a shroud, and very gloomy. Moonlight streamed across a heavy oak rocker's back, through a window with long curtains, and fell at a casket's bottom before the fireplace. There were some wreaths of flowers on it which the rays did not touch, and they covered and surrounded the velvet trappings. The close air, which was musty, was filled with their odor. A small bronze Virgin stood at the bier's end."

Aside from the fact that it contains few active verbs, can you imagine anything more jerky and unrhythmical than this story prelude? Now, by applying to it some of the simpler rules of rhythm, we can obtain this:

"The parlor was shrouded in deep gloom, save where, between the long curtains of the window, the moonlight streamed across the back of a heavy oak rocker and fell on the bottom of a casket standing before the fireplace. Wreaths of flowers, untouched by the rays, covered and surrounded the velvet trappings, their odor pervading the close, musty air. At one end of the bier stood a small bronze Virgin."

What did we do? That is hard to tell exactly. We know that we worked with it for some time, rewriting and reordering the details almost metrically [1] until we got them together in a sequence and form that satisfied our rhythmic sense much more than did the original passage. Perhaps the secret lies ultimately in projecting oneself into the mood of the situation, just as the description of a character will come forth instinctively if the character is sympathetically and intensely realized by the writer from the moment he is conceived. Obviously the rhythm of the passage above fits the somber mood of the surroundings, and we got the rhythm ultimately by projecting ourselves into that mood.

Consider again the same process applied to the following:

"St. Mary's clock up in the dark spire struck nine slow strokes that were muffled and sounded dully through the snow driving down. The blind man, shifting his pencils to his other hand, rubbed his right leg which was cold. He once or twice shuffled his feet and blew on his hands. He listened a moment for steps, shook his beard, which was gray, free of snow and slowly pushed himself up on his feet, using his cane."

Our version of this, after some metrical rewriting, turned out to be:

"The clock in St. Mary's struck nine in slow, muffled strokes that sounded dully through the driving snow. The blind man shifted his pencils to his other hand and rubbed his cold right leg. He shuffled his feet once or twice and blew on his hands. Listening a moment for steps, he shook his gray beard free of snow and pushed himself slowly to his feet with the aid of his broken cane." [2]

---

[1] Scan the revised passage for types of metrical feet.
[2] Note the predominance of anapests at the end.

Connectives are changed, details combined within one sentence, words left almost the same in number though arranged in a more metrical sequence; but over it all is a mood which carries a sense of the slow, inexorable, silent fall of the snow. We realized, as sympathetically as possible, the blind man's feeling of hopelessness.

Rhythm is the last deft touch to be applied to the plot story. But descending from this sublime feature a moment, remember that mechanical mistakes will ruin, as effectively as exquisite rhythm will transfigure, a story. Hence before your story finds its way to the instructor, take a blank sheet of paper, lay it across your written lines, leaving only the first line uncovered, and then move the paper slowly and uniformly down the page so that you can read each line as a child reads the sentences in his Second Reader. Forget that the work is your own. Read for mechanical errors. And if you find none in this manner, you have made a good ending of one task and are now ready for the next.

Finally, as a result of many years of teaching this type, we have found some specific, miscellaneous minor points which are helpful to the student in evading the pitfalls inherent in the plot story.

First, use short paragraphs based on change of incident. Dialogue is always paragraphed. In general avoid mystification— that is, fooling both the character and reader: this may be all right for detective stories, but they have a technique of their own quite different from that of ordinary stories (see Carolyn Wells's book on the subject). Dialect is hard to handle, but effective when you show direct knowledge of it. Be sure the beginning is clear: do not confuse the reader with four or five names right at the start; and make the locale perfectly clear. Above all, avoid a sarcastic tone of condescension toward your characters; this procedure will kill the emotional value of the story on the spot.

Now and then your title may give away your solution: e.g., "Saved by Our Dog." Particularly beware of the necessity of retrospect at the end to explain obscure points; everything should be made logical and complete as you go along, so that the story can end abruptly. It is possible, as we have already indicated, for the author to shift the point of view by writing the story in sections if absolutely necessary. And you can also have the leading character die at the end, as Jack London did in "To Build a Fire," but that solution is seldom genuinely logical.

The main point is to feel with your characters throughout. Clever wording will never make up for lack of sympathetic emotional creation. Get in your negative aspect—your opposing force—quickly and then suffer with your character. At the end solve the story completely, giving the reader full relaxation: don't leave your hero hanging by one arm between the ties on a trestle over the rapids while the train goes by on the other track; get him back on safe ground. With these added suggestions perhaps you can now go ahead more safely.

Turn now to the more intricate story types developed in the subsequent chapters. But always remember the old plot-story formula: *your own personal experience in life colored by your own imagination*—that is, heightened or intensified to fulfill the requirements of suspense and climax. For as Arnold Bennett once remarked, "Good fiction is autobiography dressed in the colors of all mankind."

CHAPTER XV

Expansion of the Plot Story

1. CHARACTER PLOTTED

The strict plot story has probably seemed barren, a mere skeleton. Modern taste has emphasized character. However, much of the world's great storehouse of narrative consists of the plot story. *Aesop's Fables*, and all fable and fairy-tale lore, Boccaccio's *Decameron*, Chaucer's *Canterbury Tales*, most Biblical narrative, the native American yarns—all these serve to illustrate that in the realm of story plot has been the thing. Since the nineteenth century there has been some shift. The artist's instinct for atmosphere and the growing fascination of character have led to the production of stories in which plot is made subordinate, actually deriving from atmosphere or character. Thus we have further possibilities for story development, more difficult but conveniently transitional to the complete short story.

"Character Plotted" means a plot story in which a dominant trait of character precipitates the plot—not only precipitates it, but carries it as well. Notice that here we plot the effect of only one rather isolated and dominant trait. A technical character story involves the bundle of varied traits which compose the complex individual.[1]

Fundamental features remain the same. The point of view as explained for the plot story is not changed (either "I" or the omniscient author). The sources of the story are, as before, principally the diary and autobiography. The raft structure will still provide the pattern for the plot, and also the relative length of divisions. All the Do's and Don't's of the last chapter are still

---

[1] See Chapter XVII below.

pertinent. And, not least in this slightly new type of story, the tone must be retained as a prime factor.

Most students, the moment character is asked for, write one of two things, a biography or a character sketch, neither one of which is wanted now. In Chapter XIII, we noted that biography might be used as a preliminary training for plotting characters in a story—and we still recommend it—but biography is not what we want here. Nor is a character sketch part of the requirement.[1] A character sketch describes a static, or stationary, complex character. The simple character we have to deal with now is kinetic, developing (positively or negatively) on the basis of one trait. Hence, although it may be well to write out a preliminary sketch of the character to be used—like a professional writer— that sketch, nevertheless, except for one dominant trait, will be merely background for the story to be plotted on that one characteristic trait.

We come back to tone, then, with its two aspects in the original plot story: its compelling force as derived from the moment of interest, and its single effect (pathos, humor, irony, etc.). The dominant trait of the character to be plotted generally accounts for the single effect. But the compelling force cannot meanwhile be neglected. If it is, biography or a mere descriptive sketch will be produced. For example, a girl may be a social climber. The effect sought may be pathetic. But one must not overlook the fact that the very first thing she does to start herself upward must have the other aspect of tone, the compelling force, the element of danger which will probably involve her quite painfully at the climax. To exemplify, suppose she drops a steady home-town boy for a socially arrived man of the world. She may discover at a crisis later that she has sold her birthright for a mess of pottage, and the complications she may ultimately get into will be in the reader's mind from the beginning—that is, from the moment of interest, which provided this compelling force.

Hence it is not sufficient to pick out a dominant trait and set it going in one direction or the other (up or down) merely by a series of carefully chosen incidents, in the manner of linear narration. That dominant trait must lead to a preliminary act of

[1] See Chapters VII and VIII.

impulse (the moment of interest) which will, throughout the suspense, worry both character and reader until at the climax something happens to break the mental strain. And notice the word *mental*. In this type of story, in contrast to the bare plot story, psychology (see Chapter XIV) must predominate throughout, from the moment of interest to the solution. It is no longer a question of external forces "torturing" the reader and character so much as the internal, or psychological, worry. The character, our social climber, for example, is disturbed by what she did at the moment of interest. All her succeeding *acts* may be consistent with that first act, but meanwhile her thoughts are becoming more and more troubled. From the beginning moment when she acted on impulse (in accordance with the dominant trait), her *feelings* impel her to follow up that first determining act consistently, but her *reason* will tell her she is getting in deeper and deeper; and her reason and feelings will fight it out fiercely. At the climax the battle will be terrific. The solution will show the victory of one or the other, and the conclusion (now almost absolutely necessary) the final results of the struggle. This internal struggle throughout the suspense is hard to handle; but it is the best possible training for the real character story later.

Before applying such a simple story more directly to the raft structure, we should like to dispose of the bugbear of the methods of delineating character. The critics here generally contradict each other. One will declare that "direct" delineation of character involves exposition and the speeches of the major and minor characters; that "indirect" is promoted by the actions of the characters and by environment. Another will denote four "direct" methods[1]: (1) exposition, (2) description, (3) psychoanalysis, and (4) reports of other characters; and also four "indirect" methods: (1) actions, (2) speeches, (3) environment, and (4) effect on other characters. The critics seem to agree only here and there, and are confusing. Hence we propose to drop the terms "direct" and "indirect," and arbitrarily suggest where some of these methods may be used in the development of the story.

The prelude ought to give the static character at the begin-

---

[1] These are repeated from Chapter VII, on the Character Sketch.

ning—with one distinctly dominant trait, somewhat unique if possible. For example, the character may be intensely self-sacrificing, selfish, ambitious, greedy, priggish, envious, sweet, proud. The story will go better if it is based on a human weakness. The methods used to show this trait will probably be a bit of exposition, description, and a suggestion of environment, if necessary. There should not be a long prelude—not much longer than that of the plot story.

At the moment of interest the character, as a result of the dominant trait, impulsively does something which will probably get him into serious difficulties later on if he fails to reverse himself by using his reason. A foppish boy, forgetting the advice of Polonius, may invest in clothes which he knows he cannot pay for. A priggish girl may start losing friends and grow unutterably lonely. An ambitious boy may plunge into too many activities, to the ultimate detriment of his health or the active antagonism of his friends. A selfish girl may start draining her father's pocketbook. A self-sacrificing girl may develop into a professional doormat, to the sacrifice of her self-respect. One impulsive, detrimental act at the beginning determines that character's future acts and sets the stage for his complete downfall or resuscitation at the climax and solution.

The suspense, as suggested before, is a logical development of the moment of interest, involving (1) the character's acts consistently based on feelings as indicated at the moment of interest, and (2) the subsequent mental disturbance after each act (in short, the tremendous struggle, within everybody at times, of impulsive feelings *versus* reason). The raft structure is still applicable, for each successive act and resultant worry increases in importance and intensity as the story approaches the climax. And throughout the suspense, now, the feelings-reason conflict is in evidence *before and after each successive act*—the devil and the good angel fight in the character's mind before and after, and probably even during the act. For example, the social climber at the moment of interest, breaks with her fine childhood chum in favor of the socially arrived individual with no brains and much money. The moment she does this she reflects, with feelings and reason fighting. In the course of this mental struggle she decides that in order to be consistent now she must cut all her old friends. She worries about this, but finally does it. Then she worries about it afterwards till she steps into further difficulty by hiding her family when they come to see her at college. She worries about that, too, before and afterward, but decides to go even further and get expensively gowned and made up. Each act is always preceded and followed by worry (reason *versus* feelings), and each act always cuts off the character a little further from her former, positively good associations. So at the climax she faces marital incompatibility, and her intense worry is only offset by her conspicuously brazen attitude. Such a development in the suspense is typical of this sort of story. The methods of delineation to be used will be principally the character's acts and psychology, with possibly some dialogue.

The solution may or may not save the character. In general, it ought to save. The type of solution will be either II or III, by external interference or internal inspiration.[1] For example, in the above story the childhood chum, realizing the possible danger, may go out of his way to save her. For type III, the man of the world may never propose to her at all; he has cut her for a better possibility. But best of all (the *character's* inspirational idea in type III) she herself may at the last moment drop the game and go to the home-town boy to beg forgiveness. At any rate, there should be a definite twist *against* the grain of the dominant characteristic as developed throughout the suspense. This twist preferably should be positive rather than negative. The conclusion may be any one of the four types given in Chapter XIV, section 5, though the echoed opening and the surprise twist tend to be a little forced in this sort of story.

On the basis of students' experiences we can submit some further definite suggestions. The main problem will be to cut down the time element so as to let the trait develop to the climax quickly; otherwise you are likely to lapse into a mere lengthy biography. But one single incident will not do either. Be sure to keep the incidents rising in intensity of suspense; chronology alone will not lift this story on the raft-scaffold structure. Retrospect may be used sparingly to account for past evidences of the

[1] See Chapter XIV, section 4 above.

decisive trait, although it is a rather dangerous technique. Do not mix plot and the trait; one student started with a chattering stenographer (surely plausible), but very quickly shifted to an office robbery in which the voluble girl was a subordinate figure. Similarly, do not write a full character short story; you are here merely plotting the effect of a single bad trait, not analyzing a complex character plus several minor characters. Once again we insist that you avoid an indifferent attitude toward the effect of this trait on your character; for the emotional value of your story depends on your sympathy for him, or her. At the end, give a definite twist which will save the character from perdition: there is no sense in being too persistently morbid. But above all, abstain from any moralizing paragraph, either at the beginning or the end. Let the story convey its own moral.

Finally, we repeat that we have not attempted to expound the character story involving several complex characters. We have merely suggested a device for plotting a *dominant characteristic* against the background of the plot story. To some extent this type of work will help toward the development of a character story in which not one dominant individual but several individuals are adequately presented.

The solution in "Cameos" is brilliant. Note that retrospect can be used sparingly, but it must be clear.

CAMEOS

The slim figure trudged slowly along the inner side of the busy street. If anyone had taken the trouble to notice, she was a young person with mended gloves and a threadbare coat, but nobody did.

Carly climbed the stairs to her neat but lonely room, carefully hung her coat on the back of the door, and opened a tiny bureau drawer. With the tenderness of a young mother she lifted a long red box and gazed at its contents. A cameo, it was the only source of joy to her. She had always held a desire in her heart for cameos. She remembered her dear mother had always worn a beautiful gold locket set with one of these lovely pink ladies. They were like fine stately beings to Carly, with their high-combed hair and beautiful white necks.

Thinking back, Carly remembered an incident when she had given all of her twenty-six marbles, her treasured pearl button, and her only doll for a pin Mabel had found under the porch. It was a cameo.

The lady's nose was chipped, and cracks ran like wrinkles over her face and neck. When Carly was sleeping, the curtain had blown it off the table to the floor, and the next morning a funeral service was held to bury the remains of her dear "pink lady."

Thinking about it now, she smiled at her childish reverence and wondered if the price of the object in her hands was worth the denials made. It was, for she had wanted it so.

Each day she would confide in her adopted lady as a child whispers her secrets to her doll. While walking on Sunday, she had passed a window full of odd collections of old jewelry. In the corner, covered with dust, was a cameo locket. Underneath it a sign fairly shouted "$68."

"No," she said aloud and moved on.

Each evening found her before the old shop, and each Saturday she tucked away her scant earnings. Denying herself all the pleasures and too many of the necessities of life, she had become thinner and very pale. One Saturday she entered the shop, breathlessly asked for her treasure, and hurried home squeezing it in her tiny palm. She felt weak. Maybe it was the thrill of possession and her dream come true. She called it "Lady Delia" after her mother. Exhausted but happy, she closed her eyes, only to awaken, hot and choking.

"Yes, it's a serious case. She'll need medical care." A man's voice reached Carly's ears. He seemed a thousand miles away.

"But there is no money," came the retort rather than the reply.

"What about the cameo? Who is this Lady Delia, she keeps murmuring about?"

The next time those heavy eyelids were lifted, she saw a sunny, white room where stately white ladies seemed to float about, whispering, "She's rich now. The cameo was one of the 'Menahand' set."

"Lady Delia" had paid her debt.

D. H.

In "The Alibi-Artist" there is also a clever twist at the end: an internal solution engineered by the writer.

THE ALIBI–ARTIST

Marge O'Hara was sixteen, and the youngest and favorite daughter of Tom O'Hara. She was as pretty as a picture, which aided her a great deal when it came to giving alibis. Poor Sally, her sister, only two and a half years older, usually bore the brunt of them, even when they were youngsters. How well Sally could remember the time that

Marge upset a large box filled with butternuts, and told her dad with such an angelic smile that Sally did it. The result was that Sally—not Marge—picked up every one for punishment without the aid of a broom.

Every night, when they both were attending high school, when it was time to clear away the dinner dishes, Marge slipped upstairs with the school-work alibi until after the dishes were done. Sally, the scapegoat as usual, always found her reveling in dime novels. After one or two attempts of complaint about it, she stopped, for Marge had a clever tongue that went with the smile that captivated everyone's heart.

And who suffered the time Marge carved an *S* in the bathroom moulding? Of course it was Sally! Everyone reasoned that if Marge did it, as Sally said, she would have made an *M* instead of an *S*.

When caught with two boy-friend callers on the same evening, Marge carefully explained to each one that the other belonged to Sally. Who wouldn't have believed such sparkling eyes and laughing lips!

One night, the night before Sally's spring vacation was up—she was attending college now in a neighboring city—Marge was given the opportunity to make another alibi. It was Sally's evening with the car, but Marge borrowed it for just a half hour to go over to Jane's to borrow a dance frock. In her haste she went through a red light and crashed into the side of a red roadster. Jarred and frightened, but not hurt, she jumped out. Instead of helping the driver of the red roadster, she gave a quick look, and darted down the street away from the accident.

Meanwhile Sally, fearing another trick, called Don to take her to the library to return some books before she left for college the next morning.

Marge was awakened the next morning by a touch on her shoulder. The anxious face of Tom O'Hara looked down on her.

"Why did you leave the car after having that accident last night?"

"Accident! What accident?" said Marge, stifling a make-believe yawn.

"Here—look! The picture of the car and license number. They're looking for the driver now, for the man in the other car was badly injured."

Marge took the paper that he held toward her. The headlines screamed, "Car abandoned after accident. Driver sought."

"Why, Dad," she exclaimed, "it was Sally's turn to use the car last

night." Marge had been thinking desperately, while apparently reading the account. She realized that her dad couldn't get in touch with
Sally until late that afternoon, for Sally's custom was to leave before
the regular breakfast hour, when she returned to Brookstone College
after a vacation. It was only 10 A.M.; surely she could think up a
perfect alibi before the afternoon came.

Tom O'Hara rushed out wondering what to do next. Marge picked
up the paper. "Unidentified man seriously hurt." She began to get
conscience-stricken. Suppose she were sending Sally to prison! Suppose the driver had recognized her before she fled! Hastily she donned
her hiking clothes and walked to the outskirts of the town, before
she realized that she had forgotten to have breakfast, and that it was
now past time for lunch.

She lunched at a wayside inn, discarding one alibi after another
between bites. When she reached the last drop of coffee, she was ready
to go back and tell her dad everything. She realized for the first time
that she had been selfish. She wouldn't let Sally take the blame again!

She came back to reality when the soft soothing music of the radio
stopped and the clear crisp voice of the announcer filled the room.
He was reading an interesting account of an accident that happened at
Forty-Third and Toole Streets. "This accident was a bit unusual, for
the driver of the sedan, now identified as Miss Sally O'Hara, who abandoned her car after crashing into Anthony Reswick, will be given
special permission by the Dean of Brookstone College to go to Darton,
where she will collect a $5,000 reward for the discovery of the money
stolen from the State Bank in Darton yesterday. Miss O'Hara is, as
yet, unaware of her good fortune, not knowing that Reswick was
recognized as one of the robbers of the bank when he was taken to
the hospital for treatment. The major portion of the loot was found
under the seat in the car."

Marge sank back on her chair, whispering over and over—"No
more alibis."

G. W.

"That Red-Headed Temper" hits the type precisely—in a
very humorous tone. The solution is evolved by the character
himself.

THAT RED–HEADED TEMPER

He had a temper, an awful one. If he had not had red hair, perhaps
—but he did have. The boys at school always found it great fun to
tease him about his hair until they found out that Bill had a mean

left. Bill always thanked the Lord that at least he had given him strength with which to protect himself from those who made fun of his red, flaming red hair.

His temper fitted his hair perfectly. When he was good, he was very, very good, but when he was angry—oh my!

He became older, as all people do, and went to work. He was working as a clerk in a department store near a doll counter. One day someone came in. A salesman went up to her with a cheery smile and the ever-ready, "Anything for you, Madam?" Then Bill heard the woman answer, "I would like to have that red-haired fellow over there!" Bill turned hot and then cold. How dared she! He would show her. And forgetting that he was working at a doll counter with yellow-haired, black-haired, and *red*-haired dolls, he virtually leaped over to the woman and with the roar of a lion yelled, "You would, eh!" The woman drew back in alarm. What sort of a man was this, what sort of a store? She would never come in here again! Apologies from the manager followed. Ugly looks were cast at Bill. Bill fidgeted uneasily, seeing his error. And finally, Bill's dismissal.

Lost, a job! And all because of his cursed sensitiveness regarding his red hair. He would try harder next time. He would control his temper. After looking and looking, he finally procured another job as an office boy. Then one day someone came into the office and slapping him suddenly on the back said, "Hello! Carrots." Just as a finger draws instinctively away from a burning substance, so did Bill without thinking turn around and place his left fist in the right eye of his greeter. The victim of the blow stumbled back, looked up with one eye—the other one was shut—and then with angry words on his lips rushed into the main office. The boss's son! Oh Heavens! there goes another job. And why? Temper! Red hair!

He shuffled along from place to place, but there was not a job in sight. Finally he decided to stop at an employment agency. While waiting his turn he became enveloped in thoughts of how he would always be nonchalant when someone called attention to his red hair. Suddenly, as if from a dream, and then very, oh too realistically came the words, "That flamingo-haired fellow! Hurry! You're next." It was so sudden that he had no time to put on the control he had promised himself he would. And so, picking up the thing nearest him—it happened to be a filled inkwell—he threw it at the clerk, who fortunately ducked.

Well, he might as well give up looking for a job after that. What to do! What to do! He could not control his temper. A flash! A light! But he could change the color of his hair. And he did.

A. F.

-»» B «&-

You will not readily find professional illustrations of such a
simplified type of story as "Character Plotted"; for, as we have
suggested above, the plotting of a single characteristic is not a high
creative endeavor, and also it ignores the essentially complex
character of human nature. At best this type is little more than
mechanical, a good exercise in intensifying a characterizing
trait. Nevertheless, professional writers do often use the idea of a
single trait to some extent in developing the complete character
story: consider, for example, Poe's "Ligeia." What we shall
attempt to do, then, is to present a few stories which concentrate their development on the effect of one trait in the leading
character, realizing at the same time that the innate complexity
of an acceptable character story relies on individualizing traits
beyond one single-track development. In each of these stories
now appended, some aspects of the artificial "Character Plotted"
are present.

In "The Father," which covers considerable time by rapid
leaps, the character does shift at the end. Note that the story has
been developed by several rising incidents, aimed toward a
climax.

THE FATHER [1]

Björnstjerne Björnson

The man whose story is here to be told was the wealthiest and most
influential person in his parish; his name was Thord Overaas. He
appeared in the priest's study one day, tall and earnest.

"I have gotten a son," said he, "and I wish to present him for
baptism."

"What shall his name be?"

"Finn—after my father."

"And the sponsors?"

They were mentioned, and proved to be the best men and women
of Thord's relations in the parish.

"Is there anything else?" inquired the priest, and looked up.

The peasant hesitated a little.

---

[1] This translation of "The Father" was made by Professor R. B. Anderson, of
Madison, Wisconsin, and is reprinted with his permission.

"I should like very much to have him baptized by himself," said he finally.

"That is to say on a week day?"

"Next Saturday, at twelve o'clock noon."

"Is there anything else?" inquired the priest.

"There is nothing else;" and the peasant twirled his cap, as though he were about to go.

Then the priest rose. "There is yet this, however," said he, and walking toward Thord, he took him by the hand and looked gravely into his eyes: "God grant that the child may become a blessing to you!"

One day sixteen years later, Thord stood once more in the priest's study.

"Really, you carry your age astonishingly well, Thord," said the priest; for he saw no change whatever in the man.

"That is because I have no troubles," replied Thord.

To this the priest said nothing, but after a while he asked: "What is your pleasure this evening?"

"I have come this evening about that son of mine who is to be confirmed tomorrow."

"He is a bright boy."

"I did not wish to pay the priest until I heard what number the boy would have when he takes his place in church tomorrow."

"He will stand number one."

"So I have heard; and here are ten dollars for the priest."

"Is there anything else I can do for you?" inquired the priest, fixing his eyes on Thord.

"There is nothing else."

Thord went out.

Eight years more rolled by, and then one day a noise was heard outside the priest's study, for many men were approaching, and at their head was Thord, who entered first.

The priest looked up and recognized him.

"You come well attended this evening, Thord," said he.

"I am here to request that the banns may be published for my son; he is about to marry Karen Storliden, daughter of Gudmund, who stands here beside me."

"Why, that is the richest girl in the parish."

"So they say," replied the peasant, stroking back his hair with one hand.

The priest sat awhile as if in deep thought, then entered the names in his book, without making any comments, and the men wrote their signatures underneath. Thord laid three dollars on the table.

"One is all I am to have," said the priest.

"I know that very well; but he is my only child; I want to do it handsomely."

The priest took the money.

"This is now the third time, Thord, that you have come here on your son's account."

"But now I am through with him," said Thord, and folding up his pocket-book he said farewell and walked away.

The men slowly followed him.

A fortnight later, the father and son were rowing across the lake, one calm, still day, to Storliden to make arrangements for the wedding.

"This thwart is not secure," said the son, and stood up to straighten the seat on which he was sitting.

At the same moment the board he was standing on slipped from under him; he threw out his arms, uttered a shriek, and fell overboard.

"Take hold of the oar!" shouted the father, springing to his feet and holding out the oar.

But when the son had made a couple of efforts he grew stiff.

"Wait a moment!" cried the father, and began to row toward his son.

Then the son rolled over on his back, gave his father one long look, and sank.

Thord could scarcely believe it; he held the boat still, and stared at the spot where his son had gone down, as though he must surely come to the surface again. There rose some bubbles, then some more, and finally one large one that burst; and the lake lay there as smooth and bright as a mirror again.

For three days and three nights people saw the father rowing round and round the spot, without taking either food or sleep; he was dragging the lake for the body of his son. And toward morning of the third day he found it, and carried it in his arms up over the hills to his gard.

It might have been about a year from that day, when the priest, late one autumn evening, heard someone in the passage outside of the door, carefully trying to find the latch. The priest opened the door, and in walked a tall, thin man with bowed form and white hair. The priest looked long at him before he recognized him. It was Thord.

"Are you out walking so late?" said the priest, and stood still in front of him.

"Ah, yes! it is late," said Thord, and took a seat.

The priest sat down also, as though waiting. A long, long silence followed. At last Thord said:

"I have something with me that I should like to give to the poor; I want it to be invested as a legacy in my son's name."

He rose, laid some money on the table, and sat down again. The priest counted it.

"It is a great deal of money," said he.

"It is half the price of my gard. I sold it today."

The priest sat long in silence. At last he asked, but gently:

"What do you propose to do now, Thord?"

"Something better."

They sat there for awhile, Thord with downcast eyes, the priest with his eyes fixed on Thord. Presently the priest said, slowly and softly:

"I think your son has at last brought you a true blessing."

"Yes, I think so myself," said Thord, looking up while two big tears coursed slowly down his cheeks.

"The Pensioner" covers a century of time in a few pages but sets off the man's pride and the woman's greed very aptly. Neither character is allowed to shift at the end: one dies, and the other gloats over her two thousand pounds.

THE PENSIONER [1]

William Caine

Miss Crewe was born in the year 1821. She received a sort of education, and at the age of twenty became the governess of a little girl, eight years old, called Martha Bond. She was Martha's governess for the next ten years. Then Martha came out and Miss Crewe went to be the governess of somebody else. Martha married Mr. William Harper. A year later she gave birth to a son, who was named Edward. This brings us to the year 1853.

When Edward was six, Miss Crewe came back, to be his governess. Four years later he went to school and Miss Crewe went away to be the governess of somebody else. She was now forty-two years old.

Twelve years passed and Mrs. Harper died, recommending Miss Crewe to her husband's care, for Miss Crewe had recently been smitten

[1] Reprinted from *The Graphic*, July 2, 1921, by permission of the editor and the proprietors.

by an incurable disease which made it impossible for her to be a governess any longer.

Mr. Harper, who had passionately loved his wife, gave instructions to his solicitor to pay Miss Crewe the sum of one hundred and fifty pounds annually. He had some thoughts of buying her an annuity, but she seemed so ill that he didn't. Edward was now twenty-two.

In the year 1888, Mr. Harper died after a very short illness. He had expected Miss Crewe to die any day during the past thirteen years, but since she hadn't he thought it proper now to recommend her to Edward's care. This is how he did it.

"That confounded old Crewe, Eddie. You'll have to see to her. Let her have her money as before, but for the Lord's sake don't go and buy her an annuity now. If you do, she'll die on your hands in a week!" Shortly afterwards the old gentleman passed away.

Edward was now thirty-five. Miss Crewe was sixty-seven and reported to be in an almost desperate state. Edward followed his father's advice. He bought no annuity for Miss Crewe. Her one hundred and fifty pounds continued to be paid each year into her bank; but by Edward, not by his late father's solicitors.

Edward had his own ideas of managing the considerable fortune which he had inherited. These ideas were unsound. The first of them was that he should assume the entire direction of his own affairs. Accordingly he instructed his solicitors to realize all the mortgages and railway stock and other admirable securities in which his money was invested and hand over the cash to him. He then went in for the highest rate of interest which anyone would promise him. The consequence was that, within twelve years, he was almost a poor man, his annual income having dwindled from about three thousand to about four hundred pounds.

Though he was a fool he was an honourable man, and so he continued to pay Miss Crewe her one hundred and fifty pounds each year. This left him about two hundred and fifty for himself. The capital which his so reduced income represented was invested in a Mexican brewery in which he had implicit faith. Nevertheless, he began to think that he might do well were he to try to earn a little extra money.

The only thing he could do was to paint, not at all well, in watercolours. He became the pupil, quite seriously, of a young artist whom he knew. He was now forty-seven years old, while Miss Crewe was seventy-nine. The year was 1900.

To everybody's amazement Edward soon began to make quite good progress in his painting. Yes, his pictures were not at all unpleasant little things. He sent one of them to the Academy. It was accepted. It was, as I live, sold for ten pounds. Edward was an artist.

Soon he was making between thirty and forty pounds a year. Then he was making over a hundred. Then two hundred. Then the Mexican brewery failed, General Malefico having burned it to the ground for a lark.

This happened in the spring of 1914 when Edward was sixty-one and Miss Crewe was ninety-three. Edward, after paying her money to Miss Crewe, might flatter himself on the possibility of having some fifty pounds a year for himself, that is to say, if his picture sales did not decline. A single man can, however, get along, more or less on fifty pounds more or less.

Then the Great War broke out.

It has been said that in the autumn of 1914 the Old Men came into their kingdom. As the fields of Britain were gradually stripped bare of their valid toilers, the Fathers of each village assumed, at good wages, the burden of agriculture. From their offices the juniors departed or were torn; the senior clerks carried on desperately until the Girls were introduced. No man was any longer too old at forty. Octogenarians could command a salary. The very cinemas were glad to dress up ancient fellows in uniform and post them on their doorsteps.

Edward could do nothing but paint rather agreeable water colours, and that was all. The market for his kind of work was shut. A patriotic nation was economising in order to get five per cent on the War Loans. People were not giving inexpensive little water colours away to one another as wedding gifts any longer. Only the painters of high reputation, whose work was regarded as a real investment, could dispose of their wares.

Starvation stared Edward in the face, not only his own starvation, you understand, but Miss Crewe's. And Edward was a man of honour.

He hated Miss Crewe intensely, but he had undertaken to provide for her, and provide for her he must—even if he failed to provide for himself.

He wrapped some samples of his paintings in brown paper, and began to seek for a job among the wholesale stationers. He offered himself as one who was prepared to design Christmas cards and calendars, and things of the kind.

Adversity had sharpened his wits. Even the wholesale stationers were not turning white-headed men from their portals. To Edward was accorded the privilege of displaying the rather agreeable contents of his parcel. After he had unpacked it and packed it up again some thirty times, he was offered work. His pictures were really rather agreeable. It was piecework, and he was to do it off the premises, no matter where. By toiling day and night he might be able to earn as much as £4 a week. He went away and toiled. His employers were pleased with what, each Monday, he brought them. They did not offer to increase his remuneration, but they encouraged him to produce, and took practically everything he offered. Edward was very fortunate.

During the first year of the war he lived like a beast, worked like a slave, and earned exactly enough to keep his soul in his body and pay Miss Crewe her one hundred and fifty pounds. During the second year of the war he did it again. The fourth year of the war found him still alive and still punctual to his obligations towards Miss Crewe.

Miss Crewe, however, found one hundred and fifty pounds no longer what it had been. Prices were rising in every direction. She wrote to Edward pointing this out, and asking him if he couldn't see his way to increasing her allowance. She invoked the memory of his dear mother and father, added something about the happy hours that he and she had spent together in the dear old schoolroom, and signed herself his affectionately.

Edward petitioned for an increase of pay. He pointed out to his firm of wholesale stationers that prices were rising in every direction. The firm, who knew when they had a marketable thing cheap, granted his petition. Henceforth, Edward was able to earn five pounds a week. He increased Miss Crewe's allowance by fifty pounds, and continued to live more like a beast than ever, for the price of paper and paints was soaring. He worked practically without ceasing, save to sleep (which he could not do) and to eat (which he could not afford). He was now sixty-four, while Miss Crewe was rising ninety-seven.

Edward had been ailing for a long time. On Armistice Day he struck work for an hour in order to walk about in the streets and share in the general rejoicing. He caught a severe cold, and the next day, instead of staying between his blankets (he had no sheets), he went up to the City with some designs which he had just completed. That night he was feverish. The next night he was delirious. The third night he was dead, and there was an end of him.

He had, however, managed, before he died (two days before), to send to Miss Crewe a money order for her quarter's allowance of fifty pounds. This had left him with precisely four shillings and twopence in the Post Office Savings Bank.

He was, consequently, buried by the parish.

Miss Crewe received her money. She was delighted to have it, and at once wrote to Edward her customary letter of grateful and affectionate thanks. She added in a postscript that if he *could* find it in his generous heart to let her have still a little more next quarter it would be most acceptable, because every day seemed to make it harder and harder for her to get along.

Edward was dead when this letter was delivered.

Miss Crewe sent her money order to her bank, asking that it might be placed to her deposit account. This, she reminded the bank, would bring up the amount of her deposit to exactly two thousand pounds.

2. SETTING PLOTTED

Once again, we must begin with a warning: this is *not* the "Atmosphere Story." Our purpose here is simply to present a type of narration in which the setting is superimposed forcibly upon the plot-story structure, so as to produce a plot story with setting generating the plot. This is an intensely difficult achievement, for a subordination of both characters and action to setting weakens the story tremendously, and you should attempt this experiment only to learn what sort of freak story results. It will make you "stop, look, and listen" before ever plunging over such a grade crossing in the future. It is a sheer experiment, then, for the sake of acquiring technical experience and is not to be taken too seriously.

We must first distinguish between atmosphere and setting. Setting is the *locale* of the story, atmosphere the impression made by the *locale* on both the characters and the reader. Setting is purely descriptive detail, atmosphere the dramatic effect of such detail. Atmosphere, then, corresponds to tone, in the sense of a single effect, while setting is the physical combination of details chosen to present that tone. Hence in the type of story we are now contemplating, atmosphere will generate the plot and dominate the type characters, and the atmosphere must be present from the very beginning.

Let us go a bit further in this distinction between atmosphere and setting. In section 3 of Chapter XIV we developed some twenty-odd sequences of suspense on a "lost-in-winter" moment of interest. Now one might say at once that setting was the prime factor in that story. It was, in one sense. *Objectively* the winter milieu was the cause of most of the boy's suffering. Had it not been cold, he could have slept. Had it not been for the snow, his shells and matches would have remained dry. Had the snow not covered a stump, he might never have fallen and broken his leg and gun. And so forth. But in every case the effect of the setting was *objective*. There was no apparently conscious and personal attempt on the part of the setting to obliterate the boy. The purely objective forces present in nature caused him trouble, but he himself never gave them subjective aspects by stopping to reflect furiously on the malevolent personality and spirit of nature. Whatever thinking the boy did was upon his own suffering and foolishness in ever getting into such a fix. His situation did not present itself to his mind as a struggle between his weak and helpless humanity and the mighty and relentless forces of nature. In other words nature (or setting) was not a subjective force, but an objective. In this new type of story, however, nature, or setting, becomes a purely subjective force; it has an atmosphere, or distinct impression, which affects the character from the beginning and *makes* him do something (moment of interest) which may ultimately get him into serious difficulties (the climax). Hence we shall use the word *atmosphere* from now on in this chapter, merely because it has a more subjective connotation than setting.

Let us suggest one weakness of this sort of story at once, then. The character to be affected by the atmosphere must be an unusual type to submit to such a sentimental force. He will be hypersensitive, perhaps even a queer sort of freak, gazing on the stars and not seeing the well before his feet. In the story as it will be developed you will have to make *yourself* such an individual, temporarily at least, and this may not be hard, provided you choose the proper atmosphere to affect you. But in the ultimate atmosphere story, attempted occasionally by professionals,[1] the weakness of such a character is obvious. He becomes inhuman, and the reality of the story suffers thereby.

[1] For example, read Bess Streeter Aldrich's "The Man Who Caught the Weather," *Century Magazine*, 1928.

Immediately now appear two pitfalls which you must take care to avoid. First, if you must subordinate yourself to an impression created by nature—to atmosphere—you may suddenly develop the most gushing personal reactions one could ever conceive in a normal human being. Moonlight will project you into exaggerated ecstasy, and a barren plain will plunge you into melancholy despair. This emotional joy ride may be an interesting experience in itself, but will inevitably kill the effect of the story. You must not let yourself go too far under the influence of atmosphere. The task of hitting the mean between a strictly normal and absurdly abnormal reaction makes this story difficult, and yet interesting, to write.

A second pitfall—intimately related to the other—will be the tendency to visualize nature as a shimmeringly dressed Queen of the May dancing around for your special diversion, or as a grim-visaged ogre who may at any moment snatch you up in his talons like an ant and pick off a leg or two. This transcendent personification of nature will kill the story as effectively as will too freakish reactions on your part. You cannot see a dryad in every tree and a Charybdis in every whirlpool without destroying the rationality of the story. Such a personification of the elements of nature becomes flagrantly sentimental, and must be avoided as much as possible. In conclusion, then, *if* you can walk erect and blindfolded between these two pitfalls—the overdoing of your own personality or lending too much personality to nature—you will achieve success in a difficult type of narration—and yet perhaps still be willing to relinquish the type to Poe, Stevenson, Herman Melville, and Joseph Conrad.

Having guarded against the sentimental tendencies in the story wherein setting is plotted, we need now to consider its proper structural development. In the story we are now undertaking, it is the atmosphere, representing the single effect, which must be presented in the opening. Hence the setting from which it emerges will be given in the prelude; carefully chosen details will create at once the desired tone, or atmosphere. For example, you might first give the weird outlines, shadows, croakings, and the dank mistiness of a swamp at night. Your purpose would be to create an impression of mystery and danger, both luring and

repelling, and so strong that as you stand on the edge of the unknown you are overwhelmed and completely submissive to it.
Then follows the moment of interest, or second aspect of tone:
you are irresistibly led to explore the mysterious darkness and
you start stepping from bog to bog. You have no business going
into that swamp at this time of night. You know it and it worries
you. It worries the reader too. But the atmosphere has cast its
spell over you, it draws you to itself, and for better or worse, you
are dominated by it.

For suspense, psychological factors will again dominate. Your
reason tells you to go back, but your feelings, overwhelmed by
the atmosphere, lead you on step by step. You think of quick-
sands, of poisonous snakes, of getting lost. But you feel you must
go on and on, just along the edge perhaps, entranced by the
mystery (atmosphere) of that setting. Now and then, of course,
the external forces of suspense may enter in. Your foot may slip
or you may temporarily lose track of directions. But the atmosphere has you in its grip. You may go on ultimately to destruction,
but you do not very much care. Present feelings are everything
and keep growing stronger and stronger, more and more irresistible as you proceed—just as some people are lured to leap
from a great height.

The climax in this sort of story is an objective happening, a
sudden, terrific obliteration of the power of those feelings gener-
ated progressively during the suspense—a power which has grown
gradually so strong that at the climax it may approach insanity
or the wild desire to fling oneself into the arms of the mysterious,
alluring monster, the swamp. Suppose the character actually
does this; then the moment he finds himself physically in the
grip of the swamp, he will awake with a start. The dream is over,
but the atmosphere has claimed its victim. Will he be saved or
will he die?

Here you will want to inject a bit of plot-story suspense, but
this must not be done. If it is, the atmosphere of the story will
collapse. Hence refrain from the desire to suspend that atmos-
phere-driven character for too long a time in the grip of the
swamp.

Any solution will do—but use it quickly, letting a bit of the atmosphere remain with him as he drags himself away from the scene. As for the conclusion, use types one, two, or three—especially three (see section 5 of Chapter XIV). Number four cannot be used because nature is not comic.

One particular warning: do not concentrate all your setting at the beginning. Diffuse the setting with its resultant atmosphere throughout the story. Repetition of a motif is much more effective than a single, crashing chord.

Once more, this type of story is merely an experiment for variety. The dominance of atmosphere is not a normal situation in life. The setting conceived above could be used as a support for a murder story or for the home of a distinctly bad or mysterious character. But to say that a normal human being could be influenced by the swamp to the extent of wandering into it in face of all its known dangers—to say, in other words, that character and plot may be logically dominated by setting—is to argue yourself abnormal. The atmosphere story, then, which is the *ultima Thule* of the type just described in this chapter, is a freak story, intensely hard to project successfully. The average writer shies from it. Hence this section was interpolated merely to give you another variation from the plot story and to point out the possibilities of setting if used properly to support plot or character, the chief elements of any story.

You will perhaps understand the lure intended in this story if, as we have suggested, you think of the instinctive impulse to jump from a high place like the Empire State Building or an overhanging cliff. This lure is a positively appealing force which gets you into trouble against your will; its latent destructive aspect does not appear till you have submitted to it and come to a realistic awakening. In other words, you must think up some setting which has a definite magnetic pull for you but which will really destroy you if you submit too completely to it.

We have proposed to students settings like the following in the hope that one of them will awaken an individual response: the desert, moonlight, a swamp, a haunted house, rain, the race track, small-town life, the factory, the farm, snow and ice, the sea, a storm, carnival, the stock exchange, Hollywood, spring. As a rule one of these will be suggestive; and then the student often starts with some objective fact which accounts for the special susceptibility of the character to the setting. If you have just inherited some money, you may start for the stock exchange; if a girl has just lost her job, she may seek the river, etc. You will have to spend some time developing the psychology of the lure itself; to do this it is best to write the story in the first person. But keep the time limit compressed as much as possible. Above all beware of injecting a plot situation: a man lost in the desert provides a plot story, but you are merely concerned with the desert's luring him to itself, and not at all with his tribulations after he wakes up and finds himself lost.

Avoid letting yourself become too much stirred up emotionally at the beginning, or you will have no reserve left for the climax. And there must be a climax, where the objective steps in and destroys the subjective illusion: when you step into the bog in the swamp, when you find you have proposed in the moonlight, when you find your money all gone on the stock exchange. Always avoid adopting a condescending attitude toward the effect of the setting on the character—if you choose someone besides yourself— for sympathy again is the keynote of this story.

A child story will go well in this sort of exercise: a little child is lured to the big woods where the fairies are—the suspense is perfect. And in the realm of the imagination we are never so far beyond childhood as we may think. Finally do not add a long conclusion after the fatal awakening; get out of trouble quickly— or die if you must. With these warnings you should have no particular trouble now with setting plotted.

≫ A ≪

"Up in the Clouds" illustrates the type well, within narrow limits. How could you improve the solution?

UP IN THE CLOUDS

This was the forty-sixth story of the Penobscot Building. The wind was howling and shrieking through the framework of bare girders. Two stories above, the massive steel shafts stood straight into the air with no crossbars. They seemed to be supporting the great dark clouds which spread for miles around. The day was very gloomy and depressing. Twelve-inch planks connected one girder with another, and so with every floor down to number thirty-six, which was finished off. To look straight down was like peering down an elevator shaft. Fastened to the corner was the small forced-draft stove in which the rivets were made to glow. Air-driven riveting machines, with their deafening machine-gun sound effects, were constantly alive.

Ivan Makowski worked aimlessly as he caught gleaming red rivets in his scoop, and placed them in their holes by means of tongs for the riveter to make them fast. He was already weary of this dull, endless job, although hired only that morning. The chill wind penetrated his light clothing, and its force made him cling desperately to the vertical girder. His eyes were strained by the roaring gusts, and he was dejected in heart and soul by the overcast sky. The noise caused his head to ache. He found himself frequently being yelled at by Tony, the rivet thrower, for not being alert, and became pale and thoroughly disheartened when a fellow known as "Spike," at the next girder, missed his sizzling bit of steel and received a deep, repulsive-looking burn on his right leg just above his knee. His task became more difficult to Ivan as noon neared, for he was weak from hunger, and had spent his last dime for a bowl of soup for breakfast. He remained aloft when the rest of the men went down for dinner, because he could not purchase any food.

When he had been sitting for some time on the outside beam pondering over his undesirable allotment, he glanced down. Suicide had entered his head many times before in his three-months' search for work, but a chance such as this had never been presented. Besides, he had not wished to put disgrace on his beloved wife and little son, but this would look like an accident. The streets below, thronging with hurrying midgets, seemed to beckon to him, and he stood up to leap into space. He crouched for the spring that would clear him of the projections of the building and end his miserable life.

The one o'clock whistle and the greetings of the hunger-satisfied men from the elevator so startled him that he quickly stood up and grasped the girder for support. The men had brought him a meal, and the sun was shining.

W. B.

A child story, like "Mary Jo," fits the type very successfully; but it demands a delicate touch.[1] There are other studies of the child mind on pages 335–6 and pages 393–4.

[1] Compare the tragic solution of the newspaper child story in Chapter XIII.

MARY JO

Mary Jo lived with her father and mother in a cottage near a great woods. The country around was sparsely populated, and the baby's friendly little heart longed for the companionship of other children. To make up this lack, her father had given her two thoroughbred collie puppies when she was only three years old. They played long hours together, Jack and Jill and Mary Jo. The dogs' devotion to their little mistress was very touching. Everywhere that Mary went the dogs were sure to go.

She was of an inquisitive nature, and the woods had always held a great fascination for her. But her mother had often warned her never to go into them alone.

It was one of the first warm, glorious days of spring, and little Mary Jo sat on her doorstep with Jack and Jill snoozing at her feet, and looked longingly at the great green trees across the road. Perhaps if she ventured in just a little way she could find the homes of Peter Rabbit, Johnny 'Chuck, and Jimmy Skunk. Mother had told her never to go in alone. "But," she thought, "I'll only go in a little way and I won't get lost." The more she thought about it the more overwhelming the fascination became, and finally she popped up and trotted across the road, Jack and Jill at her heels.

In she went, just a little way. Oh! the wonder of it. The moss at the foot of the great oak trees and the violets scattered everywhere. She had never imagined anything so wonderful as this cool, green, shady world with the sunshine sparkling through the leaves.

"Oh look! there's Sammy Squirrel, and the story book said that Johnny 'Chuck lived the second oak tree past Sammy. Come on, Jill, let's find Johnny."

But Johnny was not to be found so easily, and little Mary Jo wandered on and on. Once she caught a glimpse of Peter but he shot away like the wind with Jack in hot pursuit. She began to gather the violets and she picked them until her little hands were full. Suddenly she noticed that Jill was gone. She called and called, but no dog came. She sat down underneath a tree to wait for Jill, Jack beside her. She was awfully hungry and tired, even sleepy. As she sat, she looked around and thought how big the trees were and how many there were! She felt so wee and small. Even Jack didn't seem as big as he did at home, and where was Jill?

She was just falling asleep when suddenly Jack jumped up and pricked up his ears. For a second there was silence and then, "Mary

Jo! Mary Jo!" It was her father's voice. The little girl ran into her daddy's arms. He lifted her up, and over his shoulder she saw good, faithful Jill happily wagging her tail. She knew Mary Jo was lost, so she went home to get the girl's father. Together they came back to find the little girl who had set out so bravely to find the homes of Peter Rabbit, Johnny 'Chuck, and Jimmy Skunk.

V. G.

"Carnival" is a very successful story of this type. It begins slowly but works up to a tense climax.

CARNIVAL

The carnival lights flared across the velvety black sky and made the countless stars seem insignificant and cold, compared to the brilliance and life beneath them. I laughingly grasped Ted's hand, and quickly shifted from one foot to another in order to keep in time with the surge and push of the eager crowd. In the next moment Ted and I were swept off our feet by an onward rush, and when we again gained our breath we were in the very middle of a vast throng of over-excited humanity that had gathered to celebrate the opening night of Gensen's Jubilee Carnival.

People were shouting, gesticulating, pushing, laughing; children were crying. Glaring lights—loud, exhilarating music—the smell of closely packed, over-heated humanity—all sent the blood coursing through my veins in a fever of excitement.

Venders were shouting their wares; lotto dealers were coaxing, persuading; the sham airplanes were whizzing, buzzing.

Somebody lost his hat. He didn't care. Somebody won a gorgeous kewpie doll and triumphantly held it high above his head so the crowd would not destroy his prize. Everybody was pushing—no room to move.

Somebody said, "Hello, Kid," to me and thrust his face close to mine.

I had a sickening moment when I thought I had lost Ted, and then he was close beside me, laughing. Ted was laughing. I was laughing. The crowd supported me, and I threw my head back and watched the dizzying whirl of lights—colors. My head felt curiously light. I could close my eyes and see the colors—red—yellow—yellow—red.

Here was a dancing hall and we were dancing. Ted held me tight as we swayed to the throbbing music. Confetti fell about us, entangled our feet—confetti—lots of it.

Then we were at the shooting gallery. My rifle wobbled uncertainly; I couldn't hold still. Ted made a mark and won a doll for me. People still pushing.

We were getting on a ferris wheel—the biggest in the world. For a moment we caught a refreshing breath of cool summer's night breeze as the wheel carried us high above the heads of the throng. For a moment we gazed upon an amazing, thrilling panorama, and then we were again a part of that panorama. We moved on. The ferris wheel was too slow; we tried the Flying Thrills. For a while it shook a little of the laughter out of us. As we landed I had an uncertain feeling. Ted steadied me and I heard a voice darkly murmur, "It's so dangerous."

We forgot it soon and pushed on, looking for more excitement. Ted's face flushed an unnatural red, his white teeth flashed, and his eyes gleamed with the light of a daredevil. I felt of my own cheeks; they were hot.

Here was a crowd. Somebody was offering a twenty-dollar gold piece to the first couple to ride the record-breaking roller coaster. Ted and I made a rush. We were through the line.

Somebody yelled, "Don't let those kids go. They're too young."

Hands were grabbing, trying to hold us back. The iron bar clanged down; Ted's arm protected me. We were off, past rows and rows of meaningless faces. First there was a slow, tantalizing, dizzying climb, and then there was a terrifying swoop. We were falling through space —would we never stop? I convulsively grasped the bar; my breath stopped; I closed my eyes. My body went limp. We reached the bottom of the first swoop. We were starting another! Fall after fall came. I half lost consciousness. Then it was over.

Ted's eyes shone into mine.

"Great, wasn't it?" he shouted. My courage returned. I laughingly answered. I was ready for anything now. We claimed our prize and pushed our way onward. The crowd was increasing; it was growing wilder. Some stranger was jubilantly thumping me on the back, congratulating me.

Ted dragged me towards another attraction. It was "Daredevil Dick" in his death-defying leap, from a fifty-foot springboard into a small patch of water. Dick the Daredevil was challenging, challenging anyone who dared to do likewise. The crowd was laughing in derision. Ted and I were experienced divers.

I couldn't think; my head whirled; I was still laughing. I was even laughing when Ted and I reached the top of the diving board. I wondered dimly how I had gotten that bathing suit on. I was to go first, Ted next. I was standing alone, and the pool seemed an awful distance away—so small. I was scared. I heard Ted's voice calling to me to hurry. I couldn't back out. Quickly I jumped. For one terrible instant I thought I had miscalculated; then the cold water closed over me as I safely made it by a margin of a few inches. Ted made a better calculation than I had. As I came up the water seemed to sober me. The carnival lost its glamour.

Suddenly I was terribly tired, and I wanted to get away from all this glaring, cheap color, the noise, the confusion.

M. G.

-»> B «<-

Obviously, as indicated in the theoretical section of this chapter, one would not expect to find professional writers frequently producing such an artificial creation as "Setting Plotted." Nevertheless, it is quite as obvious that expert writers will now and then use setting in sections of stories in order to help carry on the complicating forces, that is, the suspense. What we shall do now is to present a few such selections in the hope of stimulating you to an interest in setting. In some cases even full stories are given.

Once in a while a newspaper appears with a feature story which is nearer the problem of this chapter than any professional short story. Such a one, for example, was printed in the *Detroit Free Press* for February 14, 1932. Doubtless the setting in rural England helped the effect.

PHANTOM HAND THAT DRAGGED GIRL TO DEATH [1]

All England Shuns the Haunted Pond Since Pretty
Florence Mocked Its Legend—
and Drowned Herself

(There was a legend about Half Hour Pond in Buckinghamshire that roused a modern young girl to laughter. A week later her body was found in the pond. Now let the newspaper conclude:)

[1] Excerpts reprinted by permission of the King Feature Syndicate and the *Detroit Free Press*.

In their imagination, the villagers saw Florence, pale and poised in the brilliant moonlight, standing with hands outspread, her blue eyes intent on the pool, while ghostly fingers—the fingers of a girl long dead—beckoned her to plunge into the inky water.

Fantastically absurd? Perhaps. But something—if not the phantom hand, then what?—did drag laughing Florence to oblivion. That is why Half Hour Pond has been deserted of late and the only sounds there are the melancholy murmur of the tree branches and the sinister cawing of the rooks.

Note the beginning of Hamlin Garland's "Lucretia Burns" in *Other Main-Travelled Roads* [1]:

Lucretia Burns had never been handsome, even in her days of early girlhood, and now she was middle-aged, distorted with work and child-bearing, and looking faded and worn as one of the boulders that lay beside the pasture fence near where she sat milking a large white cow.

She had no shawl or hat and no shoes, for it was still muddy in the little yard, where the cattle stood patiently fighting the flies and mosquitoes swarming into their skins, already wet with blood. The evening was oppressive with its heat, and a ring of just-seen thunderheads gave premonitions of an approaching storm.

She rose from the cow's side at last, and, taking her pails of foaming milk, staggered toward the gate. The two pails hung from her lean arms, her bare feet slipped on the filthy ground, her greasy and faded calico dress showed her tired and swollen ankles, and the mosquitoes swarmed mercilessly on her neck and bedded themselves in her colorless hair. . . .

She felt vaguely that the night was beautiful. The setting sun, the noise of frogs, the nocturnal insects beginning to pipe—all in some way called her girlhood back to her, though there was little in her girlhood to give her pleasure. Her large gray eyes grew round, deep, and wistful as she saw the illimitable craggy clouds grow crimson, roll slowly up, and fire at the top. A childish scream recalled her.

"Oh, my soul!" she half groaned, half swore. . . .

Compare also Garland's "Among the Corn-Rows" in *Main-Travelled Roads*. In Kipling's "At the End of the Passage" the power of the heat is terrific. Read the effect of it on the man Hummil. Consider, too the following illustrations.

---

[1] Reprinted by permission of the author.

The opening of Poe's "The Fall of the House of Usher" strikingly illustrates the almost hypnotic effects possible for atmosphere.

During the whole of a dull, dark, and soundless day in the autumn of the year, when the clouds hung oppressively low in the heavens, I had been passing along on horseback, through a singularly dreary tract of country; and at length found myself, as the shades of the evening drew on, within view of the melancholy House of Usher. I know not how it was—but, with the first glimpse of the building, a sense of insufferable gloom pervaded my spirit. I say insufferable; for the feeling was unrelieved by any of that half-pleasurable, because poetic, sentiment with which the mind usually receives even the sternest natural images of the desolate or terrible. I looked upon the scene before me—upon the mere house, and the simple landscape features of the domain—upon the bleak walls—upon the vacant eye-like windows—upon a few rank sedges—and upon a few white trunks of decayed trees—with an utter depression of soul which I can compare to no earthly sensation more properly than to the after-dream of the reveller upon opium—the bitter lapse into every-day life—the hideous dropping off of the veil. There was an iciness, a sinking, a sickening of the heart—an unredeemed dreariness of thought which no goading of the imagination could torture into aught of the sublime. What was it—I paused to think—what was it that so unnerved me in the contemplation of the House of Usher? It was a mystery all insoluble; nor could I grapple with the shadowy fancies that crowded upon me as I pondered. I was forced to fall back upon the unsatisfactory conclusion, that while, beyond doubt, there *are* combinations of very simple natural objects which have the power of thus affecting us, still the analysis of this power lies among considerations beyond our depth. It was possible, I reflected, that a mere different arrangement of the particulars of the scene, of the details of the picture, would be sufficient to modify, or perhaps, to annihilate its capacity for sorrowful impression; and, acting upon this idea, I reined my horse to the precipitous brink of a black and lurid tarn that lay in unruffled lustre by the dwelling, and gazed down—but with a shudder even more thrilling than before—upon the remodelled and inverted images of the gray sedge, and the ghastly tree-stems, and the vacant and eye-like windows.

Nevertheless, in this mansion of gloom I now proposed to myself a sojourn of some weeks. . . .

The following sketch shows the devastating negative effect possible in setting. The actual reaction is delayed to the close.

IN THE METROPOLIS [1]
Benjamin Rosenblatt

She sat in the show window of a large department store. "A prize to those who make her laugh," read a conspicuous sign over her head. An American flag was wrapped around her slim figure; a sword which she clutched with both hands rested on her lap with its point towards a placard announcing a bargain sale.

She sat motionless, her eyes wide open, her face hardly betraying a trace of life.

All day long she sat there, while multitudes passing on the sidewalk turned their heads towards her and wondered: "Is it a living woman or a wax figure?" It was this puzzle which held the pedestrian, and caused the manager of the store to chuckle at his own cleverness. When he saw in the morning this bashful country girl shuffling into the store and asking inaudibly for a job, he caught at the chance for novelty in the advertising of his sale. Her features were so immobile; she appeared, on the whole, so lifeless that his agile mind had promptly pictured her in her present setting.

Unceasingly the crowd surged before the window. Newsboys with bundles under their arms, messengers in uniform, girls with lunch boxes in their hands, even trim-looking business men—all forgot their errands for a few minutes, and directed their mingled breath towards that window. Some of the boys stood for hours, sticking out their tongues, puffing up their cheeks, grinning and grimacing in a vain effort to get a smile from that grim apparition.

Though she was alone inside the window, still it seemed to her as if she were thrown into that seething mass before her, as if jostled and mercilessly kicked about. How strange everything! How confusing to her!

In the morning, when she learned there was work for her at the store, she was so happy that she thought of writing home at once about her good luck. But in the evening, after her first day's work, she was so exhausted that the girls of the establishment who took her to their boarding-house, had to lead her under her arms. She walked and wondered: the manager had said there was absolutely no work attached to her job.

[1] From *Brief Stories* (1921). Reprinted by permission of the author.

At the supper table the girls, good-naturedly, poked fun at her; and she grew livelier. Later, some of them had a romp, and decided that the feet of the uncouth lass were surely more used to follow the cows to pasture, than to dance.

The next morning the girls hurried feverishly. They paid little attention to the "rustic clown." Some had slept too late; they looked anxious and careworn. Last evening's warmth had all evaporated, and the "wax figure" felt a strange chill and a sinking at the heart.

Again she took her seat in the show window. She was faint, not having been in the mood for breakfast, and before long dizziness overtook her. She felt as if she looked into some deep water from which a wave suddenly emerged—a huge wave that roared, groaned, moved towards her, striving to engulf her, to carry her away.

Still, she appeared on that second day conscious of things she had not observed at first. The cars that thundered back and forth seemed new, and she noted the elevated overhead. The crowds were again as large and again as busy making "faces" which frightened her into immobility, so that it became harder for the people to get her attention, and most of them wondered: "Will she ever smile?"

In the afternoon it rained. The electric lights began to twinkle early, and a sea of umbrellas moved, moved endlessly before the motionless figure in the window.

She stared at the rumbling taxis that splashed hither and thither; at the zigzag drizzle, the steady downpour, and her eyes suddenly filled. Thoughts of home were awakened within her by the rain. Her brain and heart, hitherto as if congealed by the terror of the strange world before her, now thawed and filled her with a gnawing sadness and self-pity. How is it at home now? her thoughts ran. How is it at home? It rains. There is the muddy road, the ruts and the pools. Father is indoors now, back from the field. The gray dusk falls. Mother sits with folded arms by the window and gazes longingly out into the dark.

"Are you looking for me," the figure in the window, forgetting herself, suddenly wailed. "Mother, mother dear, take me to you. I ain't used to this; I'm so lonely and afraid."

Her lips trembled visibly. A spasm shot across her face and contracted it—and many of the crowd outside who made "mouths" at her, burst into a triumphant hurrah. "She laughed!" roared a colored man so loud that it reached the manager, who forthwith decided to discharge the "figure." "I get the prize," yelled others. "I made her laugh! I made her laugh!"

Finally, in "The Cop and the Anthem" both negative reaction and positive are present: the cold makes "Soapy" do some amazing things, and the anthem leads him in precisely the opposite direction.

THE COP AND THE ANTHEM [1]

O. Henry

On his bench in Madison Square Soapy moved uneasily. When wild geese honk high of nights, and when women without sealskin coats grow kind to their husbands, and when Soapy moves uneasily on his bench in the park, you may know that winter is near at hand.

A dead leaf fell in Soapy's lap. That was Jack Frost's card. Jack is kind to the regular denizens of Madison Square, and gives fair warning of his annual call. At the corners of four streets he hands his pasteboard to the North Wind, footman of the mansion of All Outdoors, so that the inhabitants thereof may make ready.

Soapy's mind became cognizant of the fact that the time had come for him to resolve himself into a singular Committee of Ways and Means to provide against the coming rigor. And therefore he moved uneasily on his bench.

The hibernatorial ambitions of Soapy were not of the highest. In them there were no considerations of Mediterranean cruises, of soporific Southern skies, or drifting in the Vesuvian Bay. Three months on the Island was what his soul craved. Three months of assured board and bed and congenial company, safe from Boreas and bluecoats, seemed to Soapy the essence of things desirable.

For years the hospitable Blackwell's had been his winter quarters. Just as his more fortunate fellow New Yorkers had bought their tickets to Palm Beach and the Riviera each winter, so Soapy had made his humbler arrangements for his annual hegira to the Island. And now the time was come. On the previous night three Sabbath newspapers, distributed beneath his coat, about his ankles and over his lap, had failed to repulse the cold as he slept on his bench near the spurting fountain in the ancient square. So the Island looked big and timely in Soapy's mind. He scorned the provisions made in the name of charity for the city's dependents. In Soapy's opinion the Law was more benign than Philanthropy. There was an endless round of institutions, municipal and eleemosynary, on which he might set out and receive

[1] From *The Four Million*, by O. Henry, copyright, 1905, by Doubleday, Doran & Company, Inc. Reprinted by arrangement.

lodging and food accordant with the simple life. But to one of Soapy's proud spirit the gifts of charity are encumbered. If not in coin you must pay in humiliation of spirit for every benefit received at the hands of philanthropy. As Caesar had his Brutus, every bed of charity must have its toll of a bath, every loaf of bread its compensation of a private and personal inquisition. Wherefore it is better to be a guest of the law, which though conducted by rules, does not meddle unduly with a gentleman's private affairs.

Soapy, having decided to go to the Island, at once set about accomplishing his desire. There were many easy ways of doing this. The pleasantest was to dine luxuriously at some expensive restaurant; and then, after declaring insolvency, be handed over quietly and without uproar to a policeman. An accommodating magistrate would do the rest.

Soapy left his bench and strolled out of the square and across the level sea of asphalt, where Broadway and Fifth Avenue flow together. Up Broadway he turned, and halted at a glittering café, where are gathered together nightly the choicest products of the grape, the silkworm, and the protoplasm.

Soapy had confidence in himself from the lowest button of his vest upward. He was shaven, and his coat was decent and his neat black, ready-tied four-in-hand had been presented to him by a lady missionary on Thanksgiving Day. If he could reach a table in the restaurant unsuspected success would be his. The portion of him that would show above the table would raise no doubt in the waiter's mind. A roasted mallard duck, thought Soapy, would be about the thing— with a bottle of Chablis, and then Camembert, a demi-tasse, and a cigar. One dollar for the cigar would be enough. The total would not be so high as to call forth any supreme manifestation of revenge from the café management; and yet the meat would leave him filled and happy for the journey to his winter refuge.

But as Soapy set foot inside the restaurant door the head waiter's eye fell upon his frayed trousers and decadent shoes. Strong and ready hands turned him about and conveyed him in silence and haste to the sidewalk and averted the ignoble fate of the menaced mallard.

Soapy turned off Broadway. It seemed that his route to the coveted island was not to be an epicurean one. Some other way of entering limbo must be thought of.

At a corner of Sixth Avenue electric lights and cunningly displayed wares behind plate-glass made a shop window conspicuous. Soapy took a cobblestone and dashed it through the glass. People came running around the corner, a policeman in the lead. Soapy stood still, with his hands in his pockets, and smiled at the sight of brass buttons.

"Where's the man that done that?" inquired the officer excitedly.

"Don't you figure out that I might have had something to do with it?" said Soapy, not without sarcasm, but friendly, as one greets good fortune.

The policeman's mind refused to accept Soapy even as a clue. Men who smash windows do not remain to parley with the law's minions. They take to their heels. The policeman saw a man half way down the block running to catch a car. With drawn club he joined in the pursuit. Soapy, with disgust in his heart, loafed along, twice unsuccessful.

On the opposite side of the street was a restaurant of no great pretensions. It catered to large appetites and modest purses. Its crockery and atmosphere were thick; its soup and napery thin. Into this place Soapy took his accusive shoes and telltale trousers without challenge. At a table he sat and consumed beefsteak, flapjacks, doughnuts and pie. And then to the waiter he betrayed the fact that the minutest coin and himself were strangers.

"Now, get busy and call a cop," said Soapy. "And don't keep a gentleman waiting."

"No cop for youse," said the waiter, with a voice like butter cakes and an eye like the cherry in a Manhattan cocktail. "Hey, Con!"

Neatly upon his left ear on the callous pavement two waiters pitched Soapy. He arose, joint by joint, as a carpenter's rule opens, and beat the dust from his clothes. Arrest seemed but a rosy dream. The Island seemed very far away. A policeman who stood before a drug store two doors away laughed and walked down the street.

Five blocks Soapy traveled before his courage permitted him to woo capture again. This time the opportunity presented what he fatuously termed to himself a "cinch." A young woman of a modest and pleasing guise was standing before a show window gazing with sprightly interest at its display of shaving mugs and inkstands, and two yards from the window a large policeman of severe demeanor leaned against a water plug.

It was Soapy's design to assume the role of the despicable and execrated "masher." The refined and elegant appearance of his victim and the contiguity of the conscientious cop encouraged him to believe that he would soon feel the pleasant official clutch upon his arm that would insure his winter quarters on the right little, tight little isle.

Soapy straightened the lady missionary's ready-made tie, dragged his shrinking cuffs into the open, set his hat at a killing cant and sidled toward the young woman. He made eyes at her, was taken with sudden coughs and "hems," smiled, smirked and went brazenly through the impudent and contemptible litany of the "masher." With half an eye Soapy saw that the policeman was watching him fixedly. The young woman moved away a few steps, and again bestowed her absorbed attention upon the shaving mugs. Soapy followed, boldly stepping to her side, raised his hat and said:

"Ah there, Bedelia! Don't you want to come and play in my yard?"

The policeman was still looking. The persecuted young woman had but to beckon a finger and Soapy would be practically en route for his insular haven. Already he imagined he could feel the cozy warmth of the station-house. The young woman faced him and, stretching out a hand, caught Soapy's coat sleeve.

"Sure, Mike," she said joyfully, "if you'll blow me to a pail of suds. I'd have spoke to you sooner, but the cop was watching."

With the young woman playing the clinging ivy to his oak Soapy walked past the policeman overcome with gloom. He seemed doomed to liberty.

At the next corner he shook off his companion and ran. He halted in the district where by night are found the lightest streets, hearts, vows, and librettos. Women in furs and men in greatcoats moved gaily in the wintry air. A sudden fear seized Soapy that some dreadful enchantment had rendered him immune to arrest. The thought brought a little of panic upon it, and when he came upon another policeman lounging grandly in front of a transplendent theatre he caught at the immediate straw of "disorderly conduct."

On the sidewalk Soapy began to yell drunken gibberish at the top of his harsh voice. He danced, howled, raved, and otherwise disturbed the welkin.

The policeman twirled his club, turned his back to Soapy, and remarked to a citizen.

"'Tis one of them Yale lads celebratin' the goose egg they give to the Hartford College. Noisy; but no harm. We've instructions to lave them be."

Disconsolate, Soapy ceased his unavailing racket. Would never a policeman lay hands on him? In his fancy the Island seemed an unattainable Arcadia. He buttoned his thin coat against the chilling wind.

In a cigar store he saw a well-dressed man lighting a cigar at a swinging light. His silk umbrella he had set by the door on entering.

Soapy stepped inside, secured the umbrella and sauntered off with it slowly. The man at the cigar light followed hastily.

"My umbrella," he said, sternly.

"Oh, is it?" sneered Soapy, adding insult to petit larceny. "Well, why don't you call a policeman? I took it. Your umbrella! Why don't you call a cop? There stands one on the corner."

The umbrella owner slowed his steps. Soapy did likewise, with a presentiment that luck would again run against him. The policeman looked at the two curiously.

"Of course," said the umbrella man—"that is—well, you know how these mistakes occur—I—if it's your umbrella I hope you'll excuse me—I picked it up this morning in a restaurant—If you recognise it as yours, why—I hope you'll——"

"Of course it's mine," said Soapy, viciously.

The ex-umbrella man retreated. The policeman hurried to assist a tall blonde in an opera cloak across the street in front of a streetcar that was approaching two blocks away.

Soapy walked westward through a street damaged by improvements. He hurled the umbrella wrathfully into an excavation. He muttered against the men who wear helmets and carry clubs. Because he wanted to fall into their clutches, they seemed to regard him as a king who could do no wrong.

At length Soapy reached one of the avenues to the east where the glitter and turmoil was but faint. He set his face down this toward Madison Square, for the homing instinct survives even when the home is a park bench.

But on an unusually quiet corner Soapy came to a standstill. Here was an old church, quaint and rambling and gabled. Through one violet-stained window a soft light glowed, where, no doubt, the organist loitered over the keys, making sure of his mastery of the coming Sabbath anthem. For there drifted out to Soapy's ears sweet music that caught and held him transfixed against the convolutions of the iron fence.

The moon was above, lustrous and serene; vehicles and pedestrians were few; sparrows twittered sleepily in the eaves—for a while the scene might have been a country churchyard. And the anthem that the organist played cemented Soapy to the iron fence, for he had known it well in the days when his life contained such things as mothers and roses and ambitions and friends and immaculate thoughts and collars.

The conjunction of Soapy's receptive state of mind and the influences about the old church wrought a sudden and wonderful change in his soul. He viewed with swift horror the pit into which he had tumbled, the degraded days, unworthy desires, dead hopes, wrecked faculties, and base motives that made up his existence.

And also in a moment his heart responded thrillingly to this novel mood. An instantaneous and strong impulse moved him to battle with his desperate fate. He would pull himself out of the mire; he would make a man of himself again; he would conquer the evil that had taken possession of him. There was time; he was comparatively young yet; he would resurrect his old eager ambitions and pursue them without faltering. Those solemn but sweet organ notes had set up a revolution in him. Tomorrow he would go into the roaring downtown district and find work. A fur importer had once offered him a place as driver. He would find him tomorrow and ask for the position. He would be somebody in the world. He would—

Soapy felt a hand laid on his arm. He looked quickly around into the broad face of a policeman.

"What are you doin' here?" asked the officer.

"Nothin'," said Soapy.

"Then come along," said the policeman.

"Three months on the Island," said the Magistrate in the Police Court the next morning.

CHAPTER XVI

Description

DESCRIPTION HAS BEEN defined as "that form of writing which has as its main purpose to produce in the mind of the reader a picture of some thing, person, or place which has been seen or imagined by the writer." The materials of description, then, must come from direct observation, reading, or imagination. The first source is the most important. Seeing must precede the process of making a reader believe that he sees.

Two fundamental principles are involved in the writing of successful description; once these have been mastered, the way will be easy. These principles are point of view and dominant tone. Point of view can be either static or changing (progressive); but the former is safer for first attempts. Place yourself definitely in one spot—tell the reader where that spot is, at once—and then proceed to describe what you can see of the object from this spot, and *no more than that*. If the position taken is in front of a building, do not tell about what you know lies behind it or what is inside. This point is simple but important, as it serves to orient the description from the beginning: the writer is restricted to what he actually sees, and the reader is started on a stable footing.

Once the elementary principle of a stationary point of view has been mastered, it is quite simple to go on to the changing, or progressive, type. This may involve a series of shifts from one position to another or a continuous changing, as from a moving vehicle. The writer describes a building as he walks through it, a town as he drives through it, or a landscape as he flies over it, being careful always to keep the reader clearly aware of his change in position. A similar effect results when the observer remains stationary and views a passing panorama, a circus parade, droves of animals, clouds, ships, and the like. Whatever the method, the fundamental principle is still the same: the point of view, the physical relation of the observer's eye to the object, must be made definite at the start—otherwise the reader will be too confused to appreciate the descriptive features as they are presented.

Point of view is a mechanical device, comparable to focusing a camera; but dominant tone is more definitely aesthetic in emphasis, involving a large element of imaginative perception on the part of the writer. Before attempting to set down any features of the scene or object to be described, pause to decide just what dominant impression it makes upon your mind. It may be an impression of color, of size, or emotional impact inspiring a sense of mystery or contentment. Whatever it is, it carries a clue to the effect of the whole, and you should try to catch it in a single phrase, a kind of slogan or headline. "The garden is a ballet of bright-colored flowers"; "The courtroom succeeds in being, at the same time, huge and stuffy, many-windowed and gloomy"; "From top to toe Mary is a symphony in blue." The emotional tone is set at the start, supplying the keynote for the rest of the description. It should be maintained throughout and it may be repeated at the end. Every detail that is admitted should support the dominant effect, enhancing it so the reader is made to feel with the writer as nearly as possible the identical effect. Often this involves omission of some prominent aspects of the thing described; but it is better to select for a dominant artistic effect than to produce a confusing clash. Some of the opposing details, however, may be used for contrast.

After the point of view has been determined and the dominant tone established, the writer is well on the way to a successful description. A clear motivation now governs the real work of selecting the concrete details which are to compose the picture. These details must be those visible in terms of the angle, distance, and other factors involved in the point of view and must support the dominant tone either by consistency with it or by contrast. In selecting and handling the details the aspiring writer will do well to follow two principles: first, choose details appealing to as many of the five senses as possible—sensory impressions are the substance of vivid descriptive effect; second, try to make these details reinforce each other, fuse and blend into single impressions. George Eliot does not say in *Adam Bede:* "There is a crimson cloth on the table; it is a large cloth; the cloth is worn," but, "The crimson cloth over the large dining table is very threadbare." Similarly, do not say, "The girl had a strong mouth; her chin was firm and freckled." Combine these elements into something like this: "The girl's firm, freckled chin supported a strong mouth."

This concern with manner of expression immediately brings up the problem of the relative values of words. Verbs, for example, cannot be omitted, yet they may be weak or merely auxiliary. Revisions of the statements in the preceding paragraph eliminated weak verbs such as *is* and *had,* words that contribute nothing to the visual impression. Other weak verbs from this point of view are *do, seem,* and *go,* and the expressions *there is* and *there are.* As a rule the passive voice of verbs is weak; do not use *is supported by,* but the active *supported.* In blending details it is important to beware of letting them clash in connotative value. If you say a girl has light brown hair, follow this with details that the reader will feel are consistent, perhaps blue eyes, an active, slim figure, and vibrant voice. If you give her dark eyes, a stocky figure, and a southern drawl, the reader will be imaginatively confused, however possible this combination might be in real life. Stay close to the normal picture, and if details must be contradictory, make the uniqueness of the situation an aspect of the dominant tone. Try to get the most effect with the fewest details. Avoid piling them up, as the possibility of clashing connotations increases rapidly with the addition of details. Beware also of overloading with adjectives; adverbs and nouns are much more dynamic. Particularly, trite adjectives, indecisive terms such as *beautiful, pretty, wonderful, thrilling,* are to be avoided. Study the power in words, and select them always to support the dominant tone and give a unified, clean-cut picture. Description is, after all, a kind of painting, with words for pigments.

The final constructive problem in description, as in all imaginative writing, is the style; throughout it must be carefully adapted to the tone. The main thing is not to overwrite, not to write affectedly, but to be absolutely sincere in your feeling about the subject, and to present what you feel as nearly as possible as you feel it. Then style will take care of itself. Most definitions of style can be traced back to one of the oldest, that of the French thinker Buffon: "The style is the man himself"; it is the stamp of personality. Be yourself then: do not try to write fine verbiage in an attempt to waft yourself through descriptive clouds. The first thing you know you will be drifting into the pathetic fallacy, which Ruskin described so aptly in *Modern Painters* [1]: you will self-consciously have the trees moaning in agony as the cruel fingers of the storm clutch their shrinking branches. Then you will start omitting verbs and dashing down impressionistic descriptive phrases, a procedure which should be avoided. Do not label the senses as you go along,[2] but choose words carefully, to suggest, objectively, sensory impressions and imagery in the reader's mind. Metaphors (and perhaps similes) will sometimes help if not too deliberately employed. Compound epithets are often effective, especially when freshly coined: read Keats's *Ode to Psyche* for its "cool-rooted flowers" and "soft-handed slumber." Sentence beginnings must be especially watched to keep them varied: description too often becomes a mere catalogue of details in similarly constructed sentences. Beware of technical terms that have no connotative value at all and may be actually unclear. Mere *S.E.*, *N.W.*, and *E.*, as directions, will not help if the reader has no map in front of him. Watch the excessive use of the pronouns *I* and *one*. In general, beware of too much straight narrative: a little will help, but not too much. Similarly, do not relapse into a mere character sketch, and do not moralize on the value of the description at the end. Some dialogue may help, but do not use too much.

Begin the description quickly; avoid writing a dull paragraph

[1] . . . in this chapter, I want to examine the nature of the other error, that which the mind admits when affected strongly by emotion. Thus, for instance, in *Alton Locke*,—

> "They rowed her in across the rolling foam—
> The cruel, crawling foam."

The foam is not cruel, neither does it crawl. The state of mind which attributes to it these characters of a living creature is one in which the reason is unhinged by grief. All violent feelings have the same effect. They produce in us a falseness in all our impressions of external things, which I would generally characterize as the "pathetic fallacy." (From *Modern Painters*, Vol. III, Chap. 12.)

[2] That is: "I saw this," "he smelled it," "we tasted that."

showing how you happened to run across this spot because the back-seat driver insisted on going on farther and farther for the picnic site. When you have finished the first draft, read it over carefully at intervals of several hours or even days: you can thus keep improving the style, sentence by sentence. After all, description is a bit of creative art; it is supposed to produce an emotional reaction in the reader. Dominant tone, details, and stylistic smoothness all contribute to this desired effect. And, once more, vital description is possible only when there is a direct connection between the material and the writer's own, real emotions.

A few final hints and warnings may be of some value. It is possible to describe a mental state—such as fear, hope, contentment, but it is not easy. Some students have done it rather successfully, as in "A Brown Night" and "Unhappiness," included below. Note here the freedom of the point of view. Now and then a fundamental image establishes the point of view, as Stevenson compared the Bay of Monterey to a fish hook, and Hugo used a capital *A* to represent the plan of the battle of Waterloo. These illustrations are famous, but fundamental images are difficult to discover and to employ effectively. The order of development will depend to some extent on the point of view adopted. Even with a fixed point of view it is often possible to move from top to bottom (or vice versa), from one side to the other, or from the near to the remote. If you cannot follow a definite order like this, give the most significant details first to substantiate the tone, and taper off at the end with a restatement of the tone. It is possible, of course, to reverse this order for purposes of climax, but it takes a skillful writer to do it. Finally, the details must be absolutely specific and concrete; this is the only way to make descriptive writing wholly effective.

Among subjects students have chosen are: A Brook, The Beggar-Woman, The Cobbler's Shop, The Old House, Unhappiness, Autumn, The County Fair, The Guest Room, The Old Lady, Lake Erie, The River at Night, The Garbage Collector, The Kitchen, The Prairie, The Park, Freedom, The Hunchback, The Deaconess, Fear, The Young Minister.

In general, subjects can be drawn from landscapes, cities, buildings and rooms, animals, persons real and imaginary, and mental states—provided they *mean something emotionally* to the writer.

↠ A ↞

Much of the success in the following attempt to catch a mood lies in its honest effortlessness. Could there be less of the first person singular pronoun, or does its use intensify the mood? Note the clearness of the point of view.

A BROWN NIGHT

It was a "brown" night. I stood by the open window and looked out. The wind was rushing by outside and the air was filled with the roar of it. At intervals it sent side currents of air in through the window. The trees were bent with the strong relentless current, but there was no dust in the air. Overhead an even blanket of clouds covered the sky. The ground and trees and hills were brown.

I stood as close to the window as I could and let the air pour over me. Although it was late winter, I did not feel cold. I wanted to take off my pajamas and let the wind envelop me. I wanted it to pour over me, around me and through me. I loved it. It was a kind wind.

There was no sound outside except the steady roar of the swift air. I leaned out the window and my head was filled with the noise of it. I felt exhilarated but not completely so. I wanted something—I tried to think of the things which ordinarily appealed to me, but none of them seemed to fit. I seldom think about God but I wondered about Him now—vaguely. It didn't make me feel much better. I tried to analyze my feeling, but my mind worked round in circles. I felt a little crazy.

Someone opened the door, and a shaft of light cut through the dimness of the room. My mother stood in the doorway, silhouetted against the surprising whiteness of the hall.

"Haven't you gone to bed yet?" she asked.

I turned away from the window very reluctantly, for I knew there would not be another night like this one for a long time.

"Good-night," she said and shut the door again.

"Good-night," I answered and my voice sounded like someone else's.

I felt tired—more tired than I had ever felt; so I got into bed. The sheets were cool but not soft as the wind had been. I lay and listened to the faint roar outside and presently I went to sleep.

D. McC.

Do the effects in this next description suggest something of an unexpressed dominant tone? How does the writer keep out of the picture? Mentally reconstruct the paper using the present tense. How is the effect changed?

RUSH DINNER

Young women sleekly swathed in formals posed gracefully about the long room. Occasionally, one drifted smoothly, soundlessly from one group to another. The subdued glow of lamps matched the tone of the conversation, low and rich. Slim fingers held little glasses of tomato juice, the brightness of which stood in relief against vari-colored backgrounds.

In one corner three girls were grouped near a lamp with crossed legs making parallel diagonals out of the folds of the skirts. The three stemless cups with their bright liquid still untouched formed a geometric design—the first high against the silver background of a sequin collar, the center one a little lower against black, and the third another step down on a green-clad knee. Three silver slippers formed steps parallel to the glasses, connected to them by the sweeping diagonals.

The glasses were lifted, and faces came into the pattern and collapsed it.

Somewhere chimes rhythmically announced dinner. Skirts rustled softly, conversation scattered as groups disintegrated, and couples moved toward the wide doorway.

E. P.

In "The County Fair" there is a progressive point of view: the writer wanders through the fair. Is there too much narrative?

THE COUNTY FAIR

"Hoky Poky Ice Cream, Hoky Poky Ice Cream," rang out a shrill voice as the heavy wooden gates were opened and a throng of people rushed into the grounds, which had recently been prepared for the annual congregation of people. The honking of automobiles and the screeching of brakes let one know that everybody was trying to get in first place, for "the closer you are the better you see."

As we walked along the grand highway, a big tent, with flags swaying in the breeze, attracted the attention of a large crowd, who stood gaping as they stared longingly and awe-stricken at the fancy-dressed young lady who was calmly twining an ugly-looking snake around her neck.

Dirty little urchins ran back and forth through the crowd, the closer to come to the pretty lady on the platform.

"Five cents a try and the winner receives a lovely Indian blanket." In the next tent a wheel was busily spinning around and around while the participants eagerly held their little green tickets, one of which held the lucky number. On and on went the wheel until finally— number 32, and the happy winner eagerly grasped the blanket, and off she went to get a nice big "hot dog" and exclaim over her wonderful luck.

Above the clatter of boyish voices and squealing little girls, the faint sound of an accordion was heard in the distance, and as we walked toward the music we saw a large wheel circling in the air. Up, up the people went until far above our heads they stopped. As we gazed up at the highest peak of the wheel a young boy and girl were laughing and swinging, as though they were near the ground. Across from the ferris wheel, roosters, donkeys, and horses were bobbing up and down on a large merry-go-round, which went round and round to the sound of a tin-pan band playing "The Peanut Man."

In the afternoon we made a collection of pop corn, cracker jack, and pink cotton candy, and found our way to the top of the grandstand. Up and down the aisles ran white-capped boys selling their wares to the starving people who sat impatiently waiting for the sound of the bell which would bring on the races.

Down at the foot of the grandstand a group of fat women were standing chattering. Out from the group stepped a young man, and raising his hand he hushed the crowd. "Ladies and gentlemen, we will now have the women's race of all those weighing over two hundred pounds." Out on the race track walked the six women who had volunteered their services. The whistle blew, the race was on. Panting and puffing they wobbled toward the home plate, as the grandstand rose and cheered them to the finish.

Throughout the afternoon the races continued, the crowd yelled, and finally after much stampeding the crowd found their way back to the hot-dog stands, where they partook of the evening meal.

As it began to grow dark, and the first sky-rocket whizzed up into the air, and sent out sprays of red, blue, and green stars, the people rushed madly toward the race track in order to get a better view of the fireworks. As the clock in the grandstand slowly ticked its way to nine o'clock, the fireworks reached their peak and suddenly the outline of the American flag flashed in the sky, and one more day of the county fair was over.   E. E. F.

"The Circus Has Come to Town" also has a progressive point of view, but this time the writer is fixed in position and the panorama moves past. Are there any other details of a circus parade that should be added to make the scene complete—the calliope, for instance?

THE CIRCUS HAS COME TO TOWN

A rumbling seemed to come from the distance! It grew louder and louder until one could recognize the strains of a march. Suddenly the street began to fill with people—pushing, shouting, screaming, calling, and pointing. Then suddenly the cause of the tumult appeared—the circus parade!

Leading the procession was the ringmaster, a tall dark man, bowing left and right. Immediately behind him came the band, dressed fantastically in yellow, red, and purple, and composed mainly of drums. Then the clowns were upon us, with their multicolored costumes and unnaturally white faces—bowing, grimacing, uttering strange noises, and turning somersaults. The children responded by giggling, but suddenly their squeals of delight were changed to exclamations of admiration, for the sweetheart of the circus had come into view—the bare-back rider. With the sun making a halo around her golden curls, she balanced herself daintily on her prancing white horse and blew kisses to the crowd, as her ballet costume fluttered in the breeze.

"Here come the lions!" A thin piping voice rose above the clamor, as the animals turned the bend. The lions—just overgrown playful kittens—growling and tugging at the bars of their cages, made the crowd edge back. The elephants, ornamented with bright cloth and glittering jewels, heavily stamped through the hot street with a slow swaying movement.

Then there was more music, more clowns, more noise, more confusion, more glaring color, until it seemed as if one's eyes would pop and one's eardrums burst. Then the entire din seemed to disappear as suddenly as it had come. A faint rumbling came from the distance, growing softer and softer, until there was no more sound.

A. S.

The author of the next paper has developed a mental state, with perhaps too much narration. This descriptive problem involves *production* of the emotion in the reader, not the telling of a story, merely.

UNHAPPINESS

With a screeching of brakes and a great deal of black smoke, the train came to a grinding stop. To a casual observer, it would seem as though the monstrous, shining engine were impatient at having to stop at such a small, insignificant place.

Before the train had come to a complete stop, a small, dark-haired girl had stepped lightly to the platform. She glanced furtively about her with a look of terror. Her actions plainly indicated that she was afraid of being recognized.

As the train slowly began to leave the tiny station, the girl took a step or two forward, as though she wanted to follow it. But she stopped suddenly, and with agonized eyes watched the string of coaches recede into the distance. As the last one rounded a curve and disappeared from view, she turned, and with a despairing gesture, started up the narrow street.

It was dusk, and the people in the little village were preparing to eat their evening meal. Lights appeared at the windows of the tiny homes like so many stars flickering in the sky. The dark-haired girl walked with lagging steps up the deserted street. How familiar everything was, and yet she felt like a perfect stranger. Her heart ached as she looked through the window of the old Jones house. The entire family was seated around the huge dining-room table and everything looked so warm and cozy.

Not so many years ago she had lived in just such a home. If only she could erase those dreadful years and live her life again. But tears came to the girl's lovely eyes as she realized that this could never be. She had brought sorrow and unhappiness to her mother and father, and she was the one who must suffer. But she felt that it would ease that horribly lonesome feeling if she could just see them again. She could go away again with a lighter heart.

As she neared her old home, her heart began to beat so furiously that she could scarcely breathe. She unlatched the gate and walked up the path. Through the window she saw her father and mother eating their evening meal in lonesome silence. Her eyes were so blurred by tears she could scarcely distinguish the other objects in the room. With a hopeless gesture, she turned and stumbled down the path.

The 8:15 train came to a grinding stop to receive one lone passenger. The girl seated herself in the empty coach and with a look of despair on her face, she turned to gaze out of the window. The train gave a long, low whistle and disappeared into the night.

M. V.

The Problem of Revision

A typical short paper is presented now in both its first and second versions; note the superiority of the second. But study the verbs and revise the paper even further. For example, would not the second and third sentences read better as follows? "She had the calm, questioning blue eyes of childhood and a tenderly modeled face, with round, rosy cheeks. Her long, thick lashes were in perfect harmony with her wavy, red-gold hair." This paper was revised in class after the first version had been regarded by the writer as satisfactory. Try this procedure yourself.

JUNE ROSS

As I walked into the room, I was immediately confronted by the ever-admired June Ross. Per usual she was in a revery; in one of her thought moments. She had the calm questioning eyes of childhood and a tenderly modeled face, with round, rosy cheeks. Her eyes of blue, shaded by long, thick lashes, were in perfect harmony with her wavy red-gold hair. Her pert nose perched ever so lightly over a sweet, gallant, red mouth. And her charming hands that were admired by all were in full view.

In build she was strong, in stature above the medium, but so lightly was she poised, that she seemed delicate and small, not looking her twenty years. However, she was slender where slenderness is demanded, and curved where curves are necessary for beauty. She lacked almost nothing; for she had charm, youth, and prettiness, being as fresh as a budding rose.

She was Puritan by a long ancestry, but not in her habits and thoughts. She was a devotee to neatness, being inviolably spick-and-span; dressed to the cool freshness of her personality. But her personality had its special allure, being dangerous to the opposite sex, when she chose to exercise it. While I scrutinized her more closely, I noticed she was cleverly hatted, warmly skirted and jacketed. Her shoes were brilliantly shined and her stockings runless, with her gloves at just the right stage of newness worn off—shabbiness not yet set in.

Heretofore mentioned, June was a dreamer, but not unhappy, being too healthy for unhappiness, too sweet for discontent. But she was vitally restless, like a child learning to walk. A dreamer born was she, weaving enchanting fairy tales and legends, with the innocent egotism of youth. As she was a typical "home" girl, much of her time was spent in attending to the wants and desires of her family. Generally, however, she was to be found with her cunning nose stuck in a book, reading herself into the pages of every book.

How sweet and charming was her personality! Her pleasing smile and laughing eyes appealed to all who came in contact with her. She seldom overdid the length or time of her conversations, but whenever she indulged in it, it was always with much common sense behind it. She felt shy in the company of strangers, but always made a pleasing picture to all, gaining everyone's admiration and attention, through her dazzling eyes and taking smile.

M. K.

JUNE ROSS (*Revised*)

As I walked into the room, I was immediately confronted by the ever-admired June Ross, in one of her thoughtful moments. She had the calm questioning eyes of childhood and a tenderly modeled face, with round, rosy cheeks. Her eyes of blue, shaded by long, thick lashes, were in perfect harmony with her wavy, red-gold hair. Her pert nose perched ever so lightly over a sweet, gallant, red mouth.

In build she was strong, in stature above the medium, but so lightly was she poised that she seemed delicate and small, not looking her twenty years. However, she was slender where slenderness is demanded, and curved where curves are necessary for beauty. She lacked nothing; she had charm, youth, and prettiness, being as fresh as a budding rose.

She was Puritan by a long ancestry, but not in her habits and thoughts. She was a devotee of neatness, being spick-and-span, always dressed to the cool freshness of her personality. But her personality had its special lure, being dangerous to the opposite sex. On this occasion she was cleverly hatted, warmly skirted and jacketed. Her shoes were brilliantly shined and her stockings runless with her gloves at just the right stage of newness worn off—shabbiness not yet set in.

June was a dreamer, but not unhappy, being too healthy and sweet for unhappiness and discontent. But she was vitally restless, like a child learning to walk. A dreamer born was she, weaving enchanting fairy tales and legends with the innocent egotism of youth. Generally, however, she could be found with her cunning nose stuck in a book, reading herself into the pages of every book.

How sweet and charming was her personality! Her pleasing smile and laughing eyes appealed to all who came in contact with her. She felt shy in the company of strangers, but always made a pleasing

picture to all, gaining everyone's admiration through her dazzling
eyes and taking smile.

M. K.

⤃» B «⤄

For Point of View:

I have named, among many rivers that make music in my memory,
that dirty Water of Leith. Often and often I desire to look upon it
again; and the choice of a point of view is easy to me. It should be
at a certain water door, embowered in shrubbery. The river is there
dammed back for the service of the flour-mill just below.

R. L. STEVENSON, "The Manse." [1]

We will push fast through them into the shadow of the pillars at
the end of the "Bocca di Piazza," and then we forget them all; for
between those pillars there opens a great light, and, in the midst of
it, as we advance slowly, the vast tower of St. Mark seems to lift
itself visibly forth from the level field of chequered stones . . .

And . . . there rises a vision out of the earth, and all the great square
seems to have opened from it in a kind of awe, that we may see it far
away; a multitude of pillars and white domes clustered into a long low
pyramid of coloured light: . . . [Then follows the famous description,
moving from the foundation of St. Mark to the topmost pinnacles.]

JOHN RUSKIN, *The Stones of Venice.*

For Dominant Tone:

It was high noon, and the rays of the sun, that hung poised directly
overhead in an intolerable white glory, fell straight as plummets upon
the roofs and streets of Guadalajara. The adobe walls and sparse brick
sidewalks of the drowsing town radiated the heat in an oily, quivering
shimmer. The leaves of the eucalyptus trees around the Plaza drooped
motionless, limp and relaxed under the scorching, searching blaze.
The shadows of these trees had shrunk to their smallest circumference,
contracting close about the trunks. The shade had dwindled to the
breadth of a mere line. The sun was everywhere. The heat exhaling
from brick and plaster and metal met the heat that steadily descended
blanketwise and smothering, from the pale, scorched sky. Only the
lizards—they lived in chinks of the crumbling adobe and in interstices
of the sidewalk—remained without, motionless, as if stuffed, their eyes

---

[1] From *Memories and Portraits* (1895), reprinted by permission of the publishers,
Charles Scribner's Sons.

closed to mere slits, basking, stupefied with heat. At long intervals the prolonged drone of an insect developed out of the silence, vibrated a moment in a soothing, somnolent, long note, then trailed slowly into the quiet again. Somewhere in the interior of one of the 'dobe houses a guitar snored and hummed sleepily. On the roof of the hotel a group of pigeons cooed incessantly with subdued, liquid murmurs, very plaintive; a cat perfectly white, with a pink nose and thin, pink lips, dozed complacently on a fence rail, full in the sun. In a corner of the Plaza three hens wallowed in the baking hot dust, their wings fluttering, clucking comfortably.

FRANK NORRIS, The Octopus.[1]

It was a rainy Sunday in the gloomy month of November. . . . A wet Sunday in a country inn!—whoever has had the luck to experience one can alone judge of my situation. The rain pattered against the casements; the bells tolled for church with a melancholy sound. I went to the windows in quest of something to amuse the eye; but it seemed as if I had been placed completely out of the reach of all amusement. The windows of my bedroom looked out among tiled roofs and stacks of chimneys, while those of my sitting-room commanded a full view of the stable-yard. I know of nothing more calculated to make a man sick of this world than a stable-yard on a rainy day. The place was littered with wet straw that had been kicked about by travellers and stable-boys. In one corner was a stagnant pool of water, surrounding an island of muck; there were several half-drowned fowls crowded together under a cart, among which was a miserable, crest-fallen cock, drenched out of all life and spirit; his drooping tail matted, as it were, into a single feather, along which the water trickled from his back; near the cart was a half-dozing cow, chewing the cud, and standing patiently to be rained on, with wreaths of vapor rising from her reeking hide; a wall-eyed horse, tired of the loneliness of the stable, was poking his spectral head out of a window, with the rain dripping on it from the eaves; an unhappy cur, chained to a dog-house hard by, uttered something every now and then, between a bark and a yelp; a drab of a kitchen wench tramped backwards and forwards through the yard in pattens, looking as sulky as the weather itself; everything in short was comfortless and forlorn, excepting a crew of hardened ducks, assembled like boon companions round a puddle, and making a riotous noise over their liquor.

WASHINGTON IRVING, "The Stout Gentleman."

[1] Copyright, 1901, by Doubleday, Doran & Company, Inc. Reprinted by permission.

Compare Dickens's famous description of fog in *Bleak House*. Irving's description above contains plenty of significant details, but note this brief sketch of Tennyson by Carlyle.[1]

One of the finest-looking men in the world. A great shock of rough dusty-dark hair; bright-laughing hazel eyes; massive aquiline face, most massive yet most delicate; of sallow-brown complexion, almost Indian-looking; clothes cynically loose, free-and-easy;—smokes infinite tobacco. His voice is musical metallic,—fit for loud laughter and piercing wail, and all that may lie between; speech and speculation free and plenteous; I do not meet, in these late decades, such company over a pipe!

Here is Thackeray's remarkable portrait of Beatrix Esmond:

She was a brown beauty: that is, her eyes, hair, and eyebrows and eyelashes were dark: her hair curling with rich undulations, and waving over her shoulders; but her complexion was as dazzling white as snow in sunshine: except her cheeks, which were a bright red, and her lips, which were of a still deeper crimson. Her mouth and chin, they said, were too large and full, and so they might be for a goddess in marble, but not for a woman whose eyes were fire, whose look was love, whose voice was the sweetest low song, whose shape was perfect symmetry, health, decision, activity, whose foot as it planted itself on the ground was firm but flexible, and whose motion, whether rapid or slow, was always perfect grace—agile as a nymph, lofty as a queen—now melting, now imperious, now sarcastic, there was no single movement of hers but was beautiful. As he thinks of her, he who writes feels young again, and remembers a paragon.

W. M. THACKERAY, *Henry Esmond*.

For intense imagery consider:

The white man rested his chin on his crossed arms and gazed at the wake of the boat. At the end of the straight avenue of forests cut by the intense glitter of the river, the sun appeared unclouded and dazzling, poised low over the water that shone smoothly like a band of metal. The forests, sombre and dull, stood motionless and silent on each side of the broad stream. At the foot of the big, towering trees, trunkless nipa palms rose from the mud of the bank, in bunches of leaves enormous and heavy, that hung unstirring over the brown swirl

---

[1] From the *Carlyle-Emerson Correspondence* (1892), ed. by C. E. Norton. Reprinted by permission of the publishers, Houghton Mifflin Company.

of eddies. In the stillness of the air every tree, every leaf, every bough, every tendril of creeper, and every petal of minute blossoms seemed to have been bewitched into an immobility perfect and final. Nothing moved on the river but the eight paddles that rose flashing regularly, dipped together with a single splash; . . .

JOSEPH CONRAD, "The Lagoon." [1]

The following contains something of a fundamental image, but it is never wholly carried through:

From the flat red sea of sand rose great rock mesas, generally Gothic in outline, resembling vast cathedrals. They were not crowded together in disorder, but placed in wide spaces, long vistas between. This plain might once have been an enormous city, all the smaller quarters destroyed by time, only the public buildings left,—piles of architecture that were like mountains. . . . The great tables of granite set down in an empty plain were inconceivable without their attendant clouds, which were a part of them, as the smoke is a part of the censer. . . .

WILLA CATHER, *Death Comes for the Archbishop*.[2]

In the next selection,[3] one approaches a description of a mental state:

Seen from behind a windshield, the highway stretches westward in lazy curves. One's arms relax on the wheel, the elbows hugging it gently, the fingers ready to stiffen at the threat of danger. Automatically the left foot fumbles for the clutch, then sinks back to the floor. The right foot presses the accelerator as a ribbon of figures moves across the face of the speedometer: 40–50–55–58–60. The eyes, fixed on the road ahead, are confined between ditches twenty-one feet apart. There are brown fields somewhere outside the focus of one's vision; somewhere behind fences cows ruminate in the shade; the life of a thousand households is hidden by rusty screens. The motor steadily roars. Interminably the road unwinds, like a surveyor's tape, like wire from a spool, like trout line cast from a reel across still water.

In the near distance, toward the end of a straightaway, there is another automobile, a black dot traveling westward at fifty-five miles

---

[1] From *Tales of Unrest*, by Joseph Conrad, copyright, 1898, by Doubleday, Doran & Company, Inc. Reprinted by permission.

[2] Reprinted from *Death Comes for the Archbishop*, by Willa Cather, by permission of and special arrangement with Alfred A. Knopf, Inc., authorized publishers.

[3] Reprinted by arrangement with the author.

an hour instead of sixty. It seems motionless, a goal to be attained
and passed. Its movement is transferred to the landscape, which now
flows backward at the speed of a furious river, or more exactly, at
fifty-five miles per hour. One's own car, to eyes fixed on the other,
moves like a man on foot; then, with the accelerator pressed to the
floor, it is like a man running toward the moment of crisis. The
moment comes; hands are tense on the wheel, eyes straight ahead
(slow, slow: wait for these eastbound cars to pass in a rush of wind;
slow: here is a curve . . . a blind hill . . . a straightaway at last). This
is the instant of danger overcome, of triumph that lasts till the appearance of another westbound car, another adversary, another goal
to be left proudly behind at five miles an hour—or is it sixty?

MALCOLM COWLEY, *The New Republic*, February 25, 1931.

This last selection [1] suggests the possibilities of progressive description.

On the left the road comes up the hill out of a pool of mist; on the
right it loses itself in the shadow of a wood. On the farther side of
the highway a hedgerow, dusty in the moonlight, spreads an irregular
border of black from the wood to the fog. Behind the hedgerow slender
poplar trees, evenly spaced, rule off the distance with inky lines.

A movement stirs the mist at the bottom of the hill. A monotonous
rhythm grows in the silence. The mist darkens, and from it there
emerges a strange, shadowy column that reaches slowly up the hill,
moving in silence to the sombre and muffled beating of a drum. As
it draws nearer, the shadow becomes two files of marching men bearing between them a long dim burden.

The leaders advance into the moonlight. Each two men are carrying
between them a pole, and from pole to pole have been slung planks
making a continuous platform. But that which is heaped upon the
platform is hidden with muddy blankets.

The uniforms of the men—of various sorts, indicating that they are
from many commands—are in shreds and spotted with stains of mould
and earth; their heads are bound in cloths so that their faces are
covered. The single drummer at the side of the column carries slung
from his shoulder the shell of a drum. No flag flies from the staff at
the column's head, but the staff is held erect.

Slowly the head of the line advances to the shadow of the wood,
touches it and is swallowed. The leaders, the bare flag-staff, the
drummer disappear; but still from the shade is heard the muffled

[1] From *The Fabulist*, reprinted by permission of the author.

rhythm of the drum. Still the column comes out of the mist, still it climbs the hill and passes with its endless articulated burden. At last the rearmost couple disengages itself from the mist, ascends, and is swallowed by the shadow. There remain only the moonlight and the dusty hedgerow.

From the left the road runs from Belgium; to the right it crosses into France.

The dead were leaving their resting places in that lost land.

W. A. DWIGGINS, "La Dernière Mobilisation."

CHAPTER XVII

The Three Elements Together—
The Short Story

A skilful literary artist has constructed a tale. If wise, he has not fashioned his thoughts to accommodate his incidents; but having conceived, with deliberate care, a certain unique or single *effect* to be wrought out, he then invents such incidents—he then combines such events as may best aid him in establishing this preconceived effect. If his very initial sentence tend not to the outbringing of this effect, then he has failed in his first step. In the whole composition there should be no word written, of which the tendency, direct or indirect, is not to the one pre-established design. And by such means, with such care and skill, a picture is at length painted which leaves in the mind of him who contemplates it with a kindred art, a sense of the fullest satisfaction. The idea of the tale has been presented unblemished, because undisturbed; and this is an end unattainable by the novel.

POE, "Hawthorne's *Twice-Told Tales," Graham's Magazine*, (1842).

LIFTING THE PLOT STORY into the realm of the short story is a problem in plastic art. The structure remains essentially the same, so far as any fixed, mechanical plot skeleton for a short story can be given, but the product is no longer a one-dimensional affair. Plot, characters, and setting are now all integrated into one homogeneous, living whole, with one or the other of the three generally dominating the combination. Finally, shaped and modeled smoothly by the scalpel of style, the resultant product will be a solid, three-dimensional block of protoplasmic life whose height depends on plot, breadth on setting, and depth on characters. And the success of this plastic achievement depends wholly upon the skill of the artist.

Here, you may say at once, we are plunging recklessly into the work of the professional writer. Thackeray and George Eliot, for example, could never explain definitely how they put living, breathing characters down on paper. No psychological method has ever been devised for producing on paper a transcript of life that will move and convince the reader. Nevertheless, there are many who accomplish the feat—perhaps by some stroke of genius or indescribable knack. And there is no reason why you, as an elementary student of narration, should not be given a chance to discover whether you yourself cannot, by verbal dexterity, careful observation and organization, and by whatever other tricks of the trade you can master, produce an *impression* of a living character, or realistic plot. As a final test take your simple, one-dimensional plot story and see whether you can so endow it with the breath of life that the reader will come away moved and convinced. For this vitalizing process some of the following suggestions will perhaps be helpful.

The best way to vitalize the plot story is to introduce a definite, firmly conceived character, with that character's resultant point of view. The "I" of the simple plot story is no longer merely the writer but a distinct character (who may, of course, be the actual writer fully individualized), whose attitude toward the events of the story is unique, that is, his own and no one else's. Essentially, then, it makes no difference whether "I" or "he" is used: the character's individuality, and hence the point of view, remains the same. The whole story is viewed from the eyes of the one character, who may be major or minor, "I" or "he." Thus unity of impression is achieved at once, provided the character is kept consistent throughout. If such a character is not the author himself, generally it is a friend of the writer and thus thoroughly known.

Other characters may now appear in the story, but they should be viewed through the central character's eyes. They will never encroach on his monopoly of the stage, and yet their attitudes toward the events of the story must be just as individual as his. In other words, you have transformed yourself into a miniature puppet show, entering *but not moving* each puppet individually. Notice we said "entering." If you *move* your characters, inconsistently with the plot or their own individualities, the effect of plastic life will be ruined at once. The characters should actually be *in control over the writer* and act in accordance with *their own* desires and motives.

The secret, then, of producing real characters is sympathy. Negatively, the writer must hate the villain, or the feeling of hatred can never be induced in the reader. And the reality of the characters will be considerably enhanced if you use individuals from your own acquaintance, perhaps close friends, as bases for your fictional people. Thus you may even split up one friend to produce two characters, or you may fuse two or more friends to produce a single fictional personage. The result will be effective in proportion to your knowledge and understanding of your friends. In general, it is well to write out a complete dossier of the fictional character. You may also analyze your own character in the same way.

Stevenson pointed out two men in us, the natural and the spiritual. Everlasting is the struggle between Dr. Jekyll and Mr. Hyde, and man's differentiation from beast lies in this mental activity, this balancing of reason *versus* feeling, intellect *versus* emotion. Hence the plastic value of a character will be considerably strengthened if free psychological play is allowed for his balance or unbalance of will and desire, reason and feeling. You will at times, therefore, have to project yourself into the character's thoughts and feelings to such an extent that they will appear on paper as the musings and deliberations of the character himself. The proportion of space given to such psychological reactions will depend wholly on the distance the character in question is removed from the original animal instincts in all of us.

Fundamentally the characters, particularly the dominant, central personage (hero or heroine) should be good. Even the villain may be discarded in favor of a disagreeable situation, out of which the hero must extricate himself somehow, preferably by his own efforts. But the characters ought not to be "true to life," in the commonplace sense of that phrase. They must, on the contrary, be unusual, unique, even exotic, and yet at the same time live and breathe. The problem intrinsically, then, is idealizing one's own intimates or oneself into usable, unique fictional *personae.* And that can readily be done without becoming too fanciful—particularly if the dossiers are written out before-hand.

Finally, as to the details of the presentation of character, we return again a moment to Chapter XV, section 1, *Character Plotted.* If this chapter has been studied carefully, the effectiveness of a dominant trait will now be quite evident. Such a trait lends unity to the whole story, and the dominance of the central character is greatly increased by the concentration on the single trait. But Chapter XV must stop there; one cannot often develop a kinetic, changing character in a short story. The character will remain static, and his dominant trait must be thrown in relief against other characteristics and a multitude of details to make him a plastic individual, rather than a one-dimensional type. He remains still a type, but, within that type, he is now also an individual.

The details to be used in this transmutation are clothes, environment, gestures, expressions, idiosyncrasies, mental traits, speeches, remarks of other characters, and finally his actions. None of these can be neglected, nor can all the details be used mechanically or indiscriminately. Relevant action ultimately reveals the character: that is, he must be painted "on the fly," so to speak, as he rushes through the plot of the story. There is no time for stopping serenely to drop a remark or gesture here, and an expression there. All the devices must be working together, interlocking and interweaving, so that the final impression results from a skillful compression of details rather than a diffuse scattering. Chief of all, the very rhythm and vocabulary of the character's speeches must be consistent and unwavering from the moment he appears.

The plot of a short story should rest on a theme, a fundamental feature of human life. This may be an exhibition of some natural law, a phase of human nature, human passion, or character. Preferably the theme ought to involve conflict: of man against man, man against the world, man against himself—all based on a dramatic situation. An Italian theorist, Georges Polti, has noted thirty-six dramatic situations. The best are probably individual revolt, ambition, deliverance, pursuit, rivalry of superior and inferior, suffering, mistaken identity, daring enterprise, and self-sacrifice (see Glenn Clark's *A Manual of the Short Story Art*, The Macmillan Company, 1922, for the complete list).

For definite sources of plots, other than those noted previously in the book, we suggest fairy tales, the Bible, legends, myths, *The London Times* and *The Saturday Review of Literature* "personal" columns, Sunday newspapers, and Bartlett's or Stevenson's source book of quotations. The last source will often suggest a theme. Finally, however, recall Arnold Bennett's dictum, "Good fiction is autobiography dressed in the colors of all mankind." Look back into your own life and pick an incident involving a fundamental human theme.

Once you have chosen a theme—for example, ambition—every incident of the plot must serve that theme; the whole story must be built to illustrate, but not necessarily preach, the theme (see Poe's method above, p. 477). The central character, too, must exemplify the theme in his own individuality. Also the supporting cast must reinforce it, perhaps by contrasts, to diversify the effect. Thus the story acquires two dimensions, merging into and quite necessary to each other.

The mechanical structure of the plot has been given in its simplest form in Chapter XIV, sections 2, 3, 4, and 5, with a diagram in section 1. The problem now is merely to transmute this simple plot-story structure into a living three-dimensional short story; and that we have already nearly accomplished by adopting one definite character's angle of narration and establishing a fundamental theme of life. Thus the basic situation (see section 2 of Chapter XIV) will be strong and the tensity of the suspense and climax assured. Only one other factor clinches the vital reality of the plot—simple convincingness. The reader must be convinced that such incidents could really happen, and furthermore, that such incidents could happen to just such characters. The secret of convincingness lies in letting the characters govern the plot; for the moment you start moving your characters about to fit a melodramatic or super-clever plot, the reader throws up his hands in disgust and turns away to learn about life elsewhere.

Finally a word about originality in plot. It is a matter of treatment, handling age-old ideas in a new way, for there is no new plot under the sun. "Cinderella," as we have noted, is repeated yearly on Broadway and invites attention on the bookseller's shelves under many disguises. Hence, while you may orchestrate your new-old plot with the newest swing rhythms, you must realize that Homer may have sung about the same thing when he "smote 'is bloomin' lyre."

The third element of the short story, going hand in hand with plot and characters, is the setting, or as noted in Chapter XV, section 2, its emotional effect. The atmosphere must support both characters and plot—that is, ultimately, the theme of the story, so that the whole is unified and effective. And while doing this service, the atmosphere must make its own effect.

The secret of convincing atmosphere lies in thorough knowledge of your setting, the objective details of the locale. A Texan should avoid Alaska, a New Englander California (unless, of course, first-hand knowledge has been gained from travel). Study of the geography of a remote district may make possible its use for a setting, but it is impossible to fool all of the readers all the time. You may slip up on some detail as one modern novelist did in closing the gates of a certain London institution a day too late to fit the actual closing of those gates; see Mr. Lynd's essay (pp. 314–15) for other such distinguished errors. It is far better to place your story in a locale you know thoroughly, so that you can immediately forget about this feature, except for its thematic value, and turn your attention to the more important elements, plot, and characters.

We have now the three elements together: the solid three-dimensional block of life is completed. We need now only to draw out some unassimilative substances and then smooth the whole with the scalpel of style. For the time being at least, omit sarcasm, coincidence, melodrama, sex, vulgarity, intellectuality, criticism, insanity, religion, and the unhappy ending. In their places may be inserted simplicity, the unities, sympathetic visualization, subtle suggestion, and above all humor. For the factor of style re-examine section 6 of Chapter XIV, above.

The work of students themselves suggests certain points. Beware of slow and obscure beginnings. For best results, pick characters of your own age and environment.[1] Be moderate in using dialogue. Cut down the time element as much as possible. A shifting point of view is confusing, but it can be achieved from the omniscient angle; otherwise, divide the story into sections as suggested above in Chapter XIV.[2] Try not to shift tenses inconsistently, and beware of sheer coincidence. Introduce plenty of psychology at the climax, and use only a few characters throughout: never drag in an extra one for ornamental purposes. If you use only one or two characters, you can substitute pronouns for the names, after you have started, and thus speed up the tempo. To sum up, read again the suggestions and warnings in section 6 of Chapter XIV on the plot story—they apply here equally well.

Some students like to attempt picture-frame stories [3] and dramatic stories. The former is a story within a story: it is effectively realistic, but may lack an element of suspense because the narrator is in front of you, alive, telling of his exploits. The dramatic story requires art in positing a situation, giving the reader foreknowledge of facts which are unknown to some of the characters in the story. The most popular trick is disguise, but the thing can be done by overhearing or through sheer situation: one student had a boy write to his girl friend's chum, whom he had never seen, without telling his girl friend. When the chum came to visit the girl in question, things began to happen.[4] Whatever type of story you use, always try to sympathize with your main characters —live *in* them. Do not push them around like puppets; once you have created them, let them go their own ways consistently. Finally, all the cleverness in the world will not attract a reader as much as sincerely felt emotion, deep sympathy with the struggles of your brain children. But, on the other hand, restrain yourself from pushing into melodramatic shrillness. Steer safely between Scylla and Charybdis.

It should be noted that no one expects you to reproduce absolute reality in a four-hundred-word story. Even the "shorts" in

---

[1] Avoid such complicated problems as marital tangles, female vampires, gangsters, etc.

[2] See "Buck Fever" in that chapter.

[3] See Elizabeth Folsom's "Towers of Fame" in Chapter XVIII below.

[4] See "Mischief Will Out" in Chapter XIV, section 3, and "Duty" just below in this chapter.

modern magazines are flimsy, and they average a thousand words. The best you can do is to approach reality in a shorter piece; later you may extend your range and hope to achieve a more life-like fullness.

We submit now a list of superior British and American stories, divided roughly into three groups: Plot Stories, Character Stories, and Atmosphere Stories. The suggestion is that you read and study them in the light of the theory in this and previous chapters, particularly for the structure of a complete story.

BEFORE POE'S SHORT STORY

W. Irving, *Rip Van Winkle*
     The Legend of Sleepy Hollow } Folk Tales

N. Hawthorne, *Ethan Brand*
     The Great Stone Face } Apologues
     Rappacini's Daughter

1. PLOT DOMINATING

Edgar Allan Poe, *The Murders in the Rue Morgue*
     The Purloined Letter
     The Gold Bug
     The Pit and the Pendulum

Fitz James O'Brien, *What Was It? A Mystery*

Henry James, *The Turn of the Screw*

"C. E. Craddock" (Mary N. Murfree), *The Mystery of Witch-Face Mountain*

A. Bierce, *An Occurrence at Owl Creek Bridge*

H. C. Bunner, *A Sisterly Scheme*

Frank Stockton, *The Lady or the Tiger?*

R. H. Davis, *In the Fog*

Rudyard Kipling, *The Man Who Would Be King*
     The Man Who Was

Thomas Hardy, *The Three Strangers*

R. L. Stevenson, *The Sire de Malétroit's Door*

"O. Henry" (W. S. Porter), *Transients in Arcadia*
     Thimble, Thimble
     Sisters of the Golden Circle

A. Conan Doyle, *The Adventure of the Speckled Band*

Melville Davisson Post, *After He Was Dead*
     The Mystery of the Blue Villa

Irvin S. Cobb, *Snake Doctor*
W. W. Jacobs, *The Monkey's Paw*
John Russell, *The Fourth Man*
R. Connell, *The Most Dangerous Game*
C. C. Dobie, *The Leech*

2. CHARACTER DOMINATING

Edgar Allan Poe, *Ligeia*
Henry James, *Brooksmith*
T. B. Aldrich, *Marjorie Daw*
Bret Harte, *Tennessee's Partner*
G. W. Cable, *Madame Délicieuse*
Sarah O. Jewett, *A Lost Lover*
R. L. Stevenson, *Markheim*
      A Lodging for the Night
Mary E. Wilkins Freeman, *The Revolt of "Mother"*
Margaret Deland, *Good for the Soul*
R. H. Davis, *Gallegher*
Jack London, *Samuel*
Rudyard Kipling, *Wee Willie Winkie*
      Without Benefit of Clergy
      With the Main Guard
"O. Henry" (W. S. Porter), *Squaring the Circle*
      A Retrieved Reformation
      The Gift of the Magi
Edith Wharton, *Xingu*
Mary R. S. Andrews, *The Perfect Tribute*
Henry van Dyke, *The Lost Word*
Katherine Mansfield, *The Fly*
      The Life of Ma Parker
Maxwell Struthers Burt, *John O'May*
Edna Ferber, *The Gay Old Dog*
Sherwood Anderson, *The Other Woman*
      I'm a Fool
      I Want to Know Why
Dorothy Canfield, *Uncle Giles*
Peter B. Kyne, *The Three Godfathers*
Willa Cather, *Paul's Case*
James Stephens, *Darling*
Ernest Hemingway, *The Killers*

3.   ATMOSPHERE DOMINATING [1]

Edgar Allan Poe, *The Masque of the Red Death*
               The Fall of the House of Usher
               A Descent into the Maelstrom
Henry James, *A New England Winter*
Bret Harte, *The Outcasts of Poker Flat*
G. W. Cable, *Père Raphael*
"Octave Thanet" (Alice French), *Otto the Knight*
T. N. Page, *Meh Lady*
           Marse Chan
J. C. Harris, *Trouble on Lost Mountain*
             The Wonderful Tar-Baby Story
James Lane Allen, *King Solomon of Kentucky*
Hamlin Garland, *Among the Corn-Rows*
M. Hewlett, *Quattrocentisteria*
Rudyard Kipling, *On Greenhow Hill*
                At the End of the Passage
                Kaa's Hunting
                They
R. L. Stevenson, *The Merry Men*
Jack London, *To Build a Fire*
"O. Henry" (W. S. Porter), *The Fourth in Salvador*
                          The Furnished Room
                          Springtime à la Carte
Joseph Conrad, *Heart of Darkness* (Novelette)
Edwina S. Babcock, *The Excursion*
Fanny Hurst, *The Vertical City*
W. D. Steele, *What Do You Mean—Americans?*
Ruth Suckow, *A Start in Life*
             Uprooted
             Golden Wedding
Zona Gale, *A Far Cry*

A first aid in the search for plot material is the newspaper. Human-interest stories are an obvious source of ready-made plots; but "personals" also should not be forgotten. These are often rather pathetic appeals for companionship, "want ads" of the lovelorn; but concealed beneath a few lines may be lurking a real

[1] See Cynthia A. Pugh, *A Book of Short Stories*, The Macmillan Company, 1931, for other types.

tragedy, or comedy. The possibilities in personals have been noted in *Plots and Personalities*, by E. E. Slosson and June E. Downey (1922).[1] The main objective of the book is to exploit the suggestive value of the "agony" column of *The London Times*. For example,

> Jasper,—Tick—tock,
> tick—tock. Sweetie.

The authors analyze, with relation to this weird sort of stimulus, varieties of imagination, such as: the inert, the stereotyped, the melodramatic, the mathematical, and the inventive. Examine your own reactions to this item; then hunt out other personals in newspapers and see what kind of stories you can develop from them.

A good test of creative ability is suggested by Slosson and Downey. You are asked to check a series of twenty-five situations with the mark plus or minus, according to your estimate of their dramatic value. Returns are tabulated for over a hundred individuals to provide a standard for judging, as the writers indicate, whether you should hope to become a creative writer or an insurance salesman. Probably the real value of such tests, however, lies in stimulation rather than in forecasting ability. The following are typical of personals that may be found in American periodicals, the most reputable ones not excepted.

> Red Flannels—Miss you lots. See you when—
> send some snaps. Love—Sally.[2]

GRAND CENTRAL—on the level? Yes, the Lower level. Meet me below stairs Vanderbilt Ave. side, 5 of the clock on Grateful Eve. Will wear my unco for identification. Asterisk explained later. Charlotte.*

GEO. H. Unattached status not in danger. Better address? Priscilla.

IS PHILADELPHIA so dead to culture that it cannot boast of one unattached man (preferably 35–45) who would prefer stimulating conversation to idle chatter, a pleasant fireside to a night club, and outdoor life to bridge? If so, why not come out of the heather and meet a bonnie lassie? Jeannie.

---

[1] Excerpt reprinted by permission of the publishers, D. Appleton-Century Company, Inc.

[2] This and the following items in the group are reprinted from the "personals" column of *The Saturday Review of Literature*, by permission of the editor.

COLLEGE GRADUATE, teaching—lonesome. Like to exchange ideas on music, dramatics, and psychology. Versa Tile.

WELL BRED, educated, urbane, young woman (with a penchant for ideas, discourse, books, music, art, camelias, and tea by the fire among other things) seeks intellectual "rescue" via intelligent and stimulating correspondence and friendship with unattached gentleman of the new school (over 30). Box 425.

WILL BACHELOR, 24–34, intelligent, versatile, attractive, seeking diversion, possibly friendship, write entertainingly to girl (neither gold-digger, dateless, nor beautiful-dumb), Toledo-Columbus region. Enjoy sunsets, canoeing, A. Adverse, symphonies, Ann Harding, dancing, Voltaire, harmonizing, sparkling conversation, Teasdale, swimming, plays; dislike conventionally dull men, spinach. Box 503.

EX-COLLEGE boy, broke, homeless, wants work. Anywhere, anything. Jack.

CE SERA MON PLAISIR. Sonia.

⇢⇢⇢ A ⇠⇠⇠

Form the habit of clipping newspaper items which provide potential plot material, hints for characters, or other elements of the short story. Consult the files of bound newspapers and periodicals in your school library, and copy promising bits in your notebook. Just how much can be done by a clever student with a newspaper item appears in "In the Desert." The only disturbing feature of it is the stream-of-consciousness technique, which is indicated—so the author insisted—by single quotation marks rather than double.

FALSE TOOTH SAVES EXPLORERS IN AFRICA[1]

Replaces Lost Bearing from their Motorcycle Magneto

WASHINGTON, Feb. 26.—What to do when a motorcycle loses a hard-rubber magneto bearing in the heart of Africa, 1500 miles from the nearest service station? Here is how a pair of young explorers, going from Nigeria to the Red Sea, met the situation, as told by one of them in the *National Geographic Magazine*.

[1] Reprinted by permission of the *Detroit News*.

· "Next day the cap dropped off Flood's magneto breaker box and a little hard rubber bearing the size of a small pearl—and much more valuable to us—fell out in the sand.

"The motorcycle wouldn't run without it, and we didn't have an extra or anything from which to make one. We absolutely had to have it, but a three-hour search on hands and knees only convinced us that it simply wasn't there. The Sahara had swallowed it up.

"But Flood had lost his four upper front teeth and the replacements were mounted on a quickly detachable partial plate.

"'Spit out your teeth, Flood. Let's see the plate . . . Hurray! Hard rubber!!!' And I carved a bearing out of it that got us across Africa, to the nearest dentist, in Khartoum—1500 miles away."

IN THE DESERT

The motorcycle slowly plowed its way through the scorching sands. Two men, with blistering hands and sweating brows, carefully spurred this strange desert craft onwards into the trackless Sahara. The burning rays of the noonday sun, directly overhead, made sport of these tiny morsels of humanity that dared to embark on this great sea of glistening white. Heat waves shimmered on all sides. The sun dispatched its fiery beams and the sands mercilessly reflected them back.

James Wilson, the younger of the two men, sent a look of encouragement at his older companion and fellow explorer. The machine floundered in a great bank of sand, sending up showers of fine, white particles at each useless twist of the wheels.

'Good old Flood, he was standing the gaff all right. Not so bad for a beginner! Only sixteen falls from the motor the first time on it. That was encouraging, and now he could wind his way quite steadily through the thick layers of sand that reluctantly gave way before them. Not a soul had they seen in three days, and now, heaven only knew how many more days before they would see another one.'

His parched lips parted in a grim smile. 'Well, they had to make it, and their water supply was diminishing in a startling manner. Their place was worse than he had ever dreamed possible. Not even Purgatory could rival its fiery ostentations. But still there was the fascination that drew them onwards and held them from turning back. Well, their fuel supply was sufficient, and while there was life, there was hope.'

'Several miles more, and then they'd stop for a last refreshing sip from their jugs. This was indeed a hell on earth!' Sand gritted between his teeth! Sand in his eyes, in his clothing, in his hair! The sun penetrated his thick red flannel spine pad and helmet! It parched the thick leather he had once called skin.

When he caught sight of some heavy rocks that boasted small shadows, he motioned to his companion, and brought the motor to a stop. Francis Flood managed a jaunty swagger over to the rocks, but as soon as they were both crouched in the meager shade, he gave way to a mild despair.

The water jugs sounded pitifully empty, when shaken, but they would take their last drink with the assurance that, according to their map, the next water hole was less than twenty-five miles away.

They both drank sparingly, and Wilson grinned as his fellow adventurer performed his hindered, dental ablutions. 'Flood was minus his four, upper front teeth, which he had lost in an accident the preceding year and the replacements were mounted on a detachable plate. Sand, creeping in between the plate and his gums, caused him great annoyance, and at every stop, Flood removed his dental works to wash the sand from them with a little of their precious water. It was a pity that the cute French miss in Nigeria, who had taken such a liking to "le Monsieur Flood," was not there to see him replace "ze gorgess smile." That water certainly felt good to parched throats and lips!'

When they resumed their journey, Wilson let Flood take the wheel. They pushed onwards, and his thoughts rambled, as thoughts will.

'They had started on this enterprise across the Sahara to the Red Sea, merely because their adventurous spirits would not permit them to remain long in any one place. If they had only supplied themselves with a guide! They had missed the last water hole because of errors on the cheap little map they were using! They must make this one! It was indispensable that they obtain fresh water.'

Suddenly, he was shaken from his reverie. The motor had suddenly stopped! What had happened? He stumbled out of the side car, and began a hurried examination. Flood probably did not realize the jeopardous position they would be in, with no means of starting their vehicle and with no water to keep them alive until help could come.

Upon investigation, he discovered a missing bearing. The cap had dropped off the magneto breaker box, and a small hard-rubber bearing had dropped out. Feverishly he dropped to his knees. Perhaps he could still recover it! Eagerly he examined the sand around the machine. Inch by inch, he went over the ground, sifting the sand carefully through his fingers. But the Sahara had swallowed it! He got up, and reluctantly met Flood's anxious eyes.

Together they looked over the spare parts they had brought with them. No, their search was fruitless! It seemed they had thought of every possible accessory but that which they now needed. They straightened up.

Perhaps some traveler would come along, someone who could help them! But no, the horizon stretched out on all sides, without a break! Even their tracks were already covered by the ever-moving sands. He examined his store of tools again, but no hope!

Suddenly he jumped! "Spit out your teeth, Flood," he yelled! And he grabbed his friend and twirled him around in the sands.

Flood probably thought the sun had affected him, but he removed his plate and held it out for inspection. "Hurray, hard rubber!" Wilson proclaimed! And waving the dental masterpiece he danced around again.

The problem was solved! With a knife, Wilson skillfully carved the necessary hard-rubber bearing out of the ill-fated dental plate!

The motorcycle slowly plowed its way through the scorching sands. Two men, with blistering hands and sweating brows, drove on with angelic grins. The one with the more celestial smile was slightly tooth-less, but, nevertheless, his appearance bespoke great mental satisfaction and greater physical comfort.

L. G.

"Duty" is dramatic. In it we are given foreknowledge of factors not known to all the characters.[1] Would a father sacrifice a son like this—as a rule? Other ways of supplying foreknowledge are by letting a character overhear, by use of a letter, or by disguise.

DUTY

John Henry, at the age of forty, was an obscure detective in the small town of York, Pennsylvania. Promotion is slow in such unimportant places, and Henry faced a dull future of spending all his life in little routine jobs that would never get him anywhere. Celebrated crimes did not happen in such small towns, and there was very little chance of a country detective ever showing himself to be a brilliant sleuth and making a big reputation.

But the celebrated crime did happen. An old man, in a nearby town, was found brutally murdered in his home. Robbery was the motive, and the robber had escaped with all the old man's savings.

---

[1] Compare "Mischief Will Out" in Chapter XIV, section 3, and page 483 above in this chapter.

The murdered man had not been prominent, but the cruelty of the murderer, and the impossibility of discovering his identity attracted nation-wide attention.

The police failed to find any solution to the mystery, and made no progress at all. There were no clues, since the old man had had no enemies and no suspicious character had been seen lurking in the neighborhood on the night of the murder. A small penknife, however, rather unique in appearance, was found in the house. It was not the weapon with which the crime had been committed, for the old man had been clubbed to death.

After a year in which many skilled detectives had admitted their failure and given up the case, the police at York were asked if they could spare a man who could devote all his time to the case. John Henry was assigned to it, and he was elated at his opportunity for fame and success. But on his very first day on the case, he discovered to his horror that the knife that had been found in the room with the murdered man was one which he had given years before to his own son. He had given it to the boy before his wife and he had been divorced and the boy had taken the name of the man his mother had married. The knife was of foreign make, and the detective had never seen another like it.

John Henry had a strong sense of duty, and nothing could swerve him from what he knew was right, no matter who suffered. He hoped that there would be some innocent explanation of his son's knife at the scene of the murder, but there was not. Bit by bit he linked up a chain of absolutely damning evidence against the boy.

The night before the boy's arrest was one of horrible anguish for him. All night long he fought it out with himself. His son's life was in his hands, and only he could expose him to the punishment of death. He knew how easy it would be to keep silent about the matter, for no one would ever know the truth, if he did not wish them to. He had the power to let his son go unsuspected for the rest of his life, but he, John Henry, would have to answer to his conscience for the rest of his. At last he decided upon the thing which was harsh but just. It was a terrible choice for a man to make.

All during the trial John Henry was in an awful state of mind. No one, not even the boy himself, knew that he was the father of the criminal. The detective was filled with bitter regrets for what he had done, and he hated that sense of duty which was so much a part of him, that sense of duty which was sending his own flesh and blood to the electric chair. However, the bitterest part if it all came after the trial was over and the judge commended him on his splendid skill in solving a crime which had baffled the shrewdest of detectives.

Henry became a nation-wide hero, and as years went by he became known as one of the cleverest men in the detective service of New York City. All of his later career was based on his solution of that celebrated case, the secret of which John Henry kept till his dying day. He was not ashamed of having done his duty, but he was ashamed of the fame and the success which that ironical stroke of chance had brought him.

G. F.

The author of the following is a born story writer. "Charlie" is an excellent character story.

CHARLIE

The first time I ever saw Charlie was one morning in old Judge Mallock's courtroom. I was just out of school at the time, and having absorbed all of the Nick Carter stuff during my more plastic years, hadn't yet gotten entirely out of the idea that I had in me the makings of a great detective. I had, therefore, procured a job with a city guidance agency the week after I finished college, and had been sent over to court this particular week to get a few lines, as they call it.

The case of gentleman Charlie was certainly a funny one. At about ten o'clock it was called on, and I saw a tall, very dapper-looking man leisurely step up. He looked more like a Hart, Schaffner, and Marx ad than a prospective guest of the county, and I immediately decided that he must be the prosecutor. The bailiff, however, soon dispelled all doubt by addressing him somewhat roughly as Charlie and requesting that he move a trifle more rapidly. At this the defendant looked somewhat annoyed and proceeded quite casually as before to the front of the court.

Well, it developed that they had Charlie, but Charlie without the goods. There were several cases of pickpocketing on file in which (as both judge and cops well knew) Charlie had played the principal role. Charlie, however, had in each case been as a soul apart, and in no instance could they bring an indictment. They simply lacked proof.

During the whole proceeding my friend Charlie stood quite indifferently attentive, an expression half of boredom, half of disdainful amusement twitching his mouth. The cases were stated but to no avail; nothing could be definitely pinned on him. When all the statements had been completed, Mallock, who, if you remember, was one of the best fellows who ever sat on a bench, turned toward him, and after eyeing him queerly, spoke:

"You interest me strangely, young man. Obviously," he said, "you're no credit to the city—yet the city can do nothing about it. So far you've cleverly managed to stump us. If you don't mind my remarking it, I noticed that three fingers on your right hand are missing. It strikes me as peculiar that you should be able to manage in your calling without them!"

At this Charlie looked meditatively for a few minutes at the apparently disabled hand and then with a chuckle remarked, "Oh! it can be done!" Charlie was then dismissed and another case brought up.

The developments of that week were certainly rare. On the second day Mallock came into the courtroom on a tear. His own pockets had been picked on the streetcar that morning, and he swore by all that was holy that from then on he was going to do his share toward making the dipping profession an unattractive one. No cases along these lines were called that day and his firm resolution was, I have no doubt, a trifle weakened by what happened on the following one. I was at court rather early that day and had noticed, before Mallock arrived, a small package placed in the center of his desk. I went up to ask him something when he came in, and as I was speaking he took the thing and opened it.

"Hey!" he exclaimed, as a brown wallet rolled onto the floor, "what's this?"

I waited while he opened it, counted some eighteen dollars in bills, and read a note attached to them. He then started to roar and, laughingly handed me the note.

A curt, "It can be done," was all it said. "Well of all the brazen monkeys," murmured Mallock, when I gave it back; "that's the wallet that was taken out of my pocket yesterday morning and there's every dollar intact. That fellow must have followed me purposely to pull that trick. Well, I'll be damned."

T. C.

"The Cub Reporter Goes Back to Keokuk" is fundamentally a plot situation.

THE CUB REPORTER GOES BACK TO KEOKUK

The cub reporter, who had been sitting idly before his typewriter, came suddenly to life. Two rings was the cue for his entrance into the managing editor's office.

"Wonder what he wants this time," soliloquized the cub. "He's threatened to fire me often enough; so I suppose this time it's all off. I wonder if anyone in New York has been hired and fired as often as I have. I just don't seem to be able to make good in this town. Guess I should have stayed in Keokuk after all."

"You're fired," shouted the editor the minute that the timid reporter was inside of the door. "The stuff you write is absolutely impossible. Your account of the Twenty-third Street fire reads like an obituary notice. How you ever got up the nerve to palm yourself off as a reporter is above me. My advice to you is to go back to Keokuk. The *Keokuk Weekly* may be able to slip your stuff over on the incredulous backwoodsmen, but it won't go here in New York. The cashier will pay you as you go out."

Mechanically the cub left the editor's office, put on his hat and coat, and went out into the street. In his mind he lived over again the past two years of his life. It wasn't exactly a success. Two years ago, he had left Keokuk to come to New York, where he thought a brilliant future awaited him. He hated New York. The people were too smart, too sure of themselves. For two years he had lived from hand to mouth, and suffered ridicule at the hands of New Yorkers because his home happened to be in Keokuk. If he could only square accounts with New York, he would be content to go back to Keokuk, and live a quiet life forever. The indignities he had suffered were many, and he clamored for revenge.

He suddenly realized that he was hungry, and stopped before a restaurant. " $12.47 between me and the poorhouse," he said to himself, as he finished counting his money; "but I've got to eat."

"What's your order?" asked the waiter.

"Half-a-dozen on the half shell," replied the cub.

The instant he took the first bite of his oyster, he let out a yell that brought the manager and the waiters rushing towards him. Something hard had come in contact with a very sensitive tooth.

"What's the matter?" demanded the manager.

The reporter fished the hard object out of his mouth, and held it up for inspection.

"I'll give you $10.00 for it," said the manager, who immediately recognized it as an oyster pearl.

"I should say not," replied the cub. New York was at work trying to get the best of him again.

Suddenly, an idea struck him—an idea whereby he would be able to square accounts with New York. Grabbing his hat, he dashed madly out of the restaurant.

"I want to buy $12.47 worth of beads," he said to the pawnbroker of the shop around the corner from the restaurant.

"You've come to the right place," replied the pawnbroker; "I have a large assortment."

The cub picked out the beads he desired, and left the shop.

About ten minutes later he stopped before an imposing restaurant on Broadway. Before entering, however, he slipped a bead into his mouth.

"What's your order?" asked the waiter.

"Half-a-dozen on the half shell," replied the reporter carelessly.

With the first taste of the oyster he let out a yell that brought the manager hurrying toward him.

"What's the matter?" demanded the manager.

By way of reply the cub fished out of his mouth a round glistening object. "I just hit on this with a sensitive tooth," he added. "Must be an oyster pearl, I guess."

The manager's eyes almost popped out of his head. It was the largest, the most perfectly shaped oyster pearl he had ever seen.

"I'll give you $10.00 for the pearl," said the manager eagerly.

"Sold," replied the cub carelessly.

The manager was jubilant at having got the pearl at such a low price.

"Not a bad afternoon's work," said the reporter to himself, as he sat in his easy chair, counting a fat roll of bills. "Fifteen restaurants netted me just one hundred fifty dollars. Keokuk sure put one over on New York this afternoon. When I've sold all of these at $10.00 per," he soliloquized, as he took a glass jar of beads from the dresser and shook them aimlessly, "I guess I'll go back to Keokuk. I might even take a job reporting on the *Keokuk Daily*. Little Old New York, I think we're about quits. Gosh, but I'm getting tired of oysters."

E. W.

Revision often saves a story. Consider these two successive versions of "Methylene Blue" (second title "Experiment"). The first is little more than a newspaper anecdote, but the second has distinct emotional value because of the compression of time and place, maintenance of point of view, and introduction of the mother element. Make a diagram of the two versions for comparison of the plot structure, and note any differences in characterization or setting.

METHYLENE BLUE

In a biological laboratory in California a white-clad woman was sitting alone before a balance, slowly and carefully weighing out a tiny amount of a deadly poison, potassium cyanide. This she placed in a beaker of water, and while it was dissolving, filled a small hypodermic syringe with a solution of methylene blue. Then she went to a table on which were a number of cages of guinea pigs, and picked out one. In the cage she placed the cyanide solution, and stood watching the animal; it finally started to drink the poison, but had hardly touched it before it fell over dead. The woman quickly removed the body and, picking up the syringe, injected the contents into the still warm corpse. She stood back and watched; a silent minute passed, two minutes, fifteen minutes went by, and still nothing happened. With a sigh she laid down the syringe which she had been holding in her clenched hand, and put the body of the guinea pig in a receptacle.

She sat on a stool for a few moments, thinking, a look of discouragement on her face. At last she rose and selected another cage. She proceeded in the same manner as before, but when five minutes had passed without visible result, she gave another injection; but again she failed to get a result. Puzzled and discouraged, she washed her instruments and stood for some time looking out a window frowning. Then she turned, and seeing the body of the guinea pig on the table, started to dispose of it.

As she reached out her hand to pick up the animal, she noticed an almost imperceptible twitch of a leg muscle. Startled, she stood watching for a long minute. She saw an eyelid flicker; there was a small, convulsive gasp; the eyeballs became brighter; the short legs moved in a weak struggle to rise. The woman's face became enraptured. Placing the now fully alive guinea pig in the cage, she picked another victim, and with new solutions, successfully repeated the experiment three times, taking notes and working until she was so tired she could hardly stand.

One afternoon about two months after this happened, two small children were playing in a home in New York. One of them, pulling a chair up to a table, stood on it and found a tiny box of candy, with a red, printed label. He ate one of the small pieces and was about to hand the box to the other child when he suddenly felt a terrible pain in his stomach. His screams brought his mother, who called the doctor, and rushed him to the hospital. At the hospital his stomach was emptied with a pump, and emergency treatment was given.

The late afternoon papers headlined the incident, and stated that the boy's condition was worse. By evening he was thought to be dying, and as a last resort it was decided to try the new and improved methylene blue treatment which had been developed by a woman out in California. The night edition reported no improvement; the mid-night edition said that another injection had been given; the morning papers noted an improvement. At noon another small dose was given, and the complete recovery of the small victim by evening proclaimed a new and effectual treatment for cyanide poisoning.

J. H.

EXPERIMENT (*Revised*)

In a small, private biological laboratory in a house in California a white-clad woman was sitting alone before a balance, slowly and carefully weighing out a tiny amount of a deadly poison, potassium cyanide. This she placed in a beaker of water, and while it was dissolving, filled a small hypodermic syringe with a solution of methylene blue. Then she went to a table on which were a number of cages of guinea pigs, and picked out one. In the cage she placed the cyanide solution, and stood watching the animal; it finally started to drink but had hardly touched the poison before it fell over, dead. The woman quickly removed the body, and picking up the syringe, injected the contents into the still warm corpse. She stood back and watched; a silent minute passed; two minutes; fifteen minutes went by, and still nothing happened. With a sigh she laid down the syringe which she had been holding in her clenched hand, and put the body of the guinea pig in a receptacle.

She sat on a stool for a few moments, thinking, a look of discouragement on her face. At last she rose, and selected another cage. She proceeded in the same manner as before, but when five minutes had passed without visible result, she gave another injection; again there was no response. Puzzled and discouraged, she washed her instruments and stood for some time looking out of a window, frowning in the bright light of the afternoon sun. Then she turned, and seeing the body of the guinea pig on the table, started to dispose of it.

As she reached out her hand to pick up the animal, she noticed an almost imperceptible twitch of a leg muscle. Startled, she stood for a long minute, watching. An eyelid flickered; there was a small convulsive gasp; the eyeballs became brighter; the short legs moved in a weak struggle to rise. The woman's face became enraptured. Placing the now fully alive guinea pig in the cage, she picked another, and with new solutions carefully repeated the experiment three times, working and taking notes until she was so tired she could hardly stand.

Finally she stopped working, and, clearing a space on the workbench, sat down to write out her notes. She had been writing but a short time when the laboratory door opened and a young girl came in, leading a small blue-eyed boy by the hand. The woman looked up and smiled.

"When'll you be done, mother?" the little girl asked.

"I'll be through in a little while, darling."

The children stood beside her, the little girl watching her write, the boy looking up at a sparkling beaker of water that stood on the edge of the table. Unnoticed, he stood on tiptoe and reached for it; failing to touch it at first, he again stretched out his arm, and finally with a little jump managed to hit the glass and knock it off on the floor. His mother jumped up and frowned.

"Oh, Jimmie, look what you've done now."

The small eyes wrinkled, and sticking a finger in his mouth, the boy started to cry. Almost as he did so, he stiffened and fell on the floor. The woman stood staring blankly for a moment; then she knelt and felt the boy's pulse.

"Mary, send for a doctor and get an ambulance, quick," she said.

When the doctor arrived, he emptied the unconscious boy's stomach with a pump, and rushed him to the hospital, where he was given emergency treatment.

By evening it was apparent that he was rapidly failing; he had not responded to treatment and was still unconscious. The mother had suggested that her experimental method be tried, but her suggestion was refused because of the danger. However, when at ten o'clock his heart made no response to stimulants, she frantically tried to persuade the doctor to use her treatment; at last he gave in. There was a slight rally, and the boy's heart action improved somewhat, but by midnight his condition was again critical. Then another injection was given, with the same short improvement.

After that the mother was allowed to stay with the nurse at his bedside. She sat dry-eyed, staring straight ahead, not moving except as she occasionally shifted her gaze from her boy's face to the window, through which the moonlight sifted from between the leaves of the trees to keep a still watch with her.

It seemed she had been sitting thus for hours, and yet for only a moment; she could not recall the passage of time since she had sat down there. She heard the nurse's voice. She slowly turned her head.

looking at her boy's face as she did so; he looked so pale and tired, and yet so very, very peaceful. Suddenly her hand went to the side of the bed; the other lifted from her lap, falteringly. Then in a tone of awe,

"Nurse, nurse. He's opening his eyes. . . . Oh, thank God."

The blue eyes opened wide; her boy was trying to speak to her.

"Mamma, I didn't break it on purpose. Honest, I didn't, mamma."

Then he closed his eyes and fell into a deep, sound sleep.

J. H.

-≫≫ B ≪≪-

Richard Connell, author of "The Most Dangerous Game" is one of America's most successful short-story writers. He graduated from Harvard in 1915 and, after a fling at reporting and advertising, saw the World War from a front-line position. In his two years' service he participated in four battles. After that came steady productivity as a writer of spirited short stories. Nearly ten volumes have been published in collected form, from *Apes and Angels* (1924), *Variety* (1925), and *The Mad Lover* (1927) to *Playboy* (1936) and *What Ho!* (1937). "The Most Dangerous Game," [1] which we think a possible best where so many are first rate, received the O. Henry prize and has also been produced as a motion picture.

THE MOST DANGEROUS GAME
Richard Connell

"Off there to the right—somewhere—is a large island," said Whitney. "It's rather a mystery——"

"What island is it?" Rainsford asked.

"The old charts call it 'Ship-Trap Island'," Whitney replied. "A suggestive name, isn't it? Sailors have a curious dread of the place. I don't know why. Some superstition . . ."

"Can't see it," remarked Rainsford, trying to peer through the dank tropical night that was palpable as it pressed its thick warm blackness in upon the yacht.

"You've good eyes," said Whitney, with a laugh, "and I've seen you pick off a moose moving in the brown fall bush at four hundred

---

[1] Reprinted by permission of the author. All of Mr. Connell's collected stories have been published by Minton, Balch & Company. They originally appeared in a variety of magazines.

yards, but even you can't see four miles or so through a moonless Caribbean night."

"Nor four yards," admitted Rainsford. "Ugh! It's like moist velvet."

"It will be light enough in Rio," promised Whitney. "We should make it in a few days. I hope the jaguar guns have come from Purdey's. We should have some good hunting up the Amazon. Great sport, hunting."

"The best sport in the world," agreed Rainsford.

"For the hunter," amended Whitney. "Not for the jaguar."

"Don't talk rot, Whitney," said Rainsford. "You're a big-game hunter, not a philosopher. Who cares how a jaguar feels?"

"Perhaps the jaguar does," observed Whitney.

"Bah! They've no understanding."

"Even so, I rather think they understand one thing at least—fear. The fear of pain and the fear of death."

"Nonsense," laughed Rainsford. "This hot weather is making you soft, Whitney. Be a realist. The world is made up of two classes—the hunters and the hunted. Luckily, you and I are hunters. Do you think we've passed that island yet?"

"I can't tell in the dark. I hope so."

"Why?" asked Rainsford.

"The place has a reputation—a bad one."

"Cannibals?" suggested Rainsford.

"Hardly. Even cannibals wouldn't live in such a God-forsaken place. But it's got into sailor lore, somehow. Didn't you notice that the crew's nerves seem a bit jumpy today?"

"They were a bit strange, now you mention it. Even Captain Nielsen——"

"Yes, even that tough-minded old Swede, who'd go up to the devil himself and ask him for a light. Those fishy blue eyes held a look I never saw there before. All I could get out of him was: 'This place has an evil name among seafaring men, sir.' Then he said to me, very gravely: 'Don't you feel anything?'—as if the air about us was actually poisonous. Now, you mustn't laugh when I tell you this—I did feel something like a sudden chill.

"There was no breeze. The sea was as flat as a plate-glass window. We were drawing near the island then. What I felt was a—a mental chill—a sort of sudden dread."

"Pure imagination," said Rainsford. "One superstitious sailor can taint the whole ship's company with his fear."

"Maybe. But sometimes I think sailors have an extra sense that tells them when they are in danger. Sometimes I think evil is a tangible thing—with wave lengths, just as sound and light have. An evil place can, so to speak, broadcast vibrations of evil. Anyhow, I'm glad we're getting out of this zone. Well, I think I'll turn in now, Rainsford."

"I'm not sleepy," said Rainsford. "I'm going to smoke another pipe up on the after deck."

"Good night, then, Rainsford. See you at breakfast."

"Right. Good night, Whitney."

There was no sound in the night as Rainsford sat there, but the muffled throb of the engine that drove the yacht swiftly through the darkness, and the swish and ripple of the wash of the propeller.

Rainsford, reclining in a steamer chair, indolently puffed on his favorite brier. The sensuous drowsiness of the night was on him. "It's so dark," he thought, "that I could sleep without closing my eyes; the night would be my eyelids——"

An abrupt sound startled him. Off to the right he heard it, and his ears, expert in such matters, could not be mistaken. Again he heard the sound, and again. Somewhere, off in the blackness, some-one had fired a gun three times.

Rainsford sprang up and moved quickly to the rail, mystified. He strained his eyes in the direction from which the reports had come, but it was like trying to see through a blanket. He leaped upon the rail to balance himself there, to get greater elevation; his pipe, striking a rope, was knocked from his mouth. He lunged for it; a short, hoarse cry came from his lips as he realized he had reached too far and had lost his balance. The cry was pinched off short as the blood-warm waters of the Caribbean Sea closed over his head.

He struggled up to the surface and tried to cry out, but the wash from the speeding yacht slapped him in the face and the salt water in his open mouth made him gag and strangle. Desperately he struck out with strong strokes after the receding lights of the yacht, but he stopped before he had swum fifty feet. A certain cool-headedness had come to him; it was not the first time he had been in a tight place. There was a chance that his cries could be heard by someone aboard the yacht, but that chance was slender, and grew more slender as the yacht raced on. He wrestled himself out of his clothes, and shouted with all his power. The lights of the yacht became faint and ever-vanishing fireflies; then they were blotted out entirely by the night.

Rainsford remembered the shots. They had come from the right, and doggedly he swam in that direction, swimming with slow, deliberate strokes, conserving his strength. For a seemingly endless time he fought the sea. He began to count his strokes desperately; he could do possibly a hundred more and then—

Rainsford heard a sound. It came out of the darkness, a high, screaming sound, the sound of an animal in an extremity of anguish and terror.

He did not recognize the animal that made the sound. He did not try to; with fresh vitality he swam toward the sound. He heard it again; then it was cut short by another noise, crisp, staccato.

"Pistol shot," muttered Rainsford, swimming on.

Ten minutes of determined effort brought another sound to his ears —the most welcome he had ever heard—the muttering and growling of the sea breaking on a rocky shore. He was almost on the rocks before he saw them; on a night less calm he would have been shattered against them. With his remaining strength he dragged himself from the swirling waters. Jagged crags appeared to jut up into the opaqueness; he forced himself upward, hand over hand. Gasping, his hands raw, he reached a flat place at the top. Dense jungle came down to the very edge of the cliffs. What perils that tangle of trees and underbrush might hold for him did not concern Rainsford just then. All he knew was that he was safe from his enemy, the sea, and that utter weariness was on him. He flung himself down at the jungle edge and tumbled headlong into the deepest sleep of his life.

When he opened his eyes he knew from the position of the sun that it was late in the afternoon. Sleep had given him new vigor; a sharp hunger was picking at him. He looked about him, almost cheerfully.

"Where there are pistol shots, there are men. Where there are men, there is food," he thought. But what kind of men? he wondered, in so forbidding a place? An unbroken front of snarled and jagged jungle fringed the shore.

He saw no sign of a trail through the closely knit web of weeds and trees; it was easier to go along the shore, and Rainsford floundered along by the water. Not far from where he had landed, he stopped.

Some wounded thing, by the evidence a large animal, had thrashed about in the underbrush; the jungle weeds were crushed down and the moss was lacerated; one patch of weeds was stained crimson. A small, glittering object not far away caught Rainsford's eye and he picked it up. It was an empty cartridge.

"A twenty-two," he remarked. "That's odd. It must have been a fairly large animal, too. The hunter had his nerve to tackle it with a light gun. It's clear that the brute put up a fight. I suppose the first three shots I heard was when the hunter flushed his quarry and wounded it. The last shot was when he trailed it here and finished it."

He examined the ground closely and found what he had hoped to find—the print of hunting boots. They pointed along the cliff in the direction he had been going. Eagerly he hurried along, now slipping on a rotten log or a loose stone, but making headway; night was beginning to settle down on the island.

Bleak darkness was blacking out the sea and jungle when Rainsford sighted the lights. He came upon them as he turned a crook in the coast line, and his first thought was that he had come upon a village, for there were many lights. But as he forged along he saw to his great astonishment that all the lights were in one enormous building—a lofty structure with pointed towers plunging upward into the gloom. His eyes made out the shadowy outlines of a palatial château; it was set on a high bluff, and on three sides of it cliffs dived down to where the sea licked greedy lips in the shadows.

"Mirage," thought Rainsford. But it was no mirage, he found, when he opened the tall spiked iron gate. The stone steps were real enough; the massive door with a leering gargoyle for a knocker was real enough; yet about it all hung an air of unreality.

He lifted the knocker, and it creaked up stiffly, as if it had never before been used. He let it fall, and it startled him with its booming loudness. He thought he heard footsteps within; the door remained closed. Again Rainsford lifted the heavy knocker, and let it fall. The door opened then, opened as suddenly as if it were on a spring, and Rainsford stood blinking in the river of glaring gold light that poured out. The first thing Rainsford's eyes discerned was the largest man Rainsford had ever seen—a gigantic creature, solidly made and black-bearded to the waist. In his hand the man held a long-barrel revolver, and he was pointing it straight at Rainsford's heart.

Out of the snarl of beard two small eyes regarded Rainsford.

"Don't be alarmed," said Rainsford, with a smile which he hoped was disarming. "I'm no robber. I fell off a yacht. My name is Sanger Rainsford of New York City."

The menacing look in the eyes did not change. The revolver pointed as rigidly as if the giant were a statue. He gave no sign that he understood Rainsford's words, or that he had even heard them. He was dressed in uniform, a black uniform trimmed with gray astrakhan.

"I'm Sanger Rainsford of New York," Rainsford began. "I fell off a yacht. I am hungry."

The man's only answer was to raise with his thumb the hammer of his revolver. Then Rainsford saw the man's free hand go to his forehead in a military salute, and he saw him click his heels together and stand at attention. Another man was coming down the broad marble steps, an erect, slender man in evening clothes. He advanced to Rainsford and held out his hand.

In a cultivated voice marked by a slight accent that gave it added precision and deliberateness, he said: "It is a very great pleasure and honor to welcome Mr. Sanger Rainsford, the celebrated hunter, to my home."

Automatically Rainsford shook the man's hand.

"I've read your book about hunting snow leopards in Tibet, you see," explained the man. "I am General Zaroff."

Rainsford's first impression was that the man was singularly handsome; his second was that there was an original, almost bizarre quality about the general's face. He was a tall man past middle age, for his hair was a vivid white; but his thick eyebrows and pointed military mustache were as black as the night from which Rainsford had come. His eyes, too, were black and very bright. He had high cheek bones, a sharp-cut nose, a spare, dark face, the face of a man used to giving orders, the face of an aristocrat. Turning to the giant in uniform, the general made a sign. The giant put away his pistol, saluted, withdrew.

"Ivan is an incredibly strong fellow," remarked the general, "but he has the misfortune to be deaf and dumb. A simple fellow, but I'm afraid, like all his race, a bit of a savage."

"Is he Russian?"

"He is a Cossack," said the general, and his smile showed red lips and pointed teeth. "So am I."

"Come," he said, "we shouldn't be chatting here. We can talk later. Now you want clothes, food, rest. You shall have them. This is a most restful spot."

Ivan had reappeared, and the general spoke to him with lips that moved but gave forth no sound.

"Follow Ivan, if you please, Mr. Rainsford," said the general. "I was about to have my dinner when you came. I'll wait for you. You'll find that my clothes will fit you, I think."

It was to a huge, beam-ceilinged bedroom with a canopied bed big enough for six men that Rainsford followed the silent giant. Ivan laid out an evening suit, and Rainsford, as he put it on, noticed that it came from a London tailor who ordinarily cut and sewed for none below the rank of duke.

The dining room to which Ivan conducted him was in many ways remarkable. There was a medieval magnificence about it; it suggested a baronial hall of feudal times with its oaken panels, its high ceiling, its vast refectory table where twoscore men could sit down to eat. About the hall were the mounted heads of many animals—lions, tigers, elephants, moose, bears; larger or more perfect specimens Rainsford had never seen. At the great table the general was sitting, alone.

"You'll have a cocktail, Mr. Rainsford," he suggested. The cocktail was surpassingly good; and, Rainsford noted, the table appointments were of the finest, the linen, the crystal, the silver, the china.

They were eating *borsch*, the rich, red soup with whipped cream so dear to Russian palates. Half apologetically General Zaroff said: "We do our best to preserve the amenities of civilization here. Please forgive any lapses. We are well off the beaten track, you know. Do you think the champagne has suffered from its long ocean trip?"

"Not in the least," declared Rainsford. He was finding the general a most thoughtful and affable host, a true cosmopolite. But there was one small trait of the general's that made Rainsford uncomfortable. Whenever he looked up from his plate he found the general studying him, appraising him narrowly.

"Perhaps," said General Zaroff, "you were surprised that I recognized your name. You see, I read all books on hunting published in English, French, and Russian. I have but one passion in my life, Mr. Rainsford, and it is the hunt."

"You have some wonderful heads here," said Rainsford as he ate a particularly well-cooked *filet mignon*. "That Cape buffalo is the largest I ever saw."

"Oh, that fellow. Yes, he was a monster."

"Did he charge you?"

"Hurled me against a tree," said the general. "Fractured my skull. But I got the brute."

"I've always thought," said Rainsford, "that the Cape buffalo is the most dangerous of all big game."

For a moment the general did not reply; he was smiling his curious red-lipped smile. Then he said slowly: "No. You are wrong, sir. The Cape buffalo is not the most dangerous big game." He sipped his wine. "Here in my preserve on this island," he said in the same slow tone, "I hunt more dangerous game."

Rainsford expressed his surprise. "Is there big game on this island?"

The general nodded. "The biggest."

"Really?"

"Oh, it isn't here naturally, of course. I have to stock the island."

"What have you imported, general?" Rainsford asked. "Tigers?"

The general smiled. "No," he said. "Hunting tigers ceased to interest me some years ago. I exhausted their possibilities, you see. No thrill left in tigers, no real danger. I live for danger, Mr. Rainsford."

The general took from his pocket a gold cigarette case and offered his guest a long black cigarette with a silver tip; it was perfumed and gave off a smell like incense.

"We will have some capital hunting, you and I," said the general. "I shall be most glad to have your society."

"But what game——" began Rainsford.

"I'll tell you," said the general. "You will be amused, I know. I think I may say in all modesty, that I have done a rare thing. I have invented a new sensation. May I pour you another glass of port, Mr. Rainsford?"

"Thank you, general."

The general filled both glasses, and said: "God makes some men poets. Some He makes kings, some beggars. Me He made a hunter. My hand was made for the trigger, my father said. He was a very rich man with a quarter of a million acres in the Crimea, and he was an ardent sportsman. When I was only five years old, he gave me a little gun, especially made in Moscow for me, to shoot sparrows with. When I shot some of his prize turkeys with it, he did not punish me; he complimented me on my marksmanship. I killed my first bear in the Caucasus when I was ten. My whole life has been one prolonged hunt. I went into the army—it was expected of noblemen's sons—and for a time commanded a division of Cossack cavalry, but my real interest was always the hunt. I have hunted every kind of game in every land. It would be impossible for me to tell you how many animals I have killed."

The general puffed at his cigarette.

"After the débâcle in Russia I left the country, for it was imprudent for an officer of the Czar to stay there. Many noble Russians lost everything. I, luckily, had invested heavily in American securities, so I shall never have to open a tea room in Monte Carlo or drive a taxi in Paris. Naturally, I continued to hunt—grizzlies in your Rockies, crocodiles in the Ganges, rhinoceroses in East Africa. It was in Africa that the Cape buffalo hit me and laid me up for six months. As soon as I recovered, I started for the Amazon to hunt jaguars, for I had heard they were unusually cunning. They weren't." The Cossack sighed. "They were no match at all for a hunter with his wits about him, and a high-powered rifle. I was bitterly disappointed. I was lying in my tent with a splitting headache one night when a terrible thought pushed its way into my mind. Hunting was beginning to bore me! And hunting, remember, had been my life. I have heard that in America business men often go to pieces when they give up the business that has been their life."

"Yes, that's so," said Rainsford.

The general smiled. "I had no wish to go to pieces," he said. "I must do something. Now, mine is an analytical mind, Mr. Rainsford. Doubtless that is why I enjoy the problems of the chase."

"No doubt, General Zaroff."

"So," continued the general, "I asked myself why the hunt no longer fascinated me. You are much younger than I am, Mr. Rainsford, and have not hunted as much, but you perhaps can guess the answer."

"What was it?"

"Simply this: hunting had ceased to be what you call 'a sporting proposition.' It had become too easy. I always got my quarry. Always. There is no greater bore than perfection."

The general lit a fresh cigarette.

"No animal had a chance with me any more. That is no boast; it is a mathematical certainty. The animal had nothing but his legs and his instinct. Instinct is no match for reason. When I thought of this it was a tragic moment for me, I can tell you."

Rainsford leaned across the table, absorbed in what his host was saying.

"It came to me as an inspiration what I must do," the general went on.

"And what was that?"

The general smiled the quiet smile of one who has faced an obstacle and surmounted it with success.

"I had to invent a new animal to hunt," he said.

"A new animal? You are joking."

"Not at all," said the general. "I never joke about hunting. I needed a new animal. I found one. So I bought this island, built this house, and here I do my hunting. The island is perfect for my purposes— there are jungles with a maze of trails in them, hills, swamps——"

"But the animal, General Zaroff?"

"Oh," said the general, "it supplies me with the most exciting hunting in the world. No other hunting compares with it for an instant. Every day I hunt, and I never grow bored now, for I have a quarry with which I can match my wits."

Rainsford's bewilderment showed in his face.

"I wanted the ideal animal to hunt," explained the general. "So I said: 'What are the attributes of an ideal quarry?' And the answer was, of course: 'It must have courage, cunning, and above all, it must be able to reason.'"

"But no animal can reason," objected Rainsford.

"My dear fellow," said the general, "there is one that can."

"But you can't mean——" gasped Rainsford.

"And why not?"

"I can't believe you are serious, General Zaroff. This is a grisly joke."

"Why should I not be serious? I am speaking of hunting."

"Hunting? Good God, General Zaroff, what you speak of is murder."

The general laughed with entire good nature. He regarded Rainsford quizzically. "I refuse to believe that so modern and civilized a young man as you seem to be harbors romantic ideas about the value of human life. Surely your experiences in the war——" He stopped.

"Did not make me condone cold-blooded murder," finished Rainsford stiffly.

Laughter shook the general. "How extraordinarily droll you are!" he said. "One does not expect nowadays to find a young man of the educated class, even in America, with such a naïve, and, if I may say so, mid-Victorian point of view. It's like finding a snuff-box in a limousine. Ah, well, doubtless you had Puritan ancestors. So many Americans appear to have had. I'll wager you'll forget your notions when you go hunting with me. You've a genuine new thrill in store for you, Mr. Rainsford."

"Thank you, I'm a hunter, not a murderer."

"Dear me," said the general, quite unruffled, "again that unpleasant word. But I think I can show you that your scruples are quite ill founded."

"Yes?"

"Life is for the strong, to be lived by the strong, and, if needs be, taken by the strong. The weak of the world were put here to give the strong pleasure. I am strong. Why should I not use my gift? If I wish to hunt, why should I not? I hunt the scum of the earth—sailors from tramp ships—lascars, blacks, Chinese, whites, mongrels—a thorough-bred horse or hound is worth more than a score of them."

"But they are men," said Rainsford hotly.

"Precisely," said the general. "That is why I use them. It gives me pleasure. They can reason, after a fashion. So they are dangerous."

"But where do you get them?"

The general's left eyelid fluttered down in a wink. "This island is called Ship-Trap," he answered. "Sometimes an angry god of the high seas sends them to me. Sometimes, when Providence is not so kind, I help Providence a bit. Come to the window with me."

Rainsford went to the window and looked out toward the sea.

"Watch! Out there!" exclaimed the general, pointing into the night. Rainsford's eyes saw only blackness, and then, as the general pressed a button, far out to sea Rainsford saw the flash of lights.

The general chuckled. "They indicate a channel," he said, "where there's none: giant rocks with razor edges crouch like a sea monster with wide-open jaws. They can crush a ship as easily as I crush this nut." He dropped a walnut on the hardwood floor and brought his heel grinding down on it "Oh, yes," he said casually, as if in answer to a question, "I have electricity. We try to be civilized here."

"Civilized? And you shoot down men?"

A trace of anger was in the general's black eyes, but it was there for but a second, and he said, in his most pleasant manner: "Dear me, what a righteous young man you are! I assure you I do not do the thing you suggest. That would be barbarous. I treat these visitors with every consideration. They get plenty of good food and exercise. They get into splendid physical condition. You shall see for yourself tomorrow."

"What do you mean?"

"We'll visit my training school," smiled the general. "It's in the cellar. I have about a dozen pupils down there now. They're from the Spanish bark 'San Lucar' that had the bad luck to go on the rocks out there. A very inferior lot, I regret to say. Poor specimens and more accustomed to the deck than to the jungle."

He raised his hand, and Ivan, who served as waiter, brought thick Turkish coffee. Rainsford, with an effort, held his tongue in check.

"It's a game, you see," pursued the general blandly. "I suggest to one of them that we go hunting. I give him a supply of food and an excellent hunting knife. I give him three hours' start. I am to follow armed only with a pistol of the smallest calibre and range. If my quarry eludes me for three whole days, he wins the game. If I find him"—the general smiled—"he loses."

"Suppose he refuses to be hunted?"

"Oh," said the general, "I give him his option, of course. He need not play that game if he doesn't wish to. If he does not wish to hunt, I turn him over to Ivan. Ivan once had the honor of serving as official knouter to the Great White Czar, and he has his own ideas of sport. Invariably, Mr. Rainsford, invariably they choose the hunt."

"And if they win?"

The smile on the general's face widened. "To date I have not lost," he said.

Then he added, hastily: "I don't wish you to think me a braggart, Mr. Rainsford. Many of them afford only the most elementary sort of problem. Occasionally I strike a tartar. One almost did win. I eventually had to use the dogs."

"The dogs?"

"This way, please. I'll show you."

The general steered Rainsford to a window. The lights from the windows sent a flickering illumination that made grotesque patterns on the courtyard below, and Rainsford could see moving about there a dozen or so huge black shapes; as they turned toward him, their eyes glittered greenly.

"A rather good lot, I think," observed the general.

"They are let out at seven every night. If anyone should try to get into my house—or out of it—something extremely regrettable would occur to him." He hummed a snatch of a song from the Folies Bergère.

"And now," said the general, "I want to show you my new collection of heads. Will you come with me to the library?"

"I hope," said Rainsford, "that you will excuse me tonight, General Zaroff. I'm really not feeling at all well."

"Ah, indeed?" the general inquired solicitously. "Well, I suppose that's only natural, after your long swim. You need a good night's sleep. Tomorrow you'll feel like a new man, I'll wager. Then we'll hunt, eh? I've one rather promising prospect——"

Rainsford was hurrying from the room.

"Sorry you can't go with me tonight," called the general. "I expect rather a fair sport—a big, strong black. He looks resourceful—Well, good night, Mr. Rainsford; I hope that you have a good night's rest."

The bed was good and the pajamas of the softest silk, and he was tired in every fiber of his being, but nevertheless Rainsford could not quiet his brain with the opiate of sleep. He lay, eyes wide open. Once he thought he heard stealthy steps in the corridor outside his room. He sought to throw open the door; it would not open. He went to the window and looked out. His room was high up in one of the towers. The lights of the château were out now, and it was dark and silent, but there was a fragment of sallow moon, and by its wan light he could see, dimly, the courtyard; there, weaving in and out in the pattern of shadow, were black, noiseless forms; the hounds heard him at the window and looked up, expectantly, with their green eyes. Rainsford went back to the bed and lay down. By many methods he tried to put himself to sleep. He had achieved a doze when, just as morning began to come, he heard, far off in the jungle, the faint report of a pistol.

General Zaroff did not appear until luncheon. He was dressed faultlessly in the tweeds of a country squire. He was solicitous about the state of Rainsford's health.

"As for me," sighed the general, "I do not feel so well. I am worried, Mr. Rainsford. Last night I detected traces of my old complaint."

To Rainsford's questioning glance the general said: "Ennui. Boredom."

Then, taking a second helping of Crêpes Suzette, the general explained: "The hunting was not good last night. The fellow lost his head. He made a straight trail that offered no problems at all. That's the trouble with these sailors; they have dull brains to begin with, and they do not know how to get about in the woods. They do excessively stupid and obvious things. It's most annoying. Will you have another glass of Chablis, Mr. Rainsford?"

"General," said Rainsford firmly, "I wish to leave this island at once."

The general raised his thickets of eyebrows; he seemed hurt. "But, my dear fellow," the general protested, "you've only just come. You've had no hunting——"

"I wish to go today," said Rainsford. He saw the dead black eyes of the general on him, studying him. General Zaroff's face suddenly brightened.

He filled Rainsford's glass with venerable Chablis from a dusty bottle.

"Tonight," said the general, "we will hunt—you and I."

Rainsford shook his head. "No, general," he said. "I will not hunt."

The general shrugged his shoulders and delicately ate a hothouse grape. "As you wish, my friend," he said. "The choice rests entirely with you. But may I not venture to suggest that you will find my idea of sport more diverting than Ivan's?"

He nodded toward the corner to where the giant stood, scowling, his thick arms crossed on his hogshead of chest.

"You don't mean——" cried Rainsford.

"My dear fellow," said the general, "have I not told you I always mean what I say about hunting? This is really an inspiration. I drink to a foeman worthy of my steel—at last."

The general raised his glass, but Rainsford sat staring at him.

"You'll find this game worth playing," the general said enthusiastically. "Your brain against mine. Your woodcraft against mine. Your strength and stamina against mine. Outdoor chess! And the stake is not without value, eh?"

"And if I win——" began Rainsford huskily.

"I'll cheerfully acknowledge myself defeated if I do not find you by midnight of the third day," said General Zaroff. "My sloop will place you on the mainland near a town."

The general read what Rainsford was thinking.

"Oh, you can trust me," said the Cossack. "I will give you my word as a gentleman and a sportsman. Of course you, in turn, must agree to say nothing of your visit here."

"I'll agree to nothing of the kind," said Rainsford.

"Oh," said the general, "in that case—But why discuss it now? Three days hence we can discuss it over a bottle of Veuve Cliquot, unless——"

The general sipped his wine.

Then a businesslike air animated him. "Ivan," he said to Rainsford, "will supply you with hunting clothes, food, a knife, I suggest you wear moccasins; they leave a poorer trail. I suggest too that you avoid the big swamp in the southeast corner of the island. We call it Death Swamp. There's quicksand there. One foolish fellow tried it. The deplorable part of it was that Lazarus followed him. You can imagine my feelings, Mr. Rainsford. I loved Lazarus; he was the finest hound in my pack. Well, I must beg you to excuse me now. I always take a siesta after lunch. You'll hardly have time for a nap, I fear. You'll want to start, no doubt. I shall not follow till dusk. Hunting at night is so much more exciting than by day, don't you think? Au revoir, Mr. Rainsford, au revoir."

General Zaroff, with a deep courtly bow, strolled from the room.

From another door came Ivan. Under one arm he carried khaki hunting clothes, a haversack of food, a leather sheath containing a long-bladed hunting knife; his right hand rested on a cocked revolver thrust in the crimson sash about his waist . . .

Rainsford had fought his way through the bush for two hours. "I must keep my nerve. I must keep my nerve," he said through tight teeth.

He had not been entirely clear-headed when the château gates snapped shut behind him. His whole idea at first was to put distance between himself and General Zaroff, and, to this end, he had plunged along, spurred on by the sharp rowels of something very like panic. Now he had got a grip on himself, had stopped, and was taking stock of himself and the situation.

He saw that straight flight was futile; inevitably it would bring him face to face with the sea. He was in a picture with a frame of water, and his operations, clearly, must take place within that frame.

"I'll give him a trail to follow," muttered Rainsford, and he struck off from the rude path he had been following into the trackless wilderness. He executed a series of intricate loops; he doubled on his trail again and again, recalling all the lore of the fox hunt, and all the dodges of the fox. Night found him leg weary, with hands and face lashed by the branches, on a thickly wooded ridge. He knew it would be insane to blunder on through the dark, even if he had the strength. His need for rest was imperative and he thought: "I have played the fox, now I must play the cat of the fable." A big tree with a thick trunk and outspread branches was near by, and, taking care to leave not the slightest mark, he climbed up into the crotch, and stretching out on one of the broad limbs, after a fashion, rested. Rest brought him new confidence and almost a feeling of security. Even so zealous a hunter as General Zaroff could not trace him there, he told himself; only the devil himself could follow that complicated trail through the jungle after dark. But, perhaps, the general was a devil——

An apprehensive night crawled slowly by like a wounded snake, and sleep did not visit Rainsford, although the silence of a dead world was on the jungle. Toward morning when a dingy gray was varnishing the sky, the cry of some startled bird focused Rainsford's attention in that direction. Something was coming through the bush, coming slowly, carefully, coming by the same winding way Rainsford had come. He flattened himself down on the limb, and through a screen of leaves almost as thick as tapestry, he watched. The thing that was approaching him was a man.

It was General Zaroff. He made his way along with eyes fixed in utmost concentration on the ground before him. He paused, almost beneath the tree, dropped to his knees and studied the ground. Rainsford's impulse was to hurl himself down like a panther, but he saw that the general's right hand held something small and metallic—an automatic pistol.

The hunter shook his head several times, as if he were puzzled. Then he straightened up and took from his case one of his black cigarettes; its pungent incenselike smoke floated up to Rainsford's nostrils. Rainsford held his breath. The general's eyes had left the ground and were traveling inch by inch up the tree. Rainsford froze there, every muscle tensed for a spring. But the sharp eyes of the hunter stopped before they reached the limb where Rainsford lay; a smile spread over his brown face. Very deliberately he blew a smoke ring into the air; then he turned his back on the tree and walked carelessly away, back along the trail he had come. The swish of the underbrush against his hunting boots grew fainter and fainter.

The pent-up air burst hotly from Rainsford's lungs. His first thought made him feel sick and numb. The general could follow a trail through the woods at night; he could follow an extremely difficult trail; he must have uncanny powers; only by the merest chance had the Cossack failed to see his quarry.

Rainsford's second thought was even more terrible. It sent a shudder of cold terror through his whole being. Why had the general smiled? Why had he turned back?

Rainsford did not want to believe what his reason told him was true, but the truth was as evident as the sun that had by now pushed through the morning mists. The general was playing with him! The general was saving him for another day's sport! The Cossack was the cat; he was the mouse. Then it was that Rainsford knew the full meaning of terror.

"I will not lose my nerve. I will not."

He slid down from the tree, and struck off again into the woods. His face was set and he forced the machinery of his mind to function. Three hundred yards from his hiding place he stopped where a huge dead tree leaned precariously on a smaller, living one. Throwing off his sack of food, Rainsford took his knife from its sheath and began to work with all his energy.

The job was finished at last, and he threw himself down behind a fallen log a hundred feet away. He did not have to wait long. The cat was coming again to play with the mouse.

Following the trail with the sureness of a bloodhound, came General Zaroff. Nothing escaped those searching black eyes, no crushed blade of grass, no bent twig, no mark, no matter how faint, in the moss. So intent was the Cossack on his stalking that he was upon the thing Rainsford had made before he saw it. His foot touched the protruding bough that was the trigger. Even as he touched it, the general sensed his danger and leaped back with the agility of an ape. But he was not quite quick enough; the dead tree, delicately adjusted to rest on the cut living one, crashed down and struck the general a glancing blow on the shoulder as it fell; but for his alertness, he must have been smashed beneath it. He staggered, but he did not fall; nor did he drop his revolver. He stood there, rubbing his injured shoulder, and Rainsford, with fear again gripping his heart, heard the general's mocking laugh ring through the jungle.

"Rainsford," called the general, "if you are within sound of my voice, as I suppose you are, let me congratulate you. Not many men know how to make a Malay man-catcher. Luckily, for me, I too have hunted in Malacca. You are proving interesting, Mr. Rainsford. I am going now to have my wound dressed; it's only a slight one. But I shall be back. I shall be back."

When the general, nursing his bruised shoulder, had gone, Rainsford took up his flight again. It was flight now, a desperate, hopeless flight, that carried him on for some hours. Dusk came, then darkness, and still he pressed on. The ground grew softer under his moccasins; the vegetation grew ranker, denser; insects bit him savagely. Then, as he stepped forward, his foot sank into the ooze. He tried to wrench it back, but the muck sucked viciously at his foot as if it were a giant leech. With a violent effort, he tore his foot loose. He knew where he was now. Death Swamp and its quicksand.

His hands were tight closed as if his nerve were something tangible that someone in the darkness was trying to tear from his grip. The softness of the earth had given him an idea. He stepped back from the quicksand a dozen feet or so and, like some huge prehistoric beaver, he began to dig.

Rainsford had dug himself in in France when a second's delay meant death. That had been a placid pastime compared to his digging now. The pit grew deeper; when it was above his shoulders, he climbed out and from some hard saplings cut stakes and sharpened them to a fine point. These stakes he planted in the bottom of the pit with the point sticking up. With flying fingers he wove a rough carpet of weeds and branches and with it covered the mouth of the pit. Then, wet with sweat and aching with tiredness, he crouched behind the stump of a lightning-charred tree.

He knew his pursuer was coming; he heard the padding sound of feet on the soft earth, and the night breeze brought him the perfume of the general's cigarette. It seemed to Rainsford that the general was coming with unusual swiftness; he was not feeling his way along, foot by foot. Rainsford, crouching there, could not see the general, nor could he see the pit. He lived a year in a minute. Then he felt an impulse to cry aloud with joy, for he heard the sharp crackle of the breaking branches as the cover of the pit gave way; he heard the sharp scream of pain as the pointed stakes found their mark. He leaped up from his place of concealment. Then he cowered back. Three feet from the pit a man was standing, with an electric torch in his hand.

"You've done well, Rainsford," the voice of the general called. "Your Burmese tiger pit has claimed one of my best dogs. Again you score. I think, Mr. Rainsford, I'll see what you can do against my whole pack. I'm going home for a rest now. Thank you for a most amusing evening."

At daybreak Rainsford, lying near the swamp, was awakened by a sound that made him know that he had new things to learn about fear. It was a distant sound, faint and wavering, but he knew it. It was the baying of a pack of hounds.

Rainsford knew he could do one of two things. He could stay where he was and wait. That was suicide. He could flee. That was postponing the inevitable. For a moment he stood there, thinking. An idea that held a wild chance came to him, and, tightening his belt, he headed away from the swamp.

The baying of the hounds drew nearer, then still nearer, nearer, ever nearer. On a ridge Rainsford climbed a tree. Down a watercourse, not a quarter of a mile away, he could see the bush moving. Straining his eyes, he saw the lean figure of General Zaroff; just ahead of him Rainsford made out another figure whose wide shoulders surged through the tall jungle weeds; it was the giant Ivan, and he seemed pulled forward by some unseen force; Rainsford knew that Ivan must be holding the pack in leash.

They would be on him any minute now. His mind worked frantically. He thought of a native trick he had learned in Uganda. He slid down the tree. He caught hold of a springy young sapling and to it he fastened his hunting knife, with the blade pointing down the trail; with a bit of wild grapevine he tied back the sapling. Then he ran for his life. The hounds raised their voices as they hit the fresh scent. Rainsford knew now how an animal at bay feels.

He had to stop to get his breath. The baying of the hounds stopped abruptly, and Rainsford's heart stopped too. They must have reached the knife.

He shinned excitedly up a tree and looked back. His pursuers had stopped. But the hope that was in Rainsford's brain when he climbed died, for he saw in the shallow valley that General Zaroff was still on his feet. But Ivan was not. The knife driven by the recoil of the springing tree, had not wholly failed.

Rainsford had hardly tumbled to the ground when the pack took up the cry again.

"Nerve, nerve, nerve!" he panted, as he dashed along. A blue gap showed between the trees dead ahead. Ever nearer drew the hounds. Rainsford forced himself on toward that gap. He reached it. It was the shore of the sea. Across a cove he could see the gloomy gray stone of the château. Twenty feet below him the sea rumbled and hissed. Rainsford hesitated. He heard the hounds. Then he leaped far out into the sea. . . .

When the general and his pack reached the place by the sea, the Cossack stopped. For some minutes he stood regarding the blue-green expanse of water. He shrugged his shoulders. Then he sat down, took a drink of brandy from a silver flask, lit a perfumed cigarette, and hummed a bit from "Madame Butterfly."

General Zaroff had an exceedingly good dinner in his great paneled dining hall that evening. With it he had a bottle of Pol Roger and a half a bottle of Chambertin. Two slight annoyances kept him from perfect enjoyment. One was the thought that it would be difficult to replace Ivan; the other was that his quarry had escaped him; of course, the American hadn't played the game—so thought the general as he tasted his after-dinner liqueur. In his library he read, to soothe himself, from the works of Marcus Aurelius. At ten he went up to his bedroom. He was deliciously tired, he said to himself, as he locked himself in. There was a little moonlight, so, before turning on his light, he went to the window and looked down at the courtyard. He could see the great hounds, and he called: "Better luck another time," to them. Then he switched on the light.

A man, who had been hiding in the curtains of the bed, was standing there.

"Rainsford!" screamed the general. "How in God's name did you get here?"

"Swam," said Rainsford. "I found it quicker than walking through the jungle."

The general sucked in his breath and smiled. "I congratulate you," he said. "You have won the game."

Rainsford did not smile. "I am still a beast at bay," he said, in a low, hoarse voice. "Get ready, General Zaroff."

The general made one of his deepest bows. "I see," he said, "splendid! One of us is to furnish a repast for the hounds. The other will sleep in this very excellent bed. On guard, Rainsford." . . .

He had never slept in a better bed, Rainsford decided.

Maxwell Struthers Burt, distinguished Princeton and Oxford graduate, has had a long career in the field of American letters, producing both verse and fiction. His "John O'May" originally appeared in *Scribner's* in 1917 and was reprinted in *John O'May and Other Stories* in 1918. Since then Mr. Burt has published a great many books, the most recent of which have been *Festival* (1931) and *Entertaining the Islanders* (1933). We think "John O'May" one of the best character stories we have ever read. Analyze it for methods of characterization.

JOHN O'MAY [1]
Maxwell Struthers Burt

One comes across adventure, mental or physical, unexpectedly. There was a dinner at Tommy Dunstan's and I had driven five miles across country. I was late, and I came in out of the semi-darkness of an April night—a little crescent moon cutting a thin band of white in a pale-green sky—to find the others already at table. They were mostly people I knew, neighbors of Tommy and myself: nice people; fox-hunters, most of them; solid young people with money back of them; tall, slim, delightfully healthy; the women with the iridescent, small-headed, not very mellow loveliness of American women—lilies without perfume. Then I noticed O'May.

He struck me at once as alien and arresting. There was exotic coloring: a brown of sunburn, a vivid black of hair, a heather-gray of eyes. Despite the half of him hidden by the table-cloth one received an impression of slim-waistedness, of broad but distinctly well-bred shoulders, of clothes worn with the careless assurance of perfection that seems to be one of the new traits actually inherited. And there was as well, from the way in which he bent toward the woman to whom he was talking, that curious suggestion of masculinity more common in Europeans than in Americans; a suggestion of—how shall I put it?—of humorous acquiescence in a tradition observed but seen through completely . . . I wondered who the man was. My neighbors wondered too.

[1] *Scribner's Magazine* (1917). Reprinted by arrangement with the publishers, Charles Scribner's Sons.

When dinner was over Dunstan called out to me. "Billy," he said, "come here. I want you to meet Captain O'May. Captain John O'May." Captain John O'May! A name like an Irish day in April, isn't it? "Ex-Tenth Hussars"—Dunstan has the explanatory manner— "ex-Boer War, ex-coca-planter, ex-everything, aren't you, Jack?"

"Ex-everything," returned the gentleman in question, with just the faintest hint of a brogue, "ex-everything, except exacting." Then he laughed, showing very white, even teeth under a short mustache, and put out his hand.

I felt immediately the tang to him.

Captain O'May sat down; he poured himself a liqueur; he pushed the bottle toward me; I found myself listening with a bewildering suddenness to a preposterous story of baboons. I have no idea how baboons came to be mentioned; but I was swept up in the tale. It seems in South Africa they march in regiments, the males first, the females with their babies following. In front goes a gray-bearded creature, portentous and not to be laughed at. When they come to a river the leaders plunge in and, taking hands, form a line over which the wives and children go. There is much screaming and refusal. The pantaloon general cuffs the obstreperous. It is a curious sight in the great moonlight—the hairy shapes, the precision and gravity of it. All the while they swing their arms and make a hoarse marching chorus—"Rum-pah! Rum-pah!" Something like that. . . . I didn't know whether to believe what I was hearing or not; but I had a distinct vision—of sands and a river like slow quicksilver, of a night wide as unknown seas, and of outlandish processions. My mind was entirely removed from an American suburb to countries lying on the outer edge of a planet which, if only you could see it in perspective, would seem a witch-like globe, phosphorescent with romance. . . . After that I saw O'May no more for a month.

When I did see him again it was again at Dunstan's, and instantly I felt the little thrill you feel when subconsciously you have been de-siring the renewal of an acquaintanceship. I asked him over to my place for the night. He came and spent six days—borrowing my collars and shirts with a calmness that gave to that irritating act a perpetual dignity. A dinner-jacket of mine fitted him perfectly. I imagine that everyone's clothes fitted O'May.

And so, in the curiously casual manner he had, he fell into the habit of Dunstan and myself.

All that summer and autumn and winter he would appear without warning, stay a week or two, and disappear as quietly as he had come.

I liked him about; I liked his feline walk; I liked his attitude of quiescent readiness. He was so immediately willing to do anything, but at the same time so little weary of doing nothing at all. One seldom meets a man who combines stoicism with eagerness. O'May lay in wait for life. I spoke of him to my friends as "a silent Irishman"; I was not a little proud that I had discovered him. I had forgotten the baboon story, you see, or, if I thought of it at all, put it down to the conversational eagerness that follows an introduction. After three months I found, quite unexpectedly, that baboons, allegorically speaking, were poignantly characteristic of O'May.

He sucked his pipe; he looked at the fire, and then at the clock which had just struck ten; he sipped his whiskey and burst into a passion of epic narration. I was utterly unprepared. Behind the rigid mask of a British ex-soldier I saw—what I should have suspected long before, peeping out—leering out, rather—the unkillable Celt. I was delighted and astonished. Here was tang added to tang.

And O'May did not let the salt evaporate. Before strangers he was a trifle shy,—not incurably, a little persuasion would as a rule produce the desired results,—but he preferred evenings alone with me. An open fire, a bottle of King William, some tobacco handy, were all the scenery needed for extraordinary feats of mental conjuring. It was as if, having taken my measure and found me an amenable victim, he had decided to exercise upon me to their limit the very great powers cf his imagination. And the interesting part was that one never knew when he was telling the truth and when he was not. I doubt if he knew himself.

What was back of it all baffled me. I often wondered. Possibly it was the chromatic Gael, educated almost entirely by a reckless, hardbitten world. In a happier age O'May would have sung to a harp. But this much must be said, as I have said before—the total effect was magnificent. Through all the tropic dusk and welter of incredible incident adventure glowed like a monstrous firefly.

He took me to Trinidad, where he had gorgeously failed at coca-planting; he took me to Ireland, where, apparently, he had been born rather carelessly into an aristocratic but typically Hibernian family; to Africa, where he had fought, and to India, where, as a young subaltern, he had served; and every time he took me he took me differently, nor did I ever recognize again anyone met before. Life blossomed exotically. It became alchemic. One had a confused impression of coincidence and paradox.

There had been a little sister of his when first he had gone out to

India, a little sister he remembered as a wee bit slip of a thing with big blue eyes and yellow curls. A sunbeam she was in the shadows of an old, badly kept park—and then, apparently, he had forgotten all about her. You conjectured the O'Mays were an enormous family. Years later came a small tribal war up in the hills, and the regiment was ordered there, and with it a young chap just out from England. O'May hardly knew him, but found him as a tent-mate. A nice young fellow he was, son of a Devonshire baronet. Details were never lacking. One night he tacked a photograph above his cot—a photograph of a girl in evening dress—very lovely, astonishingly lovely. O'May felt his heart stirred, and there came the glimmerings of memory. "Who's that?" he asked sharply; he was excited.

"Cordelia."

"Cordelia who?"

"Cordelia O'May. My fiancée."

Cordelia O'May! Fancy it! 'Way out there, thousands of miles from anywhere, meeting your future brother-in-law in such a fashion! . . . Exactly! Fancy it!

And then there was the adventure of the nose. One falls naturally into the language of the Arabian Nights when speaking of O'May. It was a curious nose, I must admit. It presented obvious opportunity for the narrative gift. Half-way down its thin, flexible length it was broken distinctly and badly, and the lower half seemed not altogether connected with what had gone before. To O'May's countenance it added a finishing touch of *diablerie*, a supplementary leer, also an additional interest. Here, at all events, was a man to whom something of moment had once happened, even if it was no more than falling forcibly and dramatically downstairs.

One night he told me about his nose; I had suspected he would.

"It's an imitation nose," he said.

"A what?"

"An imitation nose. It doesn't belong to me—at least, the lower half doesn't. I lost it through a dirty Swede in one of old Botha's commandos."

There was no use in asking how in a cavalry skirmish one could have ascertained the nationality of one's adversary. I awaited the sequel in silence. O'May had been removed to a hospital. They thought he wouldn't live. But he did. When he was convalescent there presented itself the question of his nose. How possibly could he go through life with such a ridiculous subtraction of feature? One imagined a hospital distraught over O'May's nose. Then out of the sunshine of an African day stepped a lady—a veiled lady—a lady who refused to give her name. About the incident was all the unexpectedness and fierceness of Oriental romance. And what had the lady come for? She had come to offer the skin of her knee to help restore O'May's shattered countenance. "And so you see," he said, "it isn't my nose at all, it's the lady's."

As to the pursuit of the vivid chance, he exhibited unexpected delicacy. How could he? How as a gentleman? Had the lady wanted him to know who she was she would have told him. No, one shouldn't disturb impalpabilities such as this. The whole thing was so delicate, so tenderly intriguing—and then he laughed—"and so damned ridiculous!" and suggested just the touch of Rabelaisianism for which one was looking.

Of course O'May could not live even in a great city without becoming known. There came a period of wide and sweeping popularity. His name was on everyone's lips; everyone repeated his stories; he was asked about constantly. Older women found him stirringly alien; younger women, possessed of an air of danger sufficient to be interesting; and the men, although from the first most of them did not like him, were grimly unable to overlook his undoubted skill at games. He played polo unexpectedly well; he rode across country like the crack of a whip; and in cricket he achieved almost immortal fame. I mention cricket particularly because it is important in O'May's story; very important. By mere chance he was asked if he was interested in the placid game. . . . Oh, a little. He had played of course—at school. . . . He appeared in flannels and promptly knocked out a century. Playing myself, I marvelled at his slashing but singularly invulnerable style.

O'May accepted all this in the same unconcerned way in which he had accepted his year of leanness and obscurity; but such casual versatility is likely to bring a certain amount of disaster in its train. Before long I found that disaster had happened. O'May was not designed for unruffled good fortune. The thing grew prodigiously. I realized its seriousness when one day I called upon an old friend of mine, a woman to whom a gift for frankness had become an affectation. She attacked me on the subject of O'May. I found myself submerged in a flood of condemnation. It was a dam bursting. To combat it seemed useless. . . . But he was not a gentleman! He boasted of amorous adventure. . . . Did he mention names? . . . No, but what difference did that make? He was not the sort of person one should introduce to young women. He said he had been in the English army. Well, if he had been, for what reason had he left? He told some ridiculous story about having married for money and then having been forced by the insane jealousy of a woman he did not love to throw up his commission and obtain a divorce. Likely, wasn't it? At all events, she for one would have no more to do with him. . . .

I sipped my tea and reflected with dumb resentment on the impossibility of destroying prejudice, old or new. Of course O'May was a gentleman; everything about him, his hands, his voice, his figure, the real ideas that lay back of all his abracadabra were those of a gentleman. As to his absurd self-glorification, at his very gloomiest he was most inclined to bolster up failing vanity by means of imaginary triumphs. Besides, there was always that business of being a derelict— the inevitable disdain and bitterness. Frequently the world must have seemed a place of too many complacent people, of judgments too cruelly made, of an unrelieved monogamous placidity. The desire to shock it would be overwhelming. But how prove all these things? It involved the whole question of what a gentleman is. Why, I have an uncle who regards all Methodists as blackguards!

I went out into streets already lit with lamps. A fine rain was falling. I was angry and ashamed. I do not like to have people's characters flayed in my presence. There is a suggestion about it of the indecency of tortured bodies on the rack. Besides, I had had no idea of the size of the storm gathering in O'May's wake. The prospect alarmed me.

And then—just at this precarious period—O'May brought matters to a climax by a bit of egregious folly peculiarly his own. I don't wonder he left the English army. I have an idea that he irritated fond but distracted superiors to final angry tears.

There was a girl—I shall call her Elinor Beech—who for two or three years had basked in a reputation for beauty. Further description is unnecessary, for perfection implies finality. You saw Miss Beech, you admitted her radiance, then nothing more happened. As for myself, by the hour I talked to her gently, all the while asking in the back of my mind, "What in the world are you doing, and where in the world are you going?" For in a perfectly unconscious but coldly heated way she was going somewhere. That was evident. She possessed the bright, small, golden-haired way of looking busy and alert when she really wasn't. Poor child, life after all must have been to her a waste of level pulchritudes. For several years I had felt sorry for her, but my sorrow now changed to indignation when I perceived that in her brisk flight from flower to flower she had alighted upon the somewhat frost-bitten leaves of O'May.

To my extreme irritation, O'May welcomed the distraction. He began to fancy himself as a suitor. He blossomed out into flowers in his buttonhole and yellow buckskin gloves. To me the whole affair smacked of speculation, with the addition, of course, of fatuous gratification at the ensnarement of a much-desired beauty. I confronted O'May with these opinions. He accepted them with his usual calm. I informed him that Miss Beech belonged to what might be called "our American royalty"; and that he was twice her age, penniless, and divorced. "Divorced, you understand!" I repeated.

He looked at me mildly. "But I'm not divorced," he said.

I gasped. "Not divorced?"

"Then why in heaven's name did you tell such a lie?"

For a moment he was thoughtful but not embarrassed. "To tell you the truth, I don't know," he observed finally. "If I could remember the circumstances, no doubt I could explain satisfactorily." Then he brightened perceptibly. "But once a story's told you have to stick by it, don't you?" He seemed much relieved by this bit of superlative wisdom.

I washed my hands of him. For a while he did not come any longer to see me. Two months passed and rumors were abroad. The older Beeches, the infatuated Beech mother and father, were, it seems, at last awake to the situation. Three generations of restraint had been flung aside. Mr. Beech, a choleric man, made lawless by extreme wealth, had threatened to kick O'May. O'May had laughed delightedly and had offered him a back for this purpose, warning him, however, as an apoplectic elderly person, to indulge in the new exercise gently. It was evident that he had made himself, to a man without humor, unbearably offensive. The world overlooked the engaging debonairness of this incident in its rage at O'May as a discredited adventurer. It was clear that even if willy-nilly he married Elinor Beech, she would take no wealth with her. Mr. Beech had threatened disinheritance, and he was one of those men who pride themselves on keeping their word, no matter how foolish that word may be. He was bitter with the bitterness of the disenchanted parent.

Then summer came and for me, at least, a respite from all such vexing problems.

It was Dunstan—Dunstan, delightfully heedless of gossip—who in his vague, guileless way produced a crisis and a drama. He gave a house party early in September. I am sure O'May was not aware that his captive princess was to be present, and as for her she was either equally ignorant or else had lied adroitly to her parents. At all events, they both turned up smiling, met in the hall, hesitated, seemed to wish to blush, and then, in the pleasure of seeing each other after a separation of three months, forgot all about everything else. The rest of us, with the exception of Dunstan, who was completely innocent, proceeded to sit apprehensively upon the edge of the crater.

The objects of our speculation meanwhile went their way as if oblivious to the talk swirling about them. I think they were happy. O'May, who shared a room with me, was preoccupied and gentler than I had ever seen him. In the violet breathless dusks before dinner the two walked in the gardens, or found inadequate excuses to motor. In the evenings they did not join us at cards or dancing, but sat on the terrace watching the immense, warm stars. Once or twice I came upon them. I must admit even my disapproving imagination was touched. There was something about O'May's lean, quiet, dark-headed figure that seemed to pick him out as a mate for the tiny, radiant fairness of the girl. Nature seemed to be wiser in this instance than Mr. Beech. After all, why not? I found myself arguing the situation in my mind. The question was—Was O'May really in love? He seemed to be. One night he stood by the window and stretched wide his arms.

"A man's never old, Billy," he said, "is he? I was thinking I was, but I'm not, Lord love you!" He paused. "She's sweeter than June," he said in his softest Irish voice.

The revelation pleased me. There seemed here a chance of complete regeneration. The prospect suddenly became secure, vivacious, reillusioned. And then a Packard car—a large, plum-colored Packard car—put an end to such unsubstantialities.

I found it—the car—standing in the driveway before Dunstan's house one afternoon as I came in late from riding. A smart chauffeur dozed in the last rays of the sun. Frogs croaked from a near-by pond, upon the shimmering surface of which gossamer flying things caught, for a moment as brief as their lives, a glory of light on their wings. I was not prepared for the red, carefully plump gentleman, clad in a fawn-colored silk suit, who sat in a wicker chair on the porch, his hands clasped determinedly upon a heavy walking-stick. The elderly gentleman glared at me; the carmine of his face was heightened by the level rays of the sun.

"Are you Dunstan?" he growled.

"No, Mr. Beech," I answered amiably—my heart leaped. "You don't remember me, I see," I introduced myself. He seemed to regard the formality as an added irritation.

"Where is the fellow—the—the—what's his name?"

But at that moment I saw the unsuspecting Dunstan approaching and I fled stableward. There was not a motor to be had, but I procured a horse. The saddling seemed unbearably slow. I was afraid O'May and the girl would arrive before I could warn them. I galloped down the driveway. And then—after all this, they were late; absurdly and fatally late.

I waited by the gate at the end of the mile-long drive. A great moon swung up over the liquid darkness of the hills to the east. Would they never come? Then I heard the purr of a motor and the long gray car swept past me in a blinding arc of light. O'May's voice reached me.

"What's wrong?" he said sharply.

I stammered. "It's none of my business, but Mr. Beech—your father, Miss Beech—is waiting for you up at the house. I thought I would warn you."

There was a moment's silence before the girl's voice said, a trifle wearily:

"It's almost nine o'clock."

I moved my horse to where the dazzling light was no longer in my eyes. O'May, his hand on the wheel, was looking at the girl. Suddenly he flung up his head.

"If you're game," he said, "so am I. I'm sick of this. Let's get through with it."

He threw in the clutch and the great machine groaned and leaped forward. I followed at a hand-gallop.

I had imagined nothing out of the ordinary; nothing, that is, on the surface, or I would not, when I came back from the stable, have gone in at the front entrance. As it was I stumbled suddenly into a strange, excited little group in one corner of the shadowy hall. Dunstan, astonished and ill at ease, stood with his hands in his pockets, and near him, but not noticing him, O'May and Elinor Beech and her father. The last was expressing some opinion in a restrained but obviously passionate voice. O'May was fingering a book on the table, his eyes first on the older man, then on the girl.

I was congratulating myself on slipping past unnoticed, but Mr. Beech saw me. "Here!" he said. "Here's a man I want. I watched him gallop down to the gate—gallop right past me. Now, sir, what did you do that for?"—I realized what a fool I had been—"Why, may I ask?"

I stepped into the circle of light.

"Mr. Beech," I said, "I am not aware what particular houses you adorn, but judging from the way you are acting here they must be curious houses. Where I live, gentlemen can ride at a gallop any time they like without being asked nonsensical questions by comparative strangers."

O'May threw back his head. He never could resist such moments as this. I suppose more than anything else they were what had ruined him.

"Oh, I say!" he applauded. "Oh, by Jove! Got just what he deserved, didn't he?"

"You fool!" hissed Dunstan.

Very satisfactory, of course; very satisfactory, indeed; but can you imagine any idiocy greater? I can't. The effect upon Mr. Beech was instantaneous. For a moment he glared; then he turned once more to his daughter and spoke in a new and peculiarly deadly voice:

"I will waste no more words. My motor is waiting outside. You can come home with me, Elinor, or else never speak to me again. You understand? You know when I say a thing I mean it. As for you, sir,"—he wheeled upon O'May—"beggar that you are, I'll make you still more of one. I can do it and you know it." He looked at his watch. "You have five minutes, Elinor," he said quietly.

It was incredible. The kind of scene one does not expect. Life had suddenly slipped back to a more brutal period. Old age in a passion has a way sometimes of producing such anachronisms.

I watched attentively O'May's face and the face of the girl. I was hoping—hoping bitterly, now—that she would step forward. I for one would help O'May if she married him; so would Dunstan. Why didn't she move? Her great eyes were wide and staring. Her small, beautifully chiselled features seemed frozen to ice. God knows what processes of computation and balance were going on behind them. Possibly this was the first time in all her life she had been called upon to think. It was unbearable. Then O'May made a sudden movement.

He laid aside with the most curious care the book the leaves of which he had been absent-mindedly fluttering and stepped nearer to Mr. Beech. His whole appearance had undergone a subtle change. The fierce intentness was past; he was careless and reckless and half-smiling again. He thrust his hands deep in his trouser-pockets and jingled some keys.

"I've lost, Mr. Beech," he said, and inclined his head. "You can take your daughter home."

Dunstan gasped. The girl suddenly stepped back and put out a hand, but O'May did not notice it.

"And I've something more to tell you," he continued; "I—"

But the older man appreciated victory. "Not a word, sir," he said. He turned to go.

O'May leaned against the table. "Oh, very well," he agreed amiably, his gray eyes smiling, his brogue very thick. "Only I think ye'd do well to listen."

Mr. Beech hesitated.

"It's just this," said O'May. "At present ye think Elinor's a fool, don't ye? Well, she's not, Mr. Beech; far from it. I'm an old hand; it wasn't very difficult for me."

"What wasn't?"

"Well, a lot of things. To tell her my brother was a baronet, and had no children. To say I'd be worth a million or two in a short while. To show her pictures of the place of a distant cousin and let her believe it was one day to be mine. To try to elope with her tonight." He paused and looked about for the effect of his announcement. "Yes, just that, Mr. Beech. If it hadn't been for her common sense we'd not be here now. That's what made us late. But she wouldn't do it. She has lots of sense. She's—" he looked at her with a sudden proud, fatherly look— "she's a girl of character, Mr. Beech; take her home and be good to her."

There was silence, and then:

"You cad!" said the older man. "Go home to your divorced wife."

"My divorced wife?" asked O'May gently. "Which one, Mr. Beech?"

"Which one!"

"Yes, you didn't know I'd been divorced twice, Mr. Beech, did you?"

This was too much. I stepped forward. "There's not a word—" I began; but Mr. Beech was already on his way to the door. Over his shoulder I caught a glimpse of a delicate gold head. The girl looked back once. Her face was small and white and perplexed.

The three of us who were left remained for a moment silent by the table, then Dunstan abruptly swung on his heel and made off down a dim corridor toward a door from which came the voices of his other guests. I went out into the garden.

Late that night I found O'May in our bedroom, smoking a cigarette and regarding the moon. "Well," I said, "I hope you've made enough of an ass of yourself to satisfy even you."

He threw away his cigarette and stood up to the full length of his lean height and stretched his arms above his head.

"Oh, no," he said. "Thank God, there's always some future foolishness left in the world."

"Would you mind telling me," I demanded, "why to an already unpleasant incident you chose to add a string of insane lies?"

He shrugged his shoulders. "Certainly," he said; and for the first time I had a complete impression of a stricken face. Why, the man had been in love with the foolish little creature after all! Really in love! "It's very simple," he continued, and yawned. One recognizes those yawns. "While there was a chance, you know; but there wasn't, not a chance. I know women's faces. Not a chance. Money wins every time. Well, it's a good horse. What do you expect? But she might just as well be off with flying colors as not, mightn't she? Otherwise, all her life—the suspicion of her being an idiot. You don't know the Beeches. It'd be hell. Don't you think I gave Elinor a reputation for an eye to the main chance? She couldn't have thought that up herself, you know." He cocked an eyebrow. "Besides," he concluded, "when my imagination gets started, I'll be hanged if I know where it's going to stop."

He sighed and returned to the window. His muffled voice reached me. "And I'll be damned if it wasn't the little devil herself who tried to do the running away tonight. I had a deuce of a time bringing her home."

And that was all.

I should hate having to leave O'May here; I should hate having to leave him spattered with the laughter of people not wise enough to be kind; to abandon him drearily lonely in a city where once, for a short time at least, he had been so welcome; and, fortunately, I don't have to. Life has its own jocose methods of compensation. It slaps you down into the mud, and then comes a great wind that lifts you up, up, to the very gates, cleanswept, of heaven itself. There was to be for O'May at least one moment left of glory and illumination—a moment the spreading fame of which caused, I think, numerous people to stand agape at their own stupidity. The moment came because O'May played cricket.

Spring was on hand and with it the trip of a team to the West Indies. There had been some talk, I dare say, of leaving O'May off, but even the blackest social record cannot destroy the value of a top-batsman; and so, unruffled and unconcerned, he went along. In his smart tweed cap and beautifully fitting ready-made clothes he was a sight for the eye as he paced the deck. Something about his leanness and hardness seemed to make a voyage tropic-ward singularly appropriate. And, as far as any one could see, he was totally oblivious of the truth that, barring myself, the dozen other men of the party despised him utterly. Fortunately they were all too good sportsmen—all but one, that is—to make this dislike known. The one was a man named Whitton. In every body of men there seems to be a Whitton. Possibly the fact perpetuates a curse of Job. Whitton was short and dark and truculent, and, to his own mind, amusing—no, not amusing, subtly witty—any adjective expressing delicate humor will do. One gets tired of describing Whittons. Why he marked O'May as a victim I do not know, for I doubt if off the cricket-field they saw each other more than once or twice in a year. But, at all events, Whitton pursued O'May, and O'May with his usual perverse humor, although the rest of us expected a quarrel, showered kindnesses on Whitton's head. We were at a loss to understand until, one day—

"I can't help liking the little devil, you know," said O'May to a group of us; "he's exactly like a stud-groom we used to have at my father's place. Vulgar little brute, but something fascinating about him."

The remark was repeated, as it was intended it should be, and an abrupt change took place in Whitton's playful venom—the playfulness disappeared. O'May was more cordial than ever.

We dropped into a blue harbor that took a half-moon slice out of a green-and-white island impossibly clean. There was to be a match with the British regiment stationed there, and the attendant dances, and a vice-regal reception; for the green-and-white island was an important place and boasted a governor-general. The night of our arrival there developed a conspiracy on the part of Whitton.

I found two or three of O'May's most ardent enemies in the smoking-room of the hotel. They seemed pleased about something. Whitton was doing the talking. He was not afraid of my presence; the plan was too insolently simple to admit of interference. Whitton, in short, was to introduce O'May to the governor-general as "Captain John O'May, late Tenth Hussars—Captain John O'May!"—very loud, you understand, so that there would be not the slightest chance of not being heard.

At first I failed to grasp the significance.

Whitton laughed. "Guess!" he said.

Light dawned on me. "That's a pleasant thing to do to a teammate," I observed. "And then, you know, he might have been in the Tenth Hussars after all."

"Not a chance!" said Whitton. "He? He never was! I know a liar when I see one. I'm sick of his lies. We're all sick of his lies, aren't we?" The attendant group nodded with sinister solemnity. "Why," continued Whitton, "why, that's one of the best regiments in England. Besides, even if he did belong, he was kicked out for some dirty work."

I attempted scorn. Did they think the governor-general of a West Indian island carried the whole British army list in his head? There might have been a dozen O'Mays in the Tenth Hussars and this fellow here none the wiser.

But Whitton persisted. It was only a chance, of course, but a mighty good one. The English army was small and rather like a club. If O'May had done anything disgraceful it would be recalled to mind at once. If, on the other hand, he was merely an impostor, detection would be equally swift. They knew in a moment, those chaps; they could tell by a dozen hidden evidences not patent to foreigners.

"Whitton," I said, "you're a fool. Look out!"

"Who for?" he sneered.

"Me, for one," I said, getting up. "Besides, this governor-general will have too much sense to show you what he knows."

"Oh!" said Whitton. He laughed. "Oh! So you think we're right, too, do you?"

And as a matter of fact I did. The plot presented all the strength of a dilemma. If O'May was what he said he was there was no need to worry; if, to the contrary, he was none of these things, or only part of these things, there was nothing to do but to let him bear the consequences of his own folly and trust to his quick wit for a not too unpleasant escape from embarrassment. To attempt to prevent Whitton's plan would be only to fasten upon O'May forever the stamp of an impostor. Apparently the test was foredoomed. I contented myself with visions of revenge upon Whitton.

Two days later came the first day of the match. The Englishmen went in to bat. When dark swallowed up the grounds, we were whisked off to a dinner; the reception was to follow.

Orange lamps, like little moons, hung in strange, heavy-foliaged trees. A band blared in an illuminated kiosk. Lithe young men in regimentals were officially and inexpressibly polite.

"Why don't you get them to play some tune we know, O'May," suggested Whitton happily.

I took this to be the first gun of the skirmish.

O'May turned. "I?"

"Yes; weren't you an officer?"

O'May's long nose wrinkled. "That's not the same as a bandmaster, you know," he explained gently.

I was keeping close to him. The time to meet the governor-general was approaching. A young aide-de-camp stepped over to us and suggested that the ceremony begin. We followed in little groups. Besides myself and Whitton there were four or five others in the lot O'May joined.

"Cheer-o!" said he. "For what is the likes of me greeting the direct and anointed representative of his Britannic Majesty. What's the old blighter's name?"

"Sir Timothy-Something-or-Other," I told him vaguely.

"Quaker!" he hissed. "A dollar he's a sour-faced Quaker."

We came to a big man, long-nosed, stooping, with a grizzled mustache. He looked bored. My heart sank. Here was not one of the kindly English; rather a veteran of many climates and varied indigestion. The band seemed to me to be playing with unnecessary softness. I was presented, bowed, heard the end of an unintelligible sentence, and moved a step or two away. O'May followed. Over his shoulder I caught sight of Whitton's face. Then it seemed to me that the worst had happened; for suddenly the governor-general took a step forward, hesitated, and peered; his harsh face in the swaying shadows becoming for a moment harsher.

"Why—" said the governor-general. "Why—let me see! No! Yes! By gad!" His thin, tired face broke into an alarming grin. "Why, by all that's holy, it's Long Jack O'May!"

"Timmy Danby!" said O'May simply. "How—what in the devil are you doing here?"

In the background I stepped on Whitton's foot.

"I?" said the governor-general. "Why, I'm the governor-general!" And he spoke with apparently no realization of the absurdity of his remark. Emotion was evident on both sides. The governor-general breathed through his nose; he looked about him nervously. "All your fellows through?" he asked.

"I think so," answered O'May. "We're the last."

"Well then—I'll just say a word or two—just a word, and then— look here! What do you think? We'll find a place to sit down. I want to see you, you devil. Where've you been? In the States? One of those blighted millionaires by now, I suppose. I heard you'd got out. Rotten job, the army, anyhow." He remembered his duties and turned to the silent, staring little group about him. "I trust you'll forgive me, gentlemen," he said, "but I haven't seen Captain O'May in ten years, and he was the best subaltern I ever had. These young men will be delighted to look after you." He indicated his aides-de-camp.

I turned to go, still in a haze of unreality, but O'May called me back. "No, you don't!" he said. "Do you mind, Timmy?" But his next action was the most extraordinary of all, for he laid a detaining hand on Whitton's shoulder and faced him about and said, most lovingly, "And Jerry Whitton, too? He's one of the best pals I've got. Can I bring 'em along?"

Whitton did not understand until later, I think; nor did I, until, looking at O'May, I saw gray eyes cold and raw as Irish moors on a hunting-day.

Under a shadowy tree, a colored lantern spreading radiance through its branches, we found a table. A man servant brought us drinks.

"Long Jack!" said the governor-general.

"Old Timmy!" said O'May.

And this was the moment of which I spoke—the apotheosis of O'May. I could see him grow as he sat there; become younger. He was home— in harbor. They talked of many things—he and the governor-general —of India, of London, of men they had known; of men who had died and of men who were still alive. And in the semi-dusk, with the band sobbing a waltz and uniforms flitting in and out of orange light and shadow, with the sound of laughter reaching us, it seemed to me that O'May was no longer a derelict, no longer a man to whom the future held nothing, but once more a young subaltern, straight and taut with the pride of the great service of a great empire. I saw India, and keen-faced young men about the white and silver of a mess-table; I saw South Africa and heard cavalry marching by night across the veldt; and it wasn't merely romancing on my part, for O'May, I knew, was seeing at the same time the same things as I. It was easy to understand now his recklessness toward the present. In face of his memories it must have seemed, indeed, a matter of small moment; old Mr. Beech merely an absurdity; his daughter, after her fiery test, pitiable and unheroic. At one corner of the table Whitton watched with a troubled, embarrassed face.

"You'll move your traps tomorrow and stay with me, won't you?" asked the governor-general.

"Will I!" said O'May.

That spring I was out of town for a month. I came back to find a telephone call, three days old, from O'May. It was urgent. He was in the hospital. I hurried out. Yes, Captain was in a private ward on the third floor. An old wound in his head. They would see if I might go to him. There was something odd in the manner in which they told me this. I fidgeted. I remember how noisy a newly awakened fly was against the window-pane. A nurse came hurrying in. Yes, I could go to Captain O'May—yes, I could go, but I had best hurry. Hurry! Why, in God's name, did I have to hurry?

He was unconscious when I reached the narrow room where he was. I waited an hour; perhaps an hour and a half. The nurse busied herself with a dozen esoteric tasks. And then, suddenly, he sat up and opened his eyes and looked squarely at me.

"On the ball, Dublin!" he said, and fell back. I had never known that he had played football . . . the extraordinary man!

When I finally left, it seemed to me as if a piece of romance had been ripped, as a sword rips tapestry, from the walls. Old age for some people is impossible to contemplate; but then—

Christopher Gerould, Princeton '35, son of eminent Princeton parents, Gordon Hall and Katherine Fullerton Gerould, directly reflects the possibly bitter intensity of the current generation, at least in its attack on boredom. His story "The End of the Party," was published in *Harper's Magazine* in 1932. The author was at the time a freshman at Princeton. The story was reprinted in the O. Henry Memorial volume for 1932. We think it primarily a story of setting. It illustrates well what a young writer can do with characters and incidents taken directly from the life of his own generation.

THE END OF THE PARTY [1]
Christopher Gerould

The white concrete road sang under the tires of the roadster, sweeping into the range of the headlights, rushing smoothly towards the car, and disappearing beneath it. Beside the road trees and fences swam past, half lighted, more slowly than the road. Behind them was darkness. Overhead a few stars and a pale, white crescent moon shone without giving light.

A girl was driving the car, and a boy in evening clothes sat close beside her with his arm round the white-fur wrap on her shoulders. Another couple, heads close together, formed a dark triangle in the rumble seat.

The boy and girl in the front seat were singing off-key and loudly to keep the whipping wind from dashing the words of the song away from the singers themselves.

[1] Reprinted by permission of the author and the editors of *Harper's Magazine*.

> Auprès de ma blonde,
> Qu'il fait bon, fait bon, fait bon
> Auprès de ma blonde, qu'il fait bon dormir.

The boy broke off the song. "That's a lousy song to sing when you're going fast. It's a marching song. Let's try another."

"All right, professor, what'll it be? We know 'em all."

"Don't know. . . . Gawd, how fast are we going?"

The girl looked at the yellow glow of the speedometer on the dash. "Sixty-five. Not fast enough to get away from our friends up there." She nodded over her shoulder at the moon and stars which were cleaving evenly through the dark skies to keep their same relative positions to the car. "How're you feeling, Jed?"

"Swell. How about you?"

"I *feel* swell, but I'd hate to have to interview the family just now."

"Want to let me drive and catch some rest?"

"Never mind. I'd rather do it myself. I prefer to take my own chances on a binge."

"You may be right," Jed said. "My sense of distance goes all flooey when I'm at all tight. I can drive but I hate to. Want a cigarette?"

"Thanks." Jed took out two cigarettes and a lighter. The girl took hers and bent her head to reach the flame cupped in his hands. There was a shock and a wrenching scream. The girl jammed on the brakes, and the car skidded to a stop, facing across the road.

"What was it?" she asked. "I wasn't looking at the road." Her voice was low and frightened.

The pair in the rumble seat sat up, moving apart, and said together, "What's wrong, May?" Jed opened the door of the car and slid out on the road. He leaned against the side of the car with both hands. "Tom and I'll go back and look, May. You and Eve stay in the car."

Tom threw a rug aside and scrambled out of the rumble seat. He and Jed set off down the road.

Eve mechanically patted her hair and asked again, "What was it, May?"

May was holding on tight to the steering wheel. "I didn't see. I was lighting a cigarette. It—it must have been a dog."

"It didn't sound like a dog. It sounded like . . . Oh, God!" She began to climb out of the rumble seat, looking down the dark road where the boys had gone. She stumbled and fell on her knees. As she was getting up, May opened the door and joined her. Together they started toward the boys, whose voices and footsteps they could hear ahead of them.

Walking down the road, Tom said to Jed, "Did you see what we hit?" Jed did not answer for a moment, and when he did his voice was carefully under control.

"It was a man. I saw him out of the corner of my eye while I was holding the lighter."

"Oh, Jesus! Do you think . . .?"

"We were going sixty-five when we hit him."

They walked on in silence, looking into the shadowed ditches beside the road. Then they saw what they were looking for. A shapeless black heap of rags lay on the concrete. Jed ran to it, and, kneeling, snapped on his lighter. One side of the man's face was like raw beef, and trickles of blood ran from his mouth and nose.

Tom, bending over, put his hand inside the coat and shirt and drew it away suddenly, covered with blood. He stood up and groaned and began to walk around in a little circle on the road. Jed sat balanced on his heels for a moment, then capped his lighter and stood up. "Did you feel his heart?" he asked.

"He didn't have any chest . . . it was all soft and wet." He continued in his circle, and Jed began to swear softly under his breath, choking back ever-quickening sobs. Tom stopped walking and beat his fist against his palm again and again. "We'll have to . . ."

May's voice called from up the road, "Where are you, Jed?"

Jed did not answer. He was crying softly to himself. Tom called, "Stay where you are. We'll be with you in a minute." He looked at Jed for a moment and then walked over and slapped him in the face. "Shut up," he said, "you'll have me doing it too in a minute." Jed stopped crying and wiped his face with his sleeve. Tom took his arm, and they started up the road.

As the boys approached, Eve and May were standing huddled together twenty yards from the car. May, peering into the dark, ran to them as they came near. "Jed, what is it? What happened?" Eve came forward more slowly, and Tom put his arm around her shoulders. Jed looked at the road and said nothing.

Suddenly Tom snatched his arm away from Eve, took a handkerchief from his pocket and began to wipe his hand. He looked at Jed, who was still silent, staring at the road with his hands clasped behind him.

Tom said, "You might as well have it. We've killed a man."

"A man?" May's voice went up into the falsetto and broke. She fell down on the road. Eve grabbed Tom by the shoulders. "That's not true, Tom, is it? You're trying to scare us. It was a dog, wasn't it? A dog that ran out in front of the car? It must have been a dog." Jed was carrying May back to the roadster, staggering a little with the weight.

Tom said, "It was a man . . . he had no chest." He began to laugh quietly.

"It couldn't have been. You must be wrong. Let's go back and look again." She started down the road. Tom caught hold of her and held her tight. She began to cry. "Let go of my arm, Tom, you're hurting me." Tom bit his lips to stop laughing and pulled her back towards the car. He opened his mouth, choked, and said, "We'd better look after May. She's in a bad way." Eve stopped struggling and turned towards the car. Glancing at his hand, Tom put his arm around her shoulders.

The roadster completely blocked the road, the headlights shining into the ditch and picking out a dirty newspaper and a broken green bottle. As they approached, they heard May say ". . . no one on the road when I looked away."

Jed said heavily, "We were all drunk." Eve made a protesting noise but didn't say anything. May and Jed were sitting in the front seat. Tom pushed Eve down on the running board and stood alone in the road. "What's the nearest town, May?" he asked.

"Hilton's about four miles away."

"We'll have to go there and 'phone the police. We'd . . .we'd better take that"—he jerked his head—"along with us."

Eve began to laugh shrilly. "Five-passenger car. Where'll we put him? Let him sit on Jed's lap." She laughed with her head thrown back until she slumped off the running board to the ground. She lay there screaming and crying while Tom stooped over her.

In the roadster, May said, "We can't go to the police, Jed."

"We've got to."

"But Mother . . . Jed, we can't stay. I'd get arrested. Mother'd die if I were arrested. We've got to get away."

"It was an accident. They can't arrest you, May."

"But I was drunk. We all were, Jed. You said so yourself. They arrest you for that. I'm scared." She raised her voice. "Tom, put Eve in the car. We've got to get away."

Tom stood up, his pudgy face white, and started to say something but stopped. He looked for a moment at May and then bent again over Eve. His voice came softly as though from a distance. "You can't run away from an accident, May."

May beat her fist on the steering wheel. "We've got to get away from here. We'll be arrested and in the papers and everything." Her voice was shrill.

"They might find out who it was, if we ran away," Jed said, "and then it would be worse. We'd better go for the police. I'll say I was driving."

"But it's my car, Jed, and everyone saw me driving when we left." On the ground beside the car, Eve had stopped screaming and was crying softly. Tom lifted one of her arms over his shoulder and turned. "Help me get her in the rumble seat, Jed." Jed climbed out and lifted her by the other arm, and the two boys carried her round to the back of the car. Eve stopped crying and said, "I want to go home." She pushed the boys away and stood up, leaning swayingly against the rear fender.

Jed looked at her. "We can't run away, May. Eve's all covered with blood."

May put her head in her arms on the steering wheel, and the other three were silent, waiting for her to speak. At last she looked up with a white smile and said, "I'll be good." She opened the door of the car. "You and Tom go and get—him. Eve and I'll get in the rumble seat."

Far down the road they heard the beat of a motor. Eve, who had climbed into the rumble seat, looked at the glow of the approaching lights with a vacant face. "Maybe they've got a five-passenger car," she said, and began to giggle.

For other atmosphere, character, or plot short stories see pages 484–86 above. One of the best means for developing an eye for forms and techniques is to classify stories for yourself. Frequently you will find types combining or fusing, sometimes into queer hybrids. In section B of the next chapter is printed a story representing a type not yet touched, a picture-frame story with the now-familiar "boy-meets-girl" theme and with the narrator participating. Consider the possibilities of combinations of your own: the character story through dialogue, the setting story plus the picture-frame technique, and other deliberately chosen patterns. Such conscious craftsmanship provides a firm basis for such creative expression as you have developed by the study of forms.

CHAPTER XVIII

The Fully Developed Form

THE LONG THEME for the second half-year or term may be an essay, a linear narrative, a plot story, a short story, or even an extended description. No further suggestions should be needed, except that you should confer with the instructor a number of times in the course of your preparation, so as to be sure of making progress in the right direction. All these forms would be merely expanded from the shorter examples: in the case of the essay, an introduction of more anecdotes, allusions, associations; in the story, a plot covering more time,[1] perhaps, and including more characters; in the description, a point of view which would begin as static and become progressive so as to allow more details.[2] That all forms can be handled successfully will be evident from a study of the selections below. You will find one or two illustrations of each.

As a matter of actual fact, however, you will often find these various types of writing, and the mood of argumentation as well, mingling in one piece. One student felt so much the need of combining forms that he invented for himself what he called the *storessay*—the result was not unlike a George Ade fable—in which story and essay fused. Brief précis glimpses of a group of essays taken at random will show this mixing of tendencies. Also it may help you to see once more the place that substance takes in a piece of writing. You might yourself produce some pieces using analogous material, or taking an opposite point of view.

    1. G. K. Chesterton, "A Defence of Nonsense," from *The Defendant* (1901). Thoroughly typical of this champion of paradox,

---

[1] Similarly an autobiography, or even a diary, could be expanded to cover more time.

[2] This, however, will be obviously the most dangerous form to attempt to expand.

this essay is still clearly expository. It leans toward criticism. The author points out that there are two ways of looking at things in a world where the morning and evening which bound our days are both twilight. Sense, he finds, is the basic substance of Lewis Carroll or the nonsense rhymes of Edward Lear; nonsense is the reigning theme of some of the greatest writers, such as Aristophanes, Rabelais, and Laurence Sterne. The true idea back of nonsense is escape, escape from reason, routine, and hard fact. Religion, Chesterton says, makes men exult in the wonders of creation; it is impossible, in fact, for anything to be "completely wonderful" if it is merely and plainly sensible. Everything, like the moon, has another side to it.

2. O. O. McIntyre represented the cream of the columnist heirs to Addison's *Spectator*. Rather than producing essays, he gave us the stuff of which they may be made. His syndicated sketch for August 25, 1934, shows him turning back in memory to old, familiar home-town scenes. The treatment, as is evident, is strongly descriptive in tendency. He recalls broad, tree-lined streets, Tom Homes's hack, the Blazing Stump saloon, Banker Henking's home with a cupola, the Sewing-Machine Man who was distinguished by a flat-topped derby. Not only these visible objects, but the coolness of Back Street with the wind swirling through the hollows of the creek, and the special atmosphere that hung over the two-storied brick house where the Only Girl lived, with the sagging hammock under the birches in the back yard—these, too, come back in an imaginary return visit after twenty years.

Notice the evocative effect of accurate reference to concrete objects and places: the schoolhouse square with its high iron fence; the ol' swimmin' hole with the fallen oak over the sharp drop of Academy Hill; and "that glorious green escape," the public square, adorned with a cannon and the town pump, the latter dangling its rusty tin cup. Whole essays and stories are suggested by recollections of the old-time livery stable—McCormack's, with its "delightfully mixed aromas" of the harness room, the dark, creaky stairs, and the scales outside. Or there is Mr. Canterbury, living alone in a squalid shack, Mr. Canterbury who would chase you till exhausted if you yelled "Sardines," though no one ever knew just why.

3. Kenneth Grahame's "The Secret Drawer," in *The Golden Age* (1899), presents a study in the force of words. The finding of a secret drawer, hidden in an old bureau, calls attention to the thrill in such words as "cave, trap door, sliding panel, bullion, ingots, or Spanish dollars." Such beginnings tend to push the writer in the direction of narrative. Who was the owner of that drawer? What did he keep in it?

4. Hilaire Belloc, "The Singer," from *Hills and the Sea* (1913). Here we have the material of diary and the mood of narrative. The writer of the essay had been taking a pleasure stroll along a river in Gascony when he heard a browned plainsman singing. The song proclaimed the virtues of well-tinned copper for cooking. It might have been the ballad of a wandering coppersmith out of the middle ages. Out of this episode flows a tribute to song and to labor, to labor singing. It does not pretend to too much, and it escapes the proletarian, propagandist feeling as does the Volga Boat Song.

5. Heywood Broun, "Holding a Baby," from *Seeing Things at Night* (1921). Such a topic raises expectation of anecdote. The essay betrays man's cleverness in preserving the fiction that housework, especially the servicing of infants, is a highly technical pursuit, that only woman's intuition and her nimble fingers can manage the delicate processes involved. Actually, we learn, there are 157 ways to hold a baby. By letting the woman continue to believe that her job is beyond the utmost capacities of the stupid male, the stupid male is left free to go out for eighteen holes of masculine golf.

Now write your own essay or story or both in one, letting narration, description, and exposition blend or dominate as they are needed.

→≫ A ≪←

"Recollections" is an excellent autobiography so far as it goes. What aspect of her career did the writer slight? It contains a great many realistic details, story sources, and stylistic individualities. Study it also for informal-essay possibilities and for descriptive elements. What is it that makes the style so smooth? What do you think of the conclusion?

RECOLLECTIONS

My earliest memories are somewhat obscure. They seem to merge into dream creations, and the difference between the two is so insignificant to me, that it is hard to distinguish between them. Still, however hazy those early recollections may be, they are an intrinsic part of my mental history, and I can no more think of myself without them than I could without my nose or without my voracious appetite.

I can still remember the rough texture of my grandmother's skirt, as I stood beside her, grasping it with one small hand and waving the other in good-bye to my favorite uncle, clad in a handsome uniform, which was the mysterious source of grandma's tears. That must have been long ago, for time has so dimmed the picture that it leaves but a slight impression upon my mind, and I can only remember that scene, and the feeling of terror, and the questions I asked because I could not understand all that was happening.

I have remarked that the majority of my earliest remembrances are founded upon fear and horror, and that these tend to stay vivid for longer intervals than those of commonplace and ordinary events. I do not know the psychological reason for this, nor do I know if this is true as a general rule, but I speak from my own experience and conclusions.

One day, I remember, I swallowed my ring. It was a very pretty ring, as I recall, and I was duly proud of it. Of course, I was very conscious of the circlet at first, and in order to show off, I went about with my finger in my mouth, so that the ring would be in the place of greatest prominence. One day, I pushed my finger too far back in my mouth, and the ring slipped off and down into my throat. When my father saw what had happened, he seized my legs and shook me, upside down, until the ring, which, fortunately, had not made much progress, reluctantly fell out. I must admit that I was more horrified at the prospect of losing my pretty ornament than I was at the swallowing of it, though I did not, after that event, attempt to show off in similar ways.

We were, at the time, residing in Detroit, where I had first seen daylight, but when my grandmother fell ill we moved back into Toledo, where I began my scholastic career and where we lived until my grandmother's death. My grandparents had been the proprietors of a small farm on the outskirts of the fast-growing town, which soon encompassed their home. The city then passed statutes forbidding the keeping of cows within the city limits, and my grandfather had to turn to another field of work. He chose to be a pioneer in the laundry industry of that city, and he established the first machine-run laundry with a one-horse delivery system. Many were the times I rode proudly beside him on the front seat, and when he allowed me to hold the reins, I almost burst, like the poor little froggy of bed-time tales, from self-esteem.

The beginning of my scholastic career was the beginning of coherent memory, and I can well remember my kindergarten days. Cousin Herman, an old, old scholar of twelve years of age, took me to my seat the first day. I adored Herman, whom I thought to be the per-sonification of all wisdom and of all manly perfections, but when he wanted to leave me alone amidst all the strange children and with a strange lady at the head of the class, I rebelled. If I couldn't stay with Herman, I didn't want to go to school. In vain he consoled me with his pencils and books; in vain he cajoled me with promises of candy; I refused to part from him. It took a violent struggle, on the part of my mother and the teacher, to separate us. And the result was a violent dislike for Miss Belle, which lasted several days, when I transferred my treacherous adoration to her.

I had a group of very intimate friends—all ranging from the ages of four to fourteen, with whom I was accustomed to go to school every day. There was a Chinese shop on the way, which was the center of much childish gossip and scandal. It was operated by a small, weazened Chinese man, probably harmless enough, but who, so the tale ran, delighted in cutting off the ears and the noses of little children, es-pecially of little girls. We reasoned, that if we organized into gangs to go to school, that terrible old man would be unable to grab any of us for his evil purposes.

And so, when one day I was unable to get ready in time to leave for school with our gang, I refused emphatically to go at all. After much parental persuasion—futile, of course—and after I had confessed my reasons for not wanting to go, the question was settled, and my father accompanied me, although he held my hand especially tight when we passed the Chinese shop.

I wore my hair in two small pigtails down my back, always tied at the ends with bright bits of ribbon—preferably red, which was my favorite color. These pigtails were my greatest dismay. I detested them because they were the cause of an eternal tormentation. The little boys delighted in pulling them, and when one succeeded in untying the ribbons, he considered himself a great conqueror. I tried to cut them off one day, but my mother stopped me in time. At last I was able to convince her of the torture they caused me, and I was marched to a barbershop, where the offending appendages were easily snipped off. However, I had joyfully demanded a boyish bob, which was even more dismaying to me than the previous coiffure had been.

Now the little girls pointed me out with scorn as the "tomboy," and the little boys looked askance at the "girl with boy's hair." I must have been a queer-looking little one, with my shorn locks in contrast to the pretty curls of my female contemporaries. However, my hair soon grew in, and then I wore it behind my ears in a short bob. The ends I promptly named "my horns," because in my shadow they stuck out from behind my ears just like those famous horny accessories of the devil. And indeed, my horns came to be almost famous, in their own small way, as did those of the aforementioned evil spirit.

One of my most impressive memories is of a day when a terrific storm broke out. It was at its worst at three-thirty, when the dismissal bell rang. Frightful tales of the strength and velocity of the wind circulated throughout the school. It was rumored that several children had been blown away. Small groups of youngsters clustered at the doors waiting for the wind to abate, peering out, meanwhile, for a familiar face. I shall never forget how relieved I was when my mother came for me. I can still remember the great velvet cape she wore, and the warmth of it. She wrapped us both within the folds of the cape and I remember how strange the familiar path seemed. I could only see our feet and a small patch of ground. And I can still feel the comfortable and yet queer feeling the close darkness within the cape aroused in me. The wind seemed trying to tear us apart, and I walked, my arms tightly clasped about my mother, as if I were afraid to lose her. It seemed an eternity before we reached the bright warm haven of our big kitchen, where the wind could not enter, no matter how hard it blew.

Several doors away, there lived a little boy who was my best pal. Willie and I manufactured all sorts of games. We played together always. We would gather all the younger neighbors together, and play "father and mother" and "school." Our favorite pastime, however, was "King and Queen." We would take an old dilapidated high chair, and place that on a stool, and this in turn on a box, and both of us took turns climbing to this lofty, although precarious position, from which we alternately ruled the admiring neighborhood children. But there was one imperfection in this fascinating play. Willie was subject to attacks of nosebleed whenever he got up that high in the altitude, and our respective, if not respectful, parents would object strenuously if they saw us balancing ourselves on our thrones. Finally Willie had a very bad nosebleed, and his mother complained so violently that several days afterwards our throne was used for firewood, and we had to look elsewhere for amusement.

We were always in mischief, and one day our little gang went out for a walk. We stopped in front of a large building with many pretty flowers around. I suggested that we pick some for my grandmother, who was ill. When I convinced them that the people would never miss the few that we picked, we proceeded to do so. Just as we were getting enthusiastic, we were interrupted by a horrified cry, and when we looked, lo and behold, there was a big policeman brandishing his club at us. We all began to run, and I led the race. I soon realized that it was a lonesome race, for the others had stopped elsewhere. However, I ran all the way home, still clutching my few flowers, too frightened to do anything. When the rest of the group came straggling up, they told a tale of a preaching policeman, who had warned them against the evils of picking flowers, especially from hospitals. I gave my grandma the flowers, but I can assure you that I went on no more flower-picking excursions after that.

Spring School, which is the elementary school I attended, was a small, two-story, brick building with three portables out on the playground for additional classrooms. The portables were little wooden cabins with big stoves to warm them in the cold weather.

Across from the school there was a cemetery—a fascinating place to spend an afternoon—although I imagine that it is not quite as fascinating in the evening. Past Forest Cemetery there is the marsh, and beyond that there is a large stretch of land which we never explored to any great degree. There are, however, several factories scattered over this area, and many railroad tracks.

Our science class, on pleasant spring days, was accustomed to take excursions through the cemetery and marsh, and, especially on dry days, both the teachers and the pupils enjoyed themselves very much.

One afternoon, coming back from the latest expedition in the name of science, laden with all kinds of scientific apparatus—such as match boxes containing queer bugs, pocketsful of harmless, although frightful-looking snakes, and an occasional frog and toad—we stopped to watch the operations of some gravediggers. It seemed a fascinating work, and I had almost determined to be a gravedigger too when I grew up. Suddenly, one of the diggers struck wood! This indeed was excitement! What wild speculations we indulged in, and how we held our breaths while the object was unearthed! It was a small box, which caved in when hoisted to the surface, and which revealed—not jewels, nor yet gold—but a thick layer of dust and a few tiny bones. The diggers told us that many such coffins, for such it was, are discovered daily because many died on route westward through Ohio.

It was about this time that I had my great love affair. Our class was preparing to graduate from public school, and in the light of the proposed separation, everyone looked upon everyone else with a new insight. Because they might be discontinued forever, friendships became tenderly prized, and because the teachers would never torment us again, they became the objects of tender affection. Under this stimulus, red-haired Clarence professed his undying devotion to me. Clarence was a quiet little boy who was studying the saxophone at that time, and who blushed violently, especially to his ears, if anyone as much as looked at him.

The first indication of this sudden love came on St. Valentine's Day, when I received a big valentine, and the indications increased fast and furiously as spring approached and as graduation drew near. I am inclined to think that this great emotion came as the result of spring—for as everyone knows, "In the spring a young man's fancy lightly turns to thoughts of love, etc." At any rate, the young man appeared several times with his saxophone under what he thought was my window—it happened to be my father's—and wailed, "Every little breeze seems to whisper Louise [Lois]" until the neighbors complained violently. This *affaire d'amour* culminated on graduation night, when the bashful swain gave a girl friend a note for me. The note proclaimed the famous words, "I love you," and the blushing Clarence and I, equally blushing, studiously avoided each other for the rest of the evening. I think that this effort exhausted Clarence, because I never heard from him again.

Soon after the exciting events of graduation, my family moved to Detroit, where I began my high-school career. The years immediately following our change of residence passed rapidly, and before I knew it, the exciting events of another graduation had overtaken me. I don't believe I have ever been a great scholastic genius, but my years at high school approached nearer that goal than any other interval of my life. At any rate, I succeeded in maintaining an all-A average, which won me, at Commencement, the much coveted *Summa Cum Laude* diploma and a year's scholarship at college.

This year at Wayne University has been a great revelation to me. It will soon be a part of my recollections; but they will always be pleasant recollections of interesting friendships and of gratifying contacts, of increased knowledge and of enlightened truths.

L. G.

A humorous strain adds a lighter touch to the long essay, "Then and Now." In spite of its length, this development of a familiar theme is sustained without straining for novelty.

THEN AND NOW

Pa and Ma cry for the good old days. They cried all Saturday night when my brother and I highballed down the street in our new sport roadster for another night out, and they're still crying. . . . Now have their lamentations for the past any justification? They tell us that the modern scheme of things is all awry. But I'm glad I'm living in the Year of Grace 1937, and I have my reasons. Of course, I am willing to admit that modern life is far from perfect. It has many drawbacks and, personally, I dislike giving the short family history to census takers. They should be given life—in prison. And I abhor the commercial announcer who interrupts a symphonic offering to inform us that it is only through the extreme courtesy of the South Side Sausage and Cheese Company that we are receiving the concert, or being told what time it is every five minutes—especially through the courtesy of the Bulova (spelled B-u-l-o-v-a) Watch Company. But all in all, the present day isn't such a bad sort.

Consider, for instance, the numerous modern inventions and refinements of living. What have the good old timers to say about the telephone? The old saying, "out of sight—out of mind," does not hold true any more, and our modern wife can see to it that she is in her traveling husband's mind every minute. She pursues him at each step with a ring, and he is constantly reminded that he has a wife and doesn't so much as look at another woman, because he knows what it feels like to lie parallel to the floor and listen to the melodious cheepings of the little linnets. For the woman of today is no longer the clinging creature of yesterday, given to weeping and fainting, and is no longer coddled like a piece of fragile bric-a-brac. This sedentary woman is now replaced by an independent sort who knows her own mind and asserts herself. Should her daring husband look at another lady, does our modern young wife grin and bear it? She does not. With an open palm she smacks him across his manly cheek for a row of centennial celebrations and makes him say "Uncle," to the edification of all other sweethearts and husbands who might have ideas about straying, even mentally, and makes them see at first hand just what happens when a man relaxes in devotion to his wife.

To get back to the telephone—of course, it is trying, just as one has stepped into the tub, or is in the midst of suave and courtly wooing, to be rung up. And even the mildest person breathes gentle curses when aroused from peaceful slumber in the middle of the night, only to learn that some incoherent night owl has the wrong number. But it could be worse. Oh yes, indeed! Think of what the scientists are considering right at present—television. No longer will one be able to sneak downstairs, carelessly pajama-clad. A person will have to be mindful of what he wears. The modern girl will have to think faster than ever. If the hour is early, she will have to remember what excuse she gave to Jimmie for not being able to go out. If it was because of that dinner dance, she must don her orchid frock and try to look as if she was just leaving. When the telephone rings and only Ma is home, she must hastily take down her curlers or get the mud off her face in case the caller is that catty Mrs. Jones. But then again, suppose a young man finds out his wife is a bum cook and he gets homesick for those home-cooked meals Ma used to have. He just calls up home, Ma sets some mashed potatoes, a roast, and some pie in front of the telephone and presto—the young man thinks he's home. So there are two sides to this telephone business.

Now let us look at the old-time bathing difficulties. Taking a bath in the days of yore was an event. In fact, a special night was set aside for it and Saturday became synonymous with cleanliness. Tubs, as we know them now, were scarce, and hot water was a semi-precious fluid. One would have to plan ahead for one's ablutions. Often the water had to be specially heated and conveyed by hand to the bathing receptacle. Today we seat ourselves in a porcelain tub and turn on the spigot. Tomorrow the scientists are planning to have a mechanical bathtub. With the pressing of a little button, a bathtub filled with water will come sliding into your bedroom through the door on the track. Fancy having the bathtub glide into the room with someone else in it! No sir, the present age with its present tubs is good enough for me.

Now consider the days of no electric lights. Coming home at night to a dark house, one would raise a goose egg on the forehead because the door was in the way, and crack his shins on the rocker. If lucky and alive, one might light the lamp and pray that it wouldn't smoke. Today we press a button and at once have a decent light without disgracing ourselves. Of course, there is a fly in the ointment in the form of that pernicious type of meter reader who slips into the basement once a month, drinks the home brew, and then reads the dial *double*.

Now consider the medical treatment about the time Lydia E. Pinkham got her medical diploma. Dentists were unaware of X-rays, bridges, pivots, porcelain work, and reconstruction. The dentist would get his pliers and let the teeth fall where they might. As for the pain, one simply bore it—silently or out loud. Anaesthetics were unknown, and if amputation was necessary, one was merely strapped down and told to think of his favorite flower. Of course, even today this species of medical person is not yet entirely extinct. There is the modern bone-breaker, commonly called chiropractor. His method is to lay his victim out on a massage table, tie both legs in a knot back of the head, and adjust the ribs by hearty application of elbows and knees.

After an evening in the depths of ye olde familye album, the present-day styles give one a feeling of satisfaction that outrivals everything—even a well-scratched itch in the small of the back. Women were terribly fond of groceries in those happy days of yore, and carried palm-leaf fans, and wore hoop skirts and bustles to maintain their equilibrium on the curves. The walk of the women of yesterday was like an Adam's apple, directly opposed to that of a pendulum. (Keep in mind the "Adam's apple"; it will be mentioned again later.) The pendulum oscillates from side to side like a bank president trying to enter a revolving door, while the Adam's apple obstinately slips up and down. When skirts began to require fewer yards of material and bustles became historical matter for reference only, the eighteen-day diet captured the modern women, and men began to lose weight too. Nowadays Ma has to count calories. She must have a reducing machine installed in the home. She wouldn't think of doing any strenuous work, because she might develop muscles. So she has the decorator and cleaner come to the house every so often. When they finish, the only way Pa can tell it's home sweet home is by the leak in the bathroom faucet, and he is seriously thinking of having a blueprint made at once and having the garage tacked down. No self-esteeming wife in these days of low viscosity of animal crackers would let her husband leave the house to go to his club before having his spinach. The result is that these husbands of the aforesaid dieting women are like goose-pimples—pretty much alike. They all grab off a little chow at a hit-and-run restaurant before coming home to dinner. But comparing them to the men of yore, they are really better off. Picture the wearer of the old-fashioned stiff collar. Close observations in the album have proved, beyond any doubt, that when the Adam's apple got caught up over the stiff collar, nothing much could be done about it until bedtime.

Possession of a frock coat in a small but growing community resulted inevitably in civic leadership. So many urgent demands for attendance at funerals, weddings, christenings, etc., were imposed upon the owner that no time whatever was left for the proper conduct of his own business, and he sometimes starved to death while acting as pallbearer. Today movie stars enlighten us in saying that a well-dressed man might get along fairly well on twelve suits in this year of recession. (You notice the difference?)

The days of yore were not void of cheap publicity-seekers either. The woman of Grandma's day who attired herself in the bathing costume of the day was considered a daring hussy if she wore no stockings or pushed her roomy pantaloons above her knees. She was merely a forerunner of the flagpole sitter and the nosepusher of peanuts.

And what did the songs of yesterday consist of? A musical evening in grandma's time began with a song about a virgin and a forlorn youth plucking a guitar. Nothing came of it, however, for the lovers were on opposite shores of a river which flowed between them "for evermore." This unhappy romance disposed of, more sorrow was introduced about sweet Alice, who lay beneath a marble slab. Her virtues were recounted with a depressing assurance that she would never be seen again. If the devotees of music were able to stand any more, there were plenty of other songs about death, graveyards, suicide, unrequited love, and missing brides. Today the lovers of a song at least have a chance to reach the nuptial altar, and one can sing a modern song without breaking down.

All this happened just ahead of the eventful hour when Henry Ford built up the idea of doing away with livery-stable odors. Again consider the improvement. Every time the ancient chariot drawn by old Dobbin hit a bump on main street, the passengers on board had to be taken out immediately for replacement of various dislocated vertebrae. Now we have speed and comfort. Of course, there is the pesky train at the crossing that insists on speeding up with an approaching car in sight and after the fatal crash, when our modern motorist asks, "Where in hell am I?" St. Peter answers, "My good man, you're in heaven." To which the motorist says, "Thank goodness, I don't have to play bridge with my wife tonight."

F. S.

"Beauty" is a more serious, but no less effective, essay of its type. The allusions are well interpolated. Analyze the style and watch the transitions.

BEAUTY

"Wherever snow falls, or water flows, or birds fly, wherever day and night meet in twilight, wherever the blue heaven is hung by clouds, or sown with stars, wherever are forms with transparent boundaries, wherever are outlets into celestial space, wherever is danger, and awe, and love, there is Beauty, plenteous as rain, shed for thee, and though thou shouldst walk the world over, thou shalt not be able to find a condition inopportune or ignoble."

Two years ago last summer I sat on the veranda of an Alpine hotel and was served luncheon by a pretty red-cheeked Swiss maid. The dining room was not especially attractive, but the scenery which enveloped it on all sides seemed like a magic curtain let down from heaven. Directly in front of me rose the snow-capped peaks of old Jungfrau towering like a giant above the other mountains. Half way down could be seen the grassy slopes of smaller mountains contrasting their bright green covering with the whiteness of the snow above them. Nestling in the valley below was the little town of Interlaken with its squatty, red-roofed houses. On my right stretched another range of mountains. Lively streams came tumbling down the steep slopes looking like snow-white ribbons against the dark background. Tiny peasant cottages dotted the mountainside. A river flowed through the fertile valley below, forming an apple-green sash for its dark-green dress. Truly, my eyes were gazing on the handiwork of God!

Who has not at some period in his life gazed on a lovely landscape and marveled at the beauty of the scene. And yet the philosopher Emerson said: "The difference between landscape and landscape is small, but there is a great difference in the beholder." In other words, there are many things of great beauty in this world that the average individual never sees. Yet to the observant eye the world is full of hidden beauty.

There is beauty in courage, real, deep, self-sacrificing courage. I am thinking just now of a hot, dusty road that winds through a field in southern France. I well remember the day that I drove through the Argonne forest, along the trenches and dugouts, and finally arrived at the great memorial cemetery with its rows and rows of snow-white crosses. As I stooped to pluck a blood-red poppy that grew on one of the little graves, I could not help seeing that even in such barren waste there was great beauty. Those ugly heaps of dirt once sheltered hundreds of courageous young men who had left kith and kin to serve their country. That barren waste that stretches for miles around was once the scene of many daring drives, of long night marches, and of fearless assaults on the enemy. And as I held the crimson poppy in my hand, I could not help thinking of the red blood that flowed so freely over this same ground just ten years before. Suddenly, the ugly mounds of dirt and the muddy dugouts were transformed before my eyes into things of rare beauty; where courage is, there, too, is beauty.

There is something indescribably alluring and beautiful in falling water. Who could stand on the brink of Niagara Falls without being deeply stirred within him at the beauty of it all? The powerful current seems to carry everything before it; all one's cares and troubles, fears and doubts are swept away before it. Great sprays of foaming white water spring up into the air, and then subside into the depths below. One can hear the roar of the rapids as the water dashes upon the rocks below. It is one of those rare beauties that cannot be fitly expressed in mere words: it must be felt, and enjoyed in silence.

Not long ago we had as a visitor in our home a crusty old gentleman who feared neither God nor man. It is the custom in our home for little four-year-old Jimmie to lisp his evening prayer at mother's knee about nine o'clock each evening. Coming in one evening about this time, I found mother at the fireplace, and heard the familiar words in Jimmie's high treble: "Now I lay me down to sleep—." Tiptoeing softly across the room, I almost bumped into the old gentleman standing just outside the glass door. The hard lines of his face were relaxed, his stooped shoulders heaved slowly up and down, and he quickly brushed a tear from the corner of his eye as I looked up at him. Frankly, I was embarrassed, but the old gentleman whispered in my ear: "Oh, the simplicity and the beauty of that little fellow's faith." And with that word he bolted up the stairs to his room, and I was left standing in the middle of the floor thinking that even faith, pure, simple, childish faith is beautiful.

I shall never forget my first sight of a storm at sea. It was the third day out. About three o'clock in the afternoon the sky grew black and threatening. Great, dark clouds shut out the light of the sun. The ocean, so calm just a half an hour before, became turbulent with huge, choppy waves. The great ship lunged to and fro like a mere toy in the powerful grasp of some monster of the deep. Higher and yet higher rose the waves. Now and then a huge one washed across the deck of the ship leaving destruction in its wake. The thunder rolled above us, and the waters roared beneath. Streaks of lightning flashed across the blackened heavens. Then "down came the storm—." For two long hours my friend and I stood on the top inner deck and watched the wild waves dash. And in that sheltered nook, while the fierce winds blew and the storm raged, we stood awed by the splendor, the power, the grandeur—in short, the great beauty of a storm at sea.

I know a dear, little white-haired lady who guards, as one of her choicest treasures, an old patchwork quilt. The quilt itself is anything but beautiful. Its varied colors do not harmonize; some are faded, others are streaked, and many are worn and old. Yet to the old lady it is beautiful, yes, very beautiful, because of the memories it brings to her. The old, purple square was cut from her first long, party gown; the worn old bit of green is a piece of her mother's wedding dress; and the tiny little patch of faded white muslin is her son's first baby dress. And so the little lady cherishes the old, ugly quilt, and to her it is more beautiful than all the latest silk taffetas in the world. It is not the faded quilt that is so beautiful to my old friend, but it is the memories, the precious memories, that are beautiful to her.

There is beauty in a sunny smile. Many a person will look twice at a bright, cheery face with a happy smile, but a somber, though good-looking person, he will pass by with scarcely a thought. And who of us has not seen a very plain face made truly beautiful for its goodness' sake alone?

There is something beautiful in strength. Who has seen an athlete leap a hurdle, or a strong man lift a heavy weight, and not marveled at the beauty of great strength?

There is a certain solemn, silent beauty in the sable night. Those nights when the sky above looks like a carpet of black velvet inlaid with sparkling diamonds. The moon, like a great golden ball, floats across the heavens, and darkness reigns supreme. Who of us has not cast our eyes heavenward on such a night, and tried to peer through the vast celestial spaces into the beauties that lie beyond?

> "Beauty is truth, truth beauty,—that is all
> Ye know on earth, and all ye need to know."

J. M. T.

The easy transition from autobiography to narrative can be studied in "Mountain Country." Note the happy combination of style, local color, dialogue, and the first-person point of view. Although the story starts as linear narrative, it rises to a well-sustained climax at the end. At what point does the suspense begin? What type of solution is used? Is there a transition near the end that is hard to follow?

MOUNTAIN COUNTRY

"Well, of all the rotten, out-of-the-way places to send a good-looking girl like me," I commented sarcastically as I landed, bag and baggage, at the railway station of Wallace Run of Wallace Mountain, Pennsylvania. Standing on the rickety wooden platform, I strained my eyes in vain to see some indication of the much-lauded Wallace Run—to see some sign other than the so-called station on which, by the way, I happened to be standing. The more I saw of the place, the less I liked it. Inwardly I called down curses upon my dear guardian uncle that had sent me here, but outwardly I remained calm. Yes, outwardly I remained calm, just in case there *might* be someone in this God-forsaken place who could see that I possessed all the proper decorum that could be expected of a new village "school-marm."

Seeing as the village hadn't gotten around yet to sending out the brass band to welcome me, I plumped myself down upon my suitcase and gazed at the majestic heights of Wallace Mountain. My neck soon developed a crick, however, from over-indulgence in the scenery; so I shifted my attention and began wondering where the station master was. It was in the midst of my wondering about the fate of the station master that Bob Bronkley appeared in the distance driving his horse and wagon at a rate that was faintly—oh so faintly—reminiscent of the famed pony express. Bob Bronkley was the eldest son of the Bronkleys at whose place I was to board. But if I had any remaining illusions concerning my prospects at Wallace Run, they were quickly shattered at the sight of Bob's buck teeth and flaming red hair. It was no use—the fates were against me at the start; and so I made the best of the bargain and smiled a greeting at the bashful young farmer.

Bob clumsily helped me into the wagon and mumbled something about "hoping I'd like it at Wallace Run." I replied that it was all right, and that I'd probably have lots of time to commune with my soul.

It seems I said the wrong thing, for he looked at me rather stupidly for a moment, and from then on, until we reached the Bronkley farm, he never uttered another word. As a consequence, I was feeling terribly depressed upon our arrival, for after all I did want to succeed. However, my fears upon that score were needless, for Bob immediately told "Ma" Bronkley—and subsequently the whole village—that I was an extremely religious girl. I needed nothing more to make me heartily welcome within the village, and I soon felt quite at home.

Even the young minister came to visit me, and I received the surprise of my life. I found him a modern and up-and-coming young man, pining away in a fogey old village. Well, I took care that he didn't pine any after he met me. We soon grew to be such good friends that his horse—Dickens, by name—nibbled nearly all the palings off the top of my school fence.

Somehow, the expected ennui never came about, for at first I was too busy investigating the village, conducting school, and getting settled generally, to have any spare time. It seemed anything might happen in school, from "Porky" Davis shooting the inkwell off my desk, to "Slick" Summers kissing little Sadie Primm and starting a family feud. Those were the nights when I slept the sleep of exhaustion. I had no sooner gotten accustomed to telling by instinct that a certain pea-shooter was operating in the northeast corner of the schoolroom, and had things pretty well in hand, when things really did begin to happen.

It all started the week Abe—the skunk trapper—decided to "keep company" with me, and it all began to end the day I fell in the creek, on one of my many rambling walks, and nearly drowned myself. Not that the drowning bothered me—I considered the skunk trapper far more of a hazard—but that creek was important.

Bear Creek started in the snows at the top of the mountain, and meandered along through the woods until it reached the position of the schoolhouse, halfway down the mountain. Once there, it neatly cut across the mountain and definitely divided the upper half, where the "hillbillies" lived, from the village at the foot which contained the homes of the more respectable farmers, such as the Bronkleys. Hillbillies and respectable farmers both sent their children to my little school on the mountainside, and soon I found myself involved in an adventure that satisfied even my bloodthirstiness for thrills.

The skunk trapper was the first cause of it. As he insisted upon waiting around school to escort me home, and as my hints didn't seem to affect him any more than the scents of his favorite profession, I began to sneak out the back way and wander over the mountain, until I was certain I had evaded him. Frequently I wandered up to the hill-billies' country, and I noticed with resentment their increasing un-friendliness each time I visited them. To be truthful, I was very much puzzled at their hostility. That is, I was puzzled until I ran across one of their whisky stills.

What a reception I had! I was met by the old man, Henry, and his two sons, each carrying enough artillery to furnish an armory, and they certainly weren't pleasant to look at! Henry's face was enough to give anyone nightmares. His small, green, pig-eyes snapped from beneath heavy, black eyebrows, as he balefully regarded me. Well—he just thrust his heavy, underslung jaw in my face, leered, showing ugly, tobacco-stained teeth, and said I'd better get out.

"Git th' hell outer hyar, er yer goin' ter git shot plumb center. Yer better keep yer trap shet too, er yer'll niver live ta tell about it."

Well you can just bet that I "got the hell out of there" mighty darn quick. I half slid, half ran all the way down the mountainside, and oh, what a relief to see dear old Dickens—the minister's horse—nibbling away at my school fence.

I found the minister—his name was Charley—reclining beneath a tree, reading *The Circuit Rider's Wife*. He rose to meet me, his handsome, dark face smiling a greeting as I reached him, panting and out of breath.

"Hi there, sister," he called, "where's the marathon?"

"It isn't a marathon," I gasped, "it's a whisky still."

Charley's face grew serious.

"So they ordered you off, did they?"

"Ordered me off," I echoed indignantly. "Brother, they as much as told me I had a berth in heaven waiting for me. That's why I was in such an all-fired hurry to reach you."

"I thought they'd be notifying you soon," Charley drawled. "They ordered me off the first week I was here—thought the sheriff and I were organizing to run them off the mountain."

His voice became suddenly angry and hard. "I'd certainly take great pleasure in doing *just that*," he added emphatically. "It's a crime when a few, rotten hillbillies can make life miserable for a village of quiet, respectable people. The sheriff has been trying to get up there for days, but the Henrys keep such close watch that it's next to impossible to get anyways near them."

He lapsed into silence, and thoughtfully watched Dickens nibble my fence.

"Charley!" I shouted suddenly. "I've got an idea! Where's the sheriff?"

" 'Way on the other side of the mountain, darling," retorted Charley sarcastically. "Were you thinking of leading him to victory?"

"Come on," I yelled, "and stop weeping over the lost cause. You and I are going to follow that creek up the mountain."

"Are you crazy?" gasped Charley. "That creek leads right up into the stills. You'll be seen sure."

"Just what I want," I crowed. "If we can only keep the Henrys' attention centered on us, the sheriff will get his chance."

Well, Charley was certainly game. We two followed the creek up the mountainside—Charley reading out loud from *The Circuit Rider's Wife* in his deepest and most impressive voice. It was his idea about reading the book—it might help to divert suspicion. We wandered slowly along, stopping every now and then, so that it was quite a while before we reached the danger line.

All of a sudden, funny little chills began to run up and down my back. Charley stopped.

"Do you want to go back?" he asked.

"Not on your life," I bluffed.

On we went; the foliage was getting thicker and thicker. My heart was going as fast as a trip hammer; my breath came in short gasps. Charley had stopped reading. How far would they let us go without stopping us? Would they shoot without warning? I felt as if a hole were already boring into the back of my head, as if we were completely surrounded. I didn't dare look back. I must try to look unconcerned— as if I suspected nothing.

What was that! My tense nerves jumped. I had distinctly seen a gun barrel glinting in the sun, amid the foliage. Was it aiming at us? I saw another one—another and another! Everything was so quiet. What *would* happen?

Then I saw Old Henry rise slowly out of the foliage. His face was dark and menacing. Charley saw him too. We stopped. No one said anything; I wanted to scream.

Slowly—slowly, Henry raised his rifle until it stopped, pointing directly at Charley. His hand reached for the trigger. Was the man crazy?

Then sharp and clear, a shot rang out—but it wasn't Henry's rifle. An astonished look came over his face. His rifle clattered to the ground; he clapped his hands to his bleeding side and slowly sank.

In another minute the place was dotted with men; volleys of shots rang out, echoing and reechoing in short, sharp explosions. Voices— not those of the hillbillies—were shouting. In the next instant the sheriff was before us, waving his hand in triumph. We had succeeded; from then on Charley and I were the idols of the village.

M. G.

"Freddy Grows Up" is a clever character story. Its dialogue is particularly good, and you will note that the age of the characters corresponds to that of most young students; hence the success of the story.

FREDDY GROWS UP

Freddy Hamilton fidgeted as he and his mother waited at the station for the morning train from Chicago. He wasn't accustomed to meeting girls arriving on trains, girls like Poppy Gordon anyway. She was so darned different. He wondered if the two years in California had changed her and if she still had a crush on him. He'd have to be nice to her, though. His mother liked Mrs. Gordon. Poppy was eighteen, too—his own age. Well, he'd been around in the last couple of years. He'd show her that he was no infant.

Now the train from the west was in. The passengers began to pour in and mingle with the crowds already in the station. He caught sight of Mrs. Gordon, and, beside her, why—that must be Poppy! Yes. Same jet hair, sparkling eyes, and cherry mouth; but something was wrong. She had grown to an amazing height. He thought he had never seen a girl so tall.

"Gee," he murmured under his breath, "she must be an easy six feet!"

Poppy rushed forward. Freddy felt a terrific impact on his shoulders as she fell on him, shrieking, "Freddy, O Freddy!" She squeezed his neck and kissed him. Then she stood off a bit, hands on his shoulders and looked him over.

"Isn't he just the sweetest thing?" she demanded, turning to the two women. Then she started hugging him again. Freddy felt as if he were out in a high wind. He gave his mother a look of despair. Why didn't Mrs. Gordon make Poppy behave herself?

People were looking at them and smiling. He drew himself up to his five feet nine, looked up at this Amazon; and said coldly, "Hello, Poppy." He hoped that would squelch her. He hated this girl who made him feel so small.

They started for the car, Poppy walking beside him, hanging over him like the Leaning Tower of Pisa. First, she was admiring his clothes, pulling out his tie and his carefully folded handkerchief to match. Then she was running her fingers through his blond hair. She embarrassed him, too, with her reminiscences.

"Freddy, 'member the time you ran away from home 'cause your mother wouldn't buy you long trousers?

"Oh, and will you ever forget the day that Bobby Smith blacked your eyes when you called him a sissy? Gee, Freddy, you looked funny!"

He could have wrung her neck cheerfully. Thank heavens, the girl was leaving for boarding school tomorrow.

That afternoon they played tennis until Freddy was weary enough to drop. He looked forward to a quiet evening at the movies where the peculiarities of Poppy would be unnoticed in the grateful dusk of the theater, but it was not to be. At eight-thirty Poppy announced herself ready for the country club dance. She really looked stunning for such a tall creature. Freddy, under the stern eye of his mother, had no choice but to agree. He felt that he was being led like a lamb to the slaughter.

This impression deepened when she demanded to drive his ancient flivver, Ermentrude. He caught his breath as they sped down the street at a rate of speed that Ermentrude had never experienced before. He had heretofore been of the opinion that he had got all the speed possible out of the "ole bus" but he saw that this idea was erroneous.

"Whoops!" Poppy cried. "I sure like the feel of this boat."

The car swayed as they veered recklessly from side to side. Under the thrill of speed, he felt more drawn to this queer girl. She was extremely pretty now with her hair blowing and her eyes shining. She could drive, too. Lord, how she could drive!

Suddenly, the loud, raucous noise of a motorcycle was heard behind him.

"Slow down!" he screamed at Poppy. "It's the law."

They stopped by the side of the road while a stern-faced policeman came over to the car.

"Say, where d' ya think you're goin'? This ain't the Indianapolis Speedway, and don't tell me you didn't know you was doin' sixty!"

"I know it," laughed Poppy. "I forget sometimes. I just love to speed, don't you? I know you do." She turned her breath-taking smile full upon him.

He softened as was expected.

"Yes, Miss, I do. That's why I'm in this line of work."

She smiled some more. The cop watched her admiringly as they talked about cars and speed. He tipped his hat when he chugged away.

"Good girl!" Freddy gave a sigh of relief as he patted her shoulder.

He felt rather queer, walking out on the dance floor, but not after they had danced together. All the other girls moved like cigar-store Indians beside her. The stag line went wild over her. At one o'clock she was as fresh as she had been that morning.

On the way home, she did not prattle but snuggled down in the seat, her head on his shoulder. Freddy put one arm around her and guided Ermentrude with the other. He told her that he was wild about her and regretted that she must leave for school tomorrow. They made solemn promises to write to each other weekly. When they reached his house, they did not get out. They sat in the car and looked at the moon.

"Say, Freddy," Poppy said abruptly, "let's get married. We're crazy about each other and everyone will be so surprised. We can be married when I come home for the holidays."

In a single, ecstatic instant, Freddy thought how wonderful life would be with this girl, what fun! He smiled at her.

"Great!" he gasped and then words failed him. He folded Poppy into his arms and kissed her again and again.

She bit his ear, pulled his nose, rumpled his hair, and called him "Delicious!" He promised to come and get her at the school in three months.

During the next few days he lived in the clouds. He looked at her picture constantly. He sang love lyrics in the bathroom. Only one thing bothered him, and it kept irritating him more and more, his height! He saw himself having to look up at Poppy for the rest of his life. Everything would be complete if only he could grow about three inches. It worried him more and more.

He put a notch on the door of his room. Then, night and morning, he went through hard, stretching exercises. He measured himself daily. He gave up coffee and cigarettes. As the weeks passed, he found that he was getting thinner but not perceptibly taller. His sleep was restless and filled with nightmares. He was always dreaming of growing as tall as the trees or a church steeple. When he woke up, however, he despaired.

One day, he saw an ad in a newspaper:

"SHORT MEN, INCREASE YOUR HEIGHT APPROXIMATELY ONE INCH PER MONTH! NEW, EUROPEAN SERUM GUARANTEED TO GIVE QUICK RESULTS. ENLARGE YOUR PITUITARY GLAND. 150 State Street. Monsieur Flaubert."

Freddy steered Ermentrude to No. 150 State Street. He parked a few doors down the street and looked cautiously about. After a while he spurred his courage to the point of venturing into the office.

M. Flaubert was a giant of a man with a long flowing beard, bushy eyebrows, and superelegant manners.

After hearing Freddy's reluctant confidences, he jumped up suddenly and kissed the boy on his right ear, pounded his chest and shouted, "Mais oui! Me, I will make you beeg. Certainement!"

Freddy was quite mortified. He paid the ten-dollar fee and hurriedly slunk out of the building, hoping no one had seen him. Ten dollars was a lot of money but Poppy was worth it. His family need never know. He knew of a magazine that might buy his illustrations, and his art instructor was always offering to find a market for his water colors. He would slave day and night. He must be worthy of Poppy.

He did work hard. His whole day was spent at art school, and on returning home he would mope around all the evening, looking at Poppy's picture on his dresser. For her he would do anything.

Twice weekly he went to M. Flaubert to have a needleful of serum shot into his arm. It was extremely painful. His arm was stiff and ached dreadfully when he was drawing but he dared not complain.

One night he found he had grown half an inch taller than the notch on the door. What a thrill! "Half an inch, half an inch upward," was his slogan.

His mother remarked casually to his father, "Freddy is growing taller every day."

"Yes," his father agreed. "I grew till I was twenty-one."

Freddy's heart failed him. Suppose he kept on growing at this rate —an inch a month until he was twenty-one! He would be a freak in a sideshow, and what a freak! This did not worry him greatly, however. He was busy, watching the calendar, and writing long letters to Poppy.

Poppy did not write letters. She sent him six postal cards and five telegrams.

At last the three months were up. Freddy had achieved the coveted three inches. He thought he looked very distinguished.

His mother declared it very nice of him to take a day off to visit Poppy and bring her home. She little knew, he told himself, the surprise in store for her.

During the long train ride, he was restless and impatient. Arriving at the small town that was honored by the presence of Poppy's exclusive school, he grabbed a taxi. He was soon borne to a large early Tudor building, half hidden by trees. He took little notice of its pretentious exterior. He rang a bell and was conducted to a large hall.

A girl sat at a desk at the end of the hall, and when he asked for Miss Gordon, she handed him a note. He tore it open and read:

"Dear Freddy:

I have gone away with José. He's a honey. I just met him last week. We are getting married today. After the holidays we are going to his estate in the Argentine. It takes three days to ride around it. Isn't that romantic? José is only five feet, six, but I don't care. Tell Mother we'll be home for Xmas.

Love, Poppy."

M. B.

⇒⇒⇒ B ⇐⇐⇐

"Engato" is a young lion. The linear narrative of his exploits, which appeared from time to time in the *New Statesman and Nation* (and is now reprinted in America), is extremely interesting.

ENGATO THE HUNTER[1]

J. H. Driberg

I woke suddenly one night, conscious of some unusual movement. The moonlight was streaming through the holes in the mud walls of my house that stood for windows, and there were few shadows that could harbour an intruder. My dogs were growling from under my bed, as if they too felt some disturbing influence: but it was not the full-throated bark they used to give as a signal of danger: it was rather an irritated grumble, half growl, half whimper, at being rudely awakened from sleep. I wondered whether it was worth getting outside my mosquito-net, and had almost determined to ignore the matter when my ears caught an unusual scraping noise, an almost imperceptible "swish" as of a broom very lightly used, apparently just outside the window. The dogs heard it too, and came out into the middle of the room, but curiously stopped their growling, now that they were satisfied that something was there, and stood silently in the moonlight pointing in the direction of the noise. This required investigation, as it might have been a python whose movements would produce just that scraping effect, and I did not want my dogs to rush out and commit suicide. I was surprised not to see Engato with the dogs and still more surprised to find that he was not in the room at all. It was he, then, who had first aroused the dogs, for Engato, when a cub, was rather clumsy and thoughtless in his movements, and probably trampled over them quite regardless of their feelings when he decided to see what was happening outside.

Slipping on a coat, I went as silently as possible to the door which, as usual, stood open, and looked out on the verandah. This was about six feet in breadth and something over forty feet long, and there I saw the strangest, the most incongruous, sight that had come within my experience, so ludicrous indeed that it was with difficulty that I checked my laughter. At the far end of the verandah sat Engato, very solemn, yet obviously very inquisitive, watching intently something that was happening towards the other end, near my bedroom window. That something was a magnificent lion, with a full mane, and he too sat watching, very much at home, watching rather quizzically and wondering (no doubt) how the little cub had found its way there. And as he watched, he was gently swishing his tail to and fro across the rough earthen surface of the verandah, the cause of the mysterious noise which had brought my dogs to their feet.

The issue, I admit, is disappointing. The stage was set for drama, and it was a dramatic situation, this meeting of the wild and the tame: but I am afraid that it was the ludicrous aspect which most appealed to me—the sudden awakening, the mystery and its odd explanation, and still these two lions confronting each other silently, both obviously inquisitive and anxious to know more about each other. The wild one had the greater poise and was content to sit patiently and watch. Not so Engato. His muscles were twitching in his anxiety to make friends. He would half lurch forward and relapse again on to his hind quarters. Like a kitten attracted by a ball of wool he would crouch as for a spring, and relax again with a mild grunt of excitement. He was really terribly excited, but could not make up his mind what to do. Neither of them took any notice of me, as I stood in the shadow of the door. Suddenly Engato took a few agile bounds forward and stopped. The old lion continued to sweep my floor quite unperturbed. Engato crept forward inch by inch, and almost before I knew it he had halved the distance between them. Perhaps an involuntary movement of mine spoilt the play: or perhaps Dignity was just a little bored and thought it unbecoming to be made the sport of a mere cub, and not his cub at that. At any rate, whatever the reason, he rose to his feet very deliberately, yawned, and bounded out of sight across the narrow trench that, surrounding the house, served the double purpose of carrying off superfluous rain water and preventing the ingress of biting ants.

. . . .

Next morning I was up early, as I had to go with the local natives after a herd of elephants which were destroying crops no great distance away. They were going to hunt them in their own way with spears and had asked me to accompany them, as they knew that I liked to leave my rifle at home and to do things, sometimes, in their way. These Lango are the finest spearmen I have ever met, and the bravest. They do not hesitate to tackle any animal, however dangerous, and never even carry a shield for their protection: they laugh at their neighbors, the Acholi, who carry much larger shields than the Lango war-shields, suggesting that they are conveniently large to protect their backs when they are running away. I have seen a running buck speared at sixty yards and constant practice has given their spears a low trajectory in flight which it is very difficult to emulate.

About a dozen men turned up at dawn and we were just starting, when out rushed Engato. His blood was up after the night's adventure, and small though he was the hunting lust was on him. He insisted on coming just as firmly as I insisted on his staying behind; for I knew that it would be too much for him and, besides, I naturally did not want to risk his being trampled to death. The Lango were much amused at his persistence and were delighted when he bounded from one to the other as though asking them to take him: the wretch could wheedle as well as any domestic cat. It was inevitable, of course, that he went. He would be a mascot, they said, and bring us luck, and if he tired one of them would carry him.

Delightedly Engato lolloped behind me in the cool of the morning air. It must have been an effort for him, as we moved at a steady jog trot for about ten miles, and his only rests came when he was carried across a couple of big swamps which we had to traverse. On arriving at the spot on which we had decided overnight, we found another dozen spearmen waiting for us, and quickly made our dispositions. We chose a clearing which extended for a depth of about fifty yards before it met thick bush and grass fully fifteen feet tall, and strung out in a long line at irregular intervals. As I thought, Engato proceeded to make a thorough nuisance of himself: first he wanted to explore the bush, and when driven back from that took his revenge by biting everyone's heels—naked heels—impartially. They took it very well, however, having only themselves to blame for insisting on his coming, and laughed uproariously at his absurd antics, especially once when with poetic justice he was bitten by a large warrior ant.

Nevertheless, as zero hour approached, I became more and more nervous for his safety and tried to get him to take cover behind a tree. I might as well have tried to balance a ball of quicksilver, but the Lango got a lot of fun out of it. They did not worry a bit about their mascot, which annoyed me, perhaps unreasonably, but said that Engato was a creature of the bush and would be able to look after himself. And indeed he had to, for once the business started I was far too busy to attend to him. Several hundred Lango had located the herd, a small one, and drove it down upon us. The animals—I should not like to say how many there were: one is apt to magnify numbers on such occasions, but probably there were only eight or ten—broke from the bush about fifty yards away and came, panic-stricken at the din behind them, in our direction without at first spotting us. As luck would have it, the elephant most conveniently disposed came towards me, and the others (as is the custom) were allowed to pass through our line unmolested. As in duty bound, I flung my spear at the elephant and it happily landed in such a way as not to disgrace me: with a scream of rage it charged towards me, and, again following the Lango ritual, I had to wait till on nearing me it was wounded by a spear from my neighbour. At once the elephant turned from me and made for its last opponent, and was in this way played up and down the line till eventually it broke through a gap, and we settled down for a long chase. It is curious that the elephant, whose instinct and sagacity are generally considered above the ordinary, can apparently be trusted to behave in this way. The Lango, who have hunted by this method for centuries, have never known it to fail, and I have never seen the technique break down, though I have not had a great deal of experience of it. They assert, and I am inclined to agree, that there is absolutely no danger for the hunters, provided that no one turns and runs, as, if he does, then the elephant will refuse to be deflected by another spear.

As may be imagined, there was not much chance of looking after Engato, while all this was going on. A moment's inattention might have been fatal to oneself or to one's neighbour, and the whole essence of this kind of co-operative hunting lies in the confidence which one has in one's fellow hunters. But it did not last long, and after the elephant broke through we were glad enough to rest for a few minutes and to see what had happened to Engato. The Lango were not long in finding him: they guessed where he would be—I admit that I had not thought of it—and their shouts of laughter told me the tale quickly enough. "Oh, Engato! Oh, Great Hunter! Chief of the Forest," they cried, "come down, come down to thy kill!" For there he was cowering in the crook of a branch well out of harm's way, on the very tree behind which I had tried to persuade him to take cover. He must have scrambled up it as soon as the trumpeting elephants broke from the bush, and nothing would coax him down. The rest of the hunt does not concern us more than it concerns Engato. We killed our elephant, but Engato was a passenger, I fear. One of the men fetched him down from the tree, but he was so upset, and his nerves were in such a tangle, that he refused to walk any more, and for the rest of the long day clung, more like a monkey than a lion, to the Lango who had rescued him from his refuge.

"Towers of Fame" is a picture-frame story. The ending is the normal type usually to be found with this particular kind of story.

TOWERS OF FAME [1]

Elizabeth Irons Folsom

He raised his voice to bar interruption.

"You cannot tell anything about anyone. Romance survives where you least expect it. Would you look for it in Eric Hall, for instance? Would you suspect him of Romance?"

"Well, hardly," said one of the listeners. "Not that calculating, cold man—all indifference. Just to make your point, don't try to prove that *he* has known sentiment."

"More than most men," replied Kent. "I have a notion to tell you about him. I *will* tell you. Come closer, Janet—all of you—to hear the unbelievable."

"About Judge Eric Hall who knows only power—fame!" They laughed.

"Yes, about him."

"How do *you* happen to know?"

"He told me."

"Did he expect you to tell?"

"Heaven knows what a man expects when he babbles."

Dinner was over; coffee was being served in the big, candle-lit drawing room. The guests had made little intimate groups; some one at the piano at the far end of the room touched half strains between talk and laughter. The group in the deep window drew closer to Kent, and made themselves comfortable.

" 'Babbles' is what I said," went on the speaker, rolling a cigarette with deliberation, "but that is the wrong word. We were old friends: in fact, I was responsible for the whole thing, for I had talked about the queer town in one of the Middle Western states. Eric is the kind who always wants to know, so when he happened to be in that part of the state, he hired a car and drove out to see for himself."

"I've heard of that town," declared Janet eagerly. "There is no other like it, is there?"

Kent passed over the question.

"I'll tell it exactly as he told me. I'm sure I can. I could not forget it. He had driven ten miles through dust and wind with a thunderstorm rolling up ahead of him—purple storm with green fringe on it

[1] From *McClure's Magazine* (1923). Reprinted by permission of the author.

—the kind they have out there. He was whacking along when he caught sight of a sign by the roadside. He stopped and backed his car to read it. It said—I remember it exactly—it said:

SMOKING, DRINKING, PROFANITY, FORBIDDEN
AS YOU PASS THROUGH THIS TOWN.

YOU HAVE NO RIGHT TO POLLUTE THE AIR.

MOST PEOPLE ARE BAD. MOST PEOPLE
LIE, STEAL, AND DRINK.

"Oh! Truly!" gasped Janet.

"It was what Eric was looking for—the entrance to the town of fanatics. There was a blank-looking group of houses marked at intervals by tall, white board signs—black letters on a white ground. He drove slowly. It was Sunday and the stillness was absolute. There was a building that might be a hotel—on the veranda were vacant chairs tilted against the rail; a few shops, gray with closed doors; houses gray, too, all with doors shut tight, curtains made to screen. The main street, three or four blocks long, was deserted. At a far corner a man appeared, took a look at the coming car, and stepped out of sight. A woman who came out on her porch, slipped back, and shut the door sharply. She was gray, too—clothes and hair; the distant man had seemed gray—a brown-gray, like the dust that whirled.

"He stopped the car to read another sign, this one as large as a house front, full of preachments, repeating the words that he had first read:

MOST PEOPLE ARE BAD. THEY LIE, STEAL,
AND DRINK.

NO OUTSIDE PEOPLE OR INSTITUTIONS
WANTED HERE.

THE DANCE IS OF THE DEVIL, THE
THEATERS ARE DEVIL-BEGOTTEN.

"And again:

MOST PEOPLE ARE BAD. THEY LIE, STEAL,
AND DRINK.

"As he stood reading, he was conscious that men had appeared in the streets ahead and behind him. They fitted the houses—brown-gray, closed, shut tight. They walked slowly, eyes on the ground, but, as they passed him, he had a look from each. The looks were alike: ominous—hate snapped out at him from under briefly raised lids. Each face had a set mouth, with slashes down from its corners. Each head that turned slightly had—menace—hostile promises.

"The storm was breaking: a flash of lightning swept down the street; thunder crashed; for a moment the wind ceased—it hung aloof and the calm was thick with the brown-gray of the town—with deep silence. A desert plain, a skiff alone on the ocean, would have been more friendly, he said."

"Where is the Romance?" someone asked, as Kent stopped.

"It's at hand. It crossed the street in front of his car just as the wind came tearing like a railroad train. He saw her face for an instant before it caught her. Well, folks—I can't tell you how Eric spoke of her face. He forgot that he had ever seen a court room or a law office, or had known indifference or ambition. He said to me—I can see him as he rapped the table and forgot he was speaking—'The face of that girl, Kent!' And—can you believe it of Eric?—he went on: 'Do you remember Raphael's peasant girl? The one with parted lips and queer, asking eyes? She was exactly like her. The wind took her sunbonnet away. She had two long braids of hair. She stopped and stared at me, her long, brown-gray skirt twisting about her little flat shoes. Then she ran on, clutching her braids, and a near door slammed after her.'

"The wind was on then; the few trees bent before it.

"The rain was close. There was no protection and, acting on impulse, he drove the car back of the huge sign. It was a shield from the wind and a slight protection against the slanting rain.

"Eric said it had been years since he had seen a Western storm, where it lets loose and whoops 'er up. He was half blinded with the lightning; he could hear the smash of small buildings; the rattling scurry of débris blown by the wind. His own shelter shivered, creaked. It was braced strongly from the back, but he thought it more than likely that it would go. Across the street he heard one go down with a splintering thud.

"But as he waited, he was conscious, he said, only of the girl who was somewhere in that strange town. I'd like to have had you—you people who think you know Eric—watch him as he told me this. There was not a drop of blood in his body, to judge from the colour of his face; his fingers twitched. He talked because he had to talk to someone, I guess. He was not self-sufficient then."

"Hm-m," said someone. "I don't get him in that role, and still I do, too, in a way: the force in him could be applied as well to an—er—infatuation as to anything else. I suppose it *was* an infatuation, eh, Kent? They are strange things, but they wear off."

"Go on," said Janet.

"He said that he sat there in the car while the wind bent his board protection and the rain came in sheets. He was wet through from the spray where it struck the outer edge of the car. He sat and watched pictures of that girl's face: they came through the rain; came into the lightning; came everywhere. He was half conscious, he said, absorbed in the new thing.

"Out of that state of mind—he told a lot about that; it seemed to puzzle him as it does us now—he was startled by a new gale of wind, a close splitting of boards, the shriek of wood parting from wood at his elbow; and then the whole great shield tottered, swayed, resisted, swayed again, and came down over him. He ducked his head. A moment later he discovered that, in falling, the sign had gone into some trees standing close and was held there, in half-tent fashion, so that it protected him from the rain. Then he saw, too, someone clinging to the slanting edge of the shield. He leaped from the car and caught her as she fell.

"Her clothes were dripping with water; there was a trickle of blood down one cheek. But she was not unconscious and she struggled in his arms. He made her sit down on the running board of the car. Then he asked her if she was hurt and she shook her head. He asked her how she happened to be there back of the sign and she shook her head again. He sat down beside her and watched her. He spoke to me about 'filling his eyes with her for the rest of his life'—and other things that Eric would not have said normally—or if he had not been—er—infatuated. That was the word, wasn't it?

"They sat there a long time without speaking, and she kept her eyes closed. The wind died away, but the rain persisted—a steady downpour; the green-gray of the storm daylight changed into the black-gray of steady rain. He waited.

"When she opened her eyes, he asked again how she happened to be there. After much urging she answered him.

" 'They turned me out of the house,' she said.

" 'Turned you out!' he repeated, incredulously. 'In this storm! From your home! Why? What had you done?'

" 'I had stopped and looked at you,' she answered simply.

" 'What?' Eric put force into the word when he spoke it.

" 'I had looked at you. Stopped and looked. It was a sin. After that, I could not be allowed to live with those who were not sinners,' she explained.

" 'I never heard of such a thing!' he told her. 'Are they crazy?'

" 'The signs tell you. It is their belief. It was a sin to have looked at you—and remembered.'

"Eric's blood was racing; she had remembered! Looked at him, and remembered.

" 'Don't worry. Just tell me,' he urged.

"She told him. He did not tell me just what she said, but I could guess as I watched the light back in his eyes. Her father had opened the door and put her out in the rain as a wanton. He was very strict—father. As soon as the rain was over she would go to the other end of town where she had a friend who would take her in. No, she did not believe as her father and the people of the town believed; her mother had taken her away and she had been brought up differently, but when the mother died, he had brought her back.

" 'My mother could not bear it here,' she said. 'I am not so brave as she, or I would go.' "

"Go on," said Janet again.

"It's a good story, isn't it? Especially since we have our own opinions concerning him. No king of lovers, no Romeo, no schoolboy, could have told such a tale of first love as Eric told me. Spilled it out. Words tumbling over each other.

"In one look, in one half hour, it seemed, he had turned over all the principles upon which we live here in New York. The primal had taken him—and her, too. She was not afraid; not frightened at what she must have seen in him.

" 'And why, when he turned you out, did you come in here?' he asked finally.

"He had never before listened for an answer as he listened for that one.

" 'I came because you were here,' she said.

"Well, people—I began to see then what he was up against in the way of intoxication. He had not touched her; it had been all very aloof, but when she told him why she had come, he said he would have been wooden if he had not gathered her close and held her tight.

"Then, through the slackening rainfall, he heard footsteps outside their shelter, heard them on the soft ground close by, saw a stooped figure straighten under their tipped roof. It was one of the all-alike, brown-gray men with jammed-shut mouth and slashes down from it; with hate-filled eyes.

"This man levelled his finger at Eric. 'Now ye kin have her,' he said harshly. 'Ye kin take her along o' ye. There's no door open in this town for such as her. They're shut against her forever. This is no place for her ever again. We're done. All o' us.'

"She sprang forward. 'Father!' she cried.

"He struck her with his open hand straight across the mouth.

" 'Harlot! Plaything o' strange men!' he accused, scornfully.

"Eric said that he reached for the man, but that she spread her arms between them.

" 'No!' she exclaimed. 'He believes it! He cannot help it. No, no!'

"Then the man did not speak again. He stooped under the slanting boards and went away.

"And now comes what Eric said was the strangest part of it—the way he took it. Back of the glamour of the girl's lovely face; back of the pull of her, standing there in the slackening rain holding her wet skirts about her, her neck bare; back of the wonder of her, there rose a bank of his sane self—that self indifferent of all else. There towered a steeple of his future as he had planned it; of his ambitions; of his wealth and fame which were just beginning and for which he had worked hard. They grew—these steeples—and pushed closer. The girl watched him.

"She had not spoken to him since her father had gone away; she had stood aside while Eric got the car out upon the road; she had followed him to it and stood there clasping her bare elbows—lips parted like the Raphael girl-child, he said. She was oblivious to watchers behind drawn curtains.

" 'Now what shall you do?' he asked her. 'Does he mean it?'

" 'Yes, he means it. I shall walk to the next town. There will be something for me to do there.'

" 'I'm sorry—' he began, all the steeples crowding around him.

" 'Don't be. I'm glad. It gives me a chance to be brave as she was.'

"She put up one hand to her mouth and pressed her lips tight with it.

" 'It's odd, isn't it?' she asked.

"He says he did not need to ask what was odd. He knew. It was the sudden new thing which was his—and hers. But the steeples were nearer. And a free life was what he had planned; it alone could bring him what he wanted. But he asked:

" 'Will you come with me, as he said?'

"She shook her head.

" 'Oh, no. I am not your kind.'

" 'But I love you,' he told her then. You should have heard him speak those three words, the day he told me the story. Another man surely—not the Eric we know. He said it twice: 'I love you.'

" 'And I you,' the girl replied.

" 'Then come with me,' he pleaded.

" 'No. It will pass. It cannot be the real thing. It was too quick for that.'

"She smiled, and he tried to laugh and say, without too much earnestness:

" 'Shall I come back some day?'

"She shook her head again.

" 'Please don't.'

"He climbed slowly into the car, legs weighted, he said. He looked back as he gathered speed on the hard road. She was walking too slowly it seemed to him—her head too low—

"But everywhere were the steeples of fame and fortune to come if he were unhampered; if he could be always indifferent. The west had red streaks—He drove away."

"Oh, I hate the man!" cried Janet, indignantly. "It's just like him! What became of her?"

"There she is now, at the end of the room," said Kent, smiling at the evident astonishment of the group around him.

Eric Hall's wife was lifting her coffee cup and laughing. Her filmy sleeves fell away from perfect arms; a jewel flashed from a tiny silver band in her hair. She was clearly the loveliest, the most distinguished woman there.

They stared at her.

"But you just said that he drove away!" someone exclaimed in amazement. "That was the drama of your story!"

"He drove back and got her," finished Kent sententiously.

The following is a long description of a cold day from an essay by Leigh Hunt. The first part of the essay, preliminary to the description, is omitted.[1]

A "NOW"; DESCRIPTIVE OF A COLD DAY[1]
Leigh Hunt

Now, the moment people wake in the morning, they perceive the coldness with their faces, though they are warm with their bodies, and exclaim, "Here's a day!" and pity the poor little sweep, and the boy with the water-cresses. How anybody can go to a cold ditch, and gather water-cresses, seems marvellous. Perhaps we hear great lumps in the

[1] Hunt here quotes a line from Thomson's *Seasons:* "Now, all amid the rigours of the year," as the origin of his use of "now." This essay was printed in *Leigh Hunt's London Journal*, December 3, 1834. Compare pages 302–3 above.

street of something falling; and, looking through the window, perceive the roofs of the neighboring houses thick with snow. The breath is visible, issuing from the mouth as we lie. Now we hate getting up, and hate shaving, and hate the empty grate in one's bedroom; and water freezes in ewers, and you may set the towel upright on its own hardness; and the window-panes are frost-whitened, or it is foggy, and the sun sends a dull, brazen beam into one's room; or, if it is fine, the windows outside are stuck with icicles; or a detestable thaw has begun, and they drip; but, at all events, it is horribly cold, and delicate shavers fidget about their chambers, looking distressed, and cherish their hard-hearted enemy, the razor, in their bosoms, to warm him a little, and coax him into a consideration of their chins. Savage is a cut, and makes them think destiny really too hard.

Now breakfast is fine; and the fire seems to laugh at us as we enter the breakfast-room, and say, "Ha, ha! here's a better room than the bed-chamber!" and we always poke it before we do anything else: and people grow selfish about seats near it; and little boys think their elders tyrannical for saying, "Oh! *you* don't want the fire; your blood is young!" And truly that is not the way of stating the case, albeit young blood is warmer than old. Now the butter is too hard to spread; and the rolls and toast are at their maximum; and the former look glorious as they issue smoking out of the flannel in which they come from the baker's; and people who come with single knocks at the door are pitied; and the voices of boys are loud in the street, sliding or throwing snow-balls; and the dustman's bell sounds cold; and we wonder how anybody can go about selling fish, especially with that hoarse voice; and schoolboys hate their slates, and blow their fingers, and detest infinitely the no-fire at school; and the parish-beadle's nose is redder than ever.

Now sounds in general are dull; and smoke out of chimneys looks warm and rich; and birds are pitied, hopping about for crumbs; and the trees look wiry and cheerless, albeit they are still beautiful to imaginative eyes, especially the evergreens, and the birch with boughs like dishevelled hair. Now mud in roads is stiff, and the kennel ices over, and boys make illegal slides in the pathways, and ashes are strewed before doors; or you crunch the snow as you tread, or kick mud-flakes before you, or are horribly muddy in cities. But, if it is a hard frost, all the world is buttoned up and great-coated, except ostentatious elderly gentlemen, and pretended beggars with naked feet; and the delicious sound of "All hot" is heard from roasted apple and potato stalls, the vender himself being cold, in spite of his "hot," and stamping up and down to warm his feet; and the little boys are astonished to think how he can eat bread and cold meat for his dinner, instead of the smoking apples.

Now skaters are on the alert; the cutlers' shop-windows abound with their swift shoes; and, as you approach the scene of action (pond or canal), you hear the dull grinding noise of the skates to and fro, and see tumbles, and Banbury cake-men and blackguard boys playing "hockey"; and ladies standing shivering on the banks, admiring anybody but their brother, especially the gentleman who is cutting figures of eight, who, for his part, is admiring his own figure. Beginners affect to laugh at their tumbles, but are terribly angry, and long to thump the by-standers. On thawing days, idlers persist to the last in skating or sliding amidst the slush and bending ice, making the Humane-Society-man ferocious. He feels as if he could give them the deaths from which it is his business to save them. When you have done skating you come away, feeling at once warm and numb in the feet, from the tight effect of the skates; and you carry them with an ostentatious air of indifference, as if you had done wonders; whereas you have fairly had three slips, and can barely achieve the inside edge.

Now riders look sharp, and horses seem brittle in the legs, and old gentlemen feel so; and coachmen, cabmen, and others, stand swinging their arms across at their sides to warm themselves; and blacksmiths' shops look pleasant, and potato shops detestable; the fishmongers' still more so. We wonder how he can live in that plash of wet and cold fish, without even a window. Now clerks in offices envy the one next the fireplace; and men from behind counters hardly think themselves repaid by being called out to speak to a countess in her chariot; and the wheezy and effeminate pastry-cook, hatless and aproned, and with his hand in his breeches-pockets (as the graphic Cruikshank noticeth in his almanack) stands outside his door, chilling his household warmth with attending to the ice which is brought him, and seeing it unloaded into his cellar like coals. Comfortable look the Miss Joneses, coming this way with their muffs and furs; and the baker pities the maid-servant cleaning the steps, who, for her part, says she is not cold, which he finds it difficult to believe.

Now dinner rejoiceth the gatherers together, and cold meat is despised; and the gout defieth the morrow, thinking it but reasonable on such a day to inflame itself with "t'other bottle"; and the sofa is wheeled round to the fire after dinner, and people proceed to burn their legs in their boots, and little boys their faces; and young ladies are tormented between the cold and their complexions; and their fingers freeze at the pianoforte; but they must not say so, because it will vex their poor comfortable grand-aunt, who is sitting with her knees in the fire, and who is so anxious that they should not be spoilt.

Now the muffin-bell soundeth sweetly in the streets, reminding us, not of the man, but his muffins, and of twilight and evening and curtains and the fireside. Now play-goers get cold feet; and invalids stop up every crevice in their rooms, and make themselves worse; and the streets are comparatively silent; and the wind rises and falls in moanings; and the fire burns blue and crackles; and an easy-chair with your feet by it on a stool, the lamp or candles a little behind you, and an interesting book just opened where you left off, is a bit of heaven upon earth. People in cottages crowd close into the chimney, and tell stories of ghosts and murders; the blue flame affording something like evidence of the facts.

"The owl, with all her feathers, is a-cold,"

or you think her so. The whole country feels like a petrifaction of slate and stillness, cut across by the wind; and nobody in the mail-coach is warm but the horses, who steam pitifully when they stop. The "oldest man" makes a point of never having "seen such weather." People have a painful doubt whether they have any chins or not; ears ache with the wind; and the waggoner, setting his teeth together, goes puckering up his cheeks, and thinking the time will never arrive when he shall get to the Five Bells.

At night, people become sleepy with the fireside, and long to go to bed, yet fear it on account of the different temperature of the bedroom; which is, furthermore, apt to wake them up. Warming-pans and hot-water bottles are in request; and naughty boys eschew their nightshirts, and go to bed in their socks.

"Yes," quoth a little boy to whom we read this passage, "and make their younger brother go to bed first."

The final essay, by Professor Charles H. Grandgent, has already been quoted from in Chapter VII, on the character sketch. It would be difficult to find a better illustration of many of the distinctive features recognized in the informal, familiar essay style. Here we have the charm of matured, humane personality directly felt. In the author's love of animals, even insects, and of nature in many other aspects, we feel the differences which set man apart from the merely animal, or from mere nature. We find the love of books and words, without pedantry; the love of personal adventure, without self-display; a tireless interest in human beings, without the impulses of morbid curiosity and gossip. The people stand out freely, sympathetically, and in their own normal proportions. It is perspective which is most finely represented here—perspective which comes from a subtle and vigorous mind submitting itself to long training. The result is a style which has both enthusiasm and restraint, each in its proper function, yet which avoids coldness and self-consciousness. It is the easy, steady, conversational murmur which is the very voice of the English essay.

Incidentally, observe that the "cracks in the clouds" reveal glimpses that might serve as illustrations of most of the chapters of this book: not the character sketch alone, but diary, biography and autobiography, definition, criticism, description, and easy-moving narrative are all to be found here. The thought seems to stray and drift, yielding to the slightest suggestion of new interest. Here we have writing, good writing, as such; and the story and the essay enter in because good writing has always tended to settle into the varied molds of these forms.

CRACKS IN THE CLOUDS[1]

Charles H. Grandgent

It gives you a strange intoxication to spend a night on a mountain. Not the bracing air alone—there is also the consciousness of being above the world, in another sphere of existence; and a peculiar lightness, both of foot and of head. It is something like your experience in dreams, when you overcome gravity and float off into space or bob up against the ceiling. When I was twelve, I remember, I slept on the Righi, after having walked up. Later I had a night on the Gorner Grat, amidst the snow peaks. Moosilauke was not so pleasant, because it rained furiously and my sheets were damp; wet sheets do dampen one's enthusiasm. But good old Mt. Washington, the top of New England! Many's the night I have slept there, in the old Tip Top House or the big Summit House. When I say "many," I suppose I mean eight. Anyhow, I once put in a three days' stay there, with grand, sunny excursions above the timber line, visiting the spots I had never had time to turn out for, on the climb up or down.

[1] Reprinted from *Imitation and Other Essays*, Harvard University Press, 1933, by permission of the publishers.

That sojourn followed a wearisome ascent in a snowstorm. We had lodged in a dilapidated house at the foot, called Darby Field Cottage, to be ready for an early start up through Tuckerman's Ravine. The evening was fair, but not without premonition of trouble. There were three of us, Carl, Max, and I, on an extended tramp through the mountains. I think it was in October. In the Darby Field Cottage there were two chambers available. Carl and Max drew the spacious one, with several articles of furniture, whilst I got a tiny hall bedroom, with nothing but a cot bed. They laughed at me as we said "good-night"; but ere morn the laugh was transferred to the other side of their mouths. For my ceiling was sound, whereas their roof had a great hole directly over the bed, and it snowed hard in the night.

The snow continued in the morning, but we decided, with easy optimism, that it would "soon clear up." It didn't. The sun dimly penetrated the clouds for an hour or two, and then went out. And the snow went on, while a solid mass of mist came rolling up the ravine. By the time we had reached the head, above the Snow Arch, one couldn't see fifty feet; it was sleeting pitilessly, and a treacherous blanket of snow covered over the mile of broken rock which lay between us and the summit. There was nothing to indicate direction except Carl's compass and my recollection of the topography, both of which Max profoundly distrusted. A shivery consultation, with the help of a map, resulted in a painful retreat to the lower part of the ravine, where a trail ran across to the carriage road.

.   .   .   .

The next morning was bright, and by ten all the snow had vanished. Of those following three days I need say nothing further. When the time came for departure, we once more, of one accord, laid our course for the bar, to offer a final libation. "Going?" said the dispenser of beverages—a humorist by nature, and glad, on that mountain-top, to find an appreciative listener. "Well, I'm sorry. You boys have been good customers. And you've behaved fine. You ain't raised no row, and you ain't tried to flirt with the table girls. Come back soon! This drink is on the house." And he even consented (contrary to rules) to join us.

But I had intended to feature a sunrise; all that precedes has been circuitously leading up to it. Seeing the sun come up is part of the Summit House ceremonial. The orb emerges to the accompaniment of a gong—and very early, at an hour when the thermometer is in the depths. Guests are warned, by a placard in every chamber, not to take their bed blankets out of doors with them. The spectacle is well worth a shiver; and after it one can scuttle back into a warm bed, if

, reading. Always in a formidable library. It is my father's,
a reckless and miscellaneous collector of books. He collected
ever, not for the sake of collecting, but to read. And read
lid—a veritable Comestor! So catholic was his taste that
or next to nothing) was absent. A pretty full set of the Latin
old calf-bound volumes. The German Romanticists in all
ke-up: two complete editions of Tieck, I remember, and
ffman. All Beyle and all Voltaire. Strauss's *Life of Jesus*,
nte, Thiers; Abbott's *Life of Napoleon*, with its illustrations
very page, the hero always portrayed in flawless skin-tight
. .
my father gave me a surprise. I must have been about
were rummaging about in the garret, when in a forgotten
came across a tall heap of uniform pamphlets tied together.
ge he pulled out, dusted, examined, and then turned over
the remark that perhaps it would interest me, since I was
ding. O joy! The pamphlets were no other than Beadle's
ls! I lost no time; seated there in the attic, I greedily began
he second was traversed at second speed. The third began
. And I stuck fast in the fourth. I have never had the courage
since. But the gift was put to good use; carrying my stock
I started a Beadle Loan Library among my mates; and,
exacted no payment, I won considerable regard. I have
ered what was my father's motive in bestowing on me that
sational literature. Did he simply think it would amuse me,
ubtless amused him for a moment? Or did he believe that it
by as to cure me of hunger for cheap stuff? At any rate, it
was wise enough to foresee it. . . .
course, is pleasurable beyond aught else, but pleasure is
bain. For instance, when you are allowed to go barefoot.
vaulting ambition to walk unshod, like the village boys;
ime to time my mother yielded, with warnings against
s. If the angels fell by ambition, they can hardly have
n that sin more than I. Have you ever, unprotected, run
v-mown field? There was one such, conveniently opposite,
vn to the river. I can feel the prick of that pitiless stubble
low good was the sensation of cool water, after an experi-
at! There was one particular deep spot, below the old
. flat rock beside it. The water was over one's knees, and
uld come and nibble at one's legs. But one could fish there
out catching so much as a cold.

one has remembered the number of one's room and has not forgotten
the key. Well, one morning, as we stepped forth on the platform, we
found ourselves on a little island. Right about us was the top of the
mountain; above us, the clear heaven, wherein some bold stars had
not yielded to the light that was spreading from a red horizon; below
our islet, as far as the eye could reach in every direction, an undulating
expanse of white, an unbroken sea of cloud. The earth had sunk away
beneath the opaque ocean, and we were alone with the sky. As the
sun climbed, from time to time the white floor would split open, just
a crack, and for a moment we had a glimpse of a tiny slice of that lost
world, until the rift closed again. In great clearness and brightness we
could see it, but only for an instant. And the breaks were not always
in the same spots; here and there they shifted, allowing inspection of
this bit and that of the hidden land. Finally, of course, the huge surface
broke up and disappeared, with amazing swiftness, and the whole
world was spread out at our feet, the valleys still full of mist, the uplands glaring in the sunshine. Then from the low places the mists
would come curling upward, joining forces and threatening to isolate
us once more; but they were no match for the sun; they would either
fade into nothingness or roll off on high as fleecy clouds.

One may well imagine, if so disposed, that in some future existence
the curtain that separates us from our past will roll away, and all will
be clear to us. Meanwhile, however, in the life we know, we catch only
transient glimpses through rifts in the screen. Why the veil of forgetfulness should break here and not there, now and not then, we cannot
tell. Some flitting association, I suppose, opens a momentary circuit
connecting present and bygone. The pictures come unbidden, always
a surprise, usually a delectation.

Frequently, in summertime, I have for a moment the illusion of
lying in a field of tall grass—monumentally tall, shielding and shading
me as I lie. Quite cut off from contact with humankind, I enjoy
membership in a larger and older society, the ancient and honorable
society of insects, which thickly peoples that forest. How interesting all
their operations are, when viewed from the appropriate distance of
six inches! Grasshoppers are my favorites, with their extraordinary
combination of sedateness and agility. Have you ever noticed how
they perform an about-face during a jump? I love to hold them gently
just before they spring, and feel in my hand the tremendous push of
those powerful hindlegs. And how wise they look as they sit and chew
tobacco! The only disadvantage of intimacy with this world of Lilliput
is that the friendships you form are so one-sided: in the consciousness of

these little beings, you are just a part of the landscape, an earthquake if you move, a harmless hummock if you are still; but you must try to forget that. For you are at a time of life when all your interest is in individuals. Each tree, each bush, each plant that you know has its own self, its own character; so it is with those savages who have no word for the species but give different names to the different specimens that surround them. And you hate to believe that you have no distinctness in the eyes of creatures who are so distinct in yours.

Little things delight the little. I can see a tiny, tiny house right beside a railway track. When I visit there, I have the feeling of a toy house built for me. I must be about five, I fancy. The occupants are a small pair (although Mr. J. B. is growing a tummy), and they have no children. There are just enough rooms, and each room is just big enough to hold the requisite furniture. The windows are beautiful with shades displaying romantic castles in dark brown. The shades, of course, have to be small, to fit the windows, so the castles can not be very big. Whenever a train goes by, the whole house shakes like jelly, and the shades flap with a joyous noise. The yard is just extensive enough to surround the house and a diminutive stable. It always seems to me that this latter edifice must have been constructed over and around the horse and buggy, while these inmates stood still for the operation; otherwise such a snug fit is hardly conceivable. Overhead is a loft with a capacity of one portion of hay. The horse is rather an undersized animal, excepting his feet, which call for considerable floor space. Judging from the situation of his home, I think Mr. J. B. must at this moment have some connection with the railway, but I am not sure. He has so many professions! Blacksmith, fireman, policeman, carpenter, cook, peddler—have you ever heard of so versatile a genius? Good in all these callings; yet, I fear, with no consecutive fondness for any. The last trade, perhaps, best suits his disposition, for he has a cheery temper, with a copious current of conversation, and an aptitude for sitting in a cart behind a horse. Some pleasant memories of his earlier pursuits he must cherish, for he still from time to time exercises the functions of carpenter and cook, and officiates as special policeman. His badge, big and shiny (the one big thing in his little house), is to me, and to him, a thing of wonderment. He is most fully himself at the season of the County Fair, when he performs the double duty of guarding the peace and fabricating his justly famous chowder. Not infrequently he is invited to furnish this delicacy at municipal banquets and church sociables. Once he took me to a sociable at the opening of a new church—Baptist, I am pretty sure. I remember benches, bread

and butter, dishes, all of which had to
wishers, and immense quantities of cho
benevolent bustle and self-satisfaction,
and I am proud (God forgive me!) to
personage. One more characteristic
He has a mania for swapping things.

The kaleidoscope shifts, and anoth
sitting on a hassock in our living-roo
cousin of hers are singing together. I
it is my first perception of counter
vocabulary, and I have no idea wha
voices together, it seems to me. But it
Fine counterpoint still affects me in
musical people, I fancy, the melody
not for me. A tune is something to b
counterpoint, mysterious and elusive,
dreamlike flashes, is the thing that se

Another sudden transition. This is
many, many years our most cherishe
of William Warren, Mrs. Vincent, A
long before the days of Mason, Haw
Wilson of beloved memory. My mot
as I was able to sit in a seat; and in
there I would sit, until its demoliti
phase that when Miss Annie Clark
last act of *Lady Audley's Secret*, "I a
well-kept secret," I wondered what
of the other characters seemed to
grievances. Well, in those days (I
remember it), a part of the proscer
upright, narrow mirror on each sic
angle that I could see in it the re
spectators. It was like looking at the
puzzle me! Again and again I woul
audience" was; but I never could
indeed, there were three distinct au
more than two at a time; and the
different quarters. After the play,
making our way out, I would pee
and never-satisfied endeavor to lo

The picture which the cloud-ri

a big cl
for he v
them, h
them h
nil huma
Classics
sorts of
two of
Locke,
on near
breeches

One
eleven.
corner w
This pac
to me w
fond of
Dime No
the first.
to pall a
to try on
to school
although
often wo
heap of s
as it had
would so
did; and

Play,
sometime
It was m
and from
stone-brui
suffered fi
across a
running d
even now.
ence like
dam, with
minnows
all day wi

It was not there that I learned to swim; both incentive and water supply were insufficient. It was on a bend of the Blackstone River, not far from the Blackstone railway station, that I found sufficiency of both. There, under a great maple, whose branches spread far over the current, was the old hole which swimmers frequented, and in their company the aspiring neophytes. The art came to me in a flash. I was in the habit of clinging to a maple branch and, thus sustained, venture in considerably beyond my depth. Suddenly, one fine day, the envious sliver broke, and I was precipitated upon my own resources. These proving to be unexpectedly adequate, fear fled, never to return. . . .

For a while, I feared the altercation would go on as long as an old-fashioned baseball game. I remember one match, on a Fourth of July, between two rustic teams, not far from Worcester. I, as a "city feller," and therefore supposedly conversant with all the rules of the sport, had been asked to serve as umpire. Early in the day the contest began; up and up rose the score, like stocks in the recent boom. From morn to noon they played, from noon to dewy eve, a summer's day. Just a few minutes off for luncheon. Towards four P.M., one of the catchers having become disabled, I took his place and caught behind the bat, still continuing my function as umpire. When darkness finally parted the contestants, the score was eighty-six to sixty-eight.

Those summer days! The sweet relaxation of them, the sense of irresponsible freedom! Best of all, perhaps, the days when summer is in the offing, when we are still looking forward to it, when we sniff it in the air. I never smell violets without recalling some scene of early spring in Paris, where boys are selling bunches of those flowers in the streets. In the era of bustles, a fashionably clad young woman goes wagging her way along the sidewalk; and an urchin, as she passes, sacrifices his whole remaining stock of violets for the fun of depositing it on her rear platform and seeing her strut on, unconscious of her load. As she pursues her course, other *gamins* contribute their mite—a package of licorice pastilles, an empty corset-box, a mangy *ouistiti;* and still she struts, in happy ignorance, all through the Chausée d'Antin.

Violets and horse-chestnut blossoms—markers of the season when opera relaxes and Madame Marchesi used to hold the closing exercises of her singing classes. One of these I recall distinctly, having been invited by one of her pupils, a powerful young contralto, who on that occasion sang "O mio Fernando." . . .

June links itself not only with love and flowers and baseball, but also with Jules Verne; for on a hot, sunny day of that month I made his acquaintance. A memorable occasion; all the details are stamped on my memory. An awning over the window, sounds of the street rising muffled by their climb of three stories. It is a little hotel on Washington Street, near Dover Street, in Boston. We are halting there in process of migration. On the centre-table lies a thick, red-covered volume, which I for days have refused to touch, stupidly mistaking it for a scientific report. *A Journey to the Centre of the Earth;* hardly has boredom impelled me to open it, when the pictures reveal something of its magic. Forevermore June shall recall those never-to-be-forgotten figures—the eccentric uncle, the unwilling nephew, and Hans, the imperturbable Icelandic guide.

They emerged, you remember, on Stromboli, having been spewed out from the earth's interior. As I read of that marvelous outcoming, I never dared to imagine that I should ever behold Stromboli, however hot my secret desire. But I have seen it, by day and night. The first time was on an Italian steamer, an old boat, but scrubbed so clean that one could have eaten off her deck anywhere; and the food so delicious that one could have eaten it off the ground. There was an uncommonly large crew, under uncommonly good discipline. The captain, a fat, good-natured man, certainly did not look the part of a martinet, but he ruled his ship. I fancy nothing escaped his notice. As we were going aboard, a lady passenger remarked softly to her companion: "Dear me! I wish we had some peaches!" The captain, not far away, said nothing; but I saw him call a cabin boy and whisper something in his ear. And just before the gangplank was hauled away, the lad came bounding aboard with a crate of peaches in his arms. We had a batch of missionaries with us. A pair of them, on their way to India, had a very pretty and very precocious little child, whom everyone admired. As it was toddling about the deck, the captain suddenly blew his whistle. We all started. Instantly the mate and bo's'n appeared, and saluted. "Boys," said the captain, "I want you to see that baby!"

So we passed Stromboli. I never reached its ruddy top, nor do I believe it offers nocturnal hospitality. And I fancy the clouds that envelop its summit are all of its own making.

INDEXES

INDEXES.

I. *Index of Subjects and Topics*

Accent, 199.

Accident, 199.

Adjectives, 461.

Adverbs, 461.

Allusions (literary), 51, 280–1, 285, 289, 296, 540, 551.

Ambiguity, 199.

Amphiboly, 199.

Analogy, 202, 204, 205.

Analytical definition, 69–70, 73.

Anecdotes, 72, 118, 119, 120, 140, 235, 280, 281, 540.

Angle of narration, 481. *See also* Point of view.

Antonyms, 70.

Argument, Chapter XI.

Argumentum ad hominem, 200.

Argumentum ad populum, 200.

Argumentum ad vericundiam, 200–1.

Artistry, 322, 359–60, 400, 409, 460, 463, 477, 483.

Atmosphere, 96, 106, 131, 357, 421, 438–9, 440–2, 482.

Autobiography, 149, 150, 322, 323–4, 327–9, 343–5, 358–9, 373, 389–90, 421, 542, 554, 577.

Basic situation, 351, 356–70, 481.

Begging the question, 199, 205.

Bibliographical criticism, 164.

Bibliography, 228, 230, 231–2, 234, 260–1, 262, 264.

Biography, expository, Chapter VIII; narrative, 322, 340–1, 357–8, 389, 422, 577.

Body, 203, 258.

Brackets, 49, 260, 266, 325 n.

Brief, 203, 206–7.

Burlesque, 84.

Characterization, 117–8, Chapter VII; 325, 348, 361, 412, 414, 415, 420, 422, 423–4, 478–80, 483, 496, 519, 577.

Character plotted, 421–38, 480.

Character writing, 81, 99, 106, 109–10, 129.

Child story, 335–6, 443, 444.

Chronicle, 321, 337.

Classification, Chapter III; 260–1; of essays, 279–82.

Clearness, 12, 13, 288.

Climax, 7 (of sentence), 351, 352, 353, 354, 370, 371, 372, 373, 375, 387–400, 411–2, 413, 415, 416, 423, 425, 431, 441, 443, 446, 481, 554.

Co-education, specimen brief on, 206–7.

Coherence. *See* Sequence.

Coincidence, 482, 483.

Comparison and contrast, 6, 37, 69, 77–8, 111, 128, 176, 231, 460.

Complication. *See* Suspense.

Compound epithets, 462.

Conclusions, 51, 169, 201, 203, 260, 280, 351, 352, 354, 375, 400–10 (narrative), 412, 423, 426, 442.

Concreteness, 14, 37, 69, 72, 78, 143, 235.

Conflict, 480–1.

Connectives, 11, 29, 417, 419.

Connotation, 415, 461, 462.

Contentiousness, 169, 196.

Convincingness, 374, 481, 482. *See also* Plausibility.

Criticism, Chapter IX; 577.

Description, 96, 106, 412, 414; Chapter XVI.

Details, 100, 103, 133, 140, 280, 323, 324, 419, 440, 460–1 (in description), 462, 467, 480, 540, 542.

Detective stories, 419.

Deus ex machina, 393.

Diagrams, 10, 29, 242, 320, 348–51, 496.

Dialect, 419.

Dialogue, 100, 323, 381, 383, 388, 412–3, 419, 425, 462, 480, 483, 554, 558.

Diary, 322–3, 325 n., 330–3, 341–3, 358, 373, 389–90, 413, 421, 577.

Dictionary, 69, 70.

Digressions, 412.

Direct characterization, 117, 423.

Disguise. *See* Dramatic situation.

Division, 6, 7, Chapter III; 199, 231.

Documentation, 258–60, 268.
Dominant characteristic. *See* **Character** plotted.
Dominant tone, 100, 459–60, 461, 465, 471–2.
Dramatic situation, 380, 416, 483, 491.

Echoing conclusion, 401, 402, 404, 407–8.
Editorial, 196–7.
Emphasis, 51.
Equivocation, 198–9.
Etymology, 67, 69, 77.
Everyday-life essay, 286–92.
Evidence, 200, 205, 209, 213.
Examples, or illustrations, 69, 71, 72, 75, 78, 168, 235.
"Explication du texte," 164–5.
Exposition, in narrative, 363, 412, 416, 423.
External solution, 392, 393, 398, 425.

Fable, 421, 540.
Fairy tale, 353–4, 421, 481
Fallacies, 197, 198–203, 205, 214.
False analogy, 202.
Footnotes, 234, 242, 259–60, 265, 268.
Force, 357, 358, 359, 422.
Foreknowledge. *See* Dramatic situation.
Form, 258.
Fundamental image, in description, 474.

Genetic criticism, 164–5.

Historical criticism, 166–7, 168, 170, 174–5, 188–90.
History, 264–5, 325, 388.
Humor, 30, 84, 177, 286, 302, 306, 355, 401, 403, 415, 422, 429, 482, 548.

Ibid., 234, 260.
Ideas, 67–9.
Idiom, 289.
Illustrations. *See* Examples.
Imagery, 462, 473–4.
Imagination, types of, 487.
Impressionistic criticism, 163–4, 182.
Indirect characterization, 117, 423.
Induction, 204.
Internal solution, 392–3, 394, 399, 400, 425.
Interpretive criticism, 165, 182–3.
Introductions, 100, 139, 203, 210, 235, 258, 287, 350, 410, 419, 462–3.
Irony, 301, 378 (fate), 403 n., 404, 405, 409, 422.

Irrelevant conclusion, 201.
Issues, 204.

Journalistic style, 62.
Judicial criticism, 165–6, 168, 170, 173–4, 177–9, 183, 184–8.

Laboratory notebook, 4, 18, 321, 356.
Letter, as dramatic device. *See* Dramatic situation.
Letters, narrative, 322 n., 333–4, 345–6.
Linear narration, Chapter XIII; 554, 563. *See also* Autobiography, Diary, History, etc.
Loc. cit., 234, 260.
Local color, 554. *See also* Setting.
Logical definition, 71, 94.

Manuscript, form of, 257–8.
Melodrama, 363, 364, 481, 482, 483.
Mental state, description, 463, 467, 474–5.
Metaphors, 462.
Metrical feet, 418.
Moment of interest, 350–1, 352, 353, 354, 356–70, 370–1, 373, 375, 410, 423, 424, 441.
Moods, 302, 334, 347. *See also* Tone.
Moral (morality, and moralizing), 72, 205, 302, 352, 354, 364, 401, 407, 413, 414, 426, 462, 479.
Moving pictures, 390.

Names, as literary device, 119, 415.
Narrative anecdote, or sketch, 346.
Nature essay, 293–5.
Newspaper story, 322, 329–30, 339, 357, 366, 389, 448–9, 488–9, 496.
Non sequitur, 201–2.
Notes, 9, 228–9, 232–4.
Nouns, 461.

Objectiveness, 18, 183, 439, 441, 462.
Omissions, 49, 460.
Omniscient point of view, 360–1, 483.
Op. cit., 234, 260.
Organization, 168, 230–1, 235 n., 256, 257, 258, 261, 362, 415–6.
Originality, in plot, 481–2.
Outlines, and outlining, 8, 168, 190, 203, 206–7, 228, 230–1, 232, 233, 258, 261, 263, 280, 350–1, 362, 370–2, 373–4, 375, 416, 423–5, 440–42.
Overhearing. *See* Dramatic situation.

one has remembered the number of one's room and has not forgotten the key. Well, one morning, as we stepped forth on the platform, we found ourselves on a little island. Right about us was the top of the mountain; above us, the clear heaven, wherein some bold stars had not yielded to the light that was spreading from a red horizon; below our islet, as far as the eye could reach in every direction, an undulating expanse of white, an unbroken sea of cloud. The earth had sunk away beneath the opaque ocean, and we were alone with the sky. As the sun climbed, from time to time the white floor would split open, just a crack, and for a moment we had a glimpse of a tiny slice of that lost world, until the rift closed again. In great clearness and brightness we could see it, but only for an instant. And the breaks were not always in the same spots; here and there they shifted, allowing inspection of this bit and that of the hidden land. Finally, of course, the huge surface broke up and disappeared, with amazing swiftness, and the whole world was spread out at our feet, the valleys still full of mist, the uplands glaring in the sunshine. Then from the low places the mists would come curling upward, joining forces and threatening to isolate us once more; but they were no match for the sun; they would either fade into nothingness or roll off on high as fleecy clouds.

One may well imagine, if so disposed, that in some future existence the curtain that separates us from our past will roll away, and all will be clear to us. Meanwhile, however, in the life we know, we catch only transient glimpses through rifts in the screen. Why the veil of forgetfulness should break here and not there, now and not then, we cannot tell. Some flitting association, I suppose, opens a momentary circuit connecting present and bygone. The pictures come unbidden, always a surprise, usually a delectation.

Frequently, in summertime, I have for a moment the illusion of lying in a field of tall grass—monumentally tall, shielding and shading me as I lie. Quite cut off from contact with humankind, I enjoy membership in a larger and older society, the ancient and honorable society of insects, which thickly peoples that forest. How interesting all their operations are, when viewed from the appropriate distance of six inches! Grasshoppers are my favorites, with their extraordinary combination of sedateness and agility. Have you ever noticed how they perform an about-face during a jump? I love to hold them gently just before they spring, and feel in my hand the tremendous push of those powerful hindlegs. And how wise they look as they sit and chew tobacco! The only disadvantage of intimacy with this world of Lilliput is that the friendships you form are so one-sided: in the consciousness of these little beings, you are just a part of the landscape, an earthquake if you move, a harmless hummock if you are still; but you must try to forget that. For you are at a time of life when all your interest is in individuals. Each tree, each bush, each plant that you know has its own self, its own character; so it is with those savages who have no word for the species but give different names to the different specimens that surround them. And you hate to believe that you have no distinctness in the eyes of creatures who are so distinct in yours.

Little things delight the little. I can see a tiny, tiny house right beside a railway track. When I visit there, I have the feeling of a toy house built for me. I must be about five, I fancy. The occupants are a small pair (although Mr. J. B. is growing a tummy), and they have no children. There are just enough rooms, and each room is just big enough to hold the requisite furniture. The windows are beautiful with shades displaying romantic castles in dark brown. The shades, of course, have to be small, to fit the windows, so the castles can not be very big. Whenever a train goes by, the whole house shakes like jelly, and the shades flap with a joyous noise. The yard is just extensive enough to surround the house and a diminutive stable. It always seems to me that this latter edifice must have been constructed over and around the horse and buggy, while these inmates stood still for the operation; otherwise such a snug fit is hardly conceivable. Overhead is a loft with a capacity of one portion of hay. The horse is rather an undersized animal, excepting his feet, which call for considerable floor space. Judging from the situation of his home, I think Mr. J. B. must at this moment have some connection with the railway, but I am not sure. He has so many professions! Blacksmith, fireman, policeman, carpenter, cook, peddler—have you ever heard of so versatile a genius? Good in all these callings; yet, I fear, with no consecutive fondness for any. The last trade, perhaps, best suits his disposition, for he has a cheery temper, with a copious current of conversation, and an aptitude for sitting in a cart behind a horse. Some pleasant memories of his earlier pursuits he must cherish, for he still from time to time exercises the functions of carpenter and cook, and officiates as special policeman. His badge, big and shiny (the one big thing in his little house), is to me, and to him, a thing of wonderment. He is most fully himself at the season of the County Fair, when he performs the double duty of guarding the peace and fabricating his justly famous chowder. Not infrequently he is invited to furnish this delicacy at municipal banquets and church sociables. Once he took me to a sociable at the opening of a new church—Baptist, I am pretty sure. I remember benches, bread and butter, dishes, all of which had to be contributed by various well-wishers, and immense quantities of chowder. Mr. J. B. is all aglow with benevolent bustle and self-satisfaction, his very tummy seems to swell; and I am proud (God forgive me!) to be the guest of so important a personage. One more characteristic of Mr. J. B. deserves mention. He has a mania for swapping things. . . .

The kaleidoscope shifts, and another picture comes to view. I am sitting on a hassock in our living-room, and my mother and a female cousin of hers are singing together. I must be very young indeed, for it is my first perception of counterpoint. No such word is in my vocabulary, and I have no idea what it is. Merely the magic of two voices together, it seems to me. But it thrills me through and through. Fine counterpoint still affects me in the same way. For most non-musical people, I fancy, the melody is the more important thing, but not for me. A tune is something to be caught and remembered; while counterpoint, mysterious and elusive, recalled only without volition, in dreamlike flashes, is the thing that seems to transmute the listener.

Another sudden transition. This is the dear old Boston Museum, for many, many years our most cherished playhouse. I mean the museum of William Warren, Mrs. Vincent, Annie Clarke, and Charles Barron, long before the days of Mason, Haworth, Sadie Martinot, and George Wilson of beloved memory. My mother used to take me there as early as I was able to sit in a seat; and in after life, whenever I got a chance, there I would sit, until its demolition. So innocent was I in my first phase that when Miss Annie Clarke's deep voice proclaimed, in the last act of *Lady Audley's Secret*, "I am mad—that is me long-kept and well-kept secret," I wondered what she had to be mad about; several of the other characters seemed to me to have much more serious grievances. Well, in those days (I wonder how many theatre-goers remember it), a part of the proscenium decoration consisted of a tall, upright, narrow mirror on each side of the stage, erected at such an angle that I could see in it the reflection of a small segment of the spectators. It was like looking at the public through a crack. How it did puzzle me! Again and again I would ask my mother where "that other audience" was; but I never could make her understand. Apparently, indeed, there were three distinct audiences, although I never could see more than two at a time; and they were all watching the stage from different quarters. After the play, while in the crowd we were slowly making our way out, I would peer eagerly around in a never-ending and never-satisfied endeavor to locate those other two halls. . . .

The picture which the cloud-rifts oftenest exhibit represents me in a big chair, reading. Always in a formidable library. It is my father's, for he was a reckless and miscellaneous collector of books. He collected them, however, not for the sake of collecting, but to read. And read them he did—a veritable Comestor! So catholic was his taste that *nil humani* (or next to nothing) was absent. A pretty full set of the Latin Classics in old calf-bound volumes. The German Romanticists in all sorts of make-up: two complete editions of Tieck, I remember, and two of Hoffman. All Beyle and all Voltaire. Strauss's *Life of Jesus*, Locke, Comte, Thiers; Abbott's *Life of Napoleon*, with its illustrations on nearly every page, the hero always portrayed in flawless skin-tight breeches. . . .

One day my father gave me a surprise. I must have been about eleven. We were rummaging about in the garret, when in a forgotten corner we came across a tall heap of uniform pamphlets tied together. This package he pulled out, dusted, examined, and then turned over to me with the remark that perhaps it would interest me, since I was fond of reading. O joy! The pamphlets were no other than Beadle's Dime Novels! I lost no time; seated there in the attic, I greedily began the first. The second was traversed at second speed. The third began to pall a bit. And I stuck fast in the fourth. I have never had the courage to try one since. But the gift was put to good use; carrying my stock to school, I started a Beadle Loan Library among my mates; and, although I exacted no payment, I won considerable regard. I have often wondered what was my father's motive in bestowing on me that heap of sensational literature. Did he simply think it would amuse me, as it had doubtless amused him for a moment? Or did he believe that it would so cloy as to cure me of hunger for cheap stuff? At any rate, it did; and he was wise enough to foresee it. . . .

Play, of course, is pleasurable beyond aught else, but pleasure is sometimes pain. For instance, when you are allowed to go barefoot. It was my vaulting ambition to walk unshod, like the village boys; and from time to time my mother yielded, with warnings against stone-bruises. If the angels fell by ambition, they can hardly have suffered from that sin more than I. Have you ever, unprotected, run across a new-mown field? There was one such, conveniently opposite, running down to the river. I can feel the prick of that pitiless stubble even now. How good was the sensation of cool water, after an experience like that! There was one particular deep spot, below the old dam, with a flat rock beside it. The water was over one's knees, and minnows would come and nibble at one's legs. But one could fish there all day without catching so much as a cold.

It was not there that I learned to swim; both incentive and water supply were insufficient. It was on a bend of the Blackstone River, not far from the Blackstone railway station, that I found sufficiency of both. There, under a great maple, whose branches spread far over the current, was the old hole which swimmers frequented, and in their company the aspiring neophytes. The art came to me in a flash. I was in the habit of clinging to a maple branch and, thus sustained, venture in considerably beyond my depth. Suddenly, one fine day, the envious sliver broke, and I was precipitated upon my own resources. These proving to be unexpectedly adequate, fear fled, never to return. . . .

For a while, I feared the altercation would go on as long as an old-fashioned baseball game. I remember one match, on a Fourth of July, between two rustic teams, not far from Worcester. I, as a "city feller," and therefore supposedly conversant with all the rules of the sport, had been asked to serve as umpire. Early in the day the contest began; up and up rose the score, like stocks in the recent boom. From morn to noon they played, from noon to dewy eve, a summer's day. Just a few minutes off for luncheon. Towards four P.M., one of the catchers having become disabled, I took his place and caught behind the bat, still continuing my function as umpire. When darkness finally parted the contestants, the score was eighty-six to sixty-eight.

Those summer days! The sweet relaxation of them, the sense of irresponsible freedom! Best of all, perhaps, the days when summer is in the offing, when we are still looking forward to it, when we sniff it in the air. I never smell violets without recalling some scene of early spring in Paris, where boys are selling bunches of those flowers in the streets. In the era of bustles, a fashionably clad young woman goes wagging her way along the sidewalk; and an urchin, as she passes, sacrifices his whole remaining stock of violets for the fun of depositing it on her rear platform and seeing her strut on, unconscious of her load. As she pursues her course, other *gamins* contribute their mite—a package of licorice pastilles, an empty corset-box, a mangy *ouistiti;* and still she struts, in happy ignorance, all through the Chausée d'Antin.

Violets and horse-chestnut blossoms—markers of the season when opera relaxes and Madame Marchesi used to hold the closing exercises of her singing classes. One of these I recall distinctly, having been invited by one of her pupils, a powerful young contralto, who on that occasion sang "O mio Fernando." . . .

June links itself not only with love and flowers and baseball, but also with Jules Verne; for on a hot, sunny day of that month I made his acquaintance. A memorable occasion; all the details are stamped on my memory. An awning over the window, sounds of the street rising muffled by their climb of three stories. It is a little hotel on Washington Street, near Dover Street, in Boston. We are halting there in process of migration. On the centre-table lies a thick, red-covered volume, which I for days have refused to touch, stupidly mistaking it for a scientific report. *A Journey to the Centre of the Earth;* hardly has boredom impelled me to open it, when the pictures reveal something of its magic. Forevermore June shall recall those never-to-be-forgotten figures—the eccentric uncle, the unwilling nephew, and Hans, the imperturbable Icelandic guide.

They emerged, you remember, on Stromboli, having been spewed out from the earth's interior. As I read of that marvelous outcoming, I never dared to imagine that I should ever behold Stromboli, however hot my secret desire. But I have seen it, by day and night. The first time was on an Italian steamer, an old boat, but scrubbed so clean that one could have eaten off her deck anywhere; and the food so delicious that one could have eaten it off the ground. There was an uncommonly large crew, under uncommonly good discipline. The captain, a fat, good-natured man, certainly did not look the part of a martinet, but he ruled his ship. I fancy nothing escaped his notice. As we were going aboard, a lady passenger remarked softly to her companion: "Dear me! I wish we had some peaches!" The captain, not far away, said nothing; but I saw him call a cabin boy and whisper something in his ear. And just before the gangplank was hauled away, the lad came bounding aboard with a crate of peaches in his arms. We had a batch of missionaries with us. A pair of them, on their way to India, had a very pretty and very precocious little child, whom everyone admired. As it was toddling about the deck, the captain suddenly blew his whistle. We all started. Instantly the mate and bo's'n appeared, and saluted. "Boys," said the captain, "I want you to see that baby!"

So we passed Stromboli. I never reached its ruddy top, nor do I believe it offers nocturnal hospitality. And I fancy the clouds that envelop its summit are all of its own making.

INDEXES

I. *Index of Subjects and Topics*

Accent, 199.

Accident, 199.

Adjectives, 461.

Adverbs, 461.

Allusions (literary), 51, 280–1, 285, 289, 296, 540, 551.

Ambiguity, 199.

Amphiboly, 199.

Analogy, 202, 204, 205.

Analytical definition, 69–70, 73.

Anecdotes, 72, 118, 119, 120, 140, 235, 280, 281, 540.

Angle of narration, 481. *See also* Point of view.

Antonyms, 70.

Argument, Chapter XI.

Argumentum ad hominem, 200.

Argumentum ad populum, 200.

Argumentum ad vericundiam, 200–1.

Artistry, 322, 359–60, 400, 409, 460, 463, 477, 483.

Atmosphere, 96, 106, 131, 357, 421, 438–9, 440–2, 482.

Autobiography, 149, 150, 322, 323–4, 327–9, 343–5, 358–9, 373, 389–90, 421, 542, 554, 577.

Basic situation, 351, 356–70, 481.

Begging the question, 199, 205.

Bibliographical criticism, 164.

Bibliography, 228, 230, 231–2, 234, 260–1, 262, 264.

Biography, expository, Chapter VIII; narrative, 322, 340–1, 357–8, 389, 422, 577.

Body, 203, 258.

Brackets, 49, 260, 266, 325 n.

Brief, 203, 206–7.

Burlesque, 84.

Characterization, 117–8, Chapter VII; 325, 348, 361, 412, 414, 415, 420, 422, 423–4, 478–80, 483, 496, 519, 577.

Character plotted, 421–38, 480.

Character writing, 81, 99, 106, 109–10, 129.

Child story, 335–6, 443, 444.

Chronicle, 321, 337.

Classification, Chapter III; 260–1; of essays, 279–82.

Clearness, 12, 13, 288.

Climax, 7 (of sentence), 351, 352, 353, 354, 370, 371, 372, 373, 375, 387–400, 411–2, 413, 415, 416, 423, 425, 431, 441, 443, 446, 481, 554.

Co-education, specimen brief on, 206–7.

Coherence. *See* Sequence.

Coincidence, 482, 483.

Comparison and contrast, 6, 37, 69, 77–8, 111, 128, 176, 231, 460.

Complication. *See* Suspense.

Compound epithets, 462.

Conclusions, 51, 169, 201, 203, 260, 280, 351, 352, 354, 375, 400–10 (narrative), 412, 423, 426, 442.

Concreteness, 14, 37, 69, 72, 78, 143, 235.

Conflict, 480–1.

Connectives, 11, 29, 417, 419.

Connotation, 415, 461, 462.

Contentiousness, 169, 196.

Convincingness, 374, 481, 482. *See also* Plausibility.

Criticism, Chapter IX; 577.

Description, 96, 106, 412, 414; Chapter XVI.

Details, 100, 103, 133, 140, 280, 323, 324, 419, 440, 460–1 (in description), 462, 467, 480, 540, 542.

Detective stories, 419.

Deus ex machina, 393.

Diagrams, 10, 29, 242, 320, 348–51, 496.

Dialect, 419.

Dialogue, 100, 323, 381, 383, 388, 412–3, 419, 425, 462, 480, 483, 554, 558.

Diary, 322–3, 325 n., 330–3, 341–3, 358, 373, 389–90, 413, 421, 577.

Dictionary, 69, 70.

Digressions, 412.

Direct characterization, 117, 423.

Disguise. *See* Dramatic situation.

Division, 6, 7, Chapter III; 199, 231.

Documentation, 258–60, 268.
Dominant characteristic. *See* Character plotted.
Dominant tone, 100, 459–60, 461, 465, 471–2.
Dramatic situation, 380, 416, 483, 491.

Echoing conclusion, 401, 402, 404, 407–8.
Editorial, 196–7.
Emphasis, 51.
Equivocation, 198–9.
Etymology, 67, 69, 77.
Everyday-life essay, 286–92.
Evidence, 200, 205, 209, 213.
Examples, or illustrations, 69, 71, 72, 75, 78, 168, 235.
"Explication du texte," 164–5.
Exposition, in narrative, 363, 412, 416, 423.
External solution, 392, 393, 398, 425.

Fable, 421, 540.
Fairy tale, 353–4, 421, 481
Fallacies, 197, 198–203, 205, 214.
False analogy, 202.
Footnotes, 234, 242, 259–60, 265, 268.
Force, 357, 358, 359, 422.
Foreknowledge. *See* Dramatic situation.
Form, 258.
Fundamental image, in description, 474.

Genetic criticism, 164–5.

Historical criticism, 166–7, 168, 170, 174–5, 188–90.
History, 264–5, 325, 388.
Humor, 30, 84, 177, 286, 302, 306, 355, 401, 403, 415, 422, 429, 482, 548.

Ibid., 234, 260.
Ideas, 67–9.
Idiom, 289.
Illustrations. *See* Examples.
Imagery, 462, 473–4.
Imagination, types of, 487.
Impressionistic criticism, 163–4, 182.
Indirect characterization, 117, 423.
Induction, 204.
Internal solution, 392–3, 394, 399, 400, 425.
Interpretive criticism, 165, 182–3.
Introductions, 100, 139, 203, 210, 235, 258, 287, 350, 410, 419, 462–3.
Irony, 301, 378 (fate), 403 n., 404, 405, 409, 422.

Irrelevant conclusion, 201.
Issues, 204.

Journalistic style, 62.
Judicial criticism, 165–6, 168, 170, 173–4, 177–9, 183, 184–8.

Laboratory notebook, 4, 18, 321, 356.
Letter, as dramatic device. *See* Dramatic situation.
Letters, narrative, 322 n., 333–4, 345–6.
Linear narration, Chapter XIII; 554, 563. *See also* Autobiography, Diary, History, etc.
Loc. cit., 234, 260.
Local color, 554. *See also* Setting.
Logical definition, 71, 94.

Manuscript, form of, 257–8.
Melodrama, 363, 364, 481, 482, 483.
Mental state, description, 463, 467, 474–5.
Metaphors, 462.
Metrical feet, 418.
Moment of interest, 350–1, 352, 353, 354, 356–70, 370–1, 373, 375, 410, 423, 424, 441.
Moods, 302, 334, 347. *See also* Tone.
Moral (morality, and moralizing), 72, 205, 302, 352, 354, 364, 401, 407, 413, 414, 426, 462, 479.
Moving pictures, 390.

Names, as literary device, 119, 415.
Narrative anecdote, or sketch, 346.
Nature essay, 293–5.
Newspaper story, 322, 329–30, 339, 357, 366, 389, 448–9, 488–9, 496.
Non sequitur, 201–2.
Notes, 9, 228–9, 232–4.
Nouns, 461.

Objectiveness, 18, 183, 439, 441, 462.
Omissions, 49, 460.
Omniscient point of view, 360–1, 483.
Op. cit., 234, 260.
Organization, 168, 230–1, 235 n., 256, 257, 258, 261, 362, 415–6.
Originality, in plot, 481–2.
Outlines, and outlining, 8, 168, 190, 203, 206–7, 228, 230–1, 232, 233, 258, 261, 263, 280, 350–1, 362, 370–2, 373–4, 375, 416, 423–5, 440–42.
Overhearing. *See* Dramatic situation.

Paradox, 280.
Paragraphs, 18, 29, 49, 51, 169, 257, 351 n., 363, 410, 419, 462.
Parallelism, 100.
Paraphrase, Chapter IV; 259.
Parentheses, 49.
Pathetic fallacy, 462.
Pathos, 422.
Periodic style, 417.
Personal abstraction, 73–8, 81–93.
Personal-confession essay, 281–6.
Personality, 73–4, 81, 148, 277–8, 279–80, 281, 300, 304, 440, 576.
"Personals," 481, 486–8.
Persuasion, 196, 205, 226.
Philosophical abstraction, 78–81.
Philosophical essay, 93–7, 295–300.
Picture-frame story, 483, 539, 567–73.
Pictures, 10, 29.
Plagiarism, 234, 259, 390.
"Plants," in narrative, 392, 395.
Plausibility, 325, 391.
Plots, 323, 324, 347–56, 481–2.
Point of view, 49, 322, 356, 360–2, 365, 366, 411, 414, 419, 421, 443; in description, 459–60, 463, 464, 471, 478, 483, 496, 540, 554.
Précis, Chapter IV; 540.
Prelude, 350, 352, 353, 354, 356–70, 370–1, 423–4.
Premises, 197–8.
Progressive point of view, 459–60, 465, 467, 475–6, 540.
Pronouns, 281, 462, 483.
Proposition, 203–5, 207.
Psychology, and psychological reactions, 81, 117, 371, 372, 373, 374, 388, 412, 413, 423, 424–5, 441, 443, 479, 483.
Punctuation, 150, 231–2.

Quotations, 49, 51, 55, 72, 169, 257, 259, 280, 281, 415.

Refutation, 196, 205, 210, 212–3.
Report, 321, 388–9.
Research, 5, 16, 29, 33, 80, 229, 239, 242, 251–2, 257, 261–4, 268.
Retrospect, 324, 419, 426.
Revision, 11, 205, 417, 418, 419, 461, 463, 469–71, 496–500.
Rhythm, 417–9, 480.

Satire, 84, 86, 98, 99, 100, 104, 117, 139.
Senses, 460, 462.

Sentences, 1–4, 11, 29, 48, 49, 100, 363, 462.
Sentimentalism, 86, 113, 117, 278, 400, 439, 440.
Sequence, or coherence, 28–9, 126.
Setting, and local color, 325, 348, 355, 414–5, 438–9, 442, 482, 554.
Setting plotted, 438–58.
Sic, 260.
Similes, 462.
Slang, 281.
Solutions, 352, 353, 354, 371, 372, 373, 375, 387–400, 400–1, 403, 411–2, 413–4, 423, 425, 427, 429, 441–2.
Sources, 167, 228, 230–1, 234, 262–3, 264–5, 323–4, 356–8, 388–90, 421, 459, 481.
Static point of view, in description, 459.
Stream-of-consciousness, 135, 366, 488.
Style, 4, 10–11, 28–9, 47, 48, 51, 55, 86, 96, 100, 110, 205, 229, 280, 281, 300, 311, 324, 325, 417–9, 461–2, 477, 482.
Subjectiveness, 81, 439.
Subtopic, 232, 233.
Supra, 260.
Surprise twist, or "O. Henry ending," 401, 402, 409, 413–4, 425, 427.
Suspense, 351, 352, 353, 354, 355, 370–87, 411, 423, 424, 425, 441, 448, 481, 554.
Syllogism, 197–8, 204.
Sympathy, 117, 118, 119, 121, 139, 140, 141, 147, 414, 420, 463, 479, 483.
Synonyms, 70.
Synthetic definition, 70, 76.

Tenses, 49, 483.
Term paper, 5–9, 29, 71, Chapter XI.
Terms, technical, 10, 281, 462.
Textual criticism, 164.
Theme, of a story, 480–1.
Thesis criticism, 165, 167, 169–70, 171.
Time limit, in narration, 320, 321, 322, 327, 355, 365, 373, 379, 400, 415–6, 431, 434, 443, 496.
Title, 49, 258, 415, 419.
Tone, 100, 101, 106, 294, 311, 324–5, 356–7, 358, 359, 361–2, 363, 364, 373, 411, 415, 418–9, 422, 438, 440, 441.
Topic sentence, 49, 54.
Transitions, 7, 28–9, 150, 235, 554.
Triads, 417.
Trick solution, 392, 399, 406.

Unities, of time, place, and action, 355, 416, 482.
Unity, 117, 118, 139, 279, 347, 416, 438, 440, 477, 478, 481. *See also* Tone and Dominant tone.

Verbs, 461–2, 483.

Vignettes, 305.
Vocabulary, 112, 296, 376, 480. *See also* Words.

Words, 71, 461–2.

II. *Index of Authors, Allusions, and Titles*

ADDISON, JOSEPH, from the *Spectator*, 40–1, 129, 541; Johnson on Addison, 183–4.
ADE, GEORGE, 351–3, 540.
AIKEN, CONRAD, from "The Dark City," 369.
ALLEN, HERVEY, 180–2.
American Mercury, The, 184, 340 n., 341.
"Ancient Mariner, The," 23, 167.
ANDERSON, R. B., translator of "The Father," 431–4.
ANDERSON, SHERWOOD, from "I'm a Fool," 368; 409.
Anglo-Saxon Chronicle, 337.
Anthony Adverse, 180–2.
ARISTOTLE, 99, 197, 416. *See also* Unities.
ARNOLD, MATTHEW, 145, 165, 169, 170; from "The Study of Poetry," 184.

BARTLETT'S *Familiar Quotations*, 280, 281 n., 481.
BEERBOHM, MAX, 297.
BELLOC, HILAIRE, 542.
BENCHLEY, ROBERT, from *No Poems*, 306–7.
BENNETT, ARNOLD, 420, 481.
BERCOVICI, KONRAD, 409.
BERKELEY, BISHOP, from *The Guardian*, 39.
Bible, the, 421, 481.
BIERCE, AMBROSE, from "An Occurrence at Owl Creek Bridge," 383–4; from "The Man and the Snake," 384–5, 398–9.
BJÖRNSON, B., "The Father," 431–4.
BLACKMORE, R. D., from *Lorna Doone*, 21–3.
BOOGHER, SUSAN N., from "An Unknown Warrior," 368–9, 408.
BOSWELL, J., 129; from *The Life of Samuel Johnson*, 340.
BRONTË, CHARLOTTE, 133.
BROOKE, RUPERT, 41.
BROUN, HEYWOOD, 542.

BROWNING, ROBERT, 202–3.
BROWNLOW, E. B., 232.
BUFFON, COMTE DE, 462.
BURNEY, FANNY, from the *Diary*, 129–30.
BURT, MAXWELL STRUTHERS, "John O'May," 519–35.
BUSCHOR, ERNST, from *Greek Vase-Painting*, 94.
BUTLER, SAMUEL, 99; from "A Medicine-Taker," 112.

CAINE, WILLIAM, "The Pensioner," 434–8.
CALLAGHAN, MORLEY, from "The Red Hat," 408.
CARLYLE, T., 202; from *The French Revolution*, 337–8; 339, 340, 473.
CARROLL, LEWIS, 67–8, 135, 541.
CATHER, WILLA, from *Death Comes for the Archbishop*, 474.
CHAUCER, G., 128–9, 191–5, 421.
CHEKHOV, A., from "The Darling," 132.
CHESTERTON, G. K., 540–1.
CLARK, GLENN, 481.
COHEN-PORTHEIM, PAUL, from *The Spirit of France*, 45–6, 95.
COLERIDGE, S. T., 23, 164.
COMFORT, W. L., from "Fear," 385, 398.
CONNELL, RICHARD, "The Most Dangerous Game," 399–400, 407, 500–19.
CONRAD, JOSEPH, from "The Lagoon," 473–4.
COWLEY, ABRAHAM, from "Of Myself," 1.
COWLEY, MALCOLM, from the *New Republic*, 474–5.
CRANE, STEPHEN, from "A Desertion," 131–2.
CRAWLEY, RICHARD, translator of Thucydides on Pericles, 57–60.
CURL, M. J., from *Expository Writing*, 279.

DAY, CLARENCE, from *Life with Father*, 308–11.

DE MILLE, GEORGE E., from *Literary Criticism in America*, 184–88.

DEFOE, DANIEL, 167.

DENT, J. C., from *Thought in English Prose*, 57–60.

Detroit Free Press, the, 448–9.

DICKENS, CHARLES, 473.

DOBIE, CHARLES CALDWELL, from "The Open Window," 368.

DOBSON, AUSTIN, from *Eighteenth Century Vignettes, Second Series*, 133–5.

DOBSON, MARGARET, from *Block-Cutting and Print-Making by Hand*, 18–21.

DOW, E. W., *Principles of a Note-System for Historical Studies*, 232.

DOWNEY, JUNE E. *See* Slosson, E. E.

DOYLE, A. CONAN, from "How It Happened," 399.

DRIBERG, J. H., "Engato the Hunter," 563–6.

DRYDEN, JOHN, from *Essay of Dramatic Poesy*, 182–3.

DURANTY, W., 407.

DUTCHER, F. E., "Death of Captain Eddie," 339.

DWIGGINS, W. A., "La Dernière Mobilisation," 475–6.

EARLE, J., from *Microcosmography*, 99, 111.

EASTMAN, MAX, 41.

EATON, WALTER PRITCHARD, "Barrett Wendell," 340–1.

EDMONDS, W. D., from "Water Never Hurt a Man," 408.

"Elegy," Gray's, 167.

ELIOT, GEORGE, *Adam Bede*, 461; 478.

ELTERLEIN, ERNST VON, from *Beethoven's Symphonies*, 44.

EMERSON, R. W., 265–8.

EVANS, HARRY, "The Mighty," from *Life*, 190–1.

FERBER, EDNA, 55–6.

FINGER, C. J., from "The Lizard God," 407.

FIRKINS, O. W., 183.

FISCHER, LOUIS, "The Road to Peace," from the *Nation*, 220–6.

FLAUBERT, G., from *Madame Bovary*, 130–1.

FOERSTER and STEADMAN, from *Writing and Thinking*, 47.

FOLSOM, ELIZABETH I., "Towers of Fame," 567–73.

FRANCE, ANATOLE, 301, 302.

FRANK, WALDO, from *Virgin Spain*, 96–7.

FREYTAG, G., 348.

GARLAND, HAMLIN, from "Lucretia Burns," 449.

GASKELL, MRS. ELIZABETH C., 133.

GEROULD, CHRISTOPHER, "The End of the Party," 535–9.

GISSING, GEORGE, from "Christopherson," 368.

GOLDSMITH, O., "On National Prejudices," 81–4; "A City Night Piece," 108–9.

GRAHAME, KENNETH, 542.

GRANBERRY, E., 407.

GRANDGENT, CHARLES H., from "Cracks in the Clouds," 118, 137–8, 577–84.

GRAY, THOMAS, 167.

GRIMM BROTHERS, "The Nix of the Millpond," 353–4.

GUEDALLA, PHILIP, from *The Duke*, 338–9.

Gulliver's Travels, 167, 170.

HALL, JOSEPH, 99.

HAMILTON, CLAYTON, 360.

HARDY, THOMAS, 168, 169.

HARTE, BRET, from "The Iliad of Sandy Bar," 367.

HAWTHORNE, N., from "The Artist of the Beautiful," 359; from "Ethan Brand," 359; from "The Grey Champion," 359.

HAZLITT, WILLIAM, from *Lectures on the English Poets*, 188.

HENRY, O., 183; "Between Rounds," 402; "The Cop and the Anthem," 453–8; "The Gift of the Magi," 403; from "Little Speck in Garnered Fruit," 407; from "A Service of Love," 369, 407; from "The Skylight Room," 409; from "Squaring the Circle," 398; from "Transients in Arcadia," 367; 414.

HENTY, G. A., 390.

HERRICK, ROBERT, from "The Argument of His Book," 41.

HOLINSHED's *Chronicle*, 337.

HOMER, 482.

HUNT, LEIGH, 280; from "A 'Now': Descriptive of a Hot Day," 302–3;

from "A 'Now': Descriptive of a Cold Day," 573–6.

IRVING, WASHINGTON, from "The Stout Gentleman," 472.

JAMESON, MRS. ANNA B., from *Characteristics of Women*, 182.
JOHNSON, SAMUEL, from *The Lives of the English Poets*, 183–4; 70–1, 129–30, 140, 188, 279, 300.
JONSON, BEN, 284.
JOYCE, JAMES, from *Ulysses*, 135–7.

KEATS, JOHN, 296; from *Ode to Psyche*, 462; 554, 576.
KEMBLE, FANNY, from *Records of a Girlhood*, 344–5.
KIPLING, R., 163, 201, 369, 400, 449.
KITTREDGE, G. L., from *Chaucer and His Poetry*, 191–5.

LAMB, CHARLES, 112–3; from "Poor Relations," 113–5; 277, 302; 345–6.
"Ligeia," 431.
Literary Digest, the, 55–6.
LONDON, JACK, 386–7.
London Times, The, 481, 487.
LYND, ROBERT, 315; "Love at Its Last Gasp," 316–9; "On Making Mistakes," 312–5.

MACAULAY, LORD, from "An Admirable Crichton," 149–50.
MANSFIELD, KATHERINE, 409.
Manual of Style, A (University of Chicago), 232 n., 261.
MARLOWE, CHRISTOPHER, 176–7.
MARQUIS, DON, from "O'Meara, 'The Mayflower,' and Mrs. MacLirr," 369.
MATTHEWS, H. L., "A World of Gold Beneath a Vacant Lot," 269–74.
MAUPASSANT, GUY DE, from "Deux Amis," 409–10.
MAUROIS, ANDRÉ, 139, 148.
MAXCY, C. L., 360.
McDOWELL, TREMAINE, "A Freshman Poem by Emerson," 265–8.
McINTYRE, O. O., 541.
McMURTRIE, D. C., 231.
MELVILLE, H., from *Moby Dick*, 23–4, 42–4, 135.
MONTAIGNE, MICHEL DE, 155–62, 277, 279, 300–1, 302.

MOORE, TOM, 290.
MORLEY, CHRISTOPHER, 277, 279, 280, 312.
MUIR, JOHN, 22.
MUNTHE, DR. AXEL, from *The Story of San Michele*, 150–4.

NATHAN, G. J., 163.
New Statesman and Nation, 315, 563.
New Yorker, The, 308.
NEWTON, A. E., 22.
NORRIS, FRANK, from *The Octopus*, 471–2.

O'BRIEN, FITZ-JAMES, from "What Was It?" 385–6.
O'REILLY, MARY B., "In Berlin," 346.
O'SULLIVAN, VINCENT, from "Master of Fallen Years," 406–7.
"Out of the Night," from *McClure's Magazine*, 402.
OVERBURY, SIR THOMAS, "An Improvident Young Gallant," 110.

PARKHURST, WINTHROP, from the *Reader's Digest*, 64–5.
PEPYS, SAMUEL, from the *Diary*, 341–2.
PERICLES, 57–60.
POE, EDGAR ALLAN, 184–8; from "The Cask of Amontillado," 368; from "The Fall of the House of Usher," 450; from "Hawthorne's *Twice-Told Tales*," 477; from "The Pit and the Pendulum," 398.
POLTI, G., 480.
POMFRET, J., 312.
POPE, A., 163, 188.
POWYS, LLWELYN, from *Thirteen Worthies*, 155–62.
PURCELL, MARIAN, from "Our Fifteen-Year-Old Sophisticates," 115–6.

RANKIN, T. E., 67 n., 227 n.
Reader's Digest, 51, 63–5, 215–9, 226.
Robinson Crusoe, 167.
ROCKWELL, F. F., from *House and Garden*, 54–5.
ROGET'S *Thesaurus*, 70.
ROSENBLATT, BENJAMIN, "In the Metropolis," 451–2.
RUSHFELDT, ELISE M., from "A Coffin for Anna," 368.
RUSKIN, JOHN, from *The Eagle's Nest*, 93; from *Modern Painters*, 462; from *Stones of Venice*, 471.

SADLER, DR. WILLIAM S., from the *American Magazine*, 52–4.

SAINTE-BEUVE, C. A., from "Voltaire," 189.

Saturday Review of Literature, The, 481, 487–8.

SCHOPENHAUER, A., from *Parerga and Paralipomena*, 87–93.

SCOTT, R., from *Scott's Last Expedition*, 342–3.

SHAKESPEARE, WILLIAM, from *Antony and Cleopatra*, 50; from *As You Like It*, 39–40; 167, 189–90 (*Hamlet*); from *Henry IV, Part I*, 129; from *Macbeth*, 50; 164, 166–7, 176–7, 182–3, 391.

SHELLEY, P. B., 146–7.

SHERMAN, STUART P., 414.

SLOSSON, E. E., and DOWNEY, JUNE E., from *Plots and Personalities*, 487.

SMITH, ALEXANDER, from *Dreamthorp and Other Essays*, 1–2.

SMITH, LOGAN PEARSALL, from *Trivia*, 305–6.

STALLINGS, LAURENCE, from "Gentlemen in Blue," 408.

STEELE, WILBUR DANIEL, from "The Shame Dance," 407.

STEVENSON, BURTON, *Home Book of Quotations*, 280–1, 281 n., 481.

STEVENSON, R. L., from "A Gossip on Romance," 357 n.; from "Markheim," 399; from "The Manse," 471; from "The Sire de Malétroit's Door," 367, 400; 360, 479.

STOCKTON, F. R., from "The Lady, or the Tiger?" 406.

STOLL, E. E., from *Hamlet* (1919), 189–90.

STRACHEY, LYTTON, 139, 148.

SUDELL, RICHARD, from *The New Garden*, 24–7.

SWIFT, J., 133–5; 167, 170.

TANNER, W. M., from *Essays and Essay Writing*, 279.

THACKERAY, W. M., from *Henry Esmond*, 473; from *The Snobs of England*, 85–6; 165, 167, 168, 169, 170, 388, 391, 478.

THEOPHRASTUS, 99.

THOREAU, HENRY, from *Walden*, 304–5.

THUCYDIDES, reporting Pericles, 57–60.

Time, 51.

TROLLOPE, ANTHONY, from the *Autobiography*, 343–4.

Vanity Fair, 165, 167, 168, 169, 170, 391.

VOLTAIRE, from *Candide*, 86; 189.

WALTON, IZAAK, 22, 298.

WELLS, H. G., 406.

WHARTON, EDITH, 415.

WHITE, S. E., 22.

WIMBERLY, L. C., from "White Man's Town," 369.

WORDSWORTH, W., 281, 291, 292.

YOUNG, EDWARD, 312.

"Y. Y." (ROBERT LYND), 315, 319.

III. *Index of Student Themes*

PAGE

Advice (J. T.) 295–6

Afternoon in Spring, An (D. D.) 335–6

Alibi-Artist, The (G. W.) 427–9

Amateur Deep-Sea Diving (R. Z.) 239–41

America Should Join the League of Nations (C. J. W.) 210–2

Art of Block Printing, The (M. M.) 235–9

Barabas and Shylock (H. T.) 176–7

Beauty (J. M. T.) 552–4

Betty Gold (L. W.) 404

British Monarchy during the Eighteenth Century, The (H. E.) 213–4

Brown Night, A (D. McC.) 464

Buck Fever (M. S.) 366, 378–9, 394–5, 404

Bulbous Irises (M. Fo.) 54–5

Cameos (D. H.) 426–7

PAGE

"Came the Dawn" (V. S.) 177–9
Carnival (M. G.) 446–8
Charlie (T. C.) 493–4
Chewing-Gum Romance, A (M. Fe.) 288–9
Chippendale Furniture (F. D.) 243–6
Circus Has Come to Town, The (A. S.) 467
Classroom Soliloquy (D. McC.) 334–5
Colonel J——, Librarian (M. E.). 173–4
Combat between the Snake and the Cock, The (O. K.) 375–6
Concrete Beehive, The (L. L. M.) 171
Conviction and Prejudice (H. B. L.) 77–8
Country Doctor, The (E. S.). 105–6
Country Road, The (J. M. T.) 294–5
County Fair, the (E. E. F.) 465–6
Cub Reporter Goes Back to Keokuk, The (E. W.) 494–6

Diary of a Lady's Lap Dog, The (F. Se.) 332–3
Dr. Wilheim's Condition Unchanged (C. E.) 329–30
Doorbell Speaks, The (E. L.) 31–3
Dorm Girl, The (M. Fe.) 103–4
Duty (G. F.) 491–3

Egyptian Mummy, the (J. R.) 16–8
Eugénie, Queen of Sorrows (V. B.) 246–51
Experiment (J. Hi.) 498–500

Farmhouse at Night (B. J. H.) 293
Fishin' (M. J.) 298–300
Five Months to Live (E. W.) 405–6
Freddy Grows Up (M. B.). 559–62
Fugitive, The (G. V.). 365, 376–8, 394
Fulfillment (P. A.) 297–8

Glamour of the Past, The (A. McK.) 296–7
Glory That Is Athens, The (W. M.) 62–3
Golf Bug, The (C. B.) 104–5

Hans Bäumgart (C. B.) 122–3
History of the Shoe, The (M. H.) 325–7
Horse Sense (C. B.) 76–7
How to Play Golf (C. S. L.) 13–4
How to Solve a Cryptogram (J. L.) 14–6

If Eve Had Kept a Diary (H. O.) 330–1
In the Desert (L. Gr.) 489–91
Introvert, The 101
It's All a Mistake (M. G.) 381–3

June Ross (M. K.) 469–70

"L'État—C'est Moi" (L. W.) 123–4
Letter of 1671, A (H. S.) 333–4
Ludwig van Beethoven (L. C.) 147–8
Lynch Victim's Last Minutes, A (A. T.). 366–7, 379–80, 395

Making Chocolate Fudge (H. M. H.) 12–3

PAGE

Mary Jo (V. G.) 445–6
Methylene Blue (J. Hi.) 497–8
Middle-Class Neighborhood, A (E. MacG.) 106–8
Mischief Will Out (R. H.) 380
Mountain Country (M. G.) 555–8
My Aunt (D. McC.) 126–8
My Aunt (M. D. R.) 143–4
My Dad (H. A.) 141–3
My Dramatic Career (C. G.) 327–9
My Grandfather (C. C.) 120–1
My Views on My Length (F. Sm.) 284–5

Narrow Escape Boating, A (E. F.) 365, 376, 394

Our "Beautiful Young Idiots" (R. M.) 55–7
Overstuffed Female Parasite, The (J. N.) 102

Personality (A. G.) 73–5
Professional Courtesies (A. Fr.) 395–7

Recollections (L. Gr.) 543–8
Refutation of the Popular Opinion that City Life Increases the Number
   of Neurotics, A (B. B.) 212–3
Rush Dinner (E. P.) 465

Sergei Rachmaninoff (S. S.) 175
Shattered Romances (L. C.) 291–2
Shelley: "The Beautiful but Ineffectual Angel" (R. M.) 146–7
Sketch of an Artist, A (R. E.) 124–6
Spasm on Spectacles, A (C. H.) 282–4
Spiritualism (I. A.) 78–80
Spring Colds (L. M.) 287–8
Stamp Collector, The (C. S.) 172–3
Summary of Pericles's Panegyric (J. J.) 60–2
Superiority Complex, The (J. Ha.) 75–6

That Dobbs Girl (B. T.) 119–20
That Red-Headed Temper (A. Fa.) 429–30
Then and Now (F. Se.) 548–51
Trans-Oceanic Flights (C. M.) 209–10
Trapped in a Burning Forest (L. Ga.) 393–4
Truth about Old Maids, The (N. T.) 290–1
Types of Dancers (M. M.) 35–7
Types of Window Displays (R. E.) 37–8
Types of Women (H. R.) 30–1

Unhappiness (M. V.) 468
Up in the Clouds (W. B.) 443–4

Voodooism (H. A.) 80–1

Weddings of Other Ages (H. A.) 33–5
We Like Them Short and Sweet (J. S.) 180–1
What to Do at Your Age to Protect Your Health (H. M. H.) 52–4
Why I Hate Being the Youngest Child (F. Se.) 285–6

"X" (D. L.) 144–5